MUSIC, BODY, AND DESIRE IN MEDIEVAL CULTURE

Figurae

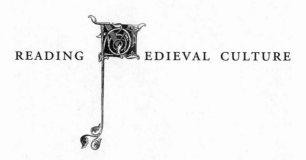

READING MEDIEVAL CULTURE

Infernal Musicians from Hieronymous Bosch, *Garden of Earthly Delights* (inner right wing), ca. 1510 (detail)

MUSIC, BODY, AND DESIRE IN MEDIEVAL CULTURE

HILDEGARD OF BINGEN TO CHAUCER

Bruce W. Holsinger

Stanford University Press, Stanford, California, 2001

Generous financial support toward the
production of this book has been provided
in the form of a Weiss / Brown Subvention
Award from The Newberry Library,
Chicago, Illinois.

Stanford University Press
Stanford, California

Printed in the United States of America
On acid-free, archival-quality paper

Library of Congress Cataloging-in-Publication Data
Holsinger, Bruce W.
    Music, body, and desire in medieval culture :
Hildegard of Bingen to Chaucer / Bruce W. Holsinger.
        p. cm. — (Figurae)
Includes bibliographical references (p.   ) and index.
ISBN 0-8047-3201-9 (cloth : acid-free paper) —
ISBN 0-8047-4058-5 (paper : acid-free paper)
        1. Music—500–1400—Philosophy and aesthetics.
2. Body, Human, in music.   3. Body, Human, in
literature.   4. Body, Human—Religious aspects—
Christianity—History of doctrines—Middle Ages,
600–1500.   I. Figurae (Stanford, Calif.)
        ML3845 .H64 2001
        780'.9'02—dc21   00-067945

Original Printing 2001

Last figure below indicates year of this printing:
10   09   08   07   06   05   04   03   02   01

Typeset by Keystone Typesetting, Inc. in
11/14 Adobe Garamond

For my parents,
Sheila and Harry Holsinger,
and for Anna Campbell Brickhouse

E io a lui: "I' mi son un che, quando
  Amor mi spira, noto, e a quel modo
  ch'e' ditta dentro vo significando."

—DANTE

Preface and Acknowledgments

Hiroshi Chu Okubo is one of the first Virtual MIDI body percussionists in the world. In preparing for a performance on Yamaha's new (and yet to be FCC-approved) Miburi R3 system, Hiroshi must attach some twenty-four electronic sensors to his head, shoulders, elbows, palms, knees, and feet until he resembles something like a patient in an intensive care unit (if a very healthy one). The sensors are then linked by cable to a set of computerized synthesizers and amplifiers, and the performance begins. A dazzling rhythmicist, Hiroshi beats out his innovative compositions and improvised riffs on the various sensors clinging to his body. The sensor on his right elbow might serve as a bass drum. His knees can be deployed as cymbals—the right, say, a high-hat, the left a tambourine. The virtuosic cascade of digital counterpoint and percussive melody that ensues almost makes us forget the technological revolutions that have enabled the postmodernist ham-bone that Hiroshi performs on his frame. Hiroshi declares the aesthetic aspirations of the performance on one of his home pages on the World Wide Web (www.angelfire.com/ok/hcomusicfactory), where the curious surfer will also find an uploaded full-color photograph of the musician in his MIDI get-up. As Hiroshi straightforwardly informs the on-line universe, "My body is the musical instrument of the future."

When I was first contacted by Hiroshi via e-mail and began familiarizing myself with the emergent technology of MIDI body percussion, I was convinced that I had found the ideal contemporary foil to the medieval musical bodies that are the subject of this study. For Hiroshi's techno musical body is, in no uncertain terms, a "posthuman" body. The various body parts employed in performance labor to produce the music that we hear, but they do so by activating metal, plastic, and wire sensors and "grip units" that together constitute a kind of "virtual" body, which in turn displaces the "real," "material" body in performance. One of the unspoken goals and effects of Hiroshi's performances, it seemed to me, was to challenge and extend the boundaries of the human, even to redefine the human body itself through a cybernetic displacement of the flesh. The result, it seemed, was a musical body that was in fact no body at all. After years of encountering medieval representations of skin, bones, sinews, throats, and chests as musical in and of themselves, I couldn't help but view Yamaha's technological revolution as prophetic of a final break with the musico-somatic naturalism of the premodern era.

Yet I have been convinced (in part by Hiroshi himself) that the self-described musical body of the late-twentieth-century MIDI body percussionist has a good deal in common with the resonant bodies of the Middle Ages. Hiroshi Chu Okubo performs at the end of a millennium that begins with Peter Damian's suggestion that the chanting of ten psalms is the musical equivalent of ten thousand lashes of the whip, the beating of the "dry skin" on his back a confessional performance upon the biblical "drum" of his flesh. Despite the vast historical and cosmological gaps that separate them, both technologies—the medieval discipline of flagellation, the postmodern deployment of the Miburi R3 synthesizer—insist upon the body, whether human or posthuman, as a performing instrument capable of producing musical sonority through self-directed and often violent movements of the frame. And they both claim music *for* the body, embracing melody, rhythm, and percussion with their torsos and limbs. If Hiroshi's body represents the musical instrument of the future, his virtuosic corporeality nevertheless constitutes a powerful reanimation of the musical bodies of the past.

I would first like to thank the staffs of the libraries in which the research for this book was carried out. They include the British Library in London; the Bodleian Library at Oxford; the King's College, Gonville and Caius College, and University Libraries in Cambridge; the Bibliothèque Nationale in Paris; and Butler Library at Columbia University. In Boulder, I owe a special thanks to the staff of Norlin Library's Interlibrary Loan Office, who have ordered over three hundred titles for me in the last four years. Other libraries, museums, and archives that provided photographs and permissions are acknowledged below. Barbara Nolan spent an afternoon in Paris introducing me to the friendly staff and cramped quarters of the Institut de Recherche et d'Histoire des Textes; the three days I spent there saved me what would have turned into many extra weeks of bibliographical research back home. Generous financial support provided by the University of Colorado in the forms of a sabbatical leave, a Junior Faculty Development Award, a Dean's Summer Research Grant, and several smaller grants have provided much-needed financial assistance and teaching relief. I owe many thanks to the Newberry Library in Chicago, which awarded my book a Weiss/Brown Publication Subvention and defrayed the prohibitive costs of photographs and reproduction permissions.

Earlier versions of various chapters were presented to audiences at Loyola University of Chicago, Harvard University, the University of Minnesota, Northwestern University, MIT, Augsburg College (Minneapolis), and Rice University and in sessions sponsored by the American Musicological Society, the conferences on Feminist Theory and Music, the Modern Language Association, the Medieval Academy of America, and the Medieval Congress at Kalamazoo. Chapter 2 is a much-revised version of an article published in *Signs*, and an earlier version of Chapter 5 was published in the first volume of *New Medieval Literatures*; I would like to thank the University of Chicago Press and Oxford University Press, respectively, for their permission to reprint this material here.

The topic of this book initially emerged during my early graduate studies in the Program in Comparative Studies in Discourse and Society (CSDS) at the University of Minnesota–Twin Cities. The extraordinary intellectual environment fostered by the students and faculty in and around CSDS—Barbara Engh, Amitava Kumar, Richard Leppert, Bruce Lincoln, John Mowitt, Gary Thomas, and many others—afforded numerous occasions for thinking and teaching against disciplinary boundaries. A number of the ideas that follow were first tried out on members of the Medieval Colloquium at Columbia University—including Suzanne Conklin Akbari, Jim Cain, Mary Agnes Edsall, Sarah Kelen, the late Claudia Rattazzi Papka, Margaret Pappano, and Sandra Pierson Prior—who provided many helpful criticisms and suggestions. I would especially like to thank the members of my dissertation committee, including Robert Hanning, Joan Ferrante,

Christopher Baswell, and Tom Payne, for their careful reading of my thesis, as well as Jean Howard, whose teaching and mentoring continue to provide a model for my own.

A number of medieval musicologists have welcomed a disciplinary interloper into their midst, providing both meticulous readings of individual chapters as well as numerous helpful suggestions and corrections in conversation and via e-mail; they include Mark Everist, Margot Fassler, Honey Meconi, Christopher Page, Judith Peraino, and Edward Roesner. Other friends, colleagues, readers, and correspondents to whom I owe special thanks include John Bowers, Philip Brett, Andrew Cowell, Carolyn Dinshaw, Richard Emmerson, Louise Fradenburg, Allen Frantzen, Karl Fugelso, Jesse Gellrich, Jeffrey Hamburger, Ralph Hexter, Donna Jackson, Willis Johnson, Jacqueline Jung, Del Kolve, Richard Leppert, Ron Martinez, Martha Mockus, Jo Ann Hoeppner Moran, Mitchell Morris, Barbara Newman, Ruth Nissé, Derek Pearsall, Patrick Pritchett, Wendy Scase, Emily Steiner, Elizabeth Randell Upton, David Wallace, Rob Walser, Elizabeth Wood, and Katherine Zieman.

At Stanford University Press, I owe particular thanks to Helen Tartar, whose early interest in this project was warm and encouraging; Kate Warne, a helpful and informative production editor; and Mary Ray Worley, whose painstaking copyediting caught numerous errors. Michael Camille, Nicholas Watson, and an anonymous third referee wrote extremely generous yet immensely helpful readers' reports that made the final round of revisions a challenging but rewarding task.

Rita Copeland—through her scholarship, teaching, and friendship—was almost single-handedly responsible for my decision to become a medievalist. In Jody Enders I have found a friend and colleague whose contribution to this project has included a six-year conversation about the aesthetics of torture in the Middle Ages. John Baldwin engaged me in a lively exchange of letters after reading a draft of Chapter 4; though he may continue to raise an eyebrow at the result, his immense knowledge of Parisian culture in the decades around 1200 proved indispensable in the final shaping of the chapter. David Townsend, collaborator extraordinaire, has been patient with a fellow Latinist always aware of his superior talents. I owe an enormous debt to Susan McClary, whose teaching and scholarship made music come alive for me again after five stultifying years in a conservatory environment and whose subsequent support of my career has been unflagging. My debt to Hiroshi Chu Okubo should already be apparent.

In the English Department at the University of Colorado at Boulder, I have been surrounded by a friendly group of junior and senior colleagues—Katherine Eggert, Jane Garrity, Jeremy Green, Jill Heydt Stevenson, Karen Jacobs, Tim Morton, Katheryn Rios, Jeffrey Robinson, Charlotte Sussman, Mark Winokur, and Sue Zemka, among others—who have provided constant intellectual and culinary support over the last five years. Only my chair, John Stevenson, can know how much his energy and empathy have meant to me. Elizabeth Robertson read the entire manuscript at a very late stage, and she has been a savvy and generous mentor since my arrival in Boulder. A wonderful group of current and former graduate students, including Rebecca Barck, Betty Benson, Kate Crassons, Beege Harding, Jana Mathews, Katherine Millersdaughter, Kirsten Otey, Ben Perry, Matt Rubery, Jamie Taylor, Amy Vines, Lorna Wheeler, and Wes Yu, remind me why I'm in this business.

There are two scholars whose influence on these pages would be impossible to exaggerate. Caroline Walker Bynum directed the dissertation out of which this book eventually developed. From the moment I first set foot in one of her graduate seminars in 1991, her passion for the Middle Ages changed my life. Despite the heavy demands on her time (and in this age of academic stardom), her untiring dedication to her students never seems to diminish. While arguing tooth and nail against some of the more irresponsible strands of my argument, she pushed me to work harder and aspire to an intellectual rigor and integrity that I can only hope someday to achieve; she was never satisfied until she believed that *I* believed every word I wrote. She inspired in me an honest awe for the past that I will never lose.

Anna Brickhouse has heard, read, and lived with more drafts of the following chapters than she would want to count. The most talented reader of literature I know, she has also been my own most perceptive and unforgiving critic, pointing out innumerable shortcomings in my arguments and showing me how to make my writing both stronger and subtler. Her intellectual generosity and love continue to inspire me, and the dedication of this book is but a pale expression of the many debts that I owe her.

She shares the dedication with my parents, whose years of love, support, and friendship have taught me more than they can know.

Contents

Part IV:

RESOUNDINGS

Illustrations and Musical Examples

MUSICAL EXAMPLES

Abbreviations

AASS   *Analecta Sanctorum quotquot toto orbe coluntur*, ed. Jean Bolland et al. 1st edition. Antwerp and Brussels, 1643–present.

CCCM   *Corpus Christianorum, continuatio medievalis*

CCSL   *Corpus Christianorum, series latina*

CF   Cistercian Fathers Series

CS   *Scriptorum de musica mediiaevi novam seriem a Gerbertina.* . . . 4 vols. Paris: Durand, 1864–76.

CSEL   *Corpus Scriptorum Ecclesiasticorum Latinorum*

CSM   *Corpus Scriptorum de Musica*

DHGE   *Dictionnaire d'histoire et de géographie ecclésiastiques*, ed. Alfred Baudrillart et al. Paris, 1912–present.

EETS   Early English Text Society

e.s.   Extra Series

o.s.   Original Series

JAMS   *Journal of the American Musicological Society*

MGG   *Die Musik in Geschichte und Gegenwart.* 9 vols. Ludwig Finscher, ed. Kassel: Bärenreiter, 1994.

MGH   *Monumenta Germaniae historica*

NG   *New Grove Dictionary of Music and Musicians*, ed. Stanley Sadie. London, 1980.

PG   *Patrologia cursus completus, series Graeca*, ed. J-P. Migne. Paris, 1857–66.

PL   *Patrologia cursus completus, series Latina*, ed. J.-P. Migne. Paris, 1844–64.

PMLA   *Publications of the Modern Language Association*

RS   Rolls Series

SC   *Sources chrétiennes*

A Note to the Reader

When quoting foreign language passages, I have retained the orthography used by the editors of the printed editions, even when these editions are themselves internally inconsistent; the originals of some passages are quoted in full in the main text, some in the notes, and others piecemeal, depending on context. I have cited existing English translations when a good one is available, though I have altered them silently in many instances; all other translations are my own. Though I have tried to keep technical musicological vocabulary to a minimum, when the use of specialized language is unavoidable, terms are explained either in the main text or in the notes.

And even man himself, if he knows that he possesses all the resources customarily associated with this art, will not doubt the great harmony with which he is equipped for this discipline: for in his throat he has a pipe for singing; in his chest, a kind of harp, adorned with strings, as it were, the fibers of his lungs; in the alternations of the beating of his pulse, fluctuating ascents and descents.

—AURELIAN OF RÉÔME, *Musica Disciplina* (ca. 850)

What is more, my beloved one, I add this, the desire of a loving heart, that when my body will be reduced to smallest particles of dust and covered with a stone, some pleasing sound giving praise and glory to you may rise from every minutest particle, and piercing the hardest stone may rise to the heavens' heights, and may sound the proclamation of a loving praise until the day of judgment, until at the blessed resurrection my body and my soul, united with one another, may be joined to praise and glorify you eternally.

—HENRY SUSO, *Horologium Sapientiae* (ca. 1330)

Introduction

Confronting a diverse array of speculation and polemic directed at pagan abuses of the flesh, Latin Christendom struggled to reconcile the sublimating aspirations of classical musical thought with its own incarnational aesthetic. Exegetes and illuminators see the body of Christ stretched so tightly on the cross that believers can pluck the passion upon his ribs and sinews, providing Italian flagellants and women visionaries in the Low Countries with a sonorous exemplum in the musical torture of the self. The heart's regulation of the pulse fashions the body into a musical microcosm keeping time with the rhythms of the universe so pervasively that medieval representations of musical experience often seem compelled to subsume the other senses. Such synesthesia causes a fifteenth-century musical theorist to write of the "redolence" of certain kinds of liturgical harmonies; it provokes a Scottish poet to describe a song exiting the leprous mouth of Criseyde as "rawk as Ruik, full hiddeous hoir and hace."[1] Sacred musical pleasures threaten always to lapse into profane musical perversions. The intermingling of same-sex voices in plainchant and polyphony allows composers and performers to explore through sonority unsanctioned forms of desire. The musical ingenuities of poets and monks cause fluttered tongues to pluck, beaten skin to resonate, a slit throat to resound. The severed head of Orpheus continues to sing as it floats down the river Heber and through countless medieval permutations. For a civilization ever alert to the perils of carnality, the human body represents nevertheless the very ground of musical experience.

Shrouded in metaphor, allegory, poetics, image, and notation, the musical bodies of the medieval era seem an intangible and perhaps unlikely object of historical inquiry. Yet careful attention to the tenuous boundary between representation and experience may allow us to cull musical metaphors for that residual kernel of bodily practice and material circumstance they often convey. We can differentiate between musical allegory and allegoresis, exposing the former as an ideological mask that works to disguise the rhetorical machinations of the latter. Verse will sometimes reveal the musical somatics of poetic invention that Chaucer evokes so movingly in the prologue to the *Legend of Good Women*: "as an harpe obeieth to the hond/And maketh it soune after his fyngerynge,/Ryght so mowe ye oute of myn herte bringe/Swich vois, ryght as yow lyst, to laughe or pleyne."[2] Visual images expose unacknowledged dimensions of musical experience; the sight of sound has always been a site of embodiment.[3] As for musical notation, here, too, resides compelling testimony to life in the body, whether the neumes are inscribed on the pedagogical hand or satirized as "flesh-hooks" by those enlisted to perform them.

This book seeks to account for the corporeality of musical culture and musical experience in the European Middle Ages. I argue that deep-seated assumptions about musical sonority as a practice of the flesh exerted a clear influence upon the composition, performance, reception, and representation of music from the twelfth through the fourteenth centuries and, further, that music played a central imaginative and ideological role in medieval representations of the human body. The book considers largely unfamiliar and often bizarre dimensions of medieval musical life that reveal themselves once we take seriously the human body as a site of musical production: to take just a few of the many examples considered herein, the understanding among ascetics and hagiographers of skin and other body parts as musical instruments to be beaten, plucked, blown through, or strummed; the allegorical notion of the crucified Christ as a harp and his exposed ribs and distended sinews as its resonant strings; or the condemnation of twelfth-century polyphony as a musical simulacrum of same-sex desire.

In its focus on medieval music as an embodied material practice, this book speaks to an already prolific bibliography of interdisciplinary scholarship that has devoted itself to excavating the history of sexuality and the body in premodern religion, art, and literature. The millennium between Augustine and Margery Kempe looks very different now than it did fifteen years ago, when historical constructions of the body and bodily practices were just beginning to emerge as serious topics of scholarly inquiry. The sexual body in Christian late antiquity, the gendering of hermeneutics and literary practices, the eucharistic miracles of medieval women, idolatry and the politics of visual representation, ideological wars over the symbolic capital of the *corpus Christi*: these are just some of the many manifestations of medieval embodiment inspiring a new cultural history that has quickly become one of the most vital subfields within fin-de-siècle medieval studies.[4] Its practitioners have demonstrated that the methodological and historical significance of their findings is rarely limited to their home disciplines. Similarly, the musical cultures of the European Middle Ages offer us a particularly rich array of somatic practices and representations that have crucial bearing on various discipline-specific histories of the body. The sonorous body performed an essential role within poetic practice, theological and devotional discourse, liturgical performance, pedagogical transmission, and visual culture throughout the medieval era. A materialist focus upon the musical body will give us new purchase on those social formations in which musical experience figured so prominently in the past.

At the same time, this book adds an earlier chapter to what some have termed the "new musicology." Those readers working in other fields will probably be unfamiliar with the polemical wars that have preoccupied major parts of this discipline in recent years. The introduction of critical theories of gender, sexuality, power, and the body into the study of Western art-music traditions has encountered fierce resistance from certain quarters, though it seems clear that the field is continuing to undergo a paradigm shift of unprecedented proportions.[5] Though this study seeks to extend many of the new musicology's findings, it does so not by applying its diverse methods and conclusions to another era, but rather by exploring certain dimensions of medieval musical life that have been largely obscured by its privileging of more recent musical epistemes. Questions of gender and sexuality aside, certain of the interdisciplinary and historicist perspectives touted as "new" in critical musicology these days—a refusal to accept "music's autonomy from society and culture," a rigorous questioning of the assumption that "music and language lie on different sides of an epistemological divide"—have long been working assumptions among medieval musicologists.[6] Indeed, as Jeffrey Hamburger has pointed out with regard to the field of art history, medievalists have always been devoted in some way to excavating what we now proudly like to call "interdisciplinary" histories.[7] Surely no medievalist would suggest that liturgical plainchant, for example, can be comprehensibly separated from its specific social, performative, and institutional contexts. Yet the Middle Ages continues to serve practitioners of the new critical musicology as a kind of metaphorical scapegoat; thus for some scholars, an "academic priesthood" resists methodological innovation; for another, postmodernist musicology has been "taking 'classical' music out of its cloister" as it "chafes at the scholastic isolation of music" by its disciplinary forebears.[8] The priesthood, the cloister, scholasticism: these are just a few of the institutions populating an era in which experiences of "music" and "society" converged centuries before the advent of Absolute Music compelled anyone to think of separating them. It is the embodied materiality of these experiences that the following chapters seek to recover.

Medieval Musical Cultures and Practices of the Flesh

Midway through the anonymous *Scholica enchiriadis*, a late ninth-century handbook devoted to the instruction of liturgical singers in the theory and practice of sacred music, the author makes the following claim about the nature of musical experience:

> Music is entirely formed and fashioned after the image of numbers. And thus it is number, by means of fixed and established proportions of notes, that brings about whatever is pleasing to the ear in singing. Whatever pleasure rhythms yield, whether in song or in rhythmic movements of whatever sort, all is the work of number. Notes pass away quickly; numbers, however, though stained by the corporeal matter of voices and moving things [*corporea vocum et motuum materia decolorantur*], remain.[9]

Adducing number and number alone as the basis for musical form, fashion, meaning, even pleasure, the author spurns the *materia corporea* of pitches, the bodily stuff that "stains" the eternal geometry undergirding heaven and earth when music sounds in human ears.

Though the *Scholica enchiriadis* makes its case with particular force, such assumptions about the tendency of the flesh to corrode the incorporeal purity of *musica* abound in early Christian and medieval writings on the subject, many of them influenced by the ancient Pythagorean notion of the numerical harmony of the universe as expounded in Plato's *Timaeus*. For

Plato, audible or sounding music was bestowed upon humans "for the sake of harmony" or concord (in the fourth-century Latin of Calcidius, "propter harmoniam tributum").[10] *Harmonia* in turn, Plato contends, was originally intended by the Muses as a rationalizing alternative to Bacchic hedonism, "as an auxiliary to the inner revolution of the Soul, when it has lost its harmony, to assist in restoring it to order and concord with itself" (47D). The harmony of the individual soul imitates the harmony of the "world soul," Plato's term for the indivisible moving force that suffuses and orders the universe. Melody, rhythm, poetry, dance, dramatic gesture: all are subsumed under the Greek *mousikē*, the holistic musical discipline that regulates the human soul but, when manifested in the body, achieves only a pale and ephemeral imitation of celestial order; in Plato's words, "by imitation of the absolutely unvarying revolutions of God we might stabilize the variable revolutions within ourselves."[11]

A long tradition of scholarship—produced by philologists, musicologists, and historians of literature, art, and aesthetics—has demonstrated the extraordinary variety of ways in which the intellectual perspectives of platonist Pythagoreanism were absorbed into the musical life and thought of the Middle Ages. In his classic study of *Stimmung* and "world harmony," Leo Spitzer contended that the speculative notion of the music of the spheres— taken to signify "the totality of the world" and the harmonious coexistence of its inhabitants—was "ever present to the mind of the Middle Ages" as an ideal to which practical music could only aspire.[12] Musicologists have shown that the period's surviving repertories often exhibit an obsessive investment in the beauty of number; thus, Margaret Bent interprets a Machaut motet as an example of "sounding number," while Pozzi Escott discerns a "hidden geometry" beneath the plainchant of Hildegard of Bingen.[13] From Augustine's assertion that music is the *scientia bene modulandi* to Marchetto of Padua's delight in the "tree of music" whose "branches are beautifully proportioned through numbers," the medieval epoch possessed an aesthetic tradition that moved many theorists, composers, and poets to locate the beauty of music and musical experience in number.[14]

Not all twentieth-century scholars have been comfortable with such assumptions about medieval musical aesthetics, however. The abiding influence of Pythagorean number theory upon the writing of the musical history of the Middle Ages has been the subject of a thorough critique by Christopher Page, who shows how often modern scholars have allowed their own predetermined notions about medieval cosmology to guide their interpretations of the cultural productions of the era's listeners and composers. An active performer and recorder of early music himself, Page writes with the conviction that such "counter-intuitive" approaches to musical meaning and pleasure in the Middle Ages have obscured aspects of medieval musical experience that cannot be accounted for in Pythagorean terms.[15] Leo Treitler has similarly argued that many such number-based interpretations of medieval music defy "common sense," and that those who advocate them have misread or misapplied the very speculative writings they have brought into their analyses.[16]

This ongoing debate clearly has far-reaching implications for our understanding of the relationship between musical theory and musical practice in the Middle Ages. Here, however, I am less interested in the relative accuracy of modern claims about medieval musical aesthetics than I am in the philosophical inconsistency at the heart of the platonist-Pythagorean musical cosmology itself, whether as reiterated by medieval writers or located in the medieval past by contemporary scholarship. And the most revealing of these contradictions lies in the tradition's steadfast refusal to account convincingly for the material foundation upon which its entire musical ontology rests: the human body. As the passage from the *Scholica enchiriadis* demonstrates, the platonist worldview adumbrated by Boethius and reiterated so often in medieval musical theory demands that the body stand precisely for the material remainder, for that which "stains" and thus can never be fully assimilated to the universal order inherent in celestial *harmonia*. When number is assumed in contemporary scholarship to be the basis of medieval musical experience and pleasure, a similar devaluation of corporeality is often the result. A paradigmatic example can be found in the work of John Stevens, who has written perhaps the most sensitive and convincing account of the aesthetics of number as it informs the basic contours of medieval music and literature. For Stevens, the relationship between words and music in medieval monophony was fundamentally arithmetical in nature: "Behind both words and notes lies 'number,' a numerical Idea waiting to be incarnated; we may come to regard this as the only common term between the verse and the melody."[17] As if paraphrasing the platonizing author of the *Scholica enchiriadis*, Stevens conceives musical "truth" as somehow prior to or beyond the body; "waiting to be incarnated," the musical Idea is protected a priori from the instability of the flesh. Thus, even as Stevens contends that an incorporeal "numerical Idea" undergirds the medieval relationship between words and music, his operative metaphor implies that it is only when this Idea is finally "incarnated"— when words and music converge in the flesh—that the relationship he posits can ever be fully realized.

The more intriguing problem, then, is not that the platonist-Pythagorean worldview necessarily "despises" or spurns the body in its aesthetic privileging of number (as we shall see in Chapter 1, this, too, may be something of an overstatement); rather, it is that those who propound it so often return to the very flesh they purportedly transcend. Even some of the most numerically obsessed medieval discussions of musical meaning and pleasure seem much more anxious and unsettled about the status of the body than do the platonic and neoplatonic works that influenced them. Perhaps this should not surprise us. After all, these writings were produced within a religious culture whose most distinctive theological tenet was its belief that God took on human flesh. How could a sublimating musical flight into disembodied number possibly represent a philosophical or experiential ideal? A useful way of imagining the relationship between classical music theory and medieval musical culture might be to envision their interaction as a kind of intellectual and theological plate tectonics, by which a dualist platonism hostile to the material world collides with an incarnational theology forced to account for the musical behaviors, pleasures, and desires of all-too-human bodies.

Nowhere are these tensions more apparent than in the legend of Pythagoras himself as the Middle Ages received it. In one of its most popular early medieval versions, recorded in the second book of Macrobius's *Commentary on the Dream of Scipio*, the story of Pythagoras's discovery of the rules of musical proportion follows a lengthy explication and defense of platonist cosmology. In book one, Macrobius aligns himself with a neoplatonic tradition that held to the idea of two deaths, agreeing that "the creature dies when the soul leaves the body, but . . . the soul itself dies when it leaves the single and individual source of its origin and is allotted to a mortal body." In Macrobius's vision of body as a site of corruption and death, a "creature" can exist only when "a soul is confined in the body," an idea he defends etymologically: "the Greek words for body are *demas*, that is a 'bond,' and *soma*, a *sema*, as it were, being a 'tomb' of the soul."[18] The soul expresses its natural desire to escape from the body by meditating on the celestial *harmonia* that cannot be heard by mortals because they are imprisoned in the flesh, which in turn knows the music of the spheres only as a distant memory: "for the soul carries with it into the body a memory of the music which it knew in the sky."[19] With these assumptions in mind, Macrobius turns, in a much-cited passage at the opening of book two, to the story of their initial musical realization by Pythagoras:

> He happened to pass the open shop of some blacksmiths who were beating a hot iron with hammers. The sound of the hammers striking in alternate and regular succession fell upon his ears with the higher note so attuned to the lower that each time the same musical interval returned, and always striking a concord. Here Pythagoras, seeing that his opportunity had been presented to him, ascertained with his eyes and hands what he had been searching for in his mind [*deprehendit oculis et manibus quod olim cogitatione quaerebat*]. He approached the smiths and stood over their work, carefully heeding the sounds that came forth from the blows of each. Thinking that the difference might be ascribed to the strength of the smiths he requested them to change hammers. Hereupon the difference in tones did not stay with the men but followed the hammers. Then he turned his whole attention to the study of their weights, and when he had recorded the difference in the weight of each, he had other hammers heavier or lighter than these made. Blows from these produced sounds that were not at all like those of the original hammers, and besides they did not harmonize. He then concluded that harmony of tones was produced according to a proportion of the weights, and made a record of all the numerical relations of the various weights producing harmony.[20]

This discovery allowed Pythagoras to elaborate his entire musical system and establish once and for all the proportions that regulate the universe: the same numbers, Macrobius observes, that Plato, "guided by Pythagoras' revelation," "constructed his World-Soul by interweaving . . . , imitating the ineffable wisdom of the divine Creator" by translating them into an incorporeal realm of geometrical harmony.[21]

Even in abstracting the music he hears into the numbers he records, however, Pythagoras depends in this account upon the testimony of his bodily senses, "ascertain[ing] with his eyes and hands what he had been searching for in his mind" by judging the muscular strength of the smiths and the actual weight of their hammers. Evidence provided by the body must be used to confirm what Macrobius presents as a purely intellectual hypothesis. And in the most revealing part of the experiment, Pythagoras follows up his serendipitous discovery by testing its validity on other, more fleshly materials: "Next he directed his investigation from hammers to stringed instruments, and stretched intestines of sheep or sinews of oxen [*intestina ovium vel bovum nervos*] by attaching to them weights of the same proportions as those determined by the hammers. Again the concord came forth which had been assured by his earlier well-conceived experiment, but with a sweeter tone, as we might expect from the nature of the instruments [*adiecta dulcedine quam natura fidium sonora praestabat*]."[22] Despite the overwhelmingly antisomatic message of the *Commentary*—the platonizing ideology that would cast the body as the "tomb," the "prison," the "first death" of the soul—Macrobius's aside contains a qualitative judgment about musical sonority based on what he assumes to be common knowledge: strings emit a "sweeter tone" than hammers and anvils, not because of the numerical relation between weights, but because they are fleshly instruments, constructed from the distended viscera of animals, the intestines and sinews of sheep and oxen that resonate whenever a stringed instrument is plucked or strummed.

Belying one of the fundamental tenets of his own musical cosmology, Macrobius's version of the legend of Pythagoras and the discovery of musical ratio reveals not only that musical form and harmony are primordially numerical, but also that musical sonority is unavoidably embodied. Macrobius's account further suggests that the "music of the spheres," supposedly an unquestioned dimension of medieval musical thought, was in fact a dazzlingly successful but ultimately contestable *ideology* of music, one that sought to contain the visceral force of music through endlessly reiterated numerical abstraction while relying upon the sonority of the very flesh it explicitly denigrated. Once we question the assumption that its medieval success was complete, we begin to discover that beneath the supposedly fixed and eternal platonic and Pythagorean frame resides a host of musical practices—erotic, political, violent, sometimes horrifying—rung on human bodies that cannot be assimilated to its rigid geometry.

Indeed, such musical practices of the flesh often entailed an active resistance to the kinds of moral and ethical imperatives that the cosmic *musica* seemingly demanded. In particular, music provided a means of performing, practicing, promoting, and enjoying same-sex desire that was unavailable through any other form of cultural or social expression. Medieval musical culture can offer unique but overlooked contributions to the history of sexuality in the West; it is no accident that three of the seven chapters in this volume are centrally concerned with medieval convergences of musical practice and sexual dissidence. While one scholar has recently chosen to lash out at what he envisions (unfairly, I think) as the tendency among "liberationist" scholars of premodern sexualities "to show that everything is about sex, same-sex sex in particular, especially when it claims to be about something else,"[23] medieval writers themselves continually confronted the fact that "sex" was both nowhere and everywhere in the musical cultures of the period, particularly in the religious cultures that are the primary object of this study. Whether or not we accept the Foucauldian premise that the delineation of "sex" and "sexuality" as discrete categories was a postmedieval phenomenon, it is surely the case that music, that *other* utterly confused category, has often served—then and now—to effectively erase sensual and epistemological boundaries between sexual and other modes of experience in the flesh. The histories of sexuality and musicality in the West are hopelessly imbricated and at times indistinguishable.[24]

"Experience" and the Musical Body

As an exploration of musical sensation in the most visceral sense, this study touches on a number of questions that have preoccupied both philosophers of music and critical musicologists in recent years.[25] What is it to "experience" music? Where and how is music located vis-à-vis the persons who listen and react to it? How do we approach music as a sensual, passionate, and emotional medium, and how might we account for its widely varied effects on and interactions with human bodies?

These are ancient questions, of course, and they can be traced back to the most influential treatments of music in the Western tradition, perhaps most famously Plato's extended excursus on musical mode and emotion in the *Republic*. For the Middle Ages, as we have just seen, musical experience has often been cast as a rationalized communion with the *musica mundana* through number.[26] Thus, as recently as 1991 we read that for medieval people "music worked by cosmic principles and was inherent in the perfectly harmonious movement of the heavenly bodies . . . mimetic and expressive properties were not commonly attributed to music. It was only in the Renaissance that music generally was seen as directly representing ideas and embodying emotion."[27] But if we discard this cherished notion that medieval people believed they absorbed and enjoyed music by a kind of harmonic convergence with the numerical order of the spheres, we are still faced with the difficult task of accounting for the embodied musical experiences of another culture. In other words, like the Pythagorean view of medieval musical cosmology, the Pythagorean view of medieval musical experience must be met head-on rather than dismissed as a defiance of twentieth-century intuition or common sense.

One of the guiding premises of this book is that any account of the emotional and affective dimensions of musical experience in the Middle Ages will be incomplete if it assumes that music is necessarily an extra-personal phenomenon that produces its psychic, somatic, and emotional effects only when it comes into contact with autonomous listeners or performers—in other words, if it assumes that "music" exists somehow outside of or apart from human persons themselves. Yet such an assumption is axiomatic in practically all contemporary philosophies of musical meaning and expression, most of which maintain an avowedly asomatic stance on musical emotion, sensation, and response. A recent treatise on music and the "passions" defines passions as "mental states," consigns music's relationship with the body to the study of physiology, and thoroughly elides the etymological roots and christological resononances of the term.[28] Similarly, in Peter Kivy's "cognitivist" theories of musical emotion and representation, our minds are required to intellectually "recognize" the emotive content in music before our embodied emotions will allow us to respond.[29] In the most general terms, the idea that music is something beyond or external to the human being sounds entirely uncontroversial. Of course the music that we hear and experience exists outside of us. How could we possibly conceive of it otherwise? When we listen to music, we do so because it has entered our bodies from outside; we may react to it by tapping a foot, dancing, or weeping, true, but music produces these bodily effects only *after* it has reached our senses from somewhere else. Human individuals, according to a recent attempt to theorize music's effects upon the body, "remain relatively autonomous in relation to the musical sounds that they utter and internalize."[30]

This is only one way of imagining the relationship between musical sonority and the human person, however, and it may be a comparatively recent one. In arguing against it repeatedly and in detail, this book proposes instead what we might call a "musicology in the flesh," a phrase I have adapted from the title of George Lakoff and Mark Johnson's study of the "embodied mind" and its implications for traditional philosophy of mind. Drawing on some of the most important recent developments in cognitive science, Lakoff (a linguist) and Johnson (a philosopher) argue that all conceptual systems, philosophical or otherwise, are both grounded in and shaped by sensory and motor systems, and thus that concepts can be formed only through and within the body. Moreover, as they suggest in a crucial extension of their well-known work in *Metaphors We Live By*, thought is shaped fundamentally by "conceptual metaphor," the "primary metaphors" that neurally "link our subjective experiences and judgments to our sensorimotor experience."[31] In other words, metaphorical language is rooted in the body and tempered and constrained by lived, corporeal experience; and metaphors in turn *actively shape bodily experience and thought,* enlisting sensorimotor inference and allowing us to construct abstract concepts (such as a philosophy of music, for example) out of experiences in the flesh.

The conclusions reached by Lakoff and Johnson regarding the embodiedness of mind, reason, and metaphor are well suited for an inquiry into the musical life of the Middle Ages, a period in which the sonorities of skin, gut, sex, and pain assumed what I argue was a central metaphorical role in even the most rationalistic attempts to account for the nature of musical life. Medieval accounts of embodied musical response pose a direct and powerful challenge to "externalist" theories of the nature and phenomenology of musical sonority. For many early Christian and medieval writers on musical experience, *musica* exists within the human body as an internal *materia* actualized when the body experiences extreme forms of pain, desire, or religious ecstasy. And despite its resolutely anticorporeal ontology, it was the platonist-Pythagorean tradition that afforded Latin Christendom the most influential models for the internal music of the human person: in platonic terms, the "tempering" of the human being that regulated the pulse, the emotions, even the development of the fetus. Like reason itself, the rationalizations of musical philosophy are "shaped crucially by the peculiarities of our human bodies, by the remarkable details of the neural structure of our brains, and by the specifics of our everyday functioning in the world."[32]

One of the primary channels of transmission through which the Middle Ages learned of the musicality of person was by way of Boethius's influential formulation of *musica humana,* or "human music." As Boethius points out in book one of the *De institutione musica,* Plato had asserted that the human being is regulated through numerical order, an idea that formed the basis for Boethius's own meditation on the microcosmic *harmonia* of the human being: "What Plato rightfully said can likewise be understood: the soul of the universe was joined together according to musical concord [*musica convenientia*]. For when we hear what is properly and harmoniously united in sound in conjunction with that which is harmoniously coupled and joined together within us and are attracted to it, then we recognize that we ourselves are put together in its likeness."[33] The concord "coupled and joined together" within the human frame represents the second of Boethius's divisions of *musica* into its celestial, human, and instrumental varieties:

> Humanam vero musicam quisquis in sese ipsum descendit intellegit. Quid est enim quod illam incorpoream rationis vivacitatem corpori misceat, nisi quaedam coaptatio et veluti gravium leviumque vocum quasi unam consonantiam efficiens temperatio? Quid est aliud quod ipsius inter se partes animae coniungat, quae, ut Aristoteli placet, ex rationabili inrationabilique coniuncta est? Quid vero, quod corporis elementa permiscet, aut partes sibimet rata coaptatione contineat? Sed de hac quoque posterius dicam.
>
> [Whoever penetrates into his own self perceives human music. For what unites the incorporeal nature of reason with the body if not a certain harmony and, as it were, a careful tuning of low and high pitches as though producing one consonance? What other than this unites the parts of the soul, which, according to Aristotle, is composed of the rational and the irrational? What is it that intermingles the elements of the body or holds together the parts of the body in an established order? I shall also speak about these things later.][34]

Though apparently he never did. Either Boethius did not extend his theory of *musica humana* or this promised section of the *De institutione musica* did not survive (though it is fascinating to imagine what the subsequent history of musical thought would look like if it had).[35] Nevertheless, Boethius clearly postulated human music as an unheard but ever-present characteristic of the human being. For him as for many of the medieval writers he influenced, *musica humana* was subordinate to and imitative of *musica mundana*, the celestial harmonies that located human beings within the cosmos and regulated them, body and soul, through their arithmetical stability.

Yet—and this is a crucial point—when medieval writers do invoke something resembling Boethius's "human music" to interpret or describe a given musical event, they often insist that the *body* they are describing, *not* the soul, produces actual sounding music, rhythms and melodies that naturally reside in bones, flesh, skin, organs, throats. If we take *musica humana* as a valid analytical category for understanding medieval musical experience, we must recognize how often individual writers, composers, and performers resist the totalizing platonist cosmology that produced it, in which the soul is the bearer of the numerical *harmonia* that keeps the human person tuned, tempered, balanced—in Boethius's words, the music that "holds together the parts of the body in an established order"—and certainly free of the frenzied and eroticized musical performances that so often appear in medieval representations. As oxymoronic as such a project might seem, then, I hope to recover a somewhat irreverent and resolutely *anti*platonizing account of the musical person, an alternative history of the harmonious human being described in Edgar de Bruyne's classic *Etudes d'esthétique médiévale* as the intellective result of a "conscious intervention of the mind in nature."[36] When Alan of Lille draws his creative analogy between sodomitical couplings and polyphonic harmonies (an instance that will provide the starting point for Chapter 4), he does so with the implicit recognition that *musica humana* can constitute a mode of bodily performance subjected only rarely to the phobic constraints of Lady Nature.

For "human music" is rivaled only by the music of the spheres as the most baffling and counterintuitive component of premodern musical thought—even to some premoderns themselves. Writing around 1300 in Paris, Johannes Grocheio reacted to the claims of Pythagoreanism with a skeptical incredulity: "Celestial bodies in movement do not make a sound, although the ancients may have thought otherwise. . . . Nor also is sound innate in the human constitution. Who has heard a constitution sounding?"[37] As Page points out, Grocheio has misconstrued the Pythagoreans: "Boethius does not say that the human constitution has audible sound located within it."[38] For Boethius, in fact, the essential thing about both *musica humana* and *musica mundana* is that we mortals *cannot* hear them.

But Grocheio wrote his *De musica* during the very decade in which Gertrude of Helfta was saluted by a "melodious harmony" emerging from one of the four gaping "wounds" in the body of Christ, a harmony that was "greatly enriched by passing through the divine heart."[39] Whatever philosophical complexity Boethius may have condensed into the phrase, *musica humana* for this medieval nun and visionary had a visceral reality that the practical empiricism of a Grocheio may not have been able to encompass. Yet perhaps Gertrude's sense of the body's musicality is not so very different from that of, say, Hugh of St. Victor, another Parisian intellectual writing over a century before Grocheio. For Hugh, "the music of the human body . . . is composed of the number nine. For there are nine orifices in the human body through which everything whereby that same body is animated and controlled flows in or out according to the natural temperament."[40] Musical wounds, hearts, and orifices: in these resides the human side of human music.

From Work to Sonority

Any study seeking to account for the social dimensions of medieval musical life must reckon in some way with a much-discussed epistemological quandary in the study of Western art music: the status of the musical work. The "work-concept" has been described by Lydia Goehr as the essential component of a Romantic ideology that has kept much musical analysis since the nineteenth century focused on the so-called music itself as the privileged object of study.[41] As Treitler has pointed out, the work-concept has resulted in a number of enduring misunderstandings of medieval notational, performance, mnemonic, and codicological practices by scholars who have been guided by relatively recent notions of the integrity and specificity of the musical artifact.[42] In a similar vein, Gary Tomlinson argues that the aim of revisionist musical scholarship should not be to contextualize surviving pieces of music and the notes they contain, but rather to "recognize the myriad situations we as historians might construct around a musical utterance and the plurality of meanings the music might thus engage."[43] Medievalists in particular are faced with basic terminological difficulties that render the proper "object" of music-historical inquiry even more difficult to specify. To take a notable example, there is a basic lack of clarity surrounding the medieval divide between practical and speculative music—between performed *cantus* (defined by Treitler and Ritva Jonsson as "music sung with words"[44]) and instrumental music, on the one hand, and *musica*, or unheard, idealized order (the *harmonia* inherited from the Pythagoreans) on the other; Boethian distinctions between the hack *cantor* and the enlightened *musicus* often function as no more than tropes in the later works on music theory that transmit them.[45]

Nevertheless, many of the medieval theoretical treatises that have guided editors in their recovery and interpretation of the surviving notated music that we commonly call "musical works" provide invaluable clues as to the complicated relationship between practical and speculative music. The musics such treatises explicate are never autonomous and self-contained aesthetic objects; rather, they are components of a thoroughly embodied musicality that integrates theory, manuscript, performer, and listener into a cultural practice invested in the experiencing of sonority. When the author of the *Ad organum faciendum* handbook compares a certain variety of "unnatural" polyphony to a human cadaver, we should not dismiss his analogy as a quaint curiosity, but take it seriously as a revealing commentary on the anthropomorphic nature of the harmonies his treatise describes. When Notker explains the letters accompanying the notation of chant from St. Gall by describing the various sorts of teeth-gnashing, throat-gargling, mouth-shaping, and note-shaving noises monks should make when singing them, he is instructing his readers—medieval and contemporary—in the effective deployment of the body in chant.[46] And when Guido of Arezzo boasts that his new method for teaching plainchant to choirboys will relieve musical *magistri* of the need to beat their students for failing to learn melodies quickly, he opens a window onto a violent pedagogical tradition that would eventually lead a fourteenth-century poet to bemoan the disciplinary wrath of his teacher by satirizing the scene of liturgical transmission as an elaborate pedagogical psychomachia. Even those medieval theoretical texts that propound the most abstract theories of musical form and meaning often betray their authors' sense of music's corporeal nature, and in so doing suggest how we in turn might locate the music they describe and transmit within the medieval genealogy of the flesh. Shifting our focus from "work" to "sonority" may thus prove as fruitful in a methodological sense as it is rigorous in a philosophical sense.

The musical body offers as well a useful perspective upon medieval notions of the relationship between music and language, a particularly formidable stumbling block for those who would apply the work-concept to the musical production of the Middle Ages. The topic of music-language relations has inspired massive scholarly production over the last twenty years, including treatments of words and music in troubadour song, studies of the interplay of sacred and profane poetics in the polytextual motet, theories about orality and the development of musical notation, and an important study of the disciplinary affiliation between music and grammar.[47] As is well known, many poets puzzled over the inseparability of poetry from its musical vehicle—in the words of Eustache Deschamps, "natural music," the internal rhythms of prosody that he regarded as superior to the mundane strains of sounding music.[48] Some of the very best scholarship on medieval literature and music recognizes that the two mediums are sometimes indistinguishable: the "musical work," if it exists at all, is very often a musico-literary work.[49]

Nevertheless, the writers treated here most often cast the human body as the site at which music and language diverge. Whether in Augustine's account of the melismatic ecstasies of the *jubilus*, Thomas of Cantimpré's description of the somatic *cantus* of Christina the Astonishing, or even Guillaume de Machaut's poetic comparison of his lady's *gent corps* to the "twenty-five strings that a harp has" (De .xxv. cordes que la harpe a),[50] writers often bemoan the inadequacy of words while celebrating the mystical ability of music to convey the extremes of experience in the flesh. While such examples certainly reflect the Christian notion of human language as a fallen representational medium, they also reveal a widespread tendency among medieval writers to attribute a kind of somatic and extralinguistic immediacy to musical sonority. The music of body becomes the music most completely divorced from the language, literature, and linguistic ways of knowing that seek to describe and contain it.

The series of broad philosophical and theoretical issues outlined above necessitates an eclectic and methodologically flexible approach to the medieval history of musical embodiment. In the chapters that follow, I have tried to find ways of combining and sometimes questioning the disciplinary perspectives afforded by literary criticism and musicology (the two fields in which this study is primarily located) upon the materials under consideration. Yet interdisciplinary scholarship can always benefit from an attention to the methodological *specificity* of the contemporary disciplines in their widely varying approaches to evidence and their distinct critical stances toward the past. Medieval musicology has important lessons to teach medievalists in other disciplines, in particular the literary practitioners of the "new philology." The renewed emphasis on manuscript studies that characterizes a number of recent books in Middle English studies, for example, demonstrates how an attention to the relationship between manuscript and performance, the transition from orality to literacy, and the materiality of the book can transform the way we think about the production, transmission, and very nature of the texts we study. But these issues have been topics of heated discussion for decades among medieval musicologists, some of whom have proposed compelling solutions to certain questions at the center of current literary-historical debate.[51]

At the same time, musicology has much to learn from literary criticism. A historical musicologist approaching the Latin poetry of Leoninus might be concerned primarily with the empirical information it yields about the composer's biography and the institutional context in which his compositions were performed. But when these writings are approached specifically *as poetry* and with attention to issues of concern to a literary critic—the play of language, intertextuality, generic convention, and so on—Leoninus's writings tell a very different story about himself and his cultural milieu, showing us a composer and poet exploiting the homoerotic potentials of Ovidian love poetry while producing music within a culture at best ambivalent regarding the expression of same-sex desire. Both approaches are valid, but each addresses a distinctive set of questions about the social and historical context that gave rise to Notre Dame polyphony (and, of course, each delimits what counts as "context" in its own particular way). Literary readings of medieval writings on music—an attention to "those moments of intensified intertextuality" in works traditionally viewed as of purely musicological interest[52]—can furnish new perspectives on their social and cultural resonance. The fact that the writings of Cicero and Quintilian on rhetorical *actio* or delivery may have inspired early Christian allegoresis of musical imagery in the Bible shows how a seeming exegetical convention can illuminate the musical performativity of the body in late antiquity (see Chapter 1). A previously unrecognized allusion to Alan of Lille's *De planctu Naturae* in a late-fourteenth-century treatise on polyphony suggests that the anxieties of its author may have been focused as much on sexual dissidence as on musical excess (Chapter 4).

Such an interdisciplinary perspective similarly informs my approach to visual materials, including sculptures, paintings, and a number of illuminations, illustrations, and drawings found in manuscripts of exegetical, liturgical, typological, and visionary writings. Some of these images could well be used (as indeed several have been) as empirical evidence about organology, performance practice, the iconographical significance of musical symbols, or the dating of manuscripts—important tasks all. Drawing on the work of art historians such as Michael Camille and Jeffrey Hamburger, however, I turn to visual materials primarily for the specific light they shed on the medieval reader's musico-somatic relation to images and to the book, asking how musical sonority created unique opportunities for participation in the experiential aspects of medieval visual culture.

It was only when completing this project that I realized how much I left out that could or should have been included. The historical range of the topic demanded selectiveness from the very beginning, and I am aware that there are entire poetic and musical repertories at whose expense others are included. The book is heavily weighted toward the musical body as it figures in religious discourse and ecclesiastical contexts—liturgy, theology, hagiography, miracle story, visionary text, and so on; even in the final two chapters, which are concerned primarily with vernacular writings, the main texts considered are a Middle English religious tale and a French mythographical treatise. This focus on religious practice bespeaks the wider cultural transformations that initially gave rise to the musical bodies of the medieval era. As we shall see, it was the patristic theologians of late antiquity who first transformed the musical speculation of the classical world into the incarnational music of Christianity, and the musical body continues to represent both a central problem and a profound opportunity for the religious cultures of the Middle Ages.

Nevertheless, the findings presented here may have important bearing on current approaches to more overtly secular texts and contexts, perhaps most obviously in the contentious field of vernacular orality and oral performance. In her study of subjectivity in troubadour poetry, Sarah Kay joins

Walter Ong, Paul Zumthor, and others in arguing for the importance of the material context of performance and the "non-linguistic manifestations of presence" to the social meaning of medieval lyric. "The song is less a text than an act that associates the performer with his audience," she suggests, an act centered around the "gesturing, singing body of the performer."[53] Perhaps the singing body of the troubadour represents a secularized instantiation of underlying cultural assumptions about the *inherently* resonant devotional body of the sort studied here.

My focus on the musical body in religious culture could be extended as well to other political dimensions of musical embodiment. Issues of social class and the musical body converge in representations of the grotesqued bagpiping bodies of peasants that D. W. Robertson found in the margins of so many religious manuscripts. Such images have often been interpreted in exegetical readings as mere *in malo* inversions of the "New Song," though they are clearly part of the same historical trajectory that includes seventeenth-century Flemish paintings depicting the peasant bagpipe as a sonorous signifier of social difference, which is very often registered in hierarchized images of dance.[54] Dance is one of the clearest medieval sites at which music and body come together; though I do not treat it at any length here, it constitutes an obvious exception to platonic attempts to restrict musical pleasure to the nonbodily. Indeed, many of the representations of music and bodily movement treated below speak to what we might call the musical predispositions of the body that are actualized in dance. Just as the music of the spheres bears an intimate relation to the dance of death,[55] Peter Chrysologus's vision of the resonant Magdalene dancing for the Pharisees or Thomas of Cantimpré's panegyric to the whirling musical body of Christina the Astonishing reveal within the history of dance an underlying will to exploit the sonorous potential of the human body.

This book is organized into four main parts. Part 1, "Backgrounds: Musical Embodiments in Christian Late Antiquity," provides an overview of the relationship between music and corporeality in early Christian writings. Beginning in Chapter 1 with a broad overview of works by Clement of Alexandria, Ambrose, Gregory of Nyssa, and others, I argue for a reevaluation of the classical legacy to Christian musical speculation by showing important affinities between Stoic naturalism and patristic musical materialism, between the delivering body in Roman rhetorical writings and the musical body postulated in Christian biblical hermeneutics. Other parts of the chapter examine the deployment of music in Greek philosophical anthropology and in Latin writings on martyrdom, bodily miracle, torture, and death. The second chapter concentrates in more detail on the writings of Augustine, whose insistent disavowal of music's corporeality in the *De musica* and his other early neoplatonic treatises yields in the later works to surprisingly materialist constructions of music's role in the creation, vivification, and resurrection of human bodies—culminating in a kind of "musical autopsy" near the end of the *City of God*. The materials treated throughout Part 1 provide a background for the rest of the book by showing that the legacy of patristic theology to the musical cultures of the Middle Ages was a musical worldview not uniformly hostile to the body, but rather deeply aware of the musicality of human flesh.

Part 2, "Liturgies of Desire," explores the interrelations among music, desire, and the body in two very different musical and poetic repertories of the twelfth and early thirteenth centuries. Chapter 3 examines the construction and performance of female corporeality in the music and writings of Hildegard of Bingen, the twelfth-century Benedictine abbess and Christian visionary whose works have enjoyed a major revival in medieval studies and beyond over the last decade. I consider Hildegard's constructions of sexuality and the female body in her medical writings, letters, and visionary tracts in relation to her musico-poetic images of female spirituality and devotion in the *Symphonia armonie celestium revelationum*, suggesting that some of the formal characteristics of her compositional style may embody her idiosyncratic views on female desire. The chapter focuses especially on Hildegard's Marian compositions, which raise the intriguing question of desire between women within monastic musical cultures.

The fourth chapter centers around the musical and literary culture of circa-1200 northern France and, in particular, the repertory known in musicological circles as Notre Dame polyphony. I explore the remarkable similarity in the twelfth century between polemics against musical innovation and diatribes against sodomy, both of which concern themselves with the feminization and inversion of the performing male body. The chapter includes the first extended analysis of the unpublished verse-epistles of Leoninus, the poet who has recently been identified as the same Leonin familiar to musicologists as one of the prime movers of the Notre Dame school. Situating these poems in the twelfth-century Ovidian revival, I consider their literary cultivation of male same-sex desire in relation to the musical homoerotics of polyphony. With this history in mind, a coda jumps ahead two centuries to what I call the "polyphonic perversity" of Chaucer's Pardoner, the desirous performances that highlight his rhetorical adeptness and distinguish his musical body from those around him.

Part 3, "Sounds of Suffering," excavates the role of bodily pain and violence in medieval musical cultures. In Chapter 5, "The Musical Body in Pain," I treat a variety of thirteenth-century Latin religious writings that speak to an enduring Christian preoccupation with the musicality of suffering. After a broadly based consideration of the violent role of music in medieval representations of ascetic practice and the Passion, I concentrate on the hagiographical writings of a Dominican friar in the Low Countries, a devotional poem by an English Franciscan and future archbishop of Canterbury, and the writings of two German nuns and visionaries. The chapter also treats a number of visual images in which devotional experiences of musicality and visuality coexist in often spectacular ways.

Chapter 6 is similarly concerned with music and violence, though it considers in more depth a specific cultural arena in which the two converged: namely, the disciplinary practice of liturgical pedagogy. I examine both negative and positive images of corporal punishment and other forms of violence in a number of Latin and vernacular writings, including saints' lives, pedagogical treatises, and a little-studied Middle English satire on the learning and performance of liturgical chant. Musical pedagogy and bodily violence meet in a particularly gruesome way in Chaucer's Prioress's Tale, the focus of the chapter. Here, in the poet's most musical tale, the vivified corpse of a "litel clergeon" sings an antiphon to the Virgin Mary even as his "throte is kut unto [the] nekke boon"; at the same time, however, Chaucer seeks to efface all suggestion of bodily violence from the narrative of the clergeon's musical learning.

Part 4, "Resoundings," explores the role of embodiment in the medieval and contemporary recovery of the musical past. Chapter 7, "Orpheus in Parts," excavates the medieval afterlife of the musical body of the Ovidian Orpheus. Of particular interest are medieval reactions to and appropriations of Orpheus's "homoerotic turn" following the death of Eurydice: his sudden erotic preference for what Ovid calls "tender boys, in the springtime and first flower of their youth"—a preference that results in the punitive dismembering of his body at the hands of the Maenads. In the neo-Ovidian poetics of Baudri of Bourgeuil, Latin and vernacular mythographies such as Pierre Bersuire's *Ovidius moralizatus* and the anonymous *Ovide moralisé*, Dante's *Purgatorio*, and Lydgate's massive *Fall of Princes*, the fragmented musical body of Orpheus is continually re-membered and reinvented, whether as a classicizing trope for homoerotic desire, a soteriological and sacramental version of the human subject, or a negative exemplum warning a Lancastrian duke of the perils of heterosexual marriage. A concluding epilogue proposes a musicology of empathy as a means of "hearing" musical bodies and confronting the many challenges they pose to our own reconstructions of the medieval past.

PART I

Backgrounds: Musical Embodiments
in Christian Late Antiquity

CHAPTER I

The Resonance of the Flesh

he inclusion of a background section focusing on early Christian culture in a book concerned primarily with the high and later Middle Ages carries certain risks, the first and most obvious of which is that of oversight and exclusion. While Part 1 will take us up to the years immediately preceding the death of Augustine in 430 C.E., Part 2 begins in the middle of the twelfth century with the visions, music, and letters of Hildegard of Bingen. The seven intervening centuries surely have much to teach us about music and embodiment, and the succeeding chapters can only glance at some of the personages and writings that would be crucial to a more complete history of the problem. One thinks of the quasi-Boethian representation of *musica humana* in Hrotsvit of Gandersheim's play *Pafnutius*—the concords "in the pulse of our veins and in the measures of our limbs, as in the parts of our fingers [*in pulsibus venarum adque in quorundam mensura menbrorum, sicut in articulus digitorum*], where we find the same mathematical proportions of measure as [exist] in harmonies"—and its ethico-pedagogical role in taming the carnal desires of the prostitute Thais.[1] These centuries embrace as well the great transitional encyclopedists and compilers such as Isidore of Seville, whose delighted musings on the panoply of musical sounds and instruments will be discussed in the epilogue; Cassiodorus, whose neo-Ovidian rendering of the Crucifixion as a flesh-strumming spectacle figures briefly in the present chapter; and that great collector of allegorical arcana, Rhabanus Maurus, who served as a crucial conveyor of somatic harps, drums, and trumpets to later exegetes and commentators. The start-up of musical notation—the study of which has produced one of the most controversial subfields in medieval musicol-

ogy—also created new ways of envisioning and practicing music's corporeality; an Italian monk named Guido of Arezzo has long been credited
(perhaps unjustly) with first deploying the hand as a mnemonic device
densely inscribed with musical notation.

A second risk entailed by beginning this study in the early Christian
period is less obvious but equally daunting. Scholars of medieval literary
history—particularly American medievalists specializing in Chaucer and
Middle English—have spent almost forty years now accounting for the
powerful legacy of D. W. Robertson Jr. and his so-called Exegetical approach to the study of medieval literature and aesthetics. While the turn
to theory in medieval literary studies brought with it a final break from
Robertsonianism some time ago, it has also had the regrettable consequence
of turning a generation of medievalists away from a vast array of Greek and
Latin writings that are still viewed by many as a reactionary albatross on the
back of the Middle Ages. With some important exceptions, historicist studies of medieval literature tend to avoid serious engagement with patristic
theology, settling for easy generalizations about early Christian culture that
the sources do not bear out. One of the purposes of the present chapter is to
revisit some of the very texts that led Robertson to his conclusions. This is
an unavoidable task, for one of the central metaphors in *A Preface to Chaucer* for the medieval doctrine of charity was the "New Song," a spiritual
harmony that symbolized what Robertson saw as the ubiquitous medieval
aspiration to transcend the flesh. It should be a truism by now that the
patristic legacy to the Middle Ages was not monolithic, but rather diverse
and contested. While the project of this book is not doctrinally Exegetical,
many of its most important sources are inevitably exegetical.

The two chapters in Part 1 piece together from selected Christian writings of late antiquity what I believe is a new story about patristic musical
cosmology and its influence upon the musical cultures of the Western
Middle Ages. For some of the most influential writers of the early Church,
the music of body provides constant fodder for theological speculation,
anxiety, and pleasure. This chapter treats a number of early Christian writings in both Greek and Latin—antipagan polemics, sermons, Psalm commentaries, philosophical anthropology, among other genres—that speak to
the extent and variety of patristic fascination with the resonance of the flesh.
The early Christian inheritance of Hellenic and Roman musical specula-

tion is more complex and troubled than scholars have previously allowed; Stoic materialism, classical notions of the musical body of the orator, and pagan representations of musical violence and torture exerted a discernible influence upon patristic and medieval constructions of musical experience. The second chapter is a briefer study of music and embodiment in the writings of Augustine, whose work has often been taken as the apogee of musical dualism. While accounting for the dualist and platonic tendencies in his early writings, I trace through the *Confessions* and some of his later works an abiding affinity for the musical *corpus.*

Patristic Christianity discovers an extraordinary variety of ways to construct the body into a performative musical agent, a sonorous yet resolutely material instrument of flesh and bone. Though two chapters cannot possibly cover all or even most patristic writings preoccupied with musical embodiment, the materials treated in Part 1 provide important theological background for the medieval composers, artists, and writers considered in subsequent chapters. At the same time, Part 1 presents what I hope is a convincing argument in its own right for questioning the received wisdom about the nature of musical thought in the patristic and medieval eras. The stakes of such a rethinking are particularly high, for the first 1,500 years of Common Era speculation on musical sensation, meaning, and experience have been largely obliterated from the history of aesthetics. A recent case in point is Edward Lippman's *History of Western Musical Aesthetics*, a monumental work written by one of the world's foremost authorities on ancient musical thought. For Lippman, however, "aesthetics" as a field of inquiry is limited, historically and philosophically, to the five centuries since the European Renaissance, centuries during which "the autonomy and coherence of the musical work of art" become axiomatic in speculation on musical phenomena: "The field of musical aesthetics clearly depends on the conception of music as an art; this in turn is connected with the modern notion of art in general."[2] This is a legitimate and eminently defensible position apropos of the history of philosophy, and I do not mean to suggest that the Middle Ages shared the Kantian sense of the autonomy of the musical work. Far from it.

Yet in identifying the social manifestations crucial to the emergence of a properly "aesthetic" sensibility—printing, the musical artwork, the academic study of composition, the notion of musical genius, and so on—

Lippman repeats a widely held assumption that presumably justifies the mere thirteen pages he gives to the pre-Christian and medieval eras (and, perhaps, explains the omission of Edgar de Bruyne, Hermann Abert, and Herbert Schueller from his citations). It was only in the Renaissance, he contends, that we can perceive in Western musical speculation "an increasing interest in expressiveness, and a concern with the physical and sensuous nature of tonal experience rather than with the primarily mathematical comprehension of music that had prevailed previously."[3]

This book is not a history of medieval musical thought, nor does it attempt to be a philosophically responsible contribution to the history of musical aesthetics. Nevertheless, I would insist that the patristic and medieval eras did indeed possess and actively practice a musical aesthetic, and that this aesthetic cannot properly be characterized as or reduced to a "mathematical comprehension of music." To the contrary, it was a profoundly incarnational aesthetic whose adherents often found a truly musical beauty in the passions and movements of human flesh—in the "expressiveness" and the "physical and sensuous nature" of musical sounds and bodies. Patristic writers on music and musical phenomena were motivated not by an overweening desire to escape the flesh, but rather by the challenge of reconciling the pleasures of musical embodiment with the incarnational religiosity they practiced.

The present chapter thus speaks to work by Peter Brown, Caroline Walker Bynum, Elizabeth Clark, Judith Perkins, and others who have been questioning the unproblematic dualism that has often been projected onto early Christian sources.[4] Patristic and medieval theology, these scholars have shown, cannot be described as possessing "a metaphysics that abhorred embodiment," as one critic has recently characterized it.[5] While it may be true that figures such as Tertullian and Jerome sometimes associated flesh with femininity, *carnalitas* with *femina*, and that they often claimed rationality as the exclusive province of men, embodiment per se represented for most patristic theologians an existential quandary that was as often embraced as spurned. Through their musical speculations, in particular, certain of them articulated their most searching inquiries into the nature and constraints of embodiment. Within many patristic constructions of the human body, we discover that music—whether in the form of *harmonia*, *cantus*, jubilation, or allegorical invention—serves as the most compelling expression of the mysteries of incarnation itself.

Clement and the Grasshopper, or
New Songs in Old Bodies

The dawn of the third century was not an auspicious moment for the Christian citizens of Roman Alexandria. The imperial reign of Septimius Severus (193–211 C.E.) witnessed a dramatic rise in anti-Christian persecution throughout the colonies of northern Africa, resulting in the quickly notorious martyrdoms of Perpetua and Felicitas in Carthage in 202, as well as a general increase in public trials, convictions, and punishments of Christian faithful. Although historians have recently questioned the extent of Severus's own role in the instigation of this wave of religious violence, bouts of local persecution in a number of northern African communities during the second half of his reign ensured that the emperor would be remembered by later chroniclers (most famously Eusebius) as a sworn enemy of Christian expression and thought.[6] In Alexandria the catechetical school was ransacked, its library burned and scattered, and many of its members forced into exile.

Into the midst of this climate of persecution Clement of Alexandria published his most scathing antipagan polemic, the *Protreptikos,* an attack on classical life, letters, and mythology that he apparently completed shortly before fleeing the city to avoid the fates of his fellow *catechumeni.* A deft rhetorician steeped in a paganism from which he himself had converted,[7] Clement begins this treatise not with an appeal to a religious sentiment that might alienate his pagan readers, but with a string of familiar musical topoi drawn from their own mythological tradition: "Amphion of Thebes and Arion of Methymna were both minstrels, and both were renowned in story. They are celebrated in song to this day in the chorus of the Greeks; the one for having allured the fishes, and the other for having surrounded Thebes with walls by the power of music. Another, a Thracian, a cunning master of his art (he also is the subject of a Hellenic legend), tamed the wild beasts by the mere might of song, and transplanted trees—oaks—by music."[8] Despite the imminent threat to his own life and livelihood, Clement speaks with easy familiarity to his intended audience, proposing a fundamental continuity between the present-day "chorus of the Greeks," who celebrate their mythological heroes "in song," and the legendary bards themselves, who embody the animistic "power of music" to erect city walls, seduce fishes and wild beasts, and transplant trees.

As soon as he has evoked the life-giving potentiality granted to music in Greek legend, however, Clement proceeds to excoriate the whole panoply of "vain fables" kept alive by his contemporaries, fables in which "animals [are] charmed by music" and "the bright face of truth . . . is regarded with unbelieving eyes." He is particularly taken with the legend of Euno-mos and the Pythic grasshopper, in which the bard performs a mournful elegy for a slain serpent. For Clement, Eunomos's "artificial" instrumental music pales in comparison to the natural song of the grasshoppers, who "were singing not to that dead dragon, but to God All-wise—a lay unfet-tered by rule, better than the numbers of Eunomos." Suddenly, however, "the Locrian breaks a string. The grasshopper sprang on the neck of the instrument, and sang on it as on a branch. And the minstrel, adapting his strain to the grasshopper's song, made up for the want of the missing string."[9] Although according to Clement the grasshopper had been per-forming the salvific song of God before jumping onto Eunomos's lyre and singing "of its own accord," the Greeks credited the bard himself with conscripting the animal into his musical service; Clement disagrees: "al-though the Greeks thought [the grasshopper] to have been responsive to music," he confidently concludes, "it was not Eunomos that drew the grass-hopper by his song."

Clement's pro-grasshopper rendition of the Eunomos legend casts the Bacchic melodies that so titillate the "frenzied rabble" as but a pale precur-sor of the "new harmony" that inspires his own devotional life. Alluding to the enduring platonic notion of the correspondence between musical mode and human emotion, he juxtaposes the *canticum novum* of the Psalms with a musical fragment from the *Odyssey*; the typology revises and rejects the strains of pagan musicality:

> What my Eunomos sings is not the measure of Terpander, nor that of Ca-pito, nor the Phrygian, nor Lydian, nor Dorian, but the immortal measure of the new harmony which bears God's name—the new, Levitical song:
> "Soother of pain, calmer of wrath, producing forgetfulness of all ills" [*Odys-sey* 4.220]. Sweet and true is the charm of persuasion which blends with this strain.[10]

"My Eunomos": Clement defines his Christian God in direct opposition to the pagan bard he displaces, the Greek musician who was naive enough to believe that he had seduced God's musical grasshopper through his own performative prowess. Yet the power of the "new song" of Christianity sounds suspiciously like the seductive melodies of Orpheus, the "cunning Thracian" Clement has already condemned: "Behold the might of the new song! It has made men out of stones, men out of beasts. Those, moreover, that were as dead, not being partakers of the true life, have come to life again, simply by becoming listeners to this song."[11] The chapter as a whole testifies as eloquently as perhaps any other early Christian writing to Averil Cameron's recent observation that early Christian discourse "made its way in the wider world less by revolutionary novelty than by the procedure of working through the familiar, by appealing from the known to the unknown."[12]

Unlike his typological predecessor, however, Christ requires neither lyre nor harp nor even grasshopper to charm souls and animate matter. Rather, the music he produces is rung on the instrument of his humanity:

> And he who is of David, and yet before him, the Word of God, despising the lyre and harp, which are but lifeless instruments, and having tuned by the Holy Spirit the universe, and especially man—who, composed of body and soul, is a universe in miniature—sings to God on this instrument of many voices [ψάλλει τῷ Θεῷ, διὰ τοῦ πολυφώνου ὀργάνου]; and to this instrument—I mean man—he sings accordant: "For thou art my harp, and pipe, and temple"—a harp for harmony, a pipe by reason of the Spirit, a temple by reason of the word; so that the first may sound, the second breathe, the third contain the Lord. . . . A beautiful, breathing instrument of music the Lord made man [Καλὸν ὁ Κύριος ὄργανον ἔμπνουν τὸν ἄνθρωπον], after his own image. And He Himself also, surely, who is the supramundane Wisdom, the celestial Word, is the all-harmonious, melodious, holy instrument of God. What, then, does this instrument—the Word of God, the Lord, the New Song—desire? To open the eyes of the blind, and unstop the ears of the deaf, and to lead the lame or the erring to righteousness, to exhibit God to the foolish, to put a stop to corruption, to conquer death, to reconcile disobedient children to their father.[13]

This vibrantly musical account of creation and incarnation replaces actual musical instruments—in this case, harp and pipe—with the putatively resonant bodies of the faithful, which are themselves "beautiful, breathing instrument[s] of music" each tuned like a "universe in miniature" to the harmonies of the cosmos. Christ's own incarnation makes him the ideal "holy instrument of God," capable of putting a harmonious end to blindness, deafness, and corruption. Christ does not simply *sing* the "New Song," but *is* the New Song by virtue of his embodied redemption of humanity.

Almost lost in this joyful enumeration of the myriad promises of the New Song is the seemingly mundane image with which the passage above concludes: the New Song will "reconcile disobedient children to their father." Following as it does the healing of the deaf, blind, and lame, the halting of foolishness and corruption, even the triumph over death, the disciplining of children appears at most an afterthought. Yet it serves to remind us that the redemptive harmony promised by Christ's humanity is from the beginning an *imposed* harmony as well, a music that commands attention and obedience from those who would stay in "tune" with the will of God. Clement acknowledges as much as he brings his extended musical metaphor to a close: "Sometimes he upbraids, and sometimes he threatens. Some men he mourns over, others he addresses with the voice of song, just as a good physician treats some of his patients with cataplasms, some with rubbing, some with fomentations; in one case cuts open with the lancet, in another cauterizes, in another amputates, in order if possible to cure the patient's diseased part or member. The Savior has many tones of voice, and many methods for the salvation of men."[14]

Even when enshrined in the polytonality of his musical voice, Christ's ability to redeem and heal in his conventional role as physician founds itself upon his frequent need to amputate, burn, or sever. It is an eerily appropriate image for an age of violent martyrdom. Clement implies that the aestheticized strains of the New Song, the mystical melodies that bind soul to body and humanity to God, bear with them as well the insistent threat of dismemberment.

The opening chapter of the *Protreptikos* represents perhaps the earliest extended treatment in Christian writings of the musicality of the human body. As its repeated analogies between the musical individual and the resonating "universe" make clear, the treatise positions its vision of the "New Song" within the ancient strain of platonic musical thought that saw the human person as a sonorous microcosm, manifesting celestial harmonies in its every breath and movement.[15] Yet if Clement found in the *harmonia* between individual and cosmos a compelling metaphor for humanity's relationship with God, the *Protreptikos* radically reshaped this philosophical convention in accord with the tenets of a religious system in which God assumed human flesh. If Clement shared with the Pythagoreans the belief that "the discord of the elements" is "tuned . . . [in] harmonious arrangement," he also insisted that God himself "harmonized this universal frame of things" by incarnating the "all-harmonious, melodious, holy instrument" of his son. Similarly, although Clement's neoplatonism led him to imagine the human person as a "universe in miniature" held together in harmonious order, the musical body adumbrated in the *Protreptikos* is not a material obstruction that will ultimately be abandoned for an incorporeal Idea, but rather the resonant body of the "celestial Word," the crucified and resurrected flesh of Christ.

The distinction is subtle but crucial. To Plotinus, the third-century Alexandrian neoplatonist, the human body was "a thing of bile and bitterness": in the *Enneads* it is the stars themselves that, when "struck in tune," resemble "the strings of a lyre" whose resonance inspires a human striving to escape the limitations of the flesh. While the human person is like a stringed instrument, for Plotinus "Melody itself" plucks the soul.[16] For Clement, by contrast, the celestial "New Song" resonates not through the soul alone, but also from the *soma* that participates materially in the harmonies inherent in "created nature." In his own words, "The instrument of God loves mankind."[17]

The New Song of the *Protreptikos* would become an influential topos for patristic and medieval theologians. It was Augustine's ultimate inspiration for his sermon of the same name, and Christian writers from Tertullian to Richard Rolle adopted it as a working metaphor for the discipline of Christian virginity.[18] Given Clement's pointed emphasis upon the resonance of the flesh, it is surprising how often the New Song has been characterized as a synecdoche for a putative patristic abhorrence of the body. In *A Preface to Chaucer*, Robertson famously adduced the *canticum novum* as a metaphor for the spiritual rejection of the "Old Song," the " 'illusory' harmony of the flesh, which is mere discord with reference to created nature."[19] The Christian worldview entailed a veritable musical escape from the body:

> To the more cultivated minds of the Middle Ages artistic works were things designed, through their "numbers," through their figurative devices, or through their very workmanship, to lead the mind toward a beauty which

transcends corporal modulations; such works were not merely attractive in themselves, but were intended to lead the mind toward something beyond.[20]

A quintessentially platonic formulation, and for some "cultivated minds" an accurate one. As we saw in the Introduction, the author of the *Scholica enchiriadis* similarly disdained such "corporal modulations," sounding bodies that corrupted the mathematical purity of that "something beyond."

Yet Clement himself was clearly captivated by the "corporal modulations" of incarnational Christianity; as its initial formulation in the *Protreptikos* suggests, the New Song constituted anything but a harmonious chorus of souls joined by a collective desire to escape the prison of the body. In the case of patristic theology especially, it is crucial to recognize the distinction drawn by many writers between *sarx* and *soma, carnis* and *corpus, flesh* and *body*; for many premodern Christian writers, flesh is more of a tendency than a physical thing. We tend to use the terms interchangeably, of course (I have done so here a number of times already), yet in premodern Christian theology the word *flesh* is not always used as a synonym for the physical stuff that constitutes the human body. As Karma Lochrie describes it, flesh is "that principle of disruption in the hyman psyche" that may signal a misuse of the body, true, but that hardly implies a spurning or hatred of the actual *corpus*.[21] Henri Crouzel similarly warns that "we must not confuse the meaning of the word body with the almost always pejorative meaning of the word flesh."[22] If the New Song of Christendom often rejected the "melody of the flesh,"[23] the melody of the *body* was consistently embraced and elaborated.

Recognizing the investment of many early Christian writers in the mysteriously resonant character of human embodiment invites a critical rethinking of much patristic speculation on the nature of music. Perhaps the most prolific and spectacular elaborations of the musical body in early Christian writings can be found in the great store of biblical commentary that would constitute the foundation for the medieval exegetical tradition, and more specifically in early commentaries on Psalms, the most musical book of the Old Testament. Dozens of Christian exegetes produced elaborate glosses of the psalm-verses that mention musical instruments ("Praise the Lord on the cithar," "Arise, psaltery and harp," or "Praise him in the sound of the trumpet"), providing a seeming wealth of information about the era's musical thought and practice.

Until relatively recently, musicologists regarded most patristic and medieval glosses of these verses (as well as their illumination in psalters and other liturgical books) as evidence for the use of actual musical instruments in the Christian liturgy. In a series of groundbreaking studies, however, James McKinnon showed that most such passages are in reality vehement polemics *against* this practice, which almost all patristic writers regarded as evil.[24] The instruments described in these commentaries are the biblical instruments of the Old Testament, not musical instruments used by the commentators' Christian contemporaries; the glosses themselves, McKinnon suggests, are "simply allegorical interpretations of the instruments mentioned in the psalms," constituting a highly "stereotyped" tradition of organological typology.[25] This helpful corrective to the earlier work of Joseph Gelineau, Bruno Stäblein, and others takes these glosses on their own terms rather than dismissing them for their failure to shed light on late-classical organology (as the editors of a popular musicology sourcebook do in terming them "fanciful" attempts to "explain away" biblical depictions of musical instruments).[26]

But are patristic commentaries and the assumptions about music they embed truly "irrelevan[t] to the question of liturgical performance practice," as McKinnon contends?[27] The answer to this question depends very much on what exactly we mean by "performance practice"—or indeed by "performance." Commenting on Psalm 32, a third-century Greek writer (long thought to be Origen) glosses the phrase "Praise the lord on the cithar, sing to him on the psaltery of ten strings" as an allegory for the human person: "Figuratively the body can be called a cithara and the soul a psaltery, which are likened musically to the wise man who fittingly employs the limbs of the body and the powers of the soul as strings. . . . The ten strings stand for ten sinews, for a string is a sinew. And the body can also be said to be the psaltery of ten strings, as it has five senses and five powers of the soul, with each power arising from a respective sense."[28] In Greek terminology, the psaltery, or *psalterion* (an ancestor of the present-day zither), was a stringed instrument held in the lap and played from above with finger or plectrum, although *psalterion* was also used as a generic term for any plucked instrument; the cithar or *kithara*, the most prestigious musical instrument for the Greeks, consisted of a sound box made of wood and two curving arms connected by a crossbar (for an example, see Figure 2 below).[29] Though these instruments in some form were certainly known to patristic and medieval theologians, less important than the technical details of their construction were their symbolic connotations (as Christopher Page puts it, "the literal sense of words like *cithara* and *psalterium* was allowed to shrivel and die").[30] For the Pseudo-Origen, the instruments are practically interchangeable, but both have significant bearing on the disposition of the human body in religious life—in other words, on the *embodied devotional performance* of the human being in the world. In his massive commentary on Psalms, the later Latin writer Cassiodorus imagines the performance of the psaltery "from above" as crucial to its incarnational resonance: "As we have often remarked, the psaltery is a beautiful likeness of the Lord's body; for just as the psaltery sounds from above, so the incarnation of the Lord celebrates heavenly commands" (Psalterium quippe ut saepe diximus corporis Domini decora similitudo est; nam sicut psalterium de summo sonat, ita et incarnatio Domini caelestia mandata concelebrat).[31] The incarnation is a celebratory "performance" by God, one in which the materiality of the body performatively reconstitutes itself through a ritualized instrumental allegory.

Clement himself penned one of the most imaginative of these early glosses during a discussion in the *Paedogogus* of proper conduct at feasts. Comparing the licentious revelry of the "irrational portion of mankind" to the music produced for "the divine service," he adapts several verses from Psalm 150 to elaborate the particulars of the bodily instrument he had earlier described at the opening of the *Protreptikos*:

> "Praise him with the sound of the trumpet," and indeed he will raise the dead with the sound of the trumpet. "Praise him on the psaltery," for the tongue is the psaltery of the Lord. "And praise him on the cithara," let the cithara be taken to mean the mouth, played by the Spirit as if by a plectrum. "Praise him with tympanum and chorus" refers to the Church meditating on the resurrection of the flesh in the resounding membrane [μελετήσασαν τῆς σαρκὸς τὴν ἀνάστασιν ἐν ἠχοῦντι τῷ δέρματι]. "Praise him on strings and the instrument" refers to our body as an instrument and its sinews as strings [ὄργανον τὸ σῶμα λέγει τὸ ἡμέτερον, καὶ χορδὰς τὰ νεῦρα αὐτοῦ] from which it derives its harmonious tension, and when strummed by the Spirit it gives off human tones [καὶ κρουόμενον τῷ Πνεύματι τοὺς φθόγγους ἀποδίδωσι τοὺς ἀνθρωπίνους]. "Praise him on the clangorous cymbals" speaks of the tongue as the cymbal of the mouth which sounds as the lips are moved.

> Therefore he called out to all mankind, "Let every breath praise the Lord,"
> because he watches over every breathing thing he has made.[32]

"Every breathing thing" is every human body through and upon which devotional music is rung. Tongue and mouth are cymbal and cithar, resonating in anticipation of the resurrection on the distended "surrounding membrane" of the cheeks, which Clement compares to the stretched and beatable head of a drum. Similarly, the body's sinews are the stretched strings of an instrument, strings that produce "human notes" when plucked and strummed. Skin, limbs, nerves, sinews, bones, teeth, cheeks, lips: the myriad body parts and organs perform as resonant containers of music to be stretched, beaten, plucked, and strummed in the fervor of devotion.

On one level, of course, all of these writers are expressing organological banalities: stringed instruments are strung with viscera; drums are covered with skin. When stretched, plucked, beaten, and strummed, the various parts of butchered animals resonate. Yet these and countless other passages from Christian exegetical literature promote the distinctive notion that *human* bodies are stringed instruments, that *human* sinews and senses are strings that make music when touched. *Pace* Robertson and others who have imputed to Christian exegesis a consistent and thoroughgoing polemic against the material body, it is in the exegetical tradition that we find the human body most actively and energetically transformed into a musical spectacle in itself. While such glosses may indeed represent a polemical rejection of musical instruments in the liturgy, this should not prevent us from reading the *allegories themselves* in the literal sense as evidence for the musical role of the body in religious practice. The instruments glossed and elaborated upon in the commentary tradition *do* in fact represent "the instruments contemporary with the commentaries' authors," as McKinnon puts it; these instruments just happen to be human bodies rather than cithars, harps, trumpets, and drums. What I am suggesting, in other words, is that the hermeneutical practice of allegoresis produces biblical allegories that in turn display a remarkable affinity for the music of the flesh. In the devotional bodily performances imagined in the early Christian exegetical tradition, the history of the body and the history of music become indistinguishable.

This performative sensibility appealed to a wide variety of early Christian writers, and its influence extended well beyond strictly exegetical works. In the midst of a sermon on the conversion of Mary Magdalene (Luke 7:36–38), St. Peter Chrysologus, a fifth-century archbishop of Ravenna, describes the "banquet of devotion" she produced during Christ's visit to the house of the Pharisee as a musical performance upon her dancing *corpus*:

> She mixed the drink with tears in proper measure [*temperat in mensuram*], and to the full delight of God she beat a melody from her heart and body [*pulsat cordis sui et corporis symphoniam*]. She produced the organ tones of her lamentations, played upon the cithar by her long and rhythmical sighs, and fitted groans to the pipe [*in fistulam*]. While she kept beating her breast in reproach to her conscience she made the cymbals resound which would please God.[33]

Here again a single body provides a wide variety of musical sounds, simultaneously beating itself like a drum, lamenting like an organ, vibrating with sighs as a cithar is strummed, and groaning like a *fistula*. The flesh is not being mortified in this representation, if by "mortified" we mean spurned or escaped; rather, the passage seeks to provoke a highly performative deployment of the body, both in its individual parts and as a whole. While Clement's *Paedogogus* metaphorizes the act of singing through the mouth in instrumental terms, Peter's description of the Magdalene emphasizes the musical resonance of chest, heart, breast, and limb. Transported into a sermon, these seeming exegetical conventions reenvision the Magdalene's dancing as a graphic biblical portrait of somatic performance.

How might we account for such representations of the body's musical parts and functions in the Christian writings of late antiquity? As we have seen, for Lippman and most other twentieth-century commentators on Christian musical cosmology, platonist Pythagoreanism has been conceived as the predominant (in many cases the only) contribution of classical philosophy to patristic and medieval musical thought. An important step toward a revisionist view of this tradition must be to broaden and complicate our historical account of the intellectual genealogy out of which Christian musical aesthetics developed. First of all, following Herbert Schueller, we must jettison the assumption that the musical cosmology of Western Christianity was subsumed within the radical dualism found in certain strands of Christian neoplatonism.[34] The Pythagoreans themselves were fascinated by the mystical realization of proportion in corporeal phenomena, and it is not necessarily accurate to equate Pythagorean notions of musical number and proportion with their fate at the hands of platonic dualists (whether Christian or otherwise). Indeed, in the pre-Socratic fragments there occurs a discussion of human gestation that compares the development of the embryo to the harmonies of a stringed instrument.[35] Number and flesh are coextensive, not contradictory as the *Scholica enchiriadis* author would claim.

Even within Plato's own oeuvre we can identify moments at which a sense of musical materialism asserts itself as a compelling alternative to the dogmatic anticorporealism of Socrates. A particularly revealing example of this occurs during Simmias's hesitant disagreement with Socrates in the *Phaedo* (a text well known to Clement of Alexandria) about the nature of the soul-body relationship.[36] Socrates has just been arguing for the eternality of the soul and the ephemerality of the body, which he envisions as a temporary obstruction that impedes the soul's progress to God. Simmias objects to this dualist way of thinking, arguing that if the soul is a *harmonia* of the body, as Socrates has posited, then the soul must perish with the flesh that it causes to resonate:

> For I suspect, Socrates, that the notion of the soul which we are all of us inclined to entertain, would also be yours, and that you too would conceive the body to be strung up [ἐντεταμένου τοῦ σώματος], and held together, by the elements of hot and cold, wet and dry, and the like, and that the soul is the harmony or due proportionate admixture of them. And, if this is true, the inference clearly is, that when the body is unstrung [ὅταν χαλάσθη τὸ σῶμα] or overstrained through disorder or other injury, then the soul, though most divine, like other harmonies of music or of works of art, of course perishes at once; although the material remains of the body may last for a considerable time, until they are either decayed or burned. Now if any one maintained that the soul, being a temperament of the elements of the body [κρᾶσιν οὖσαν τὴν ψυχὴν τῶν ἐν τῷ σώματι], first perishes in that which is called death, how shall we answer him?[37]

In a frank questioning of Socratic doctrine on human nature, Simmias (a Pythagorean disciple of Philolaus) argues *against* the eternality of the soul by deploying Socrates' own instrumental metaphor against itself: If the soul truly is the "harmony of the body," and if maintaining the harmoniousness of the "strings of the body" is the soul's very reason for existence, then, Simmias seems to imply, would not a loosening, slackening, or perishing of these fleshly "strings" cause the soul to perish? Even a "disorder or other injury" suffered by a still living being will force the soul to flee the body and perish; and in death, the strings of the body, albeit in a shattered or fragmented state, will survive.

In the *Phaedo*, Plato allows this objection to last but a moment; Socrates soon rescues his auditors from the supposedly naive belief that "the soul is a harmony capable of being led by the affections of the body."[38] Nevertheless, Simmias's fleeting inquiry into the nature of somatic *harmonia* speaks to a number of more general tensions in classical aesthetics regarding the music of the flesh, tensions that will reappear in new guises throughout early Christian musical speculation. Certain aspects of Clement of Alexandria's incarnational New Song—the redemptive music of Christ's body in the *Protreptikos*, the discrete sonorities of tongues, sinews, and lips in the *Paedogogus*—are more in the spirit of Simmias's antiplatonic (or better, perhaps, anti-Socratic) thesis on the harmonious priority of the flesh than of Socrates' dismissive rejection of the body's instrumental perdurance.[39]

Other strands of classical philosophy, though much influenced by the platonic notion of individual and celestial harmony, nevertheless provided early Christian writers with a surprisingly materialist means of conceptualizing the musicality of the human person. Certain writers seem almost Epicurean in their musical materialism, as if sharing Lucretius's belief that the quality of song results from the comparative roughness or smoothness of atoms of sound flowing through the performing body.[40] More important for the history of Christian musical sensibilities is the naturalistic zest for somatic detail that characterizes Stoic views on the nature of the body.[41] While not radically materialist like their Epicurean counterparts, Stoic thinkers worked within a "general conceptual framework which denies that anything can exist which is not a body or the state of a body." "Since persons do exist," the Stoics held, "they must be bodies," and the person is, in fact, "an ensouled, rational and mortal body."[42] Though this does not mean that the person is identical with the *sarx*, the Stoics held that corporeality in some form is essential to human identity—so much so that they invented no fewer than four discrete categories of embodiment in order to delineate the nature of the material world.[43] And perhaps the primary objective of Stoic physics, Marcia Colish points out, was to combat the dualistic tendencies found in other Greek philosophical schools.[44]

Such a naturalistic view of body as integral to the ontology of the self informs numerous Stoic or Stoic-inspired images of the musicality of the *corpus*. In Cicero's *De natura deorum*, the Stoic speaker Lucilius Balbus describes human speech—"our instrument for exhortation and persuasion, for consoling the afflicted and assuaging the fears of the terrified"—in terms of the musico-physiological mechanism that produces it:

> In the first place there is an artery passing from the lungs to the back of the mouth, which is the channel by which the voice, originating from the mind, is caught and uttered. Next, the tongue is placed in the mouth and confined by the teeth; it modulates and defines the inarticulate flow of the voice and renders its sounds distinct and clear by striking the teeth and other parts of the mouth.[45]

In a passage that dramatically anticipates Clement's psalm-gloss in the *Paedogogus*, Balbus contends that the Stoa are "fond of comparing the tongue to the plectrum of a lyre, the teeth to the strings, and the nostrils to the horns which echo the notes of the strings when the instrument is played" (plectri similem lingua nostri solent dicere, chordarum dentes, nares cornibus iis qui ad nervos resonant in cantibus).[46] These chapters of *De natura deorum* book 2 represent one of Cicero's most successful attempts to represent Stoic doctrine on theology and cosmology with accuracy.[47] In the course of claiming a Stoic genealogy to the notion of the mouth as a stringed instrument, Balbus adumbrates as well a more general vision of the musical eloquence of the oratorical body that culminates in the encyclopedic rhetorical treatise *De oratore*, in which Cicero asserts that the "instrument of persuasion" is not verbal speech alone, but the rhetorical body that performs: "For delivery is like an oration of the body" (Est enim actio quasi sermo corporis).[48] *Actio*, or delivery, is the division of classical rhetoric most often neglected by modern scholars, who have tended to focus on the formal aspects of oratory at the expense of their performance in gesture, posture, tone of voice, and movement—all of which were regarded as crucial by classical rhetoricians.[49] For Cicero, in a dramatic revision of Aristotle's explicit denigration of the topic, "delivery is the dominant component in oratory" (actio . . . in dicendo una dominatur), a claim so forceful that Quintilian felt obliged to moderate it much later.[50] In his own description of the *actio* of the orator, Cicero constructs an elaborate paratactic simile that casts rhetorical delivery as a musical performance upon the body:

> Omnis enim motus animi suum quemdam a natura habet vultum et sonum et gestum; totumque corpus hominis et eius omnis vultus omnesque voces, ut nervi in fidibus, ita sonant ut a motu animi quoque sunt pulsae. Nam voces ut chordae sunt intentae quae ad quemque tactum respondeant, acuta gravis, cita tarda, magna parva, quas tamen inter omnes est suo quaeque in genere mediocris; atque etiam illa sunt ab his delapsa plura genera, lene asperum, contractum diffusum, continenti spiritu intermisso, fractum scissum, flexo sono attenuatum inflatum. Nullum est enim horum generum quod non arte ac moderatione tractetur; hi sunt actori, ut pictori, expositi ad variandum colores.

> [For nature has assigned to every emotion a particular look and tone of voice and bearing of its own; and the whole of a person's body and every look on his face and utterance of his voice are like the strings of a harp, and sound according as they are struck by each successive emotion. For the tones of the voice are keyed up like the strings of an instrument, so as to answer to every touch, high or low, quick or slow, loud or soft, while between all of these in their several kinds there is a medium note; and there are also the various modifications derived from these, smooth or rough, limited or full in volume, tenuto or staccato, faint or harsh, diminuendo or crescendo. For there are none of these varieties that cannot be regulated by the control of art; they are the colours available for the actor, as for the painter, to secure variety.][51]

While the platonic notion of the soul as the *harmonia* of the human person may serve as Cicero's point of departure, his emphasis here is emphatically not on the human person as a despised microcosm, but on the body as the material medium of forensic performance.

Such writings furnish the most compelling classical parallels to the musical bodies of Latin Christendom. Though transmitted piecemeal to the Middle Ages, they were readily available to a wide range of patristic authors, a good number of whom were schooled in the practice of Roman rhetoric before their conversions to Christianity. Clement of Alexandria cites numerous passages from the Greek Stoa (often as part of a Middle-Platonist condemnation of Stoic pantheism) that correspond to many found in the works of Cicero;[52] Augustine responded in brilliant detail in the *City of God* to the *De natura deorum*;[53] and when Boethius came to formulate his influential notion of *musica humana*, the "human music" that "holds the parts of the body together in an established order," he must surely have been thinking in part of the sonorous body described in the *Tusculan Disputations* of Cicero, whose writings he cites explicitly elsewhere in the treatise.[54]

One of the founding ironies of this book, then, is the possibility that the patristic *canticum novum*, the "new song" that has been made to stand in for a Christian neoplatonism that spurns the body and the flesh wholesale, may derive in part from classical representations of the somatic performance of the pagan orator, the public intellectual whose flesh is integral to rhetorical expression. Though this musico-rhetorical body receives its most vivid realization in the Ciceronian canon proper, there are many other intriguing affiliations between the Roman rhetorical corpus and Christian musical commentary. The ubiquitous medieval notion of the Christian preacher as a *tuba* or trumpet could be cataloged in the ninth century as an allegorical commonplace: "*Tuba* est sonus praedicationis" (*Trumpet* is the sound of preaching).[55] But Quintilian had already propounded a similar notion in the *Institutio*, which contains a negative exemplum of *actio* that criticizes poor rhetoricians who "rock their bodies to and fro, booming inarticulately as if they had a trumpet inside them and adapting their agitated movements, not to the delivery of the words, but to their pursuit" (aut murmure incerto velut classico instincti concitatissimum corporis motum non enuntiandis sed quaerendis verbis accommodant).[56]

Even the predicatory oratory of Jesus Christ was imagined as a performance upon his musical body. For Hilary of Poitiers, the psaltery, the "most upright of all musical instruments" (unum omnium musicorum organorum rectissimum), models the body of Christ in its suasive musicality: "it is an instrument built in the shape of the Lord's body and made without a single curve or bend [*sine ullo inflexu deflexuue directum est*], an instrument moved and struck from above and brought to life to sing of supernal and heavenly teaching, not one that sounds with a base and terrestrial spirit, as do the other earthly instruments. For the Lord did not preach what is base and terrestrial while in the instrument of his own body."[57] Here, too, Quintilian furnishes the most apt pagan analogue: "Eloquence is like a harp and will never reach perfection unless all its strings be taut and in tune" (Name sicut cithara ita oratio perfecta non est, nisi ab imo ad summum omnibus intenta nervis consentiat).[58] Classical "musical oratory" has metamorphosed into the predicatory mimesis rung on the instrumental body of Christ, who preaches through and performs upon his resonant "frame" before his auditors.

"A beautiful, breathing instrument of music": Gregory of Nyssa

Thus far this chapter has argued that the music of body represents an important site of philosophical puzzlement and exegetical ingenuity for a number of early Christian writers. I turn now to the work of a single theologian, Gregory of Nyssa, for the unique perspective he gives us on the implications of musical embodiment for patristic thought on the nature of the human being more generally. Gregory's peculiar vision of the instrumental person could almost be described as a kind of musical physiology. As such, it represents what I would propose is the most extended and thoughtful attempt in early Christian cultures to come to terms with the musicality of the flesh.

Like the other great Cappadocians of the late fourth century, Basil the Great and Gregory Nazianzen, Gregory of Nyssa belonged to a provincial aristocracy whose Christian theology reached back to Origen and, through him, to the teachings of Origen's own master, Clement of Alexandria.[59] While Clement is notable among early Christian writers for the consistency and clarity of his vision, the same cannot be said of Gregory, who contradicts himself with baffling regularity both within individual works and from one work to the next.[60] One of the most inconsistent aspects of Gregory's thought is his anthropology, which represents a constant source of ambiguity throughout his works.[61] This lack of consistency characterizes Gregory's eschatology as well, perhaps especially his images of the resurrection body; while Gregory's paradigmatic body in this life was that of the Christian ascetic, his more general discussions of human bodies emphasize above all the movement and variation to which they are susceptible.[62] In Gregory's own words, "This life of our bodies, material and subject to flux, always advancing by way of motion, finds the power of its being in this, that it never rests from its motion."[63]

Nowhere in early Christian musical commentary is the influence of the classical philosophical materialism discussed above more pervasive than in Gregory's writings on human physiology. In the influential treatment of the subject in *De hominis opificio* (ca. 385), motions of the flesh become profoundly musical, and the musical instrumentality of the human person constitutes the most startling realization of the incarnational integrity of the flesh. Over and over this work condemns the doctrine "that souls existed before bodies"; a discussion against transmigration rails against those who "assert that the state of souls is prior to their life in the flesh" as well as "the fabulous doctrines of the heathen which they hold on the subject of successive incorporation" (28.3). The treatise instead imagines body and soul as altruistic companions, not combatants struggling against one another; for Gregory, the "seminal cause" of human constitution (a Stoic notion) "is neither a soul without body, nor a body without soul, but . . . from animated and living bodies, it is generated at the first as a living and animate being . . . our humanity takes it and cherishes it like a nursling with the resources she herself possesses, and it thus grows on both sides and makes its growth manifest correspondingly in either part" (30.29). Gregory repeatedly emphasizes the homogeneity of person, the "compound" that "results from the joining" of body and soul; as he puts it elsewhere, "the one does not come first, any more than the other comes after."[64]

Equal in importance to the mutuality of body and soul is the ineffability and incomprehensibility of their interrelationship: "there is not a doubt that there is in [our living bodies] the soul's vivifying influence exerted by a law which it is beyond the human understanding to comprehend." This "law" represents a constant source of mystery, defying the general scope of language and, indeed, the exactitude of prepositions:

> [T]he union of the mental with the bodily presents a connection unspeakable
> and inconceivable—not being within it (for the incorporeal is not enclosed in
> a body), nor yet surrounding it without (for that which is incorporeal does
> not include anything), but the mind approaching our nature in some inexpli-
> cable and incomprehensible way, and coming into contact with it, is to be re-
> garded as both in it and around it, neither implanted in it nor enfolded with
> it, but in a way which we cannot speak or think. (15.3)

So intimately bound up with one another are "the mental and the bodily" within the human person that practically any conceivable analogy—enclosing, enfolding, implanting, or surrounding—must be doomed to failure.

Except one. If the simultaneity, spontaneity, and homogeneity of the body-soul relationship can be neither captured within the representational limitations of human language nor analogized to recognizable processes and actions, how are we to comprehend it? Gregory's persistent struggle with this thoroughly epistemological question throughout the *De hominis opificio* explains the treatise's virtual obsession with the music of the flesh. While the treatise turns to music repeatedly and at some length, it does so only in chapters 7 through 15, the portions treating such matters as the uprightness of human form, the nature and uses of the hands, the action of the intellective soul upon the body, and the nature of sleep and dreams. Extended musical metaphors appear not in the early chapters (1 through 6), which investigate God's creation of the first human beings and their likeness to the divine image; nor in the second half of the treatise (chapters 16 through 29), which returns to the creation and original sin and compares the bodies of prelapsarian humans to the nature of redeemed bodies at the resurrection; but rather in those portions of the *De hominis* in which Gregory ponders exactly how our bodies live, breathe, sleep, sicken, and age in the present life.[65] The physical production of music provides a materialist analogy for both the psychosomatic integrity of the human person and the wonders of embodied existence.[66]

Each time the *De hominis opificio* turns to musical imagery the general thrust of the argument is the same: Gregory begins with a phrase such as "just as a musician," "like a plectrum," or "as in a musical performance," followed by a lengthy passage explaining exactly how the specific bodily function he is discussing parallels the strumming of a harp, the tuning of strings, the blowing of a flute, or a combination of the three. The basic framework for this musical imagery derives from the same store of classical musical speculation that inspired Clement—though in Gregory's case mediated through Clement, Origen, and, perhaps most importantly, his older brother Basil's speculations in the *Hexaemeron* (of which the *De hominis opificio* was written as a continuation) and the Psalm commentaries.[67] It is in the details, however, that Gregory's musical imagery is unique and innovative, for each time he turns to instrumental analogy he does so with a quite distinctive purpose in mind.

The work's initial deployment of musical metaphor occurs during a discussion of the physical differences between humans and beasts. Like Cicero in *De natura deorum*, Gregory argues that humanity's upright stature is a sign of "sovereignty" and "royal dignity" (8.1–2). Our other great distinguishing physical characteristic is our hands, which, unlike paws and hoofs, "adapt themselves to the requirement of reason" in a particular musical way:

> Now since man is a rational animal, the instrument of his body must be made suitable for the use of reason; as you may see musicians producing their music according to the form of their instruments, and not piping with harps nor harping upon flutes, so it must needs be that the organization of these instruments of ours should be adapted for reason, that when struck by the vocal organs they might be able to sound properly for the use of words. For this reason the hands were attached to the body. (8.8)

Our hands, an essential part of "these instruments of ours," give us the ability to use our other organs—particularly the mouth—for the purpose for which they were intended, just as a musician uses a harp, not a flute, for strumming. Unlike "brute" animals, who must employ their mouths for digging and chewing, humans can use theirs as they were meant to be used: for speech. If we did *not* have hands, Gregory quips, our faces would look like those of "quadrupeds," our lips "lumpy, stiff, and thick," our tongues lolling out of the sides of our mouths "like [those] of dogs and other carnivorous beasts, projecting through the gaps in [our] jagged row[s] of teeth." As he asks in conclusion, "If, then, our body had no hands, how could articulate sound have been implanted in it, seeing that the form of the parts of the mouth would not have had the configuration proper for the use of speech, so that man must of necessity have either bleated, or 'baaed,' or barked, or neighed, or bellowed like oxen or asses, or uttered some other bestial sound?" (8.8). The analogy implies that the "implanted" gift of speech or "articulate sound" is also the gift of music.

Gregory's next chapter extends this metaphor through a lengthy instrumental analogy, which, taken as a whole, must count as one of the most stunning meditations on the musicality of the human body to survive from late antiquity. Considering the ways in which God "impart[ed]" mind and reason to humanity and caused them to be manifested through the body, Gregory begins:

> Now since the mind is a thing intelligible and incorporeal, its grace would have been incommunicable and isolated, if its motion were not manifested

by some contrivance. For this cause there was still need of this instrumental organization, that it might, like a plectrum, touch the vocal organs and indicate by the quality of the notes struck, the motion within.

And as some skilled musician, who may have been deprived by some affection of his own voice, and yet wish to make his skill known, might make melody with voices of others, and publish his art by the aid of flutes or of the lyre, so also the human mind . . . touches, like some skillful musician, these animated instruments, and makes known its hidden thoughts by means of the sound produced upon them. (9.1–2)

By means of its "instrumental organization," the mind performs like a mute musician, touching and striking the organs of the throat as a plectrum strikes strings, causing them to resound with its desires. Unable to rely upon "mere soul," the mind here depends absolutely upon the music of body to reveal its "hidden thoughts." Indeed, as the chapter progresses, the analogy subsumes more and more of the bodily functions, implying that "these animated instruments," the same "beautiful, breathing instrument[s] of music" that so captivated Clement of Alexandria, do not simply resemble or operate like musical instruments, but actually *are* musical instruments:

Now the music of the human instrument is a sort of compound of flute and lyre, sounding together in combination as in a concerted piece of music. For the breath—as it is forced up from the air-receiving vessels through the windpipe, when the speaker's impulse to utterance attunes the harmony to sound, and as it strikes against the internal protuberances which divide this flute-like passage in a circular arrangement—imitates in a way the sound uttered through a flute, being driven round and round by the membranous projections. But the palate receives the sound from below in its own concavity, and dividing the sound by the two passages that extend to the nostrils, and by the cartilages about the perforated bone, as it were by some scaly protuberance, makes its resonance louder; while the cheek, the tongue, the mechanism of the pharynx by which the chin is relaxed when drawn in, and tightened when extended to a point—all these in many different ways answer to the motion of the plectrum upon the strings, varying very quickly, as occasion requires, the arrangement of the tones; and the opening and closing of the lips has the same effect as players produce when they check the breath of the flute with their fingers according to the measure of the tune. (9.3)

In a passage that loses no ground to Balbus's panegyric to oratorical sonority in Cicero's *De natura deorum*, Gregory imagines the speaking voice, a product of the "flutelike" windpipe, larynx, nostrils, palate, and nose, resonating ever more loudly as the breath of speech passes through the body. The cheek, tongue, pharynx, and chin alternately stretch and relax themselves like harp strings that "answer to the motion of the plectrum." Just as speech exits through the mouth, the lips open and close like a flautist's fingers checking the airflow. What is so remarkable about this passage is the sheer variety of musical sounds the body produces simultaneously, whether by percussively striking its internal organs, strumming its teeth with its tongue, or causing its "scaly protuberance" of cartilage to resonate with its words.

The "music of reason" Gregory treats here and elsewhere in the *De hominis opificio*, the "instrumental organization" through which humans articulate thought in speech, also represents the indivisibility of body and soul. In chapter 12, the body's musicality signifies the psychosomatic integrity of the human person in the face of "the vain and conjectural discussion of those who confine the intelligible energy to certain bodily organs." Although Gregory is secure in the knowledge that "the mind is equally in contact with each of the [bodily] parts," he admits that this relationship exists "according to a kind of combination which is indescribable" (12.1–6). Once again language fails him in his attempt to discern precisely how mind pervades and is coextensive with body, and once again he turns to music instead:

> [T]he intelligible nature neither dwells in the empty spaces of bodies, nor is extruded by encroachments of the flesh; but since the whole body is made like some musical instrument—just as it often happens in the case of those who know how to play, but are unable, because the unfitness of the instrument does not admit of their art, to show their skill (for that which is destroyed by time, or broken by a fall, or rendered useless by rust or decay, is mute and inefficient, even if it be breathed upon by one who may be an excellent artist in flute-playing)—so too the mind, passing over the whole instrument, and touching each of the parts in a mode corresponding to its intellectual activities, according to its nature, produces its proper effect on those parts which are in a natural condition, but remains inoperative and ineffective upon those which are unable to admit the movement of its art. (12.8)

Just as an expert musician "breathe[s] upon" a flute, the mind "pass[es]" over the whole instrument" of the body. Even those body parts that might be disabled, "unable to admit . . . movement" just as the rusted or decayed components of a flute in disrepair will remain "mute" when the flute is played, are touched equally by the mind. In a disabled body, "the communication of the true beauty extends proportionally through the whole series, beautifying by the superior nature that which comes next to it" (12.10).

The treatise's determined use of such imagery even in those cases where music *cannot* be produced by the body further testifies to the literalism of its musical sensibility. By the thirteenth chapter, which returns one final time to the analogy while treating the nature of sleep and dreams, the body at rest—producing "no orderly melody"—brims with musical potential:

> Again, as a musician, when he touches with the plectrum the slackened strings of a lyre, brings out no orderly melody (for that which is not stretched will not sound), but his hand frequently moves skilfully, bringing the plectrum to the position of the notes so far as place is concerned, yet there is no sound, except that he produces by the vibration of the strings a sort of uncertain and indistinct hum; so in sleep the mechanism of the senses being relaxed, the artist is either quite inactive, if the instrument is completely relaxed by satiety or heaviness; or will act slackly and faintly, if the instrument of the senses does not fully admit of the exercise of its art. (13.9)

Like the rest of the treatise, the passage argues for a kind of musical artistry of living. Human physiology is an ongoing musical performance upon and within ourselves, and the instrumental body will only cease its performance when the strumming, beating, and breathing artist—the human being— finally dies.

Gregory of Nyssa's quirky constructions of the body's musicality in *De hominis opificio* imply that music may be as integral to body as body is to the human person. Though he depends heavily upon the allegorical music of individual body parts he found in earlier Christian exegesis of the Psalms, he moves beyond this tradition by incorporating its details into a more generalized anthropological musicality and expanding them with great relish. Refining a platonic vision of individual harmony with a Stoicizing zest for naturalistic detail—the musics of windpipe, palate, nose, larynx, teeth, tongue, and lip—Gregory presents a compelling case for the musicality of everyday life; his musical vision of the bodily functions was as unhesitant and untroubled as it was detailed and consistent.

The Sonority of Torture: Ovid to Ambrose

Yet Gregory's optimistic take on the resonance of the flesh was not to be the sole patristic legacy to later musical thought. As I will argue at much greater length in Chapters 5 and 6, the premodern Christian vision of music and embodiment was also one of intense pain and privation. Here again we can find compelling classical precedents. Ovid's *Metamorphoses* is an intertextual cornucopia of melodious sadism; some of the work's most musical tales seem to suggest a primal link between violence and the origins of musical sound and instruments. In book 1, Pan pursues the nymph Syrinx; just as she is grasped by her potential ravisher, she is transformed into an armful of reed-pipes, which Pan fashions into his signature musical instrument: "And so the pipes, made of unequal reeds fitted together by a joining of wax, took and kept the name of the maiden" (atque ita disparibus calamis conpagine cerae/ inter se iunctis nomen tenuisse puellae).[68] In Ovid's frame-narrative Mercury relates the tale of Pan and Syrinx to Argus, who has asked the god to relate how the pipe, or *fistula*, was first invented; when Argus nods off, Mercury "smites with his hooked sword the nodding head just where it joins the neck, and sends it bleeding down the rocks, defiling the rugged cliff with blood"—to join the severed head of Orpheus in book 11, the bard torn apart by the spurned Maenads but whose music somehow survives the fragmentation of his body: "The poet's limbs lay scattered all around; but his head and lyre, O Hebrus, thou didst receive, and (a marvel!) while they floated in mid-stream the lyre gave forth some mournful notes, mournfully the lifeless tongue murmured, mournfully the banks replied" (membra iacent diversa locis, caput, Hebre, lyramque/excipis: et (mirum!) medio dum labitur amne,/flebile nescio quid queritur lyra, flebile lingua/ murmurat exanimis, respondent flebile ripae) (11.50–53). And Orpheus's "lifeless tongue" recalls from book 6 Philomel's "severed tongue" "palpitating on the dark earth, faintly murmuring" (6.557–58), metaphorizing the horrors of a narrative sequence of rape, filicide, and cannibalism that would endure for medieval readers in the mournful song of the nightingale and the swallow.

But perhaps Ovid's story of Apollo and Marsyas, which immediately precedes the narrative of Philomel and Procne in book 6, is most in the spirit of early Christian accounts of music, violence, and suffering. The satyr Marsyas—performing, Fulgentius would later record, upon a bone flute abandoned by Minerva for giving her "stretched cheeks" when she played[69]—loses a musical duel to Apollo, who renders a punishment that eerily fits the musical crime:

> . . . "quid me mihi detrahis?" inquit;
> "a! piget, a! non est," clamabat "tibia tanti."
> clamanti cutis est summos direpta per artus,
> nec quicquam nisi vulnus erat; cruor undique manat,
> detectique patent nervi, trepidaeque sine ulla
> pelle micant venae; salientia viscera possis
> et perlucentes numerare in pectore fibras.
>
> ["Why do you tear me from myself?" he cried. "Oh, I repent! Oh, a flute is not worth such price!" As he screams, his skin is stripped off the surface of his body, and he is all one wound: blood flows down on every side, the sinews lie bare, his veins throb and quiver with no skin to cover them: you could count the entrails as they palpitate, and the vitals showing clearly in his breast.] (*Met.* 6.385–91)

Ovid does not draw an explicit analogy between Marsyas's exposed sinews, veins, and vitals and the strings of Apollo's harp. Yet the connection is clearly implied in numerous images of the so-called Hanging Marysas surviving from Roman antiquity.[70] In a second-century Roman oscillum (see Figure 1), Apollo's harp rests with its strings running parallel to his vanquished musical challenger, whose flayed body and the tree to which he is bound together form a hybrid *cithara* across the disc from Apollo's own.

Other Roman images of Apollo and Marsyas are even more revealing. In a second-century sculpture of *Apollo citharoedus*, now residing at the Pio-Clementine Gallery at the Vatican (see Figure 2), a larger-than-life Apollo strikes a bold pose, his *cithara* resting on his hip and the fingers of his right hand plucking at invisible strings with a plectrum. What distinguishes this particular statue is the subtle relief on the right arm of the instrument. Here, an emaciated Marsyas hangs by his bound hands exactly parallel to the instrument's imaginary strings (see the detail, Figure 3).[71] The statue seems intended to convey the eternity of Marysas's punishment to the viewer. The relief is nothing less than an anthropomorphic notch on Apollo's instrument. Staring outward with a blank countenance, the god of

FIGURE 1   The Flaying of Marsyas on marble oscillum, Roman, first century
CE, Staatliche Kunstsammlung, Dresden

music delivers a shiver of pain to the flayed body of his defeated rival at
every touch of the strings.

Such pagan spectacles might seem far removed from early Christian
aesthetic sensibilities. Yet the statue of *Apollo citharoedus* spectacularly anticipates a widespread medieval tradition of representing the Crucifixion as a
violent musical performance upon the *cithara* of Christ's own body (for a

FIGURE 2 *Apollo citharoedus*, Roman, first century CE, Pio-Clementine
Gallery, Vatican, Rome

FIGURE 3   Detail of Figure 2

more extended discussion, see Chapter 5 of this volume). This allegorical tradition has its roots in the Christian writings of late antiquity and receives one of its most graphic realizations in Cassiodorus's commentary on Psalms: "The *harp* denotes the glorious passion, performed on stretched tendons and individuated bones, which made the virtue of patience resound with the song as it were of the understanding" (*Cithara* vero gloriosam significat passionem, quae tensis nervis dinumeratisque ossibus, virtutem patientiae intellectuali quodam carmine personabat).[72] An avid reader and encyclopedist, Cassiodorus surely knew the *Metamorphoses*; given the close verbal parallels between the two images of musical torture, it is entirely possible that Ovid's poetic depiction of Marsyas's flayed body—with its distended *nervi*, its stretched *venae*, and its entrails and vitals that "you could count" (possis . . . numerare)—exerted a deep influence on this and other Christian depictions of the music of the Passion.

Pagan musical torture receives a particularly compelling Christian guise in the writings of Ambrose, who bequeathed to the Middle Ages some of the most horrifying images of musical suffering. In book 2 of *De Iacob et vita beata* (ca. 386), a philosophical sermon exploring the relationship between reason and salvation, Ambrose discusses several Old Testament accounts of martyrdom as exempla for the virtue of happiness in the face of persecution. While most of the book is devoted to the story of Jacob, Ambrose turns in the final chapters to the account of martyrdom recorded in the fourth book of Maccabees, a pseudepigraphal Old Testament work he knew in the original Greek.[73] After relating the story of Eleazar, Ambrose turns to the seven Maccabees, focusing on the spectacle as seen from their mother's perspective: "Her sons fell, all wounded by the torments; in death they rolled upon the dead, bodies rolled on bodies, heads were cut off above heads, the place was filled with the corpses of her sons."[74] The violence of this account is not original to Ambrose, who found in 4 Maccabees a spectacle to satisfy the most sadistic persecutor: "She saw the flesh of her sons being consumed in the fire, and the extremities of their hands and feet scattered on the ground, and the flesh-coverings, torn off from their heads right to their cheeks, strewn about like masks. . . . When thou sawest the flesh of one son being severed after the flesh of another, and hand after hand being cut off, and head after head being flayed, and corpse cast upon corpse, and the place crowded with spectators on account of the tortures of the children, thou sheddest not a tear."[75]

In his own sermonizing rendition of these horrors, Ambrose again emphasizes the steadfastness of the mother, who knows that greater glory will be accorded to her sons after death if they appear "torn to pieces and jumbled together with dust and blood," like conquerors returning from war. Thus, she decides that coverings should not be "placed over [their] bodies" after they have expired, and that their funeral rites should not be accompanied "except by the accompaniment of her own death." According to Ambrose, in fact, the torturous death of the Maccabees resonated with a musical accompaniment all its own:

> What cithara could give forth sweeter song than her dying sons [*morientes filii*] in their final agony? For a natural but uninvited groaning burst from them, despite their unwillingness. You might look upon their mangled bodies arranged in a row as the strings of an instrument [*fila cordarum*]. You might hear in their victorious sighs the sounding of the seven-string psaltery. Not in such a fashion could those alluring songs of the Sirens—or so they were said to be—attract their listener, for they were attracting him to shipwreck; but these songs were leading him to the victory of sacrifice.[76]

Ambrose transforms the mother's sons into strings, her *filii* into *fila*, an alliterative and assonant echo that produces the mangled cadaver of the martyr as a site of musical production. Like Clement, Ambrose confidently asserts the superiority of this salvific song of body to the false strains of pagan legend, the "alluring songs" that led so many ancient warriors to their deaths.

Yet even here Ambrose betrays the influence of classical philosophy we have seen elsewhere in patristic images of musical somatics. References to the *Enneads* abound in *De Iacob*, and I would suggest that Plotinus's famous image of the soul as harp in book 1, chapter 4, may have been the primary motivation for Ambrose's representation of the marytrs' cadavers as the strings of a *cithara*.[77] As its modern editor has argued, moreover, 4 Maccabees is one of the most Stoic of the pseudepigraphal books, a philosophical influence evident in the manifest concern throughout with the inner harmony and ethical *temperatio* of the body.[78] Like Gregory in the *De hominis opificio*, the anonymous author describes the harmonies resonating between the limbs; the Maccabees march "in harmony to death for its sake," "choirlike" in their martyrdom (14:6–8), and the moment of their death inspires the very oppositional musical terms later adopted by Ambrose: "Not the melodies of the sirens nor the songs of swans with sweet sound do so charm the hearers' ears, as sounded the voices of the sons, speaking to the mother from amid the torments" (15:14–22).

For Ambrose, as for Clement of Alexandria, the human harp is not a soul striving for an Idea, but a corpse resonating in martyrdom. And the Stoic harmonies of *his* martyrs are not simply a sign of inner temperance and fortitude as they are in 4 Maccabees, but spectacular melodies resounding outward from the torn flesh of sacrificial victims. Thus, when Ambrose turns again to this story during a discussion of martyrdom in his *De officiis ministrorum*, it is not enough that the "voices" of the Maccabees "speak" to their mother, as they do in his tutor text. Even for the legendary father of Western psalmody, there was more beauty in the music of a dying body than in the chanted syllables of a psalm:

> Quid matre loquar, quae spectabat laeta filiorum quot funera tot trophaea, et morientium vocibus tanquam psallentium cantibus delectabatur, pulcherrimam ventris sui citharam in filiis cernens, et pietatis harmoniam omni lyrae numero dulciorem?
>
> [What shall I say of the mother, who joyously looked upon the corpses of her sons as so many trophies, who delighted in their dying cries as in the singing of psalms, and saw in her offspring the fairest *cithara* of her womb and the harmony of devotion, sweeter than the number of any lyre?][79]

Ambrose does not look solely beyond the body and its death; sacrifice promises redemption, but the music of violent suffering—*not* the promise of celestial music—is what appeals to the mother's ear at the moment of her sons' deaths. Though presented in a particularly graphic way, Ambrose's vision of the Maccabees typifies the profound sense of musical embodiment that proliferated in the Christian writings of late antiquity.

CHAPTER 2

Saint Augustine and the Rhythms of Embodiment

C hapter 1 argued that the music of the flesh resonates in surprising ways and in unexpected places throughout patristic theologies and cultures. For any number of early Christian writers, the musical body has an important role to play in religious life, whether in public worship or private suffering. The "New Song" of Clement of Alexandria is a song of redemption, but it is also a song of incarnation. Ambrose's "musical Maccabees" do not sing through their mouths; rather, they resound from their corpses.

This chapter focuses on the writings of Ambrose's most famous student, Augustine of Hippo, whose massive oeuvre returns again and again to the sublime paradox that is music. I include this excursus on Augustine for several reasons, not the least of which is the unparalleled influence many of his writings exerted on the theological and devotional literature of the Middle Ages. Augustine's musical thought has been much studied, and the following pages will undoubtedly strike some specialists as a highly selective exercise based on too narrow a cross-section of his writings. Yet the musical struggles faced by Augustine throughout his life bear crucially on the subsequent history of Christian musical pleasure and speculation. In their many attempts to reconcile what I argue are the numerous contradictions in Augustine's musical cosmology, many scholars have been guided by the working assumption that such a task is possible; they have found consistency in his musical thought where there is actually puzzlement, deep anxiety, even self-loathing. Indeed, Augustine's scattered writings on musical experience and meaning provide some of the most compelling examples of the wider philosophical and religious inconsistencies that much of the best recent scholarship on the saint has brought to the foreground.[1] By listening carefully to Augustine's agonizings over the music of the flesh, we can begin to perceive the many contradictions subtending the Christian realization of the musical body over the next millennium.

In this spirit, I begin not with Augustine's own words on music, but with a much later musical story that centrally concerns him. An apocryphal legend circulating in the early Middle Ages and recorded by Landulf, an eleventh-century bishop of Milan, describes the initial encounter between Augustine and his teacher, Ambrose, and its significance for the history of Christian music.[2] The brash and youthful Augustine, still "led astray by the errors of the Manichaeans," visits Ambrose's church for the purpose of debating and refuting him on matters of religious doctrine pertaining to the incarnation. Upon entering the church, however, Augustine stands "as if transfixed, pale and trembling" in the face of the Christian truths he hears. After the service, he approaches Ambrose in private; the Holy Spirit reveals to Ambrose the prodigiousness of Augustine's learning and assures him that he will soon become a "faithful and orthodox believer." Finally, rejoicing like the father of the prodigal son, "weeping and placing his ring on his son's finger" and kissing him, Ambrose baptizes Augustine in the sight of the community:

> [T]he Holy Spirit granted them eloquence and inspiration; and so, with all who were there hearing and seeing and marveling, they sang together the *Te Deum laudamus*, and so brought forth [*ediderunt*] what is now approved of by the whole church, and sung devoutly everywhere. Rejoicing together in God, like men just granted great riches and pearls of great price, they ate together and were very glad; they rejoiced with great joy, and took comfort in God.

This quasi-miraculous generation of the *Te Deum* within the spiritual energy between two holy men exemplifies the spontaneity and concord so often attributed to devotional music-making in the Christian tradition. The Latin *edere*, the verb Landulf selects to connote the collective "bringing forth" of the *Te Deum*, can be translated "to give birth," suggesting that Ambrose and Augustine together are responsible for figuratively reproducing a liturgical song that will be perpetuated through the mouths of those who continue to perform it.

Centuries before Landulf reported this account of the miraculous conception of the *Te Deum*, Augustine himself had recorded a different sort of miracle story centering around the performance of Christian music. Book 22 of the *City of God* recounts in detail over a dozen miracles he has heard about or witnessed: the healing of seemingly incurable diseases, tumors, and fistulas, as well as the exorcism of demons afflicting livestock and causing physical disorders. Although contemporary miracles do not enjoy the popularity they did in biblical times, evidence for their occurrence can be heard in the very melodies performed in Christ's name: "Christ is now sung [*cantatur*] everywhere, with such profound faith, as having been taken up to heaven with his flesh [*cum carne sublatus*]."[3] Such an incarnational song performs the most vivid bodily miracle described in the book. A young man possessed by a demon is brought into a nearby manor house for treatment, where he lay "at the point of death, and indeed looking very like a corpse." The situation appears hopeless until the lady of the house enters the room, along with her servants, "for the customary evening hymns and prayers [*hymnos et orationes*]; and they began to sing a hymn [*hymnos cantare*]":

> The youth was shaken out of his coma by their voices, as if by a sudden shock [*quasi percussus excussus est*]; and with a terrifying roar he seized hold of the altar, clutching it as if tied to it or stuck to it, not daring to move, or else without the power of movement. Then with a mighty shriek [*eiulatu*] the demon begged for mercy, and confessed when and where and how it had invaded the young man. Finally it declared that it would depart from him, and named the various limbs and parts which, so it threatened, it would maim as it left them; and while saying this, it withdrew from the man. But one of his eyes slipped down to his jaw, hanging by a small vein from the socket, as from its root, and the whole center of the eye, which had been dark, became white.[4]

The demon possessing the young man is exorcised by the musical violence of hymnody: the voices that "shook" the youth out of his coma, the melody that "shocked" him, produced a "terrifying roar" and forced the demon itself to emit an agonized *eiulatu* before it left the young man's body. Augustine's percussive imagery implies that the women's music quite literally beat the devil out of the possessed man, wrenching it from his body at the comparatively minor cost of a lost eye and several maimed limbs.

When examined side by side, these two snapshots of early Christian musical culture present remarkably dissimilar visions of the nature and significance of religious song. In Landulf's account of the meeting at Milan, Ambrose and Augustine embody an originary musical eloquence granted to them by God, a rhetorical musicality that allows them together to give spiritual birth to a specific liturgical song that by Landulf's own time is "sung together everywhere." Early Christian accounts of music-making contain many such descriptions of sublime devotional songs as sonorous panaceas promising a harmonious end to social dissension and signifying the musical immanence of salvation. In the words of Basil the Great, "A psalm is tranquility of soul and the arbitration of peace; it settles one's tumultuous and seething thoughts. It mollifies the soul's wrath and chastens its recalcitrance. A psalm creates friendships, unites the separated and reconciles those at enmity. Who can still consider one to be a foe with whom one sings the same prayer to God?"[5] Yet in *City of God* 22, musical sonority *is* "tumultuous," "seething," a Christian weapon that achieves a stark material agency as it penetrates a human body and wages an inner battle against a possessing demon.

While Landulf's story may accord with our expectations about Augustine's musical sensibilities, the narrative of musical violence in the *City of God* raises numerous and troubling questions. Are the sacred words of these "hymnos et orationes" alone responsible for the graphic denouement of the exorcism? How is it that a simple *cantus* can be invested with the extraordinary power to enter a body and engage in a violent struggle within? Conversely, what is it about the youth's body, and the human body in general, that allows the *corpus* to be musically penetrated and affected in such an extreme way? Is the body somehow predisposed to the kind of percussive musical spectacle described in such detail by Augustine? And is it truly the demon's exit from the young man's body that is responsible for leaving him disfigured, or should we suspect that the music itself has a primary role in the maiming?

Augustine's narrative does not provide answers to these questions, of course, nor should we expect it to. Its implications for his musical life more generally will become clear only once the eye-popping story above has been situated within a wider variety of musical stories, images, and memories described in his surviving writings. Here it is worth remembering that *De civitate Dei* was written near the end of Augustine's life. A very late work, its musical reflections could not be more distinct from those propounded in the writings of his younger years, to which I now turn.

"Free of all body"? The Early Writings

As he nears the conclusion of book 5 of *De musica libri sex*, an unfinished dialogue on rhythm, meter, and artistic perception that he began in the late 380s, Augustine records the following exhortation from Master to Disciple: "Let this be the end of the discussion, so we may next come with as much wisdom as we can from these sensible traces of music [*ab his vestigiis ejus sensibilibus*], all dealing with that part of it in the numbers of the times, to the real places where it is free of all body [*ubi ab omni corpore aliena est*]."[6] The injunction announces the author's move away from the changeable world of human language and song to the immutable realm of truth and number: the sixth book explores not the musical properties of poetic language, but the eternal "truth" that resides in number and proportion, the celestial geometry that, with rational study, can reveal something of the nature of God. While Augustine's actual influence on medieval musical theory and speculation is a matter of some debate,[7] there can be little doubt that the aspects of music with which he was most closely associated in later centuries were the numerical ones. Book 1 of the *De musica* formulates an oft-cited definition of music that many have taken as a reduction of the entire *scientia* to its mathematical foundations: "musica est scientia bene modulandi" ("Music is the science of measuring well").[8]

It comes as no surprise that whole sections of the *De ordine* were paraphrased by the author of the *Scholica enchiriadis* in support of his contention that number alone produces all that is beautiful and pleasurable in sounding music;[9] nor that most surveys of Western aesthetics cite Augustine primarily for his vision of the beauty residing in number, proportion, and measure, an aesthetic in which his musical speculation is given historical pride of place.[10] As a recent set of essays on the *De musica* and his other writings on music shows, Augustine's musical cosmology consists in large part of a Pythagorean emphasis on number and proportion, a practical attention to the rules of prosody and metrics, and a more or less consistent vision of biblical organology and *musica* itself as integral to the "spiritual quest of the soul."[11] Like many of the early Church fathers, he was greatly troubled by the capacity of music to arouse, and his writings on the subject often attribute this capacity to the *harmonia* of the soul rather than to the delectation of the flesh. Nevertheless, the conventional view of Augustine's musical thought as simply another expression of his "comprehensive, consistent and Christian metaphysics"[12] is only partially accurate. Even as he pondered the eternal numbers that expressed themselves imperfectly in material things, Augustine was perplexed throughout his career both by the corporeality he discerned in musical sonority and by the mysteriously musical qualities of human bodies.

Though Augustine consistently employs idealizing platonic musical terminology—*harmonia, consonantia, coaptatione*—in his representations of the mysterious rational order of the universe, the category of *musica* in his works nevertheless unites practical and theoretical concerns. Indeed, as Leo Treitler has argued, for Augustine the seemingly rarefied *scientia* of *musica speculativa* did not exclude *musica practica*, the everyday performances of Christian music in late antiquity.[13] His stated desire to "free" his discussion of music from "all body" surely is a sign of his conviction that the "numbers of the times," the transitory rhythms of earthly life, can be transcended, that in some sense there exists a place where music is "more real" and closer to God than the sounding music experienced by living persons. But he repeatedly confronts the fact that we can perceive these fixed and universal proportions only through and within the ever-changing shapes and rhythms of our emphatically mutable bodies. Again, while most studies of Augustine's musical cosmology have stressed his philosophical and aesthetic consistency, arguing for an underlying continuity from the *De musica* through the *Retractiones,*[14] I want to examine the inconsistencies in which the problem of corporeality often mires his treatments of musical beauty and experience. For it is in the numerous contradictions and discontinuities within and between his writings that Augustine reveals what can only be described as a profound obsession with the human body—and his own in particular—in theorizing the personal and philosophical significance of music.

As we have just seen, the penultimate book of the *De musica* concludes with a stridently anticorporeal injunction to move away from "body" and mutability. The opening words of book 6 continue in the same vein, seemingly repudiating the contents of the preceding five books:

We have delayed long enough and very childishly, too, through five books, in those number-traces belonging to time-intervals. And let us hope a dutiful labor will readily excuse our triviality in the eyes of benevolent men. For we only thought it ought to be undertaken so adolescents, or men of any age God has endowed with a good natural capacity, might with reason guiding be torn away, not quickly but gradually, from the fleshly senses and letters [*a sensibus carnis atquo a carnalibus litteris*] it is difficult for them not to stick to, and adhere with the love of unchangeable truth to one God and Master of all things who with no mean term whatsoever directs human minds.[15]

This rather jarring dismissal is in part a product of chronology: Augustine wrote the first five books of the treatise in Milan around 387, completing book 6 in Africa in 391.[16] Once again, however, he calls for what he later terms a "pass[ing] from corporeal to incorporeal things" (*a corporeis ad incorporea*),[17] a "tearing away" from the "fleshly senses" of earthly number and the trivial carnality of adolescence; the "truest" music is that which allows the soul to adhere to God, the ratios that are, like him, eternal, unchanging, and incorporeal. As Carol Harrison puts it, "music finds its ideal form not in performance but in knowledge of numerical theory in the mind."[18]

Such negative assessments of the body and the senses typify Augustine's early writings. The *Soliloquies*, written a year before the *De musica*, argue for the soul's absolute superiority to the flesh, a constant source of irritation to its higher companion: "although in this life the soul is already blessed because of its understanding of God, it still endures many annoyances [*multas molestias*] because of the body, and must therefore hope that all these inconveniences will no longer exist after death."[19] In the *De immortalitate animae* (387) as well, body is a cumbersome weight, constantly dragging the soul down to its level and preventing it from achieving its full potential: "You must flee from all these things connected with the senses, and you must take great care that while we manage this body, the feathers of our wings do not become stuck together through the slime that oozes from the things of sense";[20] or, in a similar passage, "The body has not intelligence, and the soul has not intelligence with the help of the body, because it turns away from the body when it wants to act with intelligence. . . . The body, therefore, cannot help the soul when it is striving towards understanding: it is enough if it does not hinder it."[21]

All of these works were written in the mid- to late 380s, a crucial turning point in Augustine's intellectual and spiritual life. Like many of his early works, they reveal the former Manichaean auditor's desire for what Peter Brown, employing an appropriately musical metaphor, terms "a light-filled harmony of souls set free from matter" that was the Manichee's vision of perfection.[22] Just as he was making an intellectual break from Manichaean dualism, Augustine was absorbing the *libri Platonicorum*, the great corpus of neoplatonic writings that were a hallmark of Milanese intellectual life.[23] It was perhaps a combination of his neoplatonic hope for a musical Idea and his Manichaean distrust of the flesh that led Augustine to postulate a musical state "free of all body" theorized in the *De musica*. The second *Soliloquy* constructs a hierarchy of soul and body founded on the relative truth and falsity of the musico-numerical forms they manifest: "Who is so blind in his mind that he could not see that the forms which are the subject of geometry dwell in the truth itself or the truth dwells in them? The forms in bodies, on the other hand, even if they appear to aspire to the others, contain some imitation or other of the truth and are, therefore, false."[24] Expressing the eternal and unchangeable inherence of number in soul rather than its particular and malleable presence in body, *musica* is clearly one of the forms "subject to geometry" that Augustine has in mind, as a rather bizarre analogy between music and what we would call the unconscious suggests: "Either there may be something in the soul which is not present to consciousness, or the art of music is not present in the soul of the trained musician when he is thinking only about geometry."[25] *Musica scientia* constitutes the very subjectivity of the *musicus*; even when the musician performs, *musica practica* can be only a pale imitation of the geometrical Idea.

Yet even in his early writings, in which he subordinates the experiential corporeality of music to its spiritual idealization, the terms of his own arguments often force Augustine to acknowledge an underlying and natural reciprocity between musicality and corporeality. In a particularly telling example, a discussion of the pulse in book 6, chapter 3, the dialogue's Master asserts that the soul contains within itself unchanging musical numbers, which it expresses in the body how and when it chooses:

> The soul produces the numbers we find in the beat of the veins [*in venarum pulsu*]. . . . For it is clear they are in the operation and we are no whit helped

with them by the memory. And if it is not sure in the case of these whether they belong to the soul operating . . . there is no doubt there are numbers in its time-intervals, and the soul so operates them that they can also be changed in many ways when the will is applied.[26]

Casting the "beat of the veins" as music produced by the soul in the body, Augustine anticipates what would become an important theme for medieval encyclopedists and medical writers.[27] Here he ascribes to the *soul* the power to regulate and "operate" the pulse; the soul's numbers—its beats, rhythms, and intervals—cause blood to flow at a chosen rate through the veins of an otherwise passive body. In the next passage, however, the Disciple, without being contradicted by his Master, asserts that these discernible variations of pulse result from the natural diversity of bodies:

> Although I do not doubt the various vein-beats and respiration-intervals are created for the equilibrium of bodies [*pro temperatione corporum*], yet who would so much as deny they are created by the soul in operation? And if the flow, according to the diversity of bodies [*pro diversitate corporum*], is faster for some, slower for others, yet, unless there is a soul to produce it, there is none.[28]

The difference is subtle: both passages clearly ascribe to the soul the production and operation of the pulse. But as soon as he confidently asserts that the soul can vary it "when the will is applied," Augustine suggests in the next breath that the pulse's *temperatio* varies from one body to another according to their own natural "diversity." Augustine wants to have it both ways, and at no point does he acknowledge his inconsistency.

"Pleasures of the Ears": The *Confessions*

If an ambiguity regarding music's corporeality subtends much of Augustine's early speculation on the subject, the *Confessions* finds him tackling the problem explicitly, repeatedly, and with a fair measure of anxiety. As it does in so many ways, the *Confessions* records an agonized yet profound transformation in Augustine's musical imagination, from a tenuous disavowal of music's corporeality to a guarded but thorough assimilation of the musical body into his cosmology. It is here that he attempts to come most directly to terms not only with the indispensability of the bodily senses to the perception and enjoyment of music, but also, and much more importantly, with the musicality of his *own* flesh.

Karl Morrison writes that throughout his life Augustine held an "abiding conviction that understanding was not linguistic," and that music was capable of providing a direct mystical access "without the mediation of any text."[29] In the *Confessions*, music constitutes "not so much an exercise of feeling oneself into a text as . . . of absorbing the sense of the words into the pith and heart of one's very being."[30] Such a nonlinguistic absorption of sense is one of the crucial ways through which Augustine imagines himself experiencing music throughout the work; at the same time, language seems inextricably linked with the various forms of bodily resonance described. Recalling his conversion in book 9, for example, he writes, "The days seemed long and many, all of us desiring the freedom and leisure to sing from the marrow of our bones [*de medullis*], 'My heart has said to you, "I have sought your face, your face [O Lord] will I require."'"[31] Similarly, book 12 begins with a description of the author's "heart . . . pulsat[ing] with the words of your Holy Scriptures" (cor meum . . . pulsatum verbis sanctae scripturae tuae) (12.1.1); later in the book, these same words become a "leafy orchard" full of "hidden fruit," and readers are bees who "fly about it in joy, breaking into song as they gaze at the fruit and feed upon it" (12.28.38). In the *Confessions*, the body quite literally pulsates with music—from the marrow and the heart, both of which encounter biblical language in musical form and internalize it within the Christian subject.

It was in a quite particular musical guise, however, that the words of Scripture would affect Augustine most deeply. Throughout the *Confessions* we find him returning again and again to the music that must have surrounded him from the moment of his baptism: the pleasurable yet paradoxical strains of Christian psalmody. Readers have long noted the complex intercalation of past and present characterizing the *Confessions*, an effect produced in part by the frequency with which a seemingly insignificant detail or image from a remembered event catapults Augustine into the past or closer to the narrative present.[32] One particularly rich example of this technique occurs in the middle of book 9, chapter 6, which recounts the events leading up to Augustine's baptism in 387. After the baptism, he remembers, "all anxiety over the past fled," and the music that celebrated the rite produced distinctly visceral effects: "How much I wept at your hymns and canticles [*hymnis et canticis tuis*], moved deeply by the sweetly-sounding voices of your church. The voices flooded into my ears, truth seeped into my heart, and my feelings of piety overflowed, and tears streamed down, and to me it seemed they were good" (9.6.14). The passage is rife with the imagery of liquefaction: the hymns "flooded into" (*influebant*) Augustine's ears, their truth was "liquefied" (*eliquabatur*) in his heart, causing his devotion to "boil over" (*exaestuabat*) and run down his cheeks (*currebant*) in the form of tears.[33]

The author's musical memory stretches more distantly into the past at the opening of the next chapter, which relates the events surrounding Ambrose's introduction of Eastern chant into the everyday religious practice of the Milanese church. Augustine recalls the highly charged political climate in which Ambrose's musical innovations took place:

> It was not long before this that the Church of Milan had begun to seek comfort and spiritual strength in this way [*genus hoc*, referring to *hymnis et canticis* in the final passage from chapter 6], in which the faithful united fervently with heart and voice [*vocibus et cordibus*]. It was only a year, or not much more, since Justina, the mother of the boy emperor Valentinian, had been persecuting your devoted servant Ambrose in the interests of the heresy into which the Arians had seduced her. In those days your faithful people used to keep watch in the church, ready to die with their bishop, your servant. (9.7.15)

The so-called Ambrosian chant, Augustine insists, came into being exactly in this context of religious persecution—indeed, as a direct response to the very real threat of death hanging over the heads of Christians in the late Roman Empire.[34] Music was deployed as a means of shielding the threatened Christian community from the city's "disturbed" (*turbata*) and dangerous state: "It was then that the singing of hymns and psalms was instituted, following the custom of eastern parts [*orientalium partium*], to revive the flagging spirits of the people during their long and cheerless watch." Since that time, Milanese chant has been adopted "throughout the rest of the world" (*per cetera orbis*)[35]; when introduced in Milan itself, however, it provided the musical setting for a momentous occasion in local history: "It was at that time too that you revealed to your bishop Ambrose in a vision the place where the bodies of the martyrs Protasius and Gervasius were hidden. All these years you had preserved them incorrupt [*incorrupta*] in your secret treasury [*thesauro*], so that when the time came you could

bring them to light to thwart the fury of a mere woman (though a ruler)"
(9.7.15–16). After the bodies are exhumed [*effossa*], Ambrose orders them
carried to his basilica "with the honor that was due to them"; during the
procession, the mere presence of the martyrs' cadavers cures a number of
faithful from demonic possession, and a blind man who touches the bier
with his handkerchief has his sight miraculously restored when he puts the
cloth to his eyes. Finally, upon hearing of the events, Justina, though not
converted, nevertheless relents somewhat "from the furor of persecution" (*a
persequendi . . . furore*), and Augustine offers a thankful prayer for the
salvation of his community:

> Thanks be to you, my God! Why have you prompted my memory so that I
> should confess to you these great events which I had forgotten to mention?
> Yet even then, when the fragrance of your perfumes allured, I did not hasten
> after you. So I wept all the more during the music of your hymns, at certain
> times breathing in to you, at last exhaling, at least in so far as human frailty
> can perceive it. (9.7.16)

The dense juxtaposition of music, martyrdom, and salvation constituting this brief chapter reveals two fundamental ways in which Augustine had
come to terms with the music of the flesh by the time he wrote the *Confessions*. In both its narrative structure and its imagery the chapter aligns the
newly introduced musical practice of the Milanese Christians with the
salvific powers of the bodies they unearth.[36] Just as the first section describes
the efficacy of the eastern chant in boosting the morale of the persecuted,
the second narrates the success of the paraded corpses in eliminating the
threat of massacre. The chapter begins and ends with Augustine's vivid
memories of psalmody's origin in a climate of persecution, a framing device
that spectacularly anticipates the denouement of Chaucer's Prioress's Tale,
treated in Chapter 6 of this volume. As in Chaucer's narrative of the "litel
clergeoun," the constitution of Christian community around the bodies of
the martyrs is celebrated and remembered through the community's collective acts of music-making.

The chapter thus registers the author's initial realization that the beauty
and power of music lie not in the transcendence of materiality in favor of a
sublime geometry "free of all body," but in the stimulation and vivification
of the flesh. On this point chronology is of the utmost importance. Au-

gustine wrote the *Confessions* between 397 and 401, beginning a decade after his baptism in 387 and at least twelve years after the bout of persecution by Justina in 385. It was also in the mid-380s that Augustine had written the *De immortalitate animae* (387), the *Soliloquies* (386), and the first five books of the *De musica* (387; book 6 was completed by 391). Looking back from the *Confessions* to his musical life in the 380s—the same years in which he vilified the *multae molestiae* of the body, proposed a move from "corporeal to incorporeal things" in musical speculation, and described the ideal musician as one who thinks "only of geometry"—Augustine reclaims musical production and reception as practices of the flesh.

Augustine never repudiated the *De musica*, and I do not mean to suggest that *Confessions* 9.7 abnegates the centrality of number and proportion to his appreciation for the beauty of sounding music. The musical bodies he delineates in his later works remain *proportional* bodies as well: Looking back on the *De musica* in the *Retractions*, Augustine would emphatically confirm the divine mystery of "the unchangeable numbers which are already in unchangeable truth itself." Yet he would do so by dubiously asserting that certain sections of the *De musica* were originally intended as a musical defense of bodily resurrection(!), that the treatise had in fact been inspired by the promise of the "corporeal numbers in incorruptible and spiritual bodies," and that these numbers will be apparent in our bodies when they become "more beautiful and more lovely" at the resurrection.[37] In the *Retractions*, in other words, Augustine seeks to recuperate the *De musica* as part of an *antidualist, incarnational* musical aesthetic, one that was in fact realized only gradually and after many years had passed since its writing. The *Confessions* clearly represents a crucial turning point for Augustine, an expression of his thankful recognition that music had at last become something he could truly feel and experience: both a fragrance that he breathed in and out and a liquid that entered his body, gushed through him like a river overflowing its banks, and erupted in his tears.

Augustine was not untroubled by his sinful indulgence in the sensual pleasures of religious music. When he famously confronts his own tendency toward musical sensuality in book 10, in fact, he has his account of the pleasures of psalmody in the preceding book demonstrably in mind. After his lengthy excursus on the memory in the earlier chapters, he begins what he calls a "discussion of the body's temptations to pleasure" in chapters 29–

34, which treat the many "pleasures of the flesh" (*concupiscentiae carnis*) to which gratification of the senses can lead (10.34.51). While "the sense of smell does not trouble [him] greatly," he must constantly "wage war" upon his appetite, the hunger and thirst that "parch and kill like a fever," while his eyes "delight in beautiful shapes of different sorts and bright and attractive colors" (10.31.43, 10.34.51). Though he struggles mightily with his vulnerability to rich food and pleasing sights, the specific temptations of music represent a kind of limiting case; while he is equally reluctant to forego the pleasures of food and drink, he both forswears and affirms the embodied pleasures of music in the course of his discussion:

> The pleasures of the ears [*voluptates aurium*] used to fascinate and subjugate me more tenaciously [than those of the nose], but you broke my bonds and set me free. I still find, I confess, a tiny bit of enjoyment in these sounds, which your praises animate, when they are sung with a sweet and skillful voice [*suavi et artificiosa voce*]; but not so much that I adhere to it, for I can arise whenever I wish [*surgam cum volo*]. (10.33.49)

"Surgam cum volo": With the self-assured defensiveness of an addict, Augustine claims he can free himself from his musical vice any time he chooses; but he immediately acknowledges the quandary into which his musical addiction has forced him: "But if I am not to turn a deaf ear to music, which is the setting for the words which give it life, I must allow it a position of some honor in my heart, and I find it difficult to assign it to its proper place. For sometimes I feel that I treat it with more honor than it deserves" (10.33.49). While much previous discussion has cast this chapter as depicting, for example, the "conflict within [Augustine's] soul engendered by his spontaneous love of music on the one hand and his Christian conscience on the other,"[38] we might learn more from his worryings over music if we see them as signs not solely of a personal conflict he wishes to resolve, but also of a fundamental contradiction upon which his larger vision of music and devotion depends.

Augustine owns up to his inconsistency at several points in the course of his confessional account of musical delectation. Although he argues on the surface for the priority of words over music, he is much more intrigued by the particular ways in which Christian song produces its *non*linguistic effects: "I am aware that when sung these sacred words stir my mind to greater religious fervor and kindle in me a more burning flame of piety than they would if they were not sung; and I know as well that there are certain modes in song and voice, corresponding to my various emotions and able to stimulate them because of some mysterious relationship between the two" (10.33.49). Here Augustine gives full credence to Hellenic theories of modes and moods; like Clement, he cannot fully abandon classical assumptions about the physiological effects of music, effects entirely unrelated to the words that are sung. Though well aware of the dangers of such modal stimulation, Augustine nevertheless cites the perils of being "too strict" in adherence to musical sobriety—as in the case of the Alexandrian bishop Athanasius, "who used to make readers recite the psalms with such slight changing of the voice that they seemed to be speaking rather than chanting" (10.33.50).

The chapter concludes by harking back to the account of baptism in book 9 and the "tears that I shed at the songs of the Church long ago, upon recovering my faith." As Augustine would have us believe, the pleasures he then took in music were merely an effect of a youthful exuberance he has now overcome: "these days I am not moved by the song, but by the matters [*rebus*] that are sung, when in a fluid voice [*liquida voce*] and with the most suitable measure [*convenientissima modulatione*]." Despite the primly confident tone of his denial, however, he quickly backtracks once again:

> So I waver between the danger that lies in gratifying the senses and the benefits which, as I know from experience, can accrue from singing. Without committing myself to an irrevocable opinion, I am inclined to approve of the custom of singing in church, in order that by indulging the ears weaker spirits may be inspired with feelings of devotion. Yet when I find the singing itself more moving than the truth which it conveys, I confess that this is a grievous sin, and at those times I would prefer not to hear the singer. (10.33.50)

Waver he certainly does. Making no attempt to disguise his inconsistency, Augustine reluctantly approves "the custom of singing in church" because "indulging the ears" of the weak is often necessary in order to lure them into the fold. Yet he terms this very indulgence "a grievous sin" when applied to his own behavior; the risk of carnal sin is worth taking, then, if it produces "feelings of devotion."[39] Although he has asserted more than once that he has recovered from his musical dependency and now finds the words more moving than the music, in this passage his sinful musical desires remain a pressing and very much present-tense concern (e.g., *accidit, canitur, moveat*).

The true scope of Augustine's disingenuousness can be appreciated if *Confessions* 10 is read alongside his equally famous but decidedly nonascetic accounts of the *jubilus*, a term most likely referring to the lengthy melisma (single syllable of text performed to a string of notes) sung on the final syllable of the Alleluia.[40] Several passages in the *Enarrationes in Psalmos* gloss biblical words and phrases such as "psallite in iubilo" (Psalm 32:3), "iubilemus" (94:1), or "iubilate" (99:1) with an account of the liturgical practice of jubilation, as in this rhapsodic comment on Psalm 94:

> One who jubilates [*iubilat*] does not speak words, but it is rather a sort of sound of joy without words; for the voice of the soul is poured out in joy [*diffusi laetitia*], showing as much as it is able the feeling without comprehending the sense. A man joying in his exultation, from certain unspeakable and incomprehensible words, bursts forth [*erumpit*] in a certain voice of exultation without words, so that it seems he does indeed rejoice with his own voice, but as if, because filled with too much joy, he cannot put into words what it is in which he delights.[41]

Taking "unspeakable" pleasure in the pure embodied experience of singing, he delights in the "feeling" of a music utterly divorced from language. The imagery evokes the liquid strains described in *Confessions* 9.7 as the soul's voice is "poured out" in joy through the mouth, the singer himself "burst[ing] forth" in exultation. This naturalistic celebration of the jubilus becomes even more explicit as the discussion concludes: "Mowers and vintagers and those who gather other products, happy in the abundance of harvest and gladdened by the very richness and fecundity of the earth, sing in joy. And between the songs [*inter cantica*] which they express in words, they insert [*inserunt*] certain sounds without words in the elevation of an exultant spirit, and this is called jubilation."[42] While Stephen J. Nichols may be correct to identify "a fundamental distrust of orality as an agent of the *vox corporis*" pervading Augustine's representations of writing and performance in the *Confessions*, this distrust results less from what Nichols terms his "scriptocentri[sm]" than from his sense that that which is "oralized," namely language, can never approach the unmediated ability of music to provide closeness to God.[43]

Augustine is emphatic on this point in another description of the jubilus earlier in the *Enarrationes*: "And if you cannot speak him, yet ought not to be silent, what remains but that you jubilate; so that the heart rejoices without words, and the great expanse of joy has not the limits of syllables [*metas non habeat syllabarum*]? 'Sing well unto him in jubilation.'"[44] Exceeding and surpassing "the limits of syllables" in musical jubilation, Augustine undermines his own confident proclamation in *Confessions* 10 that he has grown out of his youthful preference for music over words. Like Gregory of Nyssa, Augustine seems to sense something innately non- or even prelinguistic in music's flow through the human body.

Almost all of the musical passages in the *Confessions* are concerned in some way with the actual practice of hymnody. Yet perhaps the most revealing image of musical corporeality in the work is not an agonized account of its author's reactions to musical practice, but a highly technical musical analogy explicated in the emotionless monotone of the philosopher. Near the end of book 12, in the course of a lengthy commentary on Genesis 1, the discussion turns to the question of the relationship between form and matter at the Creation, particularly the implications of the phrase "In the Beginning" ("In principio"). Those who take this phrase to imply the priority of form over matter are clearly wrong; while the statement "God first created matter without form and then gave it form" is closer to the truth, however, it demands a subtle and multiple definition of priority, which comes in at least four varieties: priority in eternity, or "that which is God's, because he pre-exists all things"; priority in time, "the priority of the blossom, for instance, in relation to the fruit"; priority in choice, "the priority of the fruit, which we should choose before the blossom"; and, finally, priority in origin, "the priority of sound, for example, before song." Though priority in time and choice are "easy enough to understand," Augustine argues, "the first and last are extremely difficult":

> [I]t is only rarely and with great difficulty that a man can discern your eternity, O Lord, creating things that are subject to change yet never suffering change itself and thereby being prior to them all. It also requires acute mental perception to see, without great effort, how sound precedes song. For song is formed sound [*cantus est formatus sonus*], and although a thing may

very well exist without order, order cannot be given to a thing which does not exist. In the same way matter precedes what is made from it, though neither in the sense that it makes anything, because its role is passive rather than active, nor in the sense that it precedes it in time. We do not first emit formless sounds [*sonos . . . informes*], which do not constitute song, and then adapt them and fashion them in the form of song as we do with wood when we make a box, or with silver when we make a bowl. . . . For when a song is sung, the sound that is heard is the song itself: it is not first heard as a formless noise, which is afterwards formed into a song. For a sound is no sooner uttered than it dies away, and nothing remains of it for a singer to take up and compose into a song. Therefore the song is inseparable from the sound, which is its material [*materies eius*]. In order to become a song the sound receives form. (12.29.40)

Sound does not precede song in the sense that it has the power to make it, "because it is not sound, but the singer, who creates the song; sound is made available from the singer's body [*ex corpore*] to his mind that he may make a song from it." From this example, Augustine hopes, we should understand that, although "the matter of things was made first and was called heaven and earth," this does not mean that matter came first in time, "because there is time only where there is form, whereas this matter was formless and we are only aware of it in time together with its form" (12.29.40).

The analogy is extended, complex, and quite startling. Song is to sound as form is to matter, giving it its distinctive shape within the time and space of musical performance.[45] Although the chapter does not address the physiological effects of music, this philosophical analogy speaks volumes about music's physical origins within the body: hymns and canticles become what they are exactly when they are drawn *ex corpore*, giving form to the materiality of sound. Even as it "dies away" (praeterit), song must always carry with it the flesh that gives it life.

The Musical Cadaver: Later Years and the *City of God*

Although his post-*Confessions* writings do not display the same kind of self-conscious agonizing over the sensuality of religious music, Augustine returned more than once to the music of body in his later years. Like numerous other patristic writers, he saw the musical instruments in the

Psalms as scriptural provocations to a human musicality, as his influential gloss of Psalm 150 suggests:

> [T]here are three kinds of sound, by voice, by breath, and by striking [*voce, flatu, pulsu*]: by voice, that is by the throat and wind pipe of a singing man without any sort of instrument; by breath, as with the tibia or anything of that kind; by striking, as with the cithara or anything of that sort . . . there is voice in the chorus, breath in the trumpet, and striking in the cithara; just like mind, spirit, and body, but through similarity, not actual properties.[46]

As the last phrase reveals, Augustine was cautious about the literalism of these kinds of metaphors throughout the *Enarrationes*;[47] yet there can be little doubt that he had rejected the disembodied view of musical number and ratio characterizing his early works. Indeed, in the *De Trinitate* musical embodiment signifies the very mystery of the incarnation. For the platonizing Augustine, this sympathy between God and humanity—this "correspondence, agreement, consent, or whatever other word may be appropriate for describing how one is joined to two"—is registered not only in the nature and image of humanity in general, but even in the individual joints of the body, "in every fitting-together of the creature, or perhaps it would be better to call it, in every co-adaptation of the creature." *Coaptatione* is a crucial term for Augustine, representing a self-conscious Latinization of the Platonic notion of individual *harmonia*:

> It just now occurs to me, that what I mean by this coadaptation is what the Greeks call *harmonian*. But this is neither the time nor the place to show how important is the harmony between the single and the double, which is found particularly in us, and which has been naturally so implanted in us . . . that not even the ignorant can remain unaware of it, whether they themselves are singing, or whether they are listening to others; for by means of it the higher and lower voices [*acutiores . . . gravioresque*] blend together, and anyone who sounds a note that does not harmonize with it commits an offense not only against the musical art of which most people are ignorant, but against our very sense of hearing. It would require a long treatise, however, to prove this, but one familiar with the subject can demonstrate it to the ear itself on a properly-adjusted monochord.[48]

Once again Augustine reveals his sense of the epistemological superiority of music to language: "even the ignorant" can perceive the internal *harmonia* "implanted" within our bodies and gluing us together, harmony that he likens to an actual musical performance, the blending of high and low voices in a choir. Recommending a monochord to the doubter, he implies that the proportional relationship between notes struck from this pedagogical device can reveal something of the structure of our bodies, which in turn will lead to an enhanced understanding of the nature of the incarnation.

It is a measure of Augustine's acceptance of the body's inner *harmonia* that he employs the concept even when discussing the nature of the redeemed body at the resurrection. Sermon 243, for example, puzzles at length over why the resurrection body will require its internal organs if biological processes such as digestion and reproduction will not occur.[49] Initially he dodges the problem of the internal organs by discussing the functions of the mouth, which seem to present an easier case since "we employ the teeth not only for chewing, but also for speaking, our tongue like a plectrum striking strings that it might articulate syllables" (Dentes enim non tantum nos adjuvant ad mandendum, verum etiam ad loquendum; sicut plectru nervos, sic linguam nostram, ut syllabas sonet, percutientes).[50] Yet the teeth and tongue are an exception; unlike them, the internal organs will be recovered because "certain of our members will be present for seeing, not for using, for the excellence of beauty, not for the want of necessity." To explain how exactly the viscera will be interconnected and "by what numbers coadapted" (*quibus numeris coaptata*), Augustine turns to imagery familiar from the *De Trinitate*; this time, however, the corporeal *harmonia* is a mixture not of the many voices of a choir, but of the many strings of a cithar:

> For this [coadaptation] is called *harmonia*, which is a word used in music, when, for example, we see strings stretched [*nervos distentos*] on a cithar. If all of the strings sound the same, there is no song [*nulla est cantilenae*]. Diverse tension produces diverse sounds; but these diverse sounds joined together in order [*ratione*] produce not the beauty of things seen, but the sweetness of things heard. That which will divide this order among the human members is so marvelous, so delightful, that it will be preferred to all the visible beauty of intelligible things.[51]

The wondrousness of the resurrection body is as much a product of the harmonious music that holds it together from within as it is of the incorruptible beauty of its individual parts.

This imagery represents a paradoxical exception to Augustine's general conception of the resurrection body. As Caroline Walker Bynum has argued, Augustine consistently posits bodily salvation as "the crystalline hardness not only of stasis but of the impossibility of non-stasis." This view reflects his abiding anxiety over process, rot, and decay, an anxiety that led him to believe that "all dynamism must disappear in heaven if we are to be redeemed" and to reject Stoic notions of seminal reason that so influenced his discussions of natural process in the *De Genesi ad litteram*.[52] Here, however, in the midst of a discussion of the resurrection, Augustine employs the emphatically Stoic notion of the tongue as a plectrum and the teeth as strings in a passage that may well be paraphrased directly from Cicero's *De natura deorum*, a treatise he knew in detail but condemned with great relish in book 5 of the *City of God*.[53] This is one of the few places in his eschatological discussions where Augustine *does* attribute a certain dynamism to the resurrection body, allowing its "crystalline hardness" to give way, if only for a moment, to the naturalism of his musical imagery. In the terms of Augustine's own metaphor, if the organs of the resurrection body truly resemble the *nervos distentos* of a cithar—its stretched strings or, more literally, its distended sinews—then they *must* vibrate and fluctuate, as a crystal or a statue never could, to produce the resonant harmonies he so admires.

In his final years, as the *City of God* neared completion, Augustine would return once more (also in the context of resurrection) to the marvelous *coaptationes* vivifying the human body and expressing the divine image in its structure. The miracles described in book 22 (such as the one with which this chapter began) provide essential evidence for what is later referred to in the book as "the blessings which God has bestowed, and still bestows, even on the corrupted and condemned state of mankind" in the present life.[54] For Augustine, "even in the body, which is something we have in common with the brute creation—which is in fact weaker than the bodies of any of the lower animals—even here what evidence we find of the goodness of God, of the providence of the mighty Creator." Aside from the obvious utility and workmanship of the individual body parts, "there is a numerical congruence [*congruentia numerosa*] between them, a beauty in their equality" with one another. Here once again are the mysterious *coaptationes* of the human body, numbers that would be readily apparent to us "if we were aware of the precise proportions in which the components are combined and fitted together; and it may be that human wit could discover these proportions, if it set itself to the task, in the exterior parts." But the *coaptationes* present *within* the body, the numbers that structure our viscera, veins, and organs, must and will remain forever unknown:

> As for the parts which are hidden from view, like the complex system of veins, sinews and internal organs, the secrets of the vital parts, the proportions of these are beyond discovery. Even though some surgeons, anatomists they are called, have ruthlessly applied themselves to the carving up of dead bodies, even though they have cut into the bodies of dying men to make their examinations, and have probed into all the secrets of the human body, with little regard for humanity, in order to assist their diagnosis, to locate the trouble and find a method of cure—even after all that, no man could ever find, no man has ever dared to try to find, those numbers [*numeros*] of which I am speaking, by which the whole body [*totius corporis*], within and without, is arranged in a system of co-adaptation [*coaptatio*]. The Greeks call this adaptation *harmonia*, on the analogy of a musical instrument [*tamquam cuiusdam organi*]; and if we were aware of it, we should find in the internal organs also, which make no display of beauty, a rational loveliness [*pulchritudo rationis*] so delightful as to be preferred to all that gives pleasure to the eyes in the outward form.[55]

As in the *De musica*, musical number harmonizes the human person in the image of God. This imaginative musical autopsy demonstrates emphatically, however, that musical number now resides and inheres *within the body*, not the soul alone; even the "internal organs," though perhaps gruesome and unsightly on the outside, contain a "rational loveliness" that will reveal itself to the eyes of the redeemed.

We have come a long way indeed from the anxious author of the *De musica*, the youthful Manichaean auditor who desired to "free" music from "all body" and greeted any suggestion of musical somatics with deep suspicion. As an old man staring his own death in the face, Augustine seems to be implying the fixity of musical ratio *even within the cadaver* as an enduring promise of the body's melodious return at the last trumpet. Body can no more be freed of its music than music itself can be unmarked by the bodies that produce and contain it, whether overflowing in psalmody or lying dead on an anatomist's table.

The searching passage above seems to me a fitting encapsulation of the trajectory of Augustine's musical life, for it exemplifies the great personal and philosophical puzzle music represented from his earliest works to his latest. No matter how passionately he desired to describe and contain music and its effects, no matter how deeply he delved into the properties of bodies dead, alive, or redeemed, their music always remained elusive, indescribable, but emphatically present at the same time. Unlike Gregory of Nyssa, who saw the musics and harmonies of body in mundane processes such as sleeping, breathing, and speaking, Augustine used them to explore the miraculous metamorphoses entailed in the resurrection and incarnation. This should not surprise us, however, for even these transformations posed no greater puzzle for Augustine than did the intertwined mysteries of music and embodiment.

PART 2

Liturgies of Desire

CHAPTER 3

Sine Tactu Viri: The Musical Somatics of Hildegard of Bingen

P art 1 of this book examined a variety of writings and images from the early Christian era that speak to patristic theology's most enduring yet contested legacy to medieval musical cultures: the resonance of the flesh. The incarnational understanding of music had its roots in ancient philosophical thought, but it was the Christian writers of late antiquity who imagined the graceful, mysterious, and tortured musical bodies that later writers would animate in their own ways. As I pointed out at the beginning of Chapter 1, one of the dangers of beginning a study such as this with early Christian writings is the risk of imposing an Exegetical uniformity upon the diversity of the medieval sources. While the medieval cultures examined in the following chapters sometimes evidence the same confluence of musical pain and pleasure found in patristic cultures, what I hope will become clear is the sheer variety of contentious and even dissident ways in which they do so. The subject of this book may well constitute a kind of musico-intellectual tradition, one that embraces the singing voices of Hildegard of Bingen's nuns along with the sonorous conversion of Augustine, the musical death of Chaucer's clergeon and the resonant martyrdom of Ambrose's Maccabees; if so, however, it is a tradition that embraces immense variety and affords numerous possibilities for revision.

Each of the following chapters takes up a particular theme, cultural moment, or ideological trajectory in the medieval history of musical embodiment. The chapters included in Part 2, "Liturgies of Desire," adopt two very different approaches to the musical life of an epoch of profound cultural change in western Europe. Intellectual and religious historians still often refer to the twelfth century as a "renaissance," while literary critics associate it with the rise and eventual triumph of the vernaculars as literary languages. It was an era that humanized its deity in new ways while sponsoring horrific violence against those who refused to accept a particular version of this deity's teachings.

To historians of music, the twelfth century is perhaps best known for the emergence of liturgical polyphony at the cathedral of Notre Dame in Paris. As we shall see in Chapter 4, the polyphonic embellishment of liturgical chant created spectacularly new ways of imagining and experiencing musical and bodily relationships. Plainchant, too, allowed for forms of musical pleasure that are difficult to understand outside a certain history of sexuality. An implicit argument of both chapters in Part 2 is that, for the musical cultures of Hildegard and Leoninus, the histories of music and sexuality are in many ways inseparable; the widespread medieval anxiety of "sex in holy places," as Dyan Elliott has recently termed it, proves very often a musical anxiety.[1]

The fact that these are predominantly *homosocial* musical cultures—cultures that carefully segregated their musical performances and enjoyments into all-male and all-female environments—implies that the musical desires and pleasures they embrace will often be homoerotic. Chapters 3 and 4 (and 7, though in a different way) are intended in part to fill in the musical blank in the burgeoning medievalist subfield of lesbian, gay, bisexual, and queer studies—or, to adopt Eve Kosofsky Sedgwick's convenient term, in *antihomophobic* medieval studies. In the twenty years since the publication of John Boswell's *Christianity, Social Tolerance, and Homosexuality*, this field has grown by leaps and bounds, and the bibliography now includes contributions by historians of art, literature, law, theater, religion, and philosophy. While suggesting some of the ways in which medieval music and medieval musicians participated in the myriad same-sex practices these scholars have revealed, I hope as well to show that music constituted a mode of sexual pleasure, anxiety, and fascination all its own. Same-sex musical cultures provide a ubiquitous but virtually untapped source for those of us seeking to expand our antihomophobic inquiries into the medieval past. The nature and representation of such practices will change over time and space, of course, and we should be cautious about imputing homoeroticism to certain musical experiences simply because they were shared by members of the same sex. Yet many medieval writers were quite self-conscious about the erotics of musical performance and reception—none of them more so, perhaps, than a remarkable visionary living in midcentury on the banks of the Rhine.

Sometime before 1157, the Benedictine visionary Elisabeth of Schönau sent a letter across the river to Hildegard of Bingen, her older and more illustrious counterpart, seeking advice on how to respond to the torrent of invective that had followed Elisabeth's recent revelation of her visions to her community. According to Elisabeth's letter, "foolish words" spoken by clerics and laypersons alike had questioned the authenticity of her visions and ecstasies. Worse yet, several letters had been forged in her name prophesying the Day of Judgment, which, she attests, "I certainly never presumed to do." Anxious to tell her side of the story and thus counter the rumors Hildegard might be hearing, Elisabeth insists that she was ordered to spread the revelations she had received by "an angel of the Lord," whose words and actions left little doubt that disobedience was not an option:

> "Why do you hide gold in mud? I mean the word of God which through your mouth has been sent to earth, not to be hidden, but to be manifested to the praise and glory of our Lord and the salvation of His people." And having said this he lifted a whip over me [*elevavit super me flagellum*], which he struck me with most harshly five times as if in great anger, so that for three days I lay with my whole body shattered by this beating [*ex illa percussione*].[2]

The angel follows this violent remonstrance by urging Elisabeth to "suffer with patience and willingness" the calumny of her detractors, just as Christ "suffered the mockery of men." After reporting several further visits by the angel and more "great bodily suffering," Elisabeth asks Hildegard to "write me some words of consolation" to help her endure the ordeal.

In her rather vague reply to Elisabeth's letter, Hildegard begins by identifying herself as a "little pauper and earthen vessel" speaking not of her "own accord," but according to the will of God, who controls her just as he controls the rest of created nature.[3] Though the present-day world is "faint in all the viridity of virtues" because most of its inhabitants have abandoned the right path in favor of the "ancient deceiver," Hildegard writes, others have been specially designated by God to be the bearers of his message: "it is necessary in this time that God should nourish some people lest his instruments become idle."[4] The "instruments" of God, "vessels of clay since they are human," are those chosen to "sound the mysteries of God like a trumpet," for a trumpet "only renders the sound and does not produce it unless another breathes into it in order to bring forth the sound." Interpreting the punitive actions of Elisabeth's angel as a sign of her designated role as God's *tuba*, Hildegard enjoins her to endure the violence this role entails by willingly performing the natural music of visionary life: "God always beats [*flagellat*] those who sing through his trumpet, watching that their earthen vessel should not perish, but rather that it should please Him."[5] The letter concludes as Hildegard allies herself with Elisabeth by acknowledging with terror and humility her own visionary instrumentality: "O daughter! May God make you a mirror of life. But even I lie in the pusillanimity of fear, occasionally resounding a little like the small sound of a trumpet [*parvus sonus tubae*] from the living light, whence may God help me to remain in his ministry."[6]

Hildegard's epistolary exchange with Elisabeth casts in miniature the depth and complexity of her musical life. As a musical "instrument" and *vas* of God, Hildegard the visionary is nevertheless an earthly exile who emits sound only when breathed through by the grace of God. Music would seem to constitute the very medium of Christian subordination. Yet she insists that God chooses to "beat" only those who themselves "sing through his trumpet" (*qui in tuba ipsius canunt*), using an active verb even while describing an ostensibly passive visionary performance. Though employing a humility topos that is typical for her, Hildegard commands respect for her visionary authority through an image of herself precisely as musical *corpus*, filled with the breath of God and suffering his demands while prophetically singing herself into his trumpet.

By the time she wrote her reply to Elisabeth of Schönau, Hildegard had been composing liturgical and quasi-liturgical *cantus* for some twenty years. Born in 1098 and placed in a monastery by her parents at the age of eight, Hildegard was astonishingly prolific throughout the course of her long life.[7] Her extant oeuvre—a unique medieval legacy that has enjoyed (some would say suffered) a widespread academic and popular revival in recent years— consists of three major visionary tracts; several learned treatises on natural history, medicine, and the nature of the human body; hundreds of letters, several of them to emperors, popes, and archbishops; saints' lives; a complete religious drama with music and text, the *Ordo virtutum*; and over seventy liturgical and quasi-liturgical compositions in a collection known as the *Symphonia armonie celestium revelationum.*

This chapter explores the techniques and implications of embodiment in Hildegard's musico-poetic production, particularly in the *Symphonia.* I hope to recover a largely neglected aspect of Hildegard's cloistered musical life by examining the somatic dimensions of her musical relationship with the women she loved and with whom she worshiped. I am concerned both with what Margot Fassler has recently described as Hildegard's "rendering of communal song as an incarnational act"[8] and with the ways in which this incarnational sensibility served to construct the female musical body into a simultaneously suffering, desiring, and eroticized musical agent. As we saw in Chapters 1 and 2, early Christian writers from Clement of Alexandria to Augustine display a remarkable range of anxieties about and affinities for musical corporeality. Hildegard's works will provide an initial medieval case study that is both paradigmatic and unique: Unlike the patristic figures discussed above, she claimed a direct divine inspiration not only for her theological/visionary writings, but also for the music she heard and ordered recorded. If Landulf of Milan's idealized account of the divine origins of the *Te Deum* strikes us as wishful thinking (see Chapter 2), in Hildegard's case we can actually transcribe and perform the music and poetry, and even see the neumes, that allegedly came from God.

The origins and inspirations of Hildegard's compositions thus raise the ideological problem of belief. One of the most daunting quandaries facing scholars of premodern religiosities is the historical challenge of analyzing works that are asserted by their authors to be divinely inspired. My approach to Hildegard's music and writings could perhaps best be described as a confection of close formal analysis and skeptical historicism; with Sarah Beckwith, I believe that a materialist account of medieval visionary works "must restore the world, the body, and the text to 'mystical writings.' It must see the language of their utterance as a 'two-sided act,' to restore in fact a constitutive dialogism to the writings which have been read as the mere transcriptions of the monologues, of God Himself speaking through the expressive spirit."[9] This problem is especially keen for those of us wishing to craft cultural-materialist accounts of mystical or visionary *music* in particular. Even more so than "mystic speech," in Michel de Certeau's term, "mystic music" constitutes in its "wordlessness," its oft-cited "ineffability," a mimetic realization of transcendence itself.[10] Such mystical ("mysticizing," perhaps) assumptions about the historical unrootedness of musical sonority have distant cousins in claims for the social purity of "absolute music," in ideological reifications of the transcendent genius of great composers, and in certain quarters of psychoanalytic theory, where it is claimed that the musical womb and heartbeat of the mother constitute a prelinguistic semiotic space that precedes the symbolic (and, very often, the political).

As Beckwith and others have shown, however, medieval mystical and visionary experiences were themselves strongly rooted in material culture. Hildegard's musical compositions, whether divinely inspired or not, were grounded in her social identity as a Benedictine nun and abbess and thus should not be separated from the material circumstances of voice, body, and religious life that conditioned their composition and performance. Indeed, in its musical, textual, and performative character, the *Symphonia* provides a unique perspective on certain seeming contradictions within and between Hildegard's works—for example, what I will show is the inseparability of female sexual desire and pleasure from the devotional experience she elaborated in song.

It is crucial at this particular historical moment to continue situating these works in their own. While the appropriations of Hildegard's life and work performed in the name of "Creation Spirituality" and the New Age might seem innocuous enough, a recent essay published in a prestigious British music journal, *Early Music*, baldly and bizarrely asserts (against a mountain of contradictory codicological, epistolary, and other empirical testimony that goes entirely uncited in the article) that there exists "not a scrap of evidence that [Hildegard] actually composed any of the 77 songs in her name, or wrote them for her nuns to sing at daily service."[11] Such an assertion would seem almost laughable if it did not have behind it a long, strong tradition of historical amnesia of the sort that used to deny to Heloise her letters and Hrotsvit her plays. If it represents a new trend in Hildegard of Bingen studies, I hope the present chapter will be received as an initial attempt to nip it in the bud.

The Demands of Music

Hildegard's musical production began in the 1140s, soon after she was commanded by God to begin putting her visions and revelations into words.

The opening "Declaration" to the *Scivias* casts this moment in her life as a violent but unthreatening seizure of her entire being:

> It happened that, in the eleven hundred and forty-first year of the Incarnation of the Son of God, Jesus Christ, when I was forty-two years and seven months old, Heaven was opened and a fiery light of exceeding brilliance came and permeated my whole brain [*totum cerebrum meum*], and inflamed my whole heart and my whole breast, not like a burning but like a warming flame, as the sun warms anything its rays touch. And immediately I knew the meaning of the exposition of the Scriptures, namely the Psalter, the Gospel and the other catholic volumes of both the Old and the New Testaments, though I did not have the interpretation of the words of their texts or the division of the syllables or the knowledge of cases or tenses.[12]

Though Hildegard does not image her awakening in the language of ecstasy, as Elisabeth of Schönau does, her first direct encounter with divinity clearly takes place in her flesh. The pain of revelation permeates her "brain" (*cerebrum*), not simply her mind. She hears God describing her as one who "suffers in her inmost being and in the veins of her flesh [*in medullis et in uenis carnis suae*]"; she is distressed in mind and sense and endures "great pain of body [*multam passionem corporis*], because no security has dwelt in her, but in all her undertakings she has judged herself guilty."[13] While resistant at first to recording her visions for others to hear and read, she is "compelled at last by many illnesses" to set her "hand to the writing."[14]

This same conception of body as locus of pain and material basis for religious experience informs Hildegard's reflections on the nature of music. Barbara Newman has suggested that Hildegard may have been influenced by a strain of medieval musical thought that saw *musica practica*, or performed music, as an integral part of *musica humana*.[15] Perhaps inspired by the Carolingian theorist Regino of Prüm and the renowned contemporaneous chant reformer William of Hirsau,[16] Hildegard consistently emphasizes the expressive qualities of music along with the numerical, an emphasis especially apparent in her notion of word-music relations. Near the end of the *Scivias*, she argues that "words symbolize the body, and jubilant music reveals the spirit [*verbum corpus designat, symphonia vero spiritum manifestat*]; the celestial harmony shows the Divinity, and the words the humanity of the Son of God."[17] This subtle analogy, in which music vivifies the liturgy just as "celestial harmony" vivifies the body of Christ, establishes music's vital immanence within the flesh, suggesting that sung *cantus*, the performed union of *harmonia* and *verbum*, is itself the incarnation.[18]

A similar sense of musical sonority as the somatic vehicle of linguistic meaning informs Hildegard's discussions of music's affective qualities: "For the song of rejoicing softens hard hearts [*dura corda emollit*], and draws forth from them the tears of compunction, and invokes the Holy Spirit. . . . And their song goes through you so that you understand [the heavenly voices] perfectly; for where divine grace has worked, it banishes all dark obscurity, and makes pure and lucid those things that are obscure to the bodily senses because of the weakness of the flesh."[19] Heavenly music draws "tears of compunction" by permeating the body, filling it with melody, and rescuing the human vessel from its postlapsarian weakness. Hildegard clearly distinguishes between *corpus* and *carnis*: while the musical body can achieve a kind of visionary clarity, flesh is an obscurantist tendency, an *anti*musical component of person that threatens to preclude participation in the divine. In a performance of the *Ordo virtutum*, this metamusical struggle over body and flesh would have been realized in sonority: unlike Anima and the Virtues, who are given music to sing, the Devil is given only "hoarse croaks of false praise," spoken words that contrast brilliantly with the simple melodies sung by the other characters.[20] The materiality of musical sound constitutes the virtual theme of a miniature illustrating a vision of the resurrection of the body in the final book of the *Scivias* (see Figure 4). Chunks of bodies—severed heads, hands, feet, and tongues—rise from the grave as a figure at the feet of God blows air through the "last trumpet."[21] Though many medieval illustrations of the resurrection depict the *tuba* described in 1 Corinthians 15:52 ("for the trumpet shall sound, and the dead shall be raised incorruptible"), here the trumpet's music appears between the two medallions as a visible *materia* identical to the winds with which "the human bones [*ossa hominum*] in whatever place in the earth they lay" are "covered in their flesh [*sua carne obtecta sunt*]" in the lower medallion.[22]

Central as well to Hildegard's vision of embodied musical life was God's use of music as an instrument of discipline. The *Liber vitae meritorum*, completed some twenty years after the *Scivias*, elaborates what I would call a musical philosophy of bodily obedience. In a vision recorded in book 1, a man appears to her with "a white cloud by his mouth that looks like a trumpet" and emits an array of musical sounds that symbolize God's control of the universe: "The trumpet is full of all sounds sounding rapidly

FIGURE 4 Resurrection of the Dead and Last Judgment, from Hildegard of Bingen, *Scivias* 3.12, late twelfth century, facsimile from (lost) Rupertsberg *Scivias* (formerly Wiesbaden, Hessische Landesbibliothek MS 1)

because all things, reasonable or unreasonable, obey the divine order in full subjection [*in plenitudine subiectionis*]. They obey God out of honor and praise since he created them."[23] The music of "full subjection" to the will of God takes a specifically instrumental form in Hildegard's personifications of the sins and virtues in book 2. After the figure of Gluttony appears and justifies his desires, Abstinence responds with a musical analogy that obliquely anticipates Langland's allegorical portrait of the sin in *Piers Plowman*: "No one should strike a *cithara* [*Nemo citharam sic percutiat*] in such a way that its strings are damaged. If its strings have been damaged, what sound will it make? None. You, gluttony, fill your belly so much that all your veins are bloated and are turned into a frenzy. Where then is the sweet sound of wisdom that God gave man?"[24] Overeating, a sinful filling of one's own "gut," will inevitably result in a wasteful expansion of the stringlike veins and tendons that stretch across the human body and bind together its parts into a musical whole.

As Abstinence contends, a strict musical discipline of the body on Earth can ensure a concordant *harmonia* in heaven: "For I am a *cithara* sounding praises and piercing the hardness of heart with good will. For when a man feeds his body moderately, I reverberate like a *cithara* in heaven [*in celum cithara resono*] with his praises. When he feeds his body temperately with moderate food, I sing accompanied with musical instruments."[25] Proper diet and moderation, she suggests, lead to the musical "tempering" of the body, the strings of which will resonate correctly only if the body is properly fed. Though Hildegard reiterates the platonic notion of individualized human *harmonia*, in the *Liber vitae meritorum* these somatic harmonies are mediated through personification allegory of the sort we find in other twelfth-century texts such as Alan of Lille's *De planctu Naturae*. *Obedientia*, for example, describes her exemplary purpose as the teaching of an instrumental submission to God's authority: "I consulted with God a long time ago and he ordered all the things he wanted to do through me. I sound like a cithar [*ut cithara sonui*] at the command of his word because I obey all his commands."[26] This sequence in the *Liber* reads like a collage of the musical metaphorics of Clement, Gregory, and Augustine: the human person is a harmonious compound of body and soul, and such harmony will be maintained by God through his earthly agents, but the human herself bears responsibility for maintaining her corporeal "strings" and protecting them from damage through proper diet and moderate living.

For this *cithara* of bodily discipline and obedience threatens always to transmogrify into the *lira* of bodily torture. A complex vision near the end of the *Scivias* (book 3, vision 11) presents an array of apocalyptic images representing the imminence of the Last Judgment and the coming of the Antichrist: five beasts with ropes stretched from their mouths to the peak of a mountain represent the "five ferocious epochs of temporal rule" (the beasts face the West, "for these fleeting times will vanish with the setting sun"); to the East, a young man (Christ, the Son of Man) standing "on the corner of the wall" of a building, glowing like the dawn "from the waist down to the place that denotes the male," the same place where "a harp is lying with its strings across his body"; a bruised and bleeding figure of a woman, Ecclesia, from whose vagina protrudes "a black and monstrous head" covered in excrement (Antichrist); the violent and rending exit of the head of Antichrist from the body of Ecclesia and the attempted ascent of the besmeared head to heaven; and, finally, the defeat of Antichrist and the glowing triumph of Ecclesia, whose feet "glow white" in a sign of the eternal triumph of Christ. The vision is justly famous as Hildegard's most threatening manifestation of the Apocalypse, during which the Antichrist will threaten the very existence of the Church and humanity before falling in defeat at the end of time.[27]

Among a number of baffling components of the vision (including the *vagina dentata*–like image of the violated Ecclesia) is the curious appearance of the *lira* "lying with its strings" across the body of the Son of Man. As Hildegard's gloss implies, music contains so many moral, corporeal, and eschatological implications that it must figure prominently in the Apocalypse itself:

> ut nunc ab umbilico suo deorsum tibi appareat: quoniam a fortitudine membrorum suorum, quod est electorum ipsius, ubi modo ipse sponsus ecclesiae uiget, usque ad completionem eorundem membrorum ipsius multa admiranda et obscura signa uides, ita uidelicet ut ab umbilico usque ad locum illum ubi uir discernitur quasi aurora fulgeat: quia a perfectione illa cum iam fidelia membra sua perfectionem fortitudinis habent, usque ad tempus filii perditionis qui se uirum uirtutis esse simulabit, in rectitudine se deuote colentium fulgorem iustitiae demonstrabit. Vnde et ibidem uelut lyra cum chordis suis in transuersum iacet: quod est in persecutione illa qua filius iniquitatis multos cruciatus electis inferet gaudium canticorum eorum, qui iam

propter dira tormenta quae in corporibus suis patiuntur a corporalibus nexi-
bus soluuntur ad requiem transeuntes.

[So *now you can see him from the waist down*; for now you see Him in the
strength of His members who are His elect, and He will flourish as Bride-
groom of the Church, with many obscure signs and wonders, until their
number is complete. *And from the waist down to the place that denotes the male
he glows like the dawn*; for until the time of the son of perdition, who will
pretend to be the man of strength, His faithful members will be perfected in
fortitude and He will be splendid in the justice of His righteous worshipers.
So, in the same place, a harp is lying with its strings across his body; which signifies the joyful songs of those who will suffer dire torments in the persecution that the son of iniquity will inflict upon the chosen, torturing their
bodies so much that they are released from them and pass over into rest.][28]

In a remarkable example of apocalyptic revisionism, the vision replaces
Christ's "members" with the strings of a *lira*, strings that resonate with
the "dire torments" inflicted by the Antichrist upon his human victims.
The passage recalls Ambrose's *De Iacob et vita beata* in its envisioning of a
musico-instrumental torture of the body, though it implies that Christ
himself was the first to be subjected to such musical torture for humanity's
sins of the flesh: the five temporal epochs, symbolized by the beasts, are
"brought about by the desires of the flesh from which the taint of sin is
never absent."

Curiously, the program of illuminations in the Rupertsberg *Scivias*
does not represent the torturing *lira* or its strings. Instead (see Figure 5), the
"place that denotes the male" on the Son of Man is covered by crenellated
battlements that form part of the allegorical building whose corner he
guards; as a result, the visualization of the apocalypse elides the iconic
musical violence of the original experience. The pain-inflicting strings were
restored to the visual program of the *Scivias* by the illustrator(s) of a slightly
later copy of the treatise in Heidelberg, Universitätsbibliothek cod. Salem X
16, which was produced at the Cistercian abbey of Salem (Figure 6). As
Madeline Caviness points out, unlike the Rupertsberg illuminations, in
which Hildegard seems to have been directly involved, the pictures in the
Salem codex were clearly produced as " 'illustration,' that is, their genesis
was secondary to the text."[29] Nevertheless, in this particular illustration,
the musical implications of the vision emerge much more clearly than in the

FIGURE 5   Day of the Great Revelation, from Hildegard of Bingen, *Scivias* 3.11, late twelfth century, from Rupertsberg *Scivias*

FIGURE 6   Day of the Great Revelation, from Hildegard of Bingen, *Scivias* 3.11, late twelfth century (Heidelberg, Universitätsbibliothek cod. Salem X 16, fol.177 ͬ)

Rupertsberg codex. In the upper right register, the Son of Man and Ecclesia stand side-by-side, and the sexual aspects of the juxtaposition are made more apparent than they are in the Rupertsberg codex: just as the feces-smeared head of the Antichrist emerges threateningly from the vagina of Ecclesia, the *lira* stretches horizontally across the lap of the Son of Man, a visual displacement of his genitals. At the same time, Ecclesia's hand appears to be pierced by the *lira*, an interpolation that overlays the musical sufferings of Christ with the apocalyptic sufferings of the Church. Though produced in a religious institution distinct from Hildegard's Rupertsberg, the Salem visualization of the *Scivias* apocalypse suggests that the Cistercian illustrators were intent on representing the musical tortures of the Apocalypse.

In her own multifaceted representations of musical sensation, response, allegory, and eschatology, Hildegard was no more consistent than Augustine. If the music of body can clarify the words of the divine, it can also beat, torture, and subjectify the visionary herself. Music in Hildegard's visionary texts and letters represents a sonorous vehicle of spiritual grace and moral clarity even as it constitutes an apocalyptic threat to the body of Christ and the well-being of the Church. As we shall see, this same incarnational sensibility infuses the musical sonorities that Hildegard brought into being.

Musical Desire and the Pleasures of Performance

If the interplay of musical pleasure and musical violence informs Hildegard's vision of sacred history, it also serves to shape quotidian life in the female body. In a brief chapter entitled *De partu* or "Concerning birth" in the *Causae et curae*, a chapter that consists of just two long Latin sentences, Hildegard begins by describing the shattering horror experienced by women about to give birth, an event that causes the entire woman to "tremble in terror" (in terrore hoc tremet), emit "tears and shrieks" (lacrimis et eiulatu), and suddenly fear that the end of the world (in fine temporum terra) is nigh.[30] The opening sentence of the chapter portrays the extreme pain and almost apocalyptic emotions women can expect in childbirth. The second and concluding sentence, however, constructs a bipartite metaphor that depicts the humoral disposition of the sexual and generative female body as a result of women's essential "openness." Women's bodies, Hildegard posits, "are open like a wooden frame in which strings have been fastened for strumming; or, again, they are like windows through which the wind blows, so that the elements affect them more vehemently than men, and the humors also are more plentiful in them" (apertae sunt ut lignum, in quo cordae ad citharizandum positae sunt, et quia etiam fenestrales et ventosae [sunt], ita quod etiam elementa in eis vehementiora sunt quam in viris, et quod humores etiam in eis plus quam in viris habundant).[31] Drawing on the same tradition that inspired Ambrose to gloss the death-wails of the Maccabees as the *cithara* of their mother's womb, Hildegard transforms the somatic significance of the instrument in an explicitly sexual revision of an exegetical convention. The image conveys both the musical and "windy" nature of female sexual pleasure as well as the harplike pangs of childbirth.

This metaphor of female sexuality and reproduction (often separate categories for Hildegard) as quasi-biblical *cithara* begins to suggest the role of specifically sexual desire within Hildegard's more general musical construction of religious experience. In the *Symphonia* compositions, poetic language and sounding *cantus* converge into an extended liturgical meditation on the musicality of the female body. "Nunc gaudeant," an antiphon written to Ecclesia, describes Ecclesia's children "gathered into her breast in supernal symphony" (in superna simphonia filii eius in sinum suum collocati sunt), literally resounding within the personified *corpus* of the Church.[32] Another song records the Virgin's words to her son praising the *divinitas* that created her "and arranged all my limbs and planted in my innards every kind of music in all the flowers of the tones [*in visceribus meis omne genus musicorum in omnibus floribus tonorum*]."[33] Hildegard describes her own privileged musicality similarly in a letter to Pope Anastasius, where she casts her calling into visionary life as the musical touch of God: "He who is great without failing has now touched a little dwelling-place . . . so that it resounds with melody in many tones, yet concordant with itself [*multimodam, sed sibi consonantem melodiam sonaret*]."[34]

Hildegard's conception of music as a somatic and often gendered dimension of her visionary life exposes the limitations of strictly formalistic analysis of her compositions. In an illuminating study of one of Hildegard's antiphons, Robert Cogan, referring to Guido of Arezzo's writings on music, summarizes the problem as follows: "Candor compels us to recognize a wide-spread preference, then and now, for the Guidonian *mechanics* of musical performance and academic explanation to Hildegard's unconventional creative *fantasy*. . . . Guido aimed at certainty of concept and performance; Hildegard on the other hand still raises challenging controversial *questions*."[35] Mechanics and fantasy, certainty and controversy: Cogan suggests that a purely formal or structural approach to Hildegard's compositions would void them of the richness that she herself found in musical expression.[36] For Cogan, the answer is to see Hildegard as the "earliest appearance in the history of European music" of the "composer as star, *auteur*, quasi-mythical being," one whose compositions reflect the "timelessness of the best music" the West has produced.[37]

Hildegard was clearly known to some outside of her immediate community for her inspired music,[38] and the popular revival of her compositions in recent years demonstrates a widely felt sentiment that they can indeed speak across the centuries. Nevertheless, the *Symphonia* is anything but "timeless"; the details of its music and texts in fact reveal just how inseparable the cycle is from Hildegard's immediate institutional milieu, her visionary identity, her idiosyncratic conceptions of human and divine bodies, and her recognition of both the enormous distances and intimate proximities between the two. In no way is my argument intended somehow to question or diminish Hildegard's musical creativity and uniqueness. But as Theodor Adorno pointed out long ago, the Romantic notion of the genius of the individual composer has consistently curtailed the analysis of Western art-music as a socially meaningful, ideologically fractious, and, again, *material* practice.[39] Hildegard would have been the last to describe musical sonority as a politically innocent expression of her own creative spirit; as John Stevens puts it, arguing against a "too narrowly organic view" of the development of Hildegard's musical oeuvre, "the *Symphonia* is not, and perhaps was never conceived as, a tight artefact, a self-contained entity to be perfected and closed."[40] In Hildegard's case, the "work concept" just doesn't work.

Among the sixteen notated Marian pieces in the *Symphonia* is the responsory "O quam preciosa," which would have been performed most likely after one of the short lessons of the hours.[41] The text alternates between the longer verse, sung by the soloist, and the brief refrain, performed by the choir:

O quam preciosa virginis huius que clausam portam habet,
et cuius viscera sancta divinitas calore suo infudit,
ita quod flos in ea crevit.

Et Filius Dei per secreta ipsius
quasi aurora exivit.

Unde dulce germen, quod Filius ipsius est,
per clausuram ventris eius paradisum aperuit.

Et Filius Dei per secreta ipsius
quasi aurora exivit.

[O how precious is the virginity of this virgin who has a closed gate, and
whose womb holy divinity suffused with its warmth, so that a flower grew in
her./And the Son of God came forth like the dawn through her secret./
Hence the tender shoot, which is her Son, opened paradise through the
cloister of her womb./And the Son of God came forth like the dawn through
her secret.][42]

While the responsory celebrates the miraculous birth of Christ, the most
striking aspect of the text is surely its repeated emphasis on the Virgin's
anatomy: the "closed gate" in the initial verse and the "cloister of her womb"
in the second, as well as the *secreta* in the refrain. When read in the order of
performance, the verses and refrains create an unavoidable sense of movement through embodied architectural space: the "flower" of Christ grows
initially behind the "closed gate" described by the soloist, travels *per secreta
ipsius* as the choir performs the refrain, emerges from the womb/cloister at
the second solo verse, and repeats the journey again in the final refrain.[43]

The responsory's extended architectural metaphor suggests that the
monastery itself represents the "cloister" of the Virgin's "womb," the physical arena that the nuns inhabit and fill with music when they sing. The song
as composed, read, and performed represents a musical refashioning of
physical space, a women-identified appropriation of architectural authority. As such, it is a compelling example of what Roberta Gilchrist has
identified as medieval religious women's frequent manipulations of the
archaeology of gender: "Monastic architecture was central to the social
construction of difference between medieval religious men and women.
Religious identities, personal mobility and perceptions of sexuality were
maintained through space, boundaries and architectural embellishment."[44]
And, we might add, challenged: "O quam preciosa" allows the nuns of
Rupertsberg to participate in Christ's own passage through the Virgin's
"secret" anatomy as they travel through the monastery. Unlike Christ, how-

ever, the women pass through the *secreta* more than once as they repeat both the refrain, which transports them back into the womb, as well as the responsory in its entirety in subsequent performances. The term *secreta* would become the central image in an influential "gynecological" tract a century later, the *De secretis mulierum*; unlike the neo-Aristotelian author, however, who anxiously sought to limit the perusal of women's secrets to the exclusive domain of men, Hildegard constructs the secret of the Virgin's womb as an intimate knowledge shared among her nuns as they move musically in and out of the Virgin's body in a suggestively anatomical revision of the conception of Christ.[45]

An equally eroticizing sense of the musicality of the Virgin's reproductive body inspires "Ave generosa," one of the four *Symphonia* compositions classified as hymns. Addressed to the Virgin and written in the second person, the hymn begins with a four-strophe image of the incarnation:

Ave generosa, gloriosa et intacta puella;
tu, pupilla castitatis, tu, materia sanctitatis,
que Deo placuit!

Nam hec superna infusio in te fuit,
quod supernum verbum in te carnem induit.

Tu, candidum lilium,
quod Deus ante omnem creaturam inspexit.

O pulcherrima et dulcissima;
quam valde Deus in te delectabatur!
cum amplexione caloris sui in te posuit
ita quod filius eius de te lactatus est.

[Hail, noble, glorious, and virgin girl; You, the pupil of chastity, you, the matter of holiness who was pleasing to God!/For it happened in you through the supernal one, that the supernal Word was cloaked in flesh./You, white lily, whom God viewed before all other creatures./O most beautiful and sweetest one; how greatly was God pleased in you! With the embrace of his heat he thus made it happen that his son was suckled by you.][46]

The text articulates a conventional array of meanings that the Virgin's body held for medieval religious. Although the hymn is addressed to the Virgin herself, these strophes concentrate on God's choice of her and her role in bearing the Word. Hildegard reiterates the common notion of the Virgin's body as a vessel, the *materia* into which God infused the substance of divinity. While "intacta" and "castitas" emphasize the Virgin's freedom from sexual penetration, the word Hildegard chooses to describe the "pleasure" God himself took in her body—*delectabatur*—is a term used repeatedly in the *Causae et curae* to denote sexual pleasure (as in a discussion of conception, in which a woman during sex is described as possessing "delectationem in se").[47] The grammar seems to deny this implicitly sexual pleasure to the Virgin.[48]

In the fifth verse, however, the hymn turns away from the will and desire of God and toward the body of the Virgin herself. Music appears here for the first time in the text:

> Venter enim tuus gaudium habuit,
> cum omnis celestis symphonia de te sonuit,
> quia, virgo, filium Dei portasti,
> ubi castitas tua in Deo claruit.

> Viscera tua gaudium habuerunt, sicut
> gramen super quod ros cadit
> cum ei viriditatem infudit;
> ut et in te factum est, o mater omnis gaudii.

> Nunc omnis Ecclesia in gaudio rutilet ac in symphonia
> sonet propter dulcissimam virginem et laudabilem
> Mariam Dei genitricem. Amen.

> [For your womb held joy, when all the celestial *symphonia* rang out from you, because, virgin, you carried the son of God, whereby your chastity burned brightly in God./Your innards held joy, just as grass on which dew falls when greenness floods into it; thus did it happen in you, o mother of all joy./Now let all Ecclesia blush in joy and sound in *symphonia* for the sweetest virgin and praiseworthy Mary, mother of God. Amen.][49]

Music, the *symphonia* echoing in and resonating from the Virgin's womb in the fifth strophe, expresses her own *gaudium* at the incarnation and resonates as heavenly harmony. While Hildegard may have in mind here the *musica mundana*, the "music of the spheres" that orders the universe, the *symphonia* originates precisely from the Virgin's *venter* and *viscera*, her womb and her flesh.

Just as music is the medium of *gaudium* in the fifth verse, the liquid of dew is its bearer in the sixth: "Your flesh held joy, just as grass on which dew falls when greenness is poured into it." In medieval theological writings dew is of course a standard image derived from the biblical story of Gideon's fleece (Judges 6:36–40), and it was a common typological symbol for the Virgin's conception.[50] Hildegard's description of the Virgin's musical womb amplifies the image of dew by incorporating it into a more general celebration of her fertility. In the final strophe, she describes the figure of Ecclesia, like the Virgin, "sound[ing] in *symphonia* for the sweetest virgin and praiseworthy Mary." As a typological recapitulation of both Eve and Mary, Ecclesia is the Church on Earth, the Body of Christ, as well as the Bride of Christ, a virgin whose well-being was constantly threatened by Satan.[51] In Hildegard's image of Ecclesia as a blushing devotee of the Virgin, the celestial *symphonia* echoes within a specifically female body; the body of Ecclesia resonates with the same music that fills the Virgin's womb two verses earlier. Participating bodily in the same sonorous experience, the Virgin and Ecclesia are inextricably joined by Hildegard through the sensual bonds of the *symphonia* that resounds from them and with which they are filled.

The vivid constructions of music and women's bodies in "Ave generosa" receive a brilliant performative vehicle in the hymn's melody. In the text to the fifth strophe, music fills the Virgin's womb with *gaudium* and causes her body to resound in sonorous joy; it is just at this point, on the word *symphonia*, that the music of the hymn reaches its highest point (see Example 1). The hymn has gradually ascended from its lowest note, the e below c' on the first syllable of "puella" in the first strophe, to the emphatically syllabic c″ on "-pho-" in "symphonia."[52] This wide span of an octave and a sixth is augmented in the culminating phrase: the c″ is approached by a leap of a fourth from g', a gesture again emphasizing openness and breadth. Similarly, Hildegard begins every verse but one with a dramatic leap of a fifth from the modal a. These melodic gestures, in which the chant moves by leaps and bounds, are examples of disjunct motion (as opposed to conjunct motion, in which single steps or half steps dominate the melody). As we can see, Hildegard foregrounds disjunction at several important moments in the hymn. The consecutive fifth-fourth jump on "tu materia" in the first strophe moves dramatically from a to e' to a″; in addition to such upward leaps, the downward jumps of fourths and fifths in the fifth and sixth strophes are especially noticeable.

MUSICAL EXAMPLE I   Hildegard of Bingen, "Ave generosa" from *Symphonia* (ed. Marianne Richert Pfau, 2:22–24)

What are we to make of Hildegard's emphasis on wide melodic range and disjunction in a hymn that celebrates the melodious *gaudium* of the female body? Given the preliminary state of research into the melodic analysis of plainchant, any attempt to interpret the contours of medieval monody (especially sacred monody) as expressive of practically anything must be made with a great deal of caution.[53] The extraordinary range and melodic vividness of "Ave generosa" are not unparalleled in twelfth-century

quod De-us   an - te   om - nem   cre - a - tu-ram   in   spe-xit.

O   pul - cher - ri - ma   et   dul - cis - si - - ma

quam   val - de   De-us   in   te   de   le - cta - ba - tur

cum   am - ple-xi-o-nem   ca-lo-ris su - i   in   te po   su - it

i - ta   quod   Fi - li - us   e - ius de   te   la - cta - tus est.

Ven   ter   e - nim   tu - us   gau - di - um   ha - bu - it

cum   om   nis   ce - le-stis sim - pho-ni - a   de   te so-nu-it

qui   a   Vir   go   Fi - li - um   De   i   por - ta - sti

u   bi   ca - sti - tas   tu - a   in   De - o   cla   ru-it:

Vi - sce - ra   tu   a gau   di   um ha - bu - e - runt

1) R reads f - f - e liqu. f - f - e liqu. c b a g a.

sic - ut gra - men su - per quod ros ca - - dit

cum e - i vi - ri - di - ta - tem in - - fu - sit

ut et in te fa - ctum est o Ma - ter om - nis gau - di - i

Nunc om - nis Ec - cle - si - a in gau - di - o ru - ti - let

ac - in sim - pho - ni - a so - net

pro - pter dul - - cis - si - mam Vir - - gi - nem

et lau - da - bi - lem Ma - - - ri - am

De - i ge - ni - tri - cem.

A - - - - - - men.

2) Both D and R hav a "♭" here.

monophonic repertories: Victorine sequences and the monophonic compositions in the *Magnus liber organi* in particular often display such characteristics. As we have seen, however, Hildegard herself insisted upon the physical and emotive expressiveness of *cantus*, and it is clear that the *Symphonia* compositions evidence a sophisticated approach to musical rhetoric and text-music relations.[54] In order to draw any conclusions about the melodic expressivity of "Ave generosa," we first need to appreciate the ways in which it diverges from the melodic norms of the contemporaneous hymn repertory; in other words, the hymn must be analyzed in terms of its liturgical and generic specificity before a more general interpretation of its melody can be attempted.

Despite their idiosyncrasies, most of the *Symphonia* songs are identified explicitly by their liturgical functions in the earliest manuscripts that transmit the collection as a whole. While Hildegard's own hierarchical arrangement of these compositions is unusual,[55] the compilation itself clearly establishes the liturgical affiliations of much of the music. In the Dendermonde codex (the older of the two manuscripts in which the *Symphonia* appears, and likely compiled under the direct supervision of Hildegard in the late 1170s), the Latin tag "Ymnus de sancta maria" appears just to the right of the incipit to "Ave generosa."[56] A careful survey of the three-hundred-odd hymn melodies from German chant sources collected in Bruno Stäblein's 1956 edition—and representing Benedictine, Cistercian, Premonstratensian, and Augustinian traditions—turns up not a single hymn whose range exceeds an octave by more than two steps.[57] While the range alone of "Ave generosa" thus represents a stunning departure from hymn conventions, to Hildegard it was something of a compositional norm: an emphasis on wide range is apparent throughout the *Symphonia* ("O vos angeli," a responsory discussed below, exceeds two octaves).[58] Moreover, though Stäblein noted a preference for greater disjunction in hymn repertories north of the Alps,[59] most chants in the Germanic repertory move primarily by conjunct motion. While formulaic opening fifths are present in several of Stäblein's examples,[60] simultaneous upward leaps such as those in the first strophe of "Ave generosa" are entirely absent, and downward leaps of fourths and fifths are relatively rare. As David Hiley has recently pointed out, it is only in later centuries that wide range and disjunction become common characteristics of the hymn repertory in general.[61]

While Hildegard's immediate musical environment was Benedictine, her compositional strategies here can be suggestively juxtaposed with the ideology of *cantus* inspiring the Cistercian Reform, which took place during the 1130s and 1140s and sought to "purify" the musical performance of liturgy.[62] Though the effectiveness of the Reform has been much debated, the documents that promulgated it (at least one of them nominally written by Bernard of Clairvaux himself, who also corresponded with Hildegard) were widely disseminated.[63] For the Cistercian reformers, perhaps the most infuriating aspect of the Order's contemporary musical practices was the excessive range of the chant, which was excoriated by the author of the "Cantum quem Cisterciensis ordinis" as a violation of *natura* itself:

> What, I say, is this lawless license that joins contradictories together, and by trespassing on natural boundaries, imposes disharmony on unity and inflicts injury upon nature [*iniuriam irrogat naturae*]? It is indeed clearer than daylight that that kind of chant is offensively and irregularly composed [*male et inordinatum compositum*] which sinks so low that it cannot be heard as it ought to be, or soars so high that it cannot be sung: for it ought to be such that in its lower notes a person can hear it, and in its higher notes that a person can sing it.[64]

As the treatise makes clear, the Cistercians grounded such vitriolic pronouncements on melodic range in the musical authority of the Bible:

> Certain persons have desired the average range to be eight notes, and certain others nine notes, taking into consideration the aptitude not of lusty but average voices. On the other hand, according to those whose opinion seems to be more carefully formulated, a chant can range up to ten notes on account of the authority of the psaltery [*propter auctoritatem psalterii*], which has ten strings, and also in order that the individual notes of the octave, which are eight, and the outer notes might have an identical capacity, that is, to be raised or lowered by positioning two notes at the ends, one above and one below.[65]

The treatise contends that the physical structure of the ten-stringed *psalterium* should be taken as the absolute limit for chant melody. Permitted to expand only one tone beyond the octave in each direction, the melody will remain within the permissible and divinely sanctioned boundaries dictated by Scripture.

Like Augustine, moreover, the Cistercians who spearheaded the twelfth-century reform were well aware of music's ability to illicitly stimulate the senses. In this respect, the Cistercian Reform was not simply an effort to instill monastic simplicity into singing style, but an attempt to regulate and discipline the singing bodies of the monks by bringing music into line with the proprieties of monastic life. As a Cistercian statute of 1134 puts it, "It befits men to sing with a manly voice, and not in a womanish manner [*non more femineo*] with tinkling, or, as it is said in the vernacular, with 'false' voices, as if imitating the wantonness of minstrels [*histrionicam imitari lasciviam*]. We have therefore stipulated that the mean should be adhered to in chant, so that it may exude seriousness and devotion may be preserved."[66] Such polemics against the "feminization" of chant are echoed in other influential twelfth-century Cistercian writings. In his forty-seventh *Sermon on the Song of Songs*, Bernard commands his monks to sing "correctly and vigorously . . . not wheezing through the nose with an effeminate stammering, in a weak and broken tone, but pronouncing the words of the Holy Spirit with becoming manliness and resonance and affection; and correctly, that while you chant you ponder on nothing but what you chant."[67] The "effeminacy" of certain forms of musical excess was a common theme in aesthetically conservative writings in the twelfth century; as we shall see in Chapter 4, polemics against new forms of polyphony were similarly anxious about the supposed feminization and emasculation of the chant.

Hildegard almost certainly never read the Cistercian legislation on plainchant, and I do not mean to suggest that the *Symphonia* should necessarily be interpreted through its polemic. Yet even a brief overview of the Cistercian Reform shows us a twelfth-century monastic movement inspired by a notion of the somatic and gendered implications of plainchant melody that was radically different from Hildegard's. Chants with the melodic range of "Ave generosa" represent the precise sort of musical excess excoriated by the Cistercian reformers as "effeminate" and "womanish" even while Hildegard was composing the *Symphonia*. In stark contrast to the limiting dictates of the Cistercian treatises, Hildegard's melodies allow the many bodies she describes in the texts to open up and resound in music. When sung, Hildegard's music captures in sound her poetic meditations on the female body and the voices she clearly saw as capable of performing well beyond conventional range.

The abbess gives a highly privileged place to music in "Ave generosa" in particular, granting it the power to express the corporeality of women's religious devotion much more effectively than would be possible through poetic language alone. While the Cistercians used the biblical *psalterium* as a justification for keeping chant carefully contained in terms of both range and affect, Hildegard saw biblical instruments as an opportunity to expound on the musicality of female desire, the properties of women that, as she puts it in the *Causae et curae*, made their musical bodies appropriate *ad citharizandum*. Read in conjunction with this musical image of the female sexual body, Hildegard's insistence that the Virgin's *womb*, in particular, contains music, invites us to look elsewhere in her voluminous writings for an interpretive key to the musicality of desire and embodiment in the *Symphonia*.

"Winds of pleasure" and the Erotics of Melody

The *Symphonia* is not the only of Hildegard's works concerned with the anatomy of female desire. The scholars who have treated Hildegard's medical writings have shown that her treatment of the specifics of sexual and reproductive anatomy and process is both broader and franker than that of practically any of her contemporaries.[68] In these works, known now as the *Physica* and the *Causae et curae*, Hildegard elaborates an anatomical system dependent on well-defined and thoroughly explained causalities. A significant portion of the *Causae et curae*, in particular, is devoted to detailed explication of the ways in which sexual desire and reproduction both reflect and shape gender difference as marked on the human body. Although it has been suggested that Hildegard gave "scarcely a nod toward theological interpretation" within her naturalistic writings,[69] I will argue that her explication of female sexuality in the *Causae et curae* throws provocative light on the musical elaborations of the female body and desire such as those we find in "Ave generosa" and other of her *Symphonia* compositions.

Of particular interest is Hildegard's painstaking analysis of the physiological difference between male and female sexual pleasure, a difference she ascribes to the nature of sexual breezes circulating in the loins. For men, breezes are constricted within the narrow space of the *stirps*. In women's bodies, however, the breezes of erotic desire create pleasure through expansion and dilation: "[W]hen the wind of pleasure proceeds from the marrow of a woman it falls into her womb, which is near the navel, and moves the woman's blood to pleasure; and because it spreads out around the womb, and is therefore more mild, because of her moisture where she burns in pleasure, or from fear or shame, she is able to restrain herself from excessive pleasure more easily than a man."[70] To Hildegard, although *pudor*, or shame, is certainly one of the consequences of erotic desire, the vagina itself is the locus of the *ventus delectationis*, the "winds" of sexual pleasure. Indeed, the vagina here becomes a place where the airs and breezes that produce desire are dispersed and diffused, allowing women to achieve a kind of tranquil eroticism. In Hildegard's own words, "Pleasure in a woman is comparable to the sun, which gently, calmly, and continuously spreads the earth with its heat, so that it may bring forth fruit" (Delectatio autem in muliere soli comparatur, qui blande et leniter et assidue terram calore suo perfundit, ut fructus proferat.[71]

This physiological account of female sexual desire in the *Causae et curae* sounds compellingly like a description of the expansive melody of "Ave generosa." In this hymn, every word of which is devoted to the Virgin and Ecclesia and the sensuous, erotic, and fertile qualities of their generative bodies, the melody begins with a rising fifth that expands by the middle of the first strophe to encompass the octave. The intervallic expansion is accomplished, again, not through conjunct motion (i.e., step-by-step progression), but rather through disjunction, where a rising fifth is followed immediately by a rising fourth and intervallic leaps are emphasized throughout. As an expression of intense and loving devotion to a female body both human and quasi-divine, the melody conveys a desiring adoration for the Virgin as the simultaneously absent and present object of love described in the text. Like the *orans*, or praying figure of Ecclesia in the manuscript illuminations that accompany a number of Hildegard's visions, the music reaches and opens simultaneously,[72] infusing the musical body with an active and restless desire for the hymn's subject, the Virgin. At the same time, however, these melodic gestures open the musical body to the touch of divinity, expressing Hildegard's awareness of women's flesh as a site of erotic exchange with the divine. The music that celebrates the Virgin maternal womb possesses an eroticized spaciousness of its own; like the desirous womb itself, the *lignum*, or harp-frame, that resounds with sexual pleasure, the music is diffused, dispersed, and spread out in a kind of cartography of female desire.

Like her musical constructions of the erotics of spirituality, Hildegard's elaborate descriptions of female desire and sexuality do not depend on male penetration. Although there are certain passages in the *Causae et curae* that discuss heterosexual intercourse in a positive light,[73] it seems clear that Hildegard sees the ability of women to experience sexual desire and pleasure as an attribute of the female body itself, not the necessary result of stimulation from an external source. For both women and men, desire arises from the marrow (*ex medulla*)—not the bone marrow, but, according to Joan Cadden, the "person's core or innermost part."[74] Just as the citharlike *lignum* of the vagina can be stimulated by the "winds of pleasure," a woman can be "moved to pleasure without the touch of a man" (sine tactu viri in delectationem movetur).[75] Hildegard's wording here is quite precise: she does not write "sine tactu *hominis*" ("homo" being the generic term she uses for person), but "sine tactu *viri*," "without the touch of a *man*." By any reckoning, this is an emphatically *nonheterosexual* model of genital stimulation. Though it has been neglected in the scholarship on Hildegard's views of human sexuality, in which emphasis is most often placed on her approving descriptions of heterosexual copulation, this clear suggestion of auto-erotic stimulation in the *Causae et curae* seems truly remarkable in the context of other medieval discussions of female sexuality.

Hildegard constructs a similar musical conflation of female spiritual desire and sexual pleasure in "O viridissima virga," a song of unspecified genre that opens with an image of the Stem of Jesse, the *virga* described in the first line. The Stem of Jesse was of course a common image in the medieval visual arts; as Newman concisely describes it, "As the father of David lies sleeping, the Messiah's family tree is seen to rise from his loins, with prophets and ancestors seated on the several branches and pointing to Mary enthroned in the crown."[76] Hildegard begins the song by praising the *virga*, the stem itself, a quite literal signifier of phallocentrism: the Latin *virga* is a common word for penis in both classical and medieval sources,[77] and Hildegard appears to be celebrating male fertility and the regenerative capabilities of men:

> O viridissima virga ave,
> que in ventoso flabro
> sciscitationis sanctorum prodisti.

Cum venit tempus quod tu floruisti in
ramis tuis; ave, ave sit tibi,
quia calor solis in te suadavit
sicut odor balsami.

Nam in te floruit pulcher flos qui odorem dedit
omnibus aromatibus que arida erant.

[Hail, o greenest stem, which was brought forth in the windy blasts of the prayers of the saints./Because the time comes when your branches have bloomed; hail, hail to you, because the heat of the sun has sweated into you like the scent of balsam./For in you the beautiful flower blossomed, which gave scent to all the spices which were dry.][78]

The erotic connotations of the language become clear in the image of the "windy blast" that brings forth the *virga. Ventoso flabro* evokes the winds and breezes (the "ventus delectationis") within the genitals that represent the source of erotic desire in the *Causae et curae*; in the pleasurable winds that allow the Stem to rise, the opening image interpolates an explicit description of male arousal into the devotional fabric of the poem.

In the fourth strophe, however, a very different form of desire begins to emerge. As the text progresses, we see that Hildegard is actually celebrating the *female* body and *female* fertility:

Et illa apparuerunt omnia in viriditate plena.

Unde celi dederunt rorem super gramen et omnis
terra leta facta est, quoniam viscera ipsius frumentum
protulerunt et quoniam volucres celi nidos in ipsa habuerunt.

Deinde facta est esca hominibus, et gaudium magnum
epulantium. Unde, o suavis Virgo, in te non deficit ullum gaudium.

Hec omnia Eva contempsit.

Nunc autem laus sit altissimo.

[And they have all appeared in pregnant greenness./Whence the heavens bestowed dew on the grass and all the earth was made fruitful, because its very womb brought forth grain, and heaven's birds made their nests in it./Finally there is made food for humanity, and great joy for the feasters; whence, o

sweet Virgin, in you there is no shortage of joy./All of these things Eve despised./Now let there be praise to the highest one.][79]

The spices that were dry in the third verse appear in "pregnant greenness
[*viriditate plena*]" in the fourth. By the fifth verse, it is clear that the womb
of the Earth is the bearer of the joy, greenness, and fruitfulness described in
the text: the *ventus*, the "wind" with which the poem began, has now
become the *venter* or womb, a subtle Latinate wordplay through which
Hildegard transfers the winds of pleasure from masculine stem to feminine
womb. The dew on the grass celebrated in "Ave generosa" reappears, and, in
another pun, *virgo*, the Virgin Mary, has replaced *virga*, the phallic stem, as
well as the Earth, as the central image: the winds of pleasure now flow into
the eroticized body of the *virgo*. The heat of the sun, the aroma of balsam,
the beautiful flower, wheat from the womb served at a banquet: Hildegard
experiences the Virgin's body as a synesthesia of taste, touch, sight, smell,
and, most important, sound, for all the other senses are set within the frame
of a musical composition.

As in "Ave generosa," Hildegard's vibrant poetic imagery is musically
realized in the melody of the chant, though in a very different way (see
Example 2). A through-composed piece (i.e., one in which the full melody
does not repeat from strophe to strophe), "O viridissima virga" conveys a
sense of musical fluidity through Hildegard's adept employment of centonization. This is a process, quite common in the medieval chant repertory, in
which short melodic fragments appear several times in the course of a
composition, connecting different sections of the chant in the listener's ear.
But Hildegard's use here of *internal* centonization differs markedly from
standard examples. Instead of using the same melodic fragment over and
over as a simple reference point, she alters slightly its original form each
time it appears, a gesture that allows the music to achieve a high degree of
expressiveness. For example, while the four-note descending figures that
open strophes 3 and 8 are similar, the figures that follow (on "in te floruit" in
3 and "laus sit" in 8) are noticeably different from one another, approaching
the repeating g's (on "-it pul-" and "sit al-") from a lower neighbor on f in 3
and an upper neighbor on a in 8.

While the range of "O viridissima virga" (an octave and a third) is not
excessive by Hildegard's standards, the song is indicative of her generally
flexible approach to melody. As Pfau has noted in a number of studies

O vi-ri-dis - si - ma vir - ga

a - - ve que in ven - to - so fla - bro

sci - sci - ta - ti - o - nis san - cto - rum pro - - - di - sti.

Cum ve-nit tem - pus quod tu flo - ru - i - sti in ra - mis tu - is

a - ve a - ve sit ti - bi

qui - a ca - lor so - lis in te su - da - vit

sic - ut o - dor bal - sa - mi.

Nam in te flo - ru - it pul - cher flos qui o - do - rem de - dit

1) Pete

MUSICAL EXAMPLE 2   Hildegard of Bingen, "O viridissima virga" from *Symphonia* (ed. Marianne Richert Pfau, 2:27–29)

showing the limits of centonization for understanding the *Symphonia* compositions, Hildegard allows for great melodic freedom in her longer liturgical songs, which are characterized by "considerable melodic contractions and expansions, changes in text declamation, registral extensions and compressions, modifications in the disposition of internal articulations, and in some instances different internal tonal goals. On the whole, these pieces are

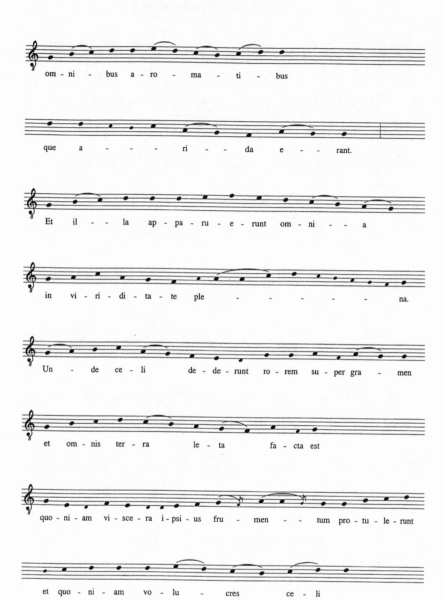

om - ni - bus a - ro - ma - ti - bus

que a - - - ri - da e - - rant.

Et il - - la ap - pa - ru - e - runt om - ni - - a

in vi - ri - di - ta - te ple - - - - - na.

Un - de ce - li de - de - runt ro - rem su - per gra - men

et om - nis ter - ra le - ta fa - cta est

quo - ni - am vi - sce - ra i - psi - us fru - men - - tum pro - tu - le - runt

et quo - ni - am vo - lu - cres ce - li

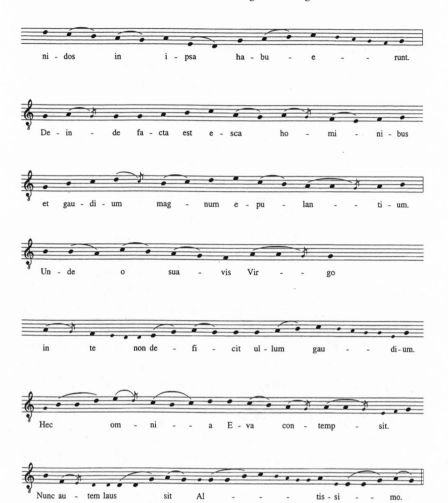

ni - dos   in   i - psa   ha - bu - e - - runt.

De - in - de fa - cta est e - sca ho - mi - ni - bus

et gau - di - um   mag - num e - pu - lan - - ti - um.

Un - de   o   sua - vis Vir - - go

in   te   non de - fi - cit ul - lum   gau - - di - um.

Hec   om - ni - - a E - va con - temp - sit.

Nunc au - tem laus   sit   Al - - - - tis - si - - mo.

not locked into fixed parallel structures. As a result, they command a dynamic model of form that emphasizes the concepts of relation over repetition, change over static identity, and process over fixed form."[80] An older tradition of scholarship characterized Hildegard's compositional strategies as unrefined and even regressive in comparison to those of her contemporaries; for the author of the *Early Music* essay cited above, they remain "capricious and uncontrolled."[81] Yet if we recognize that a composition such as "O viridissima virga" is in part a musical expression of devotional desire and female corporeality, the many contractions, expansions, extensions, compressions, modifications, and goal changes Pfau notes within the formal structure of the chant can be seen as compositional strategies Hildegard employs precisely in order to express in *cantus* the sonorous richness of the female body, the musical *viriditas* shared by the Virgin, the "womb" of the Earth, and Hildegard alike.

In fact, the text of "O viridissima virga" suggests that Hildegard may have been fully aware of the dynamism of her own music, incorporating this self-consciousness into the fabric of the *Symphonia*. Aside from its biblical and sexual connotations, the term *virga* had a particular lexical significance within medieval musical culture: along with the *punctum*, it was one of the most basic varieties of neume in the notation of plainchant. Writing at the end of the century, probably in Würzburg, the anonymous author of the *Summa musice* evokes the twelfth-century penchant for analyzing the component elements of neumes, describing the *virga* as "a simple note, elongated like a staff" (Virga est nota simplex ad modum virge oblonga).[82] The musical *virga*, then, *is* the "staff" in a quite literal way. As is well known, Hildegard herself claimed that she "had never studied neumes or any chant at all" when she began composing her music, and it is likely that she was initially unfamiliar with the more complex notational vocabulary contemporaneous with her musical production—*climacus, cephalicus, epiphonus, pressus, quilisma,* and so on.[83] Yet she is not claiming here that she did not know or have some basic familiarity with chant, merely that she had never *studied* it—an important distinction, I think. In the case of the *virga*, it seems inconceivable that Hildegard could have lived in a monastery into her forties and become acquainted with the large Benedictine repertory without learning of this most basic of notational forms. Indeed, the simplicity of the neume and its performance—a single, uninflected musical tone—would have made it an ideal image for symbolically initiating the miraculous compositional process as Hildegard describes herself experiencing it.

"O viridissima virga" is among a cluster of five Marian songs (the other four are an antiphon, an Alleluia verse, a sequence, and a responsory) that begin by evoking the image of the *virga* as a source of dynamism and change. In each of these songs, it seems possible that the musical connotations of the term are integral to the wider symbolic deployment of the *virga* as generative "stem," whether of music or of Christian genealogy. In the following excerpts, I have left *virga* deliberately untranslated in order to

show how all of these texts—which are, on the surface at least, directed to
the Virgin, the redemptive progeny of the Stem of Jesse—could also be read
as Hildegard's addresses to her own music (numbers indicate the pages from
Newman's *Symphonia* edition):

O frondens virga,
in tua nobilitate stans
sicut aurora procedit . . .
manum tuam porrige
ad erigendum nos.

[O leafy *virga*, standing in your nobility as the dawn breaks . . . stretch forth
your hand to raise us up.] (Antiphon, 120–21)

O virga mediatrix,
sancta viscera tua
mortem superaverunt
et venter tuus
omnes creaturas illuminavit

[O *virga*, mediatrix, your holy flesh overcame death, and your womb il-
lumined all creatures . . .] (Alleluia-verse, 124–25)

O viridissima virga, ave,
que in ventoso flabro sciscitationis
sanctorum prodisti.

[Hail, O greenest *virga*! You came forth in the windy blast of the questioning
of saints.] (Unspecified song, 126–27)

O virga ac diadema,
purpure regis,
que es in clausura tua
sicut lorica:
Tu frondens floruisti
in alia vicissitudine
quam Adam omne genus humanum
produceret.

[O *virga* and diadem of royal purple, you stand fast in your cloister like a
breastplate. Unfolding your leaves, you blossomed in another way than
Adam brought forth the whole human race.] (Sequence, 128–31)

O tu suavissima virga
frondens de stripe Iesse,

o quam magna virtus est
quod divinitas
in pulcherrimam filiam aspexit,
sicut aquila in solem
oculum suum ponit.

[O sweetest *virga* budding from the stock of Jesse, what a mighty work this is! God gazed on his fairest daughter as an eagle sets its eye upon the sun.]
(Responsory, 132–33)

Figure 7, which reproduces the page from the Dendermonde codex containing the responsory "O tu suavissima virga," may serve to illustrate the kind of self-reflexive reading of these songs I have in mind. The syllables "sua" and "-vi-" of *suavissima* are each set to a *virga*, which is formed by a single vertical stroke of the pen and the addition of a small head at the top.[84] At the notational foundations of every chant, the *virga* performs the life-giving and vernal musical functions described in these texts: the *virga* "stands" in leafy nobility before "stretching forth" and "rising" as the music ascends (or falling as it descends); it serves as a "mediatrix" between the human and the divine, allowing the musical "holy flesh" of the Virgin to triumph over death through *symphonia*; it originates precisely in the "windy blast" as the musical breath moves through the singing body; and it "stands fast" in the "cloister" before "unfolding" and "blossoming" into the myriad other neumes and sonorities constituting the body of chant, both on the page and in performance. In the final example above, Hildegard gives praise to the "budding" *virga* of her music in one of the most self-referential moments in the *Symphonia*: "What a mighty work this is!" The *virga* is both the medium and the object of song, both the notational apparatus of plainchant and the venerated result of divine inspiration and liturgical performance.

The various forms of desire registered in the *Symphonia* pervaded Hildegard's entire musical world, in which a group of nuns, living in intimate proximity, raised their voices together in song, allowing music—the actual *cantus* resonating between the nuns' bodies as well as the *symphonia* emerging from the womb and flesh of the Virgin and Ecclesia—to create and enliven the social, institutional, and devotional bonds both between one another and between themselves and the Virgin they worshiped. Music, always a somatic and often an erotic medium for Hildegard, establishes in

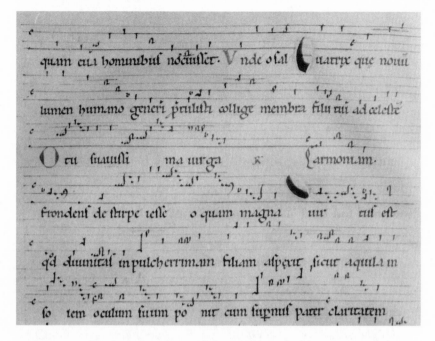

FIGURE 7   "O tu suavissima virga," from Hildegard of Bingen, *Symphonia*
(Dendermonde, St.-Pieters & Paulusabdij, cod. 9, fol. 156ᵛ)

the moment of performance a liturgical time and space that brings women
together in the *clausuram ventris*—the "cloister of the womb" of the Virgin,
as Hildegard puts it in "O quam preciosa"—that physically constitutes their
institution and contains their musical lives. How might we relate the various circulations of female desire in Hildegard's music to the Christian
tradition within which she lived, wrote, and composed?

As I have argued at greater length elsewhere, a large part of the *Symphonia*'s significance for the history of sexuality may lie in the opportunity
it provided for the musical expression of desire between women, a desire
simultaneously erotic and devotional.[85] While the twelfth century saw a
burgeoning of new discourses celebrating the importance of femininity to
religious experience, the central role of the Virgin to Christian theology,
and a new emphasis on the involvement of affectivity and the senses in
devotional practice, very few allowed for the kinds of bonds between
women—what we might term the *homoerotics of Marian devotion*—that the

Symphonia brings to the center of liturgical practice. These texts very often focus not on the corporeal specificity of Christ, but on the body of the Virgin, elaborating at length the *gaudium* she experiences, the music that expresses it, and the simultaneous openness and constriction of the womb from which this music emanates. It often seems that the *corpus Christi* functions in the *Symphonia* as the very means of elaborating the erotic musicality of the Virgin's body. When performed, Hildegard's compositions musically intermingle the bodies that sing and those that are sung about—Ecclesia, the Virgin, Hildegard, and her nuns—by binding them together in *symphonia*. Female-male-female constructions of triangulated desire often yield to female-female eroticized performance.

This is precisely what occurs in a vision recorded in the sixth book of the *Liber vitae meritorum*, where Hildegard observes a group of virgins gathered together "as if in a mirror": "On their heads they wore crowns intertwined with gold and roses and lilies and surrounded with pipes [*fistulis*] of most precious stone. Whenever the Lamb of God used his voice, this sweetest blowing of the wind coming from a secret and divine place touched these pipes [*suauissimus flatus uenti de secreto diuinitatis uenians fistulas has tangebat*] so that they resounded with every type of strumming of cithara and organ [*omni genere citharedorum citharizantium et organorum*]. No one was playing this song, except these who wore these crowns, but the others who heard this song rejoiced in it, like a previously blind person now sees the brightness of the sun."[86] Once again Hildegard associates music with wind, the eroticized *ventus delectationis* she describes in the *Causae et curae* as spreading through the womb and "moving the blood" to pleasure. Even more strikingly, the wind in this vision emerges from a *secreto*, a "secret place": though the wind begins only when the Agnus Dei speaks, Hildegard may be suggesting that it originates from the very *secretum* she describes in "O quam preciosa," the Virgin's musical womb. Whatever the case, the musical performance she envisions is the exclusive province of the virgins, "those who wore these crowns" and whose somatic *citharae*—the metaphorical stringed instruments analogized in the *Causae et curae* to the vagina, which itself is appropriate *ad citharizandum*—receive the collective touch of the *ventus* and resound together in song.

Although her musical elaborations of religious experience are often erotic, Hildegard was avowedly not an ecstatic. Unlike figures such as St. Teresa, she did not employ the language of heterosexual intercourse in writing of her own experiences of communion with the divine, and she insisted that she maintained control of her senses at all times. But we should not assume, as older scholarship on female sanctity and *Brautmystik* often did, that spiritually erotic experiences for medieval religious women somehow depended upon submission to a dominant male figure.[87] Like the *sine tactu viri* image in the *Causae et curae*, the lyrics of many of Hildegard's compositions suggest that female-female sensuality was much more central to her expressions of religious devotion than was heteroeroticism, for they consistently capture the physical, sensual essence of the Virgin, the unattainable but constantly present body that exudes *symphonia* from its womb. The *Symphonia* provided the means for women to explore what Hildegard saw as the uniquely musical abilities and pleasures of their *own* bodies by exploiting the fantastic range and melodic complexity of her music, mostly unavailable in the standard Gregorian repertory that constituted the majority of the music they sang. These were the same bodies whose capacity for sexual arousal fascinated Hildegard in the *Causae et curae*, the bodies whose pleasures she described in a technical vocabulary of her own and likened to musical instruments designed for erotic strumming.

That the *Symphonia* reveals a musical affinity between female spirituality and female sexuality suggests that the relationship between Hildegard's naturalistic writings and her spiritual works may be closer than previous scholarship has allowed. Commenting on the "themes that pervade all Hildegard's writing about the Virgin," Barbara Newman writes, "If we step back for a moment from the details, what seems most distinctive about this body of prose and song is the near-total absence of Mary as a person. She is rather a state of existence, an embodied Eden. Her flesh is the garden where God dwells; everything about her is joy, innocence, asexual eros. Her beauty is not that of a human form but that of intangible essences—light and fragrance and song."[88] Here Newman is following Peter Dronke, who similarly argues for a strict demarcation between sex and devotion: "she who wrote so openly about women's sexuality in the context of medicine nonetheless retained an asexual concept of love in her ideal realm."[89] Both scholars would have us see Hildegard's devotional verse and music addressed to the Virgin as somehow asexual, divorced from her naturalistic appreciation of the female body and erotic desire. I would agree that Hildegard's Marian compositions are a-*hetero*sexual. Yet the musical circulations of desire created within the *Symphonia* often establish the very connections between sexuality and sanctity that the study of her life and works has obscured.

Of course, like many medieval writers, Hildegard often described carnal desire as a sign of the Fall, and her monastic vow of chastity was one of the ways in which she demonstrated this view. Indeed, at one point in the *Scivias* she explicitly attacks homosexual practice in no uncertain terms.[90] As we have seen, however, Hildegard herself did not necessarily distinguish between what we might include under the rubric "sexuality" and other aspects of her life, including religious experience.[91] Quite the contrary: the imagery and vocabulary of female sexual pleasure were an integral part of her musical creativity. In a more general sense, Hildegard's musical erotics of devotion— as well as the polymorphously erotic nature of the bodies she enshrined in melody—pressures us to consider the ways in which she and other medieval religious writers sexualized the *entire* body, not simply the genitals.[92]

I want to make it very clear that I am not arguing that Hildegard herself was a lesbian; there is no empirical evidence for the kind of intimate sexual relationship between her and one of her sisters such as that found by Judith Brown in the writings of Benedetta Carlini, a Renaissance nun living in Italy (though the overwhelming emotional intensity of Hildegard's relationship with the much younger Richardis is certainly suggestive).[93] The last ten years of scholarship in gender studies and the history of sexuality have shown us that there are more complex ways of situating discourses of same-sex love within the history of sexuality without reducing them to genital essentialism. As Judith Bennett has recently pointed out, the writing of the social history of medieval lesbianism has been hampered by just such a fetishization of same-sex genital contact; instead, she suggests, those concerned with recovering this history would do better to excavate what she terms "lesbian-like" institutions and practices, ways of living and creating that provided women with the means of resisting the bodily and sexual demands of reproductive heterosexuality.[94] E. Ann Matter puts it well: "We can only find 'medieval lesbians' among the landmarks of medieval culture, on that particular continuum, not ours." Although according to Matter "the overwhelmingly patriarchal nature of medieval culture significantly modified the evidence for, or even the experience of, women whose primary emotional and erotic relation was to other women,"[95] the "continuum" to which she refers is nevertheless a *lesbian* continuum, in Adrienne Rich's term, which "includes a range—through each woman's life and throughout history—of woman-identified experience [and] not simply the fact that a woman has had or consciously desired genital sexual experience with another woman."[96] For Rich, as for Hildegard, the erotic "is unconfined to any single part of the body or solely to the body itself, an energy not only diffuse but . . . omnipresent"; like Bennett, Rich urges historians to recover the "breadths of female history and psychology which have lain out of reach as a consequence of limited, mostly clinical, definitions of 'lesbianism.' "[97]

The musicalities of premodern same-sex desire provide us with a rich perspective upon such antiessentialist histories. Chapter 4 will show that the controversial harmonies produced in twelfth-century polyphony were imagined by some of their opponents as a personified embodiment of the very sorts of sexual "inversions" castigated by contemporaneous polemicists against sodomy. In the particular case of Hildegard's music, a useful model for situating its desirous texts and melodies within the history of sexuality can be found in the recent work of Elizabeth Wood, who has coined the term "Sapphonics" to denote "a mode of articulation, a way of describing a space of lesbian possibility, for a range of erotic and emotional relationships among women who sing and women who listen."[98] The musical bodies envisioned in Hildegard's *Symphonia* are, quite emphatically, *Sapphonic* bodies. They create sonorous spaces of lesbian possibility in themselves and as they are performed by other Sapphonic bodies. They claim the medieval monastery as a Sapphonic space even as they inhabit it and fill it with the music that Hildegard's own body gave them to perform.

Despite the pleasures (and often the Sapphonic pleasures) she discovered and reproduced in musical experience, Hildegard's musical life was also very much about pain. As we have seen, she constructs several metaphors in which cithars, harps, and strings serve as instruments of discipline and torture. And she describes her initial reception of music from God as occurring within the same series of wrenching bodily afflictions that brought her the *Scivias* and other theological works. This is made particularly explicit in one of the first-person passages in the *Vita*, where Hildegard describes her initial decision to record her visions and music in terms that clearly echo the account in the *Scivias*:

Post cuius finem ita permansi uidens in quadragesimum etatis mee annum.
Tunc in eadem uisione magna pressura dolorum coacta sum palam mani-
festare, que uideram et audieram, sed ualde timui et erubui proferre, que
tamdiu silueram. . . . Sed et cantum cum melodia *in laudem Dei et sanctorum*
absque doctrina ullius hominis protuli et cantaui, cum numquam uel neu-
mam uel cantum aliquem didicissem.

[After (Jutta's) death, I continued seeing as before, till my fortieth year of
age. Then in this same vision I was constrained by the great pressure of my
pains to reveal openly what I had seen and heard. But I was very afraid, and
blushed at the thought of proclaiming what I had kept silent about for so
long. . . . Then I also composed and sang chant with melody, to the praise of
God and his saints, without being taught by anyone, since I had never studied neumes or any chant at all.][99]

The passage suggests an unavoidable convergence of musical *inventio* and
visionary suffering, one that the *Symphonia*'s imagistic catalog of the *gaudium* of musical wombs, viscera, and bodies makes it easy for us to forget.

In order to tease out the implications of Hildegard's musical suffering
for her musical practice, I turn in conclusion to the text and music of "O vos
angeli," an antiphon in the *Symphonia* that crystallizes these aspects of her
visionary cosmology:

O vos angeli
qui custoditis populos,
quorum forma fulget
in facie vestra,
et o vos archangeli
qui suscipitis
animas iustorum,
et vos virtutes,
potestates,
principatus, dominationes
et troni,
qui estis computati
in quintum secretum numerum,
et o vos cherubin
et seraphin,
sigillum secretorum Dei:

Sit laus vobis,
qui loculum antiqui cordis
in fonte asspicitis.

Videtis enim
interiorem vim Patris,
que de corde illius spirat
quasi facies.

Sit laus vobis,
qui loculum antiqui cordis
in fonte asspicitis.

[O you angels who guard the peoples, whose form gleams in your face, and
O you archangels, who receive the souls of the just, and you virtues, powers,
princedoms, dominations, and thrones, who are counted in the secret number five, and O you cherubim and seraphim, seal of the secrets of God: Praise
be to you, who behold in the fountain the little place of the ancient heart.
For you see the inner strength of the Father, which breathes from his heart
like a face. Praise be to you, who behold in the fountain the little place of the
ancient heart.][100]

As Newman shows, the antiphon's text conveys Hildegard's idiosyncratic
vision of the order of the angels, which she divides into groups of two, five,
and two: angels and archangels, who "deal most often with human beings,
represent body and soul; the cherubim and seraphim, closest to the ineffable light, signify the knowledge and love of God; and the five orders in
between (ll. 8–13) correspond to the five senses and the five wounds of
Christ."[101]

One of the most idiosyncratic characteristics of Hildegard's chants is,
again, their often immense range, a formal aspect of her musical production
interpreted above as a sonorous acknowledgment of the simultaneously
devotional and sexual pleasures, aspirations, and "openness" of the musical
body as she conceived it. "O vos angeli" has a wider range than any other
Symphonia composition. The two excerpts given in Example 3 come from
the opening and the middle of the responsory as it appears in the Dendermonde codex. In the first excerpt (3a), the melody begins with two
melismas on *O* and *vos*, the second of which immediately takes the singer
down to the song's lowest note, a neighbor g over an octave below c′, be-

fore cadencing on low a. As the poem moves from angels and archangels through the virtues and powers, the melody hovers around a until (Ex. 3b) the word *dominationes*, when it suddenly shoots up to the antiphon's highest tone, a d″ an octave and a step above the c clef line. We might take this kind of plainchant pyrotechnics as "ecstatic," as Hildegard's attempt to reach musically to the angels described in the text by employing an extremely wide range in a piece of sung music. Newman describes "O vos angeli" as depicting the "vertiginous ascent of the soul," and it may be that the melody represents the same sort of musical "reaching" we have seen in "Ave generosa."[102]

Yet the text of this antiphon is not only about the powers of angels, but also implicitly about human inability to reach God without their mediation. Without angels, archangels, virtues, dominations, powers, and thrones, the human being will remain forever frail and bound to the earth. Perhaps the antiphon's music is intended to force this realization on its performers. The highest note occurs on *dominationes*, a word that appears in the middle of a list Hildegard took from the first chapter of Paul's letter to the Colossians (1:16). In the same brief chapter, Paul is explicit about his own participation in Christian suffering: "I rejoice in my sufferings for you, and fill up that which is left of the afflictions of Christ in my flesh for his body's sake" (Col. 1:24). Singing a text devoted to the immense powers of the ranks of angels standing between humanity and God, the human being is musically compelled to recognize her own bodily inferiority within the time and space of performance.

Here again it may be useful to turn to the contemporaneous Cistercian legislation on chant for its vivid depiction of the physicality of singing. For the Cistercians, musical excess—whether in range, "effeminate" performance, or unclear articulation of words—was carnal anathema. Yet excessively wide-ranging singing also created a painful spectacle of the singing body: "To what purpose are such chants composed or kept in use, too low for notation, lower still for singing, causing a change of clef lines, torturing the vocal chords [*arterias cruciantes*], having an endless range, ascending at one time up to the skies, and descending at another down to the abyss?"[103] The passage seems to imply that notational and performance practices conspire to keep chant out of control and injurious to the bodies that perform it (indeed, a better translation of the phrase *arterias cruciantes* is probably "*crucifying* the vocal chords"). The Cistercian legislation suggests

3a.

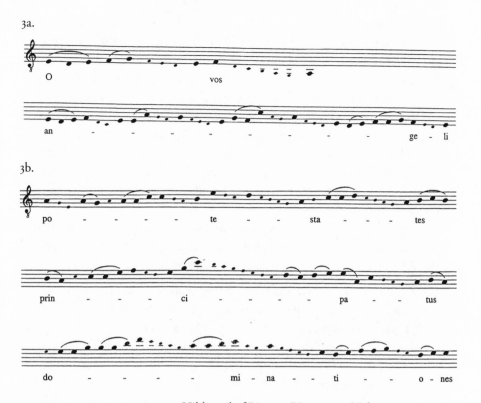

3b.

MUSICAL EXAMPLE 3   Hildegard of Bingen, "O vos angeli" from *Symphonia* (ed. Marianne Richert Pfau, 4:5–8)

that the performer, by stretching the range of a liturgical chant beyond ten notes, quite literally tortures the singing body.

Hildegard possessed her own vocabulary for the torturous demands of musical performance, one that she articulates most clearly in a famous letter she wrote near the end of her life to the prelates of Mainz. Following a bitter dispute over the burial of a formerly excommunicated nobleman, Hildegard and her monastery were placed under interdict for their failure to obey the prelates' order to exhume the body. A crucial part of the interdict was the order that all musical activity immediately cease, an order to which Hildegard replied by formulating the most forceful and direct expression of her own philosophy of music.[104] In the letter, Hildegard suggests that the incarnational "canticle of praise," the liturgy forbidden to herself and her spiritual daughters, represents the devotional voice of the body: "Consider, too, that just as the body of Jesus Christ was born of the purity of the Virgin Mary through the operation of the Holy Spirit, so, too, the canticle of praise, reflecting celestial harmony, is rooted in the Church through the Holy Spirit. The body is the vestment of the spirit, which has a living voice, and so it is proper for the body, with the soul, to use its voice to sing praises to God [*ut corpus cum anima per vocem Deo laudes decantet*]."[105] Hildegard locates a means of transcending what she calls "the music of this exile" through the *vox corporis*: "all arts pertaining to things useful and necessary for mankind have been created by the breath that God sent into man's body."[106] Music is, by definition, of the body, its cessation a kind of premature death.

Yet the same letter to the Mainz prelates contains a simultaneously practical and allegorical construction of the suffering of song, the performative pain that constitutes an indispensable component of musical life:

> Et quoniam interdum in auditu alicuius cantionis homo sepe suspirat et gemit, naturam celestis harmonie recolens, propheta . . . hortatur in psalmo ut confiteamur Domino in cithara, et in psalterio decem chordarum psallamus ei, citharam, qui inferius sonat, ad disciplinam corporis, psalterium, quod de superius sonum reddit, ad intentionem spiritus, decem chordas ad completionem legis referri cupiens.

> [And because sometimes a person sighs and groans at the sound of singing, remembering, as it were, the nature of celestial harmony, the prophet . . . urges us in the psalm to confess to the Lord with the harp and to sing a psalm to Him with the ten-stringed psaltery. His meaning is that the harp, which is plucked from below, relates to the discipline of the body; the psaltery, which is plucked from above, pertains to the exertion of the spirit; the ten chords, to the fulfillment of the law.][107]

Singing, then, is never simply a human performance of the pleasures of devotion. The incarnational performance of *symphonia* inevitably involves the "sighs and groans" that humans emit when they hear and experience *cantus*. Here, in a letter insisting on her institution's right to continue performing the liturgy, Hildegard relates the embodied performance of song to the christological music of the passion—in other words, to the tradition of musico-biblical representation that includes the "dire torments" and "torture" inflicted by the *lira* upon the Son of Man in the *Scivias*. The biblical *lira*, "plucked from below," is the human body as well as the musical *disciplina* that causes this body to suffer as it performs.

Hildegard may thus be producing within the sonic space of "O vos angeli" the precise sort of "musical crucifixion" described by the Cistercians, the "sighs and groans" and *lira*-induced tortures imagined in the Mainz letter and in the *Scivias*. Many of us who have written on Hildegard's music have assumed that she and the women for whom she composed must have been talented musicians, and that the *Symphonia* therefore reflects their virtuosic abilities as singers. But it seems equally likely (more likely, perhaps) that a composition such as "O vos angeli" may reflect her nuns' *disabilities* as singers. This antiphon asks its performers to sing *two octaves and a sixth*, an extraordinary range even for professional singers of the early twenty-first century (just ask one). Georg Friedrich Handel wrote a part in his oratorio *Aci, Galatea e Polifemo* (1708) in order to exploit the renowned range of the great eighteenth-century Italian bass Giuseppe Boschi. The total range of the part is two and one-half octaves, a full step narrower than the range of "O vos angeli."

Perhaps extreme range had a punitive purpose in the *Symphonia*. An antiphon like "O vos angeli" may have been Hildegard's way of making her nuns suffer as she suffered, forcing them to participate liturgically in religious suffering just as she participated mystically. Even as they sang to the angels, the performers of "O vos angeli" took part in the musical pain of the passion, performing their own musical "domination" as a reminder of their pathetic state as human beings in human bodies. In this sense, Hildegard's compositions obliquely anticipate Bach's sometimes sadistic stance toward the performers of his religious compositions as Richard Taruskin has recently described them.[108] Like Hildegard, Bach often forced his performers to grovel in the musical mud, as it were, foregrounding the inabilities of boy singers to reach low notes and even writing instrumental parts that exceeded the mechanically possible ranges of available instruments.

Hildegard, too, placed unreasonable demands on the bodies of her nuns, just as she felt God placing what surely seemed like unreasonable demands on her own. Hildegard belongs less in a New Age or Creation Spiritualist ethic of "healing chant" than she does in the performative company of modern artists such as Diamanda Galas, whose operatic renderings of disease and bodily suffering should be seen as part of a long tradition of musical violence in the Christian tradition (see Part 3 of this volume). Listening to Hildegard's plainchant as a mode of musical pleasure *and* suffering may well render it less enjoyable to those of us used to basking in the melodies of her sequences, humming the elaborate melismas of her responsories, or parsing and dissecting her modal techniques. Yet it may be a more honest way of conceiving her visionary life as we recuperate it for our own study, analysis, and pleasure.

CHAPTER 4

Polyphones and Sodomites:
Music and Sexual Dissidence from
Leoninus to Chaucer's Pardoner

A mong the more obscure texts collected in Edmond de Cousse-maker's *Scriptores Ecclesiastici de Musica* is a "Brief treatise concerning the different kinds and degrees of musicians" (*Tractatulus de Differentiis et Gradibus Cantorum*), recently reedited from its single manuscript source by Christopher Page.[1] Written shortly before 1400 by one Arnulf de St. Ghislain, the *Tractatulus* seeks to describe the "four principal types" of musician active in its author's social milieu, three of which types, according to Arnulf, deserve praise and commendation: first, the "lay persons," musical hedonists "drawn by a zeal for sweetness" who "lend their pleasure-loving ears to any music"; second, the teachers and theorists who "keep the glorious treasures of the art and discipline of music in the sanctuaries of their breasts" and "teach their pupils to perform what they cannot perform themselves"; and finally singers, the "first in honor . . . whom natural instinct, aided by a sweet voice, turns into very nightingales." Arnulf finds the voices of women singers particularly ravishing to the ear:

> Among [singers] there is a second group—that is to say of the favoured
> female sex—which is so much the more precious the more it is rare; when it
> freely divides tones into semitones with a sweet-sounding throat, and divides
> semitones into indivisible microtones, it delights itself with an indescribable
> melody that you would rather deem angelic than human. So it is that these
> women—goddesses, or indeed rather earthly Sirens—enchant the bewitched
> ears of their listeners and then steal away their hearts, which are for the most
> part lulled by this kind of intoxication, in secret theft, and having snatched
> them and made them subject to their will, they then enslave them and lead

them, shipwrecked by the beauty, alas! of their prison, into an earthly
Charybdis in which no kind of redemption or ransom is of any avail.[2]

Drawing on an ancient trope for musical seduction but recasting it in
contemporary terms, Arnulf ascribes a Sirenic aura to the dazzling skill with
which such women "enchant the bewitched ears" of their male listeners,
"enslave them" in a prison of song, and throw away the key.

Yet Arnulf's praise for the ravishments of the female voice follows an
equally vehement polemic in the opening lines of the *Tractatulus* against
what he sees as the most prevalent type of musician, "those who are utterly
ignorant of the art."[3] At the heart of his attack lies a revealing description of
their "notorious" performances, one that casts a certain style of polyphonic
singing as an animalistic spectacle of the musical body:

> in sue corrixationis latratu dum clamore rudiunt altius asino et brutali
> clangore terribilius intubant, cachephaton evomunt, *organizantesque per
> antifrasin faciunt in musica irregulariter barbarismum* atque execrabili sue
> presumptionis falso cecati putamine se ipsos in se iactitant cantores posse
> postponere seu preire precipuos . . . semper cum consonantibus nic-
> hilominus dissonantes et soloestico fedantes vicio in scolata musicorum
> turba quidquid profertur regularius adeo cantoribus intollerabiles.
>
> [When they bray with the din of their brawling bark louder than an ass, and
> when they trumpet more terribly than the clamour of a wild animal, they
> spew out harsh-sounding things; *and these part-singers, through antiphrasis,
> produce barbarism in music contrary to rule*; falsely blinded by a despicable
> delusion that arises from their presumption, they boast in their hearts that
> they can disregard excellent singers and surpass them . . . (they) are always
> producing dissonance amongst those who are concordant, and with their
> ineptitude they constantly pollute whatever is more correctly performed in
> the learned throng of musicians.][4]

In a brief comment on the phrase italicized above, Page rightly points out
that the use of grammatical and rhetorical terminology "to create a vocabulary for describing musical phenomena associated with no technical vocabulary of their own" characterizes a good deal of medieval theoretical writing
on music.[5] This particular conflation of musical and grammatical terminology, however, is not original to Arnulf's *Tractatulus*. In fact, the passage

derives practically word-for-word from a specific literary source, Alan of Lille's Latin neoplatonic treatise *De planctu Naturae* (ca. 1160–1170). In condemning a certain kind of musical performer, one who "pollutes" musical beauty through illicit rhetorical *inventio*, Arnulf draws on the writings of a moralist and philosopher two centuries in his grave by interpolating into his own treatise this much earlier representation of polyphonic "barbarism." Though fascinating on its own terms as evidence of the knowledge of Latin philosophical literature among late-medieval musical theorists, Arnulf's allusion also invites us to examine in more detail the historical conditions that led to Alan of Lille's own peculiarly linguistic depiction of twelfth-century "part-singers," or *organizantes*.[6]

Familiar to literary scholars as a complex allegorical dream-vision commenting in various ways on the degenerate state of humanity and poetic language, the *Complaint of Nature* was composed by Alan during his years as a young *magister* in the schools of northern France, in particular at the cathedral school of Notre Dame in Paris.[7] The passage that attracted Arnulf's allusive eye appears in the midst of an extended ekphrastic description of the natural world as depicted on Lady Nature's gown:

> Illic equus, feruenti prouectus audacia, suo insessori conmilitans, hastam frangebat cum milite. Illic asinus, clamoribus aures ociosis fastidiens *quasi per antifrasim organizans, barbarismum faciebat in musica*.[8]
>
> [There the horse, urged on by his impetuous mettle, joining his rider in battle, broke a lance with the enemy. There the ass, offending our ears with his idle braying, as though a singer of organum, by antiphrasis, introduced barbarisms into music.]

Alan's analogy here between linguistic "barbarism" and brash "organizing," or part-singing (the Latin *organizans*), points to a larger moral concern pervading the treatise as a whole, for it echoes quite explicitly the guiding metaphorical assumption of the *Complaint*: that grammatical "barbarism" in language and gender inversion in human sexual relations are one and the same.[9] As Alan writes in the fourth *prosa* of the *Complaint*, "the human race, fallen from its high estate, adopts a highly irregular metaplasm when it inverts the rules of Venus by introducing barbarisms in its arrangement of genders" (Humanum namque genus, a sua generositate degenerans, in constructione generum *barbarizans*, Venereas regulas inuertendo nimis irregulari utitur metaplasmo).[10] For Alan, the most spectacular and widespread manifestation of *barbarismus* in human relations is the abandonment of "natural" sexual roles through homosexual sodomy, which he casts as a hermaphroditic performance of gender: "A man turned woman blackens the fair name of his sex. The witchcraft of Venus turns him into a hermaphrodite" (Femina uir factus sexus denigrat honorem,/Ars magice Veneris hermafroditat eum).[11] Simultaneously man and woman, masculine and feminine, the sodomite for Alan is the veritable embodiment of sexual and grammatical ambiguity. And as Alan's musical analogy above suggests, those singers who "produce barbarism in music" through their antiphrastic spectacles create in polyphony itself a musical simulacrum of sodomitical inversion.

Taken alone, Alan's comparison between an allegorical ass and a barbarous *organizans* or "part-singer" seems more amusing than historically significant. Yet this rather oblique image of musical perversion may well represent one of the earliest surviving literary allusions to Notre Dame polyphony, the innovative and enormously influential repertory of liturgical music composed, improvised, and performed at the Parisian cathedral beginning sometime in the second half of the twelfth century. This is an impossible claim to prove, of course, nor will I attempt to do so unequivocally in this chapter. Indeed, I will return to Alan below only after sifting through a number of other works—musical, poetic, theological, and philosophical—originating in the Latinate intellectual culture of northern France and Norman England in the twelfth and early thirteenth centuries. As we shall see, Alan's seemingly off-the-cuff analogy between the musical logic of polyphony and the sexual logic of sodomy was neither incidental nor fanciful. To the contrary, this eroticizing analogy points to a more general cultural anxiety over the performing male body as a site of musical and sexual deviance, an anxiety that becomes nowhere more apparent than in a number of Latin writings contemporary with the wide-scale emergence of liturgical polyphony in the Île-de-France. This music was heard by a number of its detractors as a sonorous embodiment of a dissident mode of desire: a transgressive eroticism that left traces in the theoretical texts that sought to explain the rules of polyphony, that came to be vilified in some of the very manuscripts that transmit the polyphonic repertory, and, perhaps most surprising of all, inspired the literary production of Leonin himself, polyphony's most celebrated twelfth-century composer.

Desiring Leonin

In the midst of a treatise on mensural polyphony dating from 1279, a writer known to us as the St. Emmeram Anonymous issues a stern warning to his readers regarding the rules of polyphonic composition:

> Attendas igitur, mi dilecte, tu qui tante dulcedinis ac modulationis cupis aq-
> uas potabiles exaurire, ut ea que secuntur aure vigili uringinis suscipias,
> cordis armariolo pacifice reponendo, ne quod a paucis cognitum et honor-
> ifice reservatum est provulgatum communiter iam vilescat.[12]
>
> [You should pay attention therefore, my beloved, you who desire to drain the
> thirst-quenching waters of so much sweetness and sound, so that you may
> take up those things which follow with the alert ear of desire, and put them
> peacefully in the book-case of your heart, lest something that is understood
> by few and honorably reserved should be widely promulgated and now be-
> come worthless.]

For the Anonymous, the harmonious and liquid sweetness of polyphony is, precisely, a secret: a secret shared among the privileged few even as its fruits are consumed by the many. His warning provides an ironically apt reminder of how securely locked away so many of this repertory's foundational secrets remain. As is well known, the first extant theoretical explication of Notre Dame polyphony dates from the 1230s at the very earliest; according to the most convincing estimates, the surviving manuscripts of the *Magnus liber organi* were compiled some seventy years after the music they transmit was first performed in the cathedral.[13] In her recent critique of Friedrich Ludwig and what she calls the "myth of Notre Dame," Nicky Loseff has gone so far as to suggest that the surviving thirteenth-century sources represent "a small number of phenomena which should never have provided more than a tentative framework around which interpretations [of the earliest Notre Dame repertory] might be made."[14] Odo of Sully's famous 1198 decree is perhaps the most celebrated piece of evidence for the early performance of polyphony at Notre Dame; it sternly mandates the use of two-, three-, and four-voice organa as a kind of musical corrective to the moral outrages perpetrated by the lower clergy during the Feast of Fools.[15] Other than Odo's decree, however, primary documents attesting to the creation, perfor-mance, and cultural significance of Notre Dame polyphony in its first seventy-odd years have been hard to come by.[16]

One of the more enduring mysteries surrounding the early history of this repertory has concerned the identity of the individuals involved in its composition and initial manuscript compilation. Until quite recently, almost nothing was known about these churchmen aside from a few tantalizing remarks made by the so-called Anonymous IV (probably an English Benedictine monk of Bury St. Edmunds) in a late-thirteenth-century treatise on polyphonic rhythm and counterpoint. In a passage whose significance for the history of the Notre Dame school has been emphasized time and again since Ludwig's day, Anonymous IV names a few of the individuals who (as oral tradition and his own memory would have it) dominated the musical culture of the cathedral almost a century before he wrote:

> And note that Master Leonin, according to what was said, was the best composer of organa, who made the great book of organum from the gradual and antiphonary to elaborate the divine service. And it was in use up to the time of Perotin the Great, who shortened it [*abbreviavit*] and made very many better clausulae or puncta, since he was the best composer of discant, and better than Leonin. But this is not to be said about the subtlety of the organum.[17]

Of the many attempts to establish the identities of Leonin and Perotin over the last century, the only successful effort has been Craig Wright's acclaimed 1986 article, "Leoninus, Poet and Musician," a landmark study to which the following discussion is deeply indebted.[18] The biography of Leonin (hereafter Leoninus) that Wright was able to patch together from a number of Parisian cartularies tells us that he was born about 1135 in Paris, eventually becoming a student and, later, a *magister* of some kind at the cathedral school of Notre Dame. Leoninus was a cathedral canon, in fact, by the 1180s, and apparently very active in church affairs until at least 1201, the year from which the last surviving record dates.

Like many of those involved in the production of church music in the Middle Ages, Leoninus was also a talented poet.[19] Wright identified seven manuscripts containing his lengthy *Historie sacre gestas ab origine mundi*, an Old Testament versification along the lines of Peter Riga's more famous *Aurora*. While its manuscript survival rate and an external mention indicate that the *Historie* attracted a fair amount of attention from his contemporaries, Leoninus's shorter works—four brief moralizing poems and four longer verse-epistles—survive in a single manuscript, Paris, Bibliothèque Nationale, MS Latin 14759.[20] Although these poems remain unpublished and, since Wright's overview, unexamined, they allow us to begin elaborating what I want to suggest was an "open secret" (in D. A. Miller's term) surrounding early Notre Dame polyphony, a complex genealogy of music, poetics, and desire that sheds new light on one of the canonical treasures of Western art-music.[21]

The first two of Leoninus's letters are addressed to popes, Adrian IV and his successor, Alexander III, the first (fols. 148r–148v) to appeal for papal favors for the church of St. Benoît, the second (148v–149v) to thank Alexander for his generosity in helping Leoninus's "special friend"—a friend whose "particular love" Leoninus "enjoy[s]" (amore fruor speciali) (149r)—in his dealings with the curia in Rome. Like many letters to popes, these epistles are appropriately ingratiating, redolent with just the kind of disingenuous humility one might expect.[22]

Leoninus's second two letters are addressed to men with whom the poet seems to have been on somewhat more intimate terms. The occasional poem "De anulo dato ab henrico cardinali" was written to Henry of Marcy, a papal legate to France in the 1180s, ostensibly to thank him for a ruby-encrusted ring, an *anulus*, he had given to Leoninus as a sign of their "sacred love." In his brief discussion of this letter, Wright notes in passing that the model for Leoninus's "De anulo" was Ovid's *Amores* 2.15.[23]

Ovid's addressee in this famous poem is the "anulus" itself, the "little ring" that the speaker has just given to his lady. The speaker opens with an erotic pun on *digitus* (finger), however, that immediately asks the reader to associate the snug circle of the *anulus* with his lady's sexual anatomy:

Anule, formosae digitum vincture puellae,
    in quo censendum nil nisi dantis amor,
munus eas gratum! te laete mente receptum
    protinus articulis induat illa suis;
tam bene convenias, quam mecum convenit illi,
    et digitum iusto commodus orbe teras.

[O ring, that are to circle the finger of my fair lady, in which naught is of value but the giver's love, may you go to her a welcome gift! May she receive thee with glad heart and straightway slip thee on her finger! May you fit her as well as she fits me, and press her finger with aptly-adjusted circle.][24]

In his exhaustive study of the Latin sexual vocabulary, J. N. Adams notes that the penis/finger analogy Ovid exploits here was practically idiomatic in classical verse (to take just one example among dozens, a speaker in Martial's *Epigrams* rebukes his male friend with the words, "Cestus often complains to me with tears in his eyes of being touched by your finger [*digito tuo*]").[25] In the next lines, just as the speaker imagines his own *digitus* encircled by the ring of his lady, he also envies the ring for its proximity to her body: "Happy ring, you will be touched by the hands of my lady-love; already, ah me, I envy my own gift" (Felix, a domina tractaberis, anule, nostra; invideo donis iam miser ipse meis) (7–8). Indeed, Ovid wishes that he himself might "suddenly become that gift," a metamorphosis that would grant him a privileged closeness to his lady's body: "Then would I wish you, my lady, both to touch your breasts, and lay your left hand within your tunic—I would slip from your finger, however tight and close; I would grow loose with wondrous art and fall into your bosom" (tunc ego te cupiam, domina, et tetigisse papillas,/et laevam tunicis inseruisse manum—/elabar digito quamvis angustus et haerens,/inque sinum mira laxus ab arte cadam) (11–14).

In the final lines of *Amores* 2.15, another popular Latin metaphor that underlies the work as a whole comes to the poetic surface. *Anulus*, "little ring," is of course the diminutive form of *anus*, a common metaphor in Latin poetry—and by far the most prevalent term in classical and medieval Latin medical writings—for the anus.[26] Ovid's introduction of his own desired role as *anulus* lends a rather more complicated tone to the poem's closing lines:

> me gere, cum calidis perfundes imbribus artus,
>> damnaque sub gemma perfer euntis aquae—
> sed, puto, te nuda mea membra libidine surgent,
>> et peragam partes anulus ille viri.
> Inrita quid voveo? parvum profiscere munus;
>> illa datam tecum sentiat esse fidem!

> [Wear me when you spray yourself with the warm rain of the bath, nor shrink at the harm from water seeping beneath the gem—But I believe my naked members would swell with lust for you, and, though a ring, I would play the part of the man. Why pray for what cannot be? Little gift, go on your way; let my lady feel that with you my true love comes!] (23–28)

In a double entendre in line 26, the speaker implies that if he were the ring, but also the little *anus*, he would nevertheless swell with desire to play the part of the man—in other words, transform himself from orificial receptor to phallic penetrator in the blink of an eye. Yet Ovid concludes with a sigh of resignation and futility: "Why pray for what cannot be?" the speaker asks, a question that acknowledges not only the impossibility of his becoming the ring himself, but also, perhaps, the limits of his founding metaphor.

It is this anal-erotic subtext of *Amores* 2.15 that Leoninus appropriates as the very theme of his "De anulo." Here Ovid's sexualized ode to the ring on his lady's finger becomes a subtle panegyric to the *anulus* on Leoninus's own *digitus*, a ring given to him as a sign of love by another man:

> Anule, qui sacri datus es michi pignus amoris,
> > qui modo paruus eras, amodo magnus eris
> Paruus es et magnus: nichil impedit hec simul esse
> > Hoc opifex, hoc te dat tuus esse dator.
> Quem manus artificis arctum contraxit in orbem
> > ampliat in toto nobilis orbe manus.
> Quod faber inuidit dator hoc indulsit et idem.
> > Laudibus innumeris laus tibi maior erit.[27]

> *[Ring, given to me as a relic of sacred love,*
> > *Though small just now, henceforth you'll turn out big,*
> *You're small and big at once—naught hinders this;*
> > *your maker and your giver make you so.*
> *What workman's hand drew into narrow circle,*
> > *a noble hand expands into a world.*
> *The giver has bestowed what smith begrudged—*
> > *unnumbered praises by your praise outstripped!]*

What is perhaps most striking about these opening lines, of course, is the *lack* of the explicit erotics found in the Ovid, which almost suggests an active suppression on Leoninus's part from the very first line. The ring is given as a sign of "*sacri* amoris," of *sacred* love, and there is no imagery here corresponding to Ovid's "naked members" swelling with lust or the ring popping off his lady's finger and exploring her body (though the term *pignus*, a common medieval word for relic, does augment the physicality of the image). While the *anulus* can be both "small and big" in lines two and three—a suggestively sexual image when applied to an orifice—Leoninus immediately seems to undermine this connotation with a rather banal analogy between the circle of the ring and the orb of the world.

Yet this artful dodging around Ovid's explicit eroticism may be just the point. Any Latin-educated medieval reader of Leoninus's poems (in other words, any medieval reader of Leoninus's poems) would have immediately recognized their Ovidian intertextuality. As Ralph Hexter has shown, the Christian moralizations of the *Metamorphoses*, long assumed to be indicative of the medieval attitude toward Ovid in general, were in fact far from the norm; the graphic erotic literalism of Ovid's amatory literature—in particular the *Ars amatoria, Amores*, and *Heroides*—was well understood and even appreciated in the medieval schoolroom.[28] In the twelfth century (the *aetas Ovidiana*, in Ludwig Traube's famous formulation), the language of Ovidian love inspired, among numerous other works, many of the obscene poems collected in the *Carmina Burana*; Guillaume de Blois's Latin drama of seduction, *Alda* (ca. 1175), and several similar works originating in the Loire valley; and even an *ars amatoria* containing graphic instructions in physical lovemaking.[29] It seems clear, moreover, that the Latin moralizations of Ovid actually represent a ubiquitous *anxiety* over the illicit erotics of their source texts.[30] (It is no wonder, then, that teachers of Latin were often enjoined to keep their young students from perusing works such as the *Ars* and the *Amores*.[31]) Leoninus's poems must be set within the sexual-poetic framework of this Ovidian revival of the late eleventh and twelfth centuries, a period during which Latinate erotic puns and graphic refashionings of Ovidian bodies were the rule rather than the exception.[32]

The *Amores* presents a particularly interesting case. The collection was known to many medieval readers as the "Book without a Title," a sobriquet explained by one reader as Ovid's own: "he feared those enemies who habitually criticized his writings lest, having read the title, they would denigrate the work. . . . For here too some of the subject-matter relates to love." The writer of this *accessus*, preserved in a late-twelfth-century manuscript contemporary with Leoninus's "De anule," describes the author's purpose in the *Amores* as a deliberately provocative one: "His intention is to give pleasure."[33] Given these kinds of expectations regarding the mode and purpose of Ovid's amatory writings—and especially in the case of *Amores* 2.15, one of the most sexually direct in the collection—there would have been no need for Leoninus to resort to the explicit erotic punning he found in his source. Instead, he makes an unmistakable reference to the *Amores* in his opening line and exploits its already palpable erotics with subtle allusions and turns of phrase that bring out all the more his own poem's specifically homoerotic resonances. Thus, unlike Ovid, who envies the ring itself (*invideo*), Leoninus writes, "The giver has bestowed what smith begrudged": Leonin's *digitus,* unlike Ovid's, already has its *anulus.* While the maker, the *faber*—perhaps the artisan, perhaps even God—begrudges Leoninus the ring, the giver, Henry, has already conceded his *anulus* to Leoninus for reasons and uses of his own.

A bit later Leoninus describes the *virga,* the "rod" that both encircles and beautifies his *digitus*:

> Virga teres modicum se circumflectit in orbem,
> Et sibi conexum lumina fallit opus
> Fallit opus uisum, nec se iunctura fatetur,
> et speciem nate res simulata gerit.
> Tu michi tam iusto digitum complecteris orbe
> natus in articulis ut uideare meis.

> *[A rounded rod into a circlet's bent;*
> *the work, with self conjoined, deceives the eye.*
> *The work beguiles the sight, denies the joint;*
> *the feigned thing bears the likeness of one born.*
> *You gird my finger with so nice a loop*
> *that it seems you were born upon my joints.]* (33–38)

Once again Leoninus's own caginess is practically thematic: The *virga* bent into an *anulus* "deceives the eye," while the *iunctura,* the very union between *anulus* and *digitum,* refuses to confess itself, to allow itself to be brought to light, known, and thus scrutinized. The insistent tension here between seeing and hiding, between secrecy and disclosure, produces a readerly desire to know the hidden substance of the "joint" even as the possibility of such certainty is taken away. Finally, while Ovid's *anulus* signifies his lady's absence and the ultimate sterility of the union he desires, Leoninus's *anulus* is reproductive and fruitful: it bears an almost human image (*speciem nate*) and feels tight enough to have been born within the joints of his fingers.

The poem then turns almost irresistibly to the body and person of the *dator* himself, the giver whose hand and voice promise greater gifts by far than the small ring embracing Leoninus's *digitus*:

> Te potuit meritum michi conciliare uel unum,
>   inseruit digito quem manus illa meo.
> Vox etiam sonuit, dono michi carior omni,
>   pectore uox umquam non abitura meo:
> "Hoc tibi ne pigeat paruum pro tempore munus,
>   set certum nostri pignus amoris habe.
> Nunc tibi parua damus set si modo uiuere detur,
>   ampla feres meritis munera digna tuis."
> Quid michi continget uerbis iocundius istis,
>   quid michi tam magno munere maius erit?
>
> (59–66)

> *[One merit only could have joined you to me—*
>   *you whom that hand implanted on my finger.*
> *A voice more loved than any gift resounded,*
>   *a voice that never will depart my breast:*
> *"Be not ashamed of this gift, small for now,*
>   *but take it as the sure pledge of our love.*
> *We give you small things now, but if life's granted,*
>   *you'll take the rich gifts worthy of your merits."*
> *What sweeter than these words could come to me?*
>   *What will be greater than so great a gift?]*

The grammar here is somewhat equivocal: Leoninus is no longer addressing solely the ring that was "implanted" on his finger, but also the man who was physically joined to him by the promise entailed in the "manual" exchange. Yet it is surely no accident that the poem at just this point interpolates the sweet voice of the beloved, the voice that "resounds" (*sonuit*) in a kind of quasi-nuptial music physically embedded in Leoninus's breast just as his finger is inserted into the ring. By the end of the passage above, this resonant *vox* and its loving words have displaced the *anulus* entirely: "I'd not compare such things [i.e., words] to gems or gold, nor aught rich India holds of greater beauty" (His ego nec gemmas ausim conferre nec aurum/ pulcrius aut si quid India diues habet) (67–68). The ultimate message of the poem is clear: the tight union of ring and finger is an ideal metaphor for the love of the two men; but it is only a metaphor, and despite its erotically "fitting" connotations, the gifts of love and physical presence far outweigh whatever fleeting pleasures are yielded by the *anulus.*

Leoninus's final verse-epistle, which immediately follows "De anulo" in Latin 14759 (fols. 150r–151v), extends the homoerotic implications of the earlier poem's dialectic of presence and absence. The poem is addressed to an unnamed *amicus* urging him to join Leoninus for the Feast of Fools in Paris, a festival notorious for the various reversals—political, ecclesiastical, and sexual—officially sanctioned but anxiously policed by the church. Here again Wright adduces an Ovidian source, this time the generic epistolary model of the *Heroides.* This appropriation alone should give us pause, for Leoninus is drawing here on some of the most uncomplicatedly heteroerotic classical love poetry—a series of impassioned letters between male and female lovers that served as a model for innumerable epistolary exchanges in medieval romance—as a model for his own epistle to another man.

Like "De anulo," this poem exploits the erotic imagery found in a specific Ovidian text: *Heroides* 19, Hero's moving plea to her already drowned lover Leander. Just as Ovid's Hero speaks of the physical and emotional effects of Leander's absence—"As the body, so is the soul of tender girls frail—delay but a little longer, and I shall die!" (ut corpus, teneris ita mens infirma puellis—/deficiam, parvi temporis adde moram!)—so Leoninus looks forward to reviving both body and mind (*corpore mente . . . utroque*) with his friend's visit, to stimulating his *caro languida* ("languid flesh") with his presence.[34] Despite the public joys characterizing the Feast of Fools, Leoninus hopes that at least a little bit of private time (*privatis tempora pauca*) will be granted to the two of them. Leoninus writes of his wish to be coupled forever by the neck with his *amicus,* for whom he bears a love that can only be approximated by the string of classical male intimates he invokes: "No less did Nisus clasp Euryalus, nor Theseus his Pirithous, no more Pylades his Orestes, than I you in my breast" (Non magis Eurialum Nisus, Phoceus Horestem,/non plus Pirithous Theseus ipse suum,/quam te complector ego pectore) (53–54). Indeed, Leoninus casts his addressee as *altera . . . mei pars,* "the other part of me," *et alter ego,* "and another I" (56).

While Hero is momentarily fearful that a *novus amor,* a "new love," will clasp Leander's neck in the circle of her arms (19.104), Leoninus is secure in the knowledge that no *novus amicus* will ruin their love, for "the one love doesn't fear the other's strength" (alterius uires non timet alter amor)

(75–76). Like the *iunctura* between the *anulus* and the *digitus* in the first poem, moreover, this is anything but an innocent spiritual union being described. Just as Hero daydreams of Leander throwing his "wet arms" (*bracchia umida*) around her neck when he emerges naked from the sea (60), Leoninus writes of a love that will prove unmistakably physical once his addressee arrives in Paris:

> Festa dies aliis baculus uenit et nouus annus.
> > Qua uenies ueniet hec michi festa dies.
> Tunc ego dilecte ceruici brachia nectam,
> > pectore tunc caro pectora cara premam.
> Seria tunc dulcesque iocos archanaque mentis
> > fas erit atque statum promere cuique suum.

> (101–6)

> *[The rod comes, and the new year—others revel;*
> > *my revels come that day when you arrive.*
> *Then, love, I'll twine my arms around your neck,*
> > *then shall I press dear breast against dear breast.*
> *Then sweet jests and the mind's more solemn secrets,*
> > *and each his state, we'll have leave to disclose.]*

The direct revision of Hero's fantasy of physical union is astonishing. While his tactic in the "De anule" was an anatomical suggestiveness through the erotic code of Ovidian euphemism, here Leoninus is plainspoken: there is little reason to doubt that these "solemn secrets" in his mind are inextricable from the intimate embrace described in his poem.

It would seem, then, that the most celebrated composer behind the earliest layer of Notre Dame polyphony also wrote erotic epistles to other men—and not simply erotic, but sexual and often anatomically precise in their inscriptions of sexual and bodily relations. Indeed, while some might be tempted to affiliate Leoninus's poems with that form of nonsexual "ennobling love" of which C. Stephen Jaeger has recently written, the epistles clearly resist such categorization; in the tradition that Jaeger claims to have recovered, "any love that incorporated and included sex was not ennobling," a characterization that would obscure the sexual sophistication, wit, and humor that Leoninus himself made an integral part of his neo-Ovidian writing.[35] Leoninus's letters were founded on the often explicit *hetero*erotic imagery he found in his classical sources, true, but they refashion this imagery into a carefully coded articulation of same-sex desire; the result is a frankly sexual poetics in which a tightly contracted *anulus* squeezes a *digitus* in an orb alternately small and large. Ralph Hexter has eloquently described the kind of erotic one-upmanship that characterizes numerous medieval appropriations and refashionings of Ovid: "It is through imitating and out-Oviding Ovid that high medieval poets, particularly but not exclusively in Latin, learn to write about the body in a certain way. . . . It is above all the name and spirit of Ovid, thanks to his own reputation for erotic license, that authorizes the admission of such ribaldry into medieval Latin texts."[36] In Leoninus's verse epistles, we are surely witnessing one of the most imaginative Ovidian authorizations of bodily writing.

Nor was Leoninus the only poet associated with the Notre Dame school whose desires seem to have taken a homoerotic turn. Scattered among the *Magnus liber* sources are a number of musical settings of works by the renowned satirist Walter of Chatillôn, whose Latin epic, the *Alexandreis*, became enormously popular by the turn of the century.[37] On the final folio of an early manuscript of the *Alexandreis* (Paris, BN Latin 8358) appears a brief poem attributed to Walter describing the nature of his relationship with his patron and the epic's dedicatee, Archbishop William of Rheims (William of the White Hands):

> Roma caput rerum,
> Que tanto turbine clerum
> Inuoluis, miserum
> Contemptorem mulierum
> Suscipe Galterum.
> Si fas est dicere verum,
> Sepe subegit erum
> Dum fleret adhuc ad Homerum,
> Nec tantum tenerum
> Sed quem iam barbara seuerum
> Reddidit et ueterum
> Perfectio longa dierum.[38]

[Rome, head of the world, you who envelop your clerks in such a storm, greet Walter, miserable despiser of women. If it be allowed that the truth be spoken, he often laid his master underneath—not only while still he wept at

Homer, nor only as a young lad, but as one whom the long and bearded
completion of aged days made severe.]

Like Leoninus's verse-epistles (though admittedly with less subtlety), Walter's "Roma caput rerum" fashions the reception of classical poetry as the
vehicle for an erotics between men in a gesture that David Townsend has
recently described as an effective " 'outing' [of] the archbishop (and himself) before the Pope."[39]

Fear and Loathing in the *Magnus liber organi*

In order to begin making some historical sense of these poems, we should
note first of all that they were produced in an urban setting in the twelfth
century, and thus at the height of what John Boswell called the "Triumph of
Ganymede," the flourishing of what he saw as a "gay literature" in twelfth-
century western Europe.[40] While few would dispute the claim that the
twelfth century saw an unprecedented literary efflorescence of erotic expression, Boswell has often been criticized for what many have taken to be his
essentialist assumptions about same-sex desire, his projection of modern
terms and categories for sexual identity onto the premodern past.[41] Influenced by the genealogical historicism of Michel Foucault, critics such as
Carolyn Dinshaw, David Halperin, Valerie Traub, and Jonathan Goldberg
have brought to light a vast array of homoerotic acts, pleasures, and desires
that do not seem to have been conditioned by discrete sexual identities and
cannot easily be assimilated to a sociocultural division between "homosexuality" and "heterosexuality" (both decidedly modern terms).[42] Leoninus's
poetic production, too, represents homoeroticism as a constellation of poetic tropes, bodily gestures, and barely disguised desires. At the same time,
though, Leoninus emerges powerfully in these works as a *subject* of desire—
whether as an "embodied erotic subject" of Ovidian writing or as a "homoerotic subject" produced within the fleeting moment of poetic creation.[43]

However we choose to conceive the relationship between Leoninus's
poems as desirous "acts" and Leoninus as subject of desire, these poems were
composed within a social environment in which the homoerotic praise of
an *anulus* could simultaneously be defended (and indeed probably was) as
an innocuous offer of thanks for a ruby ring; as Leoninus himself puts it in
the "De anule," "Nothing prevents you being both at once." Leoninus

resists modernity's "epistemology of the closet," in Sedgwick's influential term—the desire to determine "whether he was or he wasn't"—just as his poetry sought to escape the policing scrutiny of his own time.[44]

For Leoninus's caginess was not simply about erotic punning; it was also about survival. It is crucial to bear in mind that these poems were written near the *end* of the twelfth century, and thus during the decades initiating what Boswell characterized as the "rise of intolerance" toward same-sex desires and practices on the part of the Church.[45] By Wright's estimates, Leoninus's "De anule" and (most likely) "Amicum venturum" both date from before 1189, and thus less than a decade after the ecumenical Third Lateran Council (1179) had mandated that clerics found guilty of "incontinence against nature" be punished with the loss of ecclesiastical office or claustration.[46] As a master and musician in Paris during this period, Leoninus would have felt particularly vulnerable to antisodomitical vilification given that one of the figures standing at the center of the "formation of a persecuting society," as R. I. Moore has termed it, was Peter the Chanter, the cantor at the cathedral in the final decades of the twelfth century.[47] Indeed, the historian John Baldwin has recently described Peter's writings as central to "the revival of homophobia at the end of the twelfth century."[48]

Peter's vehement proclamations against sodomy in his *Verbum abbreviatum*—including a condemnation of sodomites as "men, spastic and feeble, who change themselves from males to females [by] abusing feminine coitus"—proved highly influential in twelfth-century ecclesiastical circles, and particularly in Paris.[49] Walter of Chatillôn himself complained that through their passive subjection to sodomy "men make women of themselves, and stallions become mares. . . . A new marriage god shamefully joins man to man, and women no longer get inside the door" (*se mares effeminant et equa fit equus . . . virum viro turpiter iungit novus hymen,/exagitata procul non intrat femina limen*).[50] In light of his enduring desire to "lay his master underneath," Walter's fiery condemnation may well represent a defense against the rising intolerance of same-sex desire, perhaps an anxious abnegation of the attested homoerotics of his own patronage relationship. Even Leoninus may have been influenced by Peter the Chanter's antisodomitical polemics: in a comment on humanity's loss of Edenic sexual innocence, the Chanter claims that copulation for Adam and Eve was a simple matter of "finger touch[ing] finger without lust" (*digitus digitum* tangit sine voluptate).[51] This is a moralizing deployment of the very Latin pun that Leoninus covertly exploits in his erotic verse epistles. Nor did Leoninus entirely elude Peter's antisodomitical phobia; a short but pointed passage in the "Historie sacre" (BN Lat. 14759, fol. 18v) is directed against the "gens sodomitica" (sodomitical race) in a sadly ironic internalization of homophobic sentiment.

Given the climate of intolerance at the turn of the century, it should come as no surprise that a measure of anxiety over same-sex desire found its way into the later layers of the *Magnus liber organi,* at least as Anonymous IV described it. Several conductus texts in particular represent the financial corruption of the curia in Rome as an erotic affront to Ecclesia, usually by casting the alternately wide open or tightly sealed pockets and purses of clerics and curial officials as constipated anuses in need of plugging or purging. As Lester Little points out, this was a common theme in Latin venality satire of the twelfth and thirteenth centuries directed against both the practices of simony and usury among the clergy in general and the financial corruption of the curia in particular.[52]

Easily the most vivid example of this brand of satire in the pages of the *Magnus liber* (which, following Edward Roesner, I am here defining broadly to include the monophonic repertory[53]) is the conductus "Qui seminant in loculis." Bound along with numerous other monophonic conductus in the tenth fascicle of the famous Florence manuscript (Biblioteca Laurenziana, MS Pluteus 29.1, hereafter F), the poem opens by condemning those "who sow seeds in purses through frequent giving of loans" (Qui seminant in loculis/Per dandi frequens mutuum), lines that construct usury as akin to the "insemination" of infertile *loculi* through a rather unsubtle pun on *culus,* or anus.[54] Casting the *loculi* as particularly susceptible to prostitution, the author suggests that "money opens and closes" (Nummus claudit et aperit) as it "serves men" (servit . . . homini) in their curial negotiations (7–9). That this two-strophe conductus was read in the thirteenth century as a satirical attack on sodomy is suggested by a classicizing literary allusion contained in a third strophe appended to "Qui seminant" in a related manuscript source:

O nummi privilegium!
Vix invocatur alius
Propitius

Deus in adiutorium.
O nummo tributoriam
Ecclesiam.
Non hec in nostra curia
Contagia:
Nam confidenter ambulant,
Qui Curios non simulant
Nec vivunt Bachanalia.

[O the privilege of money! Scarcely more propitious is the cry, "Make haste, O God, to deliver me!" O to money we assign a tribute Church! In our curia these are not contagions: For they walk confidently who do not ape the Curii, nor live like Bacchanals.][55] (23–33)

In railing against hypocrisy, the text holds up those "who do not pretend to be a Curius" as virtuous counterexamples in the midst of widespread corruption. Crucially, these lines are lifted directly from Juvenal's second *Satire*, the most extended attack on male-male sexual relations in classical Latin verse. For Juvenal's speaker, the public spectacle of prostitution and effeminacy among Roman men and boys—and in particular the hypocritical claims they make to be virtuous like the noble "Curius" family—provokes a desire to leave his native city behind: "I would fain flee to Sarmatia and the frozen Sea when people who ape the Curii and live like Bacchanals dare talk about morals" (Ultra Sauromatas fugere hinc libet et glacialem/Oceanum, quotiens aliquid de moribus audent/qui Curios simulant et Bacchanalia vivunt). Juvenal's lengthy attack on "effeminates" (molles) also rails against "would-be [male] brides" (ingens nubentibus) who "can bear no children wherewith to keep the affection of their husbands" (nequeant parere et partu retinere maritos) (137–38). Moreover, his description in the same *Satire* of hardened country boys "throw[ing] away their trousers and their knives, their bridles and their whips, and thus carry[ing] back to Artaxata the manners of our Roman youth" (mittentur bracae cultelli frena flagellum/sic praetextatos referunt Artaxata mores) (169–70) is the same polemic that inspired Walter of Chatillôn to bemoan the fate of the many "sons of the nobility . . . sent to France to become scholars" who, through "coaxing or cash," instead "bring obscene habits back to Artaxata."[56]

In much the same spirit, a polyphonic conductus in the seventh fascicle of F, "Non habes auditum," sarcastically advises its listeners to be prepared to pay handily for favors in Rome. Describing the greed of curial officials with clear sexual overtones, the poem exploits the same *loculus/culus* pun found in "Qui seminant":

> Ad loculos oculos dirigunt
> Et manus porrigunt
> Manipulos parvulos negligunt
> Qui gestant anulos.
>
> [To pockets they direct their eyes, and as they stretch forth their hands, they neglect the little bundles, they who wear rings.][57]

Qui gestant anulos: in condemning the curial officials who "wear rings," this satirical conductus text deploys the very anus/*anulus* wordplay that inspires Leoninus's homoerotic appropriation of Ovid. The pun on "*manipulos*," "little bundles" or, by the text's logic, testicles, suggests that the *anulus*-bearing officials who turn their attention to "pockets" neglect the protruding organs of their prospective clients.

The subtle but pronounced (and sometimes playful) presence of anti-sodomitical sentiment in the *Magnus liber organi* thus confronts us with something of a paradox. While Leoninus's poetic epistles (several of them written to Popes and other curial officials) are brimming with homoeroticism, his venerated polyphonic compositions are included in the very manuscript of the *Magnus liber* containing poetic attacks on the sodomitical corruption of the Curia and the church at large. On the one hand, of course, this simply tells us that there was no monolithic attitude toward same-sex desire during this period, which comes as no surprise. But it also suggests that we have in late-twelfth-century Paris, side by side, a vibrant poetics of homoeroticism and a musical culture of polyphony, discourses that demonstrably had both participants and opponents in common.

Consider the example of Robert of Courson, a master in Paris around 1200 and a member of what Baldwin has identified as Peter the Chanter's inner circle.[58] Robert's *Summa* contains a heated polemic against the economic corruption and increasing secularization of liturgical polyphony, directed in particular at the unruly behavior of what Christopher Page calls the "shifting body of polyphonic talent" in turn-of-the-century Paris.[59] As Robert makes clear, one of the most disturbing aspects of this abuse of the liturgy lies in its potential to invert gender and "feminize" both performer and listener: "the services of Masters of organum who set minstrelish and effeminate things before young and ignorant men in order to feminize their minds are illicit" (dicimus quod illicite sunt opere magistrorum organicorum qui scurrilia et effeminata proponunt iuvenibus et rudibus ad effeminandos animos ipsorum).[60] Robert vilifies the organum of the *Magnus liber* in the same terms upon which Peter the Chanter, Juvenal, and Walter found their polemics against sodomy: as a spectacle of effeminacy and sexual inversion. Like the venality satire in the *Magnus liber*, moreover, Robert's polemic implicitly equates simony with male prostitution, casting the "minstrelish" strains of polyphony as a site of diseased lasciviousness that corrupts even the nonmusical ecclesiastical officials who arrange and pay for its performance: "If a wanton prelate gives benefices to such wanton singers in order that this kind of minstrelish and wanton music may be heard in his church, I believe that he becomes contaminated with the disease of simony" (Si prelatus lascivus lasciviis talibus cantatoribus det beneficia ut huiusmodi scurrilia et lascivia audiat in ecclesia sua, credo quod lepram symonie incurrit).[61]

If Robert's sentiments can be taken as characteristic of a more general hostility toward the dissident erotics of polyphony, then the antisodomitical sentiments inscribed on the pages of the *Magnus liber organi* may well reflect an abiding anxiety over the perceived homoerotics of the music itself, the radical proximity between sodomy and polyphony, between the feminizing sexual acts performed by sodomites and the emasculating vocal displays performed by *organistae*. In the virtuosic melismas and fleeting unisons of Notre Dame organum, we may indeed be hearing the luxurious intertwining of male bodies that so horrified the antisodomitical polemicists. Alan of Lille's bizarre analogy begins to make sense.

From Polemic to Performance: The Sodomitical Logic of Polyphony

Although Robert of Courson's comments represent an attack on specifically Parisian musical practices, they recall two slightly earlier polemics against musical excess in the liturgy penned by the Anglo-Latin writers John of Salisbury and Aelred of Rievaulx. These well-known passages have been associated with one another since they were excerpted side-by-side in William Prynne's lengthy *Histrio-Mastix*, a Renaissance antitheatrical tract published in London in 1633.[62] In book 1 of the *Policraticus*, an eclectic and influential mix of political philosophy and social commentary, John inveighs against the potential erotic charge of liturgical performance in terms that anticipate both Robert's worries over the emasculating effects of organum and Arnulf's delight in the Siren-like voices of talented women:

> ante conspectum Domini in ipsis penetralibus sanctuarii lasciuientis uocis luxu, quadam ostentatione sui, muliebribus modis notularum articulorumque caesuris, stupentes animulas emollire nituntur. Cum praecinentium et succinentium, concinentium et decinentium, intercinentium et occinentium praemolles modulationes audieris, Sirenarum concentus credas esse non hominum . . . sic acuta uel acutissima grauibus et subgrauibus temperantur ut auribus sui iudicii fere subtrahatur auctoritas. . . . Cum haec quidem modum excesserint, lumborum pruriginem quam deuotionem mentis poterunt citius excitare.

> [in the very sight of God, in the sacred recesses of the sanctuary itself, the singers attempt, with the lewdness of a lascivious singing voice and a singularly foppish manner, to feminize all their spellbound little followers with the girlish way they render the notes and end the phrases. Could you but hear the effete emotings of their before-singing and their after-singing, their singing and their counter-singing, their in-between singing and their ill-advised singing, you would think it an ensemble of Sirens, not of men. . . . The high or even the highest notes are mixed together with the low or lowest ones to such an extent that the ears are almost completely divested of their critical power. . . . Indeed, when such practices go too far, they can more easily occasion an itching of the loins than a sense of devotion in the mind.][63]

A good deal of ink has been spilled debating whether or not John is describing polyphony here; Janet Knapp, in her authoritative *New Oxford History of Music* article on the Notre Dame school, argues that there is "little doubt" that John's polemic is directed specifically at Parisian polyphony, which he would have heard during his stay in Paris before completing the *Policraticus* in the late 1140s.[64] Whether directed against polyphony or not, the passage suggests that twelfth-century musical practices were deeply fraught with sexual anxiety years before Leoninus began writing his poetry. John's graphically sexual language—his horror at the "itching of the loins" (lumborum pruriginem) to which such musical excesses can lead—envisions the spectacle of men singing before, after, against, and in-between one another as a performance of sexual inversion, an erotic (mis)use of the male body directly analogous to the sexual performances that inspired twelfth- and thirteenth-century polemics against sodomy.

For even within this brief chapter of the *Policraticus* there is indisputable evidence that John conceives of the *singing* practices he condemns as musical inducements to *sodomitical* practices. Just after concluding the famous polemic above, he begins another rant against the same musical deviants he has already vilified. Although this passage will be less familiar to musicologists who have concentrated on the earlier (and much anthologized) one, it leaves little doubt that John envisions musical dissidence in the church as a clear threat to the heterosexual imperatives of *Natura*:

> An non recolis Ciconum matres et nurus indignationem suam totam in Orpheum, qui mares modis suis effeminauerat . . . ? Exinde huiusmodi hominum quaestus plerumque felicem exitum non expectat et forte quia *non habet euentus sordida praeda bonos*. Quae uero mentes emolliunt moresque subuertunt, a nostra aetate undique asciscuntur, licet ipsa ultra quam satis est uitiis suis abundet.

> [Do you not recall that the mothers and wives of the Thracians poured out upon Orpheus all their indignation, even to the degree of arousing the ill will of the fates, because he had by his melodies rendered their males effeminate? . . . Therefore plaints of men of his type can expect for the most part no happy outcome. Possibly the reason is that *Base gain can have no happy end* (Ovid, *Amores* 1.10.48). However, influences that weaken the character and subvert morals are everywhere borrowed from our own age, for we concede that it is superabundantly supplied with vices of its own.][65]

This densely allusive passage opens with an angry reference to the legend of Orpheus—not the Orpheus happily married to Eurydice, nor the Orpheus seeking to recover his dead wife from Hell, but rather the Orpheus who returned unsuccessfully from the underworld and, as Ovid puts it in the *Metamorphoses*, "set the example for the people of Thrace of giving his love to tender boys, and enjoying the springtime and first flower of their youth" (ille etiam Thracum populis fuit auctor amorem in teneros transferre mares citraque iuventam aetatis breve ver et primos carpere flores) (*Met* 10.83-85). As we shall see in Chapter 7, this homoerotic, post-Eurydice Orpheus represented for numerous medieval poets and commentators an inspiring source of rhetorical and mythographical invention.

For John of Salisbury, however, the homoerotic Orpheus constitutes a profound sexual threat to males by musically rendering them "effeminates." Alan of Lille makes the same point in the *Complaint of Nature*: "Man alone turns with scorn from the modulated strains of my *cithara* and runs deranged to the notes of mad Orpheus's lyre [*lira*]. For the human race, fallen from its high estate, adopts a highly irregular *metaplasmus* when it inverts the rules of Venus by introducing barbarisms in its arrangement of genders. Thus man, his sex changed [*tiresiatus*] by a ruleless Venus, in defiance of due order, by his arrangement changes what is a straightforward attribute of his."[66] Here again are Arnulf's musical "barbarisms," in this case exemplified by Orpheus's own musical perversion. Finally, with his allusion to the *Amores*, John draws on the same Ovidian poetic that Leoninus refashioned in his verse epistles. While for Leoninus Ovidian lovers and friends, whether male or female, provide poetic models for articulating his own desires for another man, John of Salisbury interpolates an *Amores* passage as a moralizing warning against same-sex musical practices.

In much the same spirit but in this case almost certainly referring to polyphony, the Cistercian writer Aelred of Rievaulx casts the perverse intermingling of male voices among contemporary *scholastici*—"This one sings below, this one sings against him, another sings over them both" (Hic succinit, ille discinit, alter supercinit)—as an emasculating, even animalizing musical metamorphosis: "Sometimes—it is shameful to say—[the voice] is expelled like the neighing of horses, sometimes, manly strength set aside, it is constricted into the shrillness of a woman's voice" (Aliquando, quod pudet dicere, in equinos hinnitus cogitur, aliquando uirili uigore deposito in femineae uocis). Like Robert, Aelred casts the "lascivious gestures of the singers" (lasciuas cantantium gesticulationes) as a fleshly transgression practically akin to the peddling of sex as he excoriates "the whorish variation and dropping of the voices" (meretricias uocum alternationes et infractiones).[67]

Such polemics have often been dismissed as quaintly conservative bits of trivia that reveal nothing of value to musicologists; Sarah Fuller has called them "diatribes against presumptuous vocal display, not descriptions of music" (leaving one to wonder just what a description of music would have to look like to be considered a "description of music").[68] There are admittedly any number of problems with relying on passages such as these for purely technical musical data; in her recent study of thirteenth-century English polyphony, Nicky Loseff, following Fuller and others, has sensibly cautioned us against using them as bases for clarifying problems of dating and geography.[69]

Nevertheless, I would suggest that the histrionic rhetoric of Robert of Courson, Aelred of Rievaulx, and John of Salisbury reveals certain prevalent assumptions about the erotic implications of twelfth- and early-thirteenth-century polyphony, assumptions that were by no means limited to its detractors. Indeed, several of the most influential treatises on polyphonic voice-relations written prior to the emergence of the Notre Dame school imagine polyphony in no uncertain terms as a musical simulacrum of intimate relations between men. Here I refer not simply to the general use of substantives (e.g., *cantor* and *organizator*) to denote part-singers, but more importantly to the specific ways in which both intervallic tensions and unisons between musical lines themselves come to represent male-male desire. Throughout the interrelated group of twelfth-century treatises known as *Ad organum faciendum*, to take the most important example, the cantus and organum lines are repeatedly personified as male companions:

> Cum autem diapente et diatessaron organizamus.
> Succinte et egregie curramus.
> Donec cum dulcedine ad copulam perueniamus.
> Et eorum diligentiam confestim uideamus.
> Prestolatim colloquendo amicas duas iungamus.
> Nam tantae affinitatis sunt tantaeque amicitiae.
> Prima conducit alteram causa beniuolentiae.
> Dat ei diatessaron. et uicissim diapente.
> Vnaque in diapason uel eadem sunt repente.
>
> [When we harmonize at the fifth and fourth, let us move precisely and to good effect, till, sweetly, we reach a *copula* and see at once the service of these intervals. Let us unite two friends conversing leisurely, for so great is their bond, so great their affection, that one conducts the other out of kindness, giving it the fourth and fifth in turn; and suddenly they are together at the octave or the unison.][70]

Here the relationship between the lines is one of affection, kindness, and mutuality, as in this more intimate description of the two lines reaching a unison: "The *cantus* straightway rising, let a *copula* be made on D. C and E will prepare it like a dulcet flute. Then let the organum double the sound at D, in sweet amity, for they should be close who trade kisses" (Cantus confestim ascendens in .D. fiat copula./C. et .E. erunt spectantes quasi dulcis fistula./Et D. quarta reddat sonum dulci amicitia./Quia prope debent esse illa que dant oscula).[71] A bit later, we read of another kiss that leads to a *copula*: "The organum, sounding D, returns the kiss at F. The cantus sounds E, F, and D, to end. Hence the organum responds with a and c. They are back in *copula* with d, the eleventh note" (Organum sonando .D. ad .F. reddit osculum./Cantus sonans quintum. sextum. quartumque per ultimum./Unde sonat octaua. decima per organum. Rursum in .d. copulantur quia est undecimum).[72]

Yet equality and mutuality are not the only attributes of this personified musical dynamic. As the Milan redaction of the treatise concludes, it becomes clear that organum can capture even violent relationships in sound:

> Organum adquirit totum sursum et inferius.
> Currit ualde delectando ut miles fortissimus.
> Frangit uoces uelut princeps senior et dominus.
> Qua de cause applicando sonat multum dulcius.
> Cantus manet ut subiectus precedenti gratia.
> Quia quod praecedit tantum minus quam sequentia.
>
> [The organum takes everything above and below. Wildly exulting, it moves like a valiant warrior. It dominates the pitches as a senior prince and lord. Therefore, with its addition, the sound is much more sweet. The cantus remains in thrall by reason of its precedence, for that which goes before is so much less than that which follows.][73]

Already in early-twelfth-century descriptions of polyphony, then, polyphonic counterpoint is conceived of as dear friends who alternately kiss, embrace, dominate, and adulate one another—friends who ultimately arrive together at the *copula*.[74] The *Ad organum faciendum* treatises seem motivated in part by a desire to anthropomorphize polyphonic harmonies, whether as kissing friends or corpses.[75]

The much-debated term *copula* would eventually be absorbed into theoretical writings on polyphony as a technical term with a number of obscure and often contradictory meanings. The many studies of the thirteenth-century resonances of the term by scholars such as Fritz Reckow, Jeremy Yudkin, and, most recently, Nancy van Deusen in her study of Anonymous IV and Robert Grosseteste, demonstrate that any generalizations about the *copula* as a technical musical term are doomed to failure.[76] Yet at the particular moment at which the *Magnus liber organi* was first compiled, *copula* had a particular resonance that has gone unremarked in the secondary literature. In fact, as far as I can determine, all of the scholarship on the *copula* (even Reckow's foundational 1972 study) has overlooked the one actual appearance of the term within the *Magnus liber* sources themselves.

Included in the tenth fascicle of F is a monophonic conductus entitled "Exceptivam actionem," based on a stanzaic poem by Alan of Lille (see Figure 8). The "Rhythmus de incarnatione Christi," or "Rhythm on the Incarnation of Christ," describes the wondrous inversions of nature created by the Incarnation through technical language drawn from the seven Liberal Arts. While only a single strophe is included in F, the poem survives as a seven-strophe work in a number of related sources of Notre Dame conductus. Alan begins with Grammar, the *Verbum Patris* that caused the overturning of the natural order when God became Man:

> Exceptivam actionem
> Verbum Patris excipit,
> Dum naturam decipit,
> Causualem dictionem
> Substantivum recipit,
> Actioque passionem
> In hoc verbo concipit.
> *Ref*: In hac Verbi copula
>   Stupet omnis regula
>
> [The Word of the Father issued an extraordinary action when it deluded
> logic, when it deceived Nature; it made a fortuitous word substantive, and
> 'active' bore 'passive' in this word. (*Refrain*:) In this coupling of the Word all
> order is astounded.][77]

In these densely figurative lines, Alan implies that God subverts or overrides the internal logic of Grammar—both as a Liberal Art and as a set of linguistic conventions—by bringing his Son to life in human flesh and thus making "active" what should, according to the dictates of *Natura*, be "passive." The same theological principle inspires the Rhetoric stanza, which draws on an array of rhetorical terminology to discuss "deviat[ions] from Nature" that occur "in God's law" when "the nature of man changes its rule" (in Dei transit iura/Hominis conditio): "A new trope appears in the figure, its whole construction is new; a new shade of meaning is in the joining"

FIGURE 8   Monophonic conductus "Exceptivam actionem," from *Magnus liber organi* setting Alan of Lille, "Rhythmus de incarnatione Christi" (Florence, Biblioteca-Mediceo-Laurenziana, MS Pluteo 29.1, fol. 444 ʳ)

(Novus tropus in figura,/Nova fit constructio,/Novus color in iunctura) (21–28). The poem is a fascinating demonstration of the categorical malleability of *Natura* in the twelfth century; language takes on an "unnatural" propensity to invert itself when God takes on human flesh, and the result is an entirely new arrangement of active and passive as well as an array of unprecedented "tropes," "joinings," and rule-changes introduced into the pedagogical discourses of Man.

While Alan's poem is set monophonically in F, the stanza concerning music contains a number of logical and grammatical terms borrowed by theoretical texts to describe polyphonic voice-relations:

> Dum factoris et facture
> Mira fit coniunctio,
> Quis sit modus ligature,
> Quis ordo, que ratio,
> Que sint vincla, que iuncture,
> Qui gumphi, que unio?
> Stupet sui fracto iure
> Musica proportio.
> *Ref*: In hac Verbi copula
>   Stupet omnis regula

> [When of the maker and the made a marvellous conjunction is made, what is the mode of ligature? What the order, what the reason, what are the bonds, what the joining, what the adhesive, what the unity? Musical proportion is stupefied at the breaking of its own law. (*Refrain:*) In this *copula* of the Word all order is astounded.] (51–60)

The stanza draws a primal analogy between the Incarnation and Music itself that is brilliantly appropriate for the *Magnus liber* repertory: Jesus Christ constitutes a "marvellous conjunction" between the Maker (God) and the Made (Man) that bears an uncanny similarity to musical performance, in which the Maker—the singer—exists in a "marvellous conjunction" with that which is made—the song that emerges *ex corpore*, as Augustine had put it, and remains somehow rooted in the singing body for the always fleeting duration of performance. The technical language here is recognizable to anyone familiar with medieval musical theory: *coniunctio, modus, ligature, iuncture* (the same term, incidentally, that Leonin uses for the hidden joining of the *anulus* with the *digitum*); most important, again in the refrain, Alan refers to the *copula*, which, after this string of musical terms, clearly implies the coupling of voices in polyphony.[78] The *copulae* repeatedly mentioned in the refrain, the couplings that "astound" the natural "order" of the material world, embody what Alan sees as a fundamental homology between the Liberal Arts, one in which music is susceptible to the same deviations from Nature that invert the disciplinary precepts of Grammar and Rhetoric.

If the "Rhythmus de incarnatione Christi" scrutinizes the marvelous *coniunctiones* between the human and the divine, Alan devotes his much more famous *Complaint of Nature* in large part to condemning unnatural *copulae* in grammatical, rhetorical, and sexual relations—especially those that occur in sodomy. As he writes near the beginning of the *Complaint* in the passage discussed above, in sodomitical *copulae*

> Actiui generis sexus se turpiter horret
> Sic in passiuum degenerare genus.
> Femina uir factus sexus denigrat honorem,
> Ars magice Veneris hermafroditat eum.
> Predicat et subicit, fit duplex terminus idem.
> Gramatice leges ampliat ille nimis.
> Se negat esse uirum Nature, factus in arte
> Barbarus. Ars illi non placet, immo tropus.[79]

> [The active sex shudders in disgrace as it sees itself degenerate into the passive sex. A man turned woman blackens the fair name of his sex. The witchcraft of Venus turns him into a hermaphrodite. He is subject and predicate: one and the same term is given a double application. Man here extends too far the laws of grammar. Becoming a barbarian in grammar, he disclaims the manhood given him by nature. Grammar does not find favor with him but rather a trope.]

Just as the inverted Grammar of the Incarnation in the conductus text makes the "active" "passive," perverted grammar in the *Complaint* forces the "active sex" to "degenerate into the passive sex." According to Alan's neoplatonic logic, the "novus tropus" created in the discipline of Rhetoric by Christ's becoming Man has its ostensibly sinful counterpart in the "tropus" of "disclaim[ed] manhood" implied by sodomitical relations between men.

Perhaps this creative analogy between incarnational and sodomitical couplings should not surprise us. R. W. Southern once remarked that the "greatest triumph of medieval humanism was to make God seem human."[80] And as Mark Jordan has shown, Alan's own theology of sodomy in general is marvelously inconsistent; nowhere in the *Complaint* or, for that matter, in any of Alan's other moral or ethical writings, can we find a clear and unambiguous condemnation of same-sex copulation. "Nature herself seems to have put a capacity for metamorphosis or transmutation into things," Jordan points out, and men by nature can "change their 'offices' in copulation. The possibility for sportive copulations inheres in bodies."[81]

Nor was Alan alone in searching for such "sportive copulations" throughout the many domains of human knowledge and practice. In the anonymous but enormously popular debate poems between Ganymede and Helen dating from around 1200, the *copula* as represented in works such as the *Complaint* was simultaneously appropriated and condemned as a prescriptive affirmation of male homoeroticism. In the following exchange between Jove's rival lovers, Ganymede responds to Helen's antisodomitical diatribe with a measured defense of homosexual practice:

[Helen:]
"Nullus amor pueri tangit unquam pectus,
sed cum marem femine iungit idem lectus,
hic est nexus competens, hic est ordo rectus,
nam in sexu dispari compar est affectus."

[Ganymede:]
"Impar omne dissidet, recte par cum pari,
eleganti copula mas aptatur mari.
Si nescis: articulos decet observari,
hic et hic gramatice debent copulari."

["No love of a boy ever touches the heart, but when one bed joins man to woman, this is a bond that is productive, this is right order, for between opposite sexes there can be equal affection."

"Disparity divides things: like things are rightly joined together; for a man to be linked to a man is a more elegant coupling. In case you had not noticed, there are certain rules of grammar by which articles of the same gender must be coupled together."][82]

In an early-thirteenth-century vernacular response to Ganymede's claims, Gautier de Coincy contends that "Grammar couples *hic* and *hic*, but Nature curses this coupling" (La grammaire hic à hic acouple,/Mais nature maldit la couple).[83] And given its grammatical similarity to several of the strophes of "Exceptivam actionem," the following Golliardic parody of Alexander of Villedieu's *Doctrinale* may also have been intended as an explicitly eroticizing response to Alan of Lille's theological construction of the Incarnation's *copulae*:

> Jam tempus est cognoscere
> quid feminini generis
> composita figura;
> quid sit casus inflectere
> cum famulabus Veneris;
> quid copula, coniunctio;
> quid signat interiectio,
> dum miscet cruri crura.[84]

[Now it is time to know what the well-wrought figure of the feminine gender is: what it is to inflect case-endings with the maids of Venus; what a *copula*, a *coniunctio*, and an interjection signify, while a person mingles thigh with thigh.]

In light of the personified *copulae* between the cantus and the organum in the *Ad organum faciendum* treatises, in which the author imagines polyphonic counterpoint as a dynamic between men, the sodomitical couplings vilified but flaunted in such metapoetical works as the debate poems and the parody of the *Doctrinale* were practically begging for a musical application. I believe this series of terminological confluences finally explains the logic behind Alan's musical analogy in the *Complaint of Nature* with which this chapter began. Just as the sodomite, "Becoming a barbarian in grammar, disclaims the manhood given him by nature" (Se negat esse virum Naturae factus in arte/Barbarus), so the "singer of organum"—*organizans*, a participle of *organizare*, the verb used throughout twelfth-century theoretical writings on polyphony—"introduce[s] barbarisms into music." The sensual musical kisses and violent musical dynamics described in *Ad organum faciendum* have reached a scandalously "barbarous" but inevitably homoerotic culmination.

Coupled Voices

Even leaving aside the poetry of Leoninus, the sheer number of Latin writings that speak to the homoerotics of musical performance and reception in the second half of the twelfth century alone is, by any measure, staggering. From the vilification of same-sex singing in church as an Orphic seduction of "effeminates" to the personification of polyphonic counterpoint as intimate male friends "copulating" in music, from figurative analogies between *organistae* and sodomites to Juvenalian satires on usury set to music in the *Magnus liber*, the musical culture of northern France and Norman England during these decades was enchanted by the spectacle of same-sex polyphonic performance, and perhaps especially by the performing bodies of *organistae* at Notre Dame and other institutions that received, altered, and performed its musical legacy. These materials together constitute rich testimony to the horizon of expectation that greeted the increasing emergence of liturgical polyphony in the twelfth century, and thus they inevitably raise questions about the sensual erotics of the music. What was it about the new polyphony that provoked such extraordinary musical fantasies and raised such deep-seated musico-sexual anxieties? Are these writings merely ephemera, external to the "real meaning" of this music, and thus to the writing of its history? Or might they speak to the inherent eroticism of vocal polyphony?

Hard questions. But I would propose that the works of Alan of Lille, Robert of Courson, Aelred of Rievaulx, Walter of Chatillôn, and the other writers considered above are just as central to the social meanings of twelfth-century polyphony as are those of Anonymous IV, Johannes de Garlandia, and the other thirteenth- and fourteenth-century theorists who sought to interpret its rhythms and codify its technicalities decades after the fact. Edward Roesner, who has written one of the most learned studies of the performance practice of Notre Dame polyphony, comments thus on the problems of reconstructing the original contexts for its performance:

> Although my method of juxtaposing information drawn from sources of differing backgrounds may seem dangerously eclectic, . . . I feel that this approach is justified owing to the relative paucity of information, the consistency of most of it, and its general character which reveals little evi-

dence of local or personal performances. Even Jerome's *flores* and Anonymous IV's irregular patterns are not so much fixed *agréments* or stylized formulas as hints of the kinds of things a performer might do with this music.[85]

Such juxtapositions and dangerous eclecticism are indispensable for anyone seeking to account for the historicity of this music, whether in the service of contemporary editing and performance or for the purpose of writing anti-homophobic accounts of its historical milieu. In fact, though clearly intended as a simple description of this repertory's various genres, Roesner's own account of the general musical contours of the various polyphonic genres sounds highly suggestive after a reading of the diverse sources discussed above. *Organum purum* is defined as "sections of two-voice organum in which the duplum voice moves in long, florid melismas over sustained notes in the tenor"; in discant sections, "both duplum and tenor move rhythmically"; in discant, *organum triplum*, and *organum quadruplum*, "the necessity for co-ordination between the moving parts restrains both the rhythmic freedom of the duplum and, as a consequence, the vagueness of its notation."[86] These phrases could be applied as easily to bodies as to voices: one body/voice moves in "long, florid" gestures "over" another; two "move rhythmically" together; discant requires "co-ordination" between "moving parts," yet "restrains" the "freedom" of both even as they move as one. We do not anachronistically sexualize these metaphors if we insist on reading them as musical descriptions of same-sex desire. For Robert of Courson, Alan of Lille, and others, the polyphonic musical interrelations that we take for granted were dazzlingly new. If they themselves took the new polyphony as a homoerotic musical spectacle, sonorous performances that brought together male bodies and commingled them perversely within the time and space of the liturgy, who are we to question them?

Nor did the homoerotics of this repertory reside in sonority alone. In an intriguing discussion of mnemotechnics and Notre Dame polyphony, Anna Maria Busse Berger, pointing to the very late date of all of the surviving primary and theoretical sources transmitting the repertory, has suggested that its memorization and performance were both primarily oral in character.[87] Extending Craig Wright's suggestion that liturgical polyphony may have been "performed without the assistance of written notation"[88] at Notre Dame, Berger draws upon recent scholarship on oral-formulaic poetry and medieval memory systems to argue that, during the first decades of polyphonic composition in Paris, this music was "transmitted orally and sung from memory."[89] The modal systems described by thirteenth-century theorists, for example, bear striking resemblances to mnemotechnical systems devised by numerous medieval writers on the memory. Central to the later spread of this repertory to other musical centers in England and France was the *coexistence* of oral and written transmission of polyphony. Writing down the music was not solely a preservational task, Berger suggests, but also a mnemonic practice in its own right, by which performers "might have used the written page to help their memory":

> The written page might have triggered the memory of the melodic and rhythmic outline of the piece, a piece which the performers already knew. The written page would just function as a mnemonic aid for recalling both the general outline and details. In this case it is not necessarily relevant whether the performers imagined the written page or actually saw it. If they had memorized the piece once with the help of the written page, they would always use it as a mnemonic device when singing by heart. In fact, the original notation brings out the modal patterns and the division into *ordines* in a much more convincing way than modern notation.[90]

In other words, the physical appearance of the polyphonic page itself may have been instrumental in the memorization and reperformance of Notre Dame polyphony during its transmission from Paris to other cities and institutions.

The manuscripts that transmitted the polyphonic repertory of Notre Dame beginning in the middle decades of the thirteenth century also represent a visual and visionary survival of the desires of those men who originally performed it. As I argue in Chapter 5, the interplay of visuality and musicality was integral to the religious practices of certain thirteenth-century holy women, devotional writers, and visionaries, involving intensive meditation upon and physical identifications with the materiality of the book. As Mary Carruthers demonstrates, moreover, medieval mnemotechnics regularly relied upon lurid, erotic, even violent imagery as an aid to the stimulation of the memory.[91] That the notation of polyphony could inspire such erotic visualization is made clear in a revealing observation made by Elias Salomonis in his *Scientia artis musicae*. Written in Rome in

1274 but by a French writer, the treatise at one point comes around to the sensual misuses of books of organum by contemporary singers. I quote the passage in full for its remarkable portrait of musical, visual, and sexual pleasures converging in polyphonic performance:

> Et etiam vix dignantur aliquotiens pedem suum facere de cantu plano, anticipando, festinando, retardando, & male copulando punctos, ex quibus effectus scientiae organizandi completur: quia fortassis vident punctos taliter paratos. Hoc autem factum est ad decorem & honestatem positionis punctorum, & notae libri, non ad cantandum, ut videntur. Hoc sciant pro certo, non quaerentes, quae nostra sunt quae vident, nec Dei, nec debitum artis musicae, quia illam ignorant; sed speculando dicentes in aere miau minau, ut appareat & audiat hospes; & fortassis, quod damnabilius est, ut magis frequenter oblationes afferantur, forte ad illicitos usus convertendae, & in marsupiis recludendae.

> [And also, they scarcely deign at times to perform plainchant at its proper pace when they sing by anticipating, accelerating, retarding, and improperly coupling the notes—from which the effect of the science of organum is achieved—because they may happen to see the notes arranged in such a way on the page. But this (writing of notes) is done for the ornament and beauty of the notes on the page; for seeing, not for singing. Let them know this for certain, not inquiring whether the (practices) that they see are ours, rather than God's, or proper to the art of music, of which they are ignorant. But experimenting, they sing "meow, meow" into the air, so that a stranger may turn up and listen; and what is even more damnable, they do this so that gifts may be brought forth more often, possibly to be diverted to unlawful uses and sheathed in pockets.][92]

Like many of the other commentators on polyphony discussed above, Elias, writing more or less contemporaneously with Anonymous IV, sprinkles his polemic with the spice of sexual panic. In deviant polyphony, voices and notes are "improperly coupled" (male copulando)—and not simply through improvisatory singing practices, but *because the visual beauty of the notated page has itself served as a provocation to "unnatural" performance.* The passage concludes with an image that takes us back to the punning phobia of the *Magnus liber* conductus repertory. The performers Elias attacks sing in catlike "meows" in order to draw "gifts" from their listeners, gifts that will very likely be put to "unlawful uses and sheathed in pockets" (marsupiis recludendae). The beautifully notated page becomes a sexually charged, musico-visual spectacle that conflates singing, seeing, and desire into the act of polyphonic performance.

What better way to account for a page like the recto of folio 92 of the W² manuscript of the *Magnus liber organi* (Figure 9), on which the duplum and the tenor of a two-voice conductus, "Presul nostri," undulate back and forth, move together and apart, embrace at certain moments and separate at others? Is this an "impressionistic" description of a page that transmits the legacy of Notre Dame? Of course it is—just as the writer of the *Ad organum faciendum* was being impressionistic when he anthropomorphized *cantus* and *organum* as "dear friends" who musically "kiss," "dominate," and "copulate"; just as John of Salisbury was being impressionistic when he excoriated the "counter-singing" and "in-between singing" of the *scholastici* of his day as both a symptom and a cause of their Orphic sexualities. Berger is surely right to point out that a modern edition transcribed in modern notation cannot replicate the medieval mnemotechnics deployed to fix the polyphonic music in the performer's mind. It fails as well to convey the sensuality of the musical experience the manuscript page itself embodies. To a "musical eye" used to liturgical books notated with plainchant, books of polyphony must surely have appeared strange creatures indeed. For those performers of chant who first opened these books and began to implant their unfamiliar counterpoints in their memories, the volumes constituted a notational spectacle of new polyphonic *coniunctiones*, one that transformed the originary vocal couplings at Notre Dame into a musical site and sight of collective memory.

There could be no more vivid exemplification of the cultural homology between polyphony and male same-sex desire as it was understood around 1200 than a passage from the lengthy *Hierapigra ad purgandos prelatos*, or *Pills for the Purging of Prelates* by Gilles de Corbeil, a master of medicine at Paris before the turn of the century who, like Robert of Courson, was closely associated with the circle of Peter the Chanter (whose work he frequently cites).[93] Unlike Leoninus, Gilles was something of a prude; in the introduction to one of his medical texts, he recommends its inherent tedium as a purifying remedy for the lasciviousness of Ovid's amatory literature—the same literature, of course, that inspired the poems of Leoninus.[94] In the midst of a polemic against sodomy among the Parisian clergy in the first book of the *Hierapigra*, Gilles likens poets and rhetoricians who

FIGURE 9   Two-voice conductus "Presul nostri," from *Magnus liber organi* (Wolfenbüttel, Herzog August Bibliothek, MS 1099, fol. 92 ʳ)

violate the rules of grammar to clerical sodomites who violate the rules of nature. Their verbal and sexual unions are simply not founded on reason, Gilles asserts; rather, in their sodomitical unions "the joining of things and the coupling of voices are brandished" (librantur rerum coniunctio, copula vocum).[95]

Like Robert of Courson, Gilles condemns vocal "couplings" occurring in musical performances—likely at the very cathedral with which he himself was institutionally associated. Though railing against sexual, grammatical, and musical deviance in the same breath, Gilles nevertheless reveals to us what may be the homoerotic foundation of Western musical harmony, a widespread sense in the twelfth century that eroticized *copulae* are endemic to the very nature of vocal polyphony. Even as writers such as Gilles, Alan, and Robert condemn what they saw as the sodomitical corruption of the chant, they allow us to begin reconstructing a distinctly medieval homo-erotics of polyphonic performance and reception, a homoerotics centered around the cathedral of Notre Dame and given a poetic voice by Leoninus, its most illustrious and articulate personality.

The Pardoner's Polyphonic Perversity:
A Chaucerian Coda

Nearly two centuries after the death of Leoninus, Geoffrey Chaucer would introduce the most visibly homoerotic character in Middle English litera-ture by similarly conflating the polyphonic and the sodomitical. In the General Prologue to the *Canterbury Tales*, Chaucer juxtaposes the Par-doner's brash singing of polyphony with his ambiguously sexed and gen-dered body:

> With hym [the Summoner] ther rood a gentil PARDONER
> Of Rouncivale, his freend and his compeer,
> That streight was comen fro the court of Rome.
> Ful loude he soong "Com hider, love, to me!"
> This Sumonour bar to hym a stif burdoun;
> Was nevere trompe of half so greet a soun.
>
> . . .
>
> A voys he hadde as smal as hath a goot.
> No berd hadde he, ne nevere sholde have;

As smothe it was as it were late shave.
I trowe he were a geldyng or a mare.

(1.669–74; 688–91)

It is the latter four lines, of course, that have inspired the often polemical Chaucerian debates over the sexual identity, proclivities, acts, or desires of the Pardoner. As an unbearded "geldyng," he is marked by Chaucer (and in Chaucer's imagination) as emasculated and effeminate; as an alleged "mare," he is constructed as sexually passive, abandoning the sexually "active" role of the male partner in favor of a "feminine" sexual penetrability.[96] Among the most significant pieces of literary evidence figuring in the critical debate around the Pardoner's sexuality has been the identification by Jill Mann of an earlier analogue to Chaucer's sexualizing use of the word "mare." As we have seen, in his Latin satire "Stulti cum prudentibus," Walter of Chatillôn condemns the sexual habits of his day by proclaiming that "men make women of themselves, and stallions become mares. . . . A new marriage god shamefully joins man to man, and women no longer get inside the door."[97] The poem was demonstrably known in England, and both poets likely deployed the term "mare" to denote the sexual passivity of the men they labeled as such.

It may be more than fortuitous that Chaucer's imaginative representation of the Pardoner as a possible "mare" has its closest extant medieval analogue in a poem originating in the Parisian culture that first postulated a cultural homology between polyphonic performance and male same-sex desire. Arnulf of St. Ghislain was another late-fourteenth-century writer who turned to a twelfth-century Latin text to rail against the perverse *organizantes* of his time—those "part-singers" who, "through antiphrasis, produce barbarism in music contrary to rule." Chaucer's polyphonic Pardoner was fabulated in the same awed yet phobic spirit in which Alan of Lille and Aelred of Rievaulx castigated the contemporary singing of dissident new music.

The polyphonic musicality of the Pardoner receives little comment in the voluminous scholarship dedicated to interpreting his performance, even from those critics most concerned with writing this literary representation into the history of medieval sexuality. An explanatory note in the *Riverside Chaucer* shows that the passage has, since at least the 1950s, raised the suggestion in the scholarship "of a homosexual relationship between the Pardoner and Summoner," but the studies cited adduce their authors' unsubstantiated speculations as the only evidence.[98] Carolyn Dinshaw intriguingly describes the musical interlude as a "homosexual display," though without further comment.[99] It is surely the case that this musical interlude in the General Prologue would never have been seen by modern exegetes to carry homosexual connotations in the first place, however, had it not also been for the Pardoner's ambiguously sexed and gendered construction in the General Prologue. When mentioned at all, the polyphonic duet becomes a *symptom* of the Pardoner's sexuality, a secondary sign of a prior sexual preference, condition, identity, and so on. A brief comment by Derek Pearsall on the line illustrates this logic: "once the secret is out . . . the Summoner's 'stif burdoun' becomes an obscene *double entendre*."[100] The Pardoner's supposed sexual "secret" allows us to interpret his musical performance as one of its many performative manifestations—but only once the Pardoner himself is "outed" by Chaucer several lines later.

What we tend to forget is the simple but crucial fact that the Chaucerian narrator of the General Prologue makes his infamous "sexual guess" about the Pardoner only *after* listening to the polyphonic performance that initiates the portrait. What makes the initial introduction of the Pardoner so remarkable, even in a narrowly formalistic sense, is Chaucer's unique and unparalleled intertwining of one pilgrim's introduction with the portrait immediately preceding it. The Summoner's portrait lingers into the Pardoner's for fully six lines as their voices accompany one another in a love song. Nowhere else in the General Prologue does Chaucer allow sequential portraits to overlap at such length; at the very most we see one or two lines establishing familial or service relationships, as with the Knight and Squire or the Prioress and Second Nun: "With [the Knight] ther was his sone, a yong SQUIER" (1.79); "Another NONNE with hire hadde [the Prioress],/ That was hir chapeleyne, and preestes three" (1.163–64). The extended commingling of the Summoner's and Pardoner's portraits in the General Prologue thus imagines a *polyphonic* intimacy between the two characters by constructing in poetry a unique *polytextual* imbrication of their portraits.

The first time we see, hear, or read about the Pardoner, he is singing—and singing polyphony. Accordingly, I would propose that Chaucer's suggestion that the Pardoner is a "geldyng or a mare" is the *real* "symptom" here, a nervously phobic and distancing acknowledgment of widespread medieval anxieties about same-sex polyphonic singing. For as the preceding pages have demonstrated, the Pardoner's polyphonic love song has a history: a material history, rooted in the homoerotic musico-poetic cultures of the twelfth and thirteenth centuries and manifested in a body of Latin literature that continued to be read well past the fourteenth.

In fact, though a great historical and stylistic divide separates the polyphony of the Notre Dame school from the Ars Nova of the English fourteenth century, the sexual anxiety occasioned by male-male singing continued to characterize reactions to musical innovation well into Chaucer's day. From the twelfth through the fourteenth centuries, condemnations of musical virtuosity and flamboyance are almost always concerned simultaneously with the emasculating and eroticizing threats posed by musical excess to the performing male body.[101] Roger Bacon's *Opus tertium* (ca. 1267), for example, rails against the "abuse of singing" (abusus cantus) throughout the Church of his day by representing it as a direct affront to the ancient sobriety and virility of chant:

> in mollitiem inverecundam lapsus, mansuetam et naturalem probitatem amisit; quod novarum harmoniarum curiositas, et prosarum lubrica adinventio, multipliciumque cantilenarum inepta voluptas manifestat. Et super omnia voces in falseto harmoniam virilem et sacram falsificantes, pueriliter effusae, muliebriter dissolutae fere per totam ecclesiam comprobant illud idem. Possem ponere exempla de maximis ecclesiis cathedralibus, et aliis collegiis famosis; in quibus totum officium confunditur propter haec vitia, quae narravi.
>
> [Having lost its natural probity and grace, it has lapsed into a shameless flaccidity. It now manifests a faddish propensity for new harmonies, a prurient inventiveness in proses, and a tasteless delight in a multiplicity of cantilenae. More than anything else, this decline of the chant is manifested in those voices, adolescent in their effusiveness and feminine in their dissoluteness, which counterfeit in falsetto the sacred and manly harmony almost everywhere throughout the Church. If I wanted to, I could give specific illustrations of the state of affairs in the greatest cathedral churches and other famous collegia, institutions in which the whole Divine Liturgy is in disarray because of the evils I have mentioned.][102]

Faddishness, flaccidity, inventiveness, multiplicity, femininity: these are the terms by which the Middle Ages invented rhetoric itself. They can be found in Tertullian's polemic against classical theatricality, which may have inspired John of Salisbury's antimusical rant in the *Policraticus*, and they directly inform numerous medieval constructions of rhetorical performances of various sorts. The "emasculation of eloquence" is a ubiquitous theme in late-classical and medieval writings on the performing body, whether the *corpus* is delivering dramatic spectacle or liturgy.[103]

Writers of practical musical treatises were similarly concerned with the dissident sexualization of sacred music through performative excess. A prime example here is the *Speculum musicae*, a strident defense of the Ars Antiqua against what its author, Jacques de Liège, saw as the corrosive musical innovations of the Ars Nova. Jacques characterizes this stylistic sea change as an abandonment of musical sobriety—a sobriety represented by organum and conductus, two strictly religious forms of polyphony—in favor of the motet and chanson, secular musics that promote a "studied lasciviousness in singing," a lustful propensity to embellish and ornament profligately. Jacques was especially disturbed by the performative license taken by singers of new forms of polyphony:

> Oh, if the ancient doctors of music were to hear these discantors, what would they say, what would they do! . . . There are some who have no regard for quality; they sing too lasciviously [*nimis lascive*], they multiply voices superfluously; some of them employ the hocquetus too much, breaking, cutting and dividing their voices into too many consonants [*hoketant . . . frangunt, scandunt et dividunt*]; in the most inopportune places they dance, whirl and jump about on notes, howling like dogs. They bay and like madmen nourished by disorderly and twisted aberrations, they use a harmony alien to nature [*armonia utuntur a natura remota*].[104]

Such performative lasciviousness is the direct result of the overt and unabashed misuse of the voice in musical practice: the singers dance, whirl, and jump around from note to note and part to part, multiplying, breaking, cutting, and dividing. Such practices make an animal-like, bestial spectacle of the singing body as the singers "bay," "howling like dogs." Worst of all, the polyphones of the Ars Nova use a harmony "alien to nature" (a natura remota): Jacques imagines the very harmonies they sing—the eroticized, carnal intermingling of one or more male voices—as a violation of nature itself.

If these writers share Alan of Lille's concern with the musico-sexual violation of *natura*, others worried over the vernacularization and, by extension in their eyes, the secularization of sacred musical discourse. As imagined in the *Docta sanctorum*, a 1325 bull issued by the Avignon Pope John XXII, the sober melodies of the chant are "robbed of their virility by *discant, tripla*, and *motetus*, with a dangerous element produced by certain parts sung on texts in the vernacular."[105] Once again, polyphonic singing and polyphonic music are themselves emasculating, feminizing, dangerous; "robbed" of its "virility," Latin plainchant is emasculated by words sung in the "mother tongue" above. John is reacting in part to a century of innovation within a particular musical genre, the polytextual motet, that purposefully mingled Latin and vernacular, sacred and secular, religious and sexual. As Sylvia Huot has shown, the often irreverent literary experimentations that characterize the thirteenth-century history of the motet were inspired by the recognition that the "sacred" and the "profane" are often indistinguishable.[106]

The anxious associations between gender inversion and aberrant musical practice articulated in the twelfth century by figures such as John, Aelred, and Robert of Courson thus continue to characterize reactions to polyphonic performance well into the later Middle Ages. Shared by most of these polemicists is an underlying awareness that within new, "alien," "unnatural" musical forms resides an ever-present musical expression of desire between men. They are united by an almost palpable worry that emergent polyphonic practices are capable of both producing and displaying the eroticized body of the performing male. They speak volumes about the dissident erotics of Chaucer's Pardoner.

But, of course, this is the *Summoner's* polyphonic love song, too. It is the Summoner who sings a "stif burdoun," a strong bass over which the Pardoner's "ful loude" "Com hider" musically soars. There is no imputation of effeminacy or castration in Chaucer's depiction of *this* pilgrim's body; he is simultaneously a sexual predator, "hoot . . . and lecherous as a sparwe" (1.626), making children "aferd" by his "visage" (628) and using the "yonge girles of the diocise" at will (664); and a professional spewing a "few termes" of Latin who has joined the "compagnye" with "his freend and his compeer" (670), the Pardoner. As John Bowers puts it, the Summoner "embodie[s] the most dangerous performance of an excessive sexuality that [is] wide-ranging in its possibilities, indeterminate in its erotic choices, and available for a broad spectrum of partners."[107]

The polyphonic perversities of the Summoner and the Pardoner ultimately suggest that, within the medieval representational history of polyphony that includes Chaucer's General Prologue, male same-sex desire is more a *musical* than a *genital* phenomenon. The polyphonic bodies excoriated by the writers discussed above are heard and represented as perverse not because they belong to a despised and marginalized minority of homosexual "others," but rather because their musical perversions are seen to have corrupted the liturgy and thus to have posed a carnal threat to the sobriety and sublimity of sacred music-making. Polyphony eroticizes a religious discourse in which *every* "man," whatever his "sexual preference," participates in some way.

This resolutely universalizing sense of polyphonic perversity thus moves us beyond the essentializing question of "whether they were or they weren't" by forcing us to recognize, in Glenn Burger's words, "the ways in which the perverse is already an integral part of the dominant and not the tragic lack embodied by a subordinate minority."[108] After all, it is with this last cluster of pilgrims on the way to Canterbury that Chaucer associates himself most closely:

> Ther was also a REVE, and a MILLERE,
> A SOMNOUR, and a PARDONER also,
> A MAUNCIPLE, and myself—ther were namo.
>
> (1.542–44)

Chaucer names *himself*, David Wallace reminds us, "as the sixth and last member of a group of 'miscellaneous predators.' "[109] Expending six precious lines of his General Prologue on the polyphonic perversity of "A SOMNOUR, and a PARDONER also," Chaucer registers an unspoken awareness that their perversions may be shared by the wider "compagnye," perhaps including himself.[110]

While the "ful loude" polyphony the Pardoner performs with the Summoner in the General Prologue is the first and most obvious sign of his musical perversion, it is certainly not the last. By the end of his portrait, it becomes clear that the Pardoner understands very well the centrality of music to his own performance on any number of levels. His rhetorical prowess depends absolutely on his *musical* prowess for its effectiveness:

> Wel koude he rede a lessoun or a storie,
> But alderbest he song an offertorie;
> For wel he wiste, whan that song was songe,
> He moste preche and wel affile his tonge
> To wynne silver, as he ful wel koude;
> Therefore he song the murierly and loude.
>
> (1.709–14)

As in the Manciple's Tale, in which the beauty of the crow's music enables him to persuade Phebus of his wife's adultery, the Pardoner's rhetorical skill, his ability to talk anyone into doing anything by switching tactics and positions seemingly at will, is aided greatly by his musicality. Yet part of the perverse rhetorical charge of the Pardoner's voice is that it is only musically "loude" when he chooses it to be. The Pardoner can have "an hauteyn speche" with a voice ringing "as round as gooth a belle," but he can also preach in a voice as "smal as hath a goot": a phrase evoking the long-standing association of goats' voices with adolescent lust and the breaking of the voice.[111] The Pardoner's *vox corporis* is thus polyphonically perverse in its own right, able to adapt to many purposes by constantly sliding and shifting, altering its tamber, volume, and pitch as the situation warrants.

Like the portrait in the General Prologue, the Pardoner's Tale begins by drawing a clear association between musical and moral deviance, locating music within the carnal "riot" that opens the narrative:

> In Flaundres whilom was a compaignye
> Of yonge folk that haunteden folye,
> As riot, hasard, stywes, and tavernes,
> Where as with harpes, lutes, and gyternes,
> They daunce and pleyen at dees bothe day and nyght,
> And eten also and drynken over hir myght,
> Thurgh which they doon the devel sacrifise
> Withinne that develes temple in cursed wise
> By superfluytee abhomynable.
>
> (6.463–71)

The Pardoner casts music as the sensual vehicle of the "compaignye's" carnality—"with harpes, lutes, and gyternes" they "daunce and pleyen at dees"; "eten . . . and drynken over hir myght." Profaning the body, "that develes temple," through lust and gluttony, the "yonge folk" are musically distanced from Christian belief, practice, and community. This becomes increasingly clear when the Pardoner implicates musical lust in the desecration of the most holy body of all:

> Our blissed Lordes body they totere—
> Hem thoughte that Jewes rente hym noght ynough—
> And ech of hem at otheres synne lough.
> And right anon thanne comen tombesteres
> Fetys and smale, and yonge frutesteres,
> Syngeres with harpes, baudes, wafereres,
> Whiche been the verray develes officeres
> To kyndle and blowe the fyr of lecherye,
> That is annexed unto glotonye.
>
> (6.474–82)

Rhetorically equating deviant Christian with murderous Jew by drawing on the stereotyped complaint of host desecration, the Pardoner imagines musicians—"Syngeres with harpes"—as the "verray develes officeres" melodiously encouraging the sins of the flesh.

The musicality of perversion extends well beyond the "yonge compaignye" whose actions the Pardoner first narrates. Before turning to the story of the three thieves, he images human misuse of the flesh—an inherent human condition with a history dating back to "Adam oure fader, and his wyf also" (505)—as corporeal inversion, the exchange of the parts and functions of one end of the body with those of the other:

> Allas, a foul thyng is it, by my feith,
> To seye this word, and fouler is the dede,
> Whan man so drynketh of the white and rede
> That of his throte he maketh his pryvee
> Thurgh thilke cursed superfluitee.
>
> (6.524–28)

And at this very moment, when he is most heatedly vilifying this "foul thyng" that inverts our bodies and perverts our desires, the Pardoner returns to sonority, positing bodily *sound* as the most horrifying sign of human degeneracy:

> O wombe! O bely! O stynkyng cod,
> Fulfilled of dong and of corrupcioun!
> At either ende of thee foul is the soun.
>
> (6.534–36)

The immoral, carnal corruption of the body—its scatological foulness—is a *musical* corruption as well. Carnal sin has its own particular music, and music can and often does "embody" the transgressions of the flesh.

In the midst of his extended and hypocritical sermonizing against bodily corruption and inversion, the Pardoner thus insists that the musical perversions of the human body are not confined to a sexually dissident minority, but are the common lot of "man." The tendency of all humans to make "of [the] throte . . . a pryvee" represents a universal potential for carnal sin musically embodied in the "foul . . . soun" of corporeal inversion. In a profound sense, the Pardoner—his musical body as well as his musical understanding of *all* human bodies and perversions—is a resonating synechdoche for the perversions of musical sonority itself, the eroticized somatic echoes that bind all human bodies to one another through their own God-given musicality.

This universalizing sense of polyphonic perversity is nowhere more spectacularly realized than in the Reeve's Tale, a narrative revolving around the sexual violation of domesticity and the nuclear family by nonfamilial outsiders. But it is also a narrative of musical orifices, of the dark musico-sexual perversions that threaten the familial institution from within. In the familiar passage below, John and Aleyn lie awake listening to the somnolent bodily musics made by the miller, his wife, and their daughter:

> This millere hath so wisely bibbed ale
> That as an hors he fnorteth in his sleep,
> Ne of his tayl bihynde he took no keep.
> His wyf bar hym a burdon, a ful strong;
> Men myghte hir rowtyng heere two furlong;
> The wenche rowteth eek, par compaignye.

Aleyn the clerk, that herde this melodye,
He poked John, and seyde, "Slepestow?
Herdestow evere slyk a sang er now?
Lo, swilk a complyn is ymel hem alle;
A wilde fyr upon thair bodyes falle!"

(1.4162–72)

The miller is loudly flatulent as he sleeps, taking "no keep" "of his tayl bihynde," and his wife musically accompanies him with a strong "burdon," or bass-line.[112] When the daughter joins in "*par compaignye*," the result is a sonorous chorus of bodies that joins the members of the family together through the music they produce, only reinforcing the status of the students as outsiders.

This is harmless satire, or so we have been told. With the phrase "swilk a complyn" in line 4171, Robert Correale argues, Chaucer is parodying a liturgical hour through Aleyn's ears: he has never heard *this* sort of "Compline" before.[113] Depicting Aleyn "pok[ing]" his friend and alerting him to the bodily chorus filling the room, the Reeve, much like the narrator of the Miller's Tale, deftly puns on a sacred musical form and brings it down to earth in the snores and farts resonating from the family's bodies.[114]

Yet Chaucer's modern editors and interpreters have obscured the true musico-sexual significance of the passage. In twentieth-century editions of the *Canterbury Tales*, the term "complyn" has been inserted as an editorial emendation in line 4171. In both the Hengwrt and Ellesmere manuscripts (generally agreed to be the two most authoritative), the reading is actually "couplyng." Aleyn's apparent "parody of Compline" is in fact a graphic description of the copulatory sound of the sleeping family, as we can see once we reinsert the line as it appears in Hengwrt:

He poked John, and seyde, "Slepestow?
Herdestow evere slyk a sang er now?
Lo, swylk a *couplyng* is ymel hem alle;
A wilde fyr upon thair bodyes falle!"

Chaucer had nothing to do with Aleyn's alleged parody. In Hengwrt, Aleyn's "Lo swylk a *couplyng*" (Ellesmere reads "whilk a cowplyng") constitutes not parody, but metonymy.[115] While "complyn" may represent a clever parody of religious music in the hands of later scribes (if it does, of course, this in itself is a fascinating scribalism), Chaucer's "couplyng" is an unmistakably eroticizing term frequently used to denote sexual intercourse in contemporaneous Middle English writings. Describing the family's music to John, Aleyn conflates a musical term for the harmonious joining of two or more lines—indeed, a vernacular appropriation of the musical *copula* that figures so prominently in the Latin writings this chapter has treated—with a graphic term for the literal *copula* of sexual bodies.

Chaucer's choice of "burdon" to signify the wife's musical accompaniment of her husband further eroticizes this metonymic representation of musical and sexual practices. Aside from his description of the Summoner's "burdoun" accompaniment to the Pardoner in the General Prologue, this is Chaucer's only musical use of the word in his entire oeuvre, an explicit signal to the reader to hear the couple's music through the Pardoner's musical perversions described earlier in the fragment. It is far from clear, moreover, that this familial polyphony is being produced exclusively orally. Given the lack of punctuation in the manuscripts, the lines describing the music could be read as follows: " . . . he fnorteth in his sleep./Ne of his tayl bihynde he took no keep;/his wyf bar hym a burdon a ful strong." While the next line identifies the "rowtyng" as the musical source, the chorus could as easily be a product of the bodies' *anal* musics as of its oral musics. In a certain sense, then, the Reeve's Tale performs a musical perversion of the family, an incestuous and sodomitical intermingling of the mouths and anuses of father, mother, and daughter. Music represents an undeniably nonproductive, non*re*productive deployment of body in this tale; the result is a familial "couplyng" that produces the musical clamor that awakens the students and inspires their own attempts to "couple."

As the fourteenth-century vernacular culmination of a long tradition of polyphonic homoerotics, the representation of the Pardoner provides a discursive vocabulary for locating musical practice within and among the bodily acts, performances, and representations that constitute the sexual universe of Middle English literature. If, as Dinshaw has argued, the Pardoner constitutes "an unwelcome but insistent reminder of normative heterosexual unnaturalness"[116] throughout the *Canterbury Tales*, it may be that his music embodies the most threateningly antiprocreative, antiheterosexual dimension of his performance. Penetrating the songs, sounds, and bodies that surround him with his own dissident sonorities, the Pardoner's musical body foregrounds the inherent weakness of the strict Robertsonian

separation between the musics of the Old Man and the New. While Robertson constructed a sharp exegetical distinction between the carnal music of
bagpipes and the spiritual melody of harps, the "music of the flesh" and the
"song of the spirit," the Pardoner demonstrates as eloquently as the music
and poetry of twelfth-century Paris how proximate bagpipe and harp, perversion and salvation truly are. In the words of the *Pearl* poet, "The grete
soun of Sodomas synkkez in Myn erez."[117]

PART 3

Sounds of Suffering

The Musical Body in Pain: Passion, Percussion, and Melody in Thirteenth-Century Religious Practice

> Split the Lark—and you'll find the Music—
> Bulb after Bulb, in Silver rolled—
> Scantily dealt to the Summer Morning
> Saved for your Ear when Lutes be old.
>
> Loose the Flood—you shall find it patent—
> Gush after Gush, reserved for you—
> Scarlet Experiment! Sceptic Thomas!
> Now, do you doubt that your Bird was true?
>
> —EMILY DICKINSON (ca. 1864)[1]

In an eight-line imperative, Emily Dickinson enjoins her readers to participate in a musical spectacle of bloodshed and dismemberment. Broken in two, a lark's dying body opens to reveal the bulbous rolls of music concealed within its breast. The scarlet flood of sound produced by the reader's imaginative violence provides the "Sceptic Thomas" with direct evidence of musical "truth": a sonorous wound that here constitutes a visceral sign of epistemological and religious certitude. Conflating the lark's resonant agonies with the passion of Christ, Dickinson calls attention to the materiality of poetic language, the visceral power of verse resonating from a body undergoing a torturous passion and a sacrificial death. Only through suffering can the body of the lark gush forth the lifeblood that will ultimately outlive the artificial, instrumental music of "Lutes."

The succinct production of a nineteenth-century New Englander, "Split the Lark" speaks to a long and varied tradition of western religious poetry written to induce and encourage private devotion to the body of Christ. For Dickinson, passion meditation also provides an ideal religious medium within which to contemplate the aesthetic and somatic dimensions of her own poetic labor. As in so many of her lyrics, she casts herself implicitly as a birdlike poet, in this case one whose body must be sacrificed for the sake of truth; writerly craft allows her to produce "Gush after Gush" of poetry only after the authorial body has been "Split." What comes across clearly in the lines above is Dickinson's sense that the nonverbal component of poetic language has a "patent" lock on the artistic expression of pain. The passionate music within the writer's body possesses a quasi-religious truth-value surpassing that of language, to which it is clearly superior; pain can be manifested only through the bleeding "Flood" of language that is, for lack of a better word, "music." The poem thematizes the expressive immediacy of pain, and Dickinson turns to music as a means of suggesting the pathetic inability of language to capture this immediacy when violence and the sacred converge.[2]

A similar representational dilemma informs perhaps the most search-ing contemporary inquiry into the nature and expression of bodily pain. "Physical pain has no voice, but when it at last finds a voice, it begins to tell a story": So writes Elaine Scarry in the introduction to *The Body in Pain*, an influential contribution to the history of the body as literary and social historians have recorded it over the past fifteen years.[3] Surveying a wide range of documents, from the Old Testament to the writings of Karl Marx to survivors' accounts of torture, Scarry identifies a gap between the "felt experience" of pain and pain's appropriation by political agents:

> The failure to express pain—whether the failure to objectify its attributes or instead the failure, once these attributes are objectified, to refer them to their original site in the human body—will always work to allow its appropriation and conflation with debased forms of power; conversely, the successful ex-pression of pain will always work to expose and make impossible that appro-priation and conflation.[4]

The "voicelessness" of physical pain both disallows its immediate expres-sion by those who suffer it and presents the possibility of political engage-ment for those who articulate it in the public sphere. The latter will always be an arduous task, for Scarry identifies in pain an essential inexpressibility and nonreferentiality: "physical pain—unlike any other state of conscious-ness—has no referential content. It is not *of* or *for* anything. It is precisely because it takes no object that it, more than any other phenomenon, resists objectification in language." In fact, pain "shatters language"; its "resistance to language," Scarry argues, "is not simply one of its incidental or accidental attributes but is essential to what it is."[5]

Yet while the impossibility of the *linguistic* articulation of pain is Scarry's premise, much of the historical evidence she adduces suggests that language may not be the only necessary or even the most desirable medium in which many human subjects express the phenomenon. It may be true that pain "shatters language," that physical pain by its very nature resists linguistic "objectif[ication]" and verbal "reference." In assuming that language must be centrally involved in any valid human expression of pain, however, Scarry obscures what seems to me an equally startling observation about the nature of pain and its perception—its fundamental audibility: "To witness the moment when pain causes a reversion to the pre-language of cries and groans is to witness the destruction of language; but conversely, to be present when a person moves up out of that pre-language and projects the facts of sentience into speech is almost to have been permitted to be present at the birth of language itself."[6] Scarry locates in the subject's expression of bodily pain the infancy of language *qua* language, the non- or preverbal "cries and groans" the subject can represent in language only once she or he makes a conscious effort to do so: "Physical pain does not simply resist language but actively destroys it, bringing about an immediate reversion to a state anterior to language, to the sounds and cries a human being makes before language is learned."[7] It is these very "sounds and cries," however, these allegedly infantile noises preceding the breakthrough into language, that remain uninterrogated.

The sonorous dimensions of pain recur with surprising regularity throughout Scarry's brilliant study, whether through analytic metaphor or unconscious acknowledgment. In scenes of political torture, "the translation of pain into power is ultimately a transformation of body into voice, a transformation arising in part out of the dissonance of the two, in part out of the consonance of the two."[8] The transformation into "voice" resolves ultimately as linguistic expression, but here and elsewhere in *The Body in Pain* one can sense a musical "dissonance" and "consonance" operative in torture as it performs the series of representational tensions that Scarry seeks to excavate. For example, the music of pain subtends her analysis of the "McGill Pain Questionnaire," an influential diagnostic tool developed in the 1970s by Ronald Melzack and W. S. Torgerson, two Canadian physicians seeking to categorize "the apparently random words most often spoken by patients" experiencing extreme pain. Recognizing that most sufferers tend to limit their descriptions of their own pain to its intensity ("moderate," "severe," and so on), the doctors discovered that patients, when encouraged, select words that convey the motion of pain through time:

> When heard in isolation, any one adjective such as "throbbing pain" . . . may appear to convey very little precise information beyond the general fact that the speaker is in distress. But when "throbbing" is placed in the company of certain other commonly occurring words [used to describe pain] ("flickering," "quivering," "pulsing," "throbbing," and "beating"), it is clear that all five of them express, with varying degrees of intensity, a rhythmic on-off sensation; and thus it is also clear that one coherent dimension of the felt-experience of pain is this "temporal dimension."[9]

In Scarry's analysis, this provocative evidence leads in part to the conclusion that pain, when articulated in language, can produce narrative. In other words, for those who already experience their pain as something that moves through time, pain's narrativization seems a logical next step. Language, once again, is the goal.

These clusters of descriptive terms for pain are worth repeating. On the one hand, we have "cries," "moans," "groans," "sounds": all forms of utterance that resist language, true, but that nevertheless produce sounds that can be heard and felt. On the other hand, we have "throbbing," "beating," "pulsing," "rhythmic on-off sensation[s]," terms by which subjects seek to metaphorize their own pain once asked explicitly to do so. And what both sets of terms show us very clearly is that sonority, and sometimes *musical* sonority—melody, percussion, rhythm—plays an often crucial role in bridging the gap that Scarry identifies between pain and its expression in language. Should we necessarily discount the representational impulse—or even the referentiality—of these "cries and groans" themselves? Are cries, groans, and rhythms, the spontaneous sounds emitted or the percussive beatings felt by a body in pain, necessarily *prior* to language? Or might they constitute an *alternative* to language, even a transcendence of the spoken or written word by subjects who glorify in their pain and lack the motivation or even the desire to articulate it in language?

Here we begin to approach a sensibility of the relationship among pain, language, and sonority that seems to me distinctly medieval. Recall from Chapter 1 St. Ambrose's account of the spectacular collective death of the Maccabees, whose mother, "joyously look[ing] upon the corpses of her sons as so many trophies," "delighted in their dying cries as in the singing of

psalms," who experienced the "natural but uninvited groaning" that burst
from their perishing bodies as "sweeter song" than the seductive chorus
of the Sirens.[10] The seven Maccabees are seven strings stretched across
the *cithara* of their mother's womb, resonating as one while they die in
agony. For Ambrose, Christian martyrdom is—in modern parlance—cham-
ber music. Centuries later, in the French court in the early eighteenth century, the composer Marin Marais would compose his "Tableau de L'Operation de la Taille" for viola de gamba. The piece was an attempt to convey in
music his own personal suffering during a lithotomy, a surgical procedure
(performed in his case, of course, without anesthesia) intended to remove
stones from the urinary bladder.[11] For Marais, at least, music "relates" the
experience of pain more effectively than narrative ever could.

If pain "shatters language," then, it may also produce music. This is not
to argue that the involuntary utterances of a suffering body are in any sense
inherently musical. Scarry's book is an empathetic effort to identify with the
experience of historical victims, political prisoners, and survivors of torture;
her study of the writings of working physicians such as Melzack and Torgerson represents a crucial component of this project: "The depth of [Mel-
zack's] belief in the referential powers of the human voice only becomes
visible when one recognizes that he has found in language not only the
record of the felt-experience of pain, . . . but has found there even the secrets
of the neurological and physiological pathways themselves."[12] This "trust in
language," as Scarry herself calls it, leads to other resolutely linguistic discourses in which pain finds a "voice"—in her case studies, invariably a
linguistic voice.

The problem is as much an aesthetic one as it is a historical or epochal
one. For early Christian and other writers imbued with the notion that pain
can be redemptive, even beautiful—for those subjects, in other words, *who
believe that pain is good*, and that language might not be capable of doing
anything particularly useful with it—the "cries and groans" of bodies undergoing torture and martyrdom constitute not prelinguistic, infantile bab-
blings, but the sublime strains of psalmody. Though its representational
limitations prevent language from capturing the experiential immediacy of
pain, when the subject *does* seek to articulate the body's pain after the fact,
this articulation may well rely on the nonlinguistic medium of music.
Despite its overriding focus on language, *The Body in Pain* resounds with
what I will call the musicality of pain and its expression, whether in songlike

groans and cries of anguish, the percussiveness of bodies being beaten from within and without, even bodies throbbing in pain as a severed artery pulses out blood in a musical rhythm.

This chapter and the next examine the role of musical pain and violence in medieval religiosity. The musical body in pain has much to teach us about Christian religiosity in general, lessons that will remain unlearned if we ignore the centrality of the gruesome and the grotesque to medieval musical life. If Part 2 argued that musical and sexual pleasures were often intertwined in the Middle Ages, Part 3 shows that music and bodily pain were equally proximate dimensions of human experience. (While this organizational division between musical pleasure and pain might be seen to imply a concordant experiential distinction between the two, this distinction is by no means clear-cut; as we have already seen in the case of Hildegard, musical pain *is* very often a form of musical pleasure.) The present chapter proposes a number of approaches to the musical body in pain and tests them on a range of medieval religious writings and visual images that seem to be particularly invested in the convergence of music and suffering. After a brief excursus on the musical Hell of Hieronymous Bosch, I turn in Chapter 6 to medieval representations of musical pedagogy in order to address one of the many ideological consequences of musical violence.

Musicality and Suffering

I begin this examination of the musical body in pain with a brief look at the writings of Peter Damian, the eleventh-century theologian who has been described as "the first great protagonist of voluntary flagellation."[13] Peter's occasional speculations on flagellation provide an extremely useful heuristic model for approaching the many later forms of musical violence that will be the subject of this chapter. Describing the extreme asceticism of Saint Dominic of Loricatus, Peter proposes a firm biblical rationale for the religious music of pain and its infliction. In a letter to a Florentine hermit written sometime after 1055, he records that Dominic made a regular practice of flagellating himself while chanting the Psalms: "He was so accustomed to this way of life that hardly a day passed without chanting two psalters, beating his naked body with both hands armed with scourges."[14] For Peter, the self-infliction of penance through bodily beatings and the musical *disciplina* of psalmody are one and the same: "Just as three thousand blows normally discharge one year of penance, chanting ten psalms [*decem autem psalmorum modulatio*] accounts for a thousand blows, as is often proven. Because it is clear that the psalter contains one hundred and fifty psalms, five years of penance, counting correctly, are earned through the discipline of one psalter [*in huius psalterii disciplina*]."[15] The liturgical performance of the Psalms through the *opus Dei* creates its own kind of pain, a regularized infliction of self-punishment that creates through the human body an instrumental means of participating in the sufferings of Christ. Thus, in a letter to Petrus Cerebrosus, Peter vividly casts his own body as the tortured instrument of devotion: "if I punish myself with my own hands, or if the executioner applies the blows, I become the actual author [*auctor*] of this ordeal if I voluntarily present myself to be tested. Moreover, since the *tympanum* is made of dry skin [*pellis . . . arida*], in the words of the prophet, he truly praises God on the *tympanum* who, when weakened by fasting, beats his body with the discipline."[16]

This is perhaps the first explicit Christian theorization of the musical torture of the self, and it is reiterated enthusiastically by a nun in the abbey of Unterlinden, writing around 1240, who describes the violent production of music from the bodies of her sisters: "In Advent and Lent, all the sisters, circling around after Matins in the chapter-house, or in another appropriate location, subject themselves cruelly and hostilely to diverse sorts of whips [*flagellorum*], lacerating their bodies until shedding blood, so that the sound of whipping themselves resonates throughout the monastery, ascending to the ears of the Lord of Hosts sweeter than any melody [*suavior omni melodia*]."[17] Unlike Peter, for whom flagellation and liturgical psalmody are coterminous, the Unterlinden writer emphasizes that the reverberating sounds of bodily mortification are produced outside the actual liturgy, during a procession following Matins. In both cases, however, music offers the devotional subject a somatic experience beyond the scope of religious language; in the Unterlinden sister book, music proves so powerful an image for the body in pain that it exceeds its own capacity for metaphorization.

Later centuries would see the development of entire genres of sacred music composed for the express purpose of performance during self-flagellation. "They even had a special song, which they would sing while whipping themselves," wrote a papal chronicler, Theodoric of Nîmes, expressing what had become practically a commonplace association between torture and song.[18] These *Geisslerlieder* (*laude* in Italy) were sometimes the product of craft guilds, members of which would process through the streets of villages, towns, and cities singing sacred songs and beating themselves in torturous accompaniment. Delighting in the musical violence they created and in which they participated, these quasi-professional flagellants sought to produce painful music as public, civic spectacle.[19]

The musical body in pain is at once a paradoxical and perfectly logical phenomenon. The neoplatonic vocabularies that provided numerous premodern writers with a way of relating their disordered individuated selves to the harmonies of the universe could also serve to express the often searing agonies of life in a human body—perhaps especially a body poised at the threshold separating the human from the divine. We have seen such expressions already in a variety of verbal and visual discourses: in the exegetical writings of Ambrose, in a Roman statue of Apollo plucking the musically vanquished Marsyas, in Hildegard of Bingen's vision of two strings of torture stretched across the genitals of the Son of Man. Musical torture could take a diverse and sometimes confounding variety of forms. In the *De nugis curialium*, Walter Map describes a music-loving fish as an exemplum of studious constancy: "The *usula* is a fish of the Danube, which pierces through the weapons of its enemies to come at musical tunes [*musice . . . mela*], nor even when wounded desists, but prodigal of its life and greedy of the organ [*auarus organi*], follows up the honeyed decoys of its soul even to death. Such is the triumphal constancy of the noble and studious man, whom not cough nor consumption nor any inconveniences whatever deter from his studies. By his anxious labour he brings martyrdom upon his anguished body. . . . In this way you should be an *usula*."[20] Medieval religiosity is a veritable aquarium of *usulae*.

Accounting historically for such bizarre confluences of sonority, suffering, and embodiment demands the same sensibility toward the experiential dimension of medieval musical cultures that art historians have brought to the study of the visual cultures of the period. In his work on "the visual and the visionary" in religious painting, for example, Jeffrey Hamburger has challenged traditional views of devotional imagery as primarily a didactic form of iconographical instruction or "popular piety" for the unlearned. Indeed, visual culture in the Middle Ages functioned not simply (or even primarily) to provide illustrations of prior, more authoritative texts, but rather to construct images "as instruments of visionary experience" in themselves, sensual objects intended "to induce, channel, and focus that experience."[21] Never merely heuristic, the visuality of late-medieval devotional practices constituted a fundamentally material component of religious life.

So, too, I want to suggest, did the *musicality* of devotional practices. The term *musicality* is generally reserved to connote the musical abilities or talents—often, in music criticism, ostensibly "natural" or God-given ones—of a particular musician.[22] (In a cutthroat conservatory environment, you either "have good musicality" or you don't.) Readers of medieval music theory know of a somewhat similar distinction, more often stated than believed: that between the enlightened *musicus*—the musical sage who, as it were, holds the numbers in his head—and the hack *cantor*, the vulgar performer responsible for producing actual sounds.[23] Yet *musicality* might also serve (and will serve here) as a convenient analytical term embracing the embodied, experiential aspects of any given musically induced or inducing discourse, whether it involves identifiable notated music or not. In this sense, a devotional poem, an exegetical treatise, or indeed a manuscript illumination or statue that contains what we would usually term "representations of," "images of," or "ideas about" music will be understood to possess a certain "musicality" when it is actually used (read, viewed, tasted, touched, heard) by a reader, viewer, or listener, whose own embodied musicality is enlisted in turn as an integral part of the experience.

An excavation of what I am calling musicality is of course the unstated purpose of much recent scholarship in premodern European musicology. Christopher Page's book on what he terms "musical life and ideas" in medieval France might be read as an explication of the musicality of miracles, the musicality of demons and demonic apparitions, even the musicality of protonationalism.[24] The complex relationship between Augustinian religiosity and Victorine sequences studied by Margot Fassler centered around the theological musicality of Hugh of St. Victor, whose writings modeled a "dynamic process" for their Augustinian readers that integrated liturgical performance and sacrament into an "aesthetic matrix" of religious experience.[25] Craig Monson's recent book on the musical culture of the convent of Santa Cristina della Fondazza in Bologna finds a moving sense of devotional musicality in the nuns' practice of biblical *imitatio*, in their use of altarpieces and other visual images, and especially in their meditations on the harmonies and texts of the sacred music they themselves produced.[26]

For premodern religious cultures, musicality may be found in text, image, or physical space, in the melismas of an Alleluia or the margins of a glossed Psalter. The musical body in pain is not solely an image or a representation, if by *image* and *representation* we mean static expressions of ideas or ideologies; rather, it is a direct source of devotional experience, a means of adapting one's own musicality to the pressures of religious life and adjusting to the musical nature of sacred time.

A case in point is what I would call the bookish musicality of *Book to a Mother*, a late-fourteenth-century Middle English religious treatise written in the voice of a son instructing his mother in the practices of devotion. As its modern editor points out, one of the *Book's* operative metaphors is the imagery of the body of Christ as a text, a book to be read and meditated upon: "þis bok is Crist, Godis Sone of heuene."[27] Like many other Middle English devotional writers, such as Richard Rolle, Margery Kempe, and the writer(s) of the *Charters of Christ*, the author continually exploits the homology between the body of Christ and the biblical texts that prefigure and relate its destiny. Yet the meditational experience *Book to a Mother* seeks to provoke is not a purely textual one; while musical imagery occurs infrequently in the *Book*, when it does appear it invites nonverbal participation. Glossing a line from the Psalms we have seen before ("Praise him on the psaltery and harp"), the author extends the already established image of Christ-as-book to include music: "þis bok is þe harpe and þe sauterry of ten strynges þat Dauid biddeþ vs synge inne to oure Lord God."[28] Rather than simply reading the "bok" of "Crist," readers are asked to imagine themselves singing from it as well, participating in its musical surface (a surface itself composed of skin, of course—parchment or vellum). Immediately after this description of the "harpe" and "sauterry," the text enjoins the reader to become part of the physical page: imitating the body of Christ, "þe harp and þe sauterry," the reader's body assumes a distinctly musical character: it "bihoueþ take good kepe þat we legge not oure harpe moist for lesinge of hure soun."[29] Like the parchment that constitutes the "bok" of "Crist," the "harpe" of the human body must be kept dry, mortified, and resonant.

Book to a Mother thus integrates musicality—its own and its readers'— into the experience of reading and meditation; though music and writing converge in the body of Christ, musicality provides access to a devotional realm beyond the reach of textuality. Such deployments of musicality in medieval religious writings suggest that the ubiquitous metaphors of "body as text" or "book and body" studied by numerous scholars in recent years have a sonorous counterpart, one that will allow us to extend our analysis of the corporeality of medieval manuscript culture to include embodied musical experiences.[30] Like many medieval visual images, which "act on the viewer, inviting visual participation and devotional imitation,"[31] so the textualization of musicality induces an empathetic and extralinguistic participation from readers, a participation that often involves intensive reflection upon the violence entailed in certain forms of musical experience.[32]

The most vivid devotional uses of the musicality of pain can be found in depictions of the Crucifixion.[33] In a passage from his Psalm commentary discussed in Chapter 1, Cassiodorus glosses the phrase "Exsurge cithara" ("Arise, harp") as a musical sign of Christ's agonies on the cross: "The *harp* denotes the glorious passion, performed on stretched tendons and individuated bones, which made the virtue of patience resound with the song as it were of the understanding" (*Cithara* uero gloriosam significat passionem, quae tensis neruis dinumeratisque ossibus, uirtutem patientiae intellectuali quodam carmine personabat).[34] Such inducements of devotional musicality figure prominently as well in vernacular religious writings. In *Die Erlösung*, an anonymous Middle High German poem written around 1300, appears a rendition of the sonorities of the Crucifixion that uses the same biblical phrase to move from exegetical contemplation to devotional experience:

Iâ der werde godes vrûnt
in deme salter aber sprach
jubilîrende unde jach:
'*Surge mea cythara.*'
Nû hôret, wie man daz verstâ
dief von sinne scharpe

. . .

Die harphe und daz psalterium
sint beide ungespannen dum,
sie sint ungeslagen doup
rehte sam ein lindenloup,
daz von dem boume vellet.
Wer sie gespannen stellet
und slehet dar und aber dar,
ir sûzekeit wirt man gewar

des ordenlîchen sanges,
des sûzen seidenklanges.
In aller wîze det alsus
unser herre Cristus.
Jâ sâ der hêre heilant
an daz krûze sâzuhant
gezwicket und geslagen wart,
gespannen unde sêre gespart,
geslagen dar und aber dar.

[The worthy friend of God declared in jubilation in his psalter: "Rise, my harp." Hear now how that is to be understood in its deep and penetrating meaning. . . . The harp and the psaltery are mute when still unspanned, and, unless struck, silent like the linden leaf that falls from the tree. If anyone tightens their strings, however, and strikes them again and again, their sweetness will be heard, their regular song: the sweet sound from the strings. Thus exactly did our Lord Christ. Yes, immediately the glorious Saviour was nailed and fastened on the Cross, spanned and direly stretched, struck again and again, the sweet music of God which he makes for his faithful was heard.][35]

Like Dickinson's injunctions in "Split the Lark," the poem's imperative to "hear . . . beyond doubt" compels the reader to participate musically in Christ's suffering, to experience the sweet sound of the strings (*des sûzen seidenklanges*) as well as the percussive and assonant repetition (*dar und aber dar*) of Christ's final persecution as the "sweet music of God." While *Book to a Mother* identifies its readers musically with the page (and thus with the body of Christ), *Die Erlösung* creates a musicality of empathy through the rhythmic character of its language, which registers in prosody the percussive torturing of Christ as the poem is read or recited. All three writers seek to channel the reader's musicality into meditation upon the sufferings of Christ; the Latin and vernacular passages are not simply attempts to impose an authoritative gloss of a biblical passage upon the reader, but provocations to take the biblical fragments they incorporate as descriptions of Christ's own passionate musicality. The musicality of the Psalms resides not only in the performance of the Psalter as part of the liturgy, then, but also in individualized moments of reading and meditation, which provide uniquely musical opportunities for Christological experience.

Perhaps the most influential medieval productions of the passion's musicality occur in the *Speculum humanae salvationis*, a popular typological manual first compiled (probably by a Dominican or Franciscan[36]) in the early fourteenth century, quickly translated into the major vernaculars, and surviving in some 350 manuscripts.[37] The *Speculum* is structured as a series of forty-two pairs of events from the Old and New Testaments; although a number of its typologies are derived from the earlier *Biblia pauperum*, chapter 23 postulates an apparently original connection between the raising of the cross and the account of Lamech's sons in Genesis.[38] For the *Speculum* author, this brief biblical legend prefigures the founding sacrifice of the Christian faith:

> Jubal et Tubalcain filii Lamech fuerunt,
> Qui inventores artis ferrariae et musicae exstiterunt.
> Quando enim Tubalcain cum malleis sonos faciebat,
> Jubal ex sonitu malleorum melodiam inveniebat.
> Ad talem ergo melodiam et malleorum fabricationem
> Comparamus Christi orationem et crucifixorum malleationem:
> Quando enim crucifixores Jesum ad crucem fabricant,
> Christus dulcissimam melodiam pro ipsis Patri suo decantabat:
> "Pater, dimitte illis, quia nesciunt quid faciunt:
> Ignorant enim quod Filius tuus sum, quem crucifigunt."[39]

> [Jubal and Tubalcain were the sons of Lamech, who were known as the inventors of the arts of metal-working and music. For when Tubalcain produced sound with hammers, Jubal discovered music from the sound of the hammers. We might thus compare the hammers' melody and forging to the praying of Christ and the hammerings of his crucifiers: For just as the crucifiers of Jesus fastened him to the cross, Christ sang the sweetest melody for them to his Father: "Father, forgive them, for they know not what they do. They do not know that I, whom they crucify, am your Son."]

The treatise establishes a vivid homology between Christ's dying moans on the Cross and the origins of music. The history and performance of earthly song mysteriously embody both the sufferings of Christ and the physical labor that produced them.

In its own right, this pairing is a fascinating example of what I would call typological musicality, an attempt to import a musical resonance into a crucial New Testament sequence by using material from the Old as an inducement to musico-biblical reflection. With the *Speculum*, however, we have a unique opportunity to explore the devotional interface between musicality and visuality in medieval representations of the Passion, for in most of the surviving manuscripts, each chapter is accompanied by a pair of painted, sketched, or block-printed illustrations of its primary typology. Given the daunting number of copies in which it survives, a thorough art-historical study of the *Speculum* will be a monumental undertaking (thus far only region-specific surveys have been attempted), and any conclusions drawn on the basis of an inevitably selective sample will be somewhat skewed.[40]

The forty-odd illustrated and illuminated manuscripts of the treatise examined for the purposes of this study come from England, Spain, Italy, Germany, and France; they cover a historical span of roughly three centuries. What becomes clear from even this relatively narrow selection is the extraordinary variety of ways artists responded to the musical typology in chapter 23 (and, to a lesser extent, the David-Christ typology in chapter 25), visually exploring the treatise's parallel between musical invention and passionate suffering in ways that the author(s) could not possibly have anticipated. In the process, these (mostly anonymous) artists left behind a prolific, widespread, and spectacular production of the musicality of the body in pain.

In a fourteenth-century copy of the *Speculum* from Germany (Munich, Bayerische Staatsbibliothek, Clm. 146, fol. 25v), the illustrator sketches the parallel found in the treatise between Tubalcain's hammerings on the forge and the pounding of nails into Christ's hands and feet (see Figure 10).[41] As if to emphasize the parallel more emphatically, however, Jubal is depicted deriving music not from his brother's labors alone, but from the mallets of *two* blacksmiths who pound the anvil simultaneously—a visual interpolation unsupported by the text of the *Speculum* chapter but corresponding to the two laborers pounding nails into Christ's hands and feet. In an attempt to develop the musicality of the Passion into an active visual exercise, a "string" is stretched across the body of Christ, a workmanlike gesture on the illustrator's part that envisions the plucked strings of Jubal's harp as prefiguring the mundane mechanical problem of actually raising the Cross.[42]

In another German example, Darmstadt, Landesbibliothek 2505 (see Figure 11), Jubal's triangular psaltery subtly mirrors the shape of the cross itself. This, of course, suggests the same musical parallel between the stretched sinews of Christ and the instrument's strings we saw in Cassio-

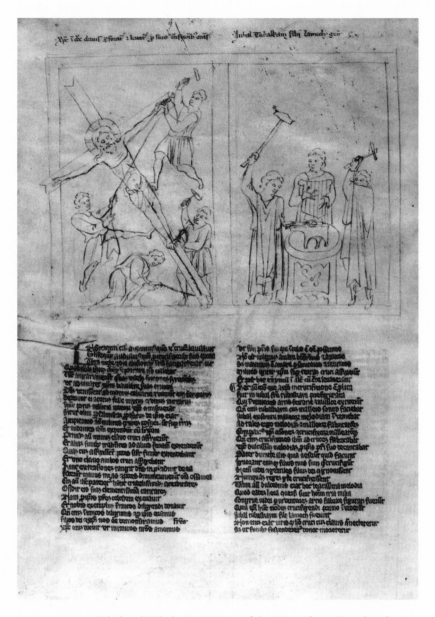

FIGURE 10   Jubal and Tubalcain/Raising of the Cross, from *Speculum humanae salvationis* chapter 23, German, fourteenth century (Munich, Bayerische Staatsbibliothek, Clm. 146, fol. 25 ᵛ)

dorus and *Die Erlösung*. The effect is grotesquely heightened by the positioning of the four holes in the psaltery's sounding board: the three smaller holes match the nail holes already in place in Christ's hands and feet, while the larger hole over Jubal's breast anticipates Christ's imminent wounding by the spear. Similarly, in the twenty-fifth chapter as it appears in BM Harley 4996, the illustrator made sure that the number of strings in David's harp corresponded exactly to the number of rows of Christ's ribs showing in the Crucifixion scene (fol. 26r).

Many illustrators exploited less explicit aspects of the parallel, as in London, British Library, Additional 16578 (produced in 1379), a beautifully colored example in which the small pegs in Jubal's psaltery are visually emphasized in painstaking detail in order to highlight their prefigurement of the nails pounded into Christ's flesh (fol. 25v). In British Library, Sloane 346, fol. 15r (fourteenth century), the crucified figures of the thieves stand behind Christ in chapter 25, itself an unusual interpolation; in this case, however, the dangling hands of the two thieves are joined together by three strings stretched tightly across their crucified bodies. Their bodies *are* thus stringed instruments more literally so than is Christ's, suggesting that the artist wished to extend the musicality of suffering to nondivine human flesh (perhaps as a subtle lesson to the decidedly nondivine readers and viewers of the treatise).

Still other manuscripts construct original musical interactions between the two typological frames of the chapter and between discrete chapters of the treatise. In the twenty-fifth chapter in Paris, BN Latin 9585 (late fourteenth century), David gazes backwards over his shoulder and across the folio's typological divide, playing on his harp and watching as the spear is thrust into Christ's side. In a deluxe fifteenth-century French copy of the *Speculum* (British Library, Harley 2838, fol. 25v), the second hammerer in chapter 23 is Tubalcain's wife,[43] and in chapter 25 David's plucking of the harp strings is clearly meant to provoke a musical identification with the crucifix on the facing folio. On British Library, Arundel 120, fol. 26v (fourteenth or fifteenth century), appears a rough line drawing that nevertheless creates a particularly moving rendition of typological musicality. Here, rather than picking out his brother's tune while positioned behind the anvil (as he usually is), Jubal stands isolated to the right of the hammering smiths gazing intently at Christ as the Cross is raised, as does the single crucifier standing on the left in the Crucifixion scene. Unlike the other hammerers,

FIGURE 11 Jubal and Tubalcain / Raising of the Cross, from *Speculum humanae salvationis* chapter 23 (Darmstadt, Landesbibliothek MS 2505, fol. 42 ᵛ)

both Jubal and the single New Testament crucifier are clean shaven, raising the possibility that Jubal's musical invention, regardless of his brother's creative labor, may be the more compelling prefiguration of the passion.

Again, none of these vivid parallels is supported by the *Speculum*'s text. Medieval illustrators and illuminators used the typological treatise as a base text for their own often ingenious visual inducements to the musicality of passion devotion. In establishing a historical intimacy between Christ's dying moans on the Cross and the very origins of music, chapter 23 of the *Speculum humanae salvationis*, along with its dazzlingly varied visual program (of which I have only scraped the surface here), suggests that any attempt to account for the role of musicality in medieval religious experience must account as well for its repeated inflictions of the sonorities of suffering.

As the examples treated thus far have shown, the musicality of bodily pain—whether performed on the body of Christ or through the actions of his ascetic imitators—figures so often in medieval devotional discourses that a single chapter cannot possibly do justice to the topic. Focusing on a number of Latin religious writings produced in the Low Countries, England, and Germany over the course of the thirteenth century, the remainder of this chapter will look in greater detail at just a handful of works that exemplify in particularly vivid ways what many devotional writers imagined as the unique propensity of musical sonority to embody and channel extreme somatic experience, particularly pain. This cluster of writings includes several works written by a Dominican preacher and hagiographer, a Franciscan devotional poem composed by a future archbishop of Canterbury, and three compilations of texts produced by a group of Rhineland nuns in the 1290s.

I have chosen to limit the following discussion to the thirteenth century for two reasons. First, the twelfth century saw a gradual but marked shift in Christian thought and discourse toward a new emphasis on the role of the human body in religious experience and personal identity. This wide-scale epistemic shift had many causes, of course, from the new emphasis on the suffering humanity of Christ adumbrated in the writings of Anselm to the "platonisms of the twelfth century" described in loving detail by Marie-Dominique Chenu.[44] The twelfth- and thirteenth-century preoccupation with the role of body in religious life can be discerned in theological debates over death and resurrection, burial practices and relic cult, and perhaps especially in new forms of devotion to the body of Christ. As Thomas Bestul and Giles Constable have recently confirmed, passion narratives and *imitatio Christi* both become increasingly graphic and violent over the course of the twelfth and thirteenth centuries.[45] Esther Cohen has even coined the term *philopassianism* to convey the extent to which late medieval Christian cultures embraced bodily pain; in theology, law, and medicine, rejection and passivity gave way to self-conscious attempts "to sense, express, and inflict as much pain as possible."[46] The thirteenth century, in particular, thus offers a spectacular array of newly violent bodily practices, many of which express what we might call the philopassianist musicality of religious suffering.

My second reason for this temporal focus lies not in sweeping changes in social and cultural history, but in certain aspects of medieval biblical exegesis. As we have seen, patristic and medieval writers often enact the musicality of the human body in their elaborations of musical imagery from the Bible, in particular Psalms, which provided patristic and medieval exegetes with the most extensive musical imagery for interpretive reflection. In the twelfth century, the era that produced the great exegetical compilations that would deeply influence the study of the Bible through the later Middle Ages, two Psalm commentaries (both heavily indebted to Cassiodorus's *Expositio psalmorum* and Augustine's *Enarrationes*) proved particularly popular: the so-called Parva glossatura, produced as part of the *Glossa ordinaria* by Anselm of Laon and his workshop before 1130; and the "Magna glossatura," Peter Lombard's *Commentarium in Psalmos Davidicos*, completed by 1138.[47] From the second half of the twelfth century on, the Lombard's Psalm gloss was the "scholastic commentary of choice,"[48] and the *Glossa ordinaria* had become a standard element in northern European monastic and secular libraries by 1200, after which the production of new manuscripts of its discrete sections became less common.[49]

The few scholars who have treated medieval commentary on the music of the Bible at any length have tended to regard it as an inherently conservative tradition, a "monolithic" reinscription of the aims and values of patristic exegesis, even a "monotonously regular" repetition of a set of predetermined tropes.[50] Although I am not primarily concerned here with the exegetical tradition per se, there is good reason to question such views of the medieval diffusion of biblical commentary, whether musical or otherwise. In her work on Peter Lombard, Marcia Colish has demonstrated the extent to which the Lombard's compilations (both the *Commentarium in Psalmos Davidicos* and the *Sentences*) were themselves remarkably innovative, featuring a diverse range of hermeneutical opinions, a careful attention to the more speculative dimensions of theology, and a shrewd grasp of the rhetorical and grammatical particularities of biblical language.[51] Our continuing haste to reject so-called Exegetical approaches to medieval literature as these approaches were practiced by D. W. Robertson and his followers should not keep us from paying careful attention to exegesis *qua* exegesis; as David Aers once caustically observed, "omission of any close reading of actual exegetical practice" is a characteristic common to both Robertsonianism and its opponents.[52] The recent renewal of interest in the medieval exegetical tradition in its own right will undoubtedly open further avenues of inquiry into the nature of exegesis as a cultural practice with particular ideological consequences.

Of particular interest here are those medieval discourses of musicality that appropriated and transformed text-based modes of exegetical interpretation. The medieval experience of an exegetical text was rarely purely textual; the codicological, visual, and liturgical contexts of a given exegetical treatise were crucial to its medieval reception.[53] A particularly germane example is Joachim of Fiore's twelfth-century *Psalterium decem chordarum*, one of the most extended medieval Latin elaborations of biblical musicality.[54] Though writ large in the poetry of the Psalms, the ten-stringed psaltery appeared to Joachim himself in an apocalyptic vision as an impossibly complex mystical symbol: of the Trinity, of the hierarchy of angels, of the gifts of the Holy Spirit and the ascent of humanity through the virtues; the instrument itself, Joachim argues elsewhere, is the *homo novus*, the human being "infused" with the virtues that enable the Beast to be conquered.[55]

Even more compelling for the purposes of the present chapter is the deployment of this imagery in the frontispiece to a late-twelfth-century manuscript of Peter Lombard's Psalm commentary likely produced at the Benedictine monastery of Zwiefalten in southeast Germany (see Figure 12).[56] The text surrounding the image comes from the commentary, which opens with a frontispiece illustrating the David-Christ typology discussed by Peter in the prologue: "Alternatively, the book is called 'Soliloquies' since its discourse is solely about Christ. For others have prophesied about Christ

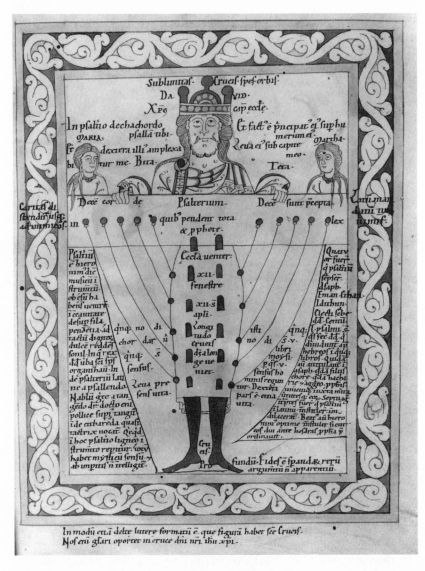

FIGURE 12   David frontispiece to Peter Lombard, *Commentarium in Psalmos*
(Stuttgart, Württembergischen Landesbibliothek, Cod. theol. et phil. 341, fol. 1 ʳ)

obscurely and through riddles. But because David spoke in the clearest terms about Christ's incarnation, passion, begetting by the Eternal Being, and resurrection, the book is entitled 'The Book of Soliloquies.' "[57] At the top of the illumination, two lines of text reading "David" and "Christus caput ecclesie" (as well as portraits of Mary and Martha) are divided by the head of the standing figure.[58] Though fragments from Peter's authoritative text seek to control the reader's experience of the image, the illumination assumes a devotional life of its own through the complex experiential inter-calation of musicality, visuality, and textuality that results when the folio as a whole is perused. The result is an image that, like the miniatures from the *Speculum humanae salvationis*, would have appeared more participatory than illustrative to its medieval viewers; it employs what Rosemary Muir Wright, in reference to illuminated manuscripts of the Apocalypse, calls "sound in pictured silence" as a means of producing a truly synesthetic experience of the page.[59]

The body of David/Christ represents the "ten-stringed psaltery" de-scribed in the Psalm verse placed in the upper left quadrant of the image ("In Psalterio dechachordo psallam tibi") and in the etymological definition (taken from Jerome) in the lower left. On the horizontal bar of the cross to which the ten strings are affixed appears the phrase "Decem corde Decem sunt precepta in quibus pendent tota lex et prophete," which both abbrevi-ates and anticipates a passage from the Lombard's gloss of Psalm 32 (lifted directly from Augustine) in the *Commentary*: "*Confitemini in Domino et cithara*, id est exhibete corpora vestra hostiam vivam mortificando carnem cum vitiies et concupiscentiis. Et, *psallite illi in psalterio decem chordarum* id est serviant membra vestra charitati, ubi tria et septem praecepta complen-tur, in quibus tota lex pendet et prophetae" (" 'Praise God on the harp,' that is, offer our bodies as a living sacrifice by mortifying the flesh with its vices and desires; and 'Praise him on the ten-stringed psaltery,' that is, that our members might serve in charity, when the three and seven precepts are ful-filled, on which hang all the law and the prophets").[60] The twelve *fenestrae* depicted below David/Christ's waist represent the twelve apostles, while the ten strings extending between the horizontal and vertical axes represent the five senses (on the viewer's left) and the five books of Moses (on the right), "by which the five human senses are governed" (per quos quinque sensus hominis reguntur). In both cases, by dispersing consecutive words and syllables across space, the image seems designed to make reading a visually assimilative process, one that integrates music, text, and image as the viewer's eyes move down or across the page.

As Mary Carruthers argues in *The Book of Memory*, "Every medieval diagram is an open-ended one . . . it is an invitation to elaborate and recompose, not a prescriptive, 'objective' schematic."[61] In the case of the diagram opening this manuscript of the Lombard's *Commentarium*, such recomposition is simultaneously verbal, visual, and, above all, musical. Like the harp in the *Speculum* miniatures, the slack strings of the *psalterium* invite the viewer to complete the typology and put it in motion by imagining the passion itself as a musical performance. Though David's calm countenance and fully clothed body ostensibly belie the agonies of the Crucifixion, the logic of the Lombard's prologue (which begins on the next folio) implies that the striking of David's harp is, precisely, the striking of the ten-stringed *psalterium* of Christ's body—and, by extension, the viewer's own. Ideally, when a relevant verse and its gloss are encountered within the manuscript, the image will be remembered, the suffering of Christ will be recalled, and the musicality of his bodily mortification will resonate internally as the text is perused and experienced. Even in "reading" the exegetical work that follows, the user of the Lombard's commentary, at least as it appears in this manuscript, participates through musicality in the Passion.

I emphasize the experiential aspect of certain strictly exegetical treatments of biblical music because this privileging of devotional experience characterizes to an even greater degree the many permutations of musical exegesis in the hands of religious poets, hagiographers, and visionaries of the later Middle Ages. Far from a stable, monolithic store of authoritative pronouncements, biblical exegesis was more open to appropriation and refashioning than the works of Ovid. Even the authoritative glosses of Augustine as compiled by the Lombard, Anselm, and others represented only a starting point; in many cases, the intentionality of the original glossator is entirely beside the point. The uses to which hagiographers and mystics of the thirteenth century put exegetical imagery for bodily musicality exemplify the same paradox that Caroline Walker Bynum, Karma Lochrie, and others have identified in medieval religious writing in general: even while castigated and condemned, the human body provides the indispensable ground and foundation of religious experience. The authoritative gloss of the *psalterium* or the *tympanum* as a symbol of *afflictio carnis*[62] encouraged religious writers both to elaborate the musical properties of the flesh they ostensibly spurned and to imagine the music of body as the quintessential expression of religious desire and agony.

There is a darker side to all of this, of course. As we shall see in Chapter 6, the ecclesiastical deployment of bodily violence played a crucial imaginative role in liturgical transmission (and in representations thereof). The musical body in pain is sometimes the body of the outsider—the heretic, the Jew, the unbeliever. While the biblical *cithara* or *lira* represents for many medieval writers a redemptive sign of Christ, the visionary Marguerite of Oingt figured these instruments producing eternal torture for the condemned: "The cauldron in which they will be trapped will be surrounded by horrible demons who will torment them as long as God lasts, in other words, until the end. Their food will be tears, pain, sighs, and gnashing of teeth. The cymbals and harps they will hear will be noisy tempests and penetrating rivers which will pierce them through their hearts."[63] Reminding us that melodious pain is not always salvific, Marguerite envisions musical instruments as an integral part of the punitive landscape of hell.

As does a late fourteenth-century illustrator of a manuscript of Dante's *Commedia*. As Virgil and the pilgrim visit the tenth *bolgia* in *Inferno* 30, they encounter among the imprisoned counterfeiters a certain Master Adam of Brescia:

> Io vidi un, fatto a guisa di lëuto,
> > pur ch'elli avesse avuta l'anguinaia
> > tronca da l'altro che l'uomo ha forcuto.
> La grave idropesì, che sì dispaia
> > le membra con l'omor che mal converte,
> > che 'l viso non risponde a la ventraia,
> faceva lui tener le labbra aperte
> > come l'etico fa, che per la sete
> > l'un verso 'l mento e l'altro in sù rinverte.

> [I saw one shaped like a lute, if only he had been cut short at the groin from the part where a man is forked. The heavy dropsy which, with its ill-digested humor, so unmates the members that the face does not answer to the paunch, made him hold his lips apart, like the hectic who, for thirst, curls the one lip toward his chin and the other upwards.][64]

Dante's simile is meant to capture the debilitating effects of dropsy upon the torso of the sinner, whose members are "unmated" and whose skin is

FIGURE 13   Falsifiers from Dante, *Inferno* 30 (Naples, Biblioteca Nazionale MS XII.C.4, fol. 26 ᵛ)

stretched so tightly that a permanent scowl is etched on his face. For the poet, Master Adam is *like* a lute.

For at least one of Dante's early readers, however, Adam of Brescia *is* a lute. A fourteenth-century illustrator of the *Inferno* took the poet at much more than his word, replacing Master Adam's entire torso with the *lëuto* described in the canto and graphically extending the punitive implications of the original image. In the lower margin of the twenty-sixth verso of MS XII.C.4 in the Biblioteca Nazionale in Naples (see Figure 13), the tuning-pegs emerging from Adam's neck practically beg to be turned by the viewer, tightening the strings running up and down his torso and thus transforming his frame into a kind of musical rack, an instrument of torture on which the condemned's body will be stretched and ultimately dismembered (or, in Dante's own terms, have his members "unmated").[65] Placing Master Adam side-by-side with the cannibalizing falsifier Gianni Schicchi, who sinks his teeth into the neck of Capocchio, the illustrator insists that music constitutes the punishment leaving the sinner in eternal pain—in Adam's own words, "the rigid justice that scourges me" (La rigida giustizia che mi fruga).[66] As we shall see, the marginal image looks forward brilliantly to the musical tortures inflicted upon the bodies of sinners in Hieronymous Bosch's *Garden of Earthly Delights*.

Little Drummers

Why is noise that is produced by striking or shaking so widely used
in order to communicate with the other world?

—RODNEY NEEDHAM[67]

Marie of Oignies did not die quietly. According to her hagiographer, Jacques de Vitry, the Beguine marked the approach of death in July of 1213 with one of the most vivid musical performances ever witnessed in the diocese of Liège. For three straight days and nights, Jacques records, Marie sang so loudly that her prior feared that those attending Mass the next day would be "scandalised by her incessant singing with such a piercing and subtle voice and think her a fool":

> God shook every tear from the eyes of His handmaid and filled her heart
> with exaltation and her lips with harmony [*modulatione*]. She began to sing
> in a high and clear voice and for three days and three nights she did not stop
> praising God and giving thanks. She rhythmically wove in sweet harmony
> the sweetest song [*dulcissimam cantilenam*] about God, the holy angels, the
> blessed Virgin, other saints, her friends and the Holy Scriptures.[68]

Jacques stresses above all Marie's role as a musical vessel, her subjection to the melodies with which God enlivens her. Indeed, to Marie herself "it seemed . . . that one of the seraphim was stretching his wings over her breast and by thus ministering and sweetly assisting her, she was inspired to sing without any difficulty."[69] Shaking tears from her eyes, filling her lips with harmony, and stretching an angel's wings across her breast, God transforms Marie's body into a resounding instrument of praise.

As the hour of her death approaches, Marie's music increases in intensity as it fills and exits her expiring body. Her blood flows ever more swiftly, her voice resounds ever more loudly:

The next morning our little drummer began to strum even higher and clearer music than usual [*tympanistria nostra altius et clarius solito incepit citharizare*]. That night an angel of the Lord had taken away all her hoarseness and put into her breast an unction of wondrous sweetness. Thus were her veins opened and her voice was renewed and for almost the whole day she did not cease from praising God and, although the doors were shut and everything blocked up, men heard a voice of great exaltation and harmonious modulation.[70]

Tympanistria nostra: though describing Marie's singing, Jacques signals his indebtedness to the same strand of exegetical imagery of percussive somatics we have seen in Peter Chrysologus's description of the Magdalene.[71] Indeed, in a twelfth-century example that suggestively anticipates the passage above, Honorius Augustodunensis glosses the phrase "Praise him with tympanum and chorus" (Laudate eum in tympano et choro) from Psalm 150 as an image of the state of human flesh after the resurrection: "The tympanum is made from dried and hardened skin, which signifies immutable flesh hardened against any corruption. Therefore praise God, because he has made your flesh, previously fragile, to be firm and because it will no longer be subject to corruption" (Tympanum fit ex corio exsiccato et firmato, quod significat carnem immutatam, ab omni corruptione firmatam. Inde laudate Deum, quod carnem vestram, prius fragilem, tanta firmitate immutavit, quod ultra nulli corruptioni subjacebit).[72] As a *tympanistria* herself, Marie is simultaneously a violent "drummer" in her own right and a devotional exemplar whose musicality manifests a promised triumph over death: "when her wedding day was close at hand, the handmaid of Christ (who had eaten nothing now for fifty-two days) began to sing the Alleluia in a sweet voice. . . . For almost the whole night she was as joyful and exultant as if she had been invited to a banquet."[73] In a sense, Marie *was* at a banquet, but instead of food she feasted on music, music that left her body empty and lifeless when she finally died: "When her tiny holy body was washed after death, it was found to be so small and shrivelled by her illness and fasting that her spine touched her belly and the bones of her back seemed to lie under the skin of her stomach as if under a thin linen cloth."[74] No longer stretched tightly like a drumhead and, in Honorius's words, "hardened against any corruption," Marie's skin now sags loosely against her bones, bereft of the music that had sustained her in her final hour.

Yet it would be wrong to see Jacques's musical somatics here as a reiteration of the aims and values of the canonized exegetical tradition to which
his university education exposed him.[75] Rather, his vivid representations of
Marie's musicality were part of a much broader hagiographical program
that radically transformed the significance for Christian life of the tropes he
appropriated. For Jacques, Marie's life was itself a kind of living, breathing,
resonating exegesis, a devotional performance that located religious authority precisely in her flesh and became nowhere more apparent than in the
musical spectacle she presented immediately before her death. In this sense,
the *vita* of Marie of Oignies represents one of the earliest and certainly one
of the most influential examples of a widespread tendency among late-
medieval *mulieres religiosae* and their biographers to cast the female body as
a spectacular site of musical suffering—a tradition that survives even into
the sixteenth century and the writings of the Golden Age visionary Mother
Juana de la Cruz (1481–1534), who, as Ronald Surtz has shown, frequently
described herself as "the Guitar of God" as a means of signaling the bodily
demands of mystical life.[76]

The female musical body in pain figures constantly in the Latin oeuvre
of Jacques's prolific contemporary, Thomas of Cantimpré, whose writings
demonstrate an enduring and multifaceted interest in the uniquely musical
character of human flesh.[77] Born near Brussels in 1201, Thomas became a
regular canon at sixteen and led a cloistered life at Cantimpré until 1232, at
which time he took vows as a Dominican at Louvain. His extant writings
include three saints' lives as well as a brief continuation of Jacques de Vitry's
vita of Marie[78]; the *Liber de natura rerum,* an encyclopedic treatise on
human anatomy and the natural world[79]; and the *Bonum universale de
apibus,* a lengthy collection of religious anecdotes and miracle stories many
of which centrally involve the musical body in pain.[80]

While for Jacques the most provocative musical sign of Marie's sanctity was the volume and continuity of her singing, Thomas's images of
musical beguines often suggest that their bodies actually contain music
within themselves: in a very real sense, music resides in the body *prior to*
performance and can be heard by others only when exuded in the throes of
devotional agony. The *vita* of Lutgard of Aywières, for example, recounts a
miraculous vision that Lutgard occasionally experienced during the singing
of Vespers:

It sometimes seemed to her (for, to be sure, Lutgard used to chant the verse
for the sake of devotion) that Christ, with the outward appearance of a lamb,
was positioning himself on her breast in such a manner that one foot was on
her right shoulder and the other on her left. He would place his mouth on
her mouth and by thus sucking would draw out from her breast the sweetness of a wondrous melody [*et sic sugendo de pectore illius mirabilis melodiae
suavitatem extraheret*]. Nor could anyone doubt that a divine miracle was
taking place in this chanting, for it was only at that verse alone that her
voice was heard to be measurelessly more filled with grace than usual and, in
like manner, so too were the hearts of all who heard her marvellously moved
to devotion.[81]

Unlike Jacques, Thomas locates the miraculousness of the beguine's music
in its *dissimilarity* to unaided singing. The music buried in the depths of
Lutgard's body somehow exceeds the *cantus* that emerges from her mouth
when she sings; bodily music—especially when "sucked" from the depths of
the human being—surpasses the religious force of conventional liturgical
song.

Though Thomas was undoubtedly familiar with the exegetical tradition that led Jacques to cast Marie of Oignies as a *tympanistria*, his vivid
depiction of Christ's sucking of melody from Lutgard's chest probably derives not from biblical commentary, but from a treatise on Christian anthropology in the tradition of Gregory of Nyssa's *De hominis opificio*. One of
the most important influences upon Thomas's hagiographical writings was
the work of William of St. Thierry, a twelfth-century Augustinian-*cum*-
Cistercian whose *Expositio super Cantica Canticorum* provided Thomas
with the language and structure of mystical growth that pervades his *vitae* of
religious women.[82] Thomas's musical imagery reflects the influence of another of William's writings, *De natura corporis et animae*, a religious and
scientific treatise on human nature that exemplifies what Chenu termed the
"wind" of inquisitiveness in the twelfth century "blowing over all of nature,
from flora and fauna to the shape given the human body, from erotic
impulses to the behavior patterns of corporate life."[83] William's first book is
a discussion of human anatomy and physiology, the second an explication
of the powers of the soul and its vivification of the body. The dynamism
William attributes to body in book 1 is typical of the Galenic tradition, from
which he does not depart in any consequential way. In book 2, however,

William achieves what Bernard McGinn has termed "a *rapprochement* between traditional Greek theological anthropology and some of the new trends of twelfth-century thought" emphasizing both the viability of nature and the integrity of the human person.[84] While the treatise thus represents a specifically twelfth-century effort to account for the role of body and soul in human identity, it is heavily indebted throughout to Gregory of Nyssa's *De hominis opificio* and indeed repeats many of its musical metaphors practically verbatim.[85]

For William, as for Gregory almost a millennium before him, soul is substantially separate from body yet shares in its pleasures, passions, and pains: "The soul is spiritual and its own substance. It is created by God. It is life-giving, rational and immortal, but changeable in regard to good and evil. It is said to be its own substance because no other spirit receives the flesh or body to share its sorrows and joys."[86] Like Gregory, too, William sees the soul's life-giving qualities and processes as beyond description, "wonderful and ineffable," and he paraphrases at length the Cappadocian's extended musical metaphor for the soul's vivification of body:

> In some way beyond the understanding of reason the intellectual soul approaches nature and, fitted into it and about it, is considered in so far as possible to be placed neither within nor enclosed by nature, nor outside and enclosing nature. Rather in a manner which cannot be expressed or understood, it is able to be completely permeated by nature and still effect its own operations. For the whole of the intellectual nature is not in any one part but in the whole. It is not located within, in the cavities of the body, nor is it forced out when one gets fat, or anything like that. For its purposes it uses the whole body as if it were a musical instrument [*veluti organum musicum totum corpus in suos creat effectus*]. One who knows how to play a musical instrument, when he finds a suitable instrument, plays well. But if the instrument is worn by rot or age or damaged by some accident, the player loses nothing of his art, but the instrument remains silent or produces poor sound. So it is with the intellectual soul. It takes possession of the whole instrument of nature, and touches each part with its intellectual operations as is its wont.[87]

Much like Augustine, William describes the "the harmony in the instrument of the human body" as immutable and eternal; like Gregory, however, he seems untroubled by the actual sounding presence of this music throughout the body. Even a body "worn by rot or age" can still be the musical instrument of the soul (if slightly out of tune). And the delicate music of body and soul is essential for the soul to make itself and its desires known: "When the intellectual soul touches the speech organs, like a plectrum, it expresses in speech its own interior motion. It is like a musician who by accident is without voice and yet wishes to make music. He displays his art through other voices, through pipes or harps [*per tibias siue lyras*]. So it is with the intellectual soul discovering various insights. Since it itself is incorporeal and has no speech of its own, it satisfies itself by expressing its thoughts through the bodily senses."[88]

Such an understanding of the musicality of the body/soul relationship similarly informs Thomas of Cantimpré's discussion of physiology in his *Liber de natura rerum*.[89] Completed in Paris before 1240, this voluminous treatise includes a lengthy treatment of human anatomy and gynecology, numerous chapters on herbs, gems, and animals, and an ethnographic excursus on the appearances and customs of foreigners.[90] In book 2, Thomas, drawing directly on William, envisions the human person as an equal compound of body and soul: "Person consists of flesh and soul and carries his goodness in both, by which he joys and exults."[91] Body and soul are inextricable and equally responsible for the happiness and well-being of person: "The goodness of soul is God with his abundance of sweetness. The goodness of flesh is the earth with its abundance of happiness."[92] While the book as a whole contains very little musical imagery, Thomas expresses the dynamic between soul and body in language that encapsulates William's much lengthier analogy: "For the body, because it is first created well-tempered and ordered, is like a musical instrument, for sweet music harmonizes in it and, drawn out, resonates, and when finished is expelled from the unused region" (Corpus autem quod prius integrum tanquam organum contemperatum et dispositum, ut melos musicum in se concineret et tractum resonaret, nunc confractum et inutile e regione iacet).[93] For Thomas, then, as for Gregory and William before him, the body contains music in a more than metaphorical sense; *musica* is itself a material substance that resonates throughout the body cavity.

Read through the *De natura rerum*, Thomas's vivid description of Christ's sucking of music from Lutgard's chest makes a perverse kind of sense: the Lamb of God is forcefully extracting from Lutgard's body a music that is already there from the beginning. In other words, the hagiographical performance that Lutgard is forced to undergo makes explicit the mysterious internal sonorities that Thomas found in the writings of William of St. Thierry. The organological treatment of the human person in Gregory of Nyssa's fourth-century *De hominis opificio* has come alive in the musical performance of a thirteenth-century beguine. Recalling the resonant bodies of Hildegard of Bingen, Thomas's conception of the music of Lutgard's saintly body appears entirely consistent with his own more naturalistic accounts of human physiology.

Like Jacques de Vitry, Thomas also personified through bodily miracle many of the biblical images of music that so captivated other medieval religious writers. In a number of the brief religious anecdotes in his *Bonum universale de apibus*, the exegetical inspiration for certain passages concerning musical performance is often transparent.[94] In a vivid account of miracles associated with preachers in book 2, Thomas begins by citing Leviticus 25:9 ("you shall send abroad the trumpet [*tubam*] throughout all your land"), which many glossators took as a statement of the rhetorical prowess of the Christian preacher.[95] For Thomas, however, the Levitical *tuba* was a literal vessel of musicality that came to life as a monk in the Low Countries:

> I saw such a trumpet, a monk in a region of Brabant, who, when he heard something of the eternal abundance and celestial joy, was ravished in the spirit, and while he was resting during the smallest hours of the night, his face shone brightly, and with closed eyes he emitted such great voices, that no musical song could be compared to the sweetness of his. And this sound was not produced by any inward articulation of the voice; rather, this harmony resonated, astonishingly, between his chest and his throat [*inter pectus et gutter harmonia illa mirabilis resonabat*].[96]

While Thomas reiterates the standard image of the preacher as trumpet, he does so not in order to emphasize the preacher's rhetorical persuasiveness, but to stress that the music the monk produces resonates from the body (*inter pectus et gutter* [sic])—indeed, that its particular beauty and miraculousness result precisely from its somatic point of origin. Elsewhere in the *Bonum universale*, Thomas writes of four monks who left Brabant for a nearby mountaintop to celebrate the Assumption of the Virgin. After covering their bare arms with dirt and prostrating themselves on the ground, the monks began to sing Vespers, at which point they were lifted from the ground and levitated until the next morning, "singing sweetly and devotedly" (*cantant simpliciter et devote*). Again, Thomas is careful to point out that their song came not from their mouths alone, but from the depths of their chests (*ab imo pectoras*), and was so beautiful that is was "impossible for us to describe or explain."[97]

Yet it was death and suffering that provoked Thomas to expound at most length on the musicality of holy persons. Relating the last words of a brother in a monastery at Bruges, Thomas sounds very much like Jacques recounting the death of Marie of Oignies:

> Early on the third day of the burdensome disease, the table was struck, and the brothers in the infirmary came running. With his brothers praying expectantly, the dying monk stretched with his hands pointed at a certain place, and, tears pouring from his eyes, he began to say in the sweetest song [*cantu lenissimo*]: "We shall see Jesus in Galilee, just as he predicted to us. Alleluia." Having said this, he died immediately.[98]

Here the monk's performance begins only after the table on which he rests has been "struck" (*percussa*) by an unnamed agent. Like Marie of Oignies, the monk is physically sustained by musical performance even while in the grips of terminal illness; at the moment of death, as the monk's soul leaves his body, music infuses him with one last burst of energy.[99]

Certainly the most spectacular musical body to be found in Thomas's extant oeuvre is that of Christina Mirabilis, whose *vita* has become something of a *cause célèbre* among scholars of medieval female sanctity due to the particularly extreme asceticism it describes. Though Christina was said to have performed a number of graphic bodily miracles—escaping fires, ovens, and boiling water unscathed; living in a river for six days; and feeding herself on oils produced by her own breasts—Thomas was particularly taken with the violent character of her musicality, an account of which I quote at length:

> She later became very familiar with the nuns of St. Catherine's who lived outside the town of St. Trond. Sometimes while she was sitting with them, she would speak of Christ and suddenly and unexpectedly she would be ravished in the spirit and her body would roll and whirl around like a hoop played with by boys [*trochus ludentem puerorum*]. She whirled around with such extreme violence that the individual limbs of her body could not be distinguished. When she had whirled around for a long time in this manner, it

seemed as if she became weakened by the violence of the rolling and all her limbs grew quiet. Then a wondrous harmony sounded between her throat and her breast which no mortal man could understand, nor could it be imitated by any artificial instrument. Her song had not only the pliancy and tones of music [*flexibilitatem musicae et tonos*] but also the words of the melody—if thus I might call them—sounded together incomprehensibly. The voice or spiritual breath, however, did not come out of her mouth or nose, but a harmony of the angelic voice resounded only from between her breast and throat [*inter guttur et pectus eius*].[100]

As in his descriptions of musical monks in the *Bonum universale*, Thomas takes care to point out that the beguine's angelic melody emerges not from her mouth or nose, but from a part of the body unassociated with music-making yet paradoxically able to produce a musical "language" of its own. In Christina's case, the musical performance of asceticism necessitates bodily violence: Christina must be "ravished" (*rapiebatur*) in the spirit and whirled around repeatedly before her body can produce the music that testifies to her sanctity.

When Thomas returns to Christina's musicality a bit later and recounts her habit of sneaking into the church at Looz after Matins, he initially describes her singing as "so marvellous to hear that it surpassed the music of all instruments and the voices of all mortals." Despite its almost divine nature, however, this music pales in comparison to the bodily sonorities that Christina produced at St. Catherine's: "Nevertheless this song was less sweet and much unequal to the sweet song of the harmony which sounded incomparably from between her throat and breast and which surpassed human understanding. This song, I say, was in Latin and wondrously adorned with harmonious oratorical devices."[101] Even a rhetorical tour-de-force in the father tongue cannot compare to the musical miracle already described.

Near the end of the *vita*, Christina happily awaits her own death by fondling and kissing her body in anticipation of rejoining it at the resurrection. Once again, Thomas of Cantimpré recalls the holy woman's resonant musicality even as she prepares to leave the body that performed it:

Then doubling her kisses, she said, "Now, O best and sweetest body, endure patiently. Now is an end of your hardship, now you will rest in the dust and will sleep for a little and then, at last, when the trumpet blows, you will rise again purified of all corruptibility and you will be joined in eternal happiness with the soul you have had as a companion in the present sadness." Thus gentling her body with words and kisses for an hour, she then uttered that wondrous song which we have already described [*jubilum, quem praediximus, mirabilem emittebat*] and was inwardly filled with such joy that one would have believed that her exterior body would burst [*rumpi exterius in corpore*].[102]

The *jubilus* Thomas has "already described," the pectoral resonance of Christina's body after her violent seizure, has now become a musical harbinger of the resurrection, prefiguring the last *tuba* that will unite Christina's disembodied soul with the body she loves and caresses in her present life. Even at the end, however, the song retains its violent character as it takes over her "exterior body" and threatens to shatter it from within.

"Philomena praevia" and the Musical Body of Christ

If Thomas's oeuvre affords a perspective upon musics produced by specifically human bodies, the text to which I now turn focuses on the musicality of the suffering body of Christ in the tradition of *Die Erlösung* and the *Speculum humanae salvationis*. Written in the mid-thirteenth century by John Pecham, a Paris-educated Franciscan and future archbishop of Canterbury,[103] "Philomena praevia" is a 280-line Latin devotional poem that represents the life and death of Christ through the desiring gaze and empathetic song of a nightingale.[104] Described early on in the poem as a figure of the human soul, the nightingale witnesses and imitates the physical and emotional torments of the Passion, dies just as Christ speaks the *Consummatum est*, and, wrapped in the *sponsi brachia*, weds herself eternally to him. Surviving in numerous manuscripts, "Philomena praevia" was translated into French shortly after its original composition and into Middle English (perhaps by John Lydgate) in the early fifteenth century.[105]

The few scholars who have treated this rich devotional text have located it primarily within the medieval nightingale tradition, the poetic and rhetorical elaborations of the nightingale that inform numerous naturalistic, religious, and philosophical writings from antiquity through the Renaissance.[106] In associating the nightingale's song with both the Incarnation and the Passion, Pecham followed a long tradition of investing the nightingale's music with a mysterious ability to negotiate the boundary between life and death, whether as a sonorous envelope supporting gestation or a provocation to violence. Yet the nightingale also served medieval writers as a means of exploring the intimacy between musical production and the flesh. Pliny, the great Roman natural historian, argued that nightingales "compete with one another" in "animated rivalry," "the loser often end[ing] her life by dying, her breath giving out before her song [*spiritu prius deficiente quam cantu*]."[107] Ambrose invests the same *cantus* with an animistic and life-giving potential: "so it seems to me this is her chief intention, to be able as much by sweet notes, as by the warmth of the body, to hatch the eggs which she warms."[108] And in the Carolingian beast-epic *Ecbasis Captivi*, a nightingale sings a polyphonic duet with a blackbird in praise of the Passion, their music registering Christ's agonies on the Cross:

> Concentu parili memoratur passio Christi.
> Passer uterque deum cesum flet verbere Iesum,
> Exanimis factus, claudens spiramina flatus;
> Commutat vocem, dum turbant tristia laudem,
> Organa divertit, dum Christi vulnera plangit,
> Solvitur in luctum recolens dominum crucifixum.
>
> [In unison the passion of Christ is sung. Each bird mourns the Lord Jesus
> flogged with the lash; each is near to death, stopping the flow of its breath;
> they alter their voices as sorrows disrupt their praise; they divide their song as
> they strike the wounds of Christ; recounting the crucifixion of the Lord, they
> are dissolved in grief.][109]

Here the suffering of Christ both inspires the song and determines its harmonic and rhythmic character: the birds' voices are initially in unison (*Concentu*) but immediately diverge into polyphonic harmony (*Organa divertit*) as they "strike" (*plangit*) the wounds of the *corpus Christi*. The effect of musical pathos heightens significantly in the final two lines through an unmistakable allusion to Job 30:31: "My harp is turned to mourning, and my instrument to the voice of the weeping" (Versa est in luctum cithara mea et organum meum in vocem flentium). While this biblical verse provoked Gregory the Great in his influential *Moralia* to expound upon the mortification of the body among *sancti viri* and compare the slack strings of a disused *cithara* to the weakness of undisciplined flesh,[110] for the *Ecbasis Captivi* author the same verse serves to create an implicit musical typology overlaying the sufferings of Job with the tortures of the Passion.

The nightingale's musicality retains similar associations with desire, pain, and death in the European literary traditions that immediately preceded the writing of "Philomena praevia." In one of the Cambridge Songs, a collection of Latin lyrics copied at the abbey of St. Augustine in Canterbury in the eleventh century, the speaker virtually compels the nightingale to sing without ceasing: "I don't want, I don't want you to rest in the leisure times. Instead, I want you to produce happy harmonies on your little tongue, so that for the praise of it you will be remembered in the palaces of kings" (Nolo, nolo ut quiescas temporis ad otia,/Sed ut letos des concentus tua uolo ligula,/Cuius laude memoreris in regum palatia).[111] In her lai *Laüstic*, Marie de France tells the tale of an unfaithful wife whose jealous husband, thinking her charmed by the music of a nightingale, traps the bird, breaks its neck, and hurls its body at his wife. Lamenting the nightingale's death, the wife wraps its corpse "in a piece of samite, embroidered in gold and writing," and sends it to her lover, who entombs it in a reliquary-like casket and "carrie[s] it with him always."[112] Alexander Neckham's *De naturis rerum* describes a knight who, "filled with excessive jealousy" by his wife's seeming unfaithfulness and supposing the nightingale to be responsible, orders the bird "to be drawn and quartered by four horses because, as he asserted, she so softened the spirit of his wife that she compelled her to illicit love."[113]

This short catalog of examples demonstrates the nightingale's tenacity as a vibrant medieval icon of music, suffering, and death within both secular poetry and Latin religious literature, two traditions that converge with particular clarity in Pecham's "Philomena praevia." In fact, I argue, the poem represents a subtle juxtaposition of two distinct and seemingly incompatible narrative sources—both of which would have been familiar to Pecham's latinate readers—and purposefully exploits rather than suppresses the ambiguities this juxtaposition creates. At the center of Pecham's musical rendering of the Crucifixion is an originary scene of sexual violence that constitutes a crucial component of the poem's passionate musicality.

"Philomena praevia" begins with a second-person address to the nightingale, whom the speaker asks to deliver a message of love to an unnamed *amicus*:

Philomena praevia temporis amoeni,
Quae recessum nuntias imbris atque coeni,
Dum mulcescis animos tuo cantu leni,
Ave prudentissima, ad me, quaeso, veni.

Veni, veni, mittam te quo non possum ire,
Ut amicum valeas cantu delinire,
Tollens eius tristia voce dulcis lyrae,
Quem heu modo nescio verbis convenire.

Ergo pia suppleas meum imperfectum
Salutando dulciter unicum dilectum,
Eique denunties qualiter affectum
Sit cor meum iugiter eius ad aspectum.

[Philomena, herald of pleasant times, who announces the retreat of storm
and mud while soothing souls with your gentle song, hail, most prudent one!
Come to me, I beg!/Come, come, that I may send you where I cannot go,
that you might soothe my friend—whom, alas!, I know not how to address
with words—with song, relieving his sorrow with the voice of your sweet
lyre./Thus, gentle one, may you make up for my imperfection by sweetly
greeting the loved one, and declare to him the nature of my desire: that my
heart might behold him forever.] (1–12)

Invoking a trope found frequently in the literature of *fin'amor*, Pecham
represents the nightingale as the go-between from the speaker/writer to the
beloved. Compensating for the speaker's voicelessness, an inability to express "with words" the extent of longing, the nightingale's *dulcis lyrae*, or
"sweet lyre," must vocalize in music the desire that initiates the poem. Like
Thomas of Cantimpré, Pecham thus attributes an extralinguistic power to
musical sonority, investing it with a unique ability to contain, channel, and
focus both the erotic love and the bodily violence that his poem elaborates.

Yet the lines immediately raise a question regarding the specific nature
of this desire by leaving the gender of the speaker vague. While the object of
the speaker's desire and the nightingale's intended message is clearly masculine—an *amicus*—there is nothing to indicate that the speaker is feminine. That this indeterminacy represented an unacceptable erotic ambiguity for some of Pecham's medieval readers can be seen in the treatment of the
third stanza by the poem's French translator, who pointedly endowed the

speaker with a woman's voice by inserting an extra phrase: "Go blithely, sweet bird, I pray,/Take him greetings from me, *his lady love*, and tell him that my joy, my happiness and my life all consist in my desire to serve him with all my heart" (Va tos légierement, doulz oysel, je te prie,/Salue moy celuy à qui je *suy amie*,/Et ly dis que ma joye, mon soulas, et ma vye/Est quant à luy servir mon coeur si s'estudye).[114] The Latin original, by contrast, exploits this ambiguity throughout, allowing for a wide range of affective musical exchanges between the speaker, the reader, the nightingale, and, as the eleventh stanza makes clear, the body of Christ, the object of the nightingale's musical veneration: "Behold, most desirous one, you have briefly heard the deeds of this bird; but if you remember, we have already noted that these songs mysteriously accord with the law of Jesus Christ" (Ecce, dilectissime, breviter audisti/Factum huius volucris, sed si meministi,/Diximus iam primitus, quia cantus isti/Mystice conveniunt legi Iesu Christi) (41–44).

Enlisting the reader's memory to keep his poem's typology in mind, Pecham deploys the secular conventions of courtly love in order to forge a kind of musical *imitatio Christi*[115]: "Igitur, carissime, audi nunc attente,/Nam si cantus volucris huius serves mente,/Eius imitatio, spiritu docente,/Te coelestem musicum faciet repente" (Thus, most beloved one, now listen carefully: for if you attend to this bird's song with your mind, the imitation of it, with a receptive spirit, will suddenly make you a heavenly *musicus*) (17–20). The nightingale's song is itself the pain and violence that Christ endures; like the nightingale, "joying in its pain" (*gaudens in pressura*) at the approach of death, the Christian soul sings "various songs" (*diversisque cantibus*) that register in music the graphic violence anticipated in the Passion: "Let the violent approach, that they might fasten this miserable one to your cross, Christ; for such a death will be sweet to me, if in dying I thus hold you in an eternal embrace" (Veniant lanistae,/Qui affigant miseram cruci tuae, Christe;/Erit enim exitus mihi dulcis iste,/Sic amplector moriens propriis ulnis te) (613–16).

Even as its soteriological narrative moves away from the discourse of courtly love and desire characterizing the opening stanzas, the poem retains a distinct patina of secular eroticism through what I would suggest is a series of direct allusions to Ovid's account of the legend of Philomel in the fifth book of the *Metamorphoses*. The language of Ovidian desire and violence permeates "Philomena praevia," suggesting that the confluence of music and bodily violence constructed in the poem be read at least in part through the erotics of Pecham's source narrative.[116] In Ovid's well-known account, the Athenian sisters Philomel and Procne are separated by the latter's marriage to Tereus, king of Thrace. Acquiescing in Procne's desire to be reunited with her sister after five years apart, Tereus sails to Athens intending to bear Philomel home with him; smitten with desire for his sister-in-law, however, Tereus tricks Philomel into a secluded hut, where he rapes her, imprisons her, and tears out her tongue to keep her from revealing the crime:

> ille indignantem et nomen patris usque vocantem
> luctantemque loqui conprensam forcipe linguam
> abstulit ense fero. radix micat ultima linguae,
> ipsa iacet terraeque tremens inmurmurat atrae,
> utque salire solet mutilatae cauda coubrae,
> palpitat et moriens dominae vestigia quaerit.

> [He seized her tongue with pincers, as it protested against the outrage, calling ever on the name of her father and struggling to speak, and cut it off with his merciless blade. The mangled root quivers, while the severed tongue lies trembling on the earth, faintly murmuring; and, as the severed tail of a mangled snake is wont to writhe, it palpitates convulsively, and with its last dying movement it seeks its mistress's feet.][117]

After Tereus has pulled it out by its roots, Philomel's tongue assumes a life of its own; though severed and mangled, the organ lies "trembling" (*tremens*) on the ground, murmuring incoherently as it attempts to rejoin the body from which it has been separated. Like many tales in the *Metamorphoses*, the episode dramatizes the transformative consequences of violent desire upon the bodies of its victims.

Ovid's image of Philomel's palpitating tongue, a horrifying symbol of heterosexual rape in the original account, reappears in the most graphically violent scene in "Philomena praevia." Rather than a sexual rape, the particular narrative into which Pecham interpolates the image is the story of the passion as manifested in the daily hours, the *opus Dei* that culminates in the nightingale's Christlike death:

> Cantilenis dulcibus praeviat auroram,
> Sed cum dies rutilat, circa primam horam,

Elevat praedulcius vocem insonoram,
In cantando nesciens pausam sive moram.

Circa vero tertiam quasi modum nescit,
Quia semper gaudium cordis eius crescit,
Vere guttur rumpitur, sic vox invalescit,
Et quo cantat altius, plus et inardescit.

Sed cum in meridie sol est in fervore,
Tunc dirumpit viscera nimio clamore.
"Oci, oci" clamitat illo suo more,
Sicque sensu deficit cantus prae labore.

Sic quassato organo huius Philomenae,
Rostro tamen palpitans fit exsanguinis pene,
Sed ad nonam veniens moritur iam plene,
Cum totius corporis dirumpuntur venae.

[It greets early morning with sweet songs, but when day begins, around the
hour of prime, its resounding voice grows sweeter still, knowing neither
pause nor delay in its singing./Around terce it sings in an unknown mode,
for its heart's joy grows always greater, until its throat almost bursts as its
voice grows stronger; the higher it sings, the more it burns./But when at
midday the sun is at its hottest, its innards burst with its excessive cry. "Kill,
kill!" it cries through its will, and thus the song loses its sense from the
toil./Thus, with the nightingale's instrument shattered, the palpitating beak
nearly drained of blood; but approaching None it soon fully dies, every vein
in its body burst.] (25–40)

Like Philomel's tongue, which "palpitates" (*palpitat*) as it attempts to rejoin its owner, the nightingale's "palpitating beak" (*Rostro . . . palpitans*)
functions as a synecdoche for the more generalized violence that has sustained and silenced its musical *imitatio*. Both Ovid and Pecham imagine
the violent curtailment of oral discourse as a metonym for death: Philomel's
tongue lies "dying" (*moriens*) on the ground just as the nightingale's beak
vibrates as the bird expires (*moritur*). Like Lutgard of Aywières, the nightingale is inherently musical, a body that contains music within its "innards"
(*viscera*); unlike the beguine's, however, the nightingale's song emerges
from its body not in an effortless surrender to the sucking of a lamb, but
through a graphically violent sequence of musical tortures that shatters its

veins and organs and leaves its body as mangled and bereft of speech as Philomel's after her victimization by Tereus.

The poem's Ovidian subtext can also be discerned in the imagery it deploys to represent the nightingale's own narrative acts. After noting that the bird's song "mysteriously accords with the law of Christ" (Mystice conveniunt legi Iesu Christi) (44), Pecham glosses it further as the very fabric of the Passion:

> Restat, ut intelligo, esse Philomenam
> Animam virtutibus et amore plenam,
> Quae, dum mente peragrat patriam amoenam,
> Satis delectabilem texit cantilenam.
>
> Ad augmentum etenim suae sanctae spei,
> Quaedam dies mystica demonstratur ei;
> Porro beneficia, quae de manu Dei
> Homo consecutus est, sunt horae diei.
>
> [You must know, as I know, that the nightingale is the soul, full of virtues and love, which, when it journeys in the mind to its happy fatherland, weaves together quite pleasing songs./And indeed, that it might increase its saintly hope, a certain mystical day is shown to it; further favors which man obtains by the hand of God are the hours of the day.] (45–52)

For Pecham, the nightingale's song is a "weaving" of events into a musical narrative that figuratively sutures the human soul into the tortures of the Passion. In a famous scene from the *Metamorphoses*, Ovid had used the same image to depict the imprisoned Philomel narrating her rape on a cloth for her sister to read: "But grief has sharp wits, and in trouble cunning comes. She hangs a Thracian web on her loom, and skilfully *weaving* purple signs on a white background, she thus tells the story of her wrongs" (grande doloris/ingenium est, miserisque venit sollertia rebus:/stamina barbarica suspendit callida tela/purpureasque notas filis *intexuit* albis,/indicium sceleris).[118] While for Ovid such "weaving" allows Philomel to regain the voice Tereus has taken from her and, ultimately, to unite with her sister in redressing a wrong, for Pecham weaving invites both nightingale and reader to participate in the devotional violence of the Crucifixion. A bit later in the poem, though, Pecham reverses the image, implying that even as the poem's *written* narrative proceeds, the musicality of the nightingale/soul becomes the vehicle of Christ's suffering: "Therefore, unravelling thus the infancy of Christ, singing vigorously the song of Prime, it passes to Terce, recalling how Christ suffered in teaching man" (Ergo sic infantiam Christi *retexendo,*/Horae primae canticum strenue canendo,/Transitum ad tertiam facit recolendo/Quantum Christus passus est, homines docendo) (133–36).

The Ovidian subtext of "Philomena praevia" points to a strong representational and experiential bond between the rape of Philomel and the Crucifixion of Christ, a proximity between sexual violence and *imitatio Christi* fundamental to the devotional experience the text seeks to instill. Though the nightingale stands in for the human *anima*, the feminine soul, the crucified body that the bird's empathetic song imitates is of course male, the *corpus Christi*. Pecham's analogy between Christ and Philomel nonetheless reflects a broader tendency among medieval devotional writers and artists to represent Christ's body as feminine or even as female, a tradition that includes twelfth-century Cistercian images of "Jesus as mother," depictions in moralized Bibles of Christ giving birth to the Church, and representations of the wound in Christ's side as a breast.[119] In "Philomena praevia," however, the feminization of Christ's body stresses not simply his maternal qualities, but his sexual victimization: like Philomel in her Ovidian incarnation, Christ is, in a sense, a victim of *raptus*, of rape. Pecham's clear allusions to Ovid locate a figurative sexual violence at the heart of Franciscan devotional practice, violence that the reader is enjoined both to commit as the viewer of Christ's suffering body and to experience as his compassionate imitator.[120] Simultaneously the reader and Christ, the nightingale mourns her Ovidian rape even as she invites Pecham's readers to experience it as they experience the Passion: as a "weaving" of "desirous melody" into mystical communion. As the discursive medium that oscillates between religious text and erotic subtext, music embodies both the sexual violation of Philomel and the corporeal suffering of Christ.

While Pecham's Ovidian erudition evokes the violent erotics of the Crucifixion, the poem's other debt is to a certain strand of liturgical commentary that equated the life and Passion of Christ with the ritual and rhythm of the liturgy. Two twelfth-century works in particular anticipate the confluence of music and violence in "Philomena praevia": the anonymous *Speculum ecclesiae* (not Edmund of Canterbury's, but a Victorine work once attributed to Hugh of St. Victor) and the *Gemma animae* of Honorius Augustodunensis. Though the influence of liturgical commentary has been neglected in studies of Pecham's poem, it merits close attention for the light it sheds on the particular spiritual and practical significance the graphic musicality of "Philomena praevia" may have held for its initial medieval audience.

In the broadest sense, liturgical commentary was devoted, in Margot Fassler's words, "to recreat[ing] the events of salvation history within the liturgy" through a minutely detailed exegesis of the individual texts, movements, and objects that constituted a given Mass or Office performance.[121] In Honorius's *Gemma animae*, the introit to the Mass signifies Christ's miraculous entry into the world through the Incarnation, the *oratio* his reconciliation with humanity, and the period of *silentia* following the Offertory his sojourn in Jerusalem before the Crucifixion.[122] Honorius interprets the singing liturgical choir as a Christianized revision of the heathens, who consciously symbolized through "the gesticulation of the body the movement of the constellations."[123] For the author of the *Speculum ecclesiae*, the fragrant *thuribulum* held aloft by the priest figures "the heart of man, the fire of charity, the eloquence of desire, which smells sweetly to God and burns with the fire of divine love" (Thuribulum est cor hominis, ignis charitas, incensum oratio, quae suaviter Deo redolet cum per ignem divini flagrescit amoris).[124] In a passage with particular bearing on "Philomena praevia," Honorius parallels Christ's musical performance on the Cross with the priest's performance of the liturgy: "In spreading his hands, [the celebrant] signifies Christ stretched on the Cross. In singing the preface, he imitates Christ's cries while hanging on the Cross. For he sang ten psalms— namely, from *Deus meus respice* through *In manus tuas commendo spiritum meum*—and thus he died" (Per manuum expansionem, designat Christi in cruce extensionem. Per cantum praefationis, exprimit clamorem Christi in cruce pendentis. Decem namque psalmos, scilicet a Deus meus respice usque In manus tuas commendo spiritum meum cantavit, et sic exspiravit).[125] Like the author and illuminators of the *Speculum humanae salvationis*, Honorius loads enormous spiritual significance into the music that Christ emitted while in pain and dying on the Cross, casting it as a prefigurement of the music performed daily and weekly in the liturgy—the same music rung upon the body of Pecham's nightingale, whose own dying moans echo those of Christ.

While Honorius's focus throughout the *Gemma animae* is on the Mass, the third chapter of the *Speculum ecclesiae* explicates in detail the canonical hours, which the author relates to Ezra's teaching of the Israelites to praise God four times in the night and four times during the day: "Thus, the Holy Fathers delegated by precept eight hours for the praising of God: midnight, early morning, prime, tierce, sext, none, vespers, and compline. For it is fitting that man, who bears a body made from four elements [*qui corpus gerit ex quatuor elementis*], should give enough of himself in a natural day to please God—four times in regard to the night, and four in regard to the day."[126] The humoral composition of the body naturally corresponds to the daily rhythm of the liturgy, a somatic framework that underlies all of the treatise's images of liturgical music. Five psalms are sung every day at Prime in order to fortify the five senses, while the melismas (*pneumae*) concluding Office antiphons signify an inexpressible desire for God: "The *pneuma* at the end bespeaks joy ineffably. After the psalms and antiphons is exclaimed the Verse, with a high voice for the excitement of souls [*ad excitandos animos*]."[127] Most important, each part of the day embodies both a stage in salvation history (the middle of the night is the virgin birth, Matins Christ's earthly life, Prime the proclamation of his resurrection, Terce the Holy Spirit's inspiration of the apostles, Sext the Crucifixion, None the *Consummatum est*, Vespers the Second Coming, and Compline the Day of Judgment) and an era of human existence: Prime represents the period separating Abraham and Moses, while Sext symbolizes the centuries between David and the nativity of Christ. None is both the *hora mori Christi* and the expulsion of Adam and Eve from Eden.[128]

In sum, the *Speculum ecclesiae* propounds the notion that in its quotidian performance of the liturgy—in music, gesture, and silence—the Christian clergy reenacts simultaneously the history of human existence as well as the life, suffering, and death of Christ, a daily and cyclical *imitatio Christi* that Pecham's "Philomena praevia" locates in the nightingale's musical communion with both Christ and the poem's readers. For Pecham, the focus of liturgical devotion is the daily Office; the liturgical imagery in "Philomena praevia" embodies both the ages of the world and the life of Christ, which the poem conflates into a single soteriological narrative:

Mane vel diliculum hominis est status,
In quo mirabiliter homo est creatus;

Hora prima, quando est Deus incarnatus;
Tertiam dic spatium sui incolatus.

Sextam, cum a perfidis voluit ligari,
Trahi, caedi, conspui, dire cruciari,
Crucifigi, denique clavis terebrari,
Caputque sanctissimum spinis coronari.

Nonam dic, cum moritur, quando consummatus
Cursus est certaminis, quando superatus
Est omnino zabulus et hinc conturbatus,
Vespera, cum Christus est sepulturae datus.

[For Matins signifies the beginning of mankind, when man was miraculously
created; the hour of Prime, when God was incarnated; and Terce, the period
of his habitation./Sext, when he desired by the faithless to be bound,
dragged, beaten, spat upon, stretched on the cross and tortured, crucified, and finally pierced with nails, his holiest head crowned with thorns./
None, when he died, when his task was done, when the devil was completely
defeated and hence ruined; Vespers, when Christ was placed in the tomb.]
(53–64)

Every day that the reader sings the Office constitutes a reliving of Christ's
progress from birth to death, a musical and textual reenactment of his
salvational existence. Heightening the musical effect of these stanzas is the
performative character of Pecham's poetics in his prolonged description of
Sext: a string of passive infinitives (*ligari, trahi, caedi, conspui, cruciari,
crucifigi*) replicates in the meter the violent rhetorical and physical blows
rung upon Christ's body during the scourging (much like the poundings of
the hammer in the *Speculum humanae salvationis*). As it contemplates the
mystical significance of the liturgical day, the nightingale/soul desires to
participate in the Passion through the music of its body, "raising the instrument of its heart and beginning its song in the early morning" (cordis
organa sursum elevando/Suum a diluculo cantum inchoando) (69–70) and
continuing until it has died in Christ's arms.

Pecham's poetic response to the Christological dimensions of liturgy
was part of a widespread infusion of liturgical commentary into a variety of
devotional genres throughout the thirteenth century. The writings of the
nuns of Helfta (as we shall see in a moment) are based fundamentally on the

formulas and conventions of works such as the *Speculum ecclesiae*. Within the sphere of Franciscan spirituality, the later chapters of the influential *Meditations on the Life of Christ* are headed by rubrics based on the Office hours that correspond quite closely to Pecham's presentation of the passion narrative.[129] Conversely, as "Philomena praevia" demonstrates, the nature and purpose of liturgical commentary was itself transformed by the increasingly corporeal character of devotional practice in the thirteenth century, moving from a distanced, authoritative mode of exegesis to the center of affective piety. This shift can also be perceived in a thirteenth-century Austrian manuscript of the *Speculum ecclesiae*, in which a cruciform miniature of David and the *psalterium* appears in the midst of the treatise's discussion of the spiritual significance of psalmody (see Figure 14).[130] Remarkably similar to the frontispiece to Peter Lombard's Psalm commentary discussed above, this illumination uses the David/Christ typology to literalize the treatise's glosses of actual liturgical music. Like Pecham's poem, the image responds to earlier liturgical commentary by making the imagined production of music from the body of Christ into a distinctly "aural" component of a reading experience.

Finally, by representing liturgical spirituality as integral to the particular devotional experience it invites, "Philomena praevia" reflects certain broad transformations within the Franciscan order during the middle third of the thirteenth century. Most scholars agree that the poem dates from early in Pecham's career: certainly before he became embroiled in the public disputes with William of St. Amour, Gerard of Abbeville, and Nicholas of Lisieux over the worthiness of the mendicant orders, and perhaps soon after he joined the Franciscan order around 1250.[131] Pecham's later interventions in high-level ecclesiastical politics as the archbishop of Canterbury are well known; his Constitutions were particularly influential (shaping, for example, the theology of Thoresby's *Lay Folks' Cathechism*).[132] While "Philomena praevia" seems far removed from such political contexts, the poem's overriding concern with liturgy was clearly part of a mid-thirteenth-century ideological program aimed at the wholesale clericalization of the Franciscan Order, a process that culminated in the Constitutions of Narbonne, compiled by Bonaventure in 1260 and approved by the Franciscan general chapter the same year.[133] The Franciscan who was more responsible than anyone else for this initiative was the Englishman Haymo of Feversham, whose term as minister general (1240–44) was characterized by a general

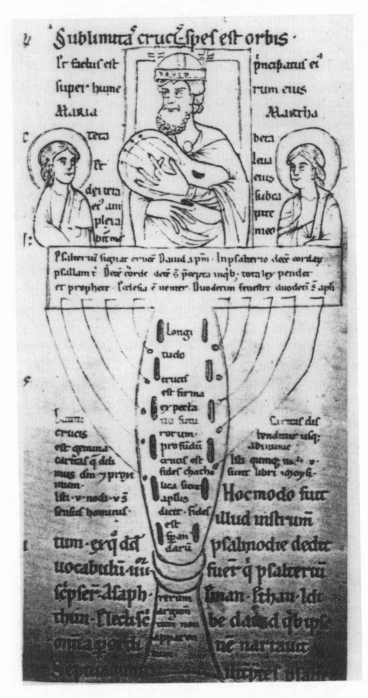

FIGURE 14   David miniature from *Speculum ecclesiae* (Lavanttal, St. Paul im Lavanttal, Stiftsbibliothek MS 45/3, fol. 164 ʳ)

hostility to lay friars (who were thereafter prohibited from becoming supe-
riors) and the imposition of strict limitations on entry into the Order by
those intending to eschew ordination.[134]

One of the more notable results of the Franciscan trend toward clericalization was what Lawrence Landini terms "the Order's preoccupation
with liturgy" through the middle decades of the thirteenth century, during
which a widespread effort at liturgical reform, spearheaded by Haymo himself, sought to instill the desire among friars to learn and perform the liturgy
as well and as often as the nonmendicant orders.[135] Written and circulated
in the midst of such a reform environment, "Philomena praevia" would
have served its aims tacitly but effectively, compelling its readers to absorb
the Christian significance of the Office while participating themselves in
the violent music of the Crucifixion. In one of the poem's final stanzas, the
nightingale's death provokes Pecham to point out the appropriate mass to
commemorate its sacrifice: "We do not sing *Requiem* for such a soul, but the
Gaudeamus mass; for if we seek God's mercy for a martyr, as the law says, we
denigrate a saint" (requiem pro anima tali non cantamus/Immo est intro-
itus missae Gaudeamus,/Quia si pro martyre Deum exoramus,/Ut de-
cretum loquitur, sancto derogamus) (269–72). Here again the poem rein-
forces the reader's knowledge of liturgy even as it interprets it anew.

The liturgical thrust of "Philomena praevia" seems as well to have
influenced its physical presentation in some of its earliest manuscripts: in
one copy of the poem (Cambridge, University Library Ee.vi.6, fols. 56–
62v), the scribe who copied it drew red flags in the margins at the appropriate stanzas and filled them in with phrases such as *hora prima* and *hora
tertia*, making the daily rhythms of the Office hours an explicit component
of the reader's experience of the poem. At the same time, the stark visual
division of the poem into eight liturgical units may well be a mnemonic
device intended to help friars bear the poem's musical message in mind
while preparing for sermonizing to the public, which Pecham considered a
crucial duty of the Franciscan Order throughout his career.[136]

The convergence of sexual violence and liturgical devotion in Pecham's
"Philomena praevia" thus performs a double function. On the one hand,
the poem draws on the literary memories of its latinate readers to recreate
the poetics of passion meditation as a kind of "musical rape" of the body of
Christ. Using a violently eroticized sequence of Ovidian images, Pecham
transfers the focus of sexual violence from the victimized body of Philomel

to the crucified musical body of Christ. And the poem performs this re-fashioning of music, passion, and sexual violence in the service of liturgical propaganda. The daily singing of the Hours establishes liturgical perfor-mance as the musical time and place of a generalized erotic violence against the *corpus Christi*, a musical body that hangs in the poem as a somatic inducement to the painful pleasures of liturgical participation.

The Nuns of Helfta and the Somatics of Liturgy

In the summer of 1294, in the course of a continuing struggle against Duke Albert of Austria and his sons, King Adolf of Nassau occupied the Thuringian countryside surrounding the village of Eisleben.[137] The conflict between Adolf and Albert was responsible for a great deal of physical devas-tation in Thuringia and Saxony throughout the final decade of the thir-teenth century, including the burning and looting of towns, the sacking of churches, and the pillaging of monasteries. One religious house particularly vulnerable to this invasion by virtue of its rural isolation was the monastery of St. Mary's at Helfta, an autonomous convent founded in 1229 and living under Cistercian rule. Though unaffiliated with the Cistercians in any official sense (the General Chapter of 1228 having prohibited the establish-ment of new nunneries), the nuns of Helfta were administered the sacra-ments by Dominican friars, who also served as liaisons between the cloister and the outside world.[138]

Although there may well have been familial connections between the Helfta nuns and soldiers on both sides of the 1294 conflict, this was no guarantee against the possibility of harm coming to St. Mary's. The general savagery that accompanied the sacking of nunneries not only threatened the physical and institutional well-being of religious houses themselves, but also posed grave threats of sexual violence and massacre against their inhab-itants. Yet the nuns of Helfta did not react to such military incursions by fortifying their monastery against marauders, nor by seeking armed assis-tance from their local feudal lord. Instead, as we are told in the *Legatus Divinae Pietatis*, which records the life and visions of Gertrude of Helfta, the nuns gathered together in the cloister and chanted:

> The community was once dreading the approach of enemies said to be
> strongly armed and advancing on the monastery. For such dire necessity, it

was decreed that the Psalter be performed by all, each Psalm separated [*distinctum*] by the verse *O lux beatissima* and the antiphon *Veni Sancte Spiritus.* . . . While they were all pouring forth their contrite prayer, she saw a vapor, as it were, being exhaled [*quasi vaporem quemdam efflare*] from each heart, as though it had been touched by the very spirit of compunction. This vapor surrounded the cloister and its vicinity, repulsing to a distance the hostile forces. And the greater the contrition of heart and the stronger the inclination to good will, the more efficacious was the vapor exhaled from those persons in repulsing the hostile forces.[139]

In a vivid scene of liturgical revisionism, the nuns perform, in one sitting, the full cycle of psalms, which would usually be dispersed through the canonical hours over the course of a week, augmenting their performance of the psaltery by repeating between each psalm the verse *O lux*, then the corresponding antiphon in its entirety. For the nuns of Helfta, *Veni Sancte Spiritus* becomes a performative means of liturgical defense against physical and institutional harm: a defense whose effectiveness was amply demonstrated by the powerful vapor "exhaled" by the nuns' bodies just as *Veni Sancte* "pour[ed] forth" from their mouths.

This episode illustrates with remarkable clarity just how thoroughly the nuns of Helfta depended upon (or at least imagined themselves dependent upon) liturgy and liturgical performance for their very survival. At the same time, though, it shows that their liturgical life was not always as predictable as we might expect. Like Hildegard, the two Helfta nuns whose writings will concern me here—Gertrude of Helfta and Mechtild of Hackeborn[140]—were deeply musical; as the *cantrix* at Helfta through much of her adult life, one of her sisters records in the *Liber specialis gratiae*, Mechtild was known as "God's nightingale" (*Philomenae suae*),[141] while the frequent references to Gertrude's musical adeptness leave little doubt that she was an accomplished musician as well. Though we cannot know whether the nuns of Helfta composed new music themselves and incorporated it into their liturgy (all their medieval liturgical books having been destroyed in the Reformation), it is clear that they made original use of whatever music they did have. Borrowing a term from Michel de Certeau, we might propose that the nuns of Helfta "poached" on the liturgy, receiving it from above while simultaneously recruiting it into their idiosyncratic visionary lives and ingeniously adapting it to their own ends. In his influential essay "Reading as

Poaching," Certeau argues that the reception of a dominant discourse can often allow those who receive it to appropriate the institutional authority of its authors and propagators: "To write is to produce the text; to read is to receive it from someone else without putting one's own mark on it, without remaking it."[142] Certeau provides a useful model for studying the liturgical practice of medieval women, which has often been seen as an inherently conservative aspect of female sanctity even by those scholars most concerned with articulating the distinctiveness of individual women's religious lives—and for good reason: in the words of I. H. Dalmais, liturgy has always entailed "a fundamental obligation to accept the religious conception of the cosmos and its rhythms."[143] Such assumptions have long informed the field of liturgical theology, for example, which is still often characterized by a structuralism that leaves little room for those aspects of liturgical practice that do not conform to normative models.[144]

In much the same vein, the scholars who have written on the Helfta nuns and the liturgy have tended to argue for an easy fit between their liturgical practices and their visionary lives. For Cyprian Vagaggini, Gertrude's *Legatus* demonstrates how "the most intense and integral liturgical life is able to enter into a perfect marriage with a mystical life of the highest sort,"[145] while Sabine Spitzlei has gone so far as to label Gertrude and Mechtild "liturgical mystics."[146] It is true that the nuns' spirituality is often difficult to distinguish from its liturgical setting. Yet what seems most striking about their particular brand of visionary mysticism is the frequency with which it transforms the structure, practice, and meaning of Christian liturgy practically beyond recognition. For Gertrude and Mechtild, the liturgy represents the material musicality of the wounded body of Christ; the passion and the imitative sufferings of the nuns converge in the musical time and space of liturgical singing, giving us an unprecedented look at the medieval visionary deployment of the musical body in pain.[147]

The overriding characteristic of the nuns' musical visions is their occurrence at specified liturgical moments. Their visions often take place during chants—antiphons, sequences, Glorias, Alleluias—and even, in some cases, during the declamation of individual words or syllables *within* single chants. Many of the visions begin with a phrase following the same basic formula: "During (matins/mass/vespers) one day in (week/feast) *x*, when (responsory/antiphon/sequence) *y* was being sung. . . ." The text then goes on to relate what exactly Mechtild or Gertrude saw, heard, tasted, or felt during the given liturgical chant or hour. During mass at All Saints', for example, Mechtild has a vision of Christ and the Virgin over the course of the performance of the antiphon *Laudem dicite Deo nostro*. During the performance of the antiphon, she records, the Virgin draws a girdle out of the wound in Christ's side encrusted with golden cymbals, which when touched together sound with wondrous music. As Mechtild sings and listens, Christ puts his hands to her hands, granting her his own ability to do good works in the world, then puts his eye and ear to her eyes and ears and thus invests her with his divine sight and hearing. Finally, when Christ puts his mouth to Mechtild's, he not only kisses her as her *sponsus*, but does so with the mouth "with which he gave worship and thanks to his Father, and with which he taught his disciples and preached to the people."[148] In the space of a single antiphon, Christ implicitly grants Mechtild his powers to preach and teach in what seems a daring gesture given the universal injunctions against women preaching throughout the medieval period.[149]

Both Mechtild's *Liber* and Gertrude's *Legatus* mimic the verbal and generic conventions of liturgical commentaries such as the *Speculum ecclesiae* and the *Gemma animae*. Instead of repeating conventional glosses from authoritative texts and thereby participating in their standardization of liturgical meaning, however, the nuns "gloss" the liturgy with their own embodied musical communions with Christ and the Virgin. Thus, while Honorius Augustodunensis (following Rhabanus Maurus) suggests that, in every celebration of the Mass, the Responsory following the reading of the Epistle symbolizes the benevolence of the apostles in their preaching,[150] Mechtild envisions Christ himself teaching her the significance of the *Sanctus* and the *Pater noster* "between the secrets" of the Mass, distracting her from the immediate locus of ecclesiastical power (the celebrant) and allowing her to derive her own authority as a liturgical commentator directly from God.[151]

For Gertrude and Mechtild, then, liturgy provided above all a privileged mode of access to God, entailing a specifically musical intimacy between their own bodies and the wounded body of Christ. The nuns are frequently found repeating and elaborating musical analogies drawn by Christ for their relationship to the divine. Near the beginning of the *Legatus*, Gertrude recounts that Mechtild, worried that her conduct was hasty and reprehensible, often sought reassurance from Christ:

The Lord replied: "I have deigned to join my heart so courteously and so inseparably with her soul that she is become one spirit with me and her will is always in perfect harmony with my own in all things and above all things, just as the members of the body are in harmony among themselves and with the will [*sicut membra proprii corporis cum suo corde concordant*]."[152]

Recalling Augustine's descriptions of death and *coaptatione* in the *City of God*, this analogy suggests that the silent music binding Mechtild's soul to Christ's heart is the same music that holds together the parts of the body in harmony: the Boethian *musica humana* but in this case deployed to signal the special musical bonds between God and a specific person. Indeed, as Christ informs Gertrude, this music distinguishes her own devotional life:

> My divine hearing, also, is moved as though by the sound of the sweetest musical instruments by each and every word uttered by your lips, whether you are murmuring soft words of love to me, or praying, either for sinners or for souls in purgatory, or correcting or instructing someone, or speaking any words for my glory . . . your words sound sweetly in my ears and move my divine heart to the very depths. The hope with which you are always panting after me I breathe in, and it is to me a scent like the sweetest fragrance of delight. Your every sigh and desire tastes to me better than any aromatic thing. Your love gives me the delight of the tenderest embrace.[153]

Gertrude's devotional musicality, the "suavissimis musicis instrumentis" of her praise, thus represents the most privileged aspect of her sanctity, framing in sound her other bodily senses and providing her with a means of celebrating the body of Christ in music. In a vision in book 2 (the only portion of the *Legatus* written in the first person), she performs the first five verses of Psalm 102 as she meditates on the wounds of Christ; at each verse she experiences one of the wounds in a unique way and thanks Christ for giving her "the grace to read in these wounds your suffering and your love."[154] Musical performance and passion meditation have converged.

Other moments of visionary musicality in the *Legatus* allow us to see how specific liturgical genres functioned within Gertrude's Christological devotion. The following extended passage presents Christ's words on the singing of the Alleluia on Easter Sunday:

> "Convenientissime poteris me per *Alleluia* collaudare in unione laudis supercaelestium qui per idem jugiter collaudant in caelis." Et adjecit Dominus:

"Nota ergo quod in illa dictione: *Alleluia,* omnes vocales inveniuntur praeter solam vocalem *O,* quae dolorem signat, et pro illa duplicatur prima, scilicet vocalis *A.* Unde per *A,* lauda me in unione illius excellentissimae laudis, qua omnes sancti conjubilando extollunt praesuavissimam delectationem divini influxus in meam deificam humanitatem, jam immortalitatis gloria sublimatam pro multimoda amaritudine passionis et mortis quam sustinui causa humanae salutis. Per *E,* lauda amoenissimam delectationem illius gratissimae vernantiae, qua oculi humanitatis meae delectantur in floridis pascuis totius summae et individuae Trinitatis. Per *U* quoque, lauda suavissimam delectationem illam, qua demulcentur aures meae deificatae humanitatis in suavisonis blanditiis semper venerandae Trinitatis, omniumque angelorum et sanctorum laudibus indefessis. Per *I* etiam extolle deliciosissimam fragrantiam aurae gratioris, qua per suavissimum sanctae Trinitatis spiramentum nares jam immortalis sanctae humanitatis meae gratissime recreantur. Per *A* deinde, quae pro *O* adjungitur, collaudando magnificum, incomprehensibilem et inaestimabilem totius divinitatis influxum in meam deificatam humanitatem, quae jam immortalis et impassibilis effecta."[155]

["You can praise me most fittingly in the *Alleluia,* joining it with the praises of the heavenly host, who pray eternally in heaven." Then God added: "Therefore, notice that in this word, *Alleluia,* all of the vowels can be found, with the sole exception of the vowel *O,* which signifies sorrow, and in place of it the first vowel, *A,* is repeated. Thus, at the first *A,* praise me along with the most exalted hallowed ones you praise, by jubilating with the saints praising the sweetest delight of the divine infusion of my holy humanity, the glory of immortality by which my human sufferings and my passion were redeemed. In the *E,* praise this wondrous joy that delights my human eyes with vernal grace in the flowering pasture of the most holy and indivisible Trinity. In the *U,* praise that sweetest pleasure, by which the ears of my divine humanity are exalted in the sweet-sounding songs embracing the ever-holy Trinity, and the praises given by all the angels and saints. In the *I,* praise the sweetest fragrance of the pleasing breezes, by which, through the sweetest breath of the holy Trinity, the nose of my immortal, holy humanity is most gracefully soothed. In the second *A* (which is substituted for the *O*) must be praised the great, unspeakable, and inestimable infusion of divinity into my sanctified humanity, which is made immediately immortal and impassible."]

What is distinctive about this passage, in a technical musical sense, is the fact that the *vowels* of the Alleluia, not the consonants, provide the basis for the visionary experience. In the singing of the word "Alleluia" during the choral respond, each vowel would have been performed to its own note or string of notes, whether syllabically (each syllable given one note), neumatically (two to four notes per syllable), or melismatically (a string of many notes sung on each syllable). Christ enjoins Gertrude, in other words, to meditate *during each discretely performed syllable* upon the meaning of his Passion, the sight of the trinity, the sound of angelic choirs, the scent of the trinity, and finally the divine redemption of Christ's body. According to the conventions of the Alleluia genre, the performance of the final *a* is the *jubilus*, in this case interpreted as a union of the human and the divine.

The passage constitutes a particularly rich Christological interpretation of liturgical singing. Along with numerous other passages throughout the *Legatus* and Mechtild's *Liber*, it suggests that the nuns gave specific liturgical genres and even specific melodic contours individuated visionary significance. The Helfta liturgical books that survived the Middle Ages were apparently all destroyed during the German Reformation, when they were thrown into beer vats during a peasants' revolt in 1525.[156] If we possessed even a few of these books with notated melodies, it could very well be possible to reconstruct in unparalleled detail the ways in which a monastic community in the Middle Ages interpreted individual plainchant melodies and melodic formulas.

Psalmody was not the sole channel of musicality between the nuns and the wounded body of Christ. In a vision that stresses the somatic rhythms of the relationship, Gertrude senses the heartbeats of Christ as she rests against his side: "Then the Lord made her lean against his heart, with the heart of her soul close to his divine heart. When her soul had sweetly rested there a while, she heard in the Lord's heart two wondrous and very sweet pulsations [*duos mirabiles et valde suaves pulsus*]," beats that Christ glosses for her as a sign of the salvation of humanity.[157] Mechtild, by contrast, hears Christ's heart emit three strong beats and one weak beat, the former signifying God's omnipotence, wisdom, and love, the latter, in Christ's words, "the goodness of my humanity" (humanitatis meae benignitatem).[158] The nuns are clearly playing here upon a venerable tradition of "pulse-music" found in numerous medieval encyclopedias, music treatises, and writings of physicians.[159] Unlike platonizing uses of the music of pulse to connote the soul's numerical regulation of the body, Gertrude and Mechtild appropriate it as a multivalent symbol of their special musical relationship to the heart of Christ, which they experience through both sung *and* instrumental musics. Thus, during the singing of an antiphon in remembrance of the death of a former abbess, Mechtild envisions a choir of souls surrounding Christ and singing a hymn to the Virgin; as the company sings, a "great trumpet" (tuba magna) suddenly emerges from Christ's heart and blends all of their voices together into sweet melody.[160] Gertrude hears within her own heart "a most sweet voice, as sweet as the lovely melody of a skillful harpist playing on his harp [*citharizantis in cithara sua*]." She soon discovers that the harpist within her is Christ; inviting Gertrude to join him, Christ reveals to her a musical pipe, a *fistula*, emerging from the wound in his side:

> During the infinitely sweet delight which this caused her, she felt herself to be drawn in an indescribable way, through the pipe we have mentioned, into the heart of the Lord, and she had the happiness of finding herself within the very being of her spouse and lord. What she there felt, saw, heard, tasted, touched, is known to her alone, and to him who deigned to admit her to such a union.[161]

The sacred heart was only one of many of Christ's body parts that the nuns invested with the ability to resound with music. In her *Spiritual Exercises*, a much shorter work than the *Legatus* composed of a series of lyrical meditations and prayers, Gertrude includes a lengthy excursus on the *jubilus* that casts God the Father as a musician performing on the instrument of his son for her benefit:

> Tu es suspector animae meae. Tu es vita spiritus mei. Tu es deus cordis mei. O amor, tu circumvolve dulcissime gutturis Iesu sponsi mei praeclarissimam lyram, ut ipse deus vitae meae, pro me sibi personet laudationis vocem primam, et sic delectatione suae laudis involvat vitam meam simul et animam. Eia o amor, nunc quod facis, fac citius. Iam enim ferre non valeo forte quod mihi infixisti vulnus.[162]

> [You are the custodian of my soul. You are the life of my spirit. You are the lord of my heart. O love, you play most sweetly on that very brightest lyre of the throat of my spouse Jesus so that he himself, God of my life, may on my behalf sound the first voice of praise for himself and may thus envelop both my life and my soul in the delight of his praise. Ah! Now O love, what you do, do quickly. For already I am not capable of bearing the serious wound you have inflicted on me.]

In Mechtild's *Liber*, Christ again appears as a stringed instrument that resonates in anticipation of the passion: "When the time of my wedding was at hand I was sold by my own heart's love as the price of the wedding banquet, and I gave myself for bread and meat and drink. I myself was the cithara and organ at the banquet by means of my gentle words." Describing his Crucifixion in an image that recalls "Philomena praevia," Christ remembers the melodious *cantus* he emitted while tortured and awaiting death: "Then fastened by the cruel nails I stretched out my arms for your dear embrace, singing on my bed of love seven songs of marvelous love."[163]

The passionate musical bonds the Helfta nuns forged between themselves and the divine served quite practical purposes as well, providing ready access to the Eucharist or opportunities for increasing spiritual knowledge. During the singing of Vespers at the Feast of the Ascension, Gertrude discovers to her horror a long scar along her left side; immediately Christ appears to her, holding the host aloft before putting it in his mouth. After passing through Christ's mouth and stomach, Gertrude observes, the Eucharist emerges from the wound in his side, and, resting there, literally glues her wound to his own. Finally, after she feels the host in her scar, Christ informs her that she can keep it alive through internal performance in one of the strangest musical images in the Helfta nuns' writings: "And the Lord said to her, 'Behold, this host will unite you to me in such a way that on one side it touches your scar [*cicatricem tuam*] and on the other my wound [*vulnus meum*], like a dressing for both of us. You must cleanse it, as it were, and renew it every day by repeating with devotion the hymn *Jesu nostra redemptio*.'"[164] By singing the hymn within her own scarred and empathetically suffering body, Christ seems to imply, Gertrude can serve herself the host; the singing of *Jesu nostra* becomes the sacrament and Gertrude the celebrant, usurping the male role of priest through internal liturgical song. Not only does Christ himself "gloss" an individual chant (in this case a hymn for the feast of the Ascension) for Gertrude's benefit, but the performed hymn actually *becomes* the Eucharist.

Yet music did not always provide the nuns with a secure mode of embodied access to God. Indeed, the nuns (particularly Gertrude) frequently use their own and others' struggles with musical learning and performance as analogies for their relationships with Christ. When Gertrude doubts her worthiness to receive the service of the divine heart, for example, Christ reassures her while also reminding her of her own skill:

"Suppose," he said, "that having a very musical and supple voice, and more-over a great love of singing, someone near you who had a very loud and harsh voice [*valde gravem et dissonam haberet vocem*] were singing very badly so that even after making great effort she could hardly sing a note correctly, would you not be indignant if she would not let you sing what you are able and most ready to render, and what she would do with so much difficulty? So, without any doubt, my divine heart, recognizing the frailty and inconstancy of human nature, always waits with ineffable longing to supply for whatever you entrust to it . . . so as to do for you whatever you are unable to do for yourself."[165]

Though here Gertrude's musical prowess registers the generosity of God, elsewhere her infrequent but troublesome *inability* to sing signifies his protection of her musical temperance: "One feast-day, when she was prevented from singing by a bad headache, she asked the Lord why he so often let this happen to her on a feast-day. She received this reply: 'Lest perchance you are carried away by the pleasure of singing the sacred melody [*per delectationem modulationis elevata*] and become less receptive of grace.' "[166] Gertrude was also musically tested by the devil, who once appeared to her "when she was reciting the Canonical Hours with less attention than usual"; mimicking her sloppy psalmody by skipping syllables (*syncopando*), the devil chides her for her devotional hypocrisy: "You can make eloquent discourse on any subject whenever you want, but when you speak to him your words are so hasty and careless that just now in this psalm you left out this number of letters, this number of syllables, and this number of words." Gertrude interprets the vision as a sign of the devil's desire to "bring grave accusations" after death "against those who tend to say the Hours of the Divine Office in a hurry and without real attention" (adversus illos qui festinanter et sine intentione horas dicere consueverunt).[167]

The nuns' concern with the pragmatics of musical pedagogy and performance similarly informs their approach to the musical page itself, as when Gertrude describes singing from the "book of Christ": "I could see that you were sweetly affected when I began to chant in choir, exerting all my powers to sing and fixing my attention on you at each note [*per singulas notas*], like a singer who has not yet learned the melody and diligently looks at the book [*diligenter respicit librum*]."[168] Analogizing her devotional intensity to the reading of musical notation by an untrained singer, Gertrude implies that musical ignorance can be devotional bliss. While for the author of *Book to a Mother* the book of Christ is a stringed musical instrument, a "sauttery," for Gertrude it is the liturgical book from which the novice must sing.

A particularly illuminating example of this confluence of music, manuscript, and visionary experience occurs in an account in book 3 of the *Legatus* of an illness that kept Gertrude from singing the Office. Though she attends the canonical Hours "so that at least thus she might exercise her body in the service of God" by listening to her sisters sing, she worries that her own failure to perform chant will make her less worthy in the eyes of God:

> "Quid, amantissime Domine mi, tu nunc habes honoris ex eo quod ego negligens et inutilis hic sedens, vix in uno vel duobus verbis, vel notis intendo?" Ad quod Dominus tandem vice quadam sic respondit: "Et quid tu haberes ex eo si amicus tuus, una vice vel bis, porrigeret tibi haustum dulcissimi et recentissimi medonis, de quo sperares te multum confortari? Multo ergo majorem delectationem scias me habere de singulis verbis et neumis, quibus nunc laudi meae intendis."

> ["How, my dearest Lord, can you derive any honor from me while I sit here negligent and useless, scarcely attending to one or two words or notes?" To which the Lord at length made this answer: "What good would you derive from it if a friend offered you only once or twice some sweet, freshly made mead from which you might hope for much relief? Know, then, that I take far greater pleasure in the individual words and neumes that you are now able to concentrate upon for my glory."][169]

In this brief exchange, Christ's analogy between music and mead points to his appreciation of Gertrude's steadfast rather than haphazard faith and devotion. Yet there is a subtle difference between Gertrude's supplication and Christ's reply: while Gertrude bemoans her inability to perform "verbis vel notis," "words or *notes*," Christ replies that he takes delight in her concentration upon "verbis et neumis," "words and *neumes*." In other words, when Gertrude is sick God takes pleasure not simply in the sung tones, the *notis*, but in the *neumis* on which she fixes her attention—a term that may connote either the "pneumae," those "very long melodies" that figure so prominently in liturgical commentaries on singing[170]; or (more likely, I think) "neumes," the musical notation transcribed on the manuscript page. The passage may suggest not only that the sick Gertrude holds a liturgical book in her lap and follows the music as her sisters sing (which in itself is a fascinating piece of evidence for everyday life at Helfta, for Gertrude would of course have known the liturgy by heart), but also that the neumes themselves have an almost iconic status within the devotional setting. This extraordinary vision casts the neumed page not as an authoritative transmission of ecclesiastical authority, but as the material ground of mystical experience, a surface of "musical skin" marked with the wounds of the Passion.

Certainly the most explicit example of "liturgical poaching" recorded at Helfta occurred during a financial dispute between the cathedral of Halberstadt and St. Mary's in 1295, which resulted in Helfta's being placed under interdict by the cathedral officials the following year.[171] To a community for which liturgy was its spiritual lifeblood, the mandated cessation of the *opus Dei* entailed by interdiction could well have been devastating. As we saw in Chapter 3, Hildegard of Bingen responded to interdict with a letter to the Prelates of Mainz that polemically described the importance of music in the life of her community.[172] In Helfta's case, we are told, Christ himself came to the rescue. During the singing of Mass the day before the interdict was scheduled to take effect, Gertrude asked the Lord, "How are you going to console us . . . in our present trial?" and inquired pointedly as to how long the interdict was to last. Rather than interpret the interdict as a punishment for the nuns' transgression, however, Jesus told her, "I act in this manner for your greater good and for your salvation. For if, at times, I raise you up by contemplation to a share in the knowledge of my secrets, I exclude you from them sometimes to preserve your humility, so that in receiving them you may find out what you are by my grace, and again, when you lack them, you may know what you are of yourself."[173] Gertrude here casts the interdict not as an imposed exclusion from the mysteries, but as an opportunity for personal and communal self-knowledge and spiritual growth, as a special privilege granted by God. Indeed, during the singing of the Offertory of the same Mass, *Recordare Virgo Mater*, Christ breathes on Gertrude as she sings and tells her that during the interdict his breath will serve as the forbidden Eucharist, and that by giving it to her he gives it to all in her community who desire it. As she gazes longingly at the host, she hears the Lord say, "This excommunication which has been imposed on you will do you no more harm than would someone trying to cut you with a wooden knife, which cannot penetrate at all, but only leave some slight impression made by its blade."[174] Christ's musical breath, which embodies the Eucharist Gertrude is instructed to share with her community, is thus received in direct defiance of an ecclesiastical authority represented as violent but rendered impotent by the very word of God—and all during the singing of a brief Offertory.

Finally, like Hildegard of Bingen's *Symphonia*, liturgy provided the Helfta nuns with a means of relating with one another through regular musical performance. Though Mechtild reacted to the very thought of lascivious secular songs by strewing glass on her bed and rolling in it with relish, desire was by no means absent from her musical unions with the nuns whose musical lives she directed.[175] On the anniversary of the death of a former abbess, Mechtild visualizes all the nuns gathered in a dance, singing the hymn *O Mater nostra* in their many voices; but Mechtild sees these individual voices enter the heart of Christ and reemerge as a single melody of marvelous beauty that binds the women together within the musical time and space of the hymn.[176] Gertrude voices a similar sentiment after the death and burial of Mechtild herself; a passage in the *Liber specialis gratiae* describes the appearance of Mechtild's soul to Gertrude in the choir: "When I chanted with you in the choir with all my desire and strength, I raised your desire upwards to God and in God when the melody ascended [*cantu ascendente*]; and when the melody descended [*cantu vero descendente*], with all goodwill I again brought down his grace upon you; and I continue to do so without ceasing."[177] In this moving tribute to her still-living sister, Mechtild conceives of music as a sonorous channel between life and death, between herself and Gertrude, and between both women and God, a medium that keeps Gertrude's presence alive for her in the heavenly notes of a hymn or an antiphon even as her own body rests in its grave.

The death of Mechtild figures as well near the beginning of book 5 of the *Legatus divinae pietatis*, where the dying nun's vision of Christ includes perhaps the clearest example of a "musical wound" in the Helfta writings: "Then he hailed her most blessed soul in an unknowable and ineffable way with each of the wounds in his most holy body; and it happened that each wound emitted four modes, wondrous and full of boundless pleasure, of saluting: namely, by a most sweet-sounding song, by a most efficacious vapor, by a most verdant dew, and by a most marvellous glowing" (Sicque incomprehensibili et inaestimabili modo salutavit animam illam beatissimam per singula vulnera sanctissimi corporis sui; ita quod unumquodque vulnus quatouor mirabiles et omni delectatione plenos emittebat modos vocandi, scilicet suavissimi soni, efficacissimi vaporis, uberrimi roris, ac amoenissimi splendoris).[178] The "most sweet-sounding song" emerging from one of his wounds, a song that "surpassed the music of all instruments," "Signified all the words which God's chosen one had given sweetly to God throughout her life, or spoken according to God's wishes for the aid of those around her."[179] This musical heart, however, can resonate with "melodious harmony" only once the body that contains it has been beaten, wounded, and crucified. Centuries before Emily Dickinson, Mechtild "splits the Lark" and "finds the Music" of the body in pain.

Excursus: The Melodious Hell of Hieronymous Bosch

The medieval theology of suffering embraced numerous dimensions of human experience: seeing, touching, smelling, hearing, and tasting were all part of Christian participation in religious agonies of various sorts. For the Middle Ages, music, despite the sublimating aesthetic tradition that often sought to contain its somatic effects and consequences, created unique opportunities for and means of religious suffering. The musicality of the body in pain provided a mode of direct identification with the sounds of Christ's suffering; it enabled flagellants to imagine and deploy their flesh as a medium of melodious asceticism; and it inspired a visual tradition that enlisted typology, memory, and meditation to internalize the techniques of musical torture within the human subject.

Before moving on to explore the pedagogical consequences of musical suffering in Chapter 6, I want to linger briefly over a premodern artifact that I believe represents both the culmination and the abandonment of medieval notions of the musical body in pain. The artifact in question is Hieronymous Bosch's well-known *Garden of Earthly Delights*, which was likely commissioned as a sort of conversation piece for Prince Henry III of Nassau around 1510. Of particular interest is Bosch's truly nasty musical tableau found in the inner right wing (see Figure 15 as well as the cover of this book). A violent ensemble is led by a devil seated among an array of musical instruments. Even to describe Bosch's gruesome ensemble is to catalog a panoply of musical forms of torture. A devil reaches with his tongue for the musical notation scored (pun intended) on the buttocks of a sinner crushed beneath a hybrid harp-lute. To the viewer's right, another

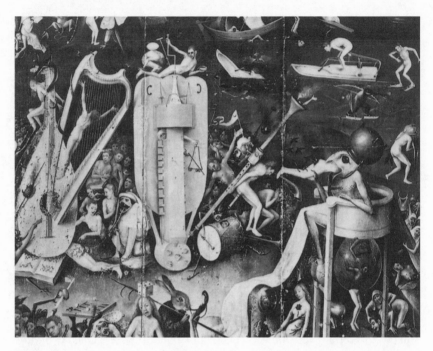

FIGURE 15   Infernal Musicians from Hieronymous Bosch, *Garden of Earthly Delights* (inner right wing), ca. 1510

devil beats a drum that imprisons a sinner gazing out of the instrument's window in horror. At a diagonal over the drum stretches the barrel of a bombardon (a kind of proto-bassoon), borne—like the cross—on the back of a sinner who is impaled anally with a flute or fife (only two finger-holes are visible). The thin stream of smoke emerging from the horn of the bombardon suggests that the sinner whose pale, reaching hand we see is being burned alive within the instrument. To the immediate left, two sinners stand or lie atop a hurdy-gurdy or *symphonia*, one of them balancing Bosch's famous cosmic egg while impaling the other, who suggestively grinds away on the instrument's crank at the expense of the veiled woman trapped beneath the keyboard. At the far left, a sinner's hands are bound tightly to the neck of a lute, which, upon closer inspection, turns out to be one-half of a hybrid lute-harp. In a spectacular motif that recalls the Roman sculpture of *Apollo citharoedus* discussed in Chapter 1 (see Figure 3), another nude sinner is literally crucified upon the harp, stretched among its strings and, we are forced to realize, tormented at every delicate touch.

The sources and politics of Bosch's *Garden of Earthly Delights* have long been a matter of scholarly debate, and the musical tableau has inspired its fair share of speculation. Wilhelm Fraenger once argued that the *Garden's* primary historical and ideological debts were to the Heresy of the Free Spirit, and that the painting as a whole represents the first large-scale artistic rendering of pre-Reformation sectarianism.[180] Though Fraenger's theory has not been generally accepted, it served to rescue the painter's magnum opus from the pietistic contortions by which art historians had long sought to squeeze the *Garden* into an orthodox Catholic box. Despite its reformist leanings, however, Fraenger's interpretation reduced the infernal concert to an uncritical excrescence of medieval musical allegory. Listening to the musicians through the platonizing ear of John the Scot, Fraenger homogenized the ensemble into a trinitarian *harmonia* and found a "message of salvation" to be the ultimate meaning of the musical instruments.[181] Particularly revealing was Fraenger's heterosexualizing take on the harp-lute hybrid, which he viewed as a musical icon of marital love and union: "What Bosch intends is to show the idea of harmony as a marriage of sounds, the harp representing the man, the lute the woman, united in a blissful duet."[182] But the human figures punished on the instruments are both clearly male (women in the *Garden* are invariably given long hair); the array of exposed, inscribed, and penetrated male buttocks scattered throughout the ensemble powerfully belies any suggestion that the image's primary erotic impulse is heterosexual. The category of the sodomitical appears inextricable from the musicality of perversion and punishment that Bosch envisions.

In recent years scholars have found more convincing ways of relating Bosch's musical tableau to its late medieval context. Some have suggested that the instruments are intended to deliver a fitting punishment to traveling minstrels for their discordant musicianship, while others have scrutinized the scene for its depiction of *Luxuria* as the "music of the flesh."[183] The entire panel bears close resemblances to medieval literary depictions of Hell such as the *Visio Tundali*, in which infernal punishments often fit earthly crimes; it is not hard to understand how Bosch might have inverted the whole idea of "musical performance" by depicting instruments playing upon humans rather than the reverse.[184] The painting may also be playing with the Rabelaisian "world-turned-upside-down" motif, as Keith Moxey has suggested, showing off the intellectual pretensions of its humanist patron by embedding deliberately confounding reversals of musical norms.[185]

My own sense of Bosch's grotesque musical concert is that the scene constitutes a brilliantly deliberate *extensio ad absurdum* of what in the painter's time was a widespread and well-known tradition of the musical body in pain. This is to say that the fleshly concert that scholars have agreed is one of the panel's most bizarre and ingenious features is perhaps its most conventional. For the visual effects of Bosch's hellish musical scene depend absolutely upon their intimate continuity with the medieval history of musical torture this chapter has discussed. Surely the harp-crucified sinner in the *Garden of Earthly Delights* is a direct descendant of the *cithara*-crucified body of Jesus Christ, the body upon which numerous allegorists and poets performed their own painful identifications with his sufferings. The visuality of the scene emphasizes this connection very clearly: the figure carrying the bombardon is leaning over and bearing the instrument at the precise angle of the harp's lower crossbar, a parallel that serves to frame the entire tableau as a kind of infernal musical crucifixion. (We might also read the image through the prophetic words of the Low Countries visionary Marguerite of Oingt: the "harps they will hear will be noisy tempests and penetrating rivers which will pierce them through their hearts"). The sinner bound to the lute recalls the punishment of Dante's Master Adam in the Naples manuscript (see Figure 13 above), whose body constitutes an instrument of torture very much in the spirit of Bosch's creation in the panel. The small demon beating on the prison-drum in the lower right strikes the same human skin that medieval allegorists imagined as sounding bodily praises to God, the *pellis arida* that Peter Damian enjoined his *tympanum*-like readers to strike as a sign of their devotion. And the notated buttocks peeking out from beneath the lute-harp have a spectacular medieval antecedent in the "Guidonian Hand," the pedagogical body part densely inscribed with musical notation that will be discussed at greater length in Chapter 6 (see Figures 16–19).

Painting on the eve of the Reformation, most likely for a lay patron, Bosch inherited a vast medieval legacy of musical bodies in pain. Whether strummed on the cross, beaten in the refectory, sketched in the margins, or sodomized with a fife, the medieval body often relished its own musical suffering. We will impoverish such sonorous performances of pain if we continue to insist that those who experienced and represented them inevitably sought to "redeem" them through negative comparison to an unheard but always present ideal (or, indeed, if we seek so to redeem them ourselves). And we must finally acknowledge that the torturous bodily concert in Bosch's hell is nothing if not conventional. The artist paints a spectacle of musical anguish forward-looking in its daring irreverence, perhaps, but thoroughly Catholic in its sensibility.[186]

Yet what is ultimately most surprising about Bosch's musical tableau is precisely its resistance to this medieval tradition's most vital contribution to the history of musical embodiment. With the important exception of the notated buttocks, Bosch's musical bodies are physically separated and discrete from those instruments inflicting the torture upon them. The harp strings penetrate and bisect the body of the crucified sinner, true, but these strings are emphatically *not* made of the sinner's own ribs and sinews. Likewise, while the lute's victim can be tortured with the instrument's strings, the amount and quality of the pain inflicted cannot approach that which is visited upon the Neapolitan illuminator's Master Adam, whose ghostly body has actually *become* the same lute that tortures him. And while eternity may be quite uncomfortable for the sinner trapped in the drum, surely it would be even more unbearable were the sinner actually to *be* the drum and his stretched skin the percussive surface performed upon by the demon. Even the musical notation inscribed on the sinner's buttocks has an almost arbitrary (or at least noninevitable) feel, as if the notes and staves could just as easily have been scored into his chest or forehead. After surveying the many medieval productions of musical pain that anticipate the horrific spectacle of melodious suffering in the *Garden of Earthly Delights*, I would propose that Bosch stopped short of enlisting the most radical and spectacular possibilities this tradition could have afforded him.

I do not mean to suggest that Bosch's refusal to register the inseparability of music and the flesh signals a definitive break with the incarnational musical sensibility of the Middle Ages.[187] As I argue in the epilogue, the musicality of the body has a long postmedieval history, and there are hundreds of examples that could be cited to argue against the notion that the early modern West loses the medieval sense of the material immanence of music. Yet the torturous musical performance in the *Garden* may in fact point to a somewhat moderated view of the music of the flesh. Bosch's hellish instruments imprison, torture, burn, pierce, and strangle the bodies unlucky enough to be cast or strung upon them. But the bodies themselves have lost the music they possessed for over a millennium.

Musical Violence and the Pedagogical Body: The Prioress's Tale and the Ideologies of "Song"

A psalm is sung at home and repeated outdoors; it is learned without effort and retained with delight. A psalm joins those with differences, unites those at odds and reconciles those who have been offended, for who will not concede to him with whom one sings to God in one voice? It is after all a great bond of unity for the full number of people to join in one chorus.

—ST. AMBROSE, *Explanatio psalmorum*[1]

If there is no longer a road from one musical sphere to the other . . . this is the phenomenon of a fractured total condition that can no more be settled by the artist's will than by mere pedagogics or by dictatorial fiat. It sears stigmata into every musical phenomenon.

—THEODOR ADORNO, "Musical Life"[2]

It would be hard to imagine two less compatible pronouncements concerning the role of music in the body politic. For Ambrose, the fourth-century Christian bishop, liturgical hymnody furnished both a naturalized model for social solidarity and the practical means of achieving it. A forceful advocate of the Milanese chant that bears his name, Ambrose understood well the indispensability of sacred music-making to the collective identity of Christians in late antique Rome.[3] Through institutional pedagogy, private practice, and public performance, music helped maintain Christian community by promoting, in his words, a "great bond of unity" in the service of worship and the hope of salvation.

Theodor Adorno, a German Jew who emigrated to the United States in 1938, imagined the relationship between music and community in quite a different light. In Adorno's view, musical sonorities evidenced a fundamental and abiding division, a "fractured total condition," between the multiple cultural spheres through which he himself had migrated, both in his native country and in exile.[4] Appropriating a Christian image of *imitatio Christi*,

Adorno describes the implications of this division as it "sears stigmata" into even the most ostensibly apolitical moments of music-making. For the Frankfurt critic, music registers social struggle, violence, and conflict in its every utterance, reflecting and reconstituting the various forms of dissension characterizing the public sphere. In this sense, Adorno makes explicit what Ambrose's formulation mystifies: that the sense of harmonious solidarity music gives to those who sing in "one chorus" often founds itself upon the violent exclusion of those whose voices are silenced.

I juxtapose these two visions of music because the contrast between them raises a number of unsettling questions about the politics of Christian music-making, questions that originate in the discursive space between harmonizing musical ideologies ("A psalm joins those with differences") and the often violent uses to which music has actually been put. As we saw in Chapter 5, music and bodily violence coexisted intimately in the religious cultures of the Christian Middle Ages, so much so that in many cases music *is* violence for all practical purposes—violence, however, that many Christian writers seek to deny or conceal. Even for Ambrose, who elsewhere relishes in the visceral musicality of martyrdom (see Chapter 1), a "psalm" represents the antithesis of violence. A psalm by its very nature heals, reconciles, and erases social difference.

Before it can do so, however, it must be *learned*, and this is perhaps the most mystifying aspect of Ambrose's formulation. "Domi psalmus *canitur*, foris *recensetur*; sine labore *percipitur*, cum voluptate *servatur*": The string of passives is emphatic. A psalm *is* sung, *is* repeated, *is* learned, *is* retained. Despite the images of home, work, and pleasure, no human agent performs in this sentence. Notable, too, is Ambrose's choice of the word "percipitur" to denote the pedagogical acquisition of the psalm. *Percipere* often functions as an agricultural term meaning to gather or harvest. A psalm is, paradoxically, harvested without labor. The *opus Dei*, the liturgical "work of God," is thus no work at all.

We know better, of course, and surely Ambrose did, too. During the ninth century there emerged a genre of Latin handbooks devoted to the pedagogical "harvesting" of plainchant, and a laborious harvest it was. In Adorno's terms, the "musical sphere" of liturgical pedagogy invents the most utilitarian medieval discourse of musical violence. Here too, however, many writers will go to great lengths to deny the need for bodily violence in the service of liturgical transmission, often by constructing the pedagogical body as a musical microcosm that need only "tune" itself to learn *cantus*. In his *Musica Disciplina*, one of the earliest surviving music-pedagogical texts from the Middle Ages, Aurelian of Réôme describes the "construction of this world and its natural order" in musical terms that embrace the body of the student: "you will find that every created thing accords with every other, interrelated in wonderful harmony."[5] Attempting to construct a philosophically consistent theory of liturgical pedagogy and performance, Aurelian contends that the individuated human subject is ideally "equipped for this discipline," "for in his throat he has a pipe for singing [*fistulam in gutture*]; in his chest, a kind of harp, adorned with strings, as it were, the fibers of the lungs; in the alternations of the beating of his pulse [*in venarum pulsumque*], fluctuating ascents and descents."[6] As we have seen, however, such instrumental bodies must always be plucked, strummed, and beaten in order to produce sound.

Focusing in particular on Chaucer's Prioress's Tale, this chapter investigates an array of Latin and vernacular writings—hagiographies, pedagogical manuals, a satire—that attest to the specifically pedagogical dimensions of musical violence. Though these works originally circulated within specific and widely varying historical circumstances that an argument of this nature cannot address responsibly, it is only by considering them as part of the same ecclesiastical tradition that we can discern the diachronic character of the violence they both depend upon and anxiously deny. Collectively, they attest to what I argue is a *longue durée* of pedagogical terror upon which the Church built the musical foundation of its liturgical tradition. In particular, the Prioress's Tale features a famous "out-of-school" narrative of musical pedagogy that leads directly to a violently musical denouement. The wider pedagogical tradition addressed here sought to produce a docile and obedient musical body, an instrumental product of pedagogical violence with a history of medieval representation whose discursive "weight," to steal a line from the Prioress, Chaucer could "nat susteene." When considered within this wider textual environment, the Prioress's Tale exposes the central role music has performed in what Nancy Armstrong and Leonard Tennenhouse have termed "the violence of representation," and suggests that music— even the naive psalmody of a medieval schoolboy—can constitute "a form of violence in its own right."[7]

The writings of Chaucer provide an ideal lens through which to begin examining the ideological implications of musical violence. Despite a venerable exegetical tradition that has insisted on the harmonious consistency of Chaucerian musical imagery,[8] even the *House of Fame*, in which Geffrey hears the disembodied "hevenyssh melody" produced by the music of the spheres, draws on Boethius's *De institutione musica* to figure musical sonority as primordially violent:

> For as flaumbe ys but lyghted smoke,
> Ryght soo soun ys air ybroke.
> But this may be in many wyse,
> Of which I wil the twoo devyse,
> As soun that cometh of pipe or harpe.
> For whan a pipe is blowen sharpe
> The air ys twyst with violence
> And rent—loo, thys ys my sentence.
> Eke whan men harpe-strynges smyte,
> Whether hyt be moche or lyte,
> Loo, with the strok the ayr tobreketh;
> And ryght so breketh it when men speketh.
> Thus wost thou wel what thing is speche.[9]

For Chaucer, as for many of the religious writers discussed in the previous chapter, musical sound—whether "sharpe" blowing through a pipe or the "smyt[ing]" of harp strings—has a discursive function inextricable from the violence of its material production. Musical forms of violence figure prominently as well in the *Canterbury Tales*: while much has been written about the musical erotics through which Chaucer figures domestic relations in the Fragment I fabliaux (Nicholas's suggestive "pleye" upon his "gay sautrie" in the Miller's Tale is the most familiar instance[10]), these innocuous musical parodies look very different when juxtaposed with the representation of music and domesticity in the Manciple's Tale. After killing his wife with his "bowe," the god repents by shattering his musical instruments prior to breaking the murder weapon itself: "he brak his mynstralcie,/Both harpe, and lute, and gyterne, and sautrie;/And eek he brak his arwes and his bowe" (267–69). The Manciple's brand of domestic "mynstralcie" represents an insidious reversal of the parodic music of marital discord critics have heard in the Miller's and Reeve's Tales.[11] And the tale's Apollo bears a disturbing resemblance to the magisterial god plucking the flayed body of Marsyas in

Ovid's *Metamorphoses* and classical statuary (see Chapter 1), pointing to the same primal link between violence and musical invention.

Even Phoebus's homicidal musicianship pales in comparison to the melodious spectacle of violence described by Chaucer's Madame Eglentyne. Narrated by a nun who sings the "service dyvyne,/Entuned in her nose ful semely" (1.122–23), the Prioress's Tale nevertheless recounts the horrifying chain of events surrounding the learning, performance, and reception of an identifiable liturgical antiphon. Like the Manciple's Tale, the story of the "litel clergeon" exploits its reader's assumption that musical sonority somehow exceeds the temporal realm in which it is produced—and thus resists political imbrication and, by extension, historicist analysis.[12] That this is an *ideology* of music is an observation that the tale goes to great lengths, through form, revision, and poesis, to deny.

Musical Learning and the Site of Song

The Prioress acknowledges the constitutive role of music in her poetic narrative at the end of her Prologue, as she asks the Virgin to "guide" her "song," the tale she is about to relate to the other pilgrims (487). With the Prologue's opening lines, however, Chaucer has already established her voice as only one of many proclaiming God's name "in this large world":

O Lord, oure Lord, thy name how merveillous
Is in this large world ysprad—quod she—
For noght oonly thy laude precious
Parfourned is by men of dignitee,
But by the mouth of children thy bountee
Parfourned is, for on the brest soukynge
Somtyme shewen they thyn heriynge.

(453–59)

In her initial description of "thy laude precious," the oral practice of Christian prayer, being "parfourned"—first by "men of dignitee," then by "the mouth of children"—the Prioress betrays the tenuousness of her own narrative authority. Her reiteration of a passive construction—the Lord's praise "parfourned is"[13]—emphasizes that the spreading of the Lord's name and the conversions it provokes are themselves products of performance, depending on the public repetition of praise; God's name and "bountee" are "ysprad" and affirmed only because they are "parfourned" repeatedly. As an example of this affirmative performance, the Prioress's "song" similarly compels her to give her own performance some kind of substantive authority to support the "labour" of "storie" (463). As is well known, the stanza paraphrases the opening lines of Psalm 8, which began matins in the Little Office of the Virgin, and may also mark an allusion to the Introit to the Mass of the Holy Innocents.[14] By interpolating these liturgical moments into the Prioress's Prologue, Chaucer identifies the clergeon as one of these "soukynge" children while grounding the Prioress's narrative voice in the hourly, daily, and yearly rhythms of Christian life in order to construct what will become an *anti*liturgical narrative.

Indeed, as Louise Fradenburg has argued, by depicting infants "on the brest soukynge," drawing the physical stuff of praise from a maternal body before projecting God's "bountee" out into the world, the Prioress, like the "childish singer" whose life she recounts, is "somehow embodied" through the very act of narration.[15] As the Prologue concludes, Chaucer explicitly (if ironically) aligns the Prioress with the first stanza's "children," relieving her of the corporeal labor necessary for praise by constructing her musical and narrative voice as utterly dependent upon maternal sustenance:

> My konnyng is so wayk, O blisful Queene,
> For to declare thy grete worthynesse
> That I ne may the weighte nat susteene;
> But as a child of twelf month oold, or lesse,
> That kan unnethes any word expresse,
> Right so fare I, and therfore I yow preye,
> Gydeth my song that I shal of yow seye.

(481–87)

Like Robert Henryson's Orpheus, who in his infancy "gart him sowke" from his mother's "palpis" "the sweit licour of all musike parfyte," the Prioress derives the substance of her narrative "song" from the maternal body of the Virgin.[16] For Fradenburg, the Virgin's body thereby provides the Prioress with "the 'open door,' the mediator, the easy passage . . . imaged through the silence of the human 'tonge' which cannot, but need not, speak."[17]

Yet speech is not the only medium through which the Prioress's "tonge" achieves its voiceless immediacy. With her final request to the Virgin, the Prioress—drawing on an ancient convention for the musicality of poetic language—casts the transition from prologue to tale, apostrophe to narrative, as a metamorphosis from speech into music, narrative "song." This metonymy identifies her precisely through her musicality with the "smale children" whose "litel scole" contrasts with the "Jewerye" at the outset:

> Ther was in Asye, in a greet citee,
> Amonges Cristene folk a Jewerye,
> Sustened by a lord of that contree
> For foule usure and lucre of vileynye,
> Hateful to Crist and to his compaignye;
> And thurgh the strete men myghte ride or wende,
> For it was free and open at eyther ende.
>
> A litel scole of Cristen folk ther stood
> Doun at the ferther ende, in which ther were
> Children an heep, ycomen of Cristen blood,
> That lerned in that scole yeer by yere
> Swich manere doctrine as men used there,
> This is to seyn, to syngen and to rede,
> As smale children doon in hire childhede.
>
> (488–501)

Polemicizing against the Jewry and its inhabitants immediately before describing the "litel scole," the stanzas imply that the "doctrine" the "smale children" learn "yeer by yere" is somewhat predetermined: "Swich manere doctrine" instilled in the children of "Cristen blood" as reading and, equally importantly, singing, will necessarily confirm the assessment of the Jews as "hateful to Crist and to his compaignye," the members of the Christian community that surrounds them.

As one of the students attending the "litel scole," the "litel clergeon" seems an ideal pedagogical subject, used to going "day to day to scole" (504) and familiar with mundane devotional practices: "th'ymage/Of Cristes mooder, hadde he in usage,/As hym was taught, to knele adoun and seye/ His *Ave Marie*, as he goth by the weye" (505–8). But the narrative carefully dissociates the clergeon's earliest education from the "doctrine" learned in school by locating it instead in a domestic space, in which his mother, a "wydwe," is his only visible instructor: "Thus hath this wydwe hir litel sone ytaught/Oure blisful Lady, Cristes mooder deere,/To worshipe ay, and he forgat it naught,/For sely child wol alday soone leere" (509–12). Already proficient in the visual and oral arts of "worshipe" taught him at home, the clergeon embodies a strange sort of resistance to the institutional discipline of the schoolroom. Ironically, the clergeon's almost willful distraction from his schoolroom studies leads to his first encounter with the music that will forever change (and eventually end) his earthly life:

> This litel child, his litel book lernynge,
> As he sat in the scole at his prymer,
> He *Alma redemptoris* herde synge,
> As children lerned hire antiphoner;
> And as he dorste, he drough hym ner and ner,
> And herkned ay the wordes and the noote,
> Til he the firste vers koude al by rote.
>
> (516–22)

Here Chaucer emphasizes the clergeon's ignorance—"noght wiste he what this Latyn was to seye,/For he so yong and tendre was of age" (523–24)—in order to stress that the *sound* of the antiphon enchants him well before he knows the meaning of the words. This is a crucial point: at least since Augustine's agonized account in the *Confessions* of the *voluptates aurium*, Christian writers on liturgy had consistently emphasized the subordination of musical sonority to the salvational language it supports (in Augustine's words, as we saw in Chapter 2, music is the "setting for the words which give it life").[18] Nevertheless, only once he learns that the *Alma redemptoris* is "maked of our blisful Lady free" (532) does the clergeon joyfully vow to memorize it in its entirety by the end of the year, a learning process described in some detail:

> "And is this song maked in reverence
> Of Cristes mooder?" seyde this innocent.
> "Now, certes, I wol do my diligence
> To konne it al er Cristemasse be went.
> Though that I for my prymer shal be shent
> And shal be beten thries in an houre,
> I wol it konne Oure Lady for to honoure!"

His felawe taughte hym homward prively,
Fro day to day, til he koude it by rote,
And thanne he song it wel and boldely,
Fro word to word, acordynge with the note.
Twies a day it passed thurgh his throte,
To scoleward and homward whan he wente;
On Cristes mooder set was his entente.

(537–50)

One of the more notable features of this much-discussed passage is its identification of the specific location in which the clergeon's assimilation of the hymn takes place: not in the "scole" where Christian children learn "to syngen and rede," but on a public road between schoolroom and home, the two previous sites of his pedagogical subjection. If Chaucer removes the clergeon's musical education from the institutional site of elementary pedagogy, he also seeks to distance the clergeon himself from the visceral reality of musical learning, the bodily labor and discipline required for the assimilation of sacred chant. The most common post-Carolingian method of instruction in the arts of chant was the so-called Guidonian Hand, named after its nominal founder, Guido of Arezzo, an eleventh-century monk who wrote widely on musical theory and pedagogy (though as far as we know Guido himself never actually described the musical hand). In this technique, the music-master employed the hand as a visual aid for learning plainchant (see Figure 16); the various joints of the fingers and regions of the palm each corresponded to a given syllable, and by pointing to different parts of his hand the master would instruct his students as to which tone to sing at the appropriate moment.[19] The hand eventually superceded the monochord as the primary pedagogical aid used in solmization, a mnemonic practice still employed today in which each note in a scale is assigned a syllable and the scale memorized accordingly.[20] As a palpable didactic method, this mode of musical instruction relied upon the corporeal and locational character of medieval memory systems that the work of Mary Carruthers has excavated.[21]

Music theorists went to great lengths to defend solmization (whether by hand or monochord) as the only proper way to learn the rudiments of plainchant, castigating—often quite harshly—the practitioners of other methods for their lack of thoroughness and discipline. In his widely copied

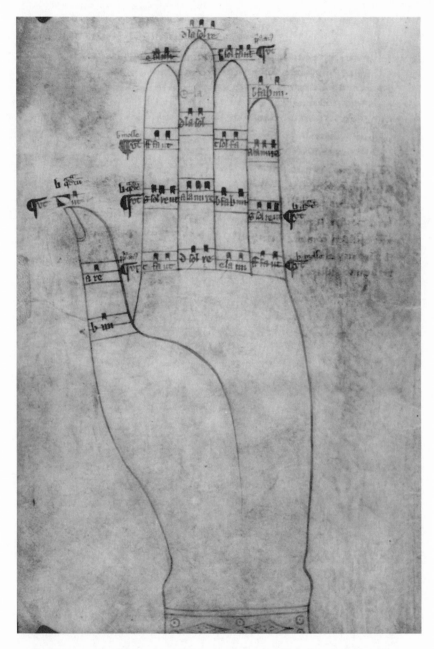

FIGURE 16   Guidonian Hand, thirteenth century (London, British Library MS. Royal 12 C VI, fol. 52 ᵛ)

Epistola de ignoto cantu, Guido of Arezzo rails against the shallowness of rote memorization in favor of the "deep" mnemonic utility of solmization: "We need not always seek out the voice of a man or the sound of some instrument to learn an unknown melody, so that, as if blind, we should appear to go forth without a leader; rather, we must commit the distinctiveness and property of individual sounds, and all descents and ascents, to the depths of the memory" (Non ergo debemus semper pro ignoto cantu vocem hominis vel alicuius instrumenti quaerere, ut quasi caeci videamur numquam sine ductore procedere; sed singulorum sonorum, omniumque depositionum et elevationem diversitates proprietatesque altae memoriae commendare).[22] For Guido and his followers, solmization entails the pedagogical and institutional power of a "leader," without whom the singers learn and perform "like the blind." The authors of the *Summa musice*, a late-twelfth-century manual for the instruction of choirboys, go even further in their condemnation of rote memorization, demoting its practitioners to the status of non-*musici*: "As I have said, and as daily examples show, there are some singers who should not be called *musici* because they do not follow the rational principles of music and they cannot learn a chant unless it is sung to them repeatedly by another, perhaps a teacher or a colleague" (Cum itaque, sicut dixi, et sicut quotidiana experimenta ostendunt, quidam sunt cantores qui musici appellari non debent eo quod musicis rationibus non utuntur, et qui cantum non possunt addiscere nisi a sepe cantante alio, ut magistro vel socio).[23]

Nor are such disciplinary prescriptions exclusive to Latin pedagogical texts. They appear in various and contradictory guises in several Middle English works roughly contemporary with the Prioress's Tale, most notably *Piers Plowman* and at least two of the poems it inspired. Despite Sloth's lengthy ecclesiastical tenure as "preest and person passynge thritty wynter" in *Piers*, he "kan . . . neyþer solve ne synge ne seintes lyves rede," his lack of musical proficiency an unmistakable sign of his sinful nature.[24] In *Mum and the Sothsegger*, youthful impatience and a lack of musical discipline characterize the "segges" in Mum's court: "Thay leden men þe long waye and louedayes breken/And maken moppes wel myry with þaire madde tales/Forto sowe siluer seede and solue ere þay singe."[25] Unlike Langland, the *Mum* author carefully distinguishes between solmization and song, implying that the former should be pursued only after a certain measure of musical proficiency has been acquired (thus the analogous reference in the next line to those who "haue ynne þaire harueste while þe hete dureth"). By contrast, the narrator of "De Veritate et Consciencia" (ca. 1415–50), a much shorter work also in the *Piers Plowman* tradition, approaches a palace where he hears "a bischop holde his correccyoun" by attempting to instruct a company "bothe lernyd" and "lewde" in the salvational arts of solmization: "*Si dedero* was ther lessoun/Who so cowde solfe þat songe shuld be save."[26]

Given such widespread insistence on the disciplinary indispensability of solmization in both canonical Latin and contemporary vernacular writings, it seems all the more appropriate that the Prioress would depict the clergeon, that paragon of "innocentz," learning the *Alma redemptoris* "day to day . . . by rote": through repetitive singing rather than Guidonian discipline. The narrative further erodes normative notions of pedagogical authority by removing the clergeon's assimilation of the hymn from the provenance of an adult song-master and thus collapsing the hierarchical relation between master and pupil into a suggestively intimate dynamic between peers: "His felawe taughte hym homward prively." Within the "scole," however, this "felawe" is institutionally segregated from the clergeon; as William Courtenay points out, "separate schools for reading and song existed by the late fourteenth century, and within the same school there might be two classes serving the needs of two different groups of students." When the older student admits, "I lerne song, I kan but smal grammeere" (536), Courtenay argues, Chaucer almost certainly means to imply that he "was being instructed in song rather than reading."[27] By placing such explicit emphasis on the division between musical and grammatical learning, Chaucer also registers a recent institutional move away from the enduring disciplinary affiliations between music and grammar that Mathias Bielitz has demonstrated.[28] As a student of grammar alone, then, the clergeon learns the antiphon incorrectly in both pedagogical and institutional terms.

Chaucer's narrative avoidance of the protocols of elementary musical pedagogy in his depiction of the clergeon is more than simply a function of his sources. To the contrary, as Carleton Brown observed over fifty years ago, one of the more notable distinctions between the Prioress's Tale and even the closest of its analogues is the fact that only in Chaucer's narrative does "the child [learn] the anthem out of school hours and not as a part of his school discipline."[29] This is a fascinating revision, and one that deserves much more comment than it has received in the criticism. For it shows us that in his meticulous refashioning of the miracle story of the singing boy martyr, Chaucer sought to avoid entirely the problem of institutionalized musical learning, the ecclesiastical discipline that might make the *Alma redemptoris* somehow less miraculous to its listeners. Absorbing the antiphon outside the "cloistre" with the gentle coaxing of a peer rather than the disciplinary ear and hand of the singing-master, the clergeon sings "Ful murily" as he learns the music "scoleward and homward"; a public roadway displaces the classroom just as pedagogical protocol gives way to "rote" memorization. The clergeon's musical learning is ostensibly anything but a product of schoolroom *disciplina*.

Yet it may be just that. For at the very moment he vows to "konne" the *Alma redemptoris*, the clergeon acknowledges the inextricability of pedagogical violence from his own musical instruction:

> "Though that I for my prymer shal be shent
> And shal be beten thries in an houre,
> I wol it konne Oure Lady for to honoure!"

The subtle "Though" distances the music rhetorically from any suggestion of disciplinary authority: the clergeon will learn the antiphon *despite the threat* of being beaten for neglecting his "prymer."[30] There is much in the passage above, however, to suggest that the clergeon learns it *as a direct result* of being beaten—indeed of the very pedagogical *disciplina* the narrative elides. First, the threat of his teacher's violence and the clergeon's rote repetition of the antiphon bear a close narrative, phonetic, and grammatical proximity to one another: the clergeon will be "beten *thries* in an houre" just as the hymn passes "*twies* a day . . . thurgh his throte," implying a hidden but inevitable intimacy between the beating of the child and his acquisition of musical knowledge. Though the tale never actually shows us the clergeon in "scole" learning to "rede," his continuous subjection to corporal punishment is naturalized as an integral part of his learning. In fact, the clergeon himself effectively *fantasizes* the violence of his pedagogical discipline— "I shal be beten"—in a percussive alliteration just as he vows that he "wol it konne"; the threat and promise of violence seem to be the very conditions for the learning of the antiphon. Finally, the *Alma redemptoris* passes through the same "throte" that will be "kitte" by the Jewish "homycide" just three stanzas later. The flow of the hymn through the clergeon's body carries the visceral threat of impending violence just as it bears the traces of corporal punishment.

Ultimately, then, the Prioress's Tale figures the clergeon's body as an object of disciplinary violence while removing him from the very institutional context that would have exposed him to it. How are we to account for this seeming contradiction? How might the musical trajectory traced in the first half of the tale—the clergeon's initial aural encounter with the *Alma redemptoris*, the sinister yet enabling threat of schoolroom violence, the assimilation of the hymn, and the clergeon's murder—shed light on the mystifying role music performs in the tale's horrific denouement? In order to begin answering these questions, we first need to consider the particular pedagogical environment from which Chaucer's revisionism removed the Prioress's "martyr"; for despite his narrative efforts to the contrary, this tradition will leave indelible traces on the body of the "litel clergeon."

Musical Learning and the Horrors of Song

The role of violence in medieval education has, until very recently, been addressed only sparingly in the scholarship.[31] Yet it is no secret that corporal punishment was a staple of early education throughout the period; it played an especially vivid and mimetic role, I want to argue, in musical pedagogy. The learning of plainchant in particular—whether through solmization or otherwise—appears with remarkable consistency throughout the Middle Ages as an inherently violent initiation into musical *scientia*.[32] Chaucer's Prioress's Tale is in fact part of a long tradition of imagining violence as an integral part of the pedagogical transmission of the medieval Latin liturgy, as we can see if we read the tale alongside a number of hagiographical *vitae*, influential pedagogical manuals, and vernacular satires that similarly represent liturgical learning as a scene of schoolroom terror.

The sixth-century pope and scholar, Gregory the Great, was revered for much of the Middle Ages as the father of "Gregorian chant," the great corpus of Latin monophony that formed the musical basis of the Roman liturgy. Twentieth-century scholarship on early chant has demolished the traditional view of Gregory as the composer or *compilator* of the earliest notated chant that survives; the so-called *Cantus Romanus* supposedly imported from Rome by the Carolingians in the ninth century has been shown by Leo Treitler and others to be a Frankish invention.[33] In later centuries, however, the need to claim Gregory as the founder of Roman chant was deeply felt, leading to what Treitler has aptly described as part of a wide-scale "process of diffusion, adaptation, invention, appropriation, and displacement . . . propagandizing, mythologizing, and rationalizing" through which the papacy and other powers sought to legitimize their own musical traditions.[34] One of the most important pieces of liturgical propaganda in this vein was the *Vita Gregorii magni*, written in the 870s by John the Deacon and compiled by order of Pope John VIII.[35] It is a text that associates violence with the very origins of liturgical psalmody, at least as John the Deacon perceived them. Describing Gregory's surviving relics in the Lateran palace, John calls particular attention to "the couch from which he gave lessons in chant, the whip with which he threatened the boys [*flagellum ipsius, quo pueris minabatur*], and the authentic antiphonal."[36] Writing in the decade that likely saw the first attempts by the papacy to place Gregory at the origins of the Roman chant tradition, John associates a living symbol of the saint's originary pedagogical violence with the liturgical book that supposedly transmits his musical legacy. The punitive spirit of Gregory's whip can still be felt in an eleventh-century Customal from St. Benigne in Dijon, which prescribes beating as an integral part of the liturgical day: "At Nocturns, and indeed at all the Hours, if the boys commit any fault in the psalmody or other singing, either by sleeping or such like transgression, let there be no sort of delay, but let them be stripped forthwith of frock and cowl, and beaten in their shirt only, with pliant and smooth osier rods provided for that special purpose."[37]

The memory of violence looms powerfully in two of the most influential medieval treatises on the learning of plainchant, both of which survive in numerous manuscripts and were regularly consulted and copied throughout the later Middle Ages. In the *Prologus* to his Antiphoner, Guido of Arezzo claims that his improved pedagogical method will allow "any intelligent and studious person [to] learn singing" quickly and easily; indeed, boasts Guido, "after he has thoroughly learned a part of it through a master, he will unhesitatingly understand the rest of it by himself without a master" (postquam partem eius per magistrum bene cognoverit, reliqua per se sine magistro indubitanter agnoscit).[38] Even as he celebrates the autodidactic promises of solmization, however, Guido recruits into his propaganda a scene of violence with which he assumes his readers will be familiar:

De quo si quis me mentiri putat, veniat, experiatur et videat, quod tale
hoc apud nos pueruli faciunt, qui pro psalmorum et vulgarium litterarum ig-
norantia saeva adhuc suscipiunt flagella, qui saepe et ipsius antiphonae,
quam per se sine magistro recte possunt cantare, verba et syllabas nesciunt
pronuntiare.[39]

[As to this, should anyone doubt that I am telling the truth, let him come,
make a trial, and see what small boys can do under our direction, boys who
until now have received whippings for their gross ignorance of the psalms
and vulgar letters, who often do not know how to pronounce the words and
syllables of the very antiphon which now, without a master, they sing correctly by themselves.]

In a revealing admission buried carefully in a subordinate clause, Guido
informs his readers of what they already know quite well: boys must be
beaten regularly in order to learn *cantus* and *grammatica*.[40] Though he
claims that solmization will obviate the need for such beatings, what comes
across quite clearly in the "advertisement" above is his blithe assumption
that they are commonplace.

A similarly revealing attempt to dissociate solmization and violence
appears in the *Enchiridion musices*, long attributed to Odo of Cluny but
now considered anonymous.[41] This tenth-century work includes an extended panegyric to the monochord, which, the author contends, affords
the student a certain measure of autonomy in the learning of plainchant.
After the author recounts the pragmatics of his method, he records a student's pathetic exuberance at the thought of his mechanical master's endless
patience:

M. Litteras monochordi, sicut per eas cantilena discurrit, ante oculos pone:
ut si nondum vim ipsarum litterarum plene cognoscis, secundum easdem litteras chordam percutiens ab ignorante magistro mirifice audias, et addiscas.

D. Vere inquam magistrum mirabilem mihi dedisti, qui a me factus me
doceat, meque docens ipse nihil sapiat. Imo propter patientiam et obedien-
tiam sui eum maxime amplector; cantabit enim mihi quando voluero, et
nunquam de mei sensus tarditate commotus verberibus vel iniuriis cruciabit.

[Master: Place before your eyes the letters of the monochord as the melody
ranges through them; then, if you do not fully recognize the force of the letters themselves, you may hear them and learn them, wonderful to relate,
from an ignorant master.

Disciple: Indeed I say that you have given me a wonderful master, who, made by me, teaches me, and teaching me, knows nothing himself. Nay, for his patience and obedience I fervently embrace him, and he will never torment me with blows or abuse when provoked by the slowness of my sense.][42]

For the disciple, the monochord promises the reversal of pedagogical discipline and the cessation of violence. Even so, the student can understand the instrument's patience only in relation to the relentless tyranny of his *magister*.

Despite the anxious protestations of Guido and the Pseudo-Odo, the spread of solmization after the Carolingian period by no means entailed the cessation of pedagogical violence. In the anonymous twelfth-century *vita* of St. Stephen of Obazine, produced in a post-Reform Cistercian environment in which chant was almost certainly learned through solmization, Stephen's "strenuous discipline" includes scrupulous surveillance of "delinquents" in the choir:

For if any raised his eyes but a little in church, or smiled but faintly, or slumbered but lightly, or negligently let fall the book which he held, or made any heedless sound, or chanted too fast or out of tune, he received forthwith either a rod on his head or an open hand upon his cheek, so loud that the sound of the blow rang in everyone's ears [*aut virginam accipiebat in capite aut palmam in facie ita ut sonus percussionis omnium auribus resultaret*]; a punishment that was especially inflicted on the younger boys, to their own correction and the terror of the rest.[43]

Stephen's hagiographer relishes in the production of violence against the choirboys, the drumlike beatings that ring in the ears of the cowering youngsters as they anticipate their own punishment. In its focus on the actual *sonus percussionis*, the "sound of beating" and its disciplinary effects, the passage anticipates the Unterlinden writer's equally violent image of the music of flagellation reaching the ears of God (see Chapter 5). Also intriguing is the fact that Stephen punishes the boys by striking them with his "open hand," the very hand symbolically inscribed with the syllables and neumes they have learned to chant—as in Figure 17, a fifteenth-century Guidonian Hand "scored" with so much music that it suggests a comparison with the wounds on Christ's palms. Such passages serve to remind us that in music, perhaps more literally than in any other medieval disci-

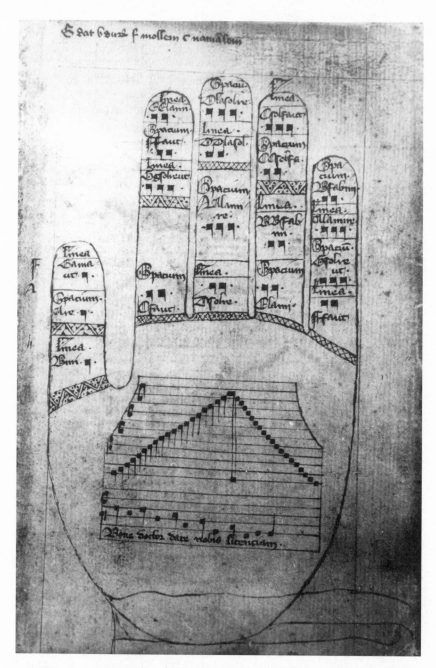

FIGURE 17 Guidonian Hand, fifteenth century (Erfurt, Stadtbibliothek, Amplon. Ca8 93, fol. 1ʳ)

FIGURE 18   Guidonian Hand, from Elias Salomonis, *Scientia artis musicae*, late thirteenth century (Milan, Biblioteca Ambrosiana, Cod. D 75 inf., fol. 6 ʳ)

pline, the *palma* that taught was also the hand that punished and inflicted pain upon the bodies of those who learned. In the most celebrated medieval representation of the Guidonian Hand, an illustration in a late-thirteenth-century copy of Elias Salomonis's *Scientia artis musicae* (Figure 18), the hand dominates the image and appears grotesquely enlarged in relation to the master's innocently smiling face. The syllables are organized and inscribed so densely along the fingers that it appears as if the giant hand is wearing a kind of musical glove.

To most of us, of course, gazing upon such an image brings to mind the practice of solmization, medieval mnemotechnics, and the history of edu-

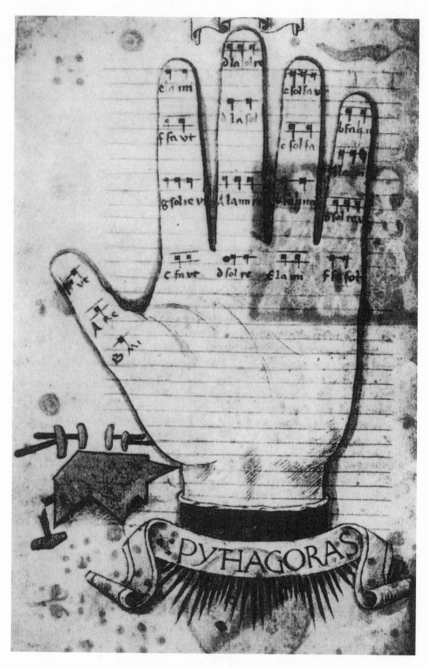

FIGURE 19 Guidonian Hand, from *Tractatus singularis super musicam planam* (anonymous) (Berlin, Staatsbibliothek zu Berlin, Mus. Ms. theor. 1599, fol. 1 ᵛ)

cation. A medieval youth learning song may have felt only fear. For indeed, the discursive history of the Guidonian Hand is bound up explicitly with the traditions of violent Christian musicality discussed at length in Chapter 5. The opening page of a fifteenth-century treatise on plainsong claims the pedagogical hand as belonging to Pythagoras himself (Figure 19). The dark rulings on the page create the semblance of a gigantic musical staff that contains the hand and marks it with the notes and syllables that the Pythagorean hand in turn must teach. At the same time, the viewer is forced to recall another famed occupation of this hand: in the lower left, its triangular extension threatening to gouge the wrist, rests an anvil surrounded by the suspended hammers of Pythagoras—the very hammers that invent music in medieval typology and thus prefigure the pounding of crucifying nails into the flesh of Christ. The Guidonian Hand provides an indispensable pedagogical apparatus for musical transmission while embodying the constant threat of musical violence.

We are fortunate to have one text that pretends to represent the torturous and painful demands of musical learning for the fourteenth-century English choirboy in particular. The "Choristers' Lament," written in the last quarter of the fourteenth century and surviving in a single manuscript,[44] provides a fascinating counterpoint to the Prioress's Tale, for it demonstrates vividly how at least one English poet contemporary with Chaucer imagined the pervasive role of violence in chant instruction. I have argued elsewhere that the "Choristers' Lament" constitutes a playful monastic response to the legalistic representations of the liturgy in Langland's *Piers Plowman*.[45] Here I am concerned with the extraordinary detail with which the poem seeks to convey the violence of the pedagogical scenario in the process of liturgical transmission. The poem opens in the voice of a student, Walter, who fearfully recounts his failed attempts to learn chant:

> "Vncomly in cloystre   i coure ful of care,
> I loke as a lurdeyn   and listne til my lare.
> þe song of þe cesolfa   dos me syken sare,
> and sitte stotiand on a song   a moneth and mare.
>
> I ga gowlend abowte   also dos a goke,
> mani is þe sorwfol song   it singge vpon mi bok.
> I am holde so harde   vnneþes dar i loke;
> al þe mirthe of þis mold   for god i forsoke."[46]

Walter bemoans his unsightly physical appearance and posture ("Vn-comly . . . i coure," "I loke as a lurdeyn"), ascribing his "goke"-like behavior to the detrimental effects caused by singing too high (the "cesolfa" is roughly the medieval equivalent of high C) and, *pace* Guido, learning too slowly for "a moneth and mare." So frightening is his songbook that Walter is afraid "vnneþes" to "loke," even lamenting his entry into religious orders because of the musical torture it has entailed. The physical appearance of the neumes on the page represents a further source of anxiety for the student, visually reminding him of the corporeal pain he endures: "Somme notes arn shorte   and somme a long noke,/Somme kroken aweyward   als a fleshoke" (11–12). The specific somatic effects of this notational "fleshoke" on Walter's body go unmentioned—though the image cannot help but remind us of the notated buttocks painted by Hieronymous Bosch in the *Garden of Earthly Delights*. Nor is the poet's perception of specific neume forms as somehow carrying pedagogical violence with them unprecedented: centuries earlier Aurelian of Réôme had compared the performance of the *tristropha*, an ornamental neume, to the (presumably familiar) sound of a slap: "with a threefold note you may make a quick beat like a lashing hand [*manus verberantis*]."[47]

Unlike Chaucer's clergeon, whose friend teaches him "by rote" as they walk to and from school, Walter learns to chant at the hands of a firm disciplinarian, who rails at him for improper singing and lambastes him for "stombl[ing] and stik[ing] faste as þu were lame" (18). So harsh is his master's discipline that Walter quite often feels "so wo þat wol ner wil he blede" (25). Not to be outdone, Walter's companion William, introduced a few stanzas later, similarly complains of the woes of musical learning, arguing that the physical pain of simply *singing* the Psalms much outweigh the various agonies recounted in the Psalms themselves: "I donke vpon dauid til my tonge talmes./I ne rendrede nowt sithen men beren palmes/Is it also mikel sorwe in song so is in salmes?" (30–32). Like Walter, William complains of the painful effects of individual notes on his singing body, concluding the poem with this spectacular image of musical violence in the cloister:

ȝet ther been oþer notes,   sol and vt and la,
and þat froward file   þat men clipis fa.
Often he dos me liken ille   and werkes me ful wa;
Miȝti him neuere hitten   inton for to ta.

ȝet þer is a streinant   witȝ to longe tailes
þerfore has vre mayster   ofte horled mi kayles
Ful litel þu kennes   qwat sorwe me ayles
It is but childes game   þat þu witȝ david dayles.

Qwan ilke note til oþer lepes   and makes hem asawt,
þat we calles a moyson   in gesolreutȝ en hawt.
Il hayl were þu boren   ȝif þu make defawt.
þanne sais oure mayster,   "Que vos ren ne vawt."

(41–52)

Here the "fa" syllable, a "froward file," "werkes" William "ful wa," to which
William responds by trying to "hitten [him] inton for to ta" (i.e., strike the
note exactly in tune); William's "kayles," moreover, have been "horled" by
his master for his poor performance of the "streinant" (probably the Ars
Nova *breve*), while the notes themselves "ilke . . . til oþer lepes and makes
hem asawt," a struggle that somehow produces "moison," or melody; finally, the "mayster," despite all his students' efforts, lambastes them as
worthless and pathetic (in French, no less). The "Choristers' Lament" thus
imagines violence as an essential part of musical learning on every level,
pervading the relationships between the pupil and the music he sings, the
pupil and the master, even the individual musical notes. Though most
likely written as a humorous parody of student complaints, the poem nevertheless speaks volumes about the daily strains on the mouths, throats,
eyes, and ears of young singers entailed by the learning of liturgical music.

Along with the Latin texts discussed above, The "Choristers' Lament"
opens a window onto a violent and ubiquitous pedagogical arena that the
Prioress's Tale ultimately fails to obscure. It would have been difficult indeed for a medieval writer at all familiar with the disciplinary norms of
musical learning successfully to dissociate the Latin psalmody of a young
singer from the corporal punishment that would have accompanied its
acquisition: for example, the "contumelias et terrores magistri" that figure
so prominently in one of the tale's later analogues.[48] Yet if the "Lament"
imagines violence as integral to elementary pedagogy within the walls of the
"cloistre," the scene of musical learning in the Prioress's Tale, though no less
fraught with violence, is emphatically public. And it is precisely the representation of the clergeon's acquisition of the *Alma redemptoris* as an event

occurring within the public sphere that asks us to puzzle over the musical progression in the remainder of the tale from pedagogy to murder and, finally, massacre. The particular pedagogical relation between music and violence shifts, subtly but unmistakably, from the institutional context discussed above to a quite distinctive form of Christian discipline.

Music and the Sacrificial Body

As the narrative focus of the Prioress's Tale moves from schoolroom to "greet citee," the threat of corporal punishment acknowledged by the clergeon devolves into a spectacular display of religious difference rung on human bodies. Just after narrating the clergeon's rote learning of the *Alma redemptoris*, the Prioress deploys the antiphon to divide the city from within, casting the essential difference between Christians who belong and Jews who do not as a kind of innate somatic dissonance:

> As I have seyd, thurghout the Juerie
> This litel child, as he cam to and fro,
> Ful murily than wolde he synge and crie
> *O Alma redemptoris* everemo.
> The swetnesse his herte perced so
> Of Cristes mooder that, to hire to preye,
> He kan nat stynte of syngyng by the weye.
>
> Oure firste foo, the serpent Sathanas,
> That hath in Jues herte his waspes nest,
> Up swal, and seide, "O Hebrayk peple, allas!
> Is this to yow a thyng that is honest,
> That swich a boy shal walken as hym lest
> In youre despit, and synge of swich sentence,
> Which is agayn youre lawes reverence?"

$$(551-64)$$

The first-person construction in the first stanza ("as I have seyd") constitutes the Prioress's Christian listeners around the musical "swetnesse" that fills and enlivens the clergeon's body "ful murily." The helplessness of the "litel child" in the face of the hymn—he "kan nat stynte of syngyng" as he passes "thurghout the Juerie"[49]—echoes the Prioress's own helplessness in the prologue under the "weighte" of song she can "nat susteene" by herself, the narrative that the "blisful Queene" is enjoined to "gyde" (481–87). The second stanza works the same way but in reverse, defining the Jews by their exclusion from the tale's audience; they are aligned with Satan through Chaucer's "Our firste foo," another first-person phrase that constructs religious difference as an a priori assumption that music immediately reifies: unlike the clergeon, whose "herte" is "perced so" by the *Alma redemptoris*, the Jews "hath in . . . herte" the painful buzzing of Satan's "waspes nest," from which the devil "up swal" to provoke his subjects to murder. Satan's injunction to the Jews only furthers the attempt here to exonerate the clergeon's song. The problem for Satan and, through him, the Jews, is not that the clergeon sings, but that he sings "of swich sentence, / Which is agayn youre lawes reverence." Though music is the very embodiment of difference in these stanzas, even the devil himself refuses to address its power and culpability within the frame of the narrative.

The contrast drawn here between the musically pierced "herte" of the clergeon and the collectively buzzing "herte" of the Jews recalls the Second Nun's description of Cecilia's asceticism as a kind of inner music: "And whil the organs maden melodie, / To God allone in herte thus sang she" (8.134–35). This link becomes increasingly clear after the clergeon is murdered and thrown "in a wardrobe. . . . Where as thise Jewes purgen hire entraille" (572–73). Just as the clergeon "wolde . . . synge and crie" the *Alma redemptoris* on his way to and from school, after the ambush his "blood out crieth" on the Jews' "cursed dede" (578), his death itself producing the music that previously had moved "thurgh his throte." In the Prioress's words:

O martir, sowded to virginitee,
Now maystow syngen, folwynge evere in oon
The white Lamb celestial—quod she—
Of which the grete evaungelist, Seint John,
In Pathmos wroot, which seith that they that goon
Biforn this Lamb and synge a song al newe,
That nevere, flesshly, wommen they ne knewe.

(579–85)

Released from life in the body, the martyred clergeon now resonates with a salvific "song" performed "Biforn this Lamb," a song registering the distance between the beatified soul and the "flesshly wommen" he has left behind. Like Cecilia, the clergeon becomes not simply a martyr, but, quite specifically, a *virgin* martyr; his musicality no longer represents the effects of earthly pedagogy, but of the "song al newe." The "New Song," an ancient Christian topos for the discipline of virginity,[50] appears in numerous Middle English texts (such as the *Ancrene Wisse* and Walter Hilton's *Scale of Perfection*) written specifically for women religious. In *The Form of Living*, Richard Rolle urges that the soul of the well-disciplined virgin, the soul "þat loueth songe and melody," keep itself "syngynge gostly" in chastity until "þe deth cum."[51] For the *Hali Meidhad* author, too, the resonance of the New Song within the hearts of virgins—"þis song" that "nane buten heo singen"—allows them to "heolden ham cleane áá from fleschliche fulðen i bodi ant i breoste."[52] The Prioress's notorious "quod she," so often read as a self-conscious attempt by Chaucer to distance himself from the Prioress's narrative voice, may also be a cue to read this stanza as the imposition of a pointedly feminine mode of bodily discipline—a reminder that virginity constitutes a musical form of subjection in its own right.

The musical resonances between Chaucer's two religious women's narratives go deeper still. Near the gruesome end of the Second Nun's Tale, after Almachius has failed to execute Cecilia by fire and water, he sends "his sonde," or messenger, to "sleen hire in the bath" (525) with his sword. Chaucer describes the messenger's vain attempts to carry out his lord's orders: "Thre strokes in the nekke he smoot hire tho,/The tormentour, but for no maner chaunce/He myghte noght smyte al hir nekke atwo" (526–28). Like the clergeon, who "with throte ykorven lay upright" as he "gan to sing" the *Alma redemptoris* after being thrown in the privy (611), Cecilia is left by Almachius's agent to "lye" "with hir nekke ycorven" (533–34); nevertheless, Cecilia "gan to preche" to her community (533–39).[53] While the explicit verbal echoes between these two final scenes of martyrdom—both involving severed necks and miraculous speech—have not gone unremarked,[54] particularly intriguing is the confluence between music, violence, and Christian martyrdom they suggest. The clergeon's self-conscious, almost stoic anticipation of being "*beten thries* in an houre" by his grammarmaster—a fear intimately bound up with the fate of his singing "throte"—is spectacularly and publicly realized in the same "*Thre strokes*" that sever Cecilia's "nekke." This image begins to reveal the implied logic of the Prioress's narrative progression from pedagogy to martyrdom to massacre:

just as the clergeon willingly resigns himself to a tripled beating at the hands of institutional authority in order to sing to the Virgin, Cecilia suffers three blows to her neck from the pagan "prefect" in order to continue singing "in herte." In each case, Chaucer represents music as integral to both a Christian martyr's defiance of non-Christian authority and a Christian community's resistance to its supposed persecutors.

With the clergeon's miraculous rescue from the "wardrobe," his resonant body becomes the focus of both community and narrative; once the murderers are discovered and bound by order of the provost (620), the tale can seemingly conclude with the "true" death and sanctification of the martyr. Even here, however, the supposed "innocentz" of the clergeon's music rings false; in the three stanzas that follow, the antiphon neatly frames the Christian massacre of the Jews:

> This child with pitous lamentacioun
> Up taken was, syngynge his song alway,
> And with honour of greet processioun
> They carien hym unto the nexte abbay.
> His mooder swownynge by his beere lay;
> Unnethe myghte the peple that was theere
> This newe Rachel brynge fro his beere.
>
> With torment and with shameful deeth echon,
> This provost dooth thise Jewes for to sterve
> That of this mordre wiste, and that anon.
> He nolde no swich cursednesse observe.
> "Yvele shal have that yvele wol deserve";
> Therfore with wilde hors he dide hem drawe,
> And after that he heng hem by the lawe.
>
> Upon this beere ay lith this innocent
> Biforn the chief auter, whil the masse laste;
> And after that, the abbot with his covent
> Han sped hem for to burien hym ful faste;
> And whan they hooly water on hym caste,
> Yet spak this child, whan spreynd was hooly water,
> And song *O Alma redemptoris mater*!
>
> (621–41)

Once again the narrative relies on bodily *music* in articulating bodily *differ-ence*. The Christians, bearing the clergeon into the enclosed space of an "abbay" and performing the requiem mass for him there, constitute and define themselves around his body and the music it produces. For the Jews, however, this same music serves to accompany the very annihilation of community and the fragmentation of body, both individual and social. The conveniently broad category of those sentenced to execution—all the Jews "that of this mordre wist"—constructs the Jews' knowledge as a community, rather than their actions as individuals, as the justification for their deaths. The Prioress attempts as well to collapse the massacre of the Jews and render it narratively insignificant; echoing the end of the first stanza ("fro his beere") in the first line of the third ("upon this beere"), she represents the mass execution as a momentary distraction from the clergeon's reclining and resonating on his "beere," the music that represents, in Fradenburg's words, "an unbroken continuity against which the violence of the Jews' execution erupts."[55] A palindromic mirroring between the first and third stanzas heightens this effect: in the first, the clergeon sings, the Christians relocate his body, then the clergeon rests on the bier, while in the third the sequence of events is exactly reversed. For the Christians the spectacle of the clergeon's sonorous corpse is the promise of everlasting life, the expectation of a collective "New Song" after the last trumpet; the spectacle of the Jews' drawn, quartered, and hung cadavers, by contrast, recalls Adorno's "sear[ed] stigmata," a sign both of the Jews' exclusion from Christian musicality and of their eternal damnation.

In this sense, the massacre scene in the Prioress's Tale represents a narrative performance of what Jacques Attali has identified as the "sacrifi-cial" function of music in premodern European cultures, a collective invest-ment in the violent musical aestheticization of the "noise" of (in this case) religious and ethnic difference: "Noise is a weapon and music, primordially, is the formation, domestication, and ritualization of that weapon as a sim-ulacrum of ritual murder."[56] Thus, with the massacre of the Jews relegated to a single stanza, the clergeon addresses the community from his resting place, explaining the revivification of his body by casting its miraculous performance as a musical site of Christian memory:

"My throte is kut unto my nekke boon,"
Seyde this child, "and as by wey of kynde

I sholde have dyed, ye, longe tyme agon.
But Jesu Crist, as ye in bookes fynde,
Wil that his glorie laste and be in mynde,
And for the worship of his Mooder deere
Yet may I synge *O Alma* loude and cleere."

(649–55)

Though lacerated and left for dead, the clergeon reveals that his musicality is the direct result of the desire or "wil" of "Jesu Crist" for his own memorialization, the "worship of his Mooder deere" in song. As in the Prioress's Prologue, such musical praise represents the audible, "cleere" confirmation of what without it would come perilously close to "makyng"—the written accounts of Christ and his "wil," in the clergeon's words, "ye in bookes fynde." As the fulfillment of divine will, music is the ultimate sign of epistemological certainty, song the visceral promise of Christian salvation.

Even this musical performance, however, must finally be mediated through language. Despite the extraordinary sight and sound of his resonant body, despite God's miraculous intervention in the community of "Cristen blood," the clergeon is obliged to gloss his own song, thereby constructing a hagiographical narrative *about himself* in order to convince the community of his "certeyn" musical sanctity:

"This welle of mercy, Cristes mooder sweete,
I loved alwey, as after my konnynge;
And whan that I my lyf sholde forlete,
To me she cam, and bad me for to synge
This anthem verraily in my deyynge,
As ye han herd, and whan that I hadde songe,
Me thoughte she leyde a greyn upon my tonge.

"Wherfore I synge, and synge moot certeyn,
In honour of that blisful Mayden free
Til fro my tonge of taken is the greyn;
And after that thus seyde she to me:
'My litel child, now wol I fecche thee,
What that the greyn is fro thy tonge ytake.
Be nat agast; I wol thee nat forsake.' "

(656–69)

Once again, belief and praise are riddled with uncertainty: the clergeon pauses to remind the listeners that they "han" in fact "herd" his song, while he himself only "thoughte" the Virgin placed the grain on his tongue. Though compelled by the Virgin to sing from the moment of his death "Til fro [his] tonge of taken is the greyn," the clergeon in fact interrupts the flow of song for three full stanzas in order to establish in explicitly *non*musical narrative ("*Seyde* this child") his own claims to miracle. In other words, the clergeon *disobeys* the careful instructions of the Virgin. At the same time, his nonmusical recitation of the Virgin's desires predetermines the cessation of song upon the abbot's removal of the "greyn": "This hooly monk, this abbot, hym meene I, / His tonge out caughte, and took awey the greyn, / and he yaf up the goost ful softely" (670–72). These lines, which mark the end of the clergeon's musical life, also signal the literal sealing of his corpse, as the community "Enclosen . . . his litel body sweete" in a marble tomb. All that is left to attest to the clergeon's musicality, embodiment, his very existence in the world, is a single "greyn."

"Travail with breath"

The grain on the clergeon's tongue has been an enduring source of contention among critics of the Prioress's Tale. Unique to Chaucer's version of the story, the grain has been glossed over the last century as a cure for an injured throat, a prayer bead, the Eucharist, a symbol of resurrection and immortality, a drop of martyr's blood, even a medieval breath freshener. The little "greyn," like the "litel clergeon" himself, seems destined for eternal fetishization.[57] At the risk of imposing yet another unitary interpretation on the "greyn," I would argue that its narrative function in the tale may be to literalize in a particularly miraculous way the Boethian notion of the unheard *musica humana*, the "human music" that "unites the incorporeal nature of reason with the body" and "holds together the parts of the body in an established order."[58] The closest anyone has come to such a reading is Sister Nicholas Maltman, who claimed to have "found the 'greyn'" in a responsory from the Sarum Breviary.[59] Performed during the Mass of the Holy Innocents and the Feast of St. Thomas of Canterbury, the responsory's imagery describes Christ's martyrdom and ascension as "grain purged from the chaff, transported into divine granaries." For Maltman, this line establishes the grain "as a symbol of the soul winnowed or purged from the body, of the spirit as distinct from the body."[60]

Closely related to the miraculously suspended life of what should "by wey of kynde" be a cadaver (650), the grain unarguably has something to do with the relationship between the clergeon's "goost" and body. But surely the grain represents not the soul "winnowed" or "transported" from the worthless "chaff" of the body, but rather the miraculous affirmation of body as the very instrument of devotion. While remaining in the clergeon's mouth the grain cannot symbolize "soul . . . *purged* from the body," but soul miraculously enduring *within* the body. The clergeon's soul sustains itself not simply by the breath and movement of a revivified corpse, but more importantly by the corpse's musicality, the sonorous burgeoning of life the *Alma redemptoris* represents. The musical body provides the soul with a means of materializing its own presence as well as the presence of God.

Yet *musica humana* was not an uncomplicatedly redemptive phenomenon for all medieval thinkers. In the midst of a chapter concerning human music in the *Summa musice*, the authors turn immediately from the soul-body relationship to the physical plight of the singing voice: "The word 'cantus' means 'a sounding action' and 'canor' 'travail with breath.' The inventors of song and the first preceptors accordingly considered the pipe of the trachea, the instrument of the human voice, to be capable of emitting a threefold music according to a triple disposition" (Cantus dicitur quasi "sonorus actus," canor autem quasi "cum anhelitu labor." Inventores itaque cantus et primi doctores consideraverunt trachiam arteriam, id est organum vocis humane, secundum triplicem dispositionem triplicem cantum posse proferre).[61] Though sharing Aurelian of Réôme's understanding of the body's musical instrumentality, the treatise makes clear that such instrumentality is not inherent, but must be acquired and refined; while a "very relaxed" throat emits a low sound and a "very tense" (constringitur) throat produces a very high sound, only a throat carefully "disposed between these two" produces an acceptable middle ground. Importantly, the "inventors of song"

> illum qui est acuto acutior non curabant propter intolerabilem eius
> laborem—in ipso etiam nulla dilectio invenitur—et cantum huiusmodi *en-*
> *harmonicum* appellabant eo quod extra diatonici cantus harmoniam positus

et cantorem et auditorem fatigat et ledit, per nullem recreationem delectationis oblectans.

[devoted no further attention to music higher than the acute because of the insupportable labour of producing it and because no pleasure is to be found in it. They called this kind of music *enharmonicus* because, situated beyond the harmoniousness of diatonic music, it exhausts and vexes both the singer and the listener, giving no pleasure of restful delight.][62]

Certain forms of *musica humana*, then, supposedly the natural, quasi-mystical "music of the human person," in the words of Hugh of St. Victor,[63] are in fact the product of an "insupportable labour" of the throat. When sung through an untrained or overworked throat, human music "exhausts and vexes both the singer and the listener." This is surely not an effect Boethius had in mind when he formulated the concept as denoting an unheard *harmonia* between body and soul.

In fact, the throaty travail described by the *Summa musice* authors may instead reflect anxieties in the Latin rhetorical tradition about injuries to the oral instrument of delivery. As the author of the pseudo-Ciceronian *Rhetorica ad Herennium* writes, "we ought to avoid piercing exclamations, for *a shock that wounds the windpipe* is produced by shouting which is excessively sharp and shrill, and the brilliance of the voice is altogether used up by one outburst" (Et acutas vocis exclamationes vitare debemus; ictus enim fit et vulnus arteriae acuta atque adtenuata nimis adclamatione, et qui splendor est vocis consumitur uno clamore universus).[64] This worry over the rhetorical expenditure of the "brilliance of the voice" is shared by the Prioress's Tale, which focuses in great detail upon a singing body quite literally "used up" by its own vocal prowess.

The Prioress's clergeon thus furnishes a particularly rich rhetorical spectacle of *musica humana* gone awry. As we have seen, his deviation from classroom discipline is the foundation of his musical learning; rather than learning how to relax his throat and sing without undue strain, the clergeon "cries and sings" "ful loude." When he passes through the Jewry bellowing the *Alma redemptoris*, the clergeon certainly "gives no pleasure of restful delight" either to himself or to the Jews (who, perhaps, respond accordingly). Yet surely the most remarkable characteristic of enharmonic singing for the *Summa musice* authors—and here again we can discern the influence of the rhetorical tradition—is that the young singer properly in tune with *musica humana* is the one who "puts the organic register aside and discards the enharmonic; one is too dark, *the other splits the throat*" (Organicum mutat enharmonicumque rescindit;/Obscurus nimis est hic, *alter guttura findit*).[65] Too much musical stress is liable to rend the throat from within.

Interpreted in these terms, the little boy's sacred hymn—and indeed the very notion of *musica humana*—does not sound like the naive preadolescent burst of song the Prioress's Tale seeks to portray. It is, rather, an excessive rhetorical performance, a "musical delivery" from the body and voice of an untrained but thoroughly indoctrinated Christian *actor*. If "human music" can threaten bodily injury, social strife, even death, the clergeon's song must ring inherently violent—violent against the "throte" through which it passes "twies a day" and against the non-Christian community disrupted and massacred by the end of the narrative. In a sense, the Prioress's Tale may assign some culpability for the clergeon's death and the massacre of the Jews to the nature and practice of Christian liturgical song: the music that the clergeon could "nat stynte of syngyng by the weye," the "song" that supposedly "joins those with differences," in St. Ambrose's mystifying formulation. Despite the tale's efforts to articulate innate and irreconcilable differences between "Cristen blood" and "cursed Jew," its spectacularly violent deployment of musical sonority undermines the very ethnic essentialisms it constructs. Rather than establishing a musical distance between self and other, the Prioress's Tale exposes the horrific acts that music is capable of provoking, sustaining, and, perhaps most insidiously, aestheticizing for its medieval listeners and modern readers.

In a recent study of medieval troubadour song, Leo Treitler has characterized the changing relationship between words and music in the West as a historical trajectory of union, loss, and desire: "Their story is like the history of two lovers—so close at first that each seems a reflection of the other but later shifting in their patterns of dominance, moving toward independence and trial separation, now one, now the other, emulating each other at different moments in their history, yearning for one another just when they appear to have achieved independence."[66] For medieval lyricists and theorists, Treitler suggests, the relationship between words and music was particularly intimate, the Middle Ages itself "an era when Language hardly troubled to distinguish between 'saying' and 'singing.'"[67] This is a much-needed corrective to recent scholarship on word-music relations that has subordinated the emotive and affective dimensions of medieval musical life to a neoplatonic aesthetic of number.

Yet as Treitler's extended analogy makes clear in no uncertain terms, an overly zealous insistence upon the inextricability of music and language in medieval *cantus* runs the risk of romanticizing this relationship and, at least on some level, of eliding the representational violence music commits when it is (to extend Treitler's metaphor) *divorced* from language. As we seek to widen the conversation between medieval musicology and literary criticism, we might also ask how these twentieth-century disciplinary affiliations (and the respective forms of methodological *disciplina* they themselves demand) have served to obscure the more disturbing implications of the historical relationship between music and poetic language. Often lost in accounts of words and music in the Middle Ages, for example, is the cultural work performed by language in domesticating musical sonority, in forcing music to "speak" in ways that can be understood and interpreted in linguistic and literary terms. It seems to me that modern approaches to word-music relations—or, for that matter, the language-based and linguistically biased accounts of human subject formation that predominate in contemporary theoretical discourse—provide little help in excavating those moments when music tears at the throats, resounds from the burning flesh, or echoes in percussive rhythms from the lacerated skin of its victims. A momentary suspension of our own belief in the warm medieval embrace of music and language, in other words, might allow us to begin reading the influential treatises of Guido of Arezzo not only for the technical light they shed on the learning and performance of medieval Latin *cantus*, but also for their active role in the promotion of bodily violence in the service of ecclesiastical tradition; or, in the case of the Prioress's Tale, to corrode the gemlike elegance and poetic precision of its rhyme royal stanzas by excavating the violent musical representations that the "natural music" of Chaucerian poesis works to obscure.[68]

PART 4

Resoundings

CHAPTER 7

Orpheus in Parts: Music, Fragmentation, Remembrance

S ince sound is a thing of sense," laments Isidore of Seville in the most musical book of the *Etymologies*, "it passes along into past time, and it is impressed on the memory. . . . For unless sounds are im-printed in the memory by man they perish, because they cannot be written down."[1] For the etymologist, sound is not simply retained in the memory, but *impressed on* the memory (inprimitur). Nor do sounds simply fade away into oblivion; rather, they die (pereunt). Perhaps the desire to impute mate-riality to sonorous phenomena is particularly keen in a culture lacking musical notation. Without the mnemonic scaffolding of written signifiers, music is susceptible to immediate loss. As we saw in Chapter 6, of course, notational musical cultures possess their own anxious means of "imprint-ing" music into the minds and bodies of aspiring performers. Neumes can become "flesh-hooks," the notated page a personified and personalized musical battle. The pedagogical hand holds the key to liturgical transmis-sion in an often painfully literal way.

Whether musical or not, sound, Isidore's "thing of sense," confronts many medieval writers with the haunting problem of its origin and material instantiation. In the *House of Fame*, Chaucer follows Boethius in casting sound as air "ybroke" and "twyst with violence and rent"; sonic violence produces music when "a pipe is blowen sharpe," and "whan men harpe-strynges smyte" (2.774–77). Thomas of Cantimpré locates the mystical origins of *cantus* within the chests of holy women, while Gertrude of Helfta hears it emerging from a gaping wound in Christ's side.[2] Part of the prob-lem, of course, is the lack of a consistent and practiced vocabulary for describing the nature, transmission, and reception of sound. Until the early modern period, there was no well-developed science of hearing (the "second sense," in Aristotle's hierarchy) to rival the voluminous discipline of optics.[3] Twentieth-century confidence in the existence of sound waves and the neurological mechanisms of hearing should not keep us from recognizing the puzzle that the materiality of sonority represented for earlier ears and eras.

Yet—and here it is worth momentarily risking a vast oversimplification—hearing, more than any of the other outer senses, confronts us with the ephemeral and *non*material nature of the object being sensed. Augustine articulates this point well in a famous discussion of time and memory in *Confessions* 11: "Suppose that we hear a noise emitted by some material body. The sound begins and we continue to hear it. It goes on until finally it ceases. Then there is silence. The sound has passed and is no longer sound. Before it began it was future and could not be measured, because it did not yet exist. Now that it has ceased it cannot be measured, because it no longer exists."[4] The chapter goes on to argue that the measuring of sound must be a purely mental process, for once sounds are "wafted away into the past" they no longer exist to *be* measured. Augustine's analogy begins with the "material body" that emits the sound, but the sound itself seemingly has no body. Yet when many classical and medieval thinkers explored the nature of hearing, they wondered how the body was suited to retain the *materia* of sound; for Ambrose, the "sinuosity" of the inner ear allowed it to "rhythmicize" the substance of sound and implant it more firmly within the aural canal, which was shaped into nooks and crannies provided by God for this purpose.[5] Here as elsewhere, sound and music adapt to the shapes, forms, and characteristics of human bodies.

Bodies in turn become sonorous. The favored term in medieval Latin writings for the inner ear was *tympanum* (which became our "eardrum"), pointing to a more general sense in which the body is literally "beaten" with sound (perhaps the inverse human equivalent of the "drumsticks" that a turkey's legs become once the bird is butchered and cooked).[6] The will to "embody" music, to attribute *corporalitas* to musical sonority and musical sound to the *corpus*, must be tempered by the recognition that sound, like the human body, perishes much too soon. As the modern aesthetician Ernst Bloch writes, "Something is lacking, and sound at least states this lack clearly. Sound has itself something dark and thirsty about it and blows about instead of stopping in one place, like paint."[7]

Isidore could not have said it better, and it is surely no coincidence that his account of sonic loss occurs within the same cluster of chapters in book 3 of the *Etymologies* in which we find a materializing inventory of musical sounds and instruments:

> Penetrating voices are those which can hold a note an unusually long time, in such a way that they continuously fill the whole place, like the sound of trumpets.
>
> A thin voice is one lacking in breath, as the voice of children or women or the sick. This is as it is in strings, for the finest strings emit fine, thin sounds.
>
> In fat voices, as those of men, much breath is emitted at once.
>
> . . .
>
> A hard voice is one which emits sound violently, like thunder, like the sound of an anvil whenever the hammer is struck against the hard iron.
>
> . . .
>
> A blind voice is one which is choked off as soon as produced, and once silent cannot be prolonged, as in crockery.
>
> A pretty voice is soft and flexible; it is so called from *vinnus*, a softly curling lock of hair.
>
> The *tibiae*, according to report, were devised in Phrygia. . . . It is thought that they are called *tibiae* because they were first made from the leg-bones of deer and fawns, and that then, by a misuse of the term, the name was used of those not made of leg-bones. Hence it is also called *tibicen*, as if for *tibiae cantus* (song of the leg-bone).
>
> [T]he form of the cithara was originally like that of the human chest, because it gives forth sound as the chest gives forth voice, and it received its name from that reason, for in Doric the chest was called *kithára*. . . . The strings [*chordae*] are so called from *cor* [heart], because the striking of the strings of the cithara is like the beating of the heart in the breast.[8]

Admittedly, Isidore includes *musica* as one of the numerical *scientiae* in book 3, "De Mathematica." Of the seven chapters devoted to music, how-ever, "De numeris musicis" is but one, and it reads like an obligatory recitation of Pythagorean truisms.

Isidore recognized that music and the somatic instruments that per-form it symbolically embrace the human being; they are an integral part of what the human is and serve as a constant reminder of the limits of what the human can achieve. The Western mythological tradition abounds with stories associating the origin and production of musical sonority with the death, fragmentation, and loss of human bodies, whether in Pan's failed pursuit of Syrinx, whose shattered body becomes his pipe, or Apollo's accidental slaying of Hyacinthus: "You shall my harp, struck by my hand, you my songs sound" (te lyra pulsa manu, te carmina nostra sonabunt) (*Met.* 10.205). The fleeting physicality of musical sound conveys the immediacy of loss in ways that language alone cannot; it provides a momentary illusion of wholeness, integrity, and restoration even as it carries the sensual reminder that that which has been lost—whether a past state of happiness, an Edenic innocence, or a loved one—can never be fully recovered. In the words of Roger Scruton, music is "a dialogue across generations, in which the dead play as great a part as the living."[9]

The Orphic Strain

No Western myth explores the interrelations among music, embodiment, and loss more movingly than the legend of Orpheus and Eurydice. Though the story has undergone an astounding variety of transformations since its earliest Hellenic redactions, for the last two millennia—from the echoic melancholy of Virgil's fourth *Georgic* to the "dire lamenting elegies" in Shakespeare's *Two Gentlemen of Verona* to Rilke's "marble ear" and "shattered glass"—Orpheus's musicality has been in some sense synonymous with his mourning for Eurydice. Though Orpheus is often paralleled with other master bards—Apollo, Pythagoras, David, even Christ—his music consistently evokes his loss and articulates his desire to overcome it.

Orpheus makes his first extended appearance in English literature in the anonymous *Sir Orfeo*, "harp[ing] at his owhen wille" as he suffers ascetic deprivation following the loss of Heurodis. Though the precise relationship between the English romance and the classical legend is unknown (among other differences, the former has a happy ending in which the bard successfully recovers his wife), the poem imagines an Orpheus whose music exists in a curiously mimetic relation to his bodily emaciation; during winter, when "his bodi was oway duine/For missays, and al to-chine," he conceals "His harp, where-on was al his gle,/ . . . in an holwe tre."[10] Similarly, in Robert Henryson's *Orpheus and Eurydice*, the death of his wife transforms Orpheus into a musical ascetic, commanding his "dulful herp, with mony dully string," to "turne all thy mirth and musik in murning,/ and seiss of all thy sutell songis sueit."[11] The harp is an animistic metonym for mourning, and Orpheus stands for a somatic musicality realized in the sonorous vessel of his body: as an infant, Orpheus synesthetically sucked the "sueit licour of all musik" from his mother's "twa palpis," just as the Lamb of God eagerly sucked *cantus* from the throat of Lutgard of Aywières.[12] Orphic song has become a physical substance, a liquid that flows from the breasts of Calliope into the eager mouth of her son. Henryson invents musical sonority as a feminized *materia* produced by the maternal body, a construction of music-as-milk that anticipates the "semiotic wombs" of poetic language postulated by Julia Kristeva.[13]

Yet the ultimate fate of Orpheus's body is determined by his *rejection* of women and the feminine. In the *Metamorphoses*, after his second loss of Eurydice, Orpheus "shunned all love of womankind" and "set the example for the people of Thrace of giving his love to tender boys, and enjoying the springtime and first flower of their youth" (ille etiam Thracum populis fuit auctor amorem in teneros transferre mares citraque iuventam aetatis breve ver et primos carpere flores) (*Met.* 10-83-85). Throughout the remainder of *Metamorphoses* 10, Orpheus sings tales of "boys beloved by gods, and maidens inflamed by unnatural love." The first tale Orpheus sings is the *raptus* of Ganymede by Jove, the second the story of Apollo and Hyacinthus. As Ovid's eleventh book opens and the frame-narrative resumes, the Maenads, overcome with anger at Orpheus's spurning of women, stone the bard to death, scattering his limbs upon the ground and forcing his soul to exit through his once-musical mouth. The severed head and resonating harp float down the Heber and into the mythological canon. Like Orpheus himself, Ovid's narrative of love, loss, and mourning fragments into the harpist's own micronarratives of transgressive desires, among which male homoeroticism occupies a privileged position.

Within antihomophobic studies of Western literature, Orpheus's turn to boys has generally been lauded as a mythic affirmation of male same-sex desire. For Gregory Woods, Orpheus is "the homosexual poet, whose [musical] skill alone can cause the supposed 'laws' of nature to be broken."[14] Leonard Barkan aptly describes him as "the *auctor* of pederasty," whose occulted embodiment of the Renaissance humanist "epistemology of inversion" authorizes the culture's intergenerational homoerotics.[15] Modern and contemporary critical theory also has its uses for this particular Orpheus. Thus, Herbert Marcuse sees Orpheus's erotic awakening to his own sex as prophetic of what he terms the "Great Refusal," the "protest against the repressive order of procreative sexuality" called for in *Eros and Civiliza-tion.*[16] Maurice Blanchot saw in the tragedy of Orpheus's failed backward gaze a paradigmatically modernist gesture: "The act of writing begins with Orpheus' gaze, and that gaze is the impulse of desire which shatters the song's destiny and concern, and in that inspired and unconcerned decision reaches the origin, consecrates the song."[17] This observation has been extended by Jacques Derrida, who revises Blanchot by insisting on locating the "Orphic turn" within the genealogy of *écriture*: "in the homosexual phase which would follow Eurydice's death. . . . Orpheus sings no more, he writes."[18]

For the Middle Ages, the implications of the homoerotic Orpheus for the writing and transmission of myth are equally complex—and just as vulnerable to easy generalization. In his 1970 study of the medieval Orpheus, John Block Friedman asserted that very little was made in the period of the homoerotic aspect of the legend, which "raised problems many medieval commentators preferred not to deal with."[19] As Kevin Brownlee has since shown, the few medieval writers who do explicitly address Orpheus's change in sexual object-choice per se seem to condemn it in no uncertain terms.[20] In a passage from *De planctu Naturae* examined in Chapter 4, Alan of Lille associates Orpheus with the deviant linguistic practices resulting in sodomitical inversion:

> Man alone turns with scorn from the modulated strains of my *cithara* and runs deranged to the notes of mad Orpheus's lyre [*lira*]. For the human race, fallen from its high estate, adopts a highly irregular *metaplasmus* when it inverts the rules of Venus by introducing barbarisms in its arrangement of genders. Thus man, his sex changed [*tiresiatus*] by a ruleless Venus, in defiance of due order, by his arrangement changes what is a straightforward attribute of his.[21]

Orphic transgression is simultaneously linguistic, musical, and sexual, a discursive conflation registered by Alan in his sexualizing revision of the *lira* and the *cithara*, the allegorical instruments that figure so prominently in the medieval panoply of musical embodiment.

Echoing Alan in *Le Roman de la Rose*, Jean de Meun condemns "those who will never keep to the straight track . . . who confirm their evil rules by abnormal exceptions when they want to follow Orpheus . . . may they, in addition to the excommunication that sends them all to damnation, suffer, before their death—since they desire to burn—the loss of their purse and testicles, the signs that they are male!" (Ne ja n'i tendront dreite rue, . . . E conferment leur regles males/Par excepcions anormales,/Quant Orpheüs veulent ensivre, . . . O tout l'escomeniement,/Qui touz les mete a danne-ment,/Puis que la se veulent aerdre,/Ainz qu'il muirent puissent il perdre/E l'aumosniere e les estalles/Don il ont signe d'estre malles!).[22] "Before their death": For Jean, the punitive fragmentation of the deviant followers of Orpheus should precede their bodily death; it should be an act of *living torture* rather than a postmortem refusal of the funeral pyre or grave. Jean's Orpheus bears a remarkable resemblance in this respect to Chaucer's Par-doner, for in both literary representations there is a clear correspondence between sexual inversion and artistic sterility. Orphic song threatens those who perform it with exile and execution.[23]

Yet even while condemning him to exile, castration, and death, Jean de Meun reveals a deep anxiety about the *creative* potential of the bard's musi-cality, contending that Orpheus "did not know how to plow or write or forge in the true forge—may he be hanged by the throat—when he showed himself badly toward Nature by contriving such rules" (Qui ne sot arer ne escrivre/Ne forgier en la dreite forge,/Penduz seit il par mi la gorge! Quant teus regles leur controuva,/Vers Nature mal se prouva).[24] Explicitly punish-ing the Orphic throat, *la gorge*, Jean focuses his phobia upon a resonant site of musical production within the body. Jean casts the throat as Orpheus's primary erogenous zone; even when castrated and lacking "the signs that they are male," Orpheus's followers threaten the "true forge" with a musi-cal perversion originating specifically from their sonorous throats. Wayne Koestenbaum's words on the erotics of the operatic body are particularly apt here: "Voice culture loves, protects, and preserves the throat, but also scape-goats the insurgent throat for saying no to genital tyranny . . . genitals are mythologized, but no one mentions the doctrines clustered in our throats, in our methods of singing and speaking. We lack a vocabulary for what the throat knows and suffers—perhaps because the throat is loath to speak about itself."[25] Koestenbaum's observation might be extended to other non-genital parts of the musical body that remain similarly undertheorized: the skin of the dancing Magdalene, the womb of Hildegard's Virgin, the wounds of Pecham's Christ. In the case of Orpheus, however, the perverse musical body is not the *sum* but the *division* of its musical parts, a distinction that will become clear for the medieval strain of Orphic revisionism once we account for the dispersion of his musical body across medieval time, space, and genre. In the *Metamorphoses*, Orpheus's deviation from heterosexual matrimony is punished by violent dismemberment. As we shall see, this classical fragmentation of Orpheus's body anticipates the larger hermeneutical process of medieval mythography itself.

One of the primary ideological forms taken by the reception of classical myth in the Middle Ages is what Ralph Hexter has termed "Lactantian segmentation"—that is, the fragmentation of larger myths into segments and the subsequent subjection of these segments to both literal *glosulae* and moralizing *allegoriae*.[26] Several of the earliest extant manuscripts of the *Metamorphoses* subdivide the Ovidian text into individual episodes, which are each given a *titulus*, summarized in prose, and, in some cases, explicated with scholiastic commentary. The subdivision of the Ovidian text prepares its management and moralization by Christian allegorists.

The classical dismemberment of Orpheus's musical body thus furnishes an uncannily appropriate synecdoche for the medieval reception of pagan myth. Just as the Maenads dismember the body of Orpheus as punishment for the homoerotic turn his desires have taken, medieval commentators fragment the corpus of classical mythology in order to manage or, indeed, exploit the moral challenge they perceive within it—especially the challenge posed by that mode of same-sex desire in which many medieval poets and allegorists located the primary erotic impulse of the Orpheus myth. Orphic fragmentation, then, adumbrates the subsequent fate of this transgressively musical body in the hands of Latin Christendom. For a Romanesque poet, this body can be appropriated through allusion in the service of a neoclassical musical erotics. For a French mythographer, it represents the unacknowledged justification for a tremendous Christianizing parataxis of myth. And for the greatest Italian poet of the Middle Ages, it allows for a momentary "refusal" of the heterosexual imperative of the exact sort celebrated by Marcuse.

The remainder of this chapter begins the interpretive task of "re-membering" the medieval bodies of Orpheus. Friedman's confidence in the medieval disinterest in the homoerotic Orpheus was very much misplaced, for the musico-sexual problem represented by the ending of the Ovidian narrative enlists the most energetic and sublime creative efforts of the story's medieval revisers. Even for those who condemned it, Orpheus's desiring body represented an inspiring source of poetic, rhetorical, and hermeneutical *inventio*. Like the music of Hildegard of Bingen, the poetics and polyphony of Leoninus, and the vernacular performance of Chaucer's Pardoner, it provides this concluding chapter with a means of locating the musical bodies of the Middle Ages within the history of sexuality without sacrificing their polymorphous eroticism to the essentializing reductiveness of genital contact. As Alan of Lille was perhaps the first to articulate explicitly, Orpheus's eroticized turn to another gender—and another generation—established Orphic musicality as a sonorous time and space that could never be fully reconciled with the *musica mundana*, the celestial harmonies keeping the universe and the bodies of its inhabitants in accord with the sexual dictates of *Natura*. In the spirit of the medieval Orphic tradition itself, the argument that follows consists of a series of hermeneutical fragments, each of them freestanding yet together constituting an interpretive whole. The succeeding epilogue that concludes this book returns for a moment—with Isidore again—to Orpheus, this time for his musical empathy with the dead.

"Orpheus alter": Baudri of Bourgeuil

Though a Benedictine monk and abbot and, later, an archbishop in eleventh-century France, Baudri of Bourgeuil was arguably the most avid reader and inventive reviser of Ovid's love poetry before Petrarch. Gerald Bond's recent studies of the Latin poet have provided the first rigorous effort to locate Baudri's poetic within what Bond terms the "Ovidian subculture" characterizing the Romanesque Latin literature of his time, adumbrating what Traube called the *aetas Ovidiana* of the succeeding century.[27] The open and often courageous homoeroticism of several of Baudri's epistolary poems led John Boswell to identify him as "one of the most famous gay men of his day," and it was his mission to combat the "impression of hypocrisy" he perceived in previous scholarly attempts to reconcile Baudri's homoerotic verse with his explicit injunctions against sodomy in other of his writings (or with the fact that he wrote love letters to women as well).[28] For Boswell, this contradiction was largely a question of genre, involving a distinction between private, erotic verse and publicly circulating letters (perhaps anticipating the similar tension characterizing the oeuvre of Leoninus discussed in Chapter 4). Bond, by contrast, places more emphasis on the complexity of the monk's erotic affiliations, which oscillate in his poems between ascetic denial and desirous plenitude, between the heteroerotic and the homoerotic.[29]

In Baudri's epistolary poems devoted to music, this sense of the indeterminacy and ineffability of sexual desire often inspires complex representations of musical sonority and performance. His numerous poetic appropriations of the musical voice of Orpheus produce a clearly homoerotic poetic that nevertheless resists sexual definition by ambiguating the categories of sex and gender through the somatics of musical experience. For a man who surely devoted hours a day to the musical labor of liturgy, musical sonority allowed for numerous meditations upon the nonascetic pleasures of the flesh.

Baudri's poetry shows a deep awareness of the hermeneutical tradition that envisioned biblical musical imagery as an allegorical model of human life. In a late poem written after an archepiscopal visit to Worcester cathedral, Baudri crafted an assonant list of songs and instruments—"Organa, cantica, cymbala, tympana, carmina, sistra,/Psalterium, cythare saltusque" (Organs, songs, cymbals, drums, songs, rattles, the psaltery, the cithar, and the dance)—into the "cultusque Dei speciosus" (the reverence and sight of God).[30] The same visit, however, inspired a fourteen-line panegyric to the cathedral's actual organ. Another English organ had been described over a century earlier by Wulfstan, the *cantor* at Winchester, in a hyperbolic passage well known to medieval musicologists as "the most remarkable account of an organ anywhere before 1000."[31] Wulfstan envisioned his cathedral's organ as a monstrous behemoth with "twice six bellows . . . joined above in a row, and below . . . four and ten" (bisseni supra sociantur in ordine folles/inferiusque . . . quattuor atque decem).[32] The instrument's operation requires the physical exertion of dozens of men: "With alternating breaths [the bellows] render a great amount of air; seventy strong men work them, moving their arms and dripping with much sweat, each eagerly encouraging his companions, to drive the air upward with all strength and make roar the full chest with its ample curve" (flatibus alternis spiracula maxima reddunt/quos agitant ualidi septuagina uiri/brachi uersantes, multo et sudore madentes/certaminque suos quique monent socios,/uiribus ut totis impellant flamina sursum/et rugiat pleno kapsa referta sinu).

For Baudri, writing a century later, the staggering immensity of the Worcester organ was as much spiritual as material. In Boethian terms, we could say that he listens to and appreciates *musica organica* while meditating upon *musica mundana*, the cosmic implications of the sonorities filling the church. If for Wulfstan the work of organal performance was located in the laboring bodies of seventy men, Baudri analogizes it to the work of God: "Vtque labor magnus calamos ex ere coaptat, / Sic Deus et mores et corpora nostra coaptet" (Just as great labor tempers the reeds with air, so God tempers both our characters and our bodies) (218/CCLI.7–8). The physical mechanism of the organ, along with the human "labor" that must be performed to make it work, constitutes part of the "symphonia mistica" (9) of devotional experience, a running together of life, breath, body, and soul into one sweetly sounding "instrument" pleasing to God.

The same tension between physically sounding and spiritually ramifying music informs Baudri's sense of song in his erotic verse. Like Hildegard, Baudri often allows the sexual and the mystical to conflate within musical space and time, and the singing body of Orpheus provides him with the most provocative means of expressing this conflation. An epistolary poem "Ad juvenem nimis elatum" (To a youth too proud; 3/XXXVIII) draws on the Ovidian Orpheus in a complex poeticization of musical allure and intergenerational desire. The poem begins with a self-conscious tautology that casts the speaker's "pleasure" as a demanding blend of present and future: "Cum michi nil placeat, nisi quod bene sit placiturum / Nec michi displiceat, nisi quod sit displiciturum" (3/XXXVIII.1–2). The plodding feel of the rhyming periphrastics emphasizes the founding desire of the poem: like several of Shakespeare's early sonnets, to maintain the body of the youthful addressee in its present state for eternity. Orpheus's undying musicality thus gives Baudri an elegantly complex means of registering the youth's erotic allure as it manifests itself in song:

> Vox tua demulcet nostras et mitigat aures,
> Que tam dulce sonat quam dulce sonat Filomela
> Incertum an pueri sit uox tua siue puelle.
> Orpheus alter eris, nisi uocem sauciet aetas,
> Aetas a pueris que dat differre puellas,
> Cum gena uestitur iuuenum lanugine prima
> Et pande nares faciem speciemque venustant.[33]

[Your voice, sounding as sweetly as the nightingale's, caresses and soothes my ears; it is uncertain whether your voice is that of a boy or that of a girl. You will be another Orpheus, unless age injures the voice, age which distinguishes girls from boys, when the cheek is clothed with the first down of young manhood and a strong nose enhances the face and appearance.] (3/XXXVIII.9–15)

For Baudri, the music the youth sings, as well as the high voice perilously close to the onset of puberty, represents the threatened source of erotic allure. The true object of the "aural gaze" here, however, is not so much *uox tua* itself, but rather its phenomenological shiftiness, its ambiguation of the already tenuous divisions between male and female, child and adult, homoerotic and heteroerotic. The singing voice has a kind of vulnerability condensed by Baudri into the verb *sauciet* (injure) and personified by Philomel, whose sexual victimization by Tereus is a subtext throughout the poem. While for John Pecham the devotional ravishment of the musical Christ promises salvation, for Baudri the process of aging is the perpetrator of musical *violentia*.

The imagery is somewhat counterintuitive. Where in Ovid a widowed Orpheus turned his desire toward preadolescent *iuuentam* (*Met*. 10.84), this poem imagines the *Orpheus alter*, the "other Orpheus," as himself an eternal youth. The confusion is only heightened by Baudri's clear assumption that age distinguishes girls from boys ("a pueris . . . puellas") rather than the reverse. Though he envisions the *male* addressee growing down on the chin and cultivating a more shapely nose, the appearance of these seemingly agreeable features will coincide with the life change that shatters the "caress" of the voice. Baudri's miniblazon implies that the objectified boy will assume the alluring manhood that will allow him to attract his own *iuvenes* through the power of music, the same *carmina* in which the Ovidian Orpheus had related the eroticism of Ganymede and other pagan youths.

Just a few lines later, however, Baudri praises the boy precisely because he *refuses* "to be Jove's Ganymede" (Laudo, Iouis quoniam Ganimedes esse refutas; 3/XXXVIII.24). In effect, the poem invests musical sonority with the *materia* of eroticism even while disallowing actual sexual practice to sully its desirability. Wistfully describing the swan song of youth, Baudri mourns in advance the loss of androgyny, the inevitable moment at which determined gender will take over the body and thus the singing voice. The poem's addressee will become Orpheus, but never Ganymede; he will be the subject of intergenerational desire, but no longer its object; he will remain a singer, but no longer be sung. Unlike Ganymede, destined to remain the eternally youthful companion of Jove, the poem's Orpheus will age and thus, despite Baudri's reservations, perpetuate the musico-sexual genealogy that the poem itself invents. Though hardly maternal, the musical body of Orpheus is nevertheless generative and productive.

An equally potent formulation of Orphic song inspires a poem written "Ad Vitalem" (195/CCXXXIII), which constructs an image of musical erotics similarly inflected by the constraints of temporality. The addressee this time is the *carmen* or "song" itself, which Baudri orders to greet Vitalis with whatever is "pleasing" to the boy. Images of bodily joining abound in this densely figurative verse: "Quem michi conplexum uiscera nostra fouent" ([This boy] embraces and caresses my flesh; 4); "Visceribus nostris pre cunctis solus inhesit" (Only he has inhered within my flesh; 5); "Solus pre cunctis me penitus tetigit" (Only he among many has touched me so deeply within; 6). Searching for comparisons that will accurately convey the unique and extraordinary qualities of the boy, Baudri moves through a dizzying series of analogies:

> Callidus ut serpens, simplex ut rauca columba
> Aetatem superat propter utrumque suam.
> Preterea puerum facundia tanta repleuit,
> Vix ut Vitalem Tullius equiperet.
> Si fidibus seruire uelit uouice canore
> Aut utrique simul, Orpheus alter erit.
> Ergo Vitalis a me nusquam dirimetur
> Sane animam donec seua dies adimat.
> Tunc quoque, si potero michi commendare uel illi,
> Amborum flatus spiritus unus erunt.

> [Cunning as a snake, simple as a cooing dove, and with these two qualities he conquers age. And more: eloquence has so inspired the boy that Cicero scarcely measures up to Vitalis. If he wanted to apprentice to the lyre or train his singing voice or both, he would be another Orpheus. Therefore, Vitalis will nowhere be separated from me, indeed till the savage day which takes his spirit away. And even then, if I can beg favor for me or for him, our two souls will become the breath of one spirit.][34] (195/CCXXXIII.11–20)

Along with his paradoxical combination of cunning and innocence, Vitalis possesses performative skills that rival those of the ancients, uniting Ciceronian rhetoric with Orphic song into a veritable personification of musical *actio* or delivery. Revising Orpheus's tragic loss of Eurydice and its homoerotic outcome, Baudri confronts his own future loss and mourning with the promise of reunion with the deceased, a reunion to occur within the posthumous breath of a single spirit.

In both poems, Baudri is held spellbound as the seduced listener to the mournfully erotic strains of these "other Orpheuses." The adult poet imaginatively subjects himself to the youthful songs and bodies of his addressees, these Orphic boys who enchant him—and whose voices must have been a constant source of aural delectation during the daily cycle of liturgical performance. Elsewhere, however, Baudri casts *himself* as Orpheus, as in an epistolary poem to Odo, an adult monastic colleague whom Baudri goes so far as to describe in the salutation as "papa futurus" (206/CCXLIV.2). Like Vitalis, Odo possesses extraordinary rhetorical prowess in Baudri's eyes (he is "Maximus orator"; 13). The poem rejects the intergenerational erotics of Orphic revisionism evident elsewhere in Baudri's oeuvre; more surprisingly, perhaps, especially in light of the ecclesiastical prestige of its addressee, it positions the future pope as the submissive object of the poem's Orphic speaker: "If you will give yourself to me . . . among singers I will be another Orpheus" (Si michi te dederis. . . . Inter cantores Orpheus alter ero; 23–24). Though constantly aware of the musical possibilities afforded by the poetic trope of other-as-Orpheus, Baudri's most personalized appropriation of Orphic voice locates the sonorous eroticism of the myth within his own musical body.

Mythographical Fragments and the *Ovide Moralisé*

Baudri crafted his artful appropriations of the musical body of Orpheus while living and working within the monastic culture of Romanesque Normandy and Brittany. A century later, another French cleric from Orléans (a bishopric that Baudri long desired but never won) turned to Ovid's Orpheus as an exemplum of the rhetorical prowess of Christian preachers. One of the great Latin mythographers of the twelfth century, Arnulf of Orléans exemplifies the hermeneutical pyrotechnics that the mythographical tradition performed in accounting for Orpheus's homoerotic turn. For

Arnulf, despite Ovid's blatant declaration, Orpheus did not really experience a psychological or practical transformation in sexual object-choice; rather, Orpheus "softened wild beasts, that is, savage men, by his song, that is, by his preaching."[35] The enduring discursive affiliation between music and rhetoric allows the mythographer to eviscerate the erotics of Orphic song and substitute the predicatory suasiveness of his oratory for his post-Eurydice musical seductions of *iuevenes*.

Arnulf's confident allegoresis would appear to exemplify the total and successful suppression of the homoerotic Orpheus from the mythographical tradition. *Pace* Friedman, however, what seems to me the most startling aspect of the treatment of Orpheus in medieval mythographies is how often writers in the tradition in fact *fail* to elide Orpheus's homoerotic turn and obscure the original justification for the dismemberment of his body. This was Boethius's unspoken strategy in the quasi-mythographical *Consolation of Philosophy*. Though intimately familiar with the version in the *Metamorphoses*, Boethius deploys the ending of the Orpheus legend as part of Lady Philosophy's strategy of keeping the mind focused on things celestial rather than things earthly; as Chaucer translated the relevant passage:

> Allas! Whanne Orpheus and his wife weren almest at the termes of the nyght (that is to seyn, at the laste boundes of helle), Orpheus loked bakward on Erudyce his wif, and lost hire, and was deed. This fable apertenith to yow alle, whosoevere desireth or seketh to lede his thought into the sovereyn day, that is to seyn, to cleernesse of soveryn good. For whoso that evere be so overcomen that he ficche his eien into the put of helle, that is to seyn, whoso sette his thoughtes in erthly thinges, al that evere he hath drawen of the noble good celestial he lesith it, whanne he looketh the helles, that is to seyn, into lowe thinges of the erthe.[36]

Though Chaucer's confusing phrase "and was deed" seems to apply to Orpheus, it may represent a mistranslation of the Latin original or French pony with which he was working; it is Eurydice who dies again when Orpheus breaks the infernal law.[37] For Boethius, however, Orpheus may as well have died after the second loss of Eurydice; the bard's erotic metamorphosis and subsequent life are entirely erased.

Ovid was too irresistible, however, and not all mythographers would follow the Boethian example of simply ignoring the sexual transgressions of Orpheus. Indeed, far from suppressing him, many mythographers greet the homoerotic Orpheus with open hermeneutical arms, allowing his dissident musical body to proliferate in their treatises through repeated rhetorical performances of allegoresis and *amplificatio*. Rather than assuming that the mythographic suppression of Orphic erotics was successful, then, I want to account for the many ways in which the mythographical tradition incorporates the very "perversions" it spends so much time excoriating. In certain mythographies, Orpheus's homoeroticism, while seemingly "disappeared," serves as a means of surrounding the Christianized Orpheus with crowds and communities of adoring men. Thus, the fourteenth-century Italian mythographer, Giovanni del Virgilio, suggests that "Orpheus . . . began to spurn women [*spernere mulieres*], giving his soul instead to God, and began to love men, that is, to act in a manly way [*viriliter agere*], on which account he was dead to the delights of the world; for such men are dead to the world."[38] Only upon his flight into monastic life, explains Giovanni, did Orpheus "truly have Eurydice back—that is, profound judgment." Even as her husband mourns her, Eurydice diffuses into homosocial and institutional bonds between cloistered men.

Within the Latin mythographical tradition, the fourteenth-century French writer Pierre Bersuire holds pride of place for the creativity with which he managed the musical problem of Orpheus's homoeroticism. In the *Ovidius Moralizatus*, probably the most influential medieval moralization of the *Metamorphoses*, Bersuire first recounts the legend of Orpheus up to the point at which he "returned to the world," then offers several allegories that try to account specifically for the relationship between Orpheus and Eurydice. In the first, Orpheus is a Christ figure who weds Eurydice, "the human soul"; in the second, Bersuire's extraordinarily misogynistic interpretation compares Orpheus's desire to regain his lost wife to a dog returning to its own vomit.[39]

Resuming the main narrative, Bersuire elides the troublesome lines from Ovid: "When Orpheus saw that he had lost the wife he had regained and had seen her die twice, he began to detest sex with all women. He sat on a mountain where there was no shade and began to play sweetly on his lyre" (Orpheus videns quod vxorem recuperatam perdiderat: et eam bis mori viderat incoepit obhorrere copulam omnium mulierum. Sedit igitur super montem vbi nulla erat vmbra: & incepit dulciter canere cum lyra).[40] Ovid's more suggestive "femineam venerem" (10.79) becomes the explicit "copulam omnium mulierum" in Bersuire, implying an interest in the sexual aspects of the legend.[41] The two allegories that follow further distance the Christianized Orpheus from the physical embraces of women:

> Orpheus significat praedicatorem & diuini verbi carminum dictatorem: qui de inferis id est de mundo veniens debet in monte scripturae vel religionis sedere carmina & melodiam sacrae scripturae canere. . . . Mulierum copulam debet fugere et carnis amplexus penitus exhorrere & contra ipsarum malicias praedicare. Quapropter saepe fit quod mulieres tales peccatores odiunt: & eos per infamiam occidunt et contra eos lapides id est verba detractoria iaciunt. Saepe enim factum est quod praedicatores qui contra malas mulieres libenter praedicant ab ipsis infamias reportant.

> [Orpheus signifies a preacher, a singer of the songs of the divine word, who after he has come from hell—that is the world—should sit on the mountain of Scripture or Religion, sing songs, sing the melody of holy scripture. . . . He should flee intercourse with women, abhor the embrace of the flesh, and preach against their evils. Therefore, it often happens that sinful women hate such men and kill them through infamy. Against them they hurl stones— that is detracting words; for it often happens that preachers who gladly preach against evil women receive infamies from them.]

> Vel dic quod orpheus significat sanctos & doctores primitiuae ecclesiae qui dulcedine cantus id est praedicationis saxa id est corda dura: arbores id est insensibiles & infideles ad fidem ecclesiae vocauerunt & magnam syluam id est magnam turbam hominum circa se collegerunt. Igitur mulieres id est tyranni & principes crudeles suos ministros tanquam lapides ad eos occidendos mittebant.

> [Or say that Orpheus signifies the holy and learned men of the primitive Church who by the sweetness of their song—that is preaching—call rocks— that is hard hearts, and trees—that is insensitive and unfaithful men—to the faith of the Church and gather a great wood—that is a great crowd of men— around themselves. Women—that is tyrants and cruel rulers—send their servants to slay them.][42]

Like Giovanni del Virgilio, Bersuire jettisons Orpheus's sexual spurning of women in favor of clerical chastity and his dissident musico-poetic performance upon the *lira* for the musical oratory of the Christian preacher. Orpheus represents the collective body of preachers in the early Church who together constitute the youthful institution; and following Arnulf of Orléans, Bersuire transforms Ovid's eroticized youths into a crowd of "insensitive and unfaithful men" who are converted by the "sweetness" of the predicatory "song" performed in the "primitive Church."

As represented by Bersuire, Orpheus is a particularly appropriate practitioner of the rhetorical *ars praedicandi*; Rita Copeland has argued that the Middle Ages was a period in which *rhetorica* was repeatedly invented "through constructions of sexual transgression," constructions by which rhetorical practice itself became located in "an emasculated or effeminate male body."[43] Unlike Alan of Lille and Jean de Meun, however, the mythographical tradition does not condemn Orpheus's followers as sodomites to be exiled, castrated, or hung by the throat, but rather enlists their rhetorical prowess into ecclesiastical service by recasting them as alluring preachers, rhetoricians, and monastic provocateurs indispensable to the Church's perdurance on Earth. For Bersuire, the Ovidian dismemberment of Orpheus provided an occasion for mythographic segmentation while reminding us of the larger ideological purpose of his treatise, which he wrote primarily as a guide for preachers.

The most complex mythographical treatment of the Orphic body (and one that I will now treat in some detail) occurs in the tenth book of the great fourteenth-century French treatise, the *Ovide moralisé*. This work has long been regarded primarily as a repository of classical myth for later vernacular authors, a ploddingly allegorical translation of its source that served fourteenth- and fifteenth-century writers such as Guillaume de Machaut and Christine de Pisan as a convenient reference work on pagan legend. More recently, scholars have begun to appreciate the work's status as a unique testament to medieval practices of rhetoric, *translatio*, and hermeneutics. For Copeland, the *Ovide moralisé* represents a "critical performance" that responds in the vernacular to the traditional forms and assumptions of academic literary criticism.[44] Renata Blumenfeld-Kosinski describes the mythography as a "hermeneutic system" in itself, one that puts allegoresis into action and shows us a "mode of reading" in the process of becoming a "mode of composition."[45]

If the raison d'être of medieval mythography is the rationalization of what to a Christian eye look like classical perversions, the musical body of Orpheus seems an ideal candidate for moralizing suppression. Yet in the *Ovide moralisé*, the homoerotic Orpheus inspires the poet to produce what is—without even a close rival—the most extended allegorization of a single Ovidian myth in the entire 72,000-line treatise. Even while doing his best to marginalize the musical homoerotics of Orpheus, the author provides us with what I would describe as an object lesson in the moral failure of medieval mythography. Interspersed among explicit polemics against the homoerotic message of the original myth, the vernacular mythographer's meditations on Orpheus inspire new and energetic flights of allegorical creativity. Book 10 in toto thus represents a botched but revealing response to Orpheus's dissident musicality, one that employs rhetorical *amplificatio*, vernacular *translatio*, and a distended instrumental allegory to ensure despite itself that the musical body of Orpheus will survive its violent allegorical fragmentation.

As is typical of the *Ovide moralisé*, the number of lines devoted to the original legend far exceeds the number in Ovid; in this case, the first twenty-five hundred lines of book 10 recount just over seven hundred lines from the *Metamorphoses*. As Blumenfeld-Kosinski points out with regard to the treatise in general, such dilations often exhibit the poet's working assumption that "sexual deviance can be an inducement to mythographical invention."[46] As book 10 progresses, Orphic musicality comes to represent an ever-growing threat to the heterosexualizing impulses of the Christian interpretive community represented and assumed by the author of the *Ovide moralisé*. The poet responds with a sustained rigor matched only by the sexual panic he consistently displays.

Even the formal organization of book 10 suggests that the vernacular mythographer regarded Orpheus's homoerotic turn as the most threatening moral aspect of the legend, and perhaps of *Metamorphoses* 10 as a whole. Each time the bard's preference for "tender boys" recurs in the Ovidian text, the French poet turns immediately to moralizing exempla and, in the process, violates the sequential rules of *histoire* and *allegorie* established elsewhere in the text. The first section of book 10 (lines 1–195) closely translates *Metamorphoses* 10.1–85 in recounting the lovers' marriage, the death of Eurydice, the tragic outcome of the descent, and the reversal in Orpheus's sexual object-choice: "Ce fu cil qui premierement/Aprist ceulz de Trace à retraire/D'amour femeline et à faire/Des joennes malles lor deduit" (That was he who first taught the Thracians to reject feminine love and take their pleasure from young men).[47]

At this first mention of Orpheus's "retraction" of love for women, the poet, rather than translating the stories that follow sequentially in the *Metamorphoses*, breaks off from the Ovidian model and begins a lengthy explication of the historical and allegorical senses of the Orpheus story as he has recounted it thus far.[48] The *historial sens*, he contends, can be summed up in the immorality of Orpheus's sexual sin. After losing his wife for the second time, his sorrow is *outre mesure* and causes him to lose all *amour de feme*, even to lose *le cors et l'ame*: "It is cruel beyond measure, such a love by which, against nature, he made one who was male female, without any hope of issue. Alas, that such a love was kept, from which one can come to an evil end" (Trop est crueulz à desmesure/Teulz amours où contre nature/Fet l'en dou malle femelin,/Sans nulle esperance de lin./Mar fet tele amour maintenir,/Dont l'en puet à mal fin venir) (10.214–19). The poet takes Orpheus's sexual violation of nature as an inevitably nonprocreative result of his failed heterosexual marriage.

Next comes a description of the rivers and inhabitants of hell, "uns abismes/Plains de tormens et plains de paine" (251–52). Acknowledging his debt to Macrobius for the account of hell's topography, the poet begins an extended harangue against gluttony and lechery with a description of the vulture gorging itself on Titius's liver (341–95). "Into this hell . . . descended Orpheus," the poet writes, "to find Eurydice, his wife" (396–98), and it becomes immediately clear how apt a synecdoche the liver-eating vulture is for the more general castigation of sensual overindulgence that follows: When humanity abandons its humility in iniquitous pursuit of "charnel plesire" (429), all hope for salvation is lost. So betrayed does Orpheus feel by Eurydice's death that he turns wholly against femininity as well as the "sensualité de l'ame" it represents. Instead, he opts for masculine virtue, and—perhaps with Arnulf of Orléans in mind—the company of other men: after losing "toute amour femeline,/Si se prist à la masculine" (590–91). Reverting to the Ovidian story line, the poet then recounts straightforwardly the "historial sens" of the tales of Cyparissus, Ganymede, Hyacinthus, Cerastes, Pygmalion, Myrrha, and Adonis.

The next awkward break occurs at line 2494, where the mythographer—without explaining his motives—inserts a compressed précis of the Orpheus legend followed by a vehement polemic against sodomy. The poet's skills as an *amplificator* are in full force here as a mere two lines of Ovid recounting Orpheus's turn to boys explode into a histrionic condemnation of the *historial sens* of the myth as a "very cruel" tale of a love "against nature and against law" that necessarily comes to an "evil end":

Mes onc puis nul jour n'ot envie
Ne desir d'amour femeline.
Cil fist par sa male douctrine
Mains folz atraire et alechier
Primes à mortelment pechier
Contre nature et contre loi,
Et pour confermer son delloi
Aus foles gens qu'il atiroit
Par son exemple, retraioit
Les males amours que mouvoient
Cil que li fol pour dieus tenoient,
Qui les joennes malles amoient
Et l'amour de femes blasmoient,
Si tesmoignoit en sa doctrine
Que miex vault l'amour masculine
Que cele aus femes ne faisoit.
Sa male douctrine plesoit
Aus folz qui o lui s'amusoient
Et de valetons abusoient,
Cil qui furent de dure orine
Plus que arbre ne sauvecine.

[From then on he never wanted nor desired feminine love. Through his evil teaching, he attracted and seduced many fools, first by mortally sinning against nature and against law; and to confirm his lawlessness to the mad people he attracted by his example, he returned the evil loves that moved him, he whom the fools held as God, whom the young males loved, denouncing the love of women. Thus, his teachings espoused that masculine love is worth more than that rendered to women. His evil teachings pleased the fools who amused themselves with him, and corrupted young men, those who were of lineage stronger than tree or wild beast.] (10.2519–39)

Even while taking literally and condemning Orphic sodomy, the poet cannot resist a tendency to allegorize: the trees and rocks that Orpheus draws around him through his music are the young men of "hard lineage" whom he has sexually corrupted.

Once this antisodomitical polemic concludes, however, the poet insists that he can put "Autre sentence en ceste letre" through a Christological "alegorie" in which Orpheus's "joennes malles" become the "Prophetes," "bon harperres," and "delitables prechierres" gathered on the eternal plain of Christ's church (10.2540–62). From a cursed sodomite condemned eternally to the fires of hell, Orpheus has become Christ in the blink of a mythographical eye. The homoerotic desires of Orpheus metamorphose into the love of Christ for human flesh, and Orpheus-Christ performs the Harrowing of Hell by leading what the poet exuberantly casts as a cosmic musical performance on the "hault mont" of Holy Church.

Actually convincing the reader that Orpheus-the-Ovidian-Sodomite is in reality Christ-the-Biblical-Redeemer is another matter. In order to do so, the poet here initiates what may be the most extended and innovative example of instrumental allegoresis in a medieval vernacular. Over the next five hundred lines, the harp of Orpheus becomes the descriptive focus of the allegory through a musical parataxis that itemizes the Christological "resonances" of each string and peg on the instrument. The harp allegory functions in concert with the Christ allegory in an attempted diversion of the reader's attention away from the literal, "contre nature" sense of the Orpheus myth by interpolating the longest allegorical interlude in book 10— indeed, as even a cursory comparison reveals, one of the most extended allegorical *amplificationes* of an Ovidian image in the entirety of the *Ovide moralisé*.[49]

The harp allegory begins at line 2578. The majestic harp possesses "Sept cordes sonans d'un acort / Sans dissence et sans desacort"; "Chacune corde," we read, "fermement / Est chevillee à double afiche, / Qui la corde tent et affiche" (is firmly attached between two pegs, which hold and fix the string) (10.2597–99). Along with his figurative description of the physical harp, the author glosses each individual string and peg on an imagined allegorical harp, constructing the "estrument" in its entirety as an organological testament to the exemplary role of Christ in human relations. The interpretation of the first two pegs signals the poet's immediate concern with the allegorical management of the flesh. The first peg is the Incarnation of Christ, on which God created a "jointure / De son fil à nostre nature / Ou ventre à la vierge pucele" (joining of his son to our nature in the womb of the young virgin). This peg is "la chambre," the somatic space of the womb in which Christ "prendre nostre humanité / Le jour de sa nativité" (2608–9). Across the harp from the Incarnation is another fleshly "jointure": the peg of "le mariage. . . . D'ome et de feme charnelment" (marriage between man and woman in the flesh). The string suspended between the incarnation and marriage, however, is the string of chastity, "li espirs qui l'ame avance/A estre franche et nete et pure" (2621–22): "Par ceste doucereuse corde/Est l'ame tenue en concorde" (2628–29). Though joined in the flesh through marriage, man and woman are chastely bound by incarnational law.

"La corde de charite," the second string, is suspended between the third peg, "de grant bonté" (2634) that God gave humanity through the Circumcision of Christ, and the fourth, "l'ordenement de provoire" (2659–60), the sacrament of ordination by which God establishes his law on Earth through his priestly agents. Here again the moral and practical associations between pegs and string make perfect sense: the circumcision of Christ embodies God's own charitable compassion in that it graphically demonstrates his consistent willingness to shed blood for humanity, while *caritas* was of course one of the virtues most closely associated with the monastic and secular clergy from at least the twelfth century.[50] Likewise, the fifth and sixth pegs, the baptism of Christ and the sacrament of baptism ("Le bastoime de nostre loi" [2698]) respectively, suspend between them the third string, "Largesce ou misericorde" (2711), which resonates with the pity that Christ manifested when he allowed himself to receive "baptesme en l'onde," which washed away "les pechiez dou monde" (2692–93). The "actual" music emitted by the string, "li douz sons de ceste corde" (2735), is a tuneful promise of succor from Christ.

With the fourth string, by contrast, the poet evokes the many violent deployments of music within medieval representations of religious suffering. The seventh peg is the Passion. Much like the author of *Die Erlösung* and other works representing the musicality of the Crucifixion (see Chapter 5), the *Ovide moralisé* poet here lapses into an uncharacteristically onomatopoetic passage in which a string of definite articles replicates for the reader the physical assault upon the body of Christ—

L'autre affiche est la passion,
La honte et la derision,
Les ramposnes et les blastenges,
Les griez affis et les laidenges,
La bateüre et la manace,
Les chraches gitez en la face

(2736–41)

—that culminates in "la mort" that he gladly suffered "pour nous" (2742–44). Human participation in the death of Christ is promised by the eighth peg, "le sacrement/De l'autier" (2748–49), the Eucharist that allegorically transforms the music of the Passion into the corporeal sacrament of the host. The fourth string, "La fort corde de pascience/Est assise entre ces affiches" (2767–68). Throughout this sequence, the poet deploys the central string and set of pegs on the allegorical harp to remind the reader that upon this harp hangs a body, one that teaches patience in the face of a clearly "musical" suffering.

The final three strings and their pegs complete the soteriological and sacramental sequence. Peg nine represents the glorious resurrection of Christ "de mort a vie" (2794), the tenth "confession,/Penitance et contricion" (2798–99), and both embrace the string "d'abstinance" (2813). Abstinence in turn is the string fixed in the harp "A tenir nous. . . . De tout pechié" (2818–19). If the believer does lapse into sin, the cleansing peg of confession sits firmly at one end of the string, the redemptive promise of resurrection at the other. Similarly, the eleventh peg, the Ascension that establishes Christ's eternal reign in heaven (2828–40), and the twelfth, the sacrament of confirmation (2841), embrace the "ferme et estable" string of justice (2851). The poet punningly casts confirmation as the sacrament that literally "pegs" the faithful to Christ: "la confirmacion,/C'est, ce croi, la douzieme *affiche*./Ceste nous conferme et *affiche*/En la foi de crestienté" (2841–44; my emphasis). The consequences of not "playing along" with the allegorical harp are made clear by the last set of pegs and string: pegs eleven, the Last Judgment (2868–84), and twelve, "la medecine et li oint" of extreme unction (2885–2903), hold between them the string of "humilité" (2906), the virtue of human awe in the face of death and eternity.

These roughly five hundred lines, taking the reader from the moment of incarnation to the Last Judgment, are the apotheosis of Christian instrumental allegory. The passage as a whole culminates the instrumental somatics first propounded in the patristic era, augmented by figures such as Rhabanus Maurus and Joachim of Fiore (whose *Psalterium decem chordarum* may in fact have directly inspired the vernacular allegory[51]), and illustrated in great detail by illuminators of texts by Peter Lombard and Dante. Among many remarkable aspects of this extended instrumental metaphor is the sheer complexity of the allegoresis, the structuring principle of which becomes clear only when the allegory is considered in its totality. What the *Ovide moralisé* poet is doing here, I would suggest, is constructing an "instrumental" model for the human subject, one in which the strings and pegs compel the reader to participate in a musico-allegorical meditation upon the embodied self. The first series of pegs traces the historical progression of Christ from the Incarnation to the Resurrection, the second the progress of the believer through the seven sacraments. The seven strings collectively represent the poet's version of the seven virtues—chastity, charity, pity, patience, abstinence, justice, and humility. The harp as a whole is a monumental symbol for human living that deploys the progression of sacred history from Incarnation to Judgment, as well as the progression of human history through the seven sacraments, in order to chart a life filled with and guided by virtues. The instrument's pegs and strings provide a simultaneously visual and sonorous exemplum of virtuous living for the Christian reader in the present: only through a tedious "reading" of this harp and an assimilative remembrance of its components can the devout human subject modeled in the treatise truly be constructed.

So perfectly idealized is the treatise's harp that the nonresisting reader easily forgets precisely how and why it began: as a response to the sodomitical lapse of Orpheus following the death of his wife. The harp allegory attempts to wrest the instrument out of Orpheus's homoerotic grasp and thus rescue it from its dissident sexual implications. The result is a pansensual synesthesia in which the figurative music of the harp can be viewed in the spectacle of the Crucifixion, tasted in the sacrament of the Eucharist, and touched in the chaste but fleshly consummation of heterosexual matrimony. Within the devotional register of the *Ovide moralisé*, the reader is made to experience the often painful course of soteriological history, the individual progression through the sacraments, and the constant demands of virtuous living: all while meditating on the poeticized harp of Orpheus upon which the beaten body of Christ is hung. The harp allegory in the *Ovide moralisé* thus performs upon the human subject a thorough *psychological* fragmentation that recasts in Christian terms the punitive dismemberment of the original, homoerotic Orpheus.

What this overview of the formal narrative and allegorical structure of book 10 suggests is that Orpheus's homoerotic musicality directly inspires much of the poet's mythographical creativity throughout this section of the *Ovide moralisé*. Only when Orpheus has lost Eurydice the second time and turned his harp to "en autre fueil" (3327) does the mythographer initiate the massive harp allegory that occupies a significant portion of the book. Organological allegory seeks to distract the reader from the homoerotics of Orpheus's performance, locating the reading subject's desire instead along the seven virtuous and sacramental strings of the harp. The musical body of Christ inspires a harmonious "temperance" through humanity's adherence to the sacraments and virtues. Yet while this paratactic allegory comes into being in the service of the moral imperative of the *Ovide moralisé*, the Orpheus-Christ figure will inevitably bear traces of his classical role as "the *auctor* of pederasty," in Barkan's terms, the somatic performer who reaches his auditors not through predicatory rhetoric alone, but through those very musico-corporeal practices—strumming, beating, plucking—to which the body of Christ is subjected throughout medieval writings and visions.

The broader human implications of these allegorical machinations become clear soon after the harp sequence concludes. Before moving from his final allegory of the Orpheus legend to the literal sense of Ovid's account of Ganymede, the author quickly recounts the Old Testament from the Fall, when Eve "menga la dapnable pome" (10.3338), to the destruction of "Gomorre et Sodome," a historical trajectory that entails the most universal loss of all, that of prelapsarian innocence and grace. The entire human condition, the mythographer implies, is implicated in Orpheus's homoerotic turn after Eurydice's death; the sodomitical severance of the marital bond recapitulates humanity's loss of innocence after the Fall, which can be redeemed only by the implicitly musical "amour et acorde" desired by "li filz Dieu." Thus, the author glosses Jove's rape of Ganymede, like Orpheus's turn to "tender boys," as an allegory for God's "love of human nature" (amour d'umaine nature), his willingness to put on human flesh and become man (3406–11).

The energetic allegoresis performed by the *Ovide moralisé* poet throughout book 10 highlights what is of course the motivating irony of medieval Christian mythography, a tradition of commentary that depends upon and amplifies the various forms of eroticism it excoriates on the literal level. In book 10, this scandal works to produce a "queer paradox" by which the mythographer cannot avoid the repeated juxtaposition of Orphic sexuality with the love of God for humanity. It could be argued that the author depends upon the scandalousness of this juxtaposition for his own claim to revisionary *auctoritas*, assuming (wrongly, I would hope) that his mythographical muscle will be enough to banish Orphic sexual dissidence from the pages of his text. In sum, the Orpheus/Christ typology in the *Ovide moralisé* represents a rigorous attempt to cleanse Orpheus's musicality of its homoerotic charge that nevertheless comes perilously close to locating Christ himself as the quintessential Orphic sodomite, the savior who sings the "New Song" luring young men into the faith.

Near the beginning of book 11 of the *Ovide moralisé*, Orpheus in pieces floats down the Heber in a miraculous portrait of musical dismemberment. The river receives "sa teste et sa lire" (11.139), resounding to the echoic accompaniment of "Les rives dou flun" (145), which join in the musical complaint. After its violent fragmentation, the body of Orpheus endures as a haunting reminder of the perils of musical and sexual dissidence. For the mythographer, however, the dismemberment of Orpheus has been preceded by the hermeneutical and sacramental fragmentation of the Christian subject; the harp allegory has already served to break down the Everyman-like reader into the discrete psychical and behavioral components that lie at the foundations of human subjectivity. Crystallized in "la langue," the singing tongue, the Orphic voice resounds well into the following decades, when it is plucked from the allegorical morass of the *Ovide moralisé* and refashioned into a *dit* by the most prolific poet-musician of the succeeding century.

The Orphic *Voix* of Guillaume de Machaut

If the homoerotics of Orpheus's musical performance are central to the allegorical machinations of *Ovide moralisé* 10, they are abandoned altogether by Guillaume de Machaut in his "Dit de la harpe," a 354-line work in which the poet appropriates the musical *auctoritas* of Orpheus to elaborate the virtues of his lady through an extended instrumental metaphor.[52] The harp, Machaut writes, is the noblest of instruments, conveying a "tres dous son" (6) that is "plaisans/A Dieu" (89–90) and clearly unsuitable for performance "en tauerne" (252). Appropriate only for the genteel company of "cheualiers, dames, et damoiselles" (255), the harp and its performers should consort with neither "villein ne garson ne merdaille" (259). Accordingly, after a lengthy account of Orpheus's unsuccessful journey to hell and briefer portraits of the harpists Apollo and David, Machaut launches into a ruminative comparison of his "dame" and her "gent corps" to the ".xxv. cordes que la harpe a" (twenty-five strings that the harp has; 3). The analogy insists through figurative language upon the status of the harp as the instrumental sine qua non of courtly desire and its literary realization.

A little-discussed part of Machaut's poetic corpus, the "Dit de la harpe" has been characterized as a "highly tedious" work, "one of Machaut's least successful efforts" at poetic invention.[53] Only Sylvia Huot has insisted upon the larger significance of the "Dit" within the poet's oeuvre, describing it as "a statement, in microcosm, of Machaut's view of himself as love poet at this later stage of his career" and pointing out its status as the most densely illuminated text in any Machaut manuscript.[54] The "Dit de la harpe" is compelling evidence for what Huot has identified as the wider epistemic shift in medieval textual culture "from song to book"; the self-conscious generic move in the poem from *lay* to *dit* marks the "transformation of musical performance into illuminated book and of love experience into poetic text," a shift that Machaut registers with particular subtlety in his appropriation of Orpheus's harp as a simultaneously oral-musical and textual-linguistic literary device.[55]

Yet there is an equally significant cultural transformation registered in the "Dit de la harpe" through Machaut's generic revisionism, which enlists the conventions of religious mythography into the service of secular love poetry. For Machaut's short poem, I would suggest, performs a thorough and dedicated revision of the harp allegory in book 10 of the *Ovide moralisé*. Machaut's more general debt to the French mythographer has long been recognized; Cornelis de Boer's useful source-study in the introduction to his edition of the *Ovide moralisé* demonstrated that the extent and variety of the later poet's borrowings are apparent throughout his oeuvre, and Blumenfeld-Kosinski shows clearly that Machaut's mythical imagination is in large part a mythographical one.[56] Though the "Dit de la harpe" has yet to be examined as part of Machaut's broader response to the *Ovide moralisé*, it is easily one of his most pointed attempts: not only is it the most transparently allegorical of the *dits*, but in its form, content, and sheer "tediousness" it constitutes an unmistakable response to the musico-allegorical book 10 that would have been easily recognized as such by many of Machaut's readers. Indeed, an underlying motivation of the "Dit de la harpe" appears to be the redirection of the reader's gaze from the Orphic body of Christ to the idealized woman who is the subject of the *dit* itself.

Though the *Ovide moralisé* is written in octosyllabic couplets as opposed to the (primarily) decasyllabics Machaut chose for the "Dit de la harpe," the vernacular mythography demonstrably furnished much of the later poem's thematic and allegorical material. The *dit*'s opening gesture echoes the very first lines of the harp metaphor in *Ovide moralisé* 10, signaling Machaut's simultaneous indebtedness to and distance from the earlier religious allegory:

> Or vueil deviser les faitures
> *Des sept cordes que la harpe a*
> Que li harperes atempra
>
> (*Ovide moralisé* 10.2593–95)

Je puis trop bien ma dame comparer
A la harpë, et son gent corps parer
De .xxv. cordes que la harpe a

> ("Dit de la harpe," 1–3)

By positioning this echo at the opening of the *dit*, Machaut crafts an allusive boast to the reader, insisting that his own allegory will far surpass the best efforts of the mythographer. *Your* harp had only seven strings, Machaut seems to be saying; *mine* will have twenty-five.

Though self-consciously allegorical, however, the instrumental parataxis of the "Dit de la harpe" distances itself from the *Ovide moralisé* in striking ways. From the beginning, as the two passages above illustrate grammatically, Machaut's focus of description and desire is the lady herself: "ma dame" and "son gent corps" are the direct objects of the first sentence, just as they are the ultimate objects of his poetic gaze throughout the *dit*. Machaut purposefully abandons the mythographer's neat triadic descriptions in favor of an idiosyncratic series of juxtapositions. Perfect Good and Loyalty are the first of twenty-five "sister strings" presented in groups of two, three, four, and five as the poem progresses. Machaut even plays a game of one-upmanship with himself by adding four or five additional strings later in the poem in what is presented as a spur-of-the-moment expansion of the original allegory.[57] Moreover, though the poem's personified "strings" are virtues, the "Dit" has already announced itself as an allegorical description of a "corps," a body. The virtues are abstractions, of course, yet prosopopoeia is nevertheless the operative allegorical mode in the "Dit"; unlike the *Ovide moralisé*, in which the virtuous strings exemplify ways of living, here they are not only attributed to a specific human individual, but are themselves living, breathing personifications whose familial relations and even rivalries are part of the poem's subject.

Perhaps the clearest sign of Machaut's revisionary stance in relation to the mythographer's Christianizing allegory is the complete absence of pegs—"affiches"—from the elaborated harp. In the *Ovide moralisé*, the pegs functioned in an almost literal sense as strong and stable reminders of Christ's bodily sacrifice as well as the sacraments in which his life is remembered and imitated. They signify the presence of the divine in human acts, and thus the possibility of human salvation provided the life course laid out on and through the body of the harp is carefully followed. For Machaut, by contrast, the pegs no longer anchor the virtues. The strings are free-floating physical and spiritual components of the human person; as his boastful addition of extra strings implies, the rigidly predetermined structure of the harp in the *Ovide moralisé* has given way to a personified panoply in which the organological relation of harp to strings feels almost arbitrary, and in fact is practically abandoned by the end. The lady-strings are not anchored by the "affiches" of the seven sacraments, nor are they governed by the soteriological imperative that anchors the primary series of pegs in the mythography.

Finally, the "Dit de la harpe" transforms an extended instrumental allegory virtually bursting with homoerotic anxieties into a straightforward celebration of heterosexual desire, a desire decidedly not "against nature." For Machaut, in fact, the category of *nature*, as well as the anathematizing label *contre nature* itself, serves only to further the heterosexualizing impulse of the poem's founding allegory:

> Si que ie di qu'on ne doit riens amer
> Fors pour bonté, et trop fait a blamer
> Ce qui est bel et de bonté n'a cure,
> Et diroit on que c'est *contre nature*
> Qu'adés bonté les choses embelist
> Plus que biauté. . . .

> [Just as I say that one should not love anything except for goodness, and that one does too much to reprimand that which is beautiful and has no concern for goodness, another would say that it is against nature that goodness always embellishes things more than beauty.] (135–40)

Machaut completes the allegorical suppression of Orphic homoeroticism unsuccessfully attempted in the *Ovide moralisé* by redeploying the harp as an eroticized metaphor for his beloved lady's body. The mythographer went out of his way to condemn the homoerotic turn of Orpheus as "contre nature et contre loi," invective repeated throughout book 10 in an attempt to cleanse the Orpheus story of its sodomitical connotations through sheer force of religious allegory. Despite his clear indebtedness to the vernacular mythography, however, Machaut enlists the label "contre nature" to serve the intricate purposes of a heterosexual love allegory.

In concluding the "Dit de la harpe," Machaut returns to Orpheus in a poetic gesture that signals his participation in the wider medieval process of Orphic fragmentation—not only of Orpheus and his lady, but also of himself. The only real crux in the relatively thin history of the poem's criticism has been the solution to the concluding anagram, which contains an authorial signature that Machaut claims can be pieced together from the following words: "Qu' esperance m'a fait riche d'amour:/Dame d'atour humble, clere de vis,/Sage d'un" (That hope has enriched me in love: Lady of humble aspect, bright of countenance, a sage man from a; 351–53). Once Machaut's name has been extracted, however, there is no single name that presents itself as the obvious solution. As many as four different ladies' names or titles can be formed, including "Dame Peronne," "Ma douce dame de Navarre," "Duchesse de Berri," and "Roine de France"; since none of these uses up all of the remaining letters, Huot argues, none can be the only correct answer. Huot suggests the intriguing possibility that Machaut may mean for the reader to spell "Orpheüs" and "Erudice" (the name's spelling in the "Dit"); the fact that even this leaves a number of letters unused may imply as well that Machaut's "lady" is "none other than the conflation of lyricism and writerly craft that makes up his poetic oeuvre."[58] Like Machaut himself, Orpheus is reconstituted and given back his bride through the reader's solving of the anagram, an interpretive process that foregrounds the poetic and musical processes integral to poetic invention.

In this sense, the poem points to the perilously Orphic nature of medieval authorship. If, as Kevin Brownlee has argued, Machaut's more general use of anagrams suggests the extent to which authorial identity and poetic activity have become "self-authorizing" in his later works,[59] the anagram in the "Dit de la harpe" may represent the exception that proves the rule. For here poetic fragmentation and remembrance—not identity and coherence—are integral to the expression of authorial subjectivity within the physical space of poetry. Like Orpheus, the author must be "re-membered" in order to emerge from the fabric of the poem. The dismemberment of Orpheus is a necessary condition for poetic invention—indeed, for the very subjectivity of the poet. If Machaut has abandoned the homoerotics of the original myth in favor of a heteroerotic adulation of his lady, he has nevertheless performed his desire upon the fragmented musical body of Orpheus.

Music, Resistance, and Subjection in Dante's *Purgatorio*

No medieval writer exploited the sonorous erotics of Orphic mourning more creatively than Dante in the *Purgatorio*, a canticle that repeatedly exposes the tense relations between pagan perversion and Christian salvation—though largely without the attendant anxiety of the *Ovide moralisé*. Dante was an acquaintance and correspondent of the mythographer Giovanni del Virgilio, whose revealing allegorization of the myth retained its homosocial flavor while jettisoning its explicit eroticism. As we saw earlier, for del Virgilio, Orpheus represented a newly chaste holy man; his loss of Eurydice directly inspired him to "spurn women, giving his soul instead to God," and begin "to love men, that is, to act in a manly way." For the mythographer's exiled contemporary, by contrast, the literal-sense erotics of the Orpheus myth remain crucial to its appropriation. If for Machaut (writing later in the fourteenth century) the body of Orpheus will provide an occasion for celebrating the *gent corps* of an idealized lady, Dante positions this same body within a poetic genealogy that embraces rather than spurns the truly *polymorphous* eroticism of the myth.

The fundamentally Orphic nature of Dante's project in the *Commedia* has been an enduring theme in the criticism. Sharing with Orpheus, Virgil, Christ, and very few others the distinct status of having survived a journey to Hell, Dante bears a compelling resemblance to the alluring bard in his search for a woman he loves—a search that nevertheless involves the constant and often overwhelming presence of same-sex desire.[60] Orphic song reaches what is in many ways its medieval apogee in the *Purgatorio*, giving rise to strings of musical and poetic echoes between source texts, cantos, and canticles that locate both pilgrim and poet within the homoerotic lineage that Orpheus represents.

Dante's clearest appropriation of an Orphic voice occurs in *Purgatorio* 30, just after the pilgrim is finally abandoned by Virgil in the Earthly

Paradise. At this point Dante inserts a famous Virgilian allusion that allows the pilgrim to produce a self-reflexive mimic of Orpheus's lament upon his second loss of Eurydice in the fourth *Georgic*:

> *Eurydicen* vox ipsa et frigida lingua,
> a miseram *Eurydicen*! anima fugiente vocabat
> *Eurydicen* toto referebant flumine ripae.
>
> ["Eurydice" called that very voice and death-cold tongue, with fleeting breath, "ah, hapless Eurydice!" "Eurydice" the shores replied, all down the stream.][61]

Virgil brilliantly emphasizes the psychic fragmentation of Orpheus at the loss of Eurydice, poetically separating "vox" and "lingua" both from one another and from the body that employs them in mourning. The passage thus adumbrates the bard's literal dismemberment that will prove so central to medieval revisitations of the story.

In the Earthly Paradise, Orpheus's Virgilian lament for his lost wife in the *Georgics* reappears as the pilgrim's lament for his male guide in Dante's direct revision of the passage above:

> Ma *Virgilio* n'avea lasciati scemi
>   di sé, *Virgilio* dolcissimo patre,
>   *Virgilio* a cui per mia salute die'mi.
>
> [But Virgil had left us bereft of himself, Virgil sweetest father, Virgil to whom I gave myself for my salvation.][62]

The pathos of Dante's echoic mourning is palpable, appropriately displaying the poet's immense powers of revisionism at one of the most transformative moments in the canticle. At the same time, the allusion is part of what Jeffrey Schnapp has described as a more general proliferation of gender substitutions in this canto and throughout the *Commedia*.[63]

Dante transforms himself into Orpheus and Eurydice into Virgil; the result is a gender reversal that entails a fleeting but crucial poetic expression of same-sex love in the *Purgatorio*. Indeed, while John Freccero reads Dante's repetition of Virgil's name as "an effacement, further and further away from the letter of Virgil's text, as Virgil fades away in the dramatic representation to make way for Beatrice," it seems clear that the tercet signals the emergence of a specifically Orphic mode of musical desire at the very moment the pilgrim feels "the great power of old love" for Beatrice.[64] Far from what Freccero terms a "mere allusion," I would argue, Dante's mournful tercet invokes a second classical text: Statius's *Achilleid,* in which the Greeks collectively mourn the absence of their hero Achilles. Perhaps himself inspired by *Georgic* 4, Statius describes a tripled repetition of Achilles' name uttered by the Greek leader Calchas:

> omnis in absentem belli manus ardet *Achillem,*
>
> nomen *Achillis* amant, et in Hectora solus *Achilles*
>
> poscitur.

> [the whole host burns for the absent *Achilles,* they love the name of *Achilles, Achilles* alone is called for against Hector.][65]

Through his veiled and doubled reference in *Purgatorio* 30, Dante recalls his earlier and more explicit allusion to the *Achilleid* in *Purgatorio* 9, where he had awakened "no differently than Achilles" (Non altrimenti Achille) immediately following his dreamed ravishment as Ganymede.[66] In this personalized retelling of the homoerotic *raptus* of Ganymede, Dante had already identified himself poetically with Orpheus, who in turn had narrated the tale of Ganymede in the *Metamorphoses.* Recalling in *Purgatorio* 30 his dreamed *raptus* just as he mourns for Virgil, Dante thus returns to the one moment in the *Commedia* that most profoundly articulates his own fleeting identity as a subject of homoerotic desire.[67]

In a single tercet, Dante thus appropriates the voice of Orpheus to mourn the jarring loss of Virgil, his guide through the vast array of infernal and purgatorial perversions; the imminent loss of Statius, his guide through the Earthly Paradise; and his own momentary identity as Achilles, the feminized subject of Ganymedean desire. And just as Beatrice reproves him for Orphically weeping at the loss of Virgil, Dante's name appears for the first and only time in the entire *Commedia*: " 'Dante, because Virgil leaves you, do not weep yet, do not weep yet, for you must weep for another sword!' " (Dante, perché Virgilio se ne vada,/non pianger anco, non piangere ancora;/ché pianger ti conven per altra spada) (*Purg.* 30.55–57). The very enunciation of the pilgrim's name entails loss: the word *Dante,* despite its uniqueness within the *Commedia,* here appears alongside *Virgilio* within the same line. While Dante's desire for Beatrice has energized his narrative and propelled his pilgrimage throughout the first two canticles, now, even

as Beatrice appears before him, Dante's Orphic loss of Virgil is in effect
the condition for his assumption of nominal identity through her mouth.
Dante is named and made a subject through the very *prohibition* of homoerotic desire, a prohibition that entails the wrenching pain of Orphic loss
and the poetic mourning of Dante's *dolcissimo patre*.

Only after this extraordinary subjective transformation is the pilgrim's
own *canto* finally "in tune" with the music of the spheres:

Sì come neve tra le vive travi
    per lo dosso d'Italia si congela,
    soffiata e stretta da li venti schiavi,
poi, liquefatta, in sé stessa trapela
    pur che la terra che perde ombra spiri,
    sì che par foco fonder la candela;
così fui sanza lagrime e sospiri
    anzi 'l cantar di quei che notan sempre
    dietro a le note de li etterni giri;
ma poi che 'ntesi ne le docli tempre
    lor compartire a me, par che se detto
    avesser: "Donna, perché sì lo stempre?"
lo gel che m'era intorno al cor ristretto,
    spirito e acqua fessi, e con angoscia
    de la bocca e de li occhi uscì del petto.

[Even as the snow, among the living rafters upon the back of Italy, is con-
gealed, blown and packed by Slavonian winds, then melting, trickles
through itself, if only the land that loses shadow breathes, so that it seems a
fire that melts the candle; so was I without tears or sighs before the song of
those who ever sing in harmony with the eternal spheres. But when I heard
how in their sweet notes they took my part, quite as if they had said, "Lady,
why do you so confound him?" the ice that was bound tight around my
heart became breath and water, and with anguish poured from my breast
through my mouth and eyes.] (*Purg.* 30.85–99)

The final tercet recalls Augustine's liquid response to the strains of Ambrosian psalmody after his baptism, when the music "flooded into" (influebant)
him and "liquified" (eliquabatur) religious truths in his heart as tears ran
down his cheek (currebant).[68] For Dante, too, musical liquefaction signals a
radical conversion, anticipating the Christian *trasumanar*, or "passing be-

yond the human," that will enable his journey through the *Paradiso*. "Taking his part," the *musica mundana* allows him to open his heart to Beatrice.

The pilgrim's crying here can and should be read as a sign of joy; the lover is reunited with his beloved, and his body responds with tears of relief. Yet these are also very clearly tears of sorrow: for Virgil, for Statius, for everything these pagan writers embody—including, perhaps, the poetic and sexual dissidence personified by Dante's other great teacher, the alleged sodomite Brunetto Latini. Dante insists upon mourning the homosocial pagan pleasures he has left behind, and in fact does so by appropriating the voice of Orpheus, the one classical mourner whose music allows him to articulate most fully the desirous complexity of his loss. Unlike that of Augustine, Dante's musical conversion comes at a great personal cost. Demanding the pilgrim's and the poet's emergence from the pagan music of Orpheus, the *musica mundana* must coerce submission to the very universal *harmonia* it supposedly embodies. Dante's Orphic poetic at the top of the purgatorial mountain constitutes an anguished mode of resistance to the order of nature, a mournful refusal—momentary but momentous—to allow the music of his own desiring body to submit to the harmonious authoritarianism of the spheres.

The Homoerotics of Marriage:
John Lydgate and the Renaissance Orpheus

In the penultimate scene of Thomas Heywood's seventeenth-century domestic tragedy *A Woman Killed with Kindness*, Anne Frankford sits on stage and mourns her lost virtue on the musical instrument that functions throughout the narrative as a metonym for her sexual body. Loyal bourgeois wife turned "base strumpet," in her own words, through an adulterous liaison with her husband's best friend, Anne requests her lute from the family servant Nick, whose wry aside even in the face of tragedy reminds the audience of the musical bawdiness that subtends the platonic commonplaces everywhere in the script:

ANNE   I know the lute. Oft have I sung to thee: We both are out of tune, both out of time.

NICK   [*Aside*] Would that had been the worst instrument that e'er you played on.[69]

Despite Anne's forecast of her own imminent death by starvation, the audience will more likely remember Nick's comic metaphor linking her musical instrument with her suitor's sexual "instrument" once the ensuing performance begins. Anne sits with the lute between her legs, and after a final
quasi apostrophe to the instrument—"My lute shall groan;/It cannot weep,
but shall lament my moan" (16.31–32)—she begins to play.

Nick is not the only on-stage witness to the ensuing musical spectacle,
however. As Anne performs, Wendoll, her companion in adultery, enters
the scene, watching in mournful ecstasy as his lover plays even as he medi-
ates the erotics of her performance to the audience:

> . . . O my sad fate!
> Here, and so far from home, and thus attended!
> O God, I have divorced the truest turtles
> That ever lived together, and being divided
> In several places, make their several moan;
> She in the fields laments, and he at home.
> So poets write that Orpheus made the trees
> And stones to dance to his melodious harp,
> Meaning the rustic and the barbarous hinds,
> That had no understanding part in them;
> So she from these rude carters tears extracts,
> Making their flinty hearts with grief to rise
> And drawn down rivers from their rocky eyes.
>
> (16.46–58)

This spectacle of musical enchantment seems at first safely heterosexual:
Anne Frankford and her husband are imagined as separated turtledoves,
fiercely loyal birds whose tragic division Wendoll himself has done much to
bring about. Crucially, however, Wendoll does not describe Anne as a
Siren-like musical seductress; the musical comparison he draws is not between Anne and a *female* performer, legendary or otherwise, but between
Anne and Orpheus. Anne performs here *as Orpheus*—and as a male listener,
Wendoll ascribes the erotics of her musical production to the success with
which she recapitulates the classical bard's seductiveness. For the early modern audience, the scene may derive a good part of its sexual charge from the
obvious fact that it is a boy who performs beneath Anne's clothes, a male

actor whose masculinity becomes most glaringly apparent on stage when Wendoll compares Anne's music to that of Orpheus. Wendoll strangely positions himself as the seduced listener—one of Ovid's "tender boys"—to a quintessentially Orphic song: a melody performed by a boy costumed as a woman but described as a man.

Orpheus's status in *A Woman Killed with Kindness* as the musical embodiment of adulterous and polymorphously erotic desire has a quite specific English genealogy, one that we will miss if we try too hard to place Heywood's Orpheus within the literary lineage of the romance Sir Orfeo or the Boethian Orpheus of Robert Henryson. The Orpheus imagined in this play has his most direct antecedent, incongruously enough, in the writings of John Lydgate. A Benedictine monk of Bury St. Edmunds who produced much of his surviving poetry as a paid propagandist for the Lancastrian upper nobility, Lydgate was long a victim of the literary prejudice against the English fifteenth century. The author's massive oeuvre is only now being reassessed for its rich perspective upon the thriving religious and political culture of vernacular writing between Chaucer and the Tudors.[70] Lydgate's *Fall of Princes* propounds what is simultaneously the most conventional and forward-looking medieval vision of the musical erotics of Orpheus, one that clearly anticipates the sorts of adulterous sexual performances the bard will be made to enact in the early modern period. I conclude this chapter with the Lydgatean Orpheus for two reasons: first, to show how the homoerotics of Orpheus's musicianship figured within the political culture of a specific historical moment; and second, to begin revealing some of the thematic and wide-ranging continuities within the history of the musical body that will be the subject of the Epilogue.

The *Fall of Princes* is a versified translation of Laurence de Premierfait's *Des Cas des Nobles Hommes et Femmes*, which in turn is a much-expanded French version of Boccaccio's *De casibus illustrium virorum*. Though for the most part loyal to his source, Lydgate's idiosyncratic interpolations within this massive text (at 36,365 lines, it is still just over half the length of the *Ovide moralisé*) show us a revisionary translator intent upon eviscerating his continental sources of their immediate political resonance in order to pander to an overbearing patron, Humphrey, Duke of Gloucester.[71] Yet it may have been Lydgate's desire to send a rather more personal message to his Lancastrian patron that inspired him to push the rhetorical, musi-

cal, and sexual boundaries of the Orpheus legend to their medieval breaking point, anticipating Heywood's Renaissance Orpheus in a surprisingly
forthright way.

Boccaccio had made short but interesting work of Orpheus in *De
casibus*, giving the bard a single sentence that covers less than two lines in
the 1520 Paris edition: "Aderat et Orpheus tum perditam eurydicen suam
tum duram inferorum legem et bacchantium mulierum atrocitatem perdite
deflens" (Orpheus approached next, bemoaning excessively first his lost
Eurydice, then the harsh law of hell and the cruelty of the Bacchante
women).[72] The postdismemberment Orpheus rematerializes in order to
mourn his lost wife in front of the writer, and the bard's erotic turn goes
unmentioned. The brevity here contrasts with the treatment of Orpheus's
body in *Genealogy of the Gods*, where Boccaccio had ruminated at length
upon the mythic and mythographic dimensions of the legend. In book 5,
chapter 12, he presents a suspiciously chastening paraphrase of the Ovidian
original: "diu flevit et celibem deducere vitam disposuit. Et ob id, ut ait
Ovidius, cum multas suas nuptias postulantes reiecisset, aliisque hominibus
celibem vitam ducere suaderet, mulierum incidit odium, et a celebrantibus
matronis orgia Bachi secus Hebrum, rastris atque ligonibus cesus atque
discerptus est" (He cried a long while and decided to lead a celibate life. And
because of that, so says Ovid, when he had rejected his many female suitors,
and persuaded other men to lead a celibate life, he incited the hatred of
women, and during an erotic Bacchic orgy by the Hebron, he was torn apart
by married women with rakes and mattocks).[73] Especially curious is the
amount of attention Boccaccio pays to the fate of Orpheus's vulnerable
head, which lands on the island of Lesbos and becomes a fragmented synecdoche of the bard's aesthetic prowess: "The serpent, or time, . . . tried to eat
the head, that is, the name and fame of Orpheus or those works performed
by his genius, since men of genius thrive by the head. . . . Nothing stands in
the way of time, and to be sure the serpent could not have gone hungry save
to this extent, that a famous man lives [on] by his lyre" (Quod autem ser-
pens, qui caput Orphei devorare volebat, . . . intelligo pro serpente an-
norum revolutiones, que caput, id est nomen Orphei, seu ea que ingenio
Orphei composita sunt, cum in capite vigeant vires ingenii, consumere, ut
reliqua faciunt, conate sint . . . nil illi posse tempus obsistere; quod quidem
huc usque non potuit egisse, quin adhuc famosus existat cum cythara

sua).[74] Detached from his body, the *caput* of Orpheus is artistic perpetuity itself, a mythic projection into the future that achieves a stellified permanence in the cosmos. Like his humanist successor, Coluccio Salutati, Boccaccio here approaches the Orpheus legend as a "comparative mythographer," in Friedman's words, mining classical and medieval sources for the hermeneutic light they shed on a confounding pagan legend.[75] By the time he began his *De casibus*, however, Boccaccio seems to have decided against Orpheus's place in the pantheon of worthies, portraying him instead as a whiner meriting no more than a sentence.

Lydgate's version of the Orpheus legend in the *Fall of Princes* occurs toward the end of book I, in which numerous illustrious figures from classical and biblical antiquity appear to the speaker's *auctor*, "Iohn Bochas," and withdraw in silence. Having just been left by Myrrha, a woman who "loued ageyn nature/Hir owne fadir," Bochas receives a mourning Orpheus, whom the poet describes as "ful ougli on to see."[76] Though hideous of face, however, Orpheus has remained an alluringly rhetorical musician despite his wife's death; Lydgate's translation clearly reveals the sensual appeal of his performance:

> Ful renommed in armys and science,
> Famous in musik and in melodie,
> And ful notable also in eloquence.
> And for his soote sugred armonie,
> Beestis, foulis, poetis specefie,
> Wodes, flodes off ther cours most strong,
> Stynt of ther cours to herkne his soote song.
>
> (1.5783–89)

A synesthesia of hearing and taste allows Orpheus to produce a "soote sugred armonie" from his harp in the world above and, in the next stanza, to recover Eurydice "with soote touchis sharpe/Which that he made vpon his heuenli harpe" (5795–96) from the world below. There is a faint echo of the *House of Fame*'s violent Boethian musicality in these "soote touchis sharpe." The sweetness of Orpheus's musical eloquence contrasts jarringly with the almost sinister, "sharpe" precision of his harp playing and the avowed ugliness of his countenance.

Like Boccaccio, Lydgate emphasizes that an unduly harsh "lawe" ultimately prevented Orpheus from recovering Eurydice, a law that "bond hym sore" yet failed to constrain his desire: "Ther may no lawe louers weel constreyne,/So inportable is ther dedli peyne" (5802–3). At this point, though, rather than meeting his readers' expectations and continuing the tragic narrative, Lydgate inserts a two-stanza aside that takes Orpheus's earth-shattering backward glance as nothing more than a lucky break from the bonds of matrimony. Rather than bemoaning his twice-dead wife, Lydgate suggests, Orpheus should have taken heart in the salutary consequences of his individual loss for the larger community of unhappily wedded men:

> Yiff summe husbondis hadde stonden in the case
> Ta lost her wyues for a look sodeyne,
> Thei wolde haue suffred and nat seid allas,
> But pacientli endured al ther peyne,
> And thanked God, that broken was the cheyne
> Which hath so longe hem in prisoun bounde,
> That thei be grace han such a fredam founde.
>
> To lyn in prisoun, it is a ful gret charge,
> And to be stokked vndir keie and lok;
> It were weel meriere a man to gon at large,
> Than with irenes be nailed to a blok:
> And there is o bond, which callid is wedlok,
> Fretyng husbondis so sore, that it is wonder,
> Which with no file may nat be broke assonder.
>
> (5804–17)

These stanzas together constitute what Lydgate, the monk of Bury, seems to have imagined as the ultimate fantasy of husbands: with a single Orphic look at their wives, married men will find a new "fredam" while feigning sorrow at their sudden widowed state. The backward glance of Orpheus represents just such an escape from matrimonial "prisoun," the avoidance of a crucifixion-like sentence of being "nailed to a blok" with "irenes" through the bond of "wedlok."

For Orpheus himself, as we would expect, the loss of wife and marriage is at first an occasion for mourning: "At his herte hir partyng sat so sore,/The green memorie, the tendre remembraunce,/That he neuer wolde wyuen more" (5825–27). Immediately, however, Lydgate enlists Orpheus to join him as an antimatrimonial polemicist, who deploys his musico-rhetorical prowess to lure husbands away from their wives and incur the punishment of women:

> This Orpheus gaff counseil ful notable
> To husbondis that han endurid peyne,
> To such as been prudent and tretable:
> Oon hell is dreedful, mor pereilous be tweyne;
> And who is onys boundyn in a cheyne,
> And may escapen out off daunger blyue—
> Yiff he resorte, God let hym neuer thryue!
>
> On this sentence women wer vengable,
> And to his writyng ful contrarious,
> Seide his counseil was not comendable.
> At the feste thei halwed to Bachus,
> Thei fill echon vpon this Orpheus;
> And, for alle his rethoriques suete,
> Thei slouh, allas, this laureat poete.

$$(5832-45)$$

This is Ovid with a Lydgatean twist. Rather than turning his love to Ovidian "tender boys, in the springtime and first flower of their youth," Orpheus becomes a kind of antinuptial counselor to previously married (but not necessarily widowed) men.

With their unapologetic antiwomen overtones, the passages above speak to a venerable Christian tradition of misogynist discourse.[77] Despite its iteration of medieval antifeminist conventions, however, Lydgate's Orpheus interlude registers as well the specific historical and literary circumstances surrounding the composition of the *Fall of Princes*. Twice Lydgate repeats the word "counseil" in the Orpheus stanzas above: first to connote the advice given to husbands, and second to indicate the violent rejection of this advice by women. And the bard is represented as "writyng" his counsel to men rather than performing it bodily; Orpheus's "rethoriques suete" is, in this one particular instance, written rather than sung.

In this respect, the Orpheus interlude bears witness to Lydgate's original inspiration for writing the *Fall of Princes*: a commission by Humphrey, the Lancastrian Duke of Gloucester, in 1431.[78] Though it would have been unusual for a Benedictine monk to spend time actually serving at the royal court, Lydgate's career was highly idiosyncratic, and his service as a Lancastrian propagandist gave him numerous occasions to meet Gloucester in person both before and during the commission. Gloucester and his wife likely accompanied Henry VI to Bury during the royal visitation in 1433–34; the abbot's register records Gloucester's presence in the abbey that Easter, and Lydgate completed the poem by 1438.

The *Fall of Princes* has generally been taken as an attempt, in Pearsall's words, "to advance the Duke's reputation as a European patron of letters and as the English representative of the new Italian humanist learning."[79] David Wallace has pointed to the poem's utter failure as a continuation of Chaucer's contribution to the *de casibus* tradition in the Monk's Tale. According to Wallace, Lydgate failed in large part because he brought his historical progression of illustrious men to an end in 1356, refusing to engage in the rash game of contemporary topical advice-giving—and thus risk falling into disfavor with his powerful patron. Lydgate's eschewal of the transformative political visions of Boccaccio and Premierfait rendered the *Fall of Princes* "dead on arrival as a critique of princely excesses."[80]

Yet Lydgate apparently could not resist at least one apt swipe at Gloucester; in deploying the musical rhetoric of Orpheus to inveigh against marriage in general, the Lancastrian propagandist knew exactly what he was doing. Gloucester's troubled marital history was a topic of intense and very public speculation in the years immediately preceding the commission.[81] Duke Humphrey married Jacqueline, Countess of Hainault (the daughter of the powerful Count William of Holland), in 1422 or 1423. Jacqueline had fled to England in 1421 in order to escape her malevolent husband, John, Duke of Brabant, and she was met at Calais by Gloucester himself. At the invitation of Henry V (whose royal ambitions in the Low Countries were well known), Jacqueline was an honored visitor at the court beginning in 1421, and it was likely during Gloucester's four-month regency in 1422 that the two were betrothed.

In a series of attempts to secure the legitimacy of his marriage to the already-wedded Jacqueline, Gloucester appealed over the next few years to both the Court of Rome and Parliament; in February 1426, however, a papal decree declared Jacqueline's desertion of John illegitimate. Jacqueline herself was back in Hainault during these years, marshaling forces to combat the military incursions of the Duke of Burgundy, a close ally of John.

Stymied in her attempts to secure aid from Gloucester, whose political ambitions had turned increasingly insular, she wrote to the English Council in 1427 begging assistance from the king himself. Though an army was funded and organized, the English rescue mission to Hainault never took place, and in September a settlement was reached between Burgundy and Gloucester that brought a tenuous resolution to the conflict. After a papal bull in January 1428 officially recognized the validity of Jacqueline's first marriage to John, Gloucester reneged on a promised loan to his now-illegitimate wife.

Gloucester's actions throughout this episode prompted outraged responses from a surprisingly diverse sector of English society. The mayor and aldermen of London appeared before Parliament and defiantly claimed Jacqueline as the Duchess of Gloucester, demanding that the nation come to her aid immediately. Remarkably, according to the *St. Alban's Chronicle*, a group of London women entered Parliament and delivered letters to Gloucester demanding that he aid Jacqueline and forswear his adulterous relationship with his current mistress, an affair bringing ruin, they claimed, to "himself, the kingdom, and the marital bond."[82] These women were referring to the well-known fact that Gloucester had been engaged in an affair (and apparently sired several illegitimate children) with Eleanor Cobham, one of Jacqueline's ladies-in-waiting who had accompanied Gloucester back to England several years earlier. John Lydgate responded directly to the affair in four lines anthologized along with other short pieces in Oxford, Bodleian Library, Ashmole 59 (fol. 592); here, he rails against the Sirens who tempted "The prynci's hert against al goddes lawe/Frome heos promesse truwe alle to withdrawe/To straunge him, and make him foule forsworne/ Unto that godely faythfull truwe pryncesse."[83]

In the *Fall of Princes*—commissioned and begun while the messy fallout from Gloucester's illegitimate marriage and even more illegitimate affair was still very much in the mind of the English public—Lydgate's intervention was subtler. Though Gloucester had married Eleanor Cobham in 1428, the poet must have been painfully aware of the disastrous consequences of the duke's previous failed effort to participate in the institution. The Orpheus interlude may have been Lydgate's attempt to appropriate the prestige of the classical bard to dissuade his patron from any further marital entanglements. It is no mistake that the Lancastrian propagandist labels Orpheus as "this laureat poete" just as he is slain; the phrase is loaded with political and literary-historical prestige for Lydgate, who deploys it both in his slavish encomia to Chaucer and, as Seth Lerer argues, in articulating his own frequent authorial fantasies of becoming the "laureat poete" himself.[84] Lydgate thinly disguises his role as an antimarital rhetorician beneath the surface of Orpheus's post-Eurydice performance as a writer of advice, of "counseil" against marriage. In effect, he refashions the homoerotic, boy-loving Orpheus into a seductive musical rhetorician who attempts to convince a Lancastrian nobleman to abandon marriage altogether—and, by his example, encourage other married men to follow his lead, to "gon at large" in a newly liberated, all-male community.

Though he cleverly exploited the homosocial implications of Orpheus's return from hell, Lydgate avoids mentioning the violent fragmentation of the bard's body by the crowd of angry women. The poem's final image of Orpheus leaves the reader with a juxtaposition of the stellified harp and an unburied and decidedly unmusical corpse:

And off his harpe yiff ye list to lere,
The god Appollo maad a translacioun
Among the ymages off the sterris cleere,
Wheroff men may haue yit inspeccioun.
But Fortune, to his confusioun,
Denyed hym, froward off hir nature,
Whan he was slayn fredam off sepulture.

(5846–52)

While the *translatio* of the constellation into the heavens assures its permanence, the body of Orpheus must remain on the surface of the earth, subject to rot and decay without the sanctuary of a tomb.

The image nevertheless provides an appropriately prophetic conclusion to the Orpheus story in the *Fall of Princes*, for Lydgate's narrative is the clearest medieval precedent for a small but rich strand of English humanistic poetry centering upon the homoerotic possibilities of the Orpheus narrative—and culminating in Anne Frankford's performance in *A Woman Killed with Kindness*. In 1595, some 157 years after the Bury monk completed the *Fall of Princes*, an anonymous poet identified only as R. B. published *Orpheus His Journey to Hell*, in which the Thracian musician represents exactly the sort of antimatrimonial inducement to husbands registered by Lydgate:

Whose songs did sort unto such deepe effect,
   as draws mens fancies from thir former wives;
Womens vaine love beginning to neglect,
   and in the fieldes with *Orpheus* spend their lives:
With which sweet life they seem'd so weel content,
As made them curse the former time they spent.[85]

Like Lydgate, the poet draws in part on standard antimarital rhetoric; by inducing husbands away from their "former wives," R. B.'s Orpheus represents the renunciation not simply of marriage, but of women. In other early modern Ovidian writings, however, Orpheus embodies what certain poets envision as an explicitly sodomitical threat to the institution of heterosexual marriage. Indeed, the Orpheus legend figures centrally in what Mario DiGangi has called the "homoerotics of marriage" in the English Renaissance, the alternative arrangements that male homosocial and homoerotic desires present to the literary and social institutionalization of marital heterosexuality.[86]

The early modern work that most directly recalls the Orpheus interlude in Lydgate's *Fall of Princes* is Humphrey Lownes's "Legend of Orpheus and Eurydice." Printed in 1597 and apparently intended "to bee solde at the West doore of Paules" (St. Paul's cathedral in London), Lownses's version of the legend imagines Orpheus's melancholic performance upon his return from Hell as an inducement to "idleness and sinne, the wicked Nurse"; the musician himself undergoes a corresponding gender transformation that will immediately lead to the sexual corruptions that follow: "Unto this Syren all the Thracians came,/Whom when they heard, as ravished they stood,/Their sences pleased, yet spoiled by the same."[87] The music's "heart-pleasing paine" constitutes a literal imprisonment for its listeners, the harp itself "Holding them bound within these silver bands,/Whose links were stronger then that net of golde/Which tangled Venus, wrought by Vulcans hand."

Lownes's Orpheus then begins to teach the Thracian men "of womens woes, of womens wrong. . . . How they intrap the fearefull innocent,/And teach them lothed paths of sinfull shame." The stanzas that follow are remarkably similar to Lydgate's extended polemic against marriage in the *Fall of Princes*: Orpheus inveighs against women's "lust-defiled soules," which are eternally "bent/To slay sweet Chastities divinest name" as they "dig the pits of humaine woe. . . . Seeking to ioyne our soules and sinne to-gether." Finally, Lownes takes the step at which Lydgate only hinted, pre-senting Orpheus as the instigator of barbaric new sexual practices among the male members of his rapt audience:

> But what, my chaster Muse doth blush to heare
> The onely fault and sinne of this his youth,
> It shames to tell unto anothers eare,
> Somtimes it profits to conceale the truth;
> > Better it were none knew the way to sinne,
> > For knowing none, then none would enter in.
>
> Hee in this path sette his defiled foote,
> which leades unto the tree of sinne and shame,
> Woe is his fruite, and wickednes his roote,
> Both there he tasted, and to both he came;
> > Such are the snares which craftie sinne doth lay,
> > That iustest men doe stumble in theyr way.
>
> Now he doth teach the soule to sinne by Art,
> And breake the Law which Nature had ordaind,
> And from her ancient customs to depart,
> which still ere this were kept untoucht, unstaind,
> > Teaching to spoyle the flower of that kinde,
> > Whose flower never yet could any find.

The desirous and desiring Orpheus assumes his Ovidian role as teacher of a previously unknown practice, creating a veritable sodomitical subculture among the men and boys seduced by his musical art. In its representation of Orpheus's naturalized transition from woman-hating melancholic to sod-omitical provocateur, the poem reveals what DiGangi and others have shown to be the complex dynamic between male homoeroticism and mi-sogyny in the premodern era. Like the French mythographer who wrote the *Ovide moralisé*, Lownes assumes an unproblematic continuum between the spurning of marriage and a turn toward the sodomitical "vice" that both poems deplore. Indeed, Lownes's "Legend of Orpheus and Eurydice" cul-minates in an almost apocalyptic response to the bard's pedagogy of sod-omy. The sun, "asham'd to see / That vice in vertues name should be pre-tended," wraps the world in darkness, and as the poem nears its conclusion the author allies himself with the Thracian women whose vengeful wrath he interpolates in a first-person threat to Orpheus: "Now will we all revenge our iniurie."

Like Lydgate, however, Lownes responds to Orpheus's violent death by exalting his dissident musicality in a markedly non-Ovidian concluding moment. The poem ends with two stanzas that represent a true innovation within the premodern Orpheus legend. In a heavenly tableau, the scattered pieces of Orpheus's fragmented corpse resonate in the sky:

> And as a tree whom *Ioves* fierce darts of thunder
> Have riven all in peeces by their force,
> So is this heavenly Poet heere brought under,
> And by their might left but a mangled corse
>   Rented in shivering pieces like a wall
>   [That] *Aquilo* hath forced downe to fall.

> And now these dainty Actors of delight,
> Sweet fingers, motors of a heavenly noyse
> Whose power hearers sences ravisht quite,
> Drownd in pleasure by that motive voyce,
>   Like *Phoebus* stately Chariot scattered lye
>   When *Phaeton* sat ruler on the skye.

The allusive stanzas are somewhat cryptic, but the implication seems startlingly clear: Orpheus's "mangled corse," the same body that tempted Thracian men from their wives and taught them the sodomitical "vice" through musical ravishment, has metamorphosed into the music of the spheres. The "shivering pieces" of Orpheus's cadaver have become "sweet fingers, motors of a heavenly noyse"; the heavens will resound eternally with the harmonies produced by these musical chunks of Orphic flesh.

Lownses's stellified Orpheus evokes the full range of musical bodies that this study has treated, from the Maccabees' resonant corpses in the sermons of St. Ambrose to the sinner crucified on the hellish harp of Hieronymous Bosch. These musical fragments make very clear that the Orphic perversions outwardly condemned by so many premodern writers on the legend are nevertheless central to the legend's mythic perpetuation, whether in the allegorical harp at the center of the *Ovide moralisé* or the Orphic lament in Dante's *Purgatorio*. Lownses's musical pieces of Orpheus show us that even the music of the spheres, that incorporeal invention of the platonic imagination, can be enveloped in the flesh. And perhaps this Orpheus could not have been invented without the antimatrimonial Orpheus of John Lydgate, the bard whose harp ends up "Among the ymages off the sterris cleere,/Wheroff men may haue yit inspeccioun." The *Fall of Princes*, the vernacular production of a fifteenth-century Benedictine, keeps alive the musico-poetic fantasies adumbrated in the Latin lyrics of that eleventh-century Benedictine, Baudri of Bourgeuil, and in the process conjures the musical rhetorician who tempts men from their wives with his erotic sonorities—the very music that causes Wendoll in Heywood's *A Woman Killed with Kindness* to reenvision and reengender an adulterous wife as a new Orpheus. The fragmentation of his legend and his body allows Orpheus to endure across the millennia as a continually revivified occasion for the musical practice of the flesh. Orpheus's dissident musical *corpus*—despite punitive dismemberment in the *Metamorphoses*, centuries of denial or explicit vilification by poets and polemicists, and anxious allegorical fragmentation at the hands of Christian mythographers—ultimately survives.

Epilogue: Toward a Musicology of Empathy

For Lydgate and many others who wrote about it, the ultimate fate of Orpheus's harp was stellification, a celestial permanence that refashioned frame and strings into an eternally visible constellation. Yet the instrument's origins could not have been more mundane. Isidore tells the story best:

> Lyra primum a Mercurio inventam fuisse dicunt, hoc modo. Cum regrediens Nilus in suos meatus varia in campis reliquisset animalia, relicta etiam testudo est. Quae cum putrefacta esset, et nervi eius remansissent extenti intra corium, percussa a Mercurio sonitum dedit; ad cuius speciem Mercurius lyram fecit et Orpheo tradidit, qui eius rei maxime erat studiosus. Vnde existimatur eadem arte non feras tantum, sed et saxa atque silvas cantus modulatione adplicuisse.
>
> [They say the lyre was invented by Mercury in the following manner. When the Nile, retreating into its channels, had left various animals in the fields, a tortoise was left behind. When it had putrefied and its sinews remained stretched within its shell, it gave out a sound on being struck by Mercury. After this pattern he made the lyre and transmitted it to Orpheus, who applied himself studiously to it and is deemed not merely to have swayed wild beasts with this art, but to have moved rocks and forests with the modulation of his song.][1]

Only through the death and putrefaction of another living being can Orpheus invent and perform his songs. The melodies that animate the inanimate, attract the desires of men and women, and lead inevitably to Orpheus's own death and remembrance by others—these songs are rung upon a corpse.

A story uncannily similar in spirit appears in a little-discussed English poem written in rhyme royal by an otherwise unknown author named John Lacy. *Wyl bucke his testament*, first printed around 1560 but composed perhaps as much as a century earlier, presents itself in large part as the last will and testament of a dying buck named Will. The poem begins with a brief first-person narrative in the voice of a hunter, who hides in a clearing, shoots a buck with an arrow, and follows the animal for four hours before the buck collapses and requests the hunter to take "his testament then, or he dyed." The hunter agrees, so the buck begins a 57-line testament that bequeaths to human beings and animals his only earthly possession: his body.[2]

Will's "grees" goes to the "frumenty potte" to help prepare the "furst course att þe lordes table." His blood and his puddings go "vnto þe puddyng wyffe," while the crow gets the "suette." His sinewed foot will "hange vpon the dure," and the top of his "tayll" will decorate the hunting-horn. "I wyll ye make steykes for your brekefast," Will requests of the hunter who has shot him, "of the lenyst fleshe þat ys of my bodye." For his executor the buck chooses "robyn redebrest," for he "louyd my fleshe yn lyffe & dethe," and this choice is his last act before he dies: "I may noo more speke, my brethe ys all gone."

With its irony and clearly parodic Eucharistic overtones ("He þat brekethe my bodye, all & some,/watter for his handes ys þe olde custome"), *Wyl bucke his testament* fits securely within a comic animal subgenre of the literary testament; the poem's mock seriousness cannot help but draw a smile from its modern readers.[3] Yet there is something peculiarly moving about this poem, perhaps not only for the inhabitants of an age that has finally found a vocabulary for discussing the dignities and rights of non-human species. For in bequeathing himself to posterity, Will Buck is concerned not with the financial or domestic well-being of his benefactors, but with the sheer pleasures that his body will provide for his human and animal survivors. These pleasures are simultaneously culinary, whimsical, decorative, and, perhaps most surprising, musical:

> I bequeth my tonge, þat neuer made lesyng,
> vnto þe fair ladye þat lyst to breke hur fast.
> He þat me helpethe vnto þe quarrye bryng
> shall haue my necke for a short repaste.

> The raucus morsell shall stycke on the þorne faste;
>
> my lyuer to rewarde your yong houndes;
>
> my small guttes to þe harpe-strynges þat makes mery sondes.

Will's tongue will help a lady break her self-denying fast. Even the dogs who · helped the hunter chase him down will get a taste of Will. And the buck's "small guttes" will be refashioned into "harpe-strynges"; rather than rotting in the ground, Will's body will make "mery sondes" even for those who have taken his life and consumed his flesh.

These two stories reveal a seldom-acknowledged fact without which neither this nor any other book about the musical cultures of the past could be conceived or written. The remains of the dead must survive in order for the living to make and enjoy music. Isidore's tortoiseshell and Will Buck's guts provide a fitting (if slightly morbid) set of images for concluding a book concerned with vivifying the musical bodies of the long dead. In seeking these bodies in the columns of the *Patrologia Latina*, the margins of manuscripts, and the writings of mythographers, the preceding chapters have been involved in a scholarly task of musical reanimation no less conditioned by the certainty of death than is Mercury's plucking of the tortoiseshell from the floodplain of the Nile. If "loss, and reparation, have shaped the desire of many twentieth-century medievalists," as Louise Fradenburg puts it, so, too, have historical persons, writings, musics, and experiences acquired much of their authority and authenticity insofar as they are, "in some profound way, *lost* to us by [their] very pastness."[4] The modern enterprise of medieval studies—of historical inquiry itself, perhaps—participates in what Armando Petrucci has recently termed "the expressive language of written death"; only by understanding "the workings of death within our own works on death" can we hope to account for the historical losses and reparations that continue to shape our study of the past.[5]

For the stories above are not simply about music and death, of course, but also about musical regeneration and survival. That the musical past inevitably conditions the musical present points up the limitations of the so-called alterity of medieval culture, in Hans Robert Jauss's influential formulation, the ostensibly impenetrable "otherness" of the medieval past, as well as the ease with which we tend to reinforce this alterity in our scholarship, emphasizing difference over continuity, "post-Cartesian" versus "premodern" ways of knowing. Like much recent work on medieval religious cultures, this book has often deployed the rhetoric of differentiation ("bizarre," "gruesome," "horrifying to modern readers," and so on) in describing the texts and images under consideration. Such language has its purposes: as suggested in the Introduction, medieval modes of embodied musical experience pose a powerful challenge to those modern philosophies, epistemologies, and musicologies that maintain the externality of the musical artifact. Perhaps we might unsettle our own assumptions about the nature of musical experience by bringing to musicological inquiry a sensitivity to what Gregory of Nyssa and others remind us is the musicality of *all* human bodies.

In a much-cited contribution to the often vitriolic "authenticity" debates in the 1980s between performers, musicologists, and critics, Richard Taruskin challenged participants to recognize what he termed "the pastness of the present and the presence of the past" within the history of musical performance. Calling into question the supposedly firm boundaries between the musical "now" and "then," Taruskin argued that much of what has been touted as "historical authenticity" in early music performance reflects the musical tastes and values of high modernism. Taruskin reserves his most withering criticism for those authenticists who would claim to be removing the "residue" of intervening history in order to reach the "original intentions" of the composer: "What is thought of as the 'dirt' when musicians speak of restoring a piece of music is what people, acting out of an infinite variety of motives over the years, have done with it."[6] Another word for the habit of mind Taruskin attacks here is, of course, platonism. The "dirt" of human history is directly analogous to the "stain" of human corporeality lamented by the *Scholica enchiriadis* as an impediment to true musical understanding and enlightenment. If nothing else, I hope the preceding chapters have shown that the musical history of the medieval era is in part a musical history of the flesh. No amount of platonizing, whether medieval or modern, can entirely efface the variety of ways the Middle Ages found to humanize and embody the fleeting effects of musical sonority. Though intervening centuries have diminished the visceral force of these musical embodiments, they have neither silenced them nor obliterated their traces from the surviving record. In insisting upon their relevance to the musical life of the present, this book represents a small part of a ubiquitous yet largely unacknowledged effort among fin-de-siècle musicologists and performers to forge new identifications with those whose musical remains we enliven and study, to invent new ways of merging and blending the musical cultures of our time with the musical cultures of the dead.

How might we characterize this effort—this desire—as it makes itself felt within contemporary musicological inquiry? I suggest we call it a "musicology of empathy." For Karl F. Morrison, its modern historian, empathy can be a mode of historical and philosophical understanding that allows human subjects "to feel the likeness that both relates and assimilates separate entities to one another, and to believe that through mediating likeness even discordant, polar opposites surrender in love each to each, parts of a single, illuminating, and fecund harmony, surprising and terrible in its power."[7] There could be no better way to describe the transhistorical listening communities that medieval music continues to forge in today's public sphere, which has seen a recording of medieval plainchant top the international pop charts and the music of Hildegard of Bingen peddled in crystal shops in Santa Fe. Music has always constituted one of the most frequent means of "nonverbal" empathetic identification. An empathetic musicology in turn will be honest and straightforward concerning our love and even desire for the music we study—what the editors of *Queering the Pitch: The New Gay and Lesbian Musicology* have called "our personal, private, and pleasurable relations with the musical"[8]—as well as the ways in which these musical relations among ourselves are constructed simultaneously with the musical bodies that populate the past. Such an empathetic effort to account for the emotive, somatic character of past musical cultures can energize the study of medieval music in particular, and not simply as a result of its compatibility with the aims of feminist, queer, or postmodern musicologies. To risk for a moment falling into Taruskin's authentistic trap, I would suggest that musical pain, pleasure, blood, sex, wounds, and skin have as convincing a claim to being an "authentic" part of the turn-of-the-millennium recovery and study of medieval music as does the careful reconstruction of a thirteenth-century hurdy-gurdy or the speculative transcription of the unwritten accidentals of musica ficta.

While remaining skeptical of homogenizing claims to universality and the transcendence of difference, a musicology of empathy will allow us to take seriously the pleasures and pains that the music of the dead—liturgical monophony, organum, motets, ancient prosody—continues to produce upon, against, and within the bodies of the living. Yet to call for an empathetic musicology is not to succumb to New Age sentimentalism at the expense of historicist rigor. Nor is it to reinforce a historical relativism that flattens all musical experiences into a nondialectical equivalency: as Gary Tomlinson has pointed out, the reactionary charge of "relativism" is often a symptom of appropriative ways of knowing that assume the transparency of others' concepts to the knower.[9]

Empathetic approaches to the musical past have in fact been adopted even by those musicologists most skeptical about twentieth-century claims of transhistorical identification and understanding. In a spirited review of a recent book by Christopher Page, Margaret Bent issues a stern warning to those scholars of early music who would rely upon the vagaries of contemporary performance as "evidence" for historical arguments. According to Bent (quoting Page), " 'The sound of medieval music, as interpreted today' lacks the authority to inform us about anything so fragile and intangible as its aesthetic apprehension in its own time." Indeed, she asserts, "it is *our* tastes that are informed by modern performances, *our* ears that we develop, not those of the Middle Ages."[10] What Bent is critiquing in Page's work, it seems to me, is its empathy, its willingness to risk bridging the gap between us and them, "our" tastes and ears and "their" tastes and ears, through a musical embrace that allows the historical past to challenge and change the scholarly present as much as the reverse. For Bent, such a strategy involves being "carried away" into naively "imagining that the music we now perform sounds as they heard it."[11] (This while obscuring the fact that much of Page's work over the last twenty years has been dedicated in large part to recovering—tracking down, editing, translating, writing about, and reshaping contemporary performances in light of—hundreds of allegedly "fragile and intangible" testimonies to the kinds of medieval "aesthetic apprehension" she herself calls for.) Nearing the conclusion of her review, Bent reveals the epistemological assumptions that underlie her objections to Page's performative empathy: "particular styles of performance," she warns, "could be quite perilous if used in turn to support claims about medieval contexts of performance, or if given the same weight as the musical identity that a piece of music keeps through extremely different performances . . . for all our work on musical texts and techniques, on performance practice and social context, we merely make music in performance with the raw materials of the notated substance."[12]

Though taking Page to task for the alleged anachronisms of a performance-based musicology, Bent herself commits a much more philosophically profound anachronism by insisting on the transhistorical integrity and "notated substance" of the medieval "musical work"—so much so that "performance," "social context," and so on assume the degraded status imputed to "body" in much platonic writing on music. Even in objecting to Page's empathetic faith in his own ear, however, Bent crafts a surprisingly empathetic identification with a particular medieval listener: "the transient sounds of early music have vanished, as poignantly for us as for Isidore of Seville, who said that sounds perish because they cannot be written down."[13] This is an ideal example of what Morrison refers to as the "negative content" of empathy: Isidore once lost it, and so, now, have we. Despite the stern asceticism of Bent's critique, her momentary burst of empathy suggests nevertheless that "we" are never as experientially removed from "them" as "we" might suppose.

Writing in a more self-critical vein, Tomlinson concludes his study of music and magic in the Italian Renaissance with what looks like a skeptical rejection of the empathetic mode. In the distant past resides "a space of the other that is inaccessible to our understanding . . . an area of difference beyond the reach of dialogue or meaningful enunciations." Tomlinson perceives an insurmountable gap, both epistemological and experiential, between himself and those whose writings and lives he studies; Renaissance musical magicians live on the other side of an immense historical gulf, "a place where magic works."[14] In the end, though, this is not "our" place.

Perhaps. Yet Tomlinson's ethnographic despair in the face of the inaccessible pastness of the musical magic of Marsilio Ficino and others is belied by the vividness and passion with which Tomlinson himself revivifies—brings back from the dead—the musical experiences and world he studies. He has put it more explicitly elsewhere: "the primary stimulus for musicology, instead of our love for this or that music, might more luminously be our love of, concern for, commitment to, belief in, alienating distance from—choose your words—the others who have made this or that music in the process of making their worlds."[15] In short, a musicology of empathy. As Morrison writes of empathetic inquiry, "Formal disciplines that require detachment also require a degree of deafness to the call within the words, 'I am you.' Other disciplines that assume the universality of passion allow the call to be heard."[16] These days, at least, musicology is somewhere in the middle. Despite its skeptical conclusion, Tomlinson's study represents one of the most successfully empathetic attempts to embrace the musical experiences of premodern listeners.

The musical body continues to resonate powerfully in our time. No clearer evidence for its perdurance can be found than in the panoply of musical corporealities populating the literary cultures of the twentieth-century United States. American poetry of the twenties and thirties alone is rife with bodies and body parts that are strummed, picked, and drummed in what might be seen as a modernist melopoesis of the body. The speaker in T. S. Eliot's "Ash-Wednesday" brings to mind the testimony of Will Buck as his corpse is consumed by foraging leopards: the only exceptions are "My guts the strings of my eyes and the indigestible portions / Which the leopards reject"; later, when all of the flesh has disappeared, "Under a juniper-tree the bones sang, scattered and shining."[17] In one of Countee Cullen's most famous works, "Heritage," the poet experiences his African ancestry in part as an "unremittant beat / Made by cruel padded feet / Walking through my body's street"; the poem's "feet," the music's "beat," and rushing blood come together to fashion the poet's body into an instrument pulsating with the musical energy of the past. Cullen's "A Song of Praise" opens with a musical throat that could have found a place on the liturgical body of Aurelian of Réôme: "You have not heard my love's dark throat, / Slow-fluting like a reed, / Release the perfect golden note / She caged there for my need."[18] Wallace Stevens retells the story of Susanna and the Elders as a musical performance of geriatric lust: "The basses of their beings throb / In witching chords, and their thin blood / Pulse pizzicati of Hosanna":

> Susanna's music touched the bawdy strings
> Of those white elders; but escaping,
> Left only Death's ironic scraping.
> Now, in its immortality, it plays
> On the clear viol of her memory,
> And makes a constant sacrament of praise.[19]

Stevens published "Peter Quince at the Clavier" in *Harmonium* in 1931, some twenty years before America would listen to Bette Davis's wry but bitter question to Bill in *All About Eve*: "And you, I take it, are the Paderew-ski who plays his concerto on me, the piano?"[20]

Such moments can seem offhand, even trivial. Like many of the images discussed in the preceding pages, they are metaphors, and they illustrate the age-old weakness of descriptive language in the face of musical phenomena. Yet language has its own ways of inducing musico-somatic experiences almost as intense as those endured by Christina Mirabilis. Here is Paul Fussell speaking of the "essentially physical" character of prosody: "since the beat in most accentual poetry is slightly faster than the normal heart beat, the apprehension of metered language physically exhilarates the hearer or reader: the heart beat, it is said, actually speeds up in an effort to 'match' the slightly faster poetic rhythm."[21] Though Fussell presents this theory of prosodic affect as in part the legacy of Romanticism, we have seen earlier examples of the "music of pulse" being induced by religious or poetic experience; it is an ancient and deeply engrained part of musico-somatic life propounded in the *De musica* of Augustine and in the writings of the nuns of Helfta, among many others. Conversely, we should not assume that internalist, embodied models of musical experience have been rendered archaic, outmoded, or quaint by the standards of more recent aesthetic paradigms.

Two final examples will demonstrate with particular clarity the perils of such an assumption. I have chosen them to conclude this book not because they reflect either the direct influence or the distant legacy of the medieval European tradition treated in preceding chapters, though in some ways they surely do. In fact, their affiliations with an alternative music-historical trajectory—and the artistic dialogues they enact with the past of another continent—put all the more pressure on the musical externalism that would deny the human body its resonance.

Figure 20 reproduces Harlem Renaissance artist Augusta Savage's *Lift Every Voice and Sing*, also referred to as *The Harp*. Savage created this work as the result of a commission for the 1939 World's Fair, and it stood in the courtyard of the Contemporary Arts Building on Rainbow Avenue in Flushing, Queens, for the duration of the event. (Cast in plaster and painted by Savage, *Lift Every Voice* was destroyed after the fair owing to lack of funds to cast it in bronze.)[22] In this sixteen-foot-long sculpture, the hand and arm of God support a standing choir, while the kneeling figure at the front bears the tune to James Weldon Johnson's 1900 poem of

FIGURE 20   Augusta Savage, *Lift Every Voice and Sing* (or *The Harp*), 1939, painted plaster

the same name, "Lift Ev'ry Voice and Sing." When I first saw a photograph of Savage's sculpture while this book was nearing completion, I was simply stunned. Here was the somatic harp of Apollo—strung not with the musically tortured corpse of the vanquished Marsyas, but with the resonant bodies of a divinely sanctioned choir. Here were Ambrose's Maccabees—the

seven sons-*cum*-strings (*filii . . . fila*) of their mother's *cithara*-like womb—
brought to artistic life by an American artist seeking to express a musical
triumph over a history of adversity and martyrdom articulated in Johnson's poem:

> Stony the road we trod,
> Bitter the chast'ning rod,
> Felt in the days when hope unborn had died;
> Yet with a steady beat,
> Have not our weary feet
> Come to the place for which our fathers sighed?
> We have come over a way that with tears has been watered.
> We have come, treading our path through the blood of the slaughtered,
> Out from the gloomy past,
> Till now we stand at last
> Where the white gleam of our bright star is cast.[23]

Sung from the surface of the sculpture, Johnson's image of the "steady beat"
of the "feet" of the enslaved creates a musical empathy with the "gloomy
past," a historical vision of sonorous victory over slaughter that Savage
in turn realizes in plaster and paint. Each member of the ensemble is
a human harp string who sings from the mouth while resounding from
the flesh.

To argue for strong parallels between such twentieth-century and premodern representations of the music of the flesh is not to collapse their
many ideological and political differences in the service of a monolithic
account of "tradition," but rather to suggest that, *despite* their differences,
these works reveal an incarnational understanding of music that has survived both vast historical spans and massive societal traumas. Augusta Savage located her artistry within a Christian trajectory that she also revised—
as did Johnson, whose verse sermon collection, *God's Trombones* (1927),
evoked the musical rhetoric of the preaching body that had been allegorized
more than a millennium before by Rhabanus Maurus and Hilary of Poitiers. These literary and historical strands of music, body, preaching, and
devotion converge in Zora Neale Hurston's 1934 novel *Jonah's Gourd Vine*,
the story of a morally lapsed but immensely talented preacher, John Buddy
Pearson, whose life course throughout this modernist work is motivated in
part by the erotic and spiritual allures of music. Near the opening of the

novel, Pearson plunges along the banks of a creek, "singing a new song and stomping the beats," listening to the "lyric crescendo" of a "tenor-singing hound dog," and "almost trumpet[ing] exultantly at the new sun." John sings a duet at a school-closing with Lucy Potts, his future wife, and "Nobody cared whether the treble was treble or the bass was bass. It was the gestures that counted."[24] Pearson delivers the final sermon of his life in a musical style that Hurston took almost verbatim from her own anthropological field notes on a preacher in a country church.[25] Devoting the entire sermon to the wounds of Christ, Pearson implicates the musical and other behaviors of his community in the sufferings of the passion: "It is not your enemies that harm you all the time. Watch that close friend. Every believer in Christ is considered His friend, and every sin we commit is a wound to Jesus. The blues we play in our homes is a club to beat up Jesus" (175). Hurston is not the first writer in the Christian tradition to represent an imagined intimacy between musical sonority and the suffering body of Christ; the sermon recalls the melodious hammer of Tubalcain, the liturgical nightingale of John Pecham, the "Split Lark" of Emily Dickinson.

Hurston frames *Jonah's Gourd Vine* with two brief but shattering visions of internal musicality. The first, in chapter 2, begins when a character named Bully issues a liberating injunction against musical instruments: " 'Us don't want no fiddles, neither no guitars, neither no banjoes. Less clap!' " For the community of Sanford, in which Hurston sets her narrative, this somatic instrumentality has specific historical and political implications that she explores by fashioning the musical body of history into a bleeding, enslaved, but ultimately redemptive symbol of musical remembrance:

> So they danced. They called for the instrument that they had brought to
> America in their skins—the drum—and they played upon it. With their
> hands they played upon the little dance drums of Africa. The drums of kid-
> skin. With their feet they stomped it, and the voice of Kata-Kumba, the
> great drum, lifted itself within them and they heard it. The great drum that
> is made by priests and sits in majesty in the juju house. The drum with the
> man skin that is dressed with human blood, that is beaten with a human
> shin-bone and speaks to gods as a man and to men as a God. Then they beat
> upon the drum and danced. It was said, "He will serve us better if we bring
> him from Africa naked and thing-less." So the buckra reasoned. They tore
> away his clothes that Cuffy might bring nothing away, but Cuffy seized his

drum and hid it in his skin under the skull bones. The shin-bones he bore
openly, for he thought, "Who shall rob me of shin-bones when they see no
drum?" So he laughed with cunning and said, "I, who am borne away to become an orphan, carry my parents with me. For Rhythm is she not my
mother and Drama is her man?" So he groaned aloud in the ships and hid
his drum and laughed. (29–30)

The passage is meant to recall the anxious legislation enacted in the American South against the use of drums by slaves, whose possession and sometimes rebellious deployment of percussive instruments was often perceived
as representing as much of a threat to slave owners as literacy itself.[26] In an
extraordinary musical rendition of enslavement and survival, a captive African hides his drum within himself, enduring the tortures of the Middle
Passage with outward groans and inward laughter. In their own percussive
performances, the post-Reconstruction citizens of Sanford forge an empathetic musical bond with Cuffy across the ocean and the centuries by re-
enacting his incarnational music with their own hands, feet, skin, and
bones. Remembering his suffering through the music rung on their bodies,
they perform collectively upon what Hurston calls "the little drum whose
body was still in Africa, but whose soul sung around a fire in Alabama" (30).

This "drum with the man skin," "beaten with a human shin-bone,"
returns in the concluding scene of *Jonah's Gourd Vine*. A few weeks after
John Pearson's death, the citizens of Sanford gather for a memorial service in
Zion Hope Church, where a "flower-banked chair . . . represented the body
of Rev. Pearson" (201). Mourning the absent body of Pearson, the congrega-
tion listens to another sermon, this one delivered by Hambo, a longtime
friend of the deceased. Like the joyous dance early in the book, the mournful rhetoric of Hambo initiates a communal participation in an internal and
eternal musical empathy with a shared African past. For Hurston, the musical animation of these mourning bodies demands that the "shin-bones" of
the living beat upon the skin-drums of the dead. The performed religiosity
she imagines enlists the man-drum that is beaten and the shin-bone that
beats into a collective memory of music, body, and desire:

> And the preacher preached a barbaric requiem poem. On the pale white
> horse of Death. On the cold icy hands of Death. On the golden streets of
> glory. Of Amen Avenue. Of Halleluyah Street. On the delight of God when
> such as John appeared among the singers about His throne. On the weeping

sun and moon. On Death who gives a cloak to the man who walked naked in the world. And the hearers wailed with a feeling of terrible loss. They beat upon the O-go-doe, the ancient drum. O-go-doe, O-go-doe, O-go-doe! Their hearts turned to fire and their shinbones leaped unknowing to the drum. Not Kata-Kumba, the drum of triumph, that speaks of great ancestors and glorious wars. Not the little drum of kid-skin, for that is to dance with joy and to call to mind birth and creation, but O-go-doe, the voice of Death—that promises nothing, that speaks with tears only, and of the past.

So at last the preacher wiped his mouth in the final way and said, "He wuz uh man, and nobody knowed 'im but God," and it was ended in rhythm. With the drumming of the feet, and the mournful dance of the heads, in rhythm, it was ended. (201–2)

Reference Matter

Notes

INTRODUCTION

1. The synesthetic aspects of medieval writings on music have been treated by Christopher Page in "Reading and Reminiscence," which includes a fascinating discussion of Johannes Tinctoris and the "smell" of music; the poet is the fifteenth-century Scottish Chaucerian Robert Henryson, "The Testament of Crisseid," line 445, in *Poems and Fables of Robert Henryson*, 120.

2. Chaucer, *Legend of Good Women*, Prologue, lines 89–93; in *The Riverside Chaucer*, 590.

3. Leppert, *Sight of Sound*. Leppert's important book begins in the seventeenth century and is concerned primarily with the visual representation of musical performance and instruments in painting, sculpture, and the plastic arts, though many of his findings could easily be extended to visual depictions of music in the Middle Ages.

4. See, in the order listed, Brown, *Body and Society*; Dinshaw, *Chaucer's Sexual Poetics*; Bynum, *Holy Feast and Holy Fast*; Camille, *Gothic Idol*; Beckwith, *Christ's Body*; and Rubin, *Corpus Christi*.

5. Some of the most important work in this area is McClary, *Feminine Endings*; Leppert, *Sight of Sound*; Leppert and McClary, *Music and Society*; Brett, Wood, and Thomas, *Queering the Pitch*; and Solie, *Musicology and Difference*. Earlier, explicit challenges to the field were issued by Tomlinson, "Web of Culture," and Kerman, *Contemplating Music*.

6. The citations are from the preface to Brett, Wood, and Thomas, *Queering the Pitch*, vii; and Kramer, *Classical Music*, 14.

7. Hamburger, review of Michael Camille, *Image on the Edge*, esp. 327.

8. Brett, Wood, and Thomas, *Queering the Pitch*, vii; Kramer, *Classical Music*, 1.

9. *Musica et scolica enchiriadis*, 113–14; see the translation in Strunk, *Source Readings*, 137.

10. Calcidius, *Timaeus a Calcidio*, 45. The *Timaeus* passages cited within the text are taken from the translation by R. G. Bury for the Loeb Classical Library.

11. *Timaeus*, 47C; on *mousiké*, see especially James Miller, *Measures of Wisdom*, 19–31; Enders, "Music, Delivery," esp. 450–51; and Lippman, *Musical Thought*, 30 and passim.

12. Spitzer, *Ideas of World Harmony*, 35. A recent contribution is Edwards, *Ratio and Invention*; see especially chapter 1, "Contrary Motions: Musical Aesthetic and the Ideal Landscape," 12–33.

13. Escott, "Gothic Cathedral"; Margaret Bent, "Deception, Exegesis."

14. Augustine, *De musica libri sex*, 1.2.2; Marchetto of Padua, *Lucidarium*, 1.2.4, 78–79.

15. Page, *Discarding Images*, chapter 1, "Cathedralism," 1–42; quote is from 14.

16. Treitler, "Troubadors Singing."

17. Stevens, *Words and Music*, 47.

18. Macrobius, *Commentarium* 11, 45; Macrobius, *Commentary*, 130.

19. Macrobius, *Commentarium* 2.3, 105; Macrobius, *Commentary*, 195.

20. Macrobius, *Commentarium* 2.1, 96–97; Macrobius, *Commentary*, 186–87.

21. Macrobius, *Commentarium* 2.2, 99, Macrobius, *Commentary*, 189–90.

22. Macrobius, *Commentarium* 2.1, 97; Macrobius, *Commentary*, 187.

23. Frantzen, *Before the Closet*, 23.

24. Two groundbreaking essays by Philip Brett and Suzanne G. Cusick in the anthology *Queering the Pitch* demonstrate very clearly the inextricability of the two categories; see Brett, "Musicality, Essentialism," and Cusick, "On a Lesbian Relationship with Music."

25. See, among many others, the introduction to McClary, *Feminine Endings*; Cusick, "Lesbian Relationship"; Kivy, *Corded Shell*; and Cook, *Music, Imagination*.

26. There are important exceptions, of course; see the provocative essays by Sears, Burnett, and Sachsin in Burnett, Fend, and Gouk, *Second Sense*, as well as Wegman, "Sense and Sensibility," and Page, "Reading and Reminiscence."

27. Wimsatt, "Chaucer and Deschamps" 134.

28. Ridley, *Music, Value, and the Passions*, 20.

29. Consider what happens to the bodily senses in the following statement: "[I]t would appear that many of the skeptical doubts with regard to

music's illustrational powers have no basis in argument or fact. And to that extent, hearing it, seeing it, or even tasting, touching, and sniffing it in music, are respectable ways of responding, *just so long as the musical text supports the illustrational interpretation*, whatever it may be" (Kivy, *Sound and Semblance*, 215–16; emphasis in the original).

30. Shepherd and Wicke, *Music and Cultural Theory*, 178.

31. Lakoff and Johnson, *Philosophy in the Flesh*, 128.

32. Ibid., 4. This may explain why I have found most discussions of music and metaphor unhelpful for this particular project: most who have written on the subject treat metaphorical descriptions of music rather than metaphorical descriptions of musical persons and bodies (see, for example, Guck, "Two Types of Metaphoric Transference," a wonderful article in which the music that is metaphorized nevertheless remains entirely external to the listener constructing the metaphors). Roger Scruton, perhaps the most brilliant writer on the subject, comes closest to explaining why: "Music is the intentional object of an experience that only rational beings can have, and only through the exercise of imagination. To describe it we must have recourse to metaphor, not because music resides in an analogy with other things, but because the metaphor describes exactly what we hear, when we hear sounds as music" (*Aesthetics of Music*, 96). Even here, however, metaphor is seen as a purely rational exercise rather than the somatic, "sensorimotor" practice that it is. The best short introduction to the problem of musical metaphor I have found is Treitler, "Interpretation of Music."

33. Boethius, *De institutione musica* 1.1, 180; Boethius, *Fundamentals of Music*, 2. "Hinc etiam internosci potest, quod non frustra a Platone dictum sit, mundi animam musica convenientia fuisse coniunctam. Cum enim eo, quod in nobis est iunctum convenienterque coaptatum, illud excipimus, quod in senis apte convenienterque coniunctum est, eoque delectamur, nos quoque ipsos eadem similitudine compactos esse cognoscimus."

34. Boethius, *De institutione musica* 1.2, 188–89; Boethius, *Fundamentals of Music*, 10. For a recent discussion of the passage see Gersh, *Concord in Discourse*, 42–45.

35. See Bower's comments in the introduction to Boethius, *Fundamentals of Music*, xxxviii; see also Chamberlain, "Philosophy of Music," in which the intriguing suggestion is made that "later" here refers to the *Consolation of Philosophy*, which "may be said to have a main theme that is musical and to embody a more complete philosophy of music than the *De musica* itself" (80).

36. De Bruyne, *Esthetics*, 53. One of the great merits of de Bruyne's chapters on musical aesthetics was his refusal to subordinate the naturalism apparent in much medieval musical speculation to the purely mathematical

abstractions that subsequent writers on the subject have tended to over-emphasize. If de Bruyne's insistence that medieval musical life was "unified by a system which coordinate[d] all its component parts in perfect concord" strikes us today as disingenuous idealism, his brief comments on the "chemico-biological" and the "anatomical and physiological" *musica* of Christian platonism seem prescient. On Boethius and *musica humana* in the *Consolation*, see Chamberlain, "Philosophy of Music," 90–95.

37. Cited and translated in Page, *Discarding Images*, 17.

38. Ibid.

39. Gertrude, *Legatus*, 5.2; see Chapter 5 of this volume.

40. Hugh of St. Victor, *Didascalicon* 2.4; cited in Gersh, *Concord in Discourse*, 270 (translation slightly altered).

41. Goehr, *Imaginary Museum*.

42. Treitler, " 'Unwritten' and 'Written Transmission,' " 132–33; see also Binkley, "The Work Is Not the Performance." For a few particularly illuminating examples of the "work-concept" being applied by a medievalist, see the comments by Margaret Bent in "Reflections," discussed in the epilogue in this volume.

43. Tomlinson, "Musical Pasts," 22. Tomlinson's comments were made in the context of a response to Lawrence Kramer's essay, "The Musicology of the Future"; see Kramer's rejoinder, "Music Criticism and the Postmodernist Turn," and Tomlinson's counterrejoinder, "Musical Pasts," 36–40.

44. Jonsson and Treitler, "Medieval Music and Language," 1.

45. See Page, "Musicus and Cantor."

46. See the discussion in McGee, *Medieval Song*, 32–33; though McGee's book is devoted to a performance-oriented study of medieval vocal technique and ornamentation, it is an exemplary demonstration of the fruits of rereading the theoretical sources for the kinds of quirky, bizarre, and generally neglected information they convey about the period's musical cultures and aesthetics.

47. The bibliography on this subject is vast; the tip of the iceberg includes Zumthor, *La poésie et la voix* and *La lettre et la voix*; Jonsson and Treitler, "Medieval Music and Language"; articles by Treitler, especially " 'Unwritten' and 'Written Transmission,' " "Homer and Gregory," "Oral, Written, and Literate Process," and "Reading and Singing"; Enders, "Music, Delivery"; Ian Parker, "Performance of Troubadour and Trouvère Songs"; the essays in Baltzer, Cable, and Wimsatt, *Union of Words and Music*; Stevens, *Words and Music*; and Bielitz, *Musik und Grammatik*. See also Winn, *Unsuspected Eloquence*, esp. 30–121, a rich study that has been virtually ignored in subsequent

treatments of word-music relations in the Middle Ages. A useful bibliographical overview of the French tradition is Switten, *Music and Poetry*.

48. On "natural music," see especially Wimsatt, *Chaucer and His French Contemporaries*.

49. See especially Huot, *From Song to Book*.

50. For a discussion of Augustine and the *jubilus*, see Chapter 2 of this volume, pp. 76–77; on Christina, see Chapter 5, pp. 223–25. The citation is from Guillaume de Machaut, "Dit de la harpe," 3.

51. See the pointed comments in Treitler, "European Music Culture," esp. 344–46.

52. The phrase comes from Page, "Reading and Reminiscence," 5.

53. Kay, *Troubadour Poetry*, 132–33.

54. Leppert, *Sight of Sound*, 38.

55. Meyer-Baer, *Music of the Spheres*.

CHAPTER 1

1. Hrotsvit of Gandersheim, *Pafnutius*, ed. Paul Winterfeld, *Hrotsvithae Opera*, 166; trans. Katharina Wilson, *The Plays of Hrotsvit of Gandersheim*, 100. On the role of music in the play, see the important article by David Chamberlain, "Musical Learning and Dramatic Action in Hrotsvit's *Pafnutius*"; Chamberlain argues that Pafnutius's teaching "harmoniz[es] Thais's bodily actions with her spiritual beliefs" (343).

2. Lippman, *Western Musical Aesthetics*, 24, 20.

3. Ibid., 19.

4. Bynum, *Resurrection of the Body*; Peter Brown, *Body and Society*; Eliza-beth A. Clark, *Origenist Controversy*; Perkins, *Suffering Self*.

5. R. Howard Bloch, *Medieval Misogyny*, 37.

6. See the comments in Sordi, *Christians and the Roman Empire*, 79–85, where it is argued that the Severan age was characterized by a "*de facto* toler-ance" toward Christians that was nevertheless punctuated by "brief intervals of local persecution" (85). But see also Keresztes, *Imperial Rome and the Chris-tians*, 2:3: "Our sources—literary, historical and martyrological documents—clearly indicate that there existed under Severus' rule at least two distinct peri-ods of intense persecutions in different parts of the Empire."

7. On this point, see Chadwick, *Early Christian Thought*, 36.

8. Clement, *Protreptikos* 1; *PG* 8, cols. 49–52; Clement, *Selected Writings*, 171. A useful discussion of Clement and music can be found in Schueller, *Idea of Music*, 214–18.

9. Clement, *Protreptikos* 1, *PG* 8, cols. 51–54; Clement, *Selected Writings*, 171.

10. Clement, *Protreptikos* 1, *PG* 8, cols. 55–56; Clement, *Selected Writings*, 171.

11. Clement, *Protreptikos* 1, *PG* 8, cols. 57–58; Clement, *Selected Writings*, 172. See Friedman, *Orpheus*, 38–85, for numerous examples of the Orpheus-Christ typology in late antiquity.

12. Cameron, *Rhetoric of Empire*, 25. The best discussion I have found of Clement's use of the classics in the service of Christian "cultural revisionism" is Dawson, *Allegorical Readers*, 199–218.

13. Clement, *Protreptikos* 1, *PG* 8, cols. 59–60; Clement, *Selected Writings*, 172.

14. Clement, *Protreptikos* 1, *PG* 8, col. 61; Clement, *Selected Writings*, 173.

15. My discussions of Roman and Hellenic musical thought throughout this chapter are indebted to Spitzer, *Classical and Christian Ideas*; Lippman, *Musical Thought*; and especially Schueller, *Idea of Music*, an encyclopedic study of musical thought from Pythagoras to Jacob of Liège.

16. Plotinus, *Enneads* 4.4.28 and 3.6.4, 313, 193. The extent of Clement's platonism has been documented in Lilla, *Clement of Alexandria*. On Plotinus and music, see Schueller, *Idea of Music*, 173–78.

17. Clement, *Protreptikos* 1, *PG* 8, cols. 59–60; Clement, *Selected Writings*, 172.

18. See, for example, McNamara, *New Song*.

19. D. W. Robertson, *Preface to Chaucer*, 127 and 132 respectively.

20. Ibid., 137.

21. Lochrie, *Margery Kempe*, 4.

22. Crouzel, *Origen*, 90. Crouzel adds the following clarification, which can be taken as axiomatic even for some of the most stridently platonizing Christian thinkers: "the earthly body, like everything perceptible, is good in itself: created by God, it is among those realities of which the Bible says that when He looked at them in their profound being: 'God saw that they were good.' In terms of the exemplarism that underlies Origen's vision of the world the body, like all the beings in this world, is the image of divine realities. If the point of man's contact with the image of God lies in the soul and not in the body, the worth of this nonetheless redounds on the body which is as it were the shrine containing this image: and that is why in accordance with I Cor. 6, 13–20, the sins of the flesh are a profanation of this body which is holy" (90–91).

23. D. W. Robertson, *Preface to Chaucer*, 129.

24. See especially McKinnon, "Meaning of the Patristic Polemic."

25. McKinnon, "Musical Instruments," 6.

26. Weiss and Taruskin, *Music in the Western World*, 28 (commenting on Origen and Honorius Augustodunensis). McKinnon's most explicit corrective to the work of Gelineau and Stäblein can be found in "Meaning of the Patristic Polemic," 71–73.

27. McKinnon, "Musical Instruments," 10.

28. (Pseudo-)Origen, *Selecta in psalmos* 32.2–3, *PG* 12, col. 1304; McKinnon, *Music in Early Christian Literature*, 38. McKinnon's invaluable book collects and translates some four hundred Greek and Latin patristic passages on music and musical performance, and I have relied on several of his translations in this chapter.

29. See Maas and Snyder, *Stringed Instruments*, 184 (for *psalterion*) and chapter 3 on the *kithara*, 53–78.

30. Page, *Voices and Instruments*, 55.

31. Cassiodorus, *Expositio Psalmorum* 48.5, *CCSL* 97, 433. Though influenced by Augustine's *Enarrationes in psalmos*, Cassiodorus's psalm commentaries are much more attuned to the physical particularities of individual instruments; the distinctions between the approaches of the two exegetes in this regard have been sensitively discussed in van Deusen, "The *Cithara* as *Symbolum*," in *Harp and the Soul*, 201–55.

32. Clement of Alexandria, *Paedogogus* 2.4, *PG* 8, col. 441; McKinnon, *Music in Early Christian Literature*, 32–33. Compare the reading of this passage in Custer, "The Psaltery, the Harp, and the Fathers," 19–20.

33. Peter Chrysologus, *Sermones* 93.4, *CCSL* 24A, 575. The passage was adduced long ago in Abert, *Die Musikanschauung des Mittelalters*, 214–15, as an example of patristic *Instrumentensymbolik*.

34. See Schueller's eleventh chapter, "The Fathers of the Church," in *Idea of Music*, 203–37.

35. These passages have been treated by Armand Delatte, "Les harmonies." See the remarks in Lippman, *Musical Thought*, 35 and 85.

36. For Clement's knowledge of the *Phaedo*, see especially the comments in Lilla, *Clement of Alexandria*, 166.

37. Plato, *Phaedo* 86B–D; Plato, *The Republic and Other Works*, 520.

38. Edward Lippman points out the exceptionalism of this passage within Plato's more general theory of music; speaking of Simmias's objection, he writes, "The conception is thoroughly Pythagorean as far as number and harmony are concerned, but it is quite the contrary in its insistence on the soul's mortality, curiously contradicting the Pythagorean belief in metempsychosis" (*Musical Thought*, 36). Some commentators have even suggested that Simmias's "pro-body" argument reflects the influence of a hetero-

dox strain of Pythagoreanism; see the notes to David Gallop's translation in Plato, *Phaedo*, 148, citing J. Burnet's classic commentary, *Plato's Phaedo*.

39. In a spirited polemic against Aristoxenus, Lactantius objects to a philosophical position that might be read as a radical realization of Simmias's argument: "What of Aristoxenus who declared absolutely that there is no soul, even while it lives in the body? He thought that just as a consonant sound or song—what the musicians call harmony—is produced on citharas [*fidibus*] by tension upon their strings [*ex intentione neruorum*], so too the power of sentience exists in human bodies from the joining together of the viscera and the vigor of the limbs. Nothing more senseless than this can be said. Certainly this man had healthy eyes, but a heart that was blind, for with it he failed to see that he lived and possessed a mind with which he had thought that very thing." Lactantius, *Diuinae institutiones* 7.13, 627; McKinnon, *Music in Early Christian Literature*, 50.

40. See Schueller, *Idea of Music*, 91.

41. On the influence of Stoicism among the early fathers more generally, see Colish, *Stoic Tradition*, vol. 2; and Spanneut, *Le stoïcisme des pères*.

42. Long, *Stoic Studies*, 227.

43. Ibid., 229.

44. Colish, *Stoic Tradition*, 1:23. The argument in the following paragraphs may be read in the context of the brilliant overview of Stoic views of the "cosmic dance" in James Miller, *Measures of Wisdom*, 157–79; though Miller is concerned here primarily with Plotinus, the same naturalistic sensibility seems to have influenced early Christian images of bodily movement as well (see esp. 352, 373–74).

45. Cicero, *De natura deorum*, 2.59.148–49; Cicero, *De Natura Deorum, Academica*, 266–67: "deinde hac cohortamur hac persuademus, hac consolamur afflictos hac deducimus perterritos a timore. . . . Primum enim a pulmonibus arteria usque ad os intimum pertinet, per quam vox principium a mente ducens percipitur et funditur. Deinde in ore sita lingua est finita dentibus; ea vocem inmoderate profusam fingit et terminat atque sonos vocis distinctos et pressos efficit cum et dentes et alias partes pellit oris."

46. Cicero, *De natura deorum* 2.59.149; Cicero, *De Natura Deorum, Academica*, 266–67. On this passage see Wille, *Musica Romana*, 506; on Ciceronian musical thought, the classic article by P. R. Coleman-Norton, "Cicero Musicus," is still valuable.

47. Colish, *Stoic Tradition*, 1:117. See also Gersh, *Middle Platonism and Neoplatonism*, 1:72.

48. Cicero, *De oratore* 3.59.222, 2:179.

49. The work of Jody Enders has begun to recover this extraordinary

mass of material for medieval studies, showing how rhetorical and antirhetorical representations of embodied delivery can contribute to largely presentist views of "performance" predominating in feminist theory and gender studies. See Enders, *Medieval Drama*; "Music, Delivery"; and "Delivering Delivery."

50. Cicero, *De oratore* 3.55.213, 2:169; Quintilian, *Institutio oratoria*, 11.3.7–11, 4:244–49.

51. Cicero, *De oratore* 3.57.216–17, 2:173. For some thoughts on the philosophical background of this tradition, see Wille, "Die Bedeutung der Music für die römische Rhetorik," in *Schriften zur Geschichte*, 207–17, as well as *Musica Romana*, 447–49.

52. Lilla, *Clement of Alexandria*, 48–49. See also Spanneut, *Le stoïcisme des pères de l'Église*, 166–76, for a discussion of Clement and Stoic anthropology more generally.

53. On Augustine's deep knowledge of Cicero, see the numerous examples cited in Stock, *Augustine the Reader*. The brief comment on Augustine and Cicero in Eco, *Art and Beauty*, 28, assumes that the writers share, not a sense of the musicality of the flesh, but rather an aesthetics of "proportion or number . . . an essentially quantitative conception of beauty." The two sensibilities should not be seen as mutually exclusive.

54. Cicero, *Tusculan Disputations* 1.19, 30–31: "As with what is called 'harmonia' in singing and stringed instruments, so from the character and shape of the body there is produced a variety of vibrations like musical notes" (velut in cantu et fidibus, quae harmonia dicitur, sic ex corporis totius natura et figura varios motus cieri tamquam in cantu sonos).

55. Rhabanus Maurus, *Allegoriae in Sacram Scripturam*, col. 1069.

56. Quintilian, *Institutio oratoria* 2.11.4–5, 1:280–81. Historians of rhetoric are beginning to realize that Quintilian's influence on medieval rhetoric was much more profound than previously supposed; see especially Ward, "Quintilian and the Rhetorical Revolution."

57. Hilary of Poitiers, *Instructio psalmorum* 7, *CSEL* 22, 8–9; McKinnon, *Music in Early Christian Literature*, 123. Compare Isidore, *Etymologies* 3.22, where he suggests that the Latin *cithara* derives from the Greek *kithara*, or "chest."

58. Quintilian, *Institutio oratoria* 2.8.15, 1:270–71. A consideration of the rhetorical category of *actio* may be the one significant omission from James Murphy's spectacular chapter on the *Ars praedicandi* in *Rhetoric in the Middle Ages*, 269–355; in the *Forma praedicandi* of Robert of Basevorn (1322), translated by Murphy at the end of the chapter, "voice modulation" and "appropriate gesture" are included among the "extrinsic ornaments" of the sermon, "which serve for beauty" (354–55).

59. Peter Brown, *Body and Society*, 285.

60. Ibid., 293 and notes; and see Bynum, *Resurrection of the Body*, 81.

61. See Oesterle, "Probleme der Anthropologie."

62. Bynum, *Resurrection of the Body*, 83.

63. Gregory of Nyssa, *De hominis opificio* 13.1, col. 158; Gregory of Nyssa, *Dogmatic Treatises*, 399–400 (hereafter cited in text).

64. Gregory of Nyssa, *Dogmatic Treatises*, 459.

65. The single exception to this rule is the final chapter (30), the treatment of bodies "from a medical point of view," in Gregory's words; but even in this chapter his images of bellows, pipes, cartilage, and the "tensing" of the sinews are very similar to the more explicitly musical images he employs earlier, and in fact it is this part of the treatise that is cited (in Latin translation) and fitted into an extended musical analogy by William of St. Thierry in his *De natura corporis et animae* (see Chapter 5 of this volume, pp. 219–21).

66. Gregory's musical imagery in the *De hominis* has been treated briefly by Eugenio Corsini, who seems to have been unaware of Leo Spitzer's work on "world harmony"; see "L'harmonie du monde." For a more general (though rather forced) consideration of Gregory's musical thought in the treatise, see Henri-Irénée Marrou, "Une théologie de la musique?" Pietro Meloni, "La chitarra di David," is a useful consideration of Gregory's instrumental allegories.

67. See especially Basil, *De titulis in psalmorum* 150.7, col. 543; *Epistola ad Marcellinum* 29, *PG* 27, col. 39 and 42; and *Hexaemeron* 15, 229; for a discussion of Basil's musical thought see Schueller, *Idea of Music*, 222–25.

68. Ovid, *Metamorphoses* 1.711–12; all citations of the *Metamorphoses* will be to Frank Justus Miller's two-volume Loeb edition and translation and will hereafter be given in text.

69. Fulgentius, *Mitologiarum* 3.9, 73: "Minerua ex osse tibias inuenit, de quibus cum in conuiuio deorum cecinisset eiusque tumentes buccas dii omnes inrisissent."

70. See Anne Weis, *The Hanging Marsyas*, especially plate 38, nos. 75 and 78; plate 39, no. 79; and plate 40, no. 82.

71. I have been unable to find a description of the statue that definitively identifies the relief figure as Marsyas, though given its obvious resemblance to the numerous representations of the "Hanging Marsyas" cataloged in Weis, *The Hanging Marsyas*, the identification seems obvious. A brief treatment of the Roman literary tradition of Apollo and Marsyas can be found in Wille, *Musica Romana*, 533–36.

72. Cassiodorus, *Expositio psalmorum* 56.9, *CCSL* 97, 511; see Pickering,

Literature and Art, 292; see the translation in Cassiodorus, *Explanation of the Psalms*, 2:43–44. Cassiodorus's writings on music have been treated at some length by Wille, *Musica Romana*, 700–709.

73. The book was never translated into Latin; see "The Fourth Book of Maccabees: Introduction," in Charles, *Pseudepigrapha*, 653–65.

74. Ambrose, *De Iacob et vita beata* 2.12.56, 68–69.

75. 4 Maccabees 15:15–21; all references are to the translation in Charles, *Pseudepigrapha*, 666–85.

76. Ambrose, *De Iacob et vita beata* 2.12.56, 68; the passage is translated in McKinnon, *Music in Early Christian Literature*, 130.

77. On Ambrose and the *Enneads*, see Soulignac, "Nouveaux parallèles," and Courcelle, "Nouveaux aspects." These passages from Ambrose might be read as well in light of Judith Perkins's recent account of the influence of Stoicism on accounts of suffering in early Christian discourse; see *Suffering Self,* esp. chapter 3, "Pain Without Effect," 77–103.

78. See Charles, *Pseudepigrapha*, 653–54. Ambrose's Stoicism as evident in both the *De Iacob et vita beata* and *De officiis ministrorum* has been discussed in Colish, *Stoic Tradition*, 2:48–70.

79. Ambrose, *De officiis ministrorum* 1.41, col. 90; McKinnon, *Music in Early Christian Literature*, 132.

CHAPTER 2

1. This is as good a place as any to begin recording a few of the many debts that all contemporary writers on Augustine owe to the ever-growing scholarly bibliography on the theologian and saint, which rivals in vastness, rigor, and imagination that on any other figure in Western history. Scholarship on the relatively narrow subject of Augustine's musical thought is less unwieldy, though I suspect I may have missed some important contributions that have gone unindexed in the various bibliographies I have consulted. Research for this chapter was greatly facilitated by the *Augustinus-Lexicon*, a massive and ongoing project under the general editorship of Cornelius Mayer, and in particular by Günther Wille's brief but magisterial article "Cantatio, canticum, cantus" (vol. 1, cols. 724–28), which led me to many of the sources discussed below.

2. The full text can be found in Landulf, *Historia Mediolanensis*, cols. 832–33; for a discussion and translation, see Weiss and Taruskin, *Music in the Western World*, 30–31.

3. Augustine, *De civitate Dei* 22.8, CCSL 48, 815. For the *City of God*, I

have used O'Meara's Penguin translation but have modified it where appropriate. On Augustine and the Resurrection, see Bynum, *Resurrection of the Body*, 94–95.

4. Augustine, *De civitate Dei* 22.8, *CCSL* 48, 820–21.

5. Basil, *Homilia in psalmum* 1.2; *PG* 29, col. 212; McKinnon, *Music in Early Christian Literature*, 65–66.

6. Augustine, *De musica libri sex*; citation from 5.13.28, col. 1162; Augustine, *On Music*, 323. On this passage see Hammerstein, *Die Musik der Engel*, 120: "Die *numeri* reichen vom Körperlichen bis zum Unkörperlichen."

7. Bowen, "St. Augustine in Medieval and Renaissance Musical Science," 29–51. See also the important study by Corbin, "*Musica* spéculative et *cantus* pratique."

8. Augustine, *De musica libri sex* 1.2.2, col. 1083; the meaning of *modulatio* changed in later centuries to correspond to actual singing practice; see Christoph von Blumroder, "Modulatio/Modulation."

9. See Bowen, "St. Augustine," 41 and notes; and the comments in the Introduction to this volume.

10. Typical here is Lippman, *Western Musical Aesthetics*, 85 and 87.

11. La Croix, *Augustine on Music*. The quotation is from Forman, "Augustine's Music: 'Keys' to the Logos," 24.

12. Ellsmere, "Augustine on Beauty, Art, and God," in *Augustine on Music*, 110.

13. Treitler, "Troubadours Singing," 19. But see the comments in Hammerstein, *Die Musik der Engel*, 120–21, where it is argued that "*musica* as discipline has, for Augustine, nothing to do with practical music" (120). A recent overview of the vocabulary of *harmonia* and *concordantia* in Augustine's writings is included in Gersh, *Concord in Discourse*, 21–28.

14. See Forman, "Augustine's Music," 17–27; and Ellsmere and La Croix, "Augustine on Art as Imitation." A notable exception is Schueller, *Idea of Music*, 239–56.

15. Augustine, *De musica libri sex* 6.1.1, col. 1161; Augustine, *On Music*, 324.

16. Forman, "Augustine's Music," 17.

17. Augustine, *De musica* 6.2.2, col. 1163.

18. Harrison, *Beauty and Revelation*, 29.

19. Augustine, *Soliloquius* 1.14, in *Soliloquies and Immortality of the Soul*, 42–43.

20. Augustine, *De immortalitate animae* 24, in *Soliloquies and Immortality of the Soul*, 158–59.

21. Augustine, *De immortalitate animae* 1, in *Soliloquies and Immortality of the Soul*, 128–29.

22. Peter Brown, *Body and Society*, 391

23. Peter Brown, *Augustine of Hippo*, 98.

24. Augustine, *Soliloquius* 2.32, in *Soliloquies and Immortality of the Soul*, 118–19.

25. Augustine, *De immortalitate animae* 5, in *Soliloquies and Immortality of the Soul*, 134–35.

26. Augustine, *De musica* 6.3, col. 1165, Augustine, *On Music*, 328.

27. Siraisi, "Music of Pulse."

28. Augustine, *De musica* 6.3, col. 1165; Augustine, *On Music*, 329.

29. Morrison, *Conversion and Text*, 20 and 32, respectively.

30. Ibid., 33.

31. Augustine, *Confessiones* 9.3.6, 184; for the *Confessions* I have used the Penguin translation by Pine-Coffin but have altered it freely. Citations of the *Confessions* hereafter will be internal.

32. See especially Peter Brown, *Augustine of Hippo*, 164; and Morrison, *Conversion and Text*, 18–20.

33. On the complex relationship between music and liquefaction in medieval thought, see Swerdlow, "Musica Dicitur A Moys." Dante may have had this very passage in mind in the Earthly Paradise (*Purgatorio* 30) when he describes his vision of Beatrice and his resultant "melting" at the music of the spheres (see Chapter 7 of this volume, pp. 329–30).

34. See Peter Brown, *Augustine of Hippo*, for an account of this persecution; also see the relevant discussions in Leeb, *Psalmodie bei Ambrosius*.

35. Augustine, *Confessiones* 9.7.15, 192. Ambrose's own comments on the effectiveness of his hymnody occur in *Sermo contra Auxentium de basilicis tradendis*, 34, in which he tells of his detractors claiming that "the people are led astray by the charms of my hymns. Certainly; I do not deny it" (*PL* 16, cols. 1017–18; cited in McKinnon, *Music in Early Christian Literature*, 132).

36. See O'Donnell, *Confessions* 3, 110–11.

37. Augustine, *Retractiones* 1.11.2, 33–35; Augustine, *Retractiones*, 60, 46.

38. Weiss and Taruskin, *Music in the Western World*, 31. The chapter as a whole has inspired voluminous commentary; the complexities of its language and tone have been treated in meticulous detail in O'Donnell's commentary, *Confessions* 3, 218–20.

39. I thus respectfully disagree with Brian Stock's reading of the chapter: "The idea of an inscrutable inner self is reinforced by what [Augustine] says about the pleasures of the ears. In this case he is unable to resist, even when he

consciously wishes to do so. As a result, he is not attracted to music by what he senses alone, but principally by a preexisting affinity for its harmonies, which is in his mind before he hears the notes. If he were not so predisposed, it would be impossible to associate the sensory effects of what he hears with higher religious sentiments, which are obviously not what he listens for. . . . He is aware that all individuals possess such 'affinities,' but he cannot say how they arise. They are an aspect of God's predestined knowledge for man" (*Augustine the Reader*, 230). By Augustine's own reckoning, it is precisely what he "senses alone" that provokes these anxieties of sensual indulgence in the first place (see the treatment in Harrison, *Beauty and Revelation*, 170–71). In Stock's interpretation, as in so many modern accounts of ancient descriptions of musical sensation, an assumption of the listener's "preexisting affinity" for *harmonia* predetermines the reading of the actual passage.

40. Though, as McKinnon notes (*Music in Early Christian Literature*, 156), there is no specific evidence supporting such an identification this early; on this question, see Gélineau, *Voices and Instruments*, 172; and Wiora, "Jubilare sine verbis."

41. Augustine, *Enarrationes in psalmos* 99.4, *CCSL* 39, 1394.

42. Ibid.

43. Nichols, "Voice and Writing," 151.

44. Augustine, *Enarrationes* 32.2, s. 1.8, *CCSL* 38, 254; McKinnon, *Music in Early Christian Literature*, 157.

45. See O'Donnell's treatment of the philosophical aspects of the chapter in *Confessions* 3, 339.

46. Augustine, *Enarrationes* 150.8, *CCSL* 40, 2196.

47. See van Deusen, "Medieval Organologies"; and McKinnon, "Musical Instruments," 4.

48. Augustine, *De Trinitate* 4.2, *CCSL* 50, 164–65; Augustine, *On the Trinity*, 133–34.

49. For a discussion of Augustine's images of the resurrection body see Bynum, *Resurrection of the Body*, 94–104.

50. Augustine, Sermon 123.4, *PL* 38, col. 1145; compare Cicero, *De Natura Deorum* 2.59: "deinde in ore sita lingua est finita dentibus; ea vocem immoderate profusam fingit et terminat atque sonos vocis distinctos et pressos efficit, cum et dentes et alias partes pellit oris; itaque plectri similem linguam nostri solent dicere, chordarum dentes, nares cordibus is quae ad nervos resonant in cantibus," 110.

51. Augustine, Sermon 123.4, *PL* 38, col. 1145.

52. Bynum, *Resurrection of the Body*, 95 and 102 respectively.

53. It is ironic that the very portions of Cicero's *De Natura Deorum* Au-

gustine rejects in the *City of God* have to do with the divination of the future; thus, Augustine relies on images from the same book he explicitly rejects for its notion of the relationship between present and future to represent the similarity between earthly body and resurrection body. Augustine could not have derived this imagery from Gregory of Nyssa; while he knew Basil's *Hexaemeron* through the Latin translation of Eustathius, he almost certainly did not know Gregory's continuation in the *De hominis opificio*, which was not translated into Latin until the early sixth century. See Courcelle, *Late Latin Writers*, 203 and 333.

54. Augustine, *De civitate Dei* 22.24, CCSL 48, 850.

55. Ibid.

CHAPTER 3

1. See Elliott, *Fallen Bodies*, especially chapter 3, "Sex in Holy Places: An Exploration of a Medieval Anxiety," 61–80.

2. Elisabeth of Schönau, "Epistola ad Hildegardem," col. 215. For the two letters discussed here I have used the translation by Kerby-Fulton and Elliott, "Self-Image and the Visionary Role."

3. Barbara Newman suggests (without explanation) that Elisabeth's letter to Hildegard discussed here was "probably not the epistle of Elisabeth printed in Migne but an earlier letter of hers"; see Barbara Newman, *Sister of Wisdom*, 36–37. Given the imagery of *flagellatio* and other verbal echoes of Elisabeth's letter, however, I have assumed (as have Elliott and Kerby-Fulton) that the two epistles do indeed represent a single exchange. On the more general relationship between Hildegard and Elisabeth, see Anne Clark, *Elisabeth of Schönau*, esp. 21–25, 34–36.

4. Hildegard, "Epistola CCIr ad Elisabeth Monialem," 456.

5. Ibid., 457.

6. Ibid.

7. Major studies of Hildegard's life and works include Barbara Newman, *Sister of Wisdom*; Flanagan, *Hildegard of Bingen*; Führkötter, *Hildegard von Bingen*; and Gronau, *Hildegard von Bingen*.

8. Fassler, "Composer and Dramatist," 149.

9. Beckwith, *Christ's Body*, 18.

10. See "Mystic Speech" in Certeau, *Heterologies*, 80–100, and the elaboration of these themes in *The Mystic Fable*. See also Treitler, "Language and the Interpretation," for a particularly compelling critique of the "ineffability" topos.

11. Witts, "How to Make a Saint," 479. The difficult issue of the prop-

erly "liturgical" nature of Hildegard's music has been examined with subtlety and care by John Stevens in "Musical Individuality."

12. Hildegard, "Protestificatio," in *Scivias, CCCM* 43, 3–4; trans. Hart and Bishop, 59.

13. Hildegard, "Protestificatio," in *Scivias*, 4–5; trans. Hart and Bishop, 60. On ecstasy in Elisabeth's visions, see Anne L. Clark, *Elisabeth of Schönau*, 85–86.

14. Hildegard, "Protestificatio," in *Scivias, CCCM* 43, 4, trans. Hart and Bishop, 60.

15. Barbara Newman's introduction in Hildegard, *Symphonia*, 20. Other useful overviews of Hildegard's musical thought include Schmidt-Görg, "Zur Musikanschauung in den Schriften"; and Ritscher, "Zur Musik," esp. 189–92. Pfau, "*Armonia*," is one of the most convincing attempts to establish a formal link between Hildegard's musical cosmology and the mechanics of her compositional style.

16. On William, see the comments in Mews, "Hildegard and the Schools," 98. As Mews argues, another possible influence upon Hildegard's thought may have been the work of Honorius Augustodunensis, author of the liturgical commentary entitled *Gemma animae* discussed in Chapter 5 of this volume.

17. Hildegard, *Scivias* 3.13.12, *CCCM* 43A, 631; trans. Hart and Bishop, 533.

18. For a brief discussion of Hildegard's images of the "heavenly liturgy," see Hammerstein, *Die Musik der Engel*, 55–57.

19. Hildegard, *Scivias* 3.13.14, *CCCM* 43A, 632; trans. Hart and Bishop, 534.

20. Fassler, "Composer and Dramatist," 170.

21. As Bynum describes it, "scattered pieces of human beings come together when the trumpet sounds." See her discussion of Hildegard and the resurrection in *Resurrection of the Body*, 239–97.

22. Hildegard, *Scivias* 3.12.vis., *CCCM* 43A, 605; trans. Hart and Bishop, 515.

23. Hildegard, *Liber vitae meritorum* 1.37, *CCCM* 90, 28; Hildegard, *Book of the Rewards*, 27.

24. Hildegard, *Liber vitae meritorum* 2.2., 75; Hildegard, *Book of the Rewards*, 74. See Langland, *Piers Plowman*, passus 5, lines 339–44, 327–28: "Gloton hadde yglubbed a galon and a gille./His guttes bigonne to goþelen as two gredy sowes;/He pissed a potel in a paternoster while,/And blew þe rounde ruwet at þe ruggebones end/That alle þat herde þat horn helde hir nose after/And wisshed it hadde ben wexed wiþ a wispe of firses."

25. Hildegard, *Liber vitae meritorum* 2.2, 75; Hildegard, *Book of the Rewards*, 74–75.

26. Hildegard, *Liber vitae meritorum* 3.10, 130–31; Hildegard, *Book of the Rewards*, 130.

27. See especially Kerby-Fulton, *Reformist Apocalypticism*, 32–33.

28. Hildegard, *Scivias* 3.11.9, *CCCM* 43A, 581–82; trans. Bishop and Hart, 496.

29. Caviness, "Artist," 113. On the Salem *Scivias*, see Meier, "Zum Verhältnis von Text." I would like to thank Richard Emmerson for drawing my attention to the illustration from the Salem codex and providing me with several helpful references.

30. Hildegard, *Causae et curae* book 2, "De partu," 105.

31. Hildegard, *Causae et curae*, 105; translated and discussed in Barbara Newman, *Sister of Wisdom*, 129.

32. Hildegard, "Nunc gaudeant," in *Symphonia: A Critical Edition*, 252–53.

33. Hildegard, "O Fili dilectissime," in *Symphonia: A Critical Edition*, 260–61; "O Fili dilectissime" lacks music in the sources, though Newman chooses to include it among Hildegard's songs.

34. Hildegard, "Epistola VIII," in *Hildegardis Bingensis Epistolarium*, *CCCM* 91, 21 (passage in the apparatus).

35. Cogan, "Hildegard's Fractal Antiphon," 2 (emphasis in the original).

36. For interpretations of Hildegard's music that emphasize its mathematical properties, see Escott, "Gothic Cathedral"; and idem, "Hildegard von Bingen."

37. Cogan, "Hildegard's Fractal Antiphon," 2 and 16 respectively.

38. See the works cited in Barbara Newman's introduction to *Symphonia: A Critical Edition*, 17; and Stevens's discussion of the letter of Tenxwind in "Musical Individuality," 163–65.

39. See especially "Bach Defended Against His Devotees," in Adorno, *Prisms*.

40. Stevens, "Musical Individuality," 174.

41. On short responsories generally, see Hiley, *Western Plainchant*, 85–88; on Hildegard's responsories, see Barbara Newman's introduction in Hildegard, *Symphonia: A Critical Edition*, 14–15.

42. "O quam preciosa," in Hildegard, *Symphonia: A Critical Edition*, 134–35 (translation slightly altered).

43. See Newman's comments on the architectural imagery in her notes to "O quam preciosa."

44. Gilchrist, *Gender and Material Culture*, 192.

45. On the dialectics of secrecy, disclosure, and desire in the *De secretis mulierum,* see Lochrie, "Don't Ask, Don't Tell."

46. "Ave generosa," in Hildegard, *Symphonia: A Critical Edition,* 122 (my translation).

47. "De conceptu," in Hildegard, *Causae et curae* 2, 104.

48. The best introduction to Hildegard's medical writings is Cadden, "It Takes All Kinds"; see also Cadden, *Sex Difference,* 78.

49. "Ave generosa," in Hildegard, *Symphonia: A Critical Edition,* 122.

50. See, for example, Rhabanus Maurus, *Allegoriae,* col. 1020: "*Ros,* plenitudo sanctitatis, ut in libro Judicum: 'Ros sit in solo vellere,' quod prae cunctis plenitudo erat sanctitatis in Maria Virgine."

51. For a detailed discussion of the significance of Ecclesia to Hildegard, see Barbara Newman, *Sister of Wisdom,* 196–249.

52. There are several systems available to medievalists for indicating the octave of a pitch; in the following and subsequent discussions, c' denotes middle C. When applied to a plainchant composition, the term "syllabic" refers to the practice of assigning a single syllable to a single note; "neumatic" passages are those in which a syllable is sung on two to four or five notes; and "melismatic" passages are those in which a long string of notes is performed on one syllable.

53. A caution missing, it must be admitted, from the 1993 essay on which this chapter is based. For a recent comment on the overall state of research into the musical analysis of medieval plainchant, see Hiley, *Western Plainchant,* 46–47.

54. See especially Pfau, "Hildegard von Bingen's 'Symphonia,'" esp. 84–89 and 213–51; Pfau, "Music and Text in Hildegard's Antiphons," in Hildegard, *Symphonia: A Critical Edition,* 74–94; and Fassler, "Composer and Dramatist."

55. On this point see Barbara Newman's comments on the Dendermonde codex in Hildegard, *Symphonia: A Critical Edition,* 58–60.

56. Hildegard, *Symphonia harmoniae caelestium revelationum: Dendermonde, St.-Pieters & Paulusabdij MS cod. 9* (facsimile), fol. 155v. This is a piece of paleographical evidence that further demolishes Witts's claim (see above) that there is "not a scrap of evidence" that Hildegard composed these songs "for her nuns to sing at daily service."

57. Stäblein, *Die mittelalterlichen Hymnenmelodien des Abendlandes.* See also Stäblein's article "Hymnus, B. Der Lateinischen Hymnus," in *MGG.*

58. Hildegard, *Lieder,* 59–62, as well as the discussion below, pp. 130–36. The range of "O vos angeli" has been noted in Ian Bent, "Hildegard von Bingen," 554.

59. As cited in Steiner, "Hymn II," 840.

60. For a few examples from the Germanic repertory specifically see Stäblein, *Hymnenmelodien*, 329, 342, 345, 351.

61. Hiley, *Western Plainchant*, 145.

62. On the Cistercian Reform, see especially Hiley, *Western Plainchant*, 609–11; Waddell, "Cistercian Antiphonary."

63. See Francis Guentner's introduction in CSM 24, 9–13.

64. "Cantum quem Cisterciensis ordinis," in Guentner, *Epistola S. Bernardi*, 31 and 53 (trans.).

65. Ibid. Compare the older position on range as formulated by (Pseudo-)Odo of Cluny in the excerpts translated in Strunk, *Source Readings*, 113.

66. Cited and translated in Page, *Owl and Nightingale*, 156. Page's seventh chapter, "Plainchant and the Beyond," provides a fascinating glimpse at the various forms of Cistercian anxiety surrounding the performance and abuse of chant.

67. Bernard of Clairvaux, *Sermons*, 10.

68. See especially Cadden, "It Takes All Kinds," the discussion in Dronke, *Women Writers*, and most recently Glaze, "Medical Writer."

69. Barbara Newman, *Sister of Wisdom*, 121. But Newman has also suggested that Hildegard's most intense concentration on both natural science and music may have occurred at roughly the same time. Especially interesting is Newman's positing of a "middle period" in the abbess's musical composition that would have included both "Ave generosa" and "O viridissima virga." According to Newman's own chronology, then, Hildegard's composition of these two songs may have taken place while she was at work on the *Causae et curae*. See Newman's introduction in Hildegard, *Symphonia: A Critical Edition*, 7 and 10. See also Dronke, "Hildegard of Bingen's *Symphonia*," 381.

70. "De viri delectatione," in Hildegard, *Causae et curae* 2, 76: "cum ventus delectationis ex medulla feminae egreditur, in matricem, quae umbilico adhaeret, cadit et sanguinem mulieris ad delectationem movet, et quia matrix circa umbilicum mulieris amplum et velut apertum locum habet, ventus ille in ventrem eius se dilatat, et ideo lenius, quamvis prae humiditate sua saepius, ibi in delectationem ardet, et ideo etiam aut prae timore aut prae pudore facilius quam vir a delectatione se continere valet."

71. "De mulieris delectatione," in Hildegard, *Causae et curae* 2, 76; Cadden, "It Takes All Kinds," 158.

72. See in particular the illuminations reproduced in Hildegard, *Scivias*, trans. Hart and Bishop, 199 and 491.

73. See Dronke's discussion in *Women Writers*, 176.

74. Cadden, "It Takes All Kinds," 157.

75. Hildegard, *Causae et curae*, 77; see Cadden, "It Takes All Kinds," 168.

76. Barbara Newman's "Commentary," in Hildegard, *Symphonia: A Critical Edition*, 276.

77. Adams, *Latin Sexual Vocabulary*, 14–15.

78. "O viridissima virga," in Hildegard, *Symphonia: A Critical Edition*, 126–27. This song has also been edited and discussed by Barbara Grant in "Five Liturgical Songs." The liturgical genre of *O viridissima virga* is unclear; according to Grant, it is "one of only two songs in the whole collection with no designation as to liturgical form or function," 563.

79. "O viridissima virga," in Hildegard, *Symphonia: A Critical Edition*, 126–27.

80. Pfau, "Form as Process." Pfau has expanded these findings in her thesis, "Hildegard von Bingen's 'Symphonia armonie celestium revelationum.'"

81. Hildegard's regression to ninth- and tenth-century sequence style has been argued in, among other places, Ian Bent, "Hildegard," 553, and Schmidt-Görg, "Die Sequenzen," 111.

82. Cited and translated from Page, *Summa musice*, in McGee, *Medieval Song*, 44 and 162. On the development and increasing standardization of notational vocabulary during the eleventh and twelfth centuries, see Huglo, "Les noms des neumes et leur origine."

83. The quoted passage appears in the *Vita Sanctae Hildegardis* 2.2, 24; Silvas, *Jutta and Hildegard*, 160–61.

84. See Peter van Poucke's comments in the introduction to the Dendermonde facsimile, Hildegard, *Symphonia harmoniae caelestium*, 11.

85. Holsinger, "Flesh of the Voice."

86. Hildegard, *Liber vitae meritorum* 6.30, 283; Hildegard, *Book of the Rewards*, 281.

87. On this point, see Lochrie, "Mystical Plots, Murderous Secrets."

88. Barbara Newman, *Sister of Wisdom*, 187.

89. Dronke, *Women Writers*, 170.

90. See Hildegard, *Scivias*, trans. Hart and Bishop, 279.

91. On this problem more generally, see, for example, Halperin, *One Hundred Years*, 24–29.

92. Bynum has made a somewhat similar argument (though with the opposite result) in a reply to Leo Steinberg's study of what he called the "sexuality of Christ" in Renaissance art; see *Fragmentation and Redemption*, 79–117. Distinguishing between sexuality and "genitality," she questions whether we are "entitled to associate genitality with sexuality" in the Middle Ages, and

whether "medieval people immediately [thought] of erections and sexual activity when they saw penises (as modern people apparently do)" (85).

93. See Brown, *Immodest Acts*; on Hildegard and Richardis, see especially the discussion in Dronke, *Women Writers*.

94. Judith Bennett, " 'Lesbian-Like.' "

95. Matter, "Introduction to MFN Gay and Lesbian Issue," 3. Matter's comments introduced a forum on "Gay and Lesbian Concerns in Medieval Studies" that appeared in the spring 1992 edition of the *Medieval Feminist Newsletter*. The short commentaries by Matter, Simon Gaunt, Carolyn Dinshaw, Sylvia Huot, Susan Schibanoff, and Mary Anne Campbell are all centrally concerned with the issues raised in Halperin, *One Hundred Years*, specifically as they relate to the study of medieval culture.

96. Rich, "Compulsory Heterosexuality," 648.

97. Ibid., 649, 650.

98. Wood, "Sapphonics," 27.

99. *Vita Sanctae Hildegardis* 2.2, 24; Silvas, *Jutta and Hildegard*, 160–61. Barbara Newman, in "Three-Part Invention," has recently argued that the *Vita* represents Hildegard's attempt at "autohagiography," "a form of saintly self-fashioning that, far from exalting the individual ego, deliberately subordinates it to existing biblical and hagiographic paradigms, letting these dominate consciousness so far as to shape not only the aspiring saint's recorded life, but the lived experience itself" (192).

100. "O vos angelis," in Hildegard, *Symphonia: A Critical Edition*, 156–57.

101. See Barbara Newman's notes to Hildegard, *Symphonia: A Critical Edition*, 283–84.

102. Ibid., 283.

103. Guentner, *Epistola S. Bernardi*, 36 and 55.

104. Dronke, *Women Writers*, 197.

105. Hildegard, "Epistola XXIII," in *Hildegardis Bingensis Epistolarium*, *CCCM* 91, 64; Hildegard, *Letters*, 1:79. On this letter see especially Dronke, *Women Writers*, 197.

106. Hildegard, "Epistola XXIII," in *Hildegardis Bingensis Epistolarium*, *CCCM* 91, 64; Hildegard, *Letters*, 1:78–79.

107. Hildegard, "Epistola XXIII," in *Hildegardis Bingensis Epistolarium*, *CCCM* 91, 65; Hildegard, *Letters*, 1:79.

108. Taruskin, *Text and Act*, 312–14, where he writes of Bach's "undermining of human agency" in the cantatas, as well as "assault[s] by composer on performer" (the discussion originally appeared in the Arts and Leisure section of the *New York Times*, January 27, 1991). See also the intriguing discus-

sion by Margot Fassler of Hildegard's *Ordo virtutum* as a musical realization of the "wounded body" of Christ in "Composer and Dramatist," esp. 173.

CHAPTER 4

1. Page, "Treatise on Musicians."

2. Ibid., 20.

3. Ibid., 17.

4. Ibid., 15 (ed.) and 17–18 (trans.).

5. Ibid., 17 n. See the useful discussion in Gallo, *Music of the Middle Ages*, 2:1–13.

6. It may also suggest that Arnulf's own description of *organizantes* is more a literary than a musical crux in the text; Page comments on the passage as follows: "Arnulf's angry reference to those musicians of category I who, *organizantes*, produce barbarous results, may well refer to singers who thought it an easy matter to improvise over a chant but who were ignorant of plainchant (as Arnulf reveals) and also unfamiliar with the classification of intervals; it is easy to imagine how such musicians might have violated the rules of consonance when they sang by failing to see when a cadence was possible or by failing to end a section on a perfect consonance" ("Treatise," 6).

7. For the details of Alan's life, see the documents collected in d'Alverny, *Textes inédits*, 11–29; and, more recently, the summary in Evans, *Alan of Lille*, 5–12.

8. Alan of Lille, *De planctu Naturae* 2.247–48, 818.

9. The definitive study of Alan's *Complaint* and its intellectual context is Ziolkowski, *Alan of Lille's Grammar of Sex*, which includes extensive and learned discussion of the kinds of sexual word games Alan plays throughout the work. See also Leupin, *Barbarolexis*, 59–78.

10. Alan of Lille, *De planctu Naturae* 8.55–57, 834 (emphasis mine).

11. Ibid., 806.

12. Yudkin, *De Musica Mensurata*, 224–25.

13. These problems have been sensitively discussed with regard to the early motet in Everist, *French Motets*, 3–14.

14. Loseff, *The Best Concords*, xvii.

15. See Craig Wright, *Music and Ceremony*, 237–40.

16. For a few notable exceptions see the relevant documents discussed in Craig Wright, *Music and Ceremony*.

17. Yudkin, *Music Treatise*, 39.

18. Craig Wright, "Leoninus." An abbreviated account of these findings appears in Craig Wright, *Music and Ceremony*, 281–88.

19. It should be noted that Wright's identification of Anonymous IV's "Leonin" with the poet "Magister Leoninus" has not won universal acceptance (though no one has yet attempted to refute it in detail). For two particularly pointed caveats, see Wathey's review of Wright, *Music and Ceremony*, esp. 312; and Page, *Discarding Images*, 5 n., in which Page notes caustically that "Wright's fluid hypothesis is already congealing into fact." This chapter will be an obvious attempt to further the congealment, though the reservations of Wathey, Page, and others are well founded: Wright's hypothesis rests in large part on identifying the Leonius discussed long ago in DuCange, "Leonius," as Anonymous IV's Leonin.

20. Craig Wright, "Leoninus," 23. There is an eighteenth-century St. Victor shelf-mark on the opening folio of the *Historie sacre* that reads "S. Victor 68"; this corresponds to the newer shelf-mark given by the BN to the St. Victor collection: Omont, *Concordances des numéros anciens et des numéros actuels des Manuscrits Latins de la Bibliothèque Nationale*, 100. Latin 14759 may have originated at St. Victor as well; based on a careful comparison of its blue, red, green, and gold filigreed initials with those cataloged in Patricia Stirnemann's useful study "Fils de la vierge," it appears to have been produced around 1200 at St. Victor (the closest match to my unpracticed eye is Stirnemann's Cat. 14, p. 62).

21. On the "open secret," see D. A. Miller, *Novel and the Police*, esp. 206.

22. Though the particular language Leoninus uses in describing his relationship with his *sodalis* is highly suggestive. For example, his pointed use of the substantive *obsequus* to denote his own role in the relationship resonates with a number of classical texts in which the term implies the sexual submissiveness of a wife in relation to her husband; see Adams, *Latin Sexual Vocabulary*, 164.

23. Craig Wright, "Leoninus," 27.

24. Ovid, *Heroides and Amores* 2.15, 426–27 (hereafter cited in text).

25. Cited in Adams, *Latin Sexual Vocabulary*, 209.

26. See Adams, *Latin Sexual Vocabulary*, 114–15.

27. Magister Leoninus, "De anulo dato ab henrico cardinali," lines 1–8, transcribed from Paris, Bibliothèque Nationale, MS Latin 14759, fol. 1149v–150r. David Townsend of the University of Toronto and I have published a collaborative edition of Leoninus's two Ovidian poems as "The Verse-Epistles of Master Leoninus"; the excerpts and line numberings given in this chapter follow our edition and an in-progress translation. Ernest Sanders has proposed that the ring given to Leoninus may have been "a reward or token of appreciation for his Magnus liber organi"; see Sanders, "Earliest Phases," 57 n. 51.

28. Hexter, *Ovid in Medieval Schooling.*

29. A useful summary can be found in Baldwin, *Language of Sex*, 20–21.

30. See in particular Chance, *Medieval Mythography.*

31. See Haskins, *Medieval Science*, 372; and Baldwin, *Language of Sex*, 22.

32. See especially Hexter, "Ovid's Body," and Baldwin, *Language of Sex*, 97–99. Also important is Bowden, "Art of Courtly Copulation," though her claims with regard to Andreas Capellanus may be somewhat exaggerated (see Monson, "Andreas Capellanus and the Problem of Irony").

33. Cited in Minnis and Scott, *Medieval Literary Theory and Criticism*, 27. For a useful survey of medieval attitudes toward the *Amores* in particular, see Stapleton, *Harmful Eloquence*, esp. 39–89. It is clear that Leoninus did not know *Amores* 2.15 in the fragmentary form in which other excerpts from the *Amores* are presented in the *Anthologia Latina*, for the poem is not listed among those culled by the anthology's compilers; see the list of citations compiled by Stapleton from Buecheler and Riese, *Carmina Latina Epigrapha: Anthologia Latina*, in *Harmful Eloquence*, 52 n. 43.

34. Leoninus, "Ad amicum venturum ad festum baculi," lines 14–15; transcribed from Paris, BN Lat. 14759, fols. 150r–151v.

35. Jaeger, *Ennobling Love*, 7.

36. Hexter, "Ovid's Body," 340.

37. On Walter's poetic contributions to the *Magnus liber*, see Robert Falck's article in *NG* 20, 190.

38. Transcribed by Crocker in his edition of Walter of Chatillôn, *Alexandreis*, xvi.

39. David Townsend's introduction to Walter of Chatillon, *Alexandreis*, xiii.

40. Boswell, *Christianity*, 243–66.

41. For Boswell's response to his critics, see his "Revolutions, Universals, and Sexual Categories."

42. See, among many others, Dinshaw, *Getting Medieval*; Halperin, *One Hundred Years*; Goldberg, *Sodometries*; Goldberg, *Queering the Renaissance*; and Traub, *Desire and Anxiety.*

43. The phrase "embodied erotic subject" is Hexter's (see "Ovid's Body," 344); I have used the notion of the "homoerotic subject" in Holsinger, "Sodomy and Resurrection."

44. Sedgwick, *Epistemology of the Closet.*

45. Boswell, *Christianity*, 269–332.

46. On sodomy and the Third Lateran Council, see in particular Greenberg, *Construction of Homosexuality*, 271 and 286; Goodich, *Unmentionable Vice*, 43–45; and Boswell, *Christianity*, 277–78.

47. On Peter the Chanter's writings on sexuality, see Boswell, *Christianity*, esp. 375–78, and Baldwin, *Masters*, 1:337–39.

48. Baldwin, *Language of Sex*, 44. Leoninus's poems are clearly part of the tradition of neoclassical poetics discussed by Peter Dronke in a section titled "Love, Praise, and Friendship" in *Medieval Latin and the Rise of European Love-Lyric*, 1:192–220; Dronke's words on the amorous hexameters of Marbod of Rennes may apply equally well to those of Leoninus: "They stylize genuine relationships, in which poetic licence (and poetic *auctoritas*) allowed a range of expressions which actual circumstances did not" (214).

49. Cited in Boswell, *Christianity*, 377.

50. Walter of Chatillôn, "Stulti cum prudentibus currunt ad coronam," stanzas 27–28, in Stehling, *Medieval Latin Poems*, 81.

51. Baldwin, *Language of Sex*, 311 n.

52. Little, *Religious Poverty*, 34.

53. This is not an uncontroversial choice on Roesner's part: "The *magnus liber* is generally regarded by present-day scholars as consisting of *organum duplum* and clausulae. However, it seems likely both from the testimony of Anonymous IV . . . and the surviving manuscript sources that the *liber* was not limited to a single genre of composition, organum or anything else, or to works for a certain number of voices, but rather included compositions in all genres cultivated by the musicians of Paris—organum, conductus, and the motet . . . Leoninus may have been known for the subtlety of *organum* [*purum*] and Perotinus for discantus, according to Anonymous IV, but there is no evidence to suggest that either wrote in only one idiom"; see the introduction to Roesner, *Les Quadrupla*, lix. Based on solid codicological and historical evidence, Roesner's concise and ground-clearing account of the original state of the *Magnus liber* sources allows us to consider the texts of the monophonic conductus discussed below as integral to the cultural work performed by the repertory: "in the Florence manuscript, the three-voice motets, a group of clausulae intended for use within the organum repertory appearing earlier in the volume, are separated from the organa by two large fascicles of conductus" (lx).

54. "Qui seminant in loculis," lines 1–2 (from F, fol. 424v), in Anderson, *Notre-Dame and Related Conductus*, 6:38. The pun was commonplace in classical verse; see Adams, "*Culus, clunes.*"

55. The added strophe appears in Oxford, Bodleian Library, Add. 86, fol. 128v; see the notes in Anderson, *Notre-Dame and Related Conductus*, 6:130.

56. Walter of Chatillôn, "Stulti cum prudentibus currunt ad coronam," in Stehling, *Medieval Latin Poems*, 80–81. Another provocative allusion to Juvenal in the *Magnus liber* conductus appears in line 4 of Philip the Chancel-

lor's "Aristippe quamvis sero" (F 10, fol. 416r, Anderson, *Notre-Dame and Related Conductus*, 6:v): "Quid Roma faciam" slightly alters the given title of the third *Satire*, "Quid Rome faciam."

57. "Non habes auditum," (F 7, fol. 353r), Anderson, *Notre-Dame and Related Conductus*, 4:xxiii.

58. See Baldwin, *Masters*, 1:19 and 25.

59. Page, *Owl and Nightingale*, 147.

60. Cited and translated in Page, *Owl and Nightingale*, 145–46.

61. Ibid.

62. Prynne, *Histrio-Mastix* [Short Title Catalogue no. 20464a]. They appear as well among a number of other passages in a short, late-fourteenth-century florilegium on music found on the final folios of Oxford, Bodleian Library MS Bodley 240, a miscellany compiled at Bury St. Edmunds.

63. John of Salisbury, *Policraticus* 1.6, *CCCM* 118, 48–49; Dalglish, "Origins of the Hocket," 7.

64. Knapp, "Polyphony at Notre Dame," 558. John's discomfort with the musical counterpoint of polyphony may reflect as well his more general anxiety about excess and opposition, a characteristic of his thinking that has been brilliantly discussed in a recent study by Catherine Brown, *Contrary Things*: "When moderation does not contemper human reading and teaching, then they fall precipitously into contraries, and opposition . . . becomes an obstacle on the road of understanding. John of Salisbury tries to remove those obstacles, to correct and re-adequate dialectical teaching and reading in an intellectual world characterized by excess and contradiction" (43).

65. John of Salisbury, *Policraticus* 1.6, *CCCM* 118, 50; John of Salisbury, *Frivolities of Courtiers*, 33.

66. Alan of Lille, *De planctu Naturae* 8.54–58, 834. On this passage see Calabrese, " 'Make a Mark That Shows.' "

67. Aelred of Rievaulx, *De Speculum Caritatis* 2.23.67, *CCCM* 1, 98.

68. Fuller, "Early Polyphony," 553.

69. Loseff, *Best Concords*, 7.

70. "Mailänder Traktat," lines 1–9, in *Ad organum faciendum*, ed. Eggebrecht and Zaminer, 111; trans. Huff, 48.

71. Ibid., lines 83–87, 113; trans. Huff, 54.

72. Ibid., lines 109–12, 114; trans. Huff, 56.

73. Ibid., lines 137–42, 115; trans. Huff, 58.

74. We should not assume that the organum described in these treatises and that of the Notre Dame school represent entirely distinct traditions: the excerpt from *Ad organum faciendum* included in the so-called Bruges Organum Treatise exists in the margins of the Garlandian mensural treatise,

"Habito de ipsa plana musica." See *Ad Organum Faciendum*, ed. Eggebrecht and Zaminer, 33–37; and Pinegar, "Exploring the Margins," esp. 216–18.

75. See *Ad organum faciendum*, trans. Huff, 46: "The organum excluded from nature is that to which neither one of the aforesaid immediates happens to be present; it is like a copy of a real animal and like a dead man, to which neither health nor sickness happens to be present under *animal*. Therefore, such organum is not organum. . . . Therefore, it is not organum except by resemblance, in the same way that *man*, as a picture and as a cadaver, is a copy of a real animal."

76. See Reckow, *Die Copula*; Yudkin, "Anonymous of St. Emmeram"; and idem, "*Copula*"; and van Deusen, *Theology and Music*, 40, 60, 64, 106, 137, and 169. A helpful summary of the scholarship on the thirteenth-century treatises' definitions of the term is provided by Knapp, "Polyphony at Notre Dame," 577–79.

77. Alan of Lille, "Exceptivam actionem," in Gordon Anderson, *Notre-Dame and Related Conductus*, 6:xci.

78. The poem thus exemplifies the various medieval conflations of rhetorical, grammatical, and musical vocabularies discussed in Gallo, *Music of the Middle Ages*, 2:1–13, where it is suggested that even Anonymous IV's discussion of the compilation of the *Magnus liber organi* is fundamentally informed by rhetorical and grammatical convention: "one can parallel the *multiplicatio* to which Anonymous IV refers with *amplificatio*, which in contemporary treatises on rhetoric and poetics indicated the combined processes of extension and embellishment in a literary text" (16).

79. Alan of Lille, *De planctu Naturae* 1.15–22, 806.

80. Southern, *Medieval Humanism*, 37.

81. Jordan, *Invention of Sodomy*, 86.

82. "A Debate between Ganymede and Helen," lines 137–44, in Stehling, *Medieval Latin Poems*, 112–13.

83. Gautier de Coincy, "Seinte Léocade," cited in Ziolkowski, *Alan of Lille's Grammar of Sex*, 35–36.

84. Cited in Ziolkowski, *Grammar of Sex*, 73–74.

85. Roesner, "Performance of Parisian Organum," 188.

86. Ibid., 174.

87. Berger, "Mnemotechnics."

88. Craig Wright, *Music and Ceremony*, 334. On the question of lost Notre Dame sources, see Baltzer, "Notre Dame Manuscripts."

89. Berger, "Mnemotechnics," 295.

90. Ibid., 297.

91. Carruthers, *Book of Memory*, esp. 131–38.

92. Elias Salomonis, *Scientia artis musicae*, cited and translated from Gerbert's *Scriptores* in McGee, *Sound of Medieval Song*, 166 and 26. I have slightly altered McGee's translation. Though uncited by Berger in "Mnemotechnics," the passage is remarkably supportive of her argument.

93. On Gilles, see Baldwin, *Masters*, 1:18, 41; Baldwin, *Language of Sex*, 10–11, 45–46; and Vieillard, *Gilles de Corbeil*.

94. See the passages edited in Vieillard, *Gilles de Corbeil*, 338–41.

95. Gilles de Corbeil, *Hierapigra ad purgandos prelatos*, ed. Vieillard, *Gilles de Corbeil*, 362.

96. McAlpine, "The Pardoner's Homosexuality."

97. Walter of Chatillôn, "Stulti cum prudentibus currunt ad coronam," stanzas 27–28, in Stehling, *Medieval Latin Poems*, 81.

98. See Chaucer, *Riverside Chaucer*, 824.

99. Dinshaw, *Chaucer's Sexual Poetics*, 153.

100. Pearsall, "Chaucer's Pardoner," 359.

101. As demonstrated by the "copious reports of flamboyant and unorthodox singing in church" cataloged by Dalglish in "Origins of the Hocket," 4–10, which led me to several of the examples discussed below. For Dalglish, such passages serve as evidence of the improvisatory character of many genres of later medieval polyphony; almost without exception, however, they simultaneously condemn deviant singing as "effeminate."

102. Bacon, *Fratri Rogeri Bacon opera quaedam hactenus inedita*, 297–98; cited and translated in Dalglish, "Origins of the Hocket," 9.

103. Enders, "Delivering Delivery"; see also Copeland, "Pardoner's Body," and the discussion of the predicatory Orpheus in Chapter 7 of this volume.

104. The full text can be found in *CS* 1:394.

105. See the text in Friedberg, *Corpus juris canonici*, 1:1256–57; cited in Dalglish, "Origins of the Hocket," 10.

106. Huot, *Allegorical Play*.

107. Bowers, "Queering the Summoner."

108. Burger, "Kissing the Pardoner," 1152. I borrow the term *universalizing* from Sedgwick, *Epistemology of the Closet*, 1, which describes "the contradiction between seeing homo/heterosexual definition on the one hand as an issue of active importance primarily for a small, distinct, relatively fixed homosexual minority (what I refer to as a minoritizing view), and seeing it on the other hand as an issue of continuing, determinative importance in the lives of people across the spectrum of sexualities (what I refer to as a universalizing view)."

109. Wallace, *Chaucerian Polity*, 80.

110. Compare Dinshaw's reading of the portrait in "Chaucer's Queer Touches," 80: "it's unclear to the narrator, just by looking at [the Pardoner], what he is; he doesn't fit into the 'felaweshipe' (I.32) of pilgrims gathered for the journey to Canterbury."

111. Rowland, "Chaucer's Idea," 143.

112. See Dieckmann, "Meaning of 'Burdoun,' " for a philological discussion of the term.

113. Correale, "Chaucer's Parody."

114. On music in the Miller's Tale, see especially Gellrich, "Parody of Medieval Music," and now Zieman, "Chaucer's *Voys*."

115. See Chaucer, *Canterbury Tales: A Facsimile and Transcription*, 212–13. As Manly and Rickert point out, "complyn" is a later fifteenth-century variant inserted by scribes "who independently sought for a better meaning than was suggested by the ancestral reading 'couplyng' " (Chaucer, *Text of the Canterbury Tales*, 3:445; for the list of variants, see 5:413). The emendation continues to prove useful, however; an otherwise rigorous article by M. Teresa Tavormina arguing that the Reeve's Tale contains a specific topical reference to a contemporaneous musician named "John Aleyn" bears the unfortunate title " 'Lo, Swilk a Complyn': Musical Topicality in the Miller's and Reeve's Tales."

116. Dinshaw, *Getting Medieval*, 136.

117. "Cleanness," line 690, in Malcolm and Waldron, *Poems of the Pearl Manuscript*, 140.

CHAPTER 5

1. Dickinson, *Complete Poems*, 412.

2. On violence in sacrificial discourses of religion, see Girard, *Violence and the Sacred*.

3. Scarry, *Body in Pain*, 3.

4. Ibid., 14.   5. Ibid., 5.

6. Ibid., 6.   7. Ibid., 4.

8. Ibid., 45.   9. Ibid., 7.

10. See Chapter 1 of this volume, 58–60.

11. See Kiefer, "Lithotomy Set to Music."

12. Scarry, *Body in Pain*, 8.

13. Henderson, "Flagellant Movement," 148. See also Russell, "Peter Damian's Whip."

14. "Epistola XLIV," in *Die Briefe des Petrus Damiani*, 2:21–22.

15. Ibid. Compare Peter's *Vita Sancti Rodulphi et S. Dominici Loricati*, chapter 11, *PL* 144, cols. 1019–21.

16. "Epistola LVI," in *Die Briefe des Petrus Damiani*, 2:157. On flagellation more generally, see the classic study by Gougaud, *Devotional and Ascetic Practices*, 179–204.

17. Ancelet-Hustache, ed., "Les 'Vitae Sororum,' " 340; cited in Bynum, *Holy Feast*, 210 (translation mine). These "sister books," all of them compiled by Dominican nuns in the thirteenth and fourteenth centuries, provide an enormously rich and virtually unmined source for examining the musical practices of late medieval women in German-speaking regions. Lewis's *By Women, for Women, about Women: The Sister-Books of Fourteenth-Century Germany* is the first full-length study of this minigenre in any language; for just a few enticing examples of these women's musical practices, see especially pages 77–80. The sister books, along with texts such as Gertrude of Helfta's *Legatus* and Mechthild of Hackeborn's *Liber* (see below), may provide the basis for more of the kind of exemplary musicological work done by Yardley in her pathbreaking article " '*Ful weel she soong the service dyvyne*': The Cloistered Musician in the Middle Ages."

18. Cited in Hübner, *Die deutschen Geisslerlieder*, 69: "habebant etiam cantum specialem, quem flagellando cantabant."

19. See the extraordinary description from a monastic writer in Padua that opens the historical account in Hübner, *Die deutschen Geisslerlieder*, 9.

20. Map, *De nugis curialium* 5.1, 406–7: "Vsula piscis est Danubii qui per tela hostium musice petit mela, nec uulneratus absistit, sed uite prodigus et auarus organi sectatur anime sue mellitas illecebras usque ad mortem. Hec est nobilis et studiosi uiri triumphalis instancia, quem a studio non deterrent tussis aut tisis aut alie qualescunque inequalitates. Angustiato corpori sollicitudine martirium asciscit. . . . Sic esto usula."

21. Hamburger, "Visual and Visionary," 174.

22. See the brilliant discussion of the term in Brett, "Musicality."

23. For an introduction to this concept, see Page, "Musicus and Cantor."

24. Page, *Owl and Nightingale*.

25. Fassler, *Gothic Song*, 14.

26. Monson, *Disembodied Voices*, especially the fascinating interpretation of one of Lucrezia Vizzana's Jesus motets as a musical reenactment of the Eucharist (97–99).

27. *Book to a Mother*, ch. 4, 31.

28. Ibid., ch. 3, 27.

29. Ibid., ch. 3b, 28.

30. See the essays collected in Frese and O'Keeffe, *Book and the Body*; Dinshaw, *Chaucer's Sexual Poetics*; and Lochrie, *Margery Kempe*.

31. Hamburger, "Visual and Visionary," 172.

32. For a discussion of music and empathy in the Western tradition that is highly relevant to the concerns of this chapter, see Morrison, *"I am You,"* 198–203 (on Gerhoch of Reichersburg and psalmody).

33. On the tradition of the Cross as harp, see the useful discussions in Pickering, *Literature and Art*, 285–307; idem, *Essays*; and Marrow, *Passion Iconography*, 123–26, 164–67, and notes.

34. Cassiodorus, *Expositio psalmorum* 56.9, *CCSL* 97, 511.

35. Maurer, *Die Erlösung*, lines 5618–23, 5633–56, 237–38; the passage is discussed by Pickering in his wonderful essay "Das Gothische Christusbild," which has been reprinted in several different forms, including Pickering, *Literature and Art*, 285–307; *Die Erlösung* is discussed and the passage above translated on 294–95. See also Pickering's wry comment on the related work of Leo Spitzer: "The absence of any real guidance in Migne may explain why in a recent study with the promising title 'Classical and Christian Ideas of World Harmony' there is, so far as I can see, no reference to Christ's Crucifixion as the Christian God's music-making, whereby a central idea of world harmony is completely missed" (293).

36. Dominican authorship has been suggested by, most recently, Wilson and Wilson, *Medieval Mirror*, 27; for the Franciscan view, see Thomas, "Zur kulturgeschichtlichen Einordnung," 192–223.

37. Breitenbach, *Speculum humanae salvationis*, 5–43.

38. Marrow, *Passion Iconography*, and Pickering, *Literature and Art*, both list a number of typological examples that loosely parallel this association, though neither posits a direct precedent for the Jubal/Christ typology specifically.

39. *Speculum humanae salvationis*, ch. 23, lines 33–42, ed. Lutz and Perdrizet, 1:48.

40. See the studies by Cardon, *Manuscripts of the Speculum humanae salvationis*; and Niesner, *Das Speculum humanae salvationis*.

41. For the dates of the manuscripts discussed in the succeeding paragraphs, I have relied on the hand-list of Latin manuscripts in Lutz and Perdrizet, *Speculum humanae salvationis*, 1:ix–xvii, rather than on the less careful estimates in individual library catalogs.

42. Compare London, British Library MS Additional 32245, fol. 41v (fifteenth century).

43. See the intriguing explanation for this particular interpolation in Pickering, *Literature and Art*, 272–73.

44. Chenu, *Nature, Man, and Society*.

45. Bestul, *Texts of the Passion*, especially chapter 2, "Medieval Narratives of the Passion of Christ," 26–68; and "The Ideal of the Imitation of Christ," in Constable, *Three Studies*, 143–248, especially 218 ff.

46. Cohen, "Towards a History of European Physical Sensibility," 47.

47. Colish, "*Psalterium Scholasticorum*," 532.

48. Ibid.

49. Introduction to Froehlich and Gibson, *Glossa Ordinaria*, 1:vii.

50. See, respectively, McKinnon, "Church Fathers and Musical Instruments," 261; and Pickering, *Literature and Art*, 294.

51. Colish, *Peter Lombard*, esp. 1:170–88 (on the *Commentarium*).

52. Aers, *Piers Plowman*, 7.

53. A similar argument has been made with regard to the Lombard's prologue in Stillinger, *Song of Troilus*, chapter 1, "*Sacra pagina*," 23–43: "I take the manuscript page of Peter Lombard's Psalm commentary as a powerful emblem of stable textual hierarchy; the sequence that transforms this hierarchy by repeatedly substituting commentary for text is an emblem—a kind of narrative synechdoche—of the gradual establishment of *auctoritas* for the living writer" (38).

54. See especially Hirsch-Reich, "The Symbolism of Musical Instruments in the *Psalterium X Chordarum* of Joachim of Fiore and Its Patristic Sources."

55. Reeves and Hirsch-Reich, Figurae *of Joachim of Fiore*, 204. In its musical allegoresis of the harp strings as the virtues, Joachim's *Psalterium* represents the most compelling possible source I have seen for the harp allegory in the *Ovide moralisé*, discussed in Chapter 7 of this volume, pp. 316–19. On Joachim's technical knowledge of the trapezoidal psaltery with central soundhole see Page, *Voices and Instruments*, 147.

56. For a description of the manuscript see Butz, *Die Romanischen Handschriften*, 59–61.

57. Lombard, *Commentarium*, col. 59.

58. On the tradition of Mary and Martha in the Middle Ages, see Constable, *Three Studies*, 3–141.

59. Rosemary Muir Wright, "Sound in Pictured Silence"; Wright's study is concerned primarily with the aurality of depicted words, but her comments bear on visual representation of musical imagery as well: "The words of the text must have hung in the air like sound waves around the design formula of the models or prototypes available to the artists who illustrated the sense of the words spoken, as distinct from their literal transposition" (251).

60. Lombard, *Commentarium*, col. 327.

61. Carruthers, *Book of Memory*, 256.

62. A typical example is Rhabanus Maurus, *Allegoriae*, col. 1067; see Richenhagen's chapter on this treatise's wide-ranging allegories of Old Testament musical instruments in *Studien zur Musikanschauung*, 147–295.

63. Marguerite d'Oingt, *Pagina meditationum*, paragraph 91, ed. Duraffour, Gardette, and Durdilly, 85: "cortine quibus erunt involuti erunt demones horribiles qui erunt circa eos ad tormentandum eos quamdiu Deus durabit, hoc est sine fine. Cibus quem comedent erunt ploratus, dolor et gemitus et stridor dentium. Tympana et vielle quas audient erunt tempestas tumultuans et flumina penetrancia que penetrabunt eos usque ad cor"; Marguerite d'Oingt, *Writings*, 38.

64. Dante, *Inferno* 30, lines 49–57, 318–19. On this scene, see Heilbronn, "Master Adam"; and, more generally, Sanguineti, "Infernal Acoustics."

65. The image is also reproduced in Rotili, *I Codici Danteschi Miniati a Napoli*, plate 23.

66. Dante, *Inferno*, 30.70.

67. Needham, "Percussion and Transition," 606.

68. Jacques de Vitry, "Vita Mariae Oigniacensis," 569; Jacques de Vitry, *Life of Marie d'Oignies*, III. For another take on this passage, see the essay on "bodily movement" in the lives and writings of the beguines by Simons, "Reading a Saint's Body," 16.

69. Jacques de Vitry, "Vita Mariae Oigniacensis," 569; Jacques de Vitry, *Life of Marie d'Oignies*, III.

70. Jacques de Vitry, "Vita Mariae Oigniacensis," 569; Jacques de Vitry, *Life of Marie d'Oignies*, 113.

71. See Chapter I of this volume.

72. Honorius Augustodunensis, *Expositio in Psalmos*, cols. 306–7.

73. Jacques de Vitry, "Vita Mariae Oigniacensis," 571; Jacques de Vitry, *Life of Marie d'Oignies*, 120.

74. Jacques de Vitry, "Vita Mariae Oigniacensis," 572: "Cum autem a morte lavaretur ejus sacrum corpusculum, inventa est ita attenuata et infirmitate jejuniisque confecta, quod dorsi ejus spina ventri ejus contingua erat; et quasi sub tenui panno lineo, sub ventris ejus pellicula ossa dorsi ejus apparebant"; Jacques de Vitry, *Life of Marie d'Oignies*, 121.

75. On the education of Jacques de Vitry and its general influence on his hagiographical writings, see McDonnell, *Beguines and Beghards*, 20–39.

76. See Surtz, *Guitar of God*, esp. chapter 3, 63–85.

77. For a sketch of Thomas's life and works see Friedman's introductory comments in "Thomas of Cantimpré *De Naturis Rerum*," 107–16.

78. For an intriguing consideration of the relationship between Jacques and Thomas as it can be interpreted through the latter's version of Marie's *vita*, see Petroff, *Body and Soul*, 147–51.

79. On the *Liber* in the medieval encyclopedic tradition, see Vollmann, "La vitalità delle enciclopedie."

80. Several musical episodes from this work are discussed in Page, *Owl and Nightingale*, 112–13 and 165–66.

81. Thomas of Cantimpré, "Vita Lutgardis," 194; trans. King, 26. The passage has been discussed in a different context in Hamburger, "Visual and Visionary," 168–69; Hamburger compares it to a miniature in a French manuscript of Joinville's *Credo* (1270).

82. See especially the notes to Thomas of Cantimpré, *Life of Christina Mirabilis*, 42–44.

83. Chenu, *Nature*, 5.

84. McGinn, *Three Treatises*, 40.

85. William knew Gregory's treatise through John the Scot's ninth-century translation rather than the more influential sixth-century translation by Denis the Little; see the extensive notes to Lemoine's edition cited below; on Gregory's musical imagery, see Chapter 1 of this volume, 46–53.

86. William of St. Thierry, *De natura*, book 2, ch. 1, 129–31; McGinn, *Three Treatises*, 125.

87. William of St. Thierry, *De natura*, 2.65, 147–49; McGinn, *Three Treatises*, 130.

88. William of St. Thierry, *De natura*, 2.68, 151; McGinn, *Three Treatises*, 131.

89. Though William's treatise is not listed among the sources for the *Liber* by Friedman, "Thomas de Cantimpré," 108–9.

90. Thomas of Cantimpré, *Liber de natura rerum*. On the *Liber*, see Michaud-Quantin, "Les Petites encyclopédies"; Walstra, "Thomas de Cantimpré"; Boese, "Zur Textüberlieferung"; and Bynum, *Fragmentation and Redemption*, 388–89 nn. 130–31.

91. Thomas of Cantimpré, *Liber de natura rerum* 2.11, 91.

92. Ibid.

93. Ibid.

94. Useful studies of the *Bonum universale de apibus* include Platelle, "Le Recueil des miracles"; Murray, "Confession as a Historical Source"; and especially the provocative discussion in Bandera, "From Mythical Bees."

95. See, for example, Rhabanus Maurus, *Allegoriae*, col. 1069.

96. Thomas of Cantimpré, *Bonum universale*, 2.41, 333.

97. Thomas of Cantimpré, *Bonum universale*, 2.40, 331–32.

98. Thomas of Cantimpré, *Bonum universale*, 2.50, 382–83.

99. Not all the connections Thomas draws in *De apibus* between music and body are connected to miraculous devotion. In book 2, ch. 49, he polemicizes against histrionics and gesticulatory singing in language very similar to Aelred of Rievaulx's and John of Salisbury's (see the discussion in Chapter 4 of this volume): "Istis merito coniuuguntur cum suis gesticulationibus et verbis turpissimis, ac scurrilibus histriones. Talibus dare, ut ait Augustinus, est daemonibus sacrificare" (375).

100. Thomas of Cantimpré, "Vita Christinae Mirabilis," ch. 35; Thomas of Cantimpré, *Life of Christina Mirabilis*, 29.

101. Thomas of Cantimpré, "Vita Christinae Mirabilis," ch. 39; Thomas of Cantimpré, *Life of Christina Mirabilis*, 31.

102. Thomas of Cantimpré, "Vita Christinae Mirabilis," ch. 49; Thomas of Cantimpré, *Life of Christina Mirabilis*, 36.

103. The most recent biography is Douie, *Archbishop Pecham*.

104. Pecham, "Philomena praevia," Line citations hereafter will be within text. On this poem see, most recently, Bestul, *Texts of the Passion*, 63.

105. For the French translation, see *Rossignol*; for the Middle English, see Lydgate, *Lydgate's Minor Poems*; Pearsall, *John Lydgate*, doubts the attribution of the translation to Lydgate on the basis of Lydgate's other poem of the same theme, which represents a freer adaptation of Pecham's Latin.

106. See Raby, "Philomena praevia temporis amoeni"; Pfeffer, *Change of Philomel*, 39–41; and *Rossignol*, 1–53.

107. Pliny, *Natural History*, 3:345.

108. *Hexaemeron* 5.24; cited in Pfeffer, *Change of Philomel*, 20.

109. *Ecbasis cuiusdam captivi per tropologiam*, lines 838–43, ed. and trans. Zeydel, 70–71.

110. Gregory, *Moralia in Iob*, 41.78; *CCSL* 143A, 1061.

111. Ziolkowski, *Cambridge Songs*, no. 10, 46–47.

112. Marie de France, *The Lais of Marie de France*, 158–59.

113. Cited by Baird and Kane in the introduction to *Rossignol*, 17.

114. *Rossignol*, 63.

115. For a recent treatment of *imitatio Christi* in thirteenth-century Franciscan spirituality, see Constable, *Three Studies*, 218–21, 234–37.

116. The clear Ovidian resonances of "Philomena praevia" have been missed even by the usually scrupulous F. J. E. Raby, "Philomena praevia temporis amoeni."

117. Ovid, *Metamorphoses* 5.555–60, 326–27.

118. Ovid, *Metamorphoses* 6.574–78, 328–29.

119. See Bynum, *Jesus as Mother*, 110–69; and "The Body of Christ in the

Later Middle Ages: A Reply to Leo Steinberg," in Bynum, *Fragmentation and Redemption*, 93–117.

120. Much like the seventeenth-century English religious lyrics treated by Richard Rambuss, "a form of love poetry written by men that revels in its desire for the male body—the naked body of Jesus, 'that beauteous form,' rendered by turns penetrable and penetrating, ravished and ravishing." See "Pleasure and Devotion," 274.

121. Fassler, *Gothic Song*, 19.

122. Honorius Augustodunensis, *Gemma animae*, ch. 84, col. 570–71.

123. Cited and translated in Page, *Voices and Instruments*, 205–6.

124. *Speculum ecclesiae*, ch. 3, col. 343.

125. Honorius Augustodunensis, *Gemma animae*, ch. 83, col. 570.

126. *Speculum ecclesiae*, ch. 3, col. 340.

127. Ibid., col. 343.

128. Ibid., col. 344.

129. See *Meditations on the Life of Christ*, 320–45.

130. For a description of the manuscript's contents see Ginhart, *Die Kunstdenkmäler*, 400.

131. On Pecham's involvement in these controversies, see Moorman, *History of the Franciscan Order*, 128–31. See also Etzkorn, "John Pecham, OFM," 71–82.

132. See Simmons and Nolloth's introduction to *The Lay Folks' Catechism*, ix–xii.

133. See especially Landini, *Causes of the Clericalization*.

134. On Haymo, see Landini, *Causes of the Clericalization*, 85–93.

135. Ibid., 137.

136. D'Avray, *Preaching of the Friars*, 47 and 56.

137. See Standaert, "Helfta," and the account in Finnegan, *Women of Helfta*, 3–4, 16.

138. The bibliography on the nuns of Helfta is large and growing; see "Women Mystics in the Thirteenth Century: The Case of the Nuns of Helfta," in Bynum, *Jesus as Mother*, 170–262 and notes; and, more recently, Finnegan, *Women of Helfta*, and Spitzlei, *Erfahrungsraum Herz*.

139. Gertrude, *Legatus*, book 3, ch. 48, 3:214: "Cum conventus timeret a facie inimicorum qui dicebantur fortiter armati prope coenobium adventuri, et pro tali necessitate in communi persolveretur Psalterium distinctum cum versu: *O lux beatissima*, et antiphona: *Veni Sancti Spiritus*. . . . Cumque sic compungerentur, vidit de cordibus singularum taliter per spiritum compunctarum quasi vaporem quemdam efflare, qui claustrum et vicinia circumdans, procul ab eis pellebat omnes adversarios: et secundum quod cujuslibet

cor erat magis compunctum et ad bonam voluntatem acclinatum, eo efficacior vapor ex illo efflans omnem contrariam potestatem remotius propellebat"; Gertrude, *Herald of Divine Love*, 216.

140. For the purposes of this chapter I have deliberately chosen not to treat Mechtild of Magdeburg, the oldest of the three nuns whose visions have survived. Though music features prominently in this Mechtild's visions as well, it is not tied to the liturgy as it is in the *Legatus* and the *Liber specialis gratiae* (for obvious reasons, perhaps, given Mechtild of Magdeburg's background as an uncloistered beguine).

141. Mechtild, *Liber*, book 7, ch. 11, 405; the full passage reads as follows: "Tunc deliciis affluens Dominus majestatis, solus satians satietas animae se amantis. Sponsam suam lumine divinitatis circumfulgens, totam et per illustrans, ipse cantor cantorum omnium, suavissima voce omnemque humanam capacitatem supergredienti melodia, Philomenae suae, quae toties ei dulciter cantando, multo magis devota intentione quam sonoritate vocis." On the nuns' musicality more generally, see the passages cited in Finnegan, *Women of Helfta*; Preger, *Geschichte der deutschen Mystik im Mittelalter*, vol. 1, 83–86; and Schroeder-Sheker, "Alchemical Harp."

142. Certeau, *Practice of Everyday Life*, 169.

143. See I. H. Dalmais's comments on time in the liturgy in Martimort, *Church at Prayer*, 1:1.

144. For a recent example that explicitly advocates a structuralist approach to the study of liturgy, see Fagerberg, *What Is Liturgical Theology?*

145. Vagaggini, *Theological Dimensions*, 802.

146. Spitzlei, *Erfahrungsraum Herz*, 77. See also Santiso, "Saint Gertrude and the Liturgy."

147. Following Jeffrey Hamburger, we might more accurately term Mechtild and Gertrude "paraliturgical" visionaries—that is, visionaries whose texts exist in a side-by-side but never entirely comfortable relationship with the liturgy; see Hamburger, *Nuns as Artists*, 135. Again, Hamburger's comments on visuality are particularly germane to the present discussion; like the musical examples, "the [visual] imagery in Mechthild's *Liber* functions less as a record than as an instrument of devotion" (134).

148. Mechtild, *Liber*, 1.1, 8–9.

149. See Bynum, *Jesus as Mother*, 184: "the mystical union these women achieved . . . enabled them to serve as counselors, mediators, and channels to the sacraments—roles which the thirteenth-century church in some ways increasingly denied to women and to laity."

150. Honorius Augustodunensis, *Gemma animae*, ch. 85, col. 572.

151. Mechtild, *Liber specialis gratiae*, 1.5, 19.

152. Gertrude, *Legatus*, 1.16, 2:211–12; Gertrude, *Herald of Divine Love*, 84.

153. Gertrude, *Legatus*, 3.50, 3:220–23: "Auditus etiam meus divinus quasi quibusdam suavissimis musicis instrumentis afficitur in omnibus et ex omnibus verbis oris tui, quibus mihi blandiris, sive pro peccatoribus, sive pro animabus purgandis orando, sive aliquos corripiendo, aut instruendo, aut qualicumque modo ad laudem meam verbum aliquod proferendo. . . . Spes quoque tua, qua jugiter ad me anhelas, aspirat olfactui meo suavissimi odoris delectamentum. Omnes quoque gemitus et desideria tua dulciter sapiunt mihi super omnia scilicet aromata. Amor quoque tuus praestat mihi delectamentum suavissimi amplexus"; Gertrude, *Herald of Divine Love*, 218.

154. Gertrude, *Legatus*, 2.4, 2:246; Gertrude, *Herald of Divine Love*, 101.

155. Gertrude, *Legatus*, 4.27, 4:264–66; Gertrude, *Herald of Divine Love*, 396–97.

156. Finnegan, *Women of Helfta*, 5.

157. Gertrude, *Legatus*, 3.51, 3:224; Gertrude, *Herald of Divine Love*, 219.

158. Mechtild of Hackeborn, *Liber specialis gratiae*, 1.5, 19; on these passages, see Bynum, *Jesus as Mother*, 214.

159. See Siraisi, "Music of Pulse."

160. Mechtild of Hackeborn, *Liber specialis gratiae*, 6.9, 389. On Mechtild and the Sacred Heart more generally, see Caron, "Invitations to the Divine Heart."

161. Gertrude, *Legatus*, 3.26, 3:126; Gertrude, *Herald of Divine Love*, 191. "Inter horum suavissimam delectationem illa sensit se inaestimabiliter mirabili modo per eamdem saepius dictam fistulam Cordi Dominico intrahi; et sic invenit se feliciter in intimis Sponsi et Domini Dei sui. Ubi quid senserit, quid viderit, quid audierit, quid gustaverit, quidve contrectaverit, ipsi soli notum est, ac illi qui eam ad tam superexcellenter sublimem admittere dignatus est sui unionem." The term *fistula* is admittedly ambiguous; as Winkworth points out, "one manner of receiving the blood under the species of wine, recorded as early as the eighth century in Rome, and certainly in use in the thirteenth century, is by sucking it from the chalice through a metal tube like a drinking-straw. This is what Gertrude seems to have in mind as she describes Christ's gifts coming to her from his heart through a sort of golden tube" (248 n. 50). The term was more commonly used, however (and I believe used here by Gertrude), to denote the "celestial pipe" allegorized by Ambrose, Rhabanus Maurus, Bernard, and others as an instrument of heavenly (and sometimes predicatory-rhetorical) music; see the useful essay by Jean Leclercq, "Caelestis fistula."

162. Gertrude, *Exercitia*, book 6, lines 47–54, 204; Gertrude, *Spiritual Exercises*, 95.

163. On this vision see Finnegan, *Women of Helfta*, 51–52.

164. Gertrude, *Legatus*, 3.18, 3:104; Gertrude, *Herald of Divine Love*, 184.

165. Gertrude, *Legatus*, 3.25, 3:120; Gertrude, *Herald of Divine Love*, 189.

166. Gertrude, *Legatus*, 3.30, 3:150; Gertrude, *Herald of Divine Love*, 199.

167. Gertrude, *Legatus*, 3.32, 3:170; Gertrude, *Herald of Divine Love*, 205.

168. Gertrude, *Legatus*, 2.16, 2:292; Gertrude, *Herald of Divine Love*, 116.

169. Gertrude, *Legatus*, 3.59, 3:242–44; Gertrude, *Herald of Divine Love*, 224.

170. Fassler, *Gothic Song*, 38–43 and passim.

171. On the 1296 interdict see Finnegan, *Women of Helfta*, 4; and Standaert, "Helfta," col. 895.

172. See above, 133–35.

173. Gertrude, *Legatus*, 3.16, 3:66; Gertrude, *Herald of Divine Love*, 170. "sed ex magna dispensatione salutis tuae, quia cum te aliquando admittendo ad mea secreta per contemplationem elevo, etiam ad custodiam humilitatis excludo quandoque: ut accipiens invenias quid sis ex me, et rursum carens agnoscas quid sis ex temetipsa."

174. Gertrude, *Legatus*, 3.16, 3:72; Gertrude, *Herald of Divine Love*, 172. "Anathema pro causa illa vobis impositum non plus vobis nocet quam si aliquid cum ligneo cultello incidi tentetur: quod omnino non possit penetrari, sed tantum parum pressum vestigium cultelli relinqueret."

175. Mechtild, *Liber*, 5.30, 365.

176. Mechtild, *Liber*, 6.9, 388–90.

177. Mechtild, *Liber*, 7.19, 414. Hammerstein, *Die Musik der Engel*, 58, remarks on the surprising sense of "musical rhetoric" in the nuns' images of rising and descending musical lines.

178. Gertrude, *Legatus*, 5.4, 5:94.

179. Gertrude, *Legatus*, 5.4, 5:94: "notabantur omnia verba quae ipsa electa Dei in omni vita sua ad Deum dulciter vel propter Deum utiliter ad salutem proximorum locuta fuerat."

180. See Fraenger, *The Millennium of Hieronymous Bosch*; and now *Hieronymous Bosch*.

181. Ibid., 86.

182. Ibid., 87.

183. For a brief discussion of both views, see Walter Gibson, *Hieronymous Bosch*, 98–99.

184. On the *Garden* and the *Visio Tundali*, see McGrath, "Satan and

Bosch," which reads the panel as "a condemnation of clerical excesses and a pointed reminder of the resultant punishments in the afterlife" (48).

185. See Moxey, *Practice of Theory*, III–47.

186. On this I am in agreement with Walter Gibson, who argues that, "Far from being an exposition of heretical doctrine, the triptych is the very essence of medieval orthodoxy in content, however bizarre its form"—though of course I would take this observation one step further and emphasize that the musical "forms" in the triptych are also traditional and, for lack of a better word, orthodox; see Walter Gibson, "*Garden of Earthly Delights,*" 19–20.

187. This seems to be the suggestion made in a rich but brief discussion of the painting by Jesse Gellrich, who sees Bosch rejecting the (supposed) medieval habit of musical totalization in favor of an arbitrary desacralizing of tradition: "medieval musical signs were understood to be naturally present in physical things," Gellrich argues; Bosch, by contrast, "cut that natural bond," and the infernal music of the *Garden of Earthly Delights* represents a decisive "movement away from the long medieval traditions of the mythology of music and the sacralization of space." (This is of course the same desacralizing movement implied in the title of John Hollander's influential study of music and poetry in England from 1500–1700, *The Untuning of the Sky*). Yet this interpretation similarly depends upon a too-ready acceptance of the Spitzerian notion that medieval representations of musical phenomena must inevitably refer and aspire to *musica mundana*—that, in Gellrich's words, "discordant oppositions are included within the total classification and given a fixed place in the underworld"; see Gellrich, *Idea of the Book*, 91–93.

CHAPTER 6

1. Ambrose, *Explanatio psalmorum* 1.9, 8: "Domi psalmus canitur, foris recensetur; sine labore percipitur, cum voluptate servatur. Psalmus dissidentes copulat, discordes sociat, offensos reconciliat; quis enim non remittat ei, cum quo unam ad deum vocem emiserit? Magnum plane unitatis vinculum, in unum chorum totius numerum plebis coire." Ambrose seems to be paraphrasing Basil of Caesaria's *Homily on the First Psalm* 1.2; see McKinnon, *Music in Early Christian Literature*, 65–66.

2. Adorno, *Sociology of Music*, 120.

3. For a discussion of the so-called Ambrosian chant and Ambrose's possible role in its development, see Leeb, *Die psalmodie bei Ambrosius*, and McKinnon, "Ambrose," *NG* 1: 313–14.

4. See Subotnik, *Developing Variations*, for a detailed consideration of Adorno's musical writings.

5. Aurelian of Réôme, *Musica Disciplina* 1, 59; trans. Ponte, 6.

6. Aurelian, *Musica Disciplina*, 59–60, trans. Ponte, 6. On "pulse-music," see Siraisi, "Music of Pulse."

7. See the introduction to Armstrong and Tennenhouse, *Violence of Representation*, 2.

8. See, among others, D. W. Robertson's discussions of the "Old Song/New Song" dichotomy in *Preface to Chaucer*; Higdon, "Diverse Melodies"; Gellrich, "Parody of Medieval Music." For a recent and notable exception, see Zieman, "Chaucer's *Voys*."

9. Chaucer, *House of Fame*, lines 769–81; see Boethius, *De institutione musica* 1.3, 189–91; Boethius, *Fundamentals of Music*, 11.

10. See Gellrich, "Parody of Medieval Music"; Correale, "Chaucer's Parody of Compline"; and Mandel, *Geoffrey Chaucer*, 151–54.

11. For a brief discussion of musical imagery in the Manciple's Tale, see Chamberlain, "Musical Signs and Symbols in Chaucer," 75–79. For Chamberlain, Phoebus's musical instruments are merely "signs of spiritual joy" that the god breaks in sorrow, and neither Phebus nor his musicality bear any responsibility for the tale's murderous denouement; rather, "the crow is envious and devilish, it sows discord, and it betrays the wife so she is slain" (79).

12. Such an assumption informs an otherwise compelling analysis of language and "maternal space" in the Prioress's Tale in Marvin, " 'I will thee not forsake.' " As Marvin writes, "For the little clergeoun of the *Prioress's Tale*, the *Alma redemptoris mater* is a maternal space drawing him to the very threshold of the symbolic. Its semiotic—the fluidity of its sounds, melodies, rhythms, intonations—brings him sweetly to grammar and symbolic meaning, which is the knife that cuts him off, separates him. The story at the heart of the *Prioress's Tale* narrativizes the stark and grievous trauma of becoming a subject—the acquisition of fundamentally impermeable limits, which, at the same time they allow a certain coherency and purposiveness of action, nevertheless *bar*, prohibit, screen off, make between self and another intolerable and irrevocable spaces" (45). Marvin's unwillingness to examine the subjectifying dimensions of music qua music is indicative of a more widespread tendency in psychoanalytic discourse to impute to musical phenomena—"sounds, melodies, rhythms, intonations"—an apolitical, even infantile character; in such analysis, music is always already *pre*symbolic, metaphorically constructed as a sonorous bridge between the maternal body and the violent "knife" of the symbolic. A psychoanalytically informed *materialist* analysis of the Prioress's Tale, by contrast, might ask how Chaucer's poetic register (which Marvin explicates with great subtlety) works precisely to convince the reader of music's

political innocence by locating it within, for lack of a better term, just such a "Kristevan maternal space."

13. The phrase translates the active Latin verb *perfecisti* from Psalm 8; see Hawkins's explanatory note to this line in *The Riverside Chaucer*.

14. For the significance of this liturgical citation, see Hawkins, "Chaucer's Prioress," 605.

15. Fradenburg, "Criticism," 91. Compare the reading in Ferster, " 'Your Praise.' "

16. "Orpheus and Eurydice," in Henryson, *Poems and Fables*, 68; see Chapter 7 of this volume, p. 299. For a reading of the Prologue and the alliance it constructs between the Prioress's and clergeon's voices, see Elizabeth Robertson, "Aspects of Female Piety," 151–52.

17. Fradenburg, "Criticism," 92.

18. Augustine, *Confessiones* 10.33.49.

19. Carol Berger, "Hand and Art of Memory," is a provocative study of the Guidonian Hand and its peculiar role in the medieval relationship between music and rhetoric. As Berger notes (115), the Guidonian Hand probably dates earlier than Guido himself. The definitive study of Guido's biography and pedagogical treatises remains Waesberghe, *De musicopaedagogico*; see also Oesch, *Guido von Arezzo*.

20. Numerous illustrations of the hand from the eleventh century through the seventeenth are reproduced in Waesberghe, *Musikerziehung*, 121–43; for the monochord, see 84–85; as well as the discussion in Adkins, "Monochord," *NG* 12:495–96.

21. Carruthers, *Book of Memory*, esp. 20–21.

22. Guido of Arezzo, "Epistola de ignoto cantu," in *CS* 2:45.

23. Page, *Summa musice*, 154 and 167.

24. Langland, *Piers Plowman II: The B-Text*, passus 5 line 416, 332.

25. *Mum and the Sothsegger*, lines 1145–48, 60.

26. "De Veritate et Consciencia," lines 101–108, in Kane, " Middle English Verse," 64. I discuss all of these passages at much greater length in Holsinger, "Langland's Musical Reader."

27. Courtenay, *Schools and Scholars*, 18–19. For an alternative (but, as Courtenay points out, probably mistaken) reading of the passage, see Orme, *Education and Society*, 232. For song schools in general, see in particular Moran, *Growth of English Schooling*, 21–62 (esp. 53–62); and Thompson, "Song Schools."

28. Bielitz, *Musik und Grammatik*. Bielitz's important study treats the relations between music and grammar in several of the works mentioned here; for Guido and Pseudo-Odo, see especially 134–223. On music and language in

Guido, see also Pirrotta, " 'Musica de sono humano.' " A somewhat different take on the disciplinary and institutional affiliations between music and grammar can be found in Riché, *Les Ecoles*, 221–52.

29. Carleton Brown, "The Prioress's Tale," in *Sources and Analogues of Chaucer's Canterbury Tales*, ed. Bryan and Dempster, 465.

30. See the remarks on the passage's obvious irony in Hawkins, "Chaucer's Prioress," 610. My view of what exactly song is doing (and being made to do) in the Prioress's Tale might be compared to that of Elizabeth Robertson in "Aspects of Female Piety," who, drawing on French feminism, argues that "song is a mode of expression particularly suited to the female speaker and others in analogously powerless positions precisely because of its mysterious power to effect change through the emotions rather than through argument" (155).

31. For a few vivid examples from late-medieval England see Orme, *Education and Society*, 61, 102, and 135. Enders, "Rhetoric, Coercion," provides a wonderful introduction to the topic.

32. The only discussion of violence in medieval musical pedagogy I have been able to find consists of two pages of Edward J. Dent's classic article "Social Aspects of Medieval Music," 180–81, which led me to a few of the sources discussed below.

33. See especially Treitler, "Homer and Gregory."

34. Treitler, "Inventing a European Music Culture," 347.

35. John the Deacon, *S. Gregorii papae vitae libri IV*, cols. 59–242. See also Helmut Hucke, "Gregory the Great," *NG* 7:699. A recent discussion of the more generally propagandistic aspects of the *Vita* can be found in Whatley, "Uses of Hagiography," 28–30.

36. John the Deacon, *S. Gregorii papae vitae*, col. 90; see van Dijk, "Papal Schola versus Charlemagne," 23.

37. Cited in Dent, "Social Aspects," 191.

38. Guido of Arezzo, *Prologus antiphonarii sui, CS* 2:35; Strunk, *Source Readings*, 118.

39. Ibid.

40. Song and grammar are closely associated in Guido's writings; see the perceptive analysis in Bielitz, *Musik und Grammatik*, and the discussion in Harrán, *Word-Tone Relations*, 54–57.

41. For an exhaustive overview of the authorship question see Huglo, "L'auteur du 'Dialogue sur la musique.' "

42. *Enchiridion Musices* 4, *CS* 1:255; Strunk, *Source Readings*, 108–9.

43. Aubrun, *Vita S. Stephani Obazinensis* 1.16, 68; cited in Dent, "Social Aspects," 191.

44. British Library, MS Arundel 292, fols. 70 ^{v} –71. The most complete description of the manuscript appears in Wirtjes's introduction to *Middle English Physiologus*, ix–xv.

45. Holsinger, "Langland's Musical Reader."

46. "The Choristers' Lament," lines 1–8, in Holsinger, "Langland's Musical Reader," 137–38; line references hereafter are cited in text from my edition (the poem has also been edited by Utley, "The Choristers' Lament").

47. Aurelian of Réôme, *Musica Disciplina*, 122; cited and discussed in McGee, *Sound of Medieval Song*, 57.

48. This is Brown's "C 10" analogue; see Bryan and Dempster, *Sources and Analogues*, 480.

49. See Spitzer's perceptive comments on this passage in *Classical and Christian Ideas*, 53.

50. Thus the title of McNamara's study, *A New Song: Celibate Women in the First Three Christian Centuries*; see 129–30 for an explicit example of the "New Song" as a topos for female virginity.

51. "The Form of Living," lines 572–74, in Rolle, *Prose and Verse*, 17.

52. *Hali Meidhad*, 11.

53. The Wycliffite resonances of Cecilia's preaching have been treated in Johnson, "Chaucer's Tale"; on the Second Nun and music, see Kolve, "Chaucer's *Second Nun's Tale*," esp. 140–41.

54. The similarity between the two scenes has been noted in, among others, Wenk, "Sources of the Prioress's Tale," 214–19.

55. Fradenburg, "Criticism," 108.

56. Attali, *Noise*, 24.

57. For an overview of scholarship on the "greyn," see Florence Ridley's notes to the Prioress's Tale in *Riverside Chaucer*, 916.

58. Boethius, *De institutione musica* 1.1; Boethius, *Fundamentals of Music*, 10.

59. Maltman, "Divine Granary," 164.

60. Ibid., 165.

61. Page, *Summa musice*, 152, 64.

62. Ibid.

63. Hugh of St. Victor, *Didascalicon*, 65.

64. *Rhetorica ad Herennium* 3.11.21, 192–93 (my emphasis).

65. Page, *Summa musice*, 152, 65 (my emphasis); Page translates *findit* as "tears at the throat," but the word can also convey the sense of splitting or cleaving an object in two.

66. Treitler, "Troubadours Singing," 15.

67. Ibid., 16.

68. On Chaucer and "natural music," a term coined by Eustache Deschamps, see Wimsatt, *Chaucer and His French Contemporaries.*

CHAPTER 7

1. Isidore, *Etymologiae* 3.15.2, 1:442. "Quarum sonus, quia sensibilis res est, et praeterfluit in praeteritum tempus inprimiturque memoriae. . . . Nisi enim ab homine memoria teneantur soni, pereunt, quia scribi non possunt"; Weiss and Taruskin, *Music in the Western World,* 41.

2. See Chapter 5 of this volume, pp. 252–53.

3. Burnett, Fend, and Gouk, *Second Sense,* 2.

4. Augustine, *Confessions* 11.27, 275.

5. See the comments by Elizabeth Sears, "Iconography of Auditory Perception," 25.

6. See Burnett, "Sound and Its Perception," 60.

7. Ernst Bloch, *Philosophy of Music,* 197.

8. Isidore, *Etymologiae* 3.20–22, 1:446–52; Strunk, *Source Readings,* 96–98.

9. Scruton, *Aesthetics of Music,* 445.

10. *Sir Orfeo,* lines 261–68, ed. Bliss (from Auchinleck), 24.

11. "Orpheus and Eurydice," lines 134–36, in Henryson, *Poems and Fables,* 133.

12. "Orpheus and Eurydice," lines 69–70, in Henryson, *Poems and Fables,* 131.

13. See the comments in Schwarz, *Listening Subjects,* 150–59.

14. Woods, *Articulate Flesh,* 30.

15. Barkan, *Transuming Passion,* 72.

16. Marcuse, *Eros and Civilization,* 171.

17. "The Gaze of Orpheus," in Blanchot, *Gaze of Orpheus,* 104.

18. See Edelman, *Homographesis,* xxi.

19. Friedman, *Orpheus in the Middle Ages,* 117.

20. Brownlee, "Orpheus's Song Re-sung."

21. Alan of Lille, *De planctu Naturae* 8.54–58, 834. On this passage see Calabrese, "Make a Mark That Shows."

22. Guillaume de Lorris and Jean de Meun, *Roman de la Rose,* lines 19,647–68, 5:10–11; Guillaume de Lorris and Jean de Meun, *Romance of the Rose,* 324. See Brownlee, "Orpheus's Song Re-sung," 201–9.

23. Calabrese, "Make a Mark That Shows."

24. Guillaume de Lorris and Jean de Meun, *Roman de la Rose* 19,652–56, 5:10; Guillaume de Lorris and Jean de Meun, *Romance of the Rose,* 324.

25. Koestenbaum, *Queen's Throat*, 161–63.

26. Hexter, "Medieval Articulations."

27. Bond, *Loving Subject*, and idem, *"Iocus amoris."*

28. Boswell, *Christianity*.

29. Bond, *Loving Subject*, esp. 48–53.

30. Baudri of Bourgueil, *Baldricus Burgulianus Carmina*, ed. Hilbert, no. 219, lines 1–3, 288; Baudri of Bourgueil, *Les Oeuvres Poétiques*, ed. Abrahams, CCLII; following the practice of Bond, I will refer (hereafter in text) to both the Hilbert and Abrahams editions of Baudri's poetry; while Hilbert's is now the standard edition, Abrahams's annotations remain indispensable for the specific historical and biographical contexts of Baudri's writings.

31. Bicknell, *History of the English Organ*, 14.

32. The full Latin text of the description and a careful translation may be found in Bicknell, *History of the English Organ*, 14–16.

33. For this poem I have relied on the translation in Stehling, *Medieval Latin Poems*, 39.

34. Translated in Stehling, *Medieval Latin Poems*, 55.

35. Arnulf of Orléans, *Allegorie super Ovidii Metamorphosin*, 222: "cantu suo i. sua predicatione feras i. efferos homines mitigavit, bruta animalia sapientes instruxit"; see the discussion in Friedman, *Orpheus in the Middle Ages*, 120. Chance, *Medieval Mythography*, cites and discusses numerous earlier examples of mythographic commentaries on the Orpheus legend.

36. Chaucer, *Boece*, book 3, metrum 12, *Riverside Chaucer*, 440.

37. See the explanatory notes to the passage in *Riverside Chaucer*, 1015. On the Boethian Orpheus, see Chance, *Medieval Mythography*, 140–41; and Friedman, *Orpheus in the Middle Ages*, 90–96.

38. Virgilio, *Allegorie Librorum Ovidii Metamorphoseos*, 89; cited and discussed in Friedman, *Orpheus in the Middle Ages*, 123.

39. Bersuire, *Ovidius moralizatus* 10, 147. "Dic allegorice quod orpheus filius solis est Christus filius dei patris: qui a principio euridicen id est animam humanam per caritatem & amorem duxit. . . . Veruntamen multi sunt qui quia retro per amorem temporalium respiciunt & tanquam canis ad vomitum mentaliter reuertuntur: & ipsam vxorem scilicet animam recuperatam nimis diligunt." The best introduction to Bersuire's mythographical method is Hexter, *"Allegari* of Pierre Bersuire."

40. Bersuire, *Ovidius moralizatus* 10, ed. Engels, 148; Bersuire, *Ovidius Moralizatus*, trans. Reynolds, 348.

41. Despite the editorial capitalization of the word in the Loeb edition, Ovid may be using the accusative of *venus* (intercourse) rather than the proper noun *Venus* for the goddess; *venus* was a ubiquitous and matter-of-fact

term for intercourse in educated Latin. See Adams, *Latin Sexual Vocabulary*, 188–89.

42. Bersuire, *Ovidius moralizatus* 10, ed. Engels, 148–49; Bersuire, *Ovidius Moralizatus*, trans. Reynolds, 349.

43. Copeland, "Pardoner's Body," 148–49.

44. Copeland, *Rhetoric, Hermeneutics*, 108.

45. Blumenfeld-Kosinski, *Reading Myth*, 90.

46. See Blumenfeld-Kosinski's fascinating comments on the tenth book of the treatise in *Reading Myth*, 91–98, 110–12, to which the following discussion is much indebted. In particular, I am interested in exploring the implications of her observation that, for the vernacular mythographer, "both the homosexual act and the Incarnation are 'contre nature' " (112).

47. *Ovide moralisé*, 10.191–94, 4:15–16 (hereafter cited in text). Friedman, *Orpheus in the Middle Ages*, 124–26, gives remarkably short shrift to the lengthy Orpheus section in the *Ovide moralisé*.

48. This break has also been noted by Blumenfeld-Kosinski, *Reading Myth*, 94.

49. See Blumenfeld-Kosinski's brief discussion of the allegory in *Reading Myth*, 111–12.

50. See, for example, Martha Newman, *Boundaries of Charity*.

51. See Chapter 5 of this volume, p. 210, and compare the harp allegory in the *Ovide moralisé* with the Joachimite passages discussed by Reeves and Hirsch-Reich in *The Figurae of Joachim of Fiore*, 199–211.

52. Machaut, "Dit de la harpe." All citations will be to this edition and will hereafter be given in text.

53. Calin, *Poet at the Fountain*, 227.

54. Huot, *From Song to Book*, 287.

55. Ibid., 291.

56. See de Boer's introduction to *Ovide moralisé*, 1:28–43; Blumenfeld-Kosinski, *Reading Myth*, chapter 4, "Myth and Fiction in the Dits of Machaut and Froissart," 137–70.

57. As Karl Young points out, Machaut's own counting of the extra strings seems to be in error:

Ie t'ay nommé les cordes de la lire
Dont il y a .xxv. tire a tire;
Et s'en y ay .iiii. mis par desseure
Qui la harpe gouuernent a toute heure.
Si puis moult bien faire comparison
De la belle qui m'a en sa prison

A la harpe qui tous instrumens passe
Qui sagement bien en ioue et compasse
...
Pour ces .xxx. dont ma dame est parée
A la harpe doit estre comparée

(277–84, 331–32)

This inconsistency may be yet another way in which Machaut is resisting the didactic orderliness of the harp portrayed in the *Ovide moralisé*, however.

58. Huot, *From Song to Book*, 290. See also the overview of criticism on the anagram in Karl Young's comments to Machaut, "Dit de la harpe," 13–14 and notes.

59. Brownlee, *Poetic Identity*, 189.

60. On Dante's Virgilian journey, see, most recently, Pike, *Passage through Hell*, 98–110; and Putnam, "Virgil's *Inferno*." I have treated the homoeroticism of the poem at length in "Sodomy and Resurrection."

61. Virgil, *Georgic* 4.525–27.

62. Dante, *Purgatorio* 30, lines 49–51 (hereafter cited in text).

63. Schnapp, "Dante's Sexual Solecisms," 211.

64. Freccero, *Dante*, 208.

65. Statius, *Achilleid* 1.473–75.

66. *Purgatorio* 9.34.

67. As argued in Holsinger, "Sodomy and Resurrection."

68. These passages are discussed in Chapter 2 of this volume, pp. 76–77.

69. Heywood, *Woman Killed with Kindness*, 16.17–21, 80; subsequent references to scene and line number will be given in text.

70. See, for example, Gibson, *Theater of Devotion*, 86–90; and the relevant sections of Lerer, *Chaucer and His Readers*.

71. See David Wallace's reading of the *Fall* in *Chaucerian Polity*, 332–34.

72. Boccaccio, *De casibus illustrium virorum* I (Paris, 1520), fol. VIIIr (p. 39 in Hall's facsimile).

73. Boccaccio, *Genealogie deorum gentilium*, 5.12.22–27, 1:244; cited in Friedman, *Orpheus in the Middle Ages*, 141.

74. Boccaccio, *Genealogie deorum gentilium*, 5.12.28–35, 1:246; Friedman, *Orpheus in the Middle Ages*, 141.

75. Friedman, *Orpheus in the Middle Ages*, 139.

76. John Lydgate, *Fall of Princes*, book 1, lines 5707–8, 5779; 1:160, 162 (hereafter cited in text).

77. A later reader of Lydgate's text felt moved to insert himself into the

poem's antifeminist genealogy by means of a marginal annotation positioned next to this stanza. Encountering Lydgate's interpolated contention that many husbands would "nat [have] seid allas" upon losing their wives with a single glance, the reader greeted the author's antimatrimonial sentiment with a complementary but more concise observation: "A trewe saying." The poem's margins consolidate and perpetuate the male readership that Orpheus, on Lydgate's interpretation, serves to initiate; see the apparatus in Lydgate, *Fall of Princes*, 163, referring to a later hand in the Rylands-Jersey manuscript.

78. On this relationship, see Hammond, "Poet and Patron"; Ebin, *John Lydgate*, 62–64; and Pearsall's chapter in *John Lydgate*, 223–52. My reading of the Orpheus interlude explores the implications of Pearsall's momentary observation that Lydgate intended this section of the *Fall* to serve as "an allegory of the hell of marriage" (237).

79. Pearsall, *John Lydgate: A Bio-Bibliography*, 33.

80. Wallace, *Chaucerian Polity*, 334.

81. The following paragraphs are based on the historical accounts presented in Vickers, *Humphrey Duke of Gloucester*, chapters 4 and 5, 125–215; and Williams, *My Lord of Bedford, 1389–1435*, esp. 118–24.

82. The passage is cited from the St. Alban's Chronicle in Vickers, *Humphrey Duke of Gloucester*, 203.

83. Cited in Vickers, *Humphrey Duke of Gloucester*, 203.

84. Lerer, *Chaucer and His Readers*, 52.

85. *Orpheus His Journey to Hell*, cited in DiGangi, *Homoerotics of Early Modern Drama*, 46.

86. DiGangi, *Homoerotics of Early Modern Drama*, 56–57.

87. "The Legend of Orpheus and Euridice," in Lownes, *Of Loves Complaint*, 22–41; all subsequent passages will be cited from this edition.

EPILOGUE

1. Isidore, *Etymologiae* 3.22, 1:452; Strunk, *Source Readings*, 98.

2. All references are to Padelford's edition in "Liedersammlungen des XVI. Jahrhunderts," 350–52.

3. On this tradition, see Rice, *European Ancestry*; cited in Boffey, "Lydgate, Henryson," 45, whose brief comment led me to the poem.

4. Fradenburg, " 'Voice Memorial,' " 173.

5. Petrucci, *Writing the Dead*, 51; Fradenburg, " 'Voice Memorial,' " 193.

6. Taruskin, *Text and Act*, 150.

7. Morrison, *"I Am You,"* 358.

8. Brett, Wood, and Thomas, *Queering the Pitch*, viii.

9. Tomlinson, *Music in Renaissance Magic*, 248–49.

10. Margaret Bent, "Reflections," 630.

11. Ibid., 631.

12. Ibid., 630–31.

13. Ibid.

14. Tomlinson, *Music in Renaissance Magic*, 247.

15. Tomlinson, "Musical Pasts," 24.

16. Morrison, *"I Am You,"* 354.

17. Eliot, *Ash-Wednesday*, 17–18.

18. "A Song of Praise" and "Heritage," in Cullen, *Color*, 4, 38.

19. Stevens, "Peter Quince at the Clavier," in *The Collected Poems*, 89–92.

20. Carey, *More about All About Eve*, 248.

21. Fussell, *Poetic Meter*, 5.

22. See Bibby, *Augusta Savage*, no. 16.

23. "Lift Ev'ry Voice and Sing," in Johnson, *Saint Peter Relates an Incident*.

24. Hurston, *Jonah's Gourd Vine*, 12, 37 (hereafter cited in text).

25. Rita Dove, "Preface," in Hurston, *Jonah's Gourd Vine*, xi.

26. See the comments in Gates and McKay, *African-American Literature*, xxix–xxx, and Katz's introduction to *Early Negro Music*, vii–viii.

Bibliography

I. PRINTED SOURCES

Ad organum faciendum: Lehrschriften der Mehrstimmigkeit in nachguidonischer Zeit. Ed. Hans Neinrich Eggebrecht and Frieder Zaminer. Neue Studien zur Musikwissenschaft 3. Mainz: B. Schott's Söhne, 1970.

Ad organum faciendum. Ed. and trans. Jay A. Huff. Music Theorists in Translation 8. Brooklyn: Institute of Medieval Music, 1971.

Aelred of Rievaulx. *Speculum caritatis.* Ed. A. Host and C. H. Talbot. *CCCM* 1. 1971.

Alan of Lille. *De planctu Naturae.* Ed. Nikolaus M. Häring. *Studi Medievali* 3rd ser., 19 (1978): 806–79.

———. *The Plaint of Nature.* Trans. James J. Sheridan. Toronto: Pontifical Institute of Medieval Studies, 1980.

———. "Rhythmus de incarnatione Christi." *PL* 210: 577–80.

Alexander Neckham. *De naturis rerum libri duo et De laudibus divinae sapientiae.* Ed. Thomas Wright. Rerum Britannicum Medii Aevi Scriptores 34. London: RS, 1863.

Ambrose, Saint. *De Iacob et vita beata.* Ed. Carol Schenkl. *CSEL* 32. 1902.

———. *De officiis ministrorum. PL* 16, 25–194.

———. *Explanatio psalmorum.* Ed. M. Petschenig. *CSEL* 64. 1919.

———. *Hexaemeron.* Ed. Il Schenkl. *CSEL* 32. Vienna: Tempsky, 1897.

Ancelet-Hustache, Jeanne, ed. "Les 'Vitae Sororum' d'Unterlinden. Edition critique du Manuscrit 508 de la Bibliothèque de Colmar." *Archives d'Histoire Doctrinale et Littéraire du Moyen Age* 5 (1930): 317–509.

Ancrene Riwle. Ed. Mabel Day. EETS, o.s. 225. London: Oxford University Press, 1952.

Anderson, Gordon, ed. *Notre-Dame and Related Conductus: Opera Omnia.* 9

vols. Henryville, Ottawa, and Binningen: Institute of Medieval Music, 1981–86.

Andrew, Malcolm, and Ronald Waldron, eds. *The Poems of the Pearl Manuscript.* Berkeley and Los Angeles: University of California Press, 1978.

Arnulf of Orléans. *Allegorie Librorum Ovidii Metamorphoseos.* Ed. Fausto Ghisalberti. *Arnolfo d'Orléans, un Cultore di Ovidio nel Secolo XII.* Memorie del Reale Istituto Lombardo di Scienze e Lettere 24. Milan: Ulrico Hoepli, 1932.

Aubrun, Michel, ed. *Vita S. Stephani Obazinensis.* Publications de l'Institut d'Études du Massif Central IV. Clermont-Ferrand: Institute d'Études du Massif Central, 1970.

Augustine, Saint. *Confessiones.* Ed. Martin Skutella. *CCSL* 27. Turnhout: Brepols, 1990.

——. *Confessions.* Trans. R. S. Pine-Coffin. New York: Penguin, 1987.

——. *De civitate Dei.* 2 vols. *CCSL* 47 and 48. Turnhout: Brepols, 1955.

——. *The City of God.* Trans. John O'Meara. New York: Penguin, 1987.

——. *De musica libri sex. PL* 32, 1082–194.

——. *De Trinitate.* 2 vols. Ed. W. J. Mountain. *CCSL* 50 and 50A. 1968.

——. *On the Trinity.* Trans. Stephen McKenna. Fathers of the Church 45. Washington: Catholic University of America Press, 1963.

——. *Enarrationes in psalmos.* 2 vols. Ed. Eligius Dekkers and Johannes Fraipon. *CCSL* 38–40. Turnhout: Brepols, 1990.

——. *On Music.* Trans. Robert Taliaferro. *Writings of Saint Augustine*, vol. 2. Fathers of the Church. New York: CIMA Publishing, 1947.

——. *Retractiones.* Ed. Almut Mutzenbecker. *CCSL* 57. 1984.

——. *Retractions.* Trans. Sister Mary Inez Bogan. Fathers of the Church 60. Washington: Catholic University Press, 1968.

——. *Sermones. PL* 38.

——. *Soliloquies and Immortality of the Soul.* Ed. and trans. Gerald Watson. Warminster: Aris and Phillips, 1990.

Aurelian of Réôme. *Musica Disciplina.* Ed. Lawrence Gushee. CSM 21. N.p.: American Institute of Musicology, 1975.

——. *Musica Disciplina.* Trans. Joseph Perry Ponte. Colorado Springs: Colorado College Music Press, 1968.

Bacon, Roger. *Fratri Rogeri Bacon Opera quaedam hactenus inedita.* Ed. John S. Brewer. London: Longman, Green, 1859.

Baldwin of Ford. *Traités.* Ed. Robert Thomas. *Pain de Cîteaux* 35–40. Chimay, 1973–75.

——. *Spiritual Tractates.* 2 vols. Trans. David N. Bell. CF 38. Kalamazoo: Cistercian Publications, 1986.

Basil the Great, Saint. *De titulis in psalmorum. PG* 27: 649–1344.

———. *Hexaemeron.* Trans. Sister Agnes Clare Way. Fathers of the Church 46. New York and Washington: Catholic University of America Press, 1963.

Baudri of Bourgueil. *Baldricus Burgulianus Carmina.* Ed. Karlheinz Hilbert. Heidelberg: Carl Winter Universitätsverlag, 1979.

———. *Les Oeuvres Poétiques de Baudri de Bourgueil (1046–1130). Édition critique publiée d'après le manuscrit du Vatican.* Ed. Phyllis Abrahams. Paris: Librairie Ancienne Honoré Champion, 1926.

Bernard of Clairvaux. *Sermons on the Song of Songs,* vol. 3. Trans. Killian Walsh and Irene Edmonds. CF 31. Kalamazoo, Mich.: Cistercian Publications, 1979.

Bersuire, Pierre [Petrus Berchorius]. *Ovidius Moralizatus.* Trans. William Donald Reynolds. "The 'Ovidius Moralizatus' of Petrus Berchorius: An Introduction and Translation." Ph.D. diss., University of Illinois at Urbana-Champaign, 1971.

———. *Reductorium morale, Liber XV, cap. ii–xv: "Ovidius Moralizatus" naar de Parijse druk van 1509.* Ed. Joseph Engels. Utrecht: Instituut voor Laat Latijn der Rijksuniversiteit, 1962.

Biblia Sacra iuxta vulgatam versionem. 3rd ed. Stuttgart: Deutsche Bibelgesellschaft, 1969.

Bland, C. C. Swinton, trans. *Miracles of the Blessed Virgin Mary.* New York: Routledge, 1928.

Boccaccio, Giovanni. *De casibus illustrium virorum. A Facsimile Reproduction of the Paris Edition of 1520.* Ed. Louis Brewer Hall. Gainesville, Fla.: Scholars' Facsimiles and Reprints, 1962.

———. *Genealogie Deorum Gentilium Libri.* Ed. Vincenzo Romano. 2 vols. Bari: Laterza and Figli, 1951.

Boethius. *De Institutione Arithmetica libri duo, De Institutione Musica libri quinque, accedit Geometria quae fertur Boetii.* Ed. Godofredus Friedlein. Leipzig: Teubner, 1867.

———. *Fundamentals of Music.* Trans. Calvin M. Bower. New Haven, Conn.: Yale University Press, 1989.

Bollandus, J., and G. Henschenius. *Acta sanctorum . . . editio novissima.* Ed. J. Carandet et al. Paris: Palmé, etc., 1863– .

Book to a Mother. Ed. Adrian James McCarthy. Salzburg Studies in English Literature 92. Salzburg: Institut für Anglistik und Amerikanistik, 1981.

Caesarius of Heisterbach. *Dialogus miraculorum.* 2 vols. Ed. Joseph Strange. Cologne: Heberle, 1851.

Calcidius. *Timaeus a Calcidio translatus commentarioque instructus.* Ed. J. H.

Waszink, Corpus Platonicum Medii Aevi, Plato Latinus 4. London and Leiden: Warburg Institute and E. J. Brill, 1962.

Cassiodorus. *Explanation of the Psalms*. 3 vols. Trans. P. G. Walsh. Ancient Christian Writers 51–53. New York: Paulist Press, 1991.

———. *Expositio Psalmorum*. 2 vols. Ed. M. Adriaen. *CCSL* 97 and 98. Turnhout: Brepols, 1958.

Charles, R. H., ed. *Pseudepigrapha*. Vol. 2 of *The Apocrypha and Pseudepigrapha of the Old Testament in English*. Oxford: Clarendon Press, 1913.

Chaucer, Geoffrey. *The Canterbury Tales: A Facsimile and Transcription of the Hengwrt Manuscript, with Variants from the Ellesmere Manuscript*. Ed. Paul Ruggiers. Norman: University of Oklahoma Press, 1979.

———. *The Riverside Chaucer*, 3rd ed. Ed. Larry D. Benson. Boston: Houghton Mifflin, 1987.

———. *The Text of the Canterbury Tales*. 8 vols. Ed. John M. Manly and Edith Rickert. Chicago: University of Chicago Press, 1940.

Chrysologus, Peter. *Sermones*. 3 vols. Ed. Alexander Olivar. *CCSL* 24, 24A, and 24B. 1975–82.

Cicero. *De natura deorum*. Ed. W. Ax. Bibliotheca Scriptorum Graecorum et Romanorum. Stuttgart: Teubner, 1980.

———. *De Natura Deorum, Academica*. Ed. and trans. Horace Rackham. Loeb Classical Library. London: William Heinemann, 1933.

———. *De oratore*. 2 vols. Ed. and trans. Horace Rackham. Loeb Classical Library. Cambridge: Harvard University Press, 1948.

———. *Tusculan Disputations* I. Ed. and trans. A. E. Douglas. Warminster, Wiltshire: Aris and Phillips, 1985.

Clement of Alexandria. *Clement of Alexandria: Selected Writings*. Trans. Alexander Roberts and James Donaldson. Grand Rapids, Mich.: Eerdmans, 1994.

———. *Opera*. *PG* 8.

Cullen, Countee. *Color*. New York and London: Harper and Brothers, 1925.

Damian, Peter. *Die Briefe des Petrus Damiani*. 4 vols. Ed. Kurt Reindel. Die Briefe der Deutschen Kaiserzeit 4. Munich: MGH, 1988–93.

———. *Vita Sancti Rudolphi et S. Dominici Loricati*. *PL* 144: 1007–24.

Dante Alighieri. *The Divine Comedy*. 3 vols. Ed. G. Petrocci, trans. Charles Singleton. Princeton, N.J.: Princeton University Press, 1970–77.

Dickinson, Emily. *The Complete Poems of Emily Dickinson*. Ed. Thomas H. Johnson. Boston: Little, Brown, 1960.

Dittmer, Luther. *Firenze, Biblioteca-Mediceo-Laurenziana, Pluteo 29.1: Facsim-

ile Reproduction of the Manuscript. 2 vols. Publications of Mediaeval Music Manuscripts 10–11. Brooklyn: Institute of Mediaeval Music, 1966–67.

Ecbasis cuiusdam captivi per tropologiam: Escape of a Certain Captive Told in a Figurative Manner. Studies in the Germanic Languages and Literatures 46. Ed. and trans. Edwin H. Zeydel. Chapel Hill: University of North Carolina Press, 1964.

Eliot, T. S. *Ash-Wednesday.* New York and London: Putnam's Sons, 1930.

Elisabeth of Schönau. "Epistola ad Hildegardem." *PL* 197: 214–16.

Friedberg, Emil, ed. *Corpus juris canonici, ed. a. 1582 cum glossa in aedibus populi Romani, iussu Gregorii XIII.* 2 vols. Leipzig: B. Tauchnizt, 1879–81.

Froehlich, Karlfried, and Margaret T. Gibson, eds. *Biblia Latina cum Glossa Ordinaria: Facsimile Reprint of the Editio Princeps Adolph Rusch of Strassburg 1480/81.* 3 vols. Turnhout: Brephols, 1992.

Fulgentius. *Opera.* Ed. Rudolf Helm. Leipzig: Teubner, 1898.

Gertrude of Helfta. *Exercitia.* Ed. Jacques Hourlier and Albert Schmitt. SC 127. Paris: Éditions du Cerf, 1967.

——. *Spiritual Exercises.* Trans. Gertrud Jaron Lewis and Jack Lewis. CF 49. Kalamazoo, Mich.: Cistercian Publications, 1989.

——. *Legatus divinae pietatis.* 4 vols. Ed. Pierre Doyére. SC 139, 143, 255, 331. Paris: Éditions du Cerf, 1967–86.

——. *The Herald of Divine Love.* Trans. Margaret Winkworth. Classics of Western Spirituality. New York: Paulist Press, 1993.

Gregory the Great. *Moralia in Iob.* 3 vols. Ed. Marcus Adriaen. *CCSL* 143, 143A, and 143B. Turnhout: Brepols, 1979–85.

Gregory of Nyssa. *De hominis opificio. PG* 44: 123–257.

——. *Gregory of Nyssa: Dogmatic Treatises, etc.* Trans. William Moore and Henry Austine Wilson. Peabody, Mass.: Hendrickson Publishers, 1994.

Guentner, Francis, ed. and trans. *Epistola S. Bernardi de Revisione Cantus Cisterciensis et Cantum Quem Cisterciensis Ordinis Ecclesiae Cantare.* CSM 24. N.p.: American Institute of Musicology, 1974.

Guillaume de Lorris and Jean de Meun. *Le Roman de la Rose.* 5 vols. Ed. Ernest Langlois. Paris: Librairie ancienne Édouard Champion, 1924.

——. *The Romance of the Rose.* Trans. Charles Dahlberg. Hanover and London: University Press of New England, 1983.

Hali Meidhad. Ed. Bella Millett. EETS 284. London, 1982.

Henryson, Robert. *The Poems and Fables of Robert Henryson.* Ed. H. Harvey Wood. Edinburgh: Oliver and Boyd, 1968.

Heywood, Thomas. *A Woman Killed with Kindness.* Ed. Brian Scobie. New York: Norton, 1985.

Hilary of Poitiers. *Tractatus super Psalmos.* Ed. Anton Zingerle. *CCSL* 22. Leipzig: Freytag, 1891.

Hildegard of Bingen. *Causae et curae.* Ed. Paul Kaiser. Leipzig: Teubner, 1903.

——. *Epistolae. PL* 197: 145–382.

——. *Hildegardis Bingensis Epistolarium.* 2 vols. Ed. Lieven Van Acker. *CCCM* 91, 91A. Turnhout: Brepols, 1991 and 1993.

——. *The Letters of Hildegard of Bingen.* 2 vols. Trans. Joseph L. Baird and Radd K. Ehrman. New York and Oxford: Oxford University Press, 1994 and 1998.

——. *Liber vitae meritorum.* Ed. Angela Carlevaris. *CCCM* 90. Turnhout: Brepols, 1995.

——. *The Book of the Rewards of Life (Liber Vitae Meritorum).* Trans. Bruce W. Hozeski. New York: Garland, 1994.

——. *Lieder.* Ed. Prudentiana Barth, Maria-Immaculata Ritscher, and Joseph Schmidt-Görg. Salzburg: Otto Müller Verlag, 1969.

——. *Scivias.* Ed. Adelgundis Führkötter and Angela Carlevaris. *CCCM* 43 and 43A. Turnhout: Brepols, 1978.

——. *Scivias.* Trans. Mother Columba Hart and Jane Bishop. Classics of Western Spirituality. New York: Paulist Press, 1990.

——. *Sequences and Hymns.* Ed. and trans. Christopher Page. Devon: Antico, 1983.

——. *Symphonia harmoniae caelestium revelationum: Dendermonde St.-Pieters & Paulusabdij Ms. Cod. 9.* Ed. Peter van Poucke. Peer: Alamire, 1991.

——. *Symphonia: A Critical Edition of the Symphonia armonie celestium revelationum.* Ed. and trans. Barbara Newman. Ithaca and London: Cornell University Press, 1988.

Holsinger, Bruce, and David Townsend, eds. "The Ovidian Verse-Epistles of Master Leoninus." *Journal of Medieval Latin* 10 (2000), forthcoming.

Honorius Augustodunensis. *Expositio in Psalmos. PL* 172: 269–312.

——. *Gemma animae. PL* 172: 541–738.

Hrotsvit of Gandersheim. *Hrotsvithae opera.* Ed. Paul Winterfeld. Munich: MGH, 1978.

——. *The Plays of Hrotsvit of Gandersheim.* Trans. Katharina Wilson. New York: Garland, 1989.

Hugh of St. Victor. *Didascalicon.* Trans. Jerome Taylor. New York: Columbia University Press, 1961.

Hughes, Andrew, and Margaret Bent, eds. *The Old Hall Manuscript.* 3 vols. New York: American Institute of Musicology, 1969.

Hurston, Zora Neale. *Jonah's Gourd Vine.* New York: HarperCollins, 1990.

Isidore of Seville. *Etymologiae.* 2 vols. Ed. José Oroz Reta and Manuel Marcos Casquero. Madrid: Biblioteca de Autores Cristianos, 1982.

Jacques de Vitry. "Vita Mariae Oignacensis." *AASS* June, vol. 5 (1867).

——. *The Life of Marie d'Oignies.* Trans. Margot King. Toronto: Peregrina Publishing, 1987.

John of Salisbury. *Frivolities of Courtiers and Footprints of Philosophers* [*Policraticus* books 1–3 and selections from books 7 and 8]. Trans. Joseph B. Pike. Minneapolis: University of Minnesota Press, 1938.

——. *Policraticus.* Ed. K. S. B. Keats-Rohan. *CCCM* 118. Turnhout: Brepols, 1993.

——. *Policraticus.* 2 vols. Ed. Clemens C. I. Webb. Oxford: Clarendon Press, 1909.

John the Deacon. *S. Gregorii Magni vita. PL* 75: 59–242.

Johnson, James Weldon. *Saint Peter Relates an Incident.* New York: Viking Press, 1935.

Kane, George. "The Middle English Verse in MS Wellcome 1493." *London Mediaeval Studies* 2 (1951).

Kempe, Margery. *The Book of Margery Kempe.* Ed. S. B. Meech and H. E. Allen. EETS, o.s. 212. London: Oxford University Press, 1940.

Lactantius. *Diuinae institutiones.* Ed. Samuel Brandt. *CSEL* 19–2. 1890.

Landulf. *Historia Mediolanensis. PL* 147: 803–954.

Langland, William. *Piers Plowman: The B-Text.* Ed. George Kane and E. Talbot Donaldson. London: Athlone Press, 1975.

The Lay Folks' Catechism. Ed. T. F. Simmons and H. E. Nolloth. EETS, o.s. 118. London: K. Paul, Trench and Trübner, 1901.

The Life of Beatrice of Nazareth. Trans. Roger De Ganck. CF 50. Kalamazoo, Mich.: Cistercian Publications, 1991.

Lombard, Peter. *Commentarium in Psalmos Davidicos. PL* 191: 61–1296.

Lownes, Humfrey. *Of Loves Complaint, With The Legend of Orpheus and Eurydice.* London: I. R., 1597.

Lydgate, John. *The Fall of Princes.* Ed. Henry Bergen. 4 vols. EETS, e.s. 121, 122, 123, and 124. London: Oxford University Press, 1924–27.

——. *Lydgate's Minor Poems: The Two Nightingale Poems.* Ed. Otto Glauning. EETS, e.s. 80. London: Trübner and Co., 1900.

Machaut, Guillaume de. "The *Dit de la Harpe* of Guillaume de Machaut," ed. Karl Young. In *Essays in Honor of Albert Feuillerat,* ed. Henri M. Peyre. Yale Romanic Studies, 1st. ser., no. 22, pp. 1–20. New Haven, Conn.: Yale University Press, 1943.

Macrobius. *Commentarium in Somnium Scipionis.* 2 vols. Ed. Jacob Willis.

Bibliotheca Scriptorum Graecorum et Romanorum. Leipzig: Teubner, 1970.

———. *Commentary on the Dream of Scipio.* Trans. William Harris Stahl. New York: Columbia University Press, 1970.

Mannyng, Robert. *Handlyng Synne.* 2 vols. Ed. F. J. Furnivall. EETS, o.s. 119, 123. London: K. Paul, Trench and Trübner, 1901–3.

Map, Walter. *De nugis curialum (Courtiers' Trifles).* Ed. and trans. M. R. James. Oxford: Clarendon Press, 1983.

Marchetto of Padua. *The Lucidarium of Marchett of Padua.* Ed. and trans. Jan W. Herlinger. Chicago: University of Chicago Press, 1985.

Marguerite d'Oingt. *Les Oeuvres de Marguerite d'Oingt.* Ed. Antonin Duraffour, Pierre Gardette, and Paulette Durdilly. Paris: Société d'Edition "Les Belles Lettres," 1965.

———. *The Writings of Marguerite of Oingt, Medieval Prioress and Mystic.* Trans. Renate Blumenfeld-Kosinski. Newburyport, Mass.: Focus Information Group, 1990.

Marie de France. *The Lais of Marie de France.* Trans. Joan Ferrante and Robert Hanning. Durham, N.C.: Labyrinth Press, 1982.

Martianus Capella. *De nuptiis Philologiae et Mercurii.* Ed. James Willis. Bibliotheca Scriptorum Graecorum et Romanorum Teubneriana. Leipzig: Teubner, 1983.

Maurer, Friedrich, ed. *Die Erlösung: eine geistliche Dichtung des 14. Jahrhunderts.* Leipzig: P. Reclam, 1934.

McGinn, Bernard, trans. *Three Treatises on Man: A Cistercian Anthropology.* CF 24. Kalamazoo, Mich.: Cistercian Publications, 1977.

McKinnon, James, ed. and trans. *Music in Early Christian Literature.* Cambridge: Cambridge University Press, 1987.

Mechtild of Hackeborn. *Liber specialis gratiae.* Vol. 2 of *Revelationes Gertrudianae ac Mechtilidanae.* Ed. Monks of Solesmes. Paris, 1877.

Meditations on the Life of Christ: An Illustrated Manuscript of the Fourteenth Century. Ed. and trans. Isa Ragusa and Rosalie B. Green. Princeton, N.J.: Princeton University Press, 1961.

Mum and the Sothsegger. Ed. Mabel Day and Robert Steele. EETS, o.s. 199. London, 1936.

Musica enchiriadis and Scolica enchiriadis. Trans. Raymond Erickson. New Haven, Conn., and London: Yale University Press, 1995.

Musica et scolica enchiriadis una cum aliquibus tractatulis adiunctis. Ed. Hans Schmid. Munich: Verlag der Bayerischen Akademie der Wissenschaften, 1981.

Neckham, Alexander. *De naturis rerum*. Ed. Thomas Wright. RS 34. London: Longman, Green, 1863.

Origen (Pseudo-). *Selecta in psalmos*. *PG* 12: 1053–686.

Ovid. *Heroides and Amores*. Ed. and trans. Grant Showerman. Loeb Classical Library. London: Heinemann, 1921.

——. *Metamorphoses*. 2 vols. Ed. and trans. Frank Justus Miller. Loeb Classical Library. London: Heinemann, 1916.

Ovide moralisé. 5 vols. Ed. Cornelis DeBoer. *Verhandelingen der koninklijke Akademie van Wetenschappen Te Amsterdam*. Afdeeling Letterkunde, nieuwe reeks, 15, 21, 30.3, 37, 43. Amsterdam: Müller, 1915–36.

Padelford, Frederick Morgan. "Liedersammlungen des XVI. Jahrhunderts, besonders aus der Zeit Heinrichs VIII. IV: 7. The Songs in Manuscript Rawlinson C. 813." *Anglia* 31 (1908): 309–97.

Page, Christopher. "Johannes de Grocheio on Secular Music: A Corrected Text and a New Translation." *Plainsong and Medieval Music* 2 (1993): 17–41.

——. "A Treatise on Musicians from ?c. 1400: The *Tractatulus de differentiis et gradibus cantorum* by Arnulf de St Ghislain." *Journal of the Royal Musical Association* 117 (1992): 15–21.

——, ed. and trans. *The* Summa music*: A Thirteenth-Century Manual for Singers*. Cambridge: Cambridge University Press, 1991.

Paliska, Claude V., trans. *Hucbald, Guido and John on Music*. New Haven, Conn.: Yale University Press, 1978.

Pecham, John. "Philomena praevia." Ed. Guido Maria Dreves. *Analecta Hymnica* 50 (1907): 602–16.

Plato. *Phaedo*. Trans. David Gallop. Oxford: Clarendon Press, 1975.

——. *The Republic and Other Works*. Trans. B. Jowett. Garden City, N.Y.: Anchor Books, 1973.

——. *Timaeus*. Ed. and trans. R. G. Bury. Loeb Classical Library. London: William Heinemann, 1929.

Pliny. *Natural History*. 10 vols. Ed. and trans. Horace Rackham. Loeb Classical Library. Cambridge: Harvard University Press, 1967.

Plotinus. *The Enneads*. Trans. Stephen MacKenna. New York: Penguin, 1991.

Prynne, William. *Histrio-Mastix: The Players Scourge or Actors Tragedie*. London: E. A. and W. I. for Michael Sparke, 1633.

Quintilian. *Institutio oratoria*. 4 vols. Ed. and trans. H. E. Butler. Loeb Classical Library. Cambridge: Harvard University Press, 1963.

Rhabanus Maurus. *Allegoriae in Sacram Scripturam*. *PL* 112: 849–1088.

Rhetorica ad Herennium. Ed. and trans. Harry Caplan. Cambridge: Harvard University Press, 1964.

Roesner, Edward, ed. *Les Quadrupla et Tripla de Paris.* Vol. 1 of *Le Magnus Liber Organi de Notre-Dame de Paris.* Monaco: L'Oiseau-Lyre, 1993.

Rolle, Richard. *Prose and Verse.* Ed. S. J. Ogilvie-Thomson. EETS 293. London, 1988.

Rossignol: An Edition and Translation. Ed. and trans. J. L. Baird and John R. Kane. Ohio: Kent State University Press, 1978.

Silvas, Anna, ed. and trans. *Jutta and Hildegard: The Biographical Sources.* Turnhout: Brepols, 1998.

Sir Orfeo. Ed. A. J. Bliss. Oxford: Clarendon Press, 1966.

Speculum ecclesiae. PL 177: 335–80.

Speculum humanae salvationis. 2 vols. Ed. J. Lutz and P. Perdrizet. Leipzig: Karl W. Hiersemann, 1907.

Stäblein, Bruno. *Die mittelalterlichen Hymnenmelodien des Abendlandes.* Monumenta monodica medii aevi, vol. 1. Kassel: Bärenreiter Verlag, 1956.

Statius. *Achilleid.* Ed. and trans. J. H. Mozley. Loeb Classical Library. Cambridge: Harvard University Press, 1989.

Stehling, Thomas, trans. *Medieval Latin Poems of Male Love and Friendship.* New York: Garland, 1984.

Stevens, Wallace. *The Collected Poems of Wallace Stevens.* New York: Vintage, 1982.

Strunk, Oliver, ed. *Source Readings in Music History: Antiquity and the Middle Ages.* New York: W. W. Norton, 1965.

Suso, Henry. *Wisdom's Watch Upon the Hours.* Trans. Edmund Colledge. Fathers of the Church. Washington: Catholic University of America Press, 1994.

Thomas of Cantimpré. *Bonum universale de apibus.* Ed. George Covener. Douai: Belleri, 1627.

——. *Liber de natura rerum.* 2 vols. Ed. Helmut Boese. Berlin and New York: Walter de Gruyter, 1973.

——. "Vita Christinae Mirabilis." *AASS* July, vol. 5: 637–60.

——. *The Life of Christina Mirabilis.* Trans. Margot King. Toronto: Peregrina Publishing, 1989.

——. "Vita Lutgardis." *AASS* June, vol. 4: 187–210.

——. *The Life of Lutgard of Aywières.* Trans. Margot King. Toronto: Peregrina Publishing, 1991.

Utley, Francis Lee, ed. "The Choristers' Lament." *Speculum* 21 (1946): 194–202.

Virgil. *Georgics.* Ed. and trans. H. Rushton Fairclough. Loeb Classical Library. Cambridge: Harvard University Press, 1978.

Virgilio, Giovanni del. *Allegorie Librorum Ovidii Metamorphoseos.* Ed. Fausto Ghisalberti. *Giornale Dantesco* 34 (1931).

Vita sanctae Hildegardis. Ed. Monica Klaes. *CCCM* 126. Turnhout: Brepols, 1993.

———. Trans. Adelgundis Führkötter and James McGrath. Collegeville, Minn.: Liturgical Press, 1995.

Vita Stephani Obazinensi. AASS March, vol. 1.

Walter of Chatillon. *Alexandreis.* Ed. Marvin L. Crocker. Padua: In aedibus antenoreis, 1978.

———. *Alexandreis.* Trans. David Townsend. Philadelphia: University of Pennsylvania Press, 1996.

Weiss, Piero, and Richard Taruskin, eds. *Music in the Western World: A History in Documents.* New York: Macmillan, 1984.

William of Conches. *Glosae super Platonem.* Ed. Édouard Jeauneau. Textes Philosophiques du Moyen Age, 13. Paris: Librairie Philosophique J. Vrin, 1965.

William of St. Thierry. *De natura corporis et animae.* Ed. Michel Lemoine. Paris: Société d'Edition 'Les Belles Lettres,' 1988.

Wirtjes, Hanneke, ed. *The Middle English Physiologus.* EETS, o.s. 299. Oxford: Oxford University Press, 1991.

Yudkin, Jeremy, ed. and trans. *De Musica Mensurata: The Anonymous of St. Emmeram.* Bloomington and Indianapolis: Indiana University Press, 1990.

———, trans. *The Music Treatise of Anonymous IV.* Musicological Studies and Documents 41. Stuttgart: American Institute of Musicology/Hänssler-Verlag, 1985.

Ziolkowski, Jan M., ed. and trans. *The Cambridge Songs (Carmina Cantabrigiensia).* New York and London: Garland, 1994.

2. SECONDARY STUDIES

Abert, Hermann. *Die Musikanschauung des Mittelalters und ihre Grundlagen.* Tutzing: Hans Schneider, 1964 [reprint].

Adams, J. N. "*Culus, clunes* and their synonyms in Latin." *Glotta* 59 (1981): 231–45.

———. *The Latin Sexual Vocabulary.* Baltimore: Johns Hopkins University Press, 1982.

Adkins, Cecil. "Monochord." *NG* 12: 496.

Adorno, Theodor. *Prisms.* Trans. Samuel Weber and Shierry Weber. Cambridge: Harvard University Press, 1981.

———. *Introduction to the Sociology of Music.* Trans. E. B. Ashton. New York: Continuum, 1989.

Aers, David. *Piers Plowman and Christian Allegory.* London: Edward Arnold, 1975.

Alford, John A. "The Grammatical Metaphor: A Survey of Its Uses in the Middle Ages." *Speculum* 57 (1982): 728–60.

Alverny, Marie Therese d'. *Alain de Lille: Textes inédits.* Etudes de philosophie médiévale 52. Paris: Librairie philosophique J. Vrin, 1965.

Archer, John. "The Structure of Anti-Semitism in the *Prioress's Tale.*" *Chaucer Review* 19 (1984): 46–54.

Armstrong, Nancy, and Leonard Tennenhouse, eds. *The Violence of Representation: Literature and the History of Violence.* London and New York: Routledge, 1989.

Attali, Jacques. *Noise: The Political Economy of Music.* Trans. Brian Massumi. Minneapolis: University of Minnesota Press, 1985.

Avray, D. L. d'. *The Preaching of the Friars: Semons Diffused from Paris before 1300.* Oxford: Clarendon Press, 1985.

Bakhtin, Mikhail. *Rabelais and His World.* Trans. Hélène Iswolsky. Bloomington: Indiana University Press, 1984.

Baldwin, John W. *Masters, Princes, and Merchants: The Social Views of Peter the Chanter and His Circle.* 2 vols. Princeton, N.J.: Princeton University Press, 1970.

———. *The Language of Sex: Five Voices from Northern France around 1200.* Chicago and London: University of Chicago Press, 1994.

Baltzer, Rebecca. "Notre Dame Manuscripts and Their Owners: Lost and Found." *Journal of Musicology* 5 (1987): 380–99.

Baltzer, Rebecca, Thomas Cable, and James I. Wimsatt, eds. *The Union of Words and Music in Medieval Poetry.* Austin: University of Texas Press, 1991.

Bandera, C. "From Mythical Bees to Medieval Anti-Semitism." *Stanford French Review* 10 (1986): 29–49.

Barkan, Leonard. *Transuming Passion: Ganymede and the Erotics of Humanism.* Stanford: Stanford University Press, 1991.

Barolini, Teodolinda. *The Undivine Comedy: Detheologizing Dante.* Princeton, N.J.: Princeton University Press, 1992.

Barthes, Roland. *Image, Music, Text.* Trans. Stephen Heath. New York: Hill and Wang, 1977.

Beckwith, Sarah. *Christ's Body: Identity, Culture, and Society in Late Medieval Writings.* London and New York: Routledge, 1993.

Beichner, "The Medieval Representative of Music, Jubal or Tubalcain?" *Texts and Studies in the History of Medieval Education* 2. Notre Dame, Ind.: University of Notre Dame Press, 1954.

Bennett, Judith. " 'Lesbian-like' and the Social History of Lesbianisms." *Journal of the History of Sexuality* 9 (2000): 1–24.

Bent, Ian. "Hildegard von Bingen." *NG* 8: 553–56.

Bent, Margaret. "Deception, Exegesis, and Sounding Number in Machaut's Motet 15." *Early Music History* 10 (1991): 15–27.

——. "Reflections on Christopher Page's *Reflections*." *Early Music* 21 (1993): 625–33.

Berger, Anna Maria Busse. "Mnemotechnics and Notre Dame Polyphony." *Journal of Musicology* 14 (1996): 263–98.

Berger, Carol. "The Hand and the Art of Memory." *Musica Disciplina* 35 (1981): 87–120.

Bestul, Thomas. *Texts of the Passion: Latin Devotional Literature and Medieval Society.* Philadelphia: University of Pennsylvania Press, 1996.

Bibby, Deirdre L. *Augusta Savage and the Art Schools of Manhattan.* New York: Schomburg Center for Research in Black Culture, New York Public Library, 1988.

Bicknell, Stephen. *The History of the English Organ.* Cambridge: Cambridge University Press, 1996.

Bielitz, Mathias. *Musik und Grammatik: Studien zur mittelalterlichen Musiktheorie.* Beiträge zur Musikforschung 4. Munich and Salzburg: Musikverlag Emil Katzbichler, 1977.

Binkley, Thomas E. "The Work Is Not the Performance." In *Companion to Medieval and Renaissance Music,* ed. David Fallows and Tess Knighton, pp. 36–43. London: Dent, 1992.

Blades, James. "Percussion Instruments of the Middle Ages and Renaissance: Their History in Literature and Painting." *Early Music* 1 (1973): 11–18.

Blamires, Alcuin. *Woman Defamed and Woman Defended: An Anthology of Medieval Texts.* Oxford: Clarendon Press, 1992.

Blanchot, Maurice. *The Gaze of Orpheus and Other Literary Essays.* Trans. Lydia Davis. Barrytown, N.Y.: Station Hill Press, 1981.

Bloch, Ernst. *Essays on the Philosophy of Music.* Trans. Peter Palmer. Cambridge: Cambridge University Press, 1985.

Bloch, R. Howard. *Medieval Misogyny and the Invention of Western Romantic Love.* Chicago and London: University of Chicago Press, 1991.

Block, Edward A. "Chaucer's Millers and Their Bagpipes." *Speculum* 29 (1954): 239–43.

Blumenfeld-Kosinski, Renate. *Reading Myth: Classical Mythology and Its Inter-pretations in Medieval French Literature.* Stanford: Stanford University Press, 1997.

Blumroder, Christoph von. "Modulatio/Modulation." In *Terminologie der musikalischen Komposition,* ed. Hans Eggebrecht. Stuttgart: Steiner, 1996.

Boenig, Robert. "The Miller's Bagpipe: A Note on the *Canterbury Tales* A 565–566." *English Language Notes* 21 (1983): 1–6.

———. "Musical Irony in the Pardoner's Tale." *Chaucer Review* 24 (1990): 253–58.

Boese, Helmut. "Zur Textüberlieferung von Thomas Cantimpratensis' *Liber de natura rerum.*" *Archivum fratrum praedicatorum* 39 (1969): 53–68.

Boffey, Julia. "Lydgate, Henryson, and the Literary Testament." *Modern Language Quarterly* 53 (1992): 41–56.

Bond, Gerald. "*Iocus amoris*: The Poetry of Baudri of Bourgueil and the For-mation of the Ovidian Subculture." *Traditio* 42 (1986): 143–93.

———. *The Loving Subject: Desire, Eloquence, and Power in Romanesque France.* Philadelphia: University of Pennsylvania Press, 1995.

Boswell, John. *Christianity, Social Tolerance, and Homosexuality: Gay People in Western Europe from the Beginning of the Christian Era to the Fourteenth Century.* Chicago: University of Chicago Press, 1980.

———. "Revolutions, Universals, and Sexual Categories." In *Hidden from His-tory: Reclaiming the Gay and Lesbian Past.* Ed. Martin Duberman, Martha Vicinus, and George Chauncey Jr., pp. 17–36. New York: Penguin, 1989.

Bowden, Betsy. "The Art of Courtly Copulation." *Medievalia et Humanistica* 9 (1979): 67–85.

Bowen, William R. "St. Augustine in Medieval and Renaissance Musical Sci-ence." In *Augustine on Music: An Interdisciplinary Collection of Essays,* ed. Robert R. La Croix, pp. 29–51. Lewiston, N.Y.: Edwin Mellen, 1988.

Blowers, John. "Queering the Summoner: Same-Sex Union in Chaucer's *Canterbury Tales.*" In *Speaking Images: Essays in Honor of V. A. Kolve,* ed. Charlotte C. Morse and R. F. Yeager. Asherville, N.C.: Pegasus Press, forthcoming 2001.

Breitenbach, Edgar. *Speculum humanae salvationis: Eine typengeschichtliche Untersuchung.* Studien zur deutsche Kunstgeschichte 272. Strasbourg: J. H. E. Heitz, 1930.

Brett, Philip. "Musicality, Essentialism, and the Closet." In *Queering the Pitch: The New Gay and Lesbian Musicology,* ed. Philip Brett, Elizabeth Wood, and Gary Thomas, pp. 9–26. New York: Routledge, 1994.

Brett, Philip, Elizabeth Wood, and Gary Thomas, eds. *Queering the Pitch: The New Gay and Lesbian Musicology.* New York: Routledge, 1994.

Brown, Carleton. "A Study of the Miracle of Our Lady Told by Chaucer's Prioress." *Chaucer Society*, 2nd ser., no. 45 (1910).

Brown, Catherine. *Contrary Things: Exegesis, Dialectic, and the Poetics of Didacticism*. Stanford: Stanford University Press, 1998.

Brown, Judith C. *Immodest Acts: The Life of a Lesbian Nun in Renaissance Italy*. New York: Oxford University Press, 1986.

Brown, Peter. *Augustine of Hippo: A Biography*. New York: Dorset Press, 1967.

———. *The Body and Society: Men, Women, and Sexual Renunciation in Early Christianity*. New York: Columbia University Press, 1988.

Brownlee, Kevin. "Orpheus's Song Re-Sung: Jean de Meun's Reworking of *Metamorphoses* X." *Romance Philology* 36 (1982/83): 201–9.

———. *Poetic Identity in Guillaume de Machaut*. Madison: University of Wisconsin Press, 1984.

Brownlee, Kevin, Marina S. Brownlee, and Stephen G. Nichols, eds. *The New Medievalism*. Baltimore and London: Johns Hopkins University Press, 1991.

Brück, Anton. Ph., ed. *Hildegard von Bingen 1179–1979: Festschrift zum 800. Todestag der Heiligen*. Mainz: Selbstverlag der Gesellschaft für mittelrheinische Kirchengeschichte, 1979.

Bruyne, Edgar de. *Etudes d'esthétique médiévale*. 3 vols. Bruges: De Tempel, 1946.

———. *The Esthetics of the Middle Ages*. Trans. Eileen B. Hennessy. New York: Frederick Ungar, 1969.

Bryan, W. F., and Germaine Dempster, eds. *Sources and Analogues of Chaucer's Canterbury Tales*. Chicago: University of Chicago Press, 1941.

Burger, Glenn. "Kissing the Pardoner." *PMLA* 107 (1992): 1143–56.

Burnett, Charles. "Sound and Its Perception in the Middle Ages." In *The Second Sense: Studies in Hearing and Musical Judgement from Antiquity to the Seventeenth Century*, ed. Charles Burnett, Michael Fend, and Penelope Gouk, pp. 43–70. Warburg Institute Surveys and Texts 22. London: Warburg Institute, 1991.

Burnett, Charles, and Peter Dronke, eds. *Hildegard of Bingen: The Context of Her Thought and Art*. London: Warburg Institute, 1998.

Burnett, Charles, Michael Fend, and Penelope Gouk, eds. *The Second Sense: Studies in Hearing and Musical Judgement from Antiquity to the Seventeenth Century*. Warburg Institute Surveys and Texts 22. London: Warburg Institute, 1991.

Butz, Annegret. *Die Romanischen Handschriften der Württembergischen Landesbibliothek Stuttgart*, part 2: Verschiedene Provinzen. Vol. 2 of *Katalog der Illuminierten Handschriften der Württembergischen Landesbibliothek Stuttgart.* Stuttgart: Anton Hiersemman, 1987.

Bynum, Caroline Walker. *Jesus as Mother: Studies in the Spirituality of the High Middle Ages.* Berkeley: University of California Press, 1982.

———. *Holy Feast and Holy Fast: The Religious Significance of Food to Medieval Women.* Berkeley: University of California Press, 1987.

———. *Fragmentation and Redemption: Essays on Gender and the Human Body in Medieval Religion.* New York: Zone Books, 1991.

———. *The Resurrection of the Body in Western Christianity, 200–1336.* New York: Columbia University Press, 1995.

Cadden, Joan. "It Takes All Kinds: Sexuality and Gender Difference in Hildegard of Bingen's 'Book of Compound Medicine.'" *Traditio* 40 (1984): 149–74.

———. *Meanings of Sex Difference in the Middle Ages: Medicine, Science, and Culture.* Cambridge: Cambridge University Press, 1993.

Calabrese. Michael. "'Make a Mark That Shows': Orphean Song, Orphean Sexuality, and the Exile of Chaucer's Pardoner." *Viator* 24: 269–86.

Calin, William. *A Poet at the Fountain: Essays on the Narrative Verse of Guillaume de Machaut.* Lexington: University Press of Kentucky, 1974.

Cameron, Averil. *Christianity and the Rhetoric of Empire.* Berkeley: University of California Press, 1991.

Camille, Michael. *The Gothic Idol: Ideology and Image-Making in Medieval Art.* Cambridge: Cambridge University Press, 1989.

Cardon, Bert. *Manuscripts of the Speculum humanae salvationis in the Southern Netherlands (c. 1410–c. 1470): A Contribution to the Study of 15th Century Book Illumination and of the Function and Meaning of Historical Symbolism.* Corpus van verluchte Handschriften / Corpus of Illuminated Manuscripts, 9: Low Countries Series, 6. Leuven: Peeters, 1996.

Carey, Gary. *More about All About Eve: A Colloquy by Gary Carey with Joseph L. Mankiewicz.* New York: Random House, 1972.

Caron, Ann Marie. "Invitations to the Sacred Heart: The Mystical Writings of Mechtild of Hackeborn." *American Benedictine Review* 45 (1994): 321–38.

Carruthers, Mary. *The Book of Memory.* Cambridge: Cambridge University Press, 1990.

Carter, H. H. *A Dictionary of Middle English Musical Terms.* Bloomington: Indiana University Press, 1961.

Caviness, Madeline. "Artist: 'To See, Hear, and Know All at Once.'" In *Voice of the Living Light: Hildegard of Bingen and Her World,* ed. Barbara Newman, pp. 110–24. Berkeley: University of California Press, 1998.

Certeau, Michel de. *Heterologies: Discourse on the Other.* Minneapolis: University of Minnesota Press, 1986.

——. *The Practice of Everyday Life.* Trans. Steven Rendall. Berkeley: University of California Press, 1988.

——. *The Mystic Fable.* Trans. Michael B. Smith. Chicago: University of Chicago Press, 1992.

Chadwick, Henry. *Early Christian Thought and the Classical Tradition.* Oxford: Clarendon Press, 1984.

Chamberlain, David. "Music in Chaucer: His Knowledge and Use of Medieval Ideas about Music." Ph.D. diss., Princeton University, 1967.

——. "The Nun's Priest's Tale and Boethius's *De Musica.*" *Modern Philology* 68 (1970): 188–91.

——. "Philosophy of Music in the *Consolatio* of Boethius." *Speculum* 45 (1970): 80–97.

——. "Musical Learning and Dramatic Action in Hrotsvit's *Pafnutius.*" *Studies in Philology* 77 (1980): 319–43.

——. "Musical Signs and Symbols in Chaucer: Convention and Originality." In *Signs and Symbols in Chaucer's Poetry,* ed. John Hermann and John Burke, pp. 43–80. Birmingham: University of Alabama Press, 1981.

Chance, Jane. *Medieval Mythography: From Roman North Africa to the School of Chartres, AD 433 to 1177.* Gainesville: University Press of Florida, 1994.

Chenu, Marie-Dominique. *Nature, Man, and Society in the Twelfth Century: Essays on New Theological Perspectives in the Latin West.* Ed. and trans. Jerome Taylor and Lester K. Little. Chicago: University of Chicago Press, 1983.

Clark, Anne L. *Elisabeth of Schönau: A Twelfth-Century Visionary.* Philadelphia: University of Pennsylvania Press, 1992.

Clark, Elizabeth A. *The Origenist Controversy: The Cultural Construction of an Early Christian Debate.* Princeton, N.J.: Princeton University Press, 1992.

Cogan, Robert. "Hildegard's Fractal Antiphon." *Sonus* 11 (1990): 1–19.

Cohen, Esther. "Towards a History of European Physical Sensibility: Pain in the Later Middle Ages." *Science in Context* 8 (1995): 47–74.

Coleman-Norton, P. R. "Cicero Musicus." *JAMS* 1 (1948): 3–22.

Colish, Marcia L. *The Stoic Tradition from Antiquity to the Early Middle Ages.* 2 vols. Leiden: E. J. Brill, 1985.

——. "*Psalterium Scholasticorum*: Peter Lombard and the Emergence of Scholastic Psalms Exegesis." *Speculum* 67 (1992): 531–48.

——. *Peter Lombard.* 2 vols. Leiden: E. J. Brill, 1994.

Constable, Giles. *Three Studies in Medieval Religious and Social Thought.* Cambridge: Cambridge University Press, 1995.

Cook, Nicholas. *Music, Imagination, and Culture*. Oxford: Oxford University Press, 1990.

Copeland, Rita. *Rhetoric, Hermeneutics, and Translation in the Middle Ages: Academic Traditions and Vernacular Texts*. Cambridge: Cambridge University Press, 1991.

———. "The Pardoner's Body and the Disciplining of Rhetoric." In *Framing Medieval Bodies*, ed. Sarah Kay and Miri Rubin, pp. 138–59. Manchester and New York: Manchester University Press, 1994.

Corbin, Solange. "*Musica* spéculative et *cantus* pratique: Le rôle de saint Augustine dans la transmission des sciences musicales." *Cahiers de civilisation médiévale* 5 (1962): 1–12.

Correale, Robert M. "Chaucer's Parody of Compline in the *Reeve's Tale*." *Chaucer Review* 1 (1967): 161–66.

Corsini, Eugenio. "L'harmonie du monde et l'home microcosme danse le *De hominis opificio*." *Epektasis: Mélanges patristiques offerts au Cardinal Jean Daniélou*. Ed. Jacques Fontaine and Charles Kannengiesser, pp. 455–62. Paris: Beauchesne, 1972.

Courcelle, Pierre. "Nouveaux aspects du platonisme chez saint Ambroise." *Revue des études latines* 34 (1956): 220–39.

———. *Late Latin Writers and Their Greek Sources*. Trans. Harry E. Wedeck. Cambridge: Harvard University Press, 1969.

Courtenay, William J. *Schools and Scholars in Fourteenth-Century England*. Princeton, N.J.: Princeton University Press, 1987.

Coussemaker, Edmond de. *Histoire de l'harmonie au moyen âge*. Hildesheim: G. Olms, 1966.

Crocker, Richard, and David Hiley, eds. *The Early Middle Ages to 1300*. Vol. 2 of *The New Oxford History of Music*. Oxford and New York: Oxford University Press, 1990.

Crouzel, Henri. *Origen*. Trans. A. S. Worrall. San Francisco: Harper and Row, 1989.

Cusick, Suzanne. "On a Lesbian Relationship with Music: A Serious Effort Not to Think Straight." In *Queering the Pitch: The New Gay and Lesbian Musicology*, ed. Philip Brett, Elizabeth Wood, and Gary Thomas, pp. 67–83. New York: Routledge, 1994.

Custer, John S. "The Psaltery, the Harp, and the Fathers: A Biblical Image and Its Interpreters." *The Downside Review* 114 (1996): 19–31.

Dalglish, William. "The Origins of the Hocket." *JAMS* 31 (1978): 3–20.

Davidson, Audrey. "*Alma Redemptoris Mater*: The Little Clergeon's Song." *Studies in Medieval Culture* 4 (1974): 459–66.

———, ed. *The Ordo Virtutum of Hildegard of Bingen: Critical Studies*. Early

Drama, Art, and Music Monograph Series 18. Kalamazoo, Mich.: Medieval Institute Publications, 1992.

Dawson, David. *Allegorical Readers and Cultural Revision in Ancient Alexandria.* Berkeley: University of California Press, 1992.

Delatte, Armand. "Les harmonies danse l'embryologie Hippocratique." *Mélanges Paul Thomas,* pp. 160–71. Bruge: Imprimerie Sainte Catherine, 1930.

Dent, Edward J. "Social Aspects of Medieval Music." In *The Oxford History of Music,* introductory volume, ed. Percy Carter Buck. Oxford: Oxford University Press, 1929.

Dieckmann, Emma. "The Meaning of 'Burdoun' in Chaucer." *Modern Philology* 26 (1929): 279–82.

DiGangi, Mario. *The Homoerotics of Early Modern Drama.* Cambridge: Cambridge University Press, 1997.

Dijk, S. J. P. van. "Papal Schola versus Charlemagne." In *Organicae voces: Festschrift Joseph Smits van Waesberghe,* pp. 21–38. Amsterdam: Instituut voor Middeleeuwse Musiekwetenschnap, 1963.

Dinshaw, Carolyn. *Chaucer's Sexual Poetics.* Madison: University of Wisconsin Press, 1989.

——. "Chaucer's Queer Touches/A Queer Touches Chaucer." *Exemplaria* 7 (1995): 75–92.

——. *Getting Medieval: Sexualities and Communities, Pre- and Postmodern.* Durham, N.C.: Duke University Press, 1999.

Dobiache-Rojdestvensky, Olga. *Les Poésies des Goliards.* Paris: Les Éditions Rieder, 1931.

Douie, D. L. *Archbishop Pecham.* Oxford: Clarendon Press, 1952.

Dronke, Peter. "The Composition of Hildegard of Bingen's *Symphonia.*" *Sacris Erudiri* 29 (1969–70): 381–93.

——. *Poetic Individuality in the Middle Ages.* Oxford: Clarendon Press, 1970.

——. *Fabula: Explorations into the Uses of Myth in Medieval Platonism.* Leiden: E. J. Brill, 1974.

——. *Women Writers of the Middle Ages.* Cambridge: Cambridge University Press, 1984.

Ebin, Lois. *John Lydgate.* Boston: Twayne Publishers, 1985.

Eco, Umberto. *Art and Beauty in the Middle Ages.* Trans. Hugh Bredin. New Haven and London: Yale University Press, 1986.

Edelman, Lee. *Homographesis: Essays in Gay Literary and Cultural Theory.* New York and London: Routledge, 1994.

Edwards, Robert R. *Ratio and Invention: A Study of Medieval Lyric and Narrative.* Nashville: Vanderbilt University Press, 1989.

Ellinwood, L. "Ars musica." *Speculum* 20 (1945): 290–99.

Elliott, Dyan. *Fallen Bodies: Pollution, Sexuality, and Demonology in the Middle Ages.* Philadelphia: University of Pennsylvania Press, 1999.

Elliott, Dyan, and Kathryn Kerby-Fulton. "Self-Image and the Visionary Role in Two Letters from the Correspondence of Elizabeth of Schönau and Hildegard of Bingen." *Vox Benedictina* 2 (1985): 214–23.

Ellsmere, Patricia. "Augustine on Beauty, Art and God." In *Augustine on Music,* ed. Robert R. La Croix, pp. 97–112. Lewiston, N.Y.: Edwin Mellen, 1988.

Ellsmere, Patricia, and Richard La Croix. "Augustine on Art as Imitation." In *Augustine on Music,* ed. Robert R. La Croix, pp. 1–16. Lewiston, N.Y.: Edwin Mellen, 1988.

Enders, Jody. "Music, Delivery, and the Rhetory of Memory in Guillaume de Machaut's Remède de Fortune." *PMLA* 107 (1992): 450–64.

———. *Rhetoric and the Origins of Medieval Drama.* Ithaca and London: Cornell University Press, 1992.

———. "Rhetoric, Coercion, and the Memory of Violence." In *Criticism and Dissent in the Middle Ages,* ed. Rita Copeland, pp. 24–55. Cambridge: Cambridge University Press, 1996.

———. "Delivering Delivery: Theatricality and the Emasculation of Eloquence." *Rhetorica* 15 (1997): 253–78.

———. *The Medieval Theater of Cruelty.* Ithaca and London: Cornell University Press, 1998.

Escott, Pozzi. "The Gothic Cathedral and Hidden Geometry of St. Hildegard." *Sonus* 11 (1984): 14–31.

———. "Hildegard von Bingen: Universal Proportion." *Sonus* 11 (1990): 33–40.

Etzkorn, Girard. "John Pecham, OFM: A Career of Controversy." In *Monks, Nuns, and Friars in Mediaeval Society,* ed. Edward B. King, Jacqueline T. Schaefer, and William B. Wadley, pp. 71–82. Sewanee Medieval Studies 4. Sewanee, Tenn.: University of the South, 1989.

Evans, Gillian. *Alan of Lille: The Frontiers of Theology in the Later Twelfth Century.* Cambridge: Cambridge University Press, 1983.

Everist, Mark. *French Motets in the Thirteenth Century: Music, Poetry and Genre.* Cambridge: Cambridge University Press, 1994.

Fagerberg, David. *What Is Liturgical Theology? A Study in Methodology.* Collegeville, Minn.: Liturgical Press, 1992.

Fassler, Margot. *Gothic Song: Victorine Sequences and Augustinian Reform in Twelfth-Century Paris.* Cambridge: Cambridge University Press, 1993.

———. "Composer and Dramatist: 'Melodious Singing and the Freshness of Remorse.'" In *Voice of the Living Light: Hildegard of Bingen and Her*

World, ed. Barbara Newman, pp. 149–75. Berkeley: University of California Press, 1998.

Ferster, Judith. " 'Your Praise Is Performed by Men and Children': Language and Gender in the Prioress's Prologue and Tale." *Exemplaria* 2 (1990): 149–68.

Finnegan, Mary Jeremy. *The Women of Helfta: Scholars and Mystics.* Athens and London: University of Georgia Press, 1991.

Flanagan, Sabina. *Hildegard of Bingen: A Visionary Life.* London: Routledge, 1989.

Forman, Robert. "Augustine's Music: 'Keys' to the Logos." In *Augustine on Music*, ed. Robert R. La Croix, pp. 17–28. Lewiston, N.Y.: Edwin Mellen, 1988.

Fradenburg, Louise. "Criticism, Anti-Semitism, and the Prioress's Tale." *Exemplaria* 1 (1989): 69–115.

———. " 'Voice Memorial': Loss and Reparation in Chaucer's Poetry." *Exemplaria* 2 (1990): 167–202.

———. " 'Be not far from me': Psychoanalysis, Medieval Studies and the Subject of Religion." *Exemplaria* 7 (1995): 41–54.

Fraenger, Wilhelm. *The Millennium of Hieronymous Bosch: Outlines of a New Interpretation.* Trans. Eithne Wilkins and Ernst Kaiser. Chicago: University of Chicago Press, 1951.

———. *Hieronymous Bosch.* Basel: Gordon and Breach, 1994.

Frantzen, Allen. *Before the Closet: Same-Sex Love from Beowulf to Angels in America.* Chicago: University of Chicago Press, 1998.

Freccero, John. *Dante: The Poetics of Conversion.* Cambridge: Harvard University Press, 1986.

Frese, Dolores Warwick. "The Homoerotic Underside in Chaucer's *Miller's Tale* and *Reeve's Tale*." *Michigan Academician* 10 (1977): 143–50.

Frese, Dolores Warwick, and Katherine O'Brien O'Keeffe, eds. *The Book and the Body.* Notre Dame, Ind.: University of Notre Dame Press, 1997.

Friedman, John Block. *Orpheus in the Middle Ages.* Cambridge: Harvard University Press, 1970.

———. "Thomas of Cantimpré *De Naturis Rerum*: Prologue, Book III and Book XIX." *Cahiers d'études médiévales* 2: *La science de la nature: théories et pratiques*, pp. 107–16. Montreal: Bellarmin, 1974.

Führkötter, Adelgundis. *Hildegard von Bingen.* Salzburg: Otto Müller Verlag, 1972.

Fuller, Sarah. "Early Polyphony." In *The Early Middle Ages to 1300*, ed. Richard Crocker and David Hiley, pp. 485–556. Oxford and New York: Oxford University Press, 1990.

Fussell, Paul. *Poetic Meter and Poetic Form*. Rev. ed. New York: Random House, 1979.

Gallo, F. Alberto. *Music of the Middle Ages*. 2 vols. Trans. Karen Eales. Cambridge: Cambridge University Press, 1985.

Gardiner, Anne Barbeau. "The Medieval Kiss." *PMLA* 108 (1993): 333–34.

Gates, Henry Louis, Jr., and Nelli Y. McKay, eds. *The Norton Anthology of African American Literature*. New York and London: W. W. Norton, 1997.

Gélineau, J. *Voices and Instruments in Christian Worship*. Trans. Clifford Howell. Collegeville: University of Minnesota Press, 1964.

Gellrich, Jesse. " 'Nicholas' 'Kynges Noote,' and 'Melodye.' " *English Language Notes* 8 (1971): 249–52.

——. "The Parody of Medieval Music in *The Miller's Tale*." *Journal of English and Germanic Philology* 73 (1974): 176–88.

——. *The Idea of the Book in the Middle Ages: Language Theory, Mythology, and Fiction*. Ithaca and London: Cornell University Press, 1985.

Gersh, Stephen. *Middle Platonism and Neoplatonism: The Latin Tradition*. 2 vols. Notre Dame, Ind.: University of Notre Dame Press, 1986.

——. *Concord in Discourse: Harmonics and Semiotics in Late Classical and Early Medieval Platonism*. Berlin and New York: Mouton de Gruyter, 1996.

Gibson, Gail McMurray. *The Theater of Devotion: East Anglian Drama and Society in the Late Middle Ages*. Chicago and London: University of Chicago Press, 1989.

Gibson, Nigel. *Music in the Age of Chaucer*. Woodbridge: Boydell and Brewer, 1979.

Gibson, Walter S. "The Garden of Earthly Delights by Hieronymous Bosch: The Iconography of the Central Panel." *Nederlands kunsthistorisch jaarboek* 24 (1973): 1–26.

——. *Hieronymous Bosch*. New York: Praeger Publishers, 1973.

Gilchrist, Roberta. *Gender and Material Culture: The Archaeology of Religious Women*. London and New York: Routledge, 1994.

Ginhart, Karl, ed. *Die Kunstdenkmäler des Benediktinerstiftes St. Paul im Lavanthal und seiner Filialkirchen*. Österreichische Kunsttopographie 37. Vienna: Anton Schroll and Co.

Girard, René. *Violence and the Sacred*. Trans. Patrick Gregory. Baltimore and London: Johns Hopkins University Press, 1977.

Glaze, Florence Eliza. "Medical Writer: 'Behold the Human Creature.' " In *Voice of the Living Light: Hildegard of Bingen and Her World*, ed. Barbara Newman, pp. 125–48. Berkeley: University of California Press, 1998.

Goehr, Lydia. *The Imaginary Museum of Musical Works: An Essay in the Philosophy of Music.* Oxford: Clarendon Press, 1992.

Goldberg, Jonathan. *Sodometries: Renaissance Texts, Modern Sexualities.* Stanford: Stanford University Press, 1992.

——, ed. *Queering the Renaissance.* Durham, N.C.: Duke University Press, 1994.

Goodich, Michael. *The Unmentionable Vice: Homosexuality in the Later Medieval Period.* Santa Barbara, Calif.: ABC-Clio, 1979.

Gougaud, Louis. *Devotional and Ascetic Practices in the Middle Ages.* Trans. G. C. Bateman. London: Burnes, Oates and Washbourne, 1927.

Grant, Barbara. "Five Liturgical Songs by Hildegard von Bingen (1098–1179)." *Signs* 5 (1980): 557–67.

Green, Richard Firth. "The Sexual Normality of Chaucer's Pardoner." *Mediaevalia* 8 (1985): 351–59.

——. "The Pardoner's Pants (and Why They Matter)." *Studies in the Age of Chaucer* 15 (1993): 131–45.

Greenberg, David F. *The Construction of Homosexuality.* Chicago: University of Chicago Press, 1988.

Gronau, Eduard. *Hildegard von Bingen 1098–1179: Prophetische Lehrerin der Kirche an der Schwelle und am Ende der Neuzeit.* Stein am Rhein: Christiana Verlag, 1991.

Guck, Marion A. "Two Types of Metaphoric Transference." In *Music and Meaning,* ed. Jenefer Robinson, pp. 201–12. Ithaca, N.Y.: Cornell University Press, 1997.

Halperin, David. *One Hundred Years of Homosexuality and Other Essays on Greek Love.* New York: Routledge, 1990.

Hamburger, Jeffrey. "The Visual and the Visionary: The Image in Late Medieval Monastic Devotions." *Viator* 20 (1989): 161–82.

——. *The Rothschild Chronicles: Art and Mysticism in Flanders and the Rhineland Circa 1300.* New Haven, Conn.: Yale University Press, 1990.

——. Review of Michael Camille, *Image on the Edge: The Margins of Medieval Art.* In *Art Bulletin* 75 (1993): 319–27.

——. *Nuns as Artists: The Visual Culture of a Medieval Convent.* Berkeley: University of California Press, 1997.

Hammerstein, Reinhold. *Die Musik der Engel: Untersuchungen zur Musikanschauung des Mittelalters.* Bern and Munich: Francke Verlag, 1962.

Hammond, E. P. "Poet and Patron in the *Fall of Princes.*" *Anglia* 38 (1914): 121–36.

Hanawalt, Barbara, ed. *Chaucer's England: Literature in Historical Context.* Minneapolis: University of Minnesota Press, 1992.

Hansen, Elaine Tuttle. *Chaucer and the Fictions of Gender*. Berkeley: University of California Press, 1992.

Harrán, Don. *Word-Tone Relations in Musical Thought from Antiquity to the Seventeenth Century*. Musicological Studies and Documents 40. Stuttgart: American Institute of Musicology/Hänssler-Verlag, 1986.

Harrison, Carol. *Beauty and Revelation in the Thought of Saint Augustine*. Oxford: Clarendon Press, 1992.

Harrison, Frank Lloyd. *Music in Medieval Britain*. London: Routledge and Kegan Paul, 1958.

Haskins, Charles Homer. *Studies in the History of Medieval Science*. Cambridge: Harvard University Press, 1924.

Hatch, Christopher, and David W. Bernstein, eds. *Music Theory and the Exploration of the Past*. Chicago and London: University of Chicago Press, 1993.

Hawkins, Sherman. "Chaucer's Prioress and the Sacrifice of Praise." *Journal of English and Germanic Philology* 63 (1964): 599–624.

Heilbronn, Denise. "Master Adam and the Fat-Bellied Lute (Inf. XXX)." *Dante Studies* 51 (1983): 51–65.

Henderson, John. "The Flagellant Movement and Flagellant Confraternities in Central Italy, 1260–1400." In *Religious Motivation: Biographical and Sociological Problems for the Church Historian*, ed. Derek Baker, pp. 147–60. Papers read at the Sixteenth Summer Meeting and the Seventeenth Winter Meeting of the Ecclesiastical History Society. Oxford: Blackwell, 1978.

Hexter, Ralph. *Ovid in Medieval Schooling: Studies in Medieval School Commentaries on Ovid's Ars Amatoria, Epistulae ex Ponto, and Epistulae Heroidum*. Münchener Beiträge zur Mediävistik und Renaissance-Forschung. Munich: Arbeo-Gesellschaft, 1986.

——. "Medieval Articulations of Ovid's *Metamorphoses*: From Lactantian Segmentation to Arnulfian Allegory." *Mediaevalia* 13 (1987): 63–82.

——. "The *Allegari* of Pierre Bersuire: Interpretation and the *Reductorium Morale*." *Allegorica* 10 (1989): 51–84.

——. "Ovid's Body." In *Constructions of the Classical Body*, ed. James I. Porter, pp. 327–54. Ann Arbor: University of Michigan Press, 1999.

Higdon, David. "Diverse Melodies in Chaucer's *General Prologue*." *Criticism* 14 (1972): 97–108.

Hiley, David. *Western Plainchant: An Introduction*. Oxford: Clarendon Press, 1993.

Hill, Boyd H., Jr. "The Grain and the Spirit in Medieval Anatomy." *Speculum* 39 (1965): 63–73.

Hirsch-Reich, Beatrice. "The Symbolism of Musical Instruments in the *Psalterium X Chordarum* of Joachim of Fiore and Its Patristic Sources." *Studia Patristica* 9 (1966): 540–51.

Hollander, John. *The Untuning of the Sky: Ideas of Music in English Poetry 1500–1700*. Princeton, N.J.: Princeton University Press, 1961.

Holsinger, Bruce. "The Flesh of the Voice: Embodiment and the Homo-erotics of Devotion in the Music of Hildegard of Bingen (1098–1179)." *Signs* 19 (1993): 92–125.

———. "Sodomy and Resurrection: The Homoerotic Subject of the Divine Comedy." In *Premodern Sexualities*, ed. Louise Fradenburg and Carla Freccero, pp. 243–74. New York: Routledge, 1996.

———. "Langland's Musical Reader: Liturgy, Law, and the Constraints of Per-formance." *Studies in the Age of Chaucer* 21 (1999): 99–141.

Hübner, Arthur. *Die deutschen Geisslerlieder: Studien zum geistlichen Volksliede des Mittelalters*. Berlin and Leipzig: Walter de Gruyter, 1931.

Hughes, Andrew. *Medieval Music: The Sixth Liberal Art*. Toronto Medieval Bibliographies 4. Toronto: University of Toronto Press, 1974.

———. *Style and Symbol: Medieval Music 800–1453*. Musicological Studies 5. Ot-tawa: Institute of Medieval Music, 1989.

Huglo, Michel. "Les noms des neumes et leur origine." *Etudes grégoriennes* 1 (1954): 53–67.

———. "L'auteur du 'Dialogue sur la musique' attribué à Odon." *Revue de musi-cologie* 55 (1969): 119–71.

Huot, Sylvia. *From Song to Book: The Poetics of Writing in Old French Lyric and Lyrical Narrative Poetry*. Ithaca and London: Cornell University Press, 1987.

———. *Allegorical Play in the Old French Motet: The Sacred and the Profane in Thirteenth-Century Polyphony*. Stanford: Stanford University Press, 1997.

Ingarden, Roman. *The Work of Music and the Problem of Its Identity*. Trans. Adam Czerniawski. Berkeley: University of California Press, 1986.

Jacoff, Rachel, and Jeffrey T. Schnapp, eds. *The Poetry of Allusion: Virgil and Ovid in Dante's Commedia*. Stanford: Stanford University Press, 1991.

Jaeger, C. Stephen. *Ennobling Love: In Search of a Lost Sensibility*. Phila-delphia: University of Pennsylvania Press, 1999.

Johnson, Lynn Staley. "Chaucer's Tale of the Second Nun and the Strategies of Dissent." *Studies in Philology* 89 (1992): 314–33.

Jones, G. Fenwick. "Wittenwiler's *Becki* and the Medieval Bagpipes." *Journal of English and Germanic Philology* 48 (1949): 209–28.

Jonsson, Ritva, and Leo Treitler. "Medieval Music and Language: A Reconsideration of the Relationship." In *Music and Language*. Vol. 1 of *Studies in the History of Music*, pp. 1–23. New York: Broude Brothers, 1983.

Jordan, Mark D. *The Invention of Sodomy in Christian Theology*. Chicago and London: University of Chicago Press, 1997.

Kaske, Robert E. "The 'Canticum Canticorum' in the 'Miller's Tale.'" *Studies in Philology* 59 (1962): 479–500.

Katz, Bernard, ed. *The Social Implications of Early Negro Music in the United States*. New York: Arno Press and the *New York Times*, 1969.

Kay, Sarah. *Subjectivity in Troubadour Poetry*. Cambridge: Cambridge University Press, 1990.

Kay, Sarah, and Miri Rubin, eds. *Framing Medieval Bodies*. Manchester and New York: Manchester University Press, 1994.

Kerby-Fulton, Kathryn. *Reformist Apocalypticism and Piers Plowman*. Cambridge: Cambridge University Press, 1990.

Keresztes, Paul. *Imperial Rome and the Christians from the Severi to Constantine the Great*. 2 vols. Lanham, Md.: University Press of America, 1989.

Kerman, Joseph. *Contemplating Music: Challenges to Musicology*. Cambridge: Harvard University Press, 1985.

Kiefer, Joseph H. "Lithotomy Set to Music: An Historical Interlude." *Transactions of the American Association of Genito-Urinary Surgeons* 55 (1963): 132–37.

Kivy, Peter. *The Corded Shell: Reflections on Musical Expression*. Princeton, N.J.: Princeton University Press, 1980.

——. *Sound and Semblance: Reflections on Musical Representation*. Princeton, N.J.: Princeton University Press, 1984.

——. *Sound Sentiment: An Essay on the Musical Emotions*. Philadelphia: Temple University Press, 1989.

Knapp, Janet. "Polyphony at Notre Dame of Paris." In *The Early Middle Ages to 1300*, ed. Richard Crocker and David Hiley, pp. 557–635. Oxford and New York: Oxford University Press, 1990.

Knapp, Peggy. *Chaucer and the Social Contest*. New York: Routledge, 1990.

Koestenbaum, Wayne. "The Queen's Throat: (Homo)sexuality and the Art of Singing." In *inside/out: Lesbian Theories, Gay Theories*, ed. Diana Fuss, pp. 205–34. New York and London: Routledge, 1991.

——. *The Queen's Throat: Opera, Homosexuality, and the Mystery of Desire*. New York: Vintage Books, 1993.

Kolve, V. A. "Chaucer's *Second Nun's Tale* and the Iconography of Saint Cecilia." In *New Perspectives in Chaucer Criticism*, ed. Donald Rose, pp. 137–74. Norman, Okla.: Pilgrim Books, 1981.

——. *Chaucer and the Imagery of Narrative: The First Five Canterbury Tales.* Stanford: Stanford University Press, 1984.

Kramer, Lawrence. "The Musicology of the Future." *Repercussions* 1 (1992): 5–18.

——. "Music Criticism and the Postmodernist Turn: In Contrary Motion with Gary Tomlinson." *Current Musicology* 53 (1993): 25–35.

——. *Classical Music and Postmodern Knowledge.* Berkeley: University of California Press, 1995.

La Croix, Robert R., ed. *Augustine on Music: An Interdisciplinary Collection of Essays.* Lewiston, N.Y.: Edwin Mellen, 1988.

Lakoff, George, and Mark Johnson. *Philosophy in the Flesh: The Embodied Mind and Its Challenge to Western Thought.* New York: Basic Books, 1999.

Landini, Lawrence. *The Causes of the Clericalization of the Order of Friars Minor, 1209–1260.* Ph.D. diss., Gregorian Pontifical University, Chicago, 1968.

Leclercq, Jean. "Caelestis fistula." In *Verbum et Signum,* ed. Hans Fromm, Wolfgang Harms, and Uwe Ruberg, pp. 57–68. Beträge zur Mediávitschen Bedeutungsforschung vol. 1. Munich: Wilhelm Fink, 1975.

Leeb, Helmut. *Die Psalmodie bei Ambrosius.* Wiener Beiträge zur Theologie 18. Vienna: Verlag Herder, 1967.

Leppert, Richard. *The Sight of Sound: Music, Representation, and the History of the Body.* Berkeley and Los Angeles: University of California Press, 1993.

Leppert, Richard, and Susan McClary, eds. *Music and Society: The Politics of Composition, Performance, and Reception.* Cambridge: Cambridge University Press, 1987.

Lerer, Seth. *Chaucer and His Readers: Imagining the Author in Late-Medieval England.* Princeton, N.J.: Princeton University Press, 1993.

Leupin, Alexandre. *Barbarolexis: Medieval Writing and Sexuality.* Trans. Kate M. Cooper. Cambridge: Harvard University Press, 1989.

Lewis, Gertrud Jaron. *By Women, for Women, about Women: The Sister-Books of Fourteenth-Century Germany.* Studies and Texts 125. Toronto: Pontifical Institute of Medieval Studies, 1996.

Lilla, Salvatore R. C. *Clement of Alexandria: A Study in Christian Platonism and Gnosticism.* Oxford: Oxford University Press, 1971.

Lippman, Edward. *Musical Thought in Ancient Greece.* New York and London: Columbia University Press, 1964.

——. *A History of Western Musical Aesthetics.* Lincoln and London: University of Nebraska Press, 1992.

Little, Lester K. *Religious Poverty and the Profit Economy in Medieval Europe.* Ithaca, N.Y.: Cornell University Press, 1978.

Lochrie, Karma. *Margery Kempe and Translations of the Flesh*. Philadelphia: University of Pennsylvania Press, 1991.

——. "Don't Ask, Don't Tell: Murderous Plots and Medieval Secrets." *GLQ: A Journal of Lesbian and Gay Studies* 1 (1995): 405–17.

——. "Mystical Plots, Murderous Secrets." In *Constructing Medieval Sexuality*, ed. Peggy McCracken Lochrie and James A. Schultz, pp. 180–200. Medieval Cultures 11. Minneapolis: University of Minnesota Press, 1997.

Long, A. A. *Stoic Studies*. Cambridge: Cambridge University Press, 1996.

Loseff, Nicky. *The Best Concords: Polyphonic Music in Thirteenth-Century Britain*. New York and London: Garland, 1994.

Maas, Martha, and Jane McIntosh Snyder. *Stringed Instruments of Ancient Greece*. New Haven and London: Yale University Press, 1989.

Maltman, Sister Nicholas. "The Divine Granary, or the End of the Prioress's 'greyn.'" *Chaucer Review* 17 (1982): 163–70.

Mandel, Jerome. *Geoffrey Chaucer: Building the Fragments of the Canterbury Tales*. Rutherford, N.J.: Fairleigh Dickinson University Press, 1992.

Marcuse, Herbert. *Eros and Civilization: A Philosophical Inquiry into Freud*. Boston: Beacon, 1966.

Marrou, Henri-Irénée. "Une théologie de la musique chez Grégoire de Nysse?" In *Epektasis: Mélanges patristiques offerts au Cardinal Jean Daniélou*, ed. Jacques Fontaine and Charles Kannengiesser, pp. 501–8. Paris: Beauchesne, 1972.

Marrow, James. *Passion Iconography in Northern European Art of the Later Middle Ages and Early Renaissance: A Study of the Transformation of Sacred Metaphor into Descriptive Narrative*. Kortrijk, Belgium: Van Ghmmert, 1979.

Martimort, Aimé-George, et al., eds. *The Church at Prayer: An Introduction to the Liturgy*. 4 vols. London: Chapman, 1985.

Marvin, Corey J. "'I Will Thee Not Forsake': The Kristevan Maternal Space in Chaucer's Prioress's Tale and John of Garland's Stella maris." *Exemplaria* 8 (1996): 35–58.

Matter, E. Ann. *The Voice of My Beloved: The Song of Songs in Western Medieval Christianity*. Philadelphia: University of Pennsylvania Press, 1991.

Mayer, Cornelius, and Karl Heinz Chelius, eds. *Aaron-Conuersio*. Vol. 1 of *Augustinus-Lexicon*. Basel: Schwabe and Co., 1994.

McAlpine, Monica. "The Pardoner's Homosexuality and How It Matters." *PMLA* 95 (1980): 8–22.

McClary, Susan. *Feminine Endings: Music, Gender, and Sexuality*. Minneapolis: University of Minnesota Press, 1991.

McDonnell, Ernest W. *The Beguines and Beghards in Medieval Culture with*

Special Emphasis on the Belgian Scene. New Brunswick, N.J.: Rutgers University Press, 1954.

McGee, Timothy J. *The Sound of Medieval Song: Ornamentation and Vocal Style according to the Treatises.* Oxford: Clarendon Press, 1998.

McGrath, Robert L. "Satan and Bosch: The *Visio Tundali* and the Monastic Vices." *Gazette des Beaux-Arts* 71 (1968): 45–50.

McKinnon, James. "The Church Fathers and Musical Instruments." Ph.D. diss., Columbia University, New York, 1965.

——. "The Meaning of the Patristic Polemic against Musical Instruments." *Current Musicology* 1 (1965): 69–82.

——. "Musical Instruments in Medieval Psalm Commentaries and Psalters." *Journal of the American Musicological Society* 21 (1968): 3–20.

——. "Ambrose." *NG* 1: 313–14.

McNamara, Jo Ann. *A New Song: Celibate Women in the First Three Christian Centuries.* Published as *Women and History* 6/7. New York: Institute for Research in History and Haworth Press, 1983.

Meier, Christel. "Zum Verhältnis von Text und Illustration in überlieferten Werk Hildegards von Bingen." In *Hildegard von Bingen 1179–1979: Festschrift zum 800. Todestag der Heiligen,* ed. Anton. Ph. Brück, pp. 159–170. Mainz: Selbstverlag der Gesellschaft für mittelrheinische Kirchengeschichte, 1979.

Meloni, Pietro. "Li chitarra di David." *Sandalion* 5 (1982): 233–61.

Meredith, Anthony. *Gregory of Nyssa.* London and New York: Routledge, 1999.

Mews, Constant. "Hildegard and the Schools." In *Hildegard of Bingen: The Context of Her Thought and Art,* pp. 89–110. London: Warburg Institute, 1998.

Meyer-Baer, Kathi. *Music of the Spheres and the Dance of Death: Studies in Musical Iconology.* Princeton, N.J.: Princeton University Press, 1970.

Michaud-Quantin, Pierre. "Les Petites encyclopédies du XIIIe siècle." *Cahiers d'histoire mondiale* 9 (1966): 580–95.

Miles, Stephen. "Critical Musicology and the Problem of Mediation." *Notes* 53 (1997): 722–50.

Miller, B. D. H. "Chaucer's *General Prologue,* A673: Further Evidence." *Notes and Queries* 7 (1960): 404–6.

Miller, D. A. *The Novel and the Police.* Berkeley: University of California Press, 1988.

Miller, James. *Measures of Wisdom: The Cosmic Dance in Classical and Christian Antiquity.* Toronto: University of Toronto Press, 1986.

Minnis, A. J., and A. B. Scott, eds. *Medieval Literary Theory and Criticism, c. 1100–c. 1375: The Commentary Tradition.* Oxford: Clarendon Press, 1988.

Monson, Craig. *Disembodied Voices: Music and Culture in an Early Modern Italian Convent.* Berkeley: University of California Press, 1995.

Monson, Don A. "Andreas Caperanus and the Problem of Irony." *Speculum* 63 (1988): 539–72.

Moorman, John. *A History of the Franciscan Order from Its Origins to the Year 1517.* Oxford: Clarendon Press, 1968.

Moran, Jo Ann Hoeppner. *The Growth of English Schooling 1340–1548: Learning, Literacy, and Laicization in Pre-Reformation York Diocese.* Princeton, N.J.: Princeton University Press, 1985.

Morrison, Karl. *"I Am You": The Hermeneutics of Empathy in Western Literature, Theology, and Art.* Princeton, N.J.: Princeton University Press, 1988.

———. *Conversion and Text: The Cases of Augustine of Hippo, Herman-Judah, and Constantine Tsatsos.* Charlottesville: University Press of Virginia, 1992.

Moxey, Keith. *The Practice of Theory: Poststructuralism, Cultural Politics, and Art History.* Ithaca, N.Y.: Cornell University Press, 1994.

Murphy, James J. *Rhetoric in the Middle Ages: A History of Rhetorical Theory from St. Augustine to the Renaissance.* Berkeley: University of California Press, 1974.

Murray, Alexander. "Confession as a Historical Source in the Thirteenth Century." In *The Writing of History in the Middle Ages: Essays Presented to Richard William Southern*, pp. 275–322. Oxford: Clarendon Press, 1981.

Needham, Rodney. "Percussion and Transition." *Man* 2 (1967): 606–14.

Newman, Barbara. *Sister of Wisdom: St. Hildegard's Theology of the Feminine.* Berkeley: University of California Press, 1987.

———. "Three-Part Invention: The *Vita S. Hildegardis* and Mystical Hagiography." In *Hildegard of Bingen: The Context of Her Thought and Art*, ed. Charles Burnett and Peter Dronke. London: Warburg Institute, 1998.

———, ed. *Voice of the Living Light: Hildegard of Bingen and Her World.* Berkeley: University of California Press, 1998.

Newman, Martha. *The Boundaries of Charity: Cistercian Culture and Ecclesiastical Reform, 1098–1180.* Stanford: Stanford University Press, 1996.

Nichols, Stephen J. "Voice and Writing in Augustine and in the Troubador Lyric." In *Vox intexta: Orality and Textuality in the Middle Ages*, ed. A. N. Doane and Carol Braun Pasternack, pp. 137–61. Madison: University of Wisconsin Press, 1991.

Niesner, Manuela. *Das Speculum humanae salvationis der Stiftsbibliothek Kremsmünster: Edition der mittelhochdeutschen Versübersetzung und Studien zum Verhältnis von Bild und Text.* Cologne, Weimar, and Vienna, 1995.

Oakden, J. P. *Alliterative Poetry in Middle English: The Dialectical and Metrical Survey.* Manchester, England: Manchester University Press, 1930.

O'Donnell, James J. *Augustine, Confessions 3: Commentary on Books 8–13.* Oxford: Clarendon Press, 1992.

Oesch, Hans. *Guido von Arezzo: Biographisches und Theoretisches unter besonderer Berücksichtigung der sogenannten odonischen Traktate.* Bern: P. Haupt, 1954.

Oesterle, H. J. "Probleme der Anthropologie bei Gregor von Nyssa." *Hermes* 113 (1985): 101–14.

Olson, Clair C. "Chaucer and the Music of the Fourteenth Century." *Speculum* 16 (1941): 64–91.

Olson, Glending. "Deschamps' *Art de Dictier* and Chaucer's Literary Environment." *Speculum* 48 (1973): 714–23.

Omont, H. *Concordances des numéros anciens et des numéros actuels des Manuscrits Latins de la Bibliothèque Nationale.* Paris: Ernest Leroux, 1903.

Orme, Nicholas. *Education and Society in Medieval and Renaissance England.* London: Hambledon Press, 1989.

Orsten, Elizabeth M. "Madame Eglentyne in Her Day and in Ours: Anti-Semitism in *The Prioress's Tale* and a Modern Parallel." *Florilegium* 11 (1992): 82–100.

Orton, P. R. "Chaucer's *General Prologue,* A673: Burdoun and Some Sixteenth-Century Puns." *English Language Notes* 23 (1985): 3–4.

Page, Christopher. *Voices and Instruments of the Middle Ages: Instrumental Practice and Songs in France 1100–1300.* London: J. M. Dent, 1987.

——. *The Owl and the Nightingale: Musical Life and Ideas in France, 1100–1300.* Berkeley and Los Angeles: University of California Press, 1989.

——. "Musicus and Cantor." In *A Companion to Medieval and Renaissance Music,* ed. Tess Knighton and David Fallows, pp. 74–78. New York: Schirmer Books, 1992.

——. *Discarding Images: Reflections on Music and Culture in Medieval France.* Oxford: Clarendon Press, 1993.

——. "Reading and Reminiscence: Tinctoris on the Beauty of Music." *JAMS* 49 (1996): 1–31.

Parker, Ian. "The Performance of Troubadour and Trouvère Songs: Some Facts and Conjectures." *Early Music* 5 (1977): 184–207.

Parker, Roscoe. "Pilates Voys." *Speculum* 25 (1950): 237–44.

Patterson, Lee. *Chaucer and the Subject of History.* Madison: University of Wisconsin Press, 1991.

Pearsall, Derek. *John Lydgate.* London: Routledge and Kegan Paul, 1970.

———. "Chaucer's Pardoner: The Death of a Salesman." *Chaucer Review* 17 (1983): 358–65.

———. *John Lydgate (1371–1449): A Bio-bibliography.* University of Victoria: English Literary Studies, 1997.

Perkins, Judith. *The Suffering Self: Pain and Narrative Representation in the Early Christian Era.* London and New York: Routledge, 1995.

Pesce, Dolores. "The Significance of Text in Thirteenth-Century Latin Motets." *Acta musicologica* 58 (1986): 91–117.

Petroff, Elizabeth. *Body and Soul: Essays on Medieval Women and Mysticism.* New York: Oxford University Press, 1994.

Petrucci, Armando. *Writing the Dead: Death and Writing Strategies in the Western Tradition.* Trans. Michael Sullivan. Stanford: Stanford University Press, 1998.

Pfau, Marianne Richert. "*Armonia* in the Songs of Hildegard von Bingen: Manifestations of Compositional Order." *Acta* 15 (1988): 69–84.

———. "Form as Process in the Sequences of Hildegard of Bingen." Paper presented at the Annual Meeting of the American Musicological Society, Austin, Tex., 1989.

———. "Hildegard von Bingen's 'Symphonia armonie celestium revelationum': An Analysis of Musical Process, Modality, and Text-Music Relations." Ph.D. diss., State University of New York–Stony Brook, 1990.

———. "Mode and Melody Types in Hildegard von Bingen's Symphonia." *Sonus* 11 (1990): 53–71.

Pfeffer, Wendy. *The Change of Philomel: The Nightingale in Medieval Literature.* New York: Peter Lang, 1985.

Pickering, F. P. "Das gotische Christusbild: Zu den Quellen mittelalterlicher Passionsdarstellungen." *Euphorion* 47 (1953): 16–37.

———. *Literature and Art in the Middle Ages.* Coral Gables, Fla.: University of Miami Press, 1970.

———. *Essays on Medieval German Literature and Iconography.* Cambridge: Cambridge University Press, 1980.

Pike, David L. *Passage through Hell: Modernist Descents, Medieval Underworlds.* Ithaca and London: Cornell University Press, 1997.

Pinegar, Sandra. "Exploring the Margins: A Second Source for Anonymous 7." *Journal of Musicological Research* 12 (1992): 213–43.

Pirrotta, Nino. " 'Musica de sono humano' and the Musical Poetics of Guido of Arezzo." In *Medieval Poetics*, ed. Paul Clogan. Medievalia et Humanistica n.s. 7. Cambridge: Cambridge University Press, 1976.

Platelle, Henri. "Le Recueil des miracles de Thomas de Cnatimpré et la vie religieuse dans les Pays-Bas et le nord de la France au XIIIe siècle." *Assis-*

tance et Assistés jusqu'à 1610. Actes du 97e congrès National des Sociétés Savantes, Nantes, 1972. Paris: Bibliothèque Nationale, 1979. pp. 469–98.

Preger, Wilhelm. *Geschichte der deutschen Mystik im Mittelalter.* 3 vols. Leipzig: Dörffling und Franke, 1874–93.

Putnam, Michael J. "Virgil's *Inferno.*" In *The Poetry of Allusion: Virgil and Ovid in Dante's Commedia,* ed. Rachel Jacoff and Jeffrey T. Schnapp, pp. 94–112. Stanford: Stanford University Press, 1991.

Raby, F. J. E. "Philomena praevia temporis amoeni." In *Moyen Age Époques Moderne et Contemporaine.* Vol. 2 of *Mélanges Joseph de Ghellink, S.J.,* pp. 435–48. Gembloux: J. Duculot, 1951.

Rambuss, Richard. "Pleasure and Devotion: The Body of Jesus and Seventeenth-Century Religious Lyric." In *Queering the Renaissance,* ed. Jonathan Goldberg, pp. 253–79. Durham, N.C.: Duke University Press, 1994.

Rawski, Conrad H. "Petrarch's Dialogue on Music." *Speculum* 46 (1971): 302–17.

Reckow, Fritz. *Die Copula: Über einige Zusammenhänge zwischen Setzweise, Formbildung, Rhythmus und Vortragsstil in der Mehrstimmigkeit von Notre-Dame.* Mainz: Akademie der Wissenschaften und der der Literatur, 1972.

Reeves, Marjorie, and Beatrice Hirsch-Reich. *The Figurae of Joachim of Fiore.* Oxford: Clarendon Press, 1972.

Reimer, Bennett, and Jeffrey E. Wright, eds. *On the Nature of Musical Experience.* Niwot: University Press of Colorado, 1992.

Rice, Winthrop Huntington. *The European Ancestry of Villon's Satirical Testaments.* Syracuse University Monographs 1. New York: Corporate, 1941.

Rich, Adrienne. "Compulsory Heterosexuality and Lesbian Existence." *Signs* 5 (1980): 631–60.

Riché, Pierre. *Les Ecoles et l'enseignement dans l'Occident chrétien de la fin du Ve siècle au milieu du XIe siècle.* Paris: Aubier Montaigne, 1979.

Richenhagen, Albert. *Studien zur Musikanschauung des Hrabanus Maurus.* Kölner Beiträge zur Musikforschung 162. Regensburg: Gustave Bosse Verlag, 1989.

Ridley, Aaron. *Music, Value, and the Passions.* Ithaca and London: Cornell University Press, 1995.

Ridley, Florence H. *The Prioress and the Critics.* Berkeley and Los Angeles: University of California Press, 1965.

Ritscher, M. Immaculata. "Zur Musik der hl. Hildegard von Bingen." In Brück, ed., *Hildegard von Bingen 1179–1979: Festschrift zum 800. Todestag der Heiligen,* ed. Anton. Ph. Brück, pp. 189–210. Mainz: Selbstverlag der Gesellschaft für mittelrheinische Kirchengeschichte, 1979.

Robertson, D. W. *A Preface to Chaucer.* Princeton, N.J.: Princeton University Press, 1962.

Robertson, Elizabeth. "Aspects of Female Piety in the Prioress's Tale." In *Chaucer's Religious Tales,* ed. C. David Benson and Elizabeth Robertson. Cambridge: D. S. Brewer, 1990.

Roesner, Edward. "The Performance of Parisian Organum." *Early Music* 7 (1979): 174–89.

Rotili, Mario. *I Codici Danteschi Miniati a Napoli.* Miniatura e Arti Minori in Campania 7. Naples: Libreria Scientifica Editrice, 1972.

Rowland, Beryl. "Chaucer's Idea of the Pardoner." *Chaucer Review* 14 (1979): 140–54.

Rubin, Miri. *Corpus Christi: The Eucharist in Late Medieval Culture.* Cambridge: Cambridge University Press, 1991.

Russell, K. C. "Peter Damian's Whip." *American Benedictine Review* 41 (1990): 20–35.

Salter, Elizabeth. *English and International: Studies in the Literature, Art and Patronage of Medieval England.* Ed. Derek Pearsall and Nicolette Zeeman. Cambridge: Cambridge University Press, 1988.

Sanders, Ernest H. "The Earliest Phases of Measured Polyphony." In *Music Theory and the Exploration of the Past,* ed. Christopher Hatch and David W. Bernstein, pp. 41–58. Chicago and London: University of Chicago Press, 1993.

Sanguineti, Edoardo. "Infernal Acoustics: Sacred Song and Earthly Song." *Lectura Dantis* 6 (1990): 69–79.

Santiso, Maria Teresa. "Saint Gertrude and the Liturgy." *Liturgy* 26 (1992): 53–84.

Scarry, Elaine. *The Body in Pain: The Making and Unmaking of the World.* New York: Oxford University Press, 1985.

Schmidt-Görg, Joseph. "Die Sequenzen der heiligen Hildegard." In *Studien zur Musikgeschichte des Rheinlandes,* ed. Willi Kahl et al., pp. 109–17. Cologne: Arno Volk-Verlag, 1956.

———. "Zur Musikanschauung in den Schriften der hl. Hildegard vong Bingen. In *Der Mensch und die Kunste: Festschrift für Heinrich Lützeler.* Düsseldorf: Verlag L. Schwann, 1962.

Schnapp, Jeffrey. "Dante's Sexual Solecisms: Gender and Genre in the Commedia." In *The New Medievalism,* ed. Kevin Brownlee, Marina S. Brownlee, and Stephen G. Nichols, pp. 201–25. Baltimore and London: Johns Hopkins University Press, 1991.

Schroeder-Sheker, Terese. "The Alchemical Harp of Mechtild of Hackeborn." *Vox Benedictina* 6 (1989): 40–55.

Schueller, Herbert M. *The Idea of Music: An Introduction to Musical Aesthetics in Antiquity and the Middle Ages*. Kalamazoo, Mich.: Medieval Institute Publications, 1988.

Schwarz, David. *Listening Subjects: Music, Psychoanalysis, Culture*. Durham, N.C., and London: Duke University Press, 1997.

Scott, Kathleen. "Sow-and-Bagpipe Imagery in the Miller's Portrait." *Review of English Studies* 18 (1967): 287–90.

Scruton, Roger. *The Aesthetics of Music*. Oxford: Clarendon Press, 1997.

Sears, Elizabeth. "The Iconography of Auditory Perception in the Early Middle Ages: On Psalm Illustration and Psalm Exegesis." In *The Second Sense: Studies in Hearing and Musical Judgement from Antiquity to the Seventeenth Century*, ed. Charles Burnett, Michael Fend, and Penelope Gouk, pp. 19–42. Warburg Institute Surveys and Texts 22. London: Warburg Institute, 1991.

Sedgewick, G. G. "The Progress of Chaucer's Pardoner, 1880–1940." *Modern Language Quarterly* 1 (1940): 431–58.

Sedgwick, Eve Kosofsky. *Between Men: English Literature and Male Homosocial Desire*. New York: Columbia University Press, 1985.

———. *Epistemology of the Closet*. Berkeley and Los Angeles: University of California Press, 1990.

———. *Tendencies*. Durham, N.C.: Duke University Press, 1993.

Shepherd, John, and Peter Wicke. *Music and Cultural Theory*. Cambridge: Polity Press, 1997.

Simons, Walter. "Reading a Saint's Body: Rapture and Bodily Movement in the Vitae of Thirteenth-Century Beguines." In *Framing Medieval Bodies*, ed. Sarah Kay and Miri Rubin, pp. 10–23. Manchester and New York: Manchester University Press, 1994.

Siraisi, Nancy. "The Music of Pulse in the Writings of Italian Academic Physicians (Fourteenth and Fifteenth Centuries)." *Speculum* 50 (1975): 689–710.

Solie, Ruth, ed. *Musicology and Difference: Gender and Sexuality in Music Scholarship*. Berkeley: University of California Press, 1993.

Sordi, Marta. *The Christians and the Roman Empire*. Trans. Annabel Bedini. Norman and London: University of Oklahoma Press, 1986.

Soulignac, A. "Nouveaux parallèles entre saint Ambroise et Plotin." *Archives de philosophie*, n.s. 19 (1956): 148–56.

Southern, R. W. *Medieval Humanism*. New York: Harper and Row, 1970.

Spanneut, Michel. *Le stoïcism des pères de l'Église de Clément de Rome à Clément d'Alexandrie*. Paris: Éditions du Seuil, 1957.

Spitzer, Leo. *Classical and Christian Ideas of World Harmony: Prolegomena to an Interpretation of the Word "Stimmung."* Baltimore: Johns Hopkins University Press, 1963.

Spitzlei, Sabine B. *Erfahrungsraum Herz: Zur Mystik des Zisterzienserinnenklosters Helfta im 13. Jahrhundert.* Stuttgart: Bad Cannstatt, 1991.

Stäblein, Bruno. "Hymnus, B. Der Lateinischen Hymnus." In *Die Musik in Geschichte und Gegenwart*, vol. 6., ed. Ludwig Finscher, pp. 993–1018. Kassel: 1994.

Standaert, M. "Helfta." In *DHGE* 22: 894–96.

Stapleton, M. L. *Harmful Eloquence: Ovid's Amores from Antiquity to Shakespeare.* Ann Arbor: University of Michigan Press, 1996.

Steiner, Ruth. "Hymn II. Monophonic Latin." *NG* 8: 838–41.

Stevens, John. "Dante and Music." *Italian Studies* 23 (1968): 1–18.

——. *Words and Music in the Middle Ages: Song, Narrative, Dance, and Drama 1050–1350.* Cambridge: Cambridge University Press, 1986.

——. "The Musical Individuality of Hildegard's Songs: A Liturgical Shadowland." In *Hildegard of Bingen: The Context of Her Thought and Art*, pp. 163–88. London: Warburg Institute, 1998.

Stillinger, Thomas. *The Song of Troilus: Lyric Authority in the Medieval Book.* Philadelphia: University of Pennsylvania Press, 1992.

Stirnemann, Patricia. "Fils de la vierge: L'initiale à filigranes parisienne: 1140–1314." *Revue de l'Art* 90 (1990): 58–73.

Stock, Brian. *Augustine the Reader: Meditation, Self-Knowledge, and the Ethics of Interpretation.* Cambridge and London: Belknap Press of Harvard University Press, 1996.

Strohm, Paul. *Social Chaucer.* Cambridge: Harvard University Press, 1989.

Subotnik, Rose Rosengard. *Developing Variations: Style and Ideology in Western Music.* Minneapolis: University of Minnesota Press, 1991.

Surtz, Ronald E. *The Guitar of God: Gender, Power, and Authority in the Visionary World of Mother Juana de la Cruz (1481–1534).* Philadelphia: University of Pennsylvania Press, 1990.

Swerdlow, Noel. "Musica Dicitur A Moys, Quod est Aqua." *JAMS* 20 (1967): 3–9.

Switten, Margaret. *Music and Poetry in the Middle Ages: A Guide to Research on French and Occitan Song, 1100–1400.* New York and London: Garland, 1995.

Tanay, Dorit. "Music in the Age of Ockham: The Interrelations between Music, Mathematics, and Philosophy in the Fourteenth Century." Ph.D. diss., University of California, Berkeley, 1989.

Taruskin, Richard. *Text and Act: Essays on Music and Performance.* New York: Oxford University Press, 1995.

Thomas, Marcel. "Zur kulturgeschichtlichen Einordnung der Armenbibel mit *Speculum humanae salvationis.*" *Archiv für Kulturgeschichte* 52 (1970): 192–223.

Thompson, A. Hamilton. "Song Schools in the Middle Ages." *Church-Music Society Occasional Papers* 14. London: Society for Promoting Christian Knowledge, 1942.

Tischler, Hans. "Intellectual Trends in Thirteenth-Century Paris as Reflected in the Texts of Motets." *Music Review* 29 (1968): 1–11.

Tomlinson, Gary. "The Web of Culture: A Context for Musicology." *19th Century Music* 7 (1984): 350–62.

———. "Musical Pasts and Postmodern Musicologies: A Response to Lawrence Kramer." *Current Musicology* 53 (1993): 18–24, 36–40.

———. *Music in Renaissance Magic: Toward a Historiography of Others.* Chicago and London: University of Chicago Press, 1993.

Traub, Valerie. *Desire and Anxiety: Circulations of Sexuality in Shakespearean Drama.* New York: Routledge, 1992.

Treitler, Leo. "Homer and Gregory: The Transmission of Epic Poetry and Plainchant." *Musical Quarterly* 60 (1974): 333–72.

———. "Oral, Written, and Literate Process in the Transmission of Medieval Music." *Speculum* 56 (1981): 471–91.

———. "Reading and Singing: On the Genesis of Occidental Music-Writing." *Early Music History* 4 (1984): 135–208.

———. "The Troubadours Singing Their Poems." In *The Union of Words and Music in Medieval Poetry*, ed. Rebecca Baltzer, Thomas Cable, and James I. Wimsatt, pp. 15–48. Austin: University of Texas Press, 1991.

———. "The 'Unwritten' and 'Written Transmission' of Medieval Chant and the Start-up of Musical Notation." *Journal of Musicology* 10 (1992): 131–91.

———. "Inventing a European Musical Culture—Then and Now." In *The Past and Future of Medieval Studies*, ed. John Van Engen, pp. 344–61. Notre Dame, Ind.: University of Notre Dame Press, 1994.

———. "Language and the Interpretation of Music." In *Music and Meaning*, ed. Jenefer Robinson, pp. 23–56. Ithaca, N.Y.: Cornell University Press, 1997.

Vagaggini, Cyprian. *Theological Dimensions of the Liturgy: A General Treatise on the Theology of the Liturgy.* Trans. Leonard Doyle and W. A. Jurgens. Collegeville, Minn.: Liturgical Press, 1976.

Van Deusen, Nancy. "Medieval Organologies: Augustine vs. Cassiodor on the Subject of Musical Instruments." In *Augustine on Music*, ed. Robert R. La Croix, pp. 53–96. Lewiston, N.Y.: Edwin Mellen, 1988.

———. *The Harp and the Soul: Essays in Medieval Music.* Lewiston, N.Y.: Edwin Mellen, 1989.

——. *Theology and Music at the Early University: The Case of Robert Grosseteste and Anonymous IV*. Leiden: E. J. Brill, 1995.

Vickers, K. H. *Humphrey Duke of Gloucester: A Biography*. London: Archibald Constable and Company, 1907.

Vieillard, C. *Gilles de Corbeil: Essai sur la Société Médicale et Religieuse au XIIe siècle*. Paris: Librairie Ancienne Honoré Champion, 1909.

Vollmann, Benedikt Konrad. "La vitalità delle enciclopedie di scienza naturale: Isidore di Siviglia, Tommaso di Cantimpré, e le redazioni del cosiddetto 'Tommaso III.' " In *L'enciclopedismo medievale*, ed. Michelangelo Picone, pp. 135–45. Ravenna: Longo, 1994.

Waddell, Chrysogonus. "The Origin and Early Evolution of the Cistercian Antiphonary: Reflections on Two Cistercian Chant Reforms." In *The Cistercian Spirit: A Symposium in Memory of Thomas Merton*, ed. M. Basil Pennington, pp. 190–223. Spencer, Mass.: Cistercian Publications, 1970.

Waesberghe, Joseph Smits van. *De musico-paedagogico et theoretico Guidona Aretino*. Florence: L. S. Olschki, 1953.

——. *Musikerziehung: Lehre und Theorie der Musik im Mittelalter*. Musikgeschicte in Bildern vol. 3.3. Leipzig: VEB Deutscher Verlag für Musik, 1969.

Wallace, David. *Chaucerian Polity: Absolutist Lineages and Associational Forms in England and Italy*. Stanford: Stanford University Press, 1997.

Walstra, G. J. J. "Thomas de Cantimpré, *De naturis rerum*: Etat de la question." *Vivarium* 5 (1967): 146–71 and 6 (1968): 46–61.

Ward, John O. "Quintilian and the Rhetorical Revolution of the Middle Ages." *Rhetorica* 13 (1995): 231–84.

Wathey, Andrew. Review of Wright, *Music and Ceremony*. In *Early Music History* 10 (1991): 305–13.

——. "Musicology, Archives and Historiography." In *Musicology and Archival Research*, ed. Barbara Haggh, Frank Daelemans, and André Vanrie, pp. 4–26. Archives et Bibliothèques de Belgique, n.s. 46. Brussels: Bibliothèques de Belgique, 1994.

Wegman, Rob. "Sense and Sensibility in Late-Medieval Music: Thoughts on Aesthetics and 'authenticity.' " *Early Music* 23 (1995): 298–312.

Weis, Anne. *The Hanging Marsyas and Its Copies: Roman Innovations in a Hellenistic Sculptural Tradition*. Archaeologica 103. Rome: Giorgio Bretschneider Editore, 1992.

Wenk, J. C. "On the Source of the Prioress's Tale." *Mediaeval Studies* 17 (1955): 214–19.

Whatley, Gordon. "The Uses of Hagiography: The Legend of Pope Gregory and the Emperor Trajan in the Middle Ages." *Viator* 15 (1984): 25–63.

Wilkins, Nigel. *Music in the Age of Chaucer.* Cambridge: D. S. Brewer, 1979; 2nd ed. 1995 with "Chaucer Songs."

Wille, Günther. *Musica Romana: Die Bedeutung der Musik im Leben der Römer.* Amsterdam: P. Schippers N.V., 1967.

——. *Schriften zur Geschichte der antiken Musik, mit einer Bibliographie zur antiken Musik 1957–1987.* Quellen und Studien zur Musikgeschichte von der Antike bis in die Gegenwart 26. Frankfurt am Main: Peter Lang, 1997.

Williams, E. Carleton. *My Lord of Bedford 1389–1435: Being a Life of John of Lancaster, First Duke of Bedford, Brother of Henry V and Regent of France.* London: Longmans, Green, 1963.

Wilson, Adrian, and Joyce Lancaster Wilson. *A Medieval Mirror: Speculum humanae salvationis 1324–1500.* Berkeley: University of California Press, 1984.

Wilson, Edward. "*The Testament of the Buck* and the Sociology of the Text." *Review of English Studies* 45 (1994): 157–84.

Wimsatt, James I. "Chaucer and Deschamps' 'Natural Music.'" In *Union of Words and Music,* ed. Rebecca Baltzer, Thomas Cable, and James I. Wimsatt, pp. 132–50. Austin: University of Texas Press, 1991.

——. *Chaucer and His French Contemporaries: Natural Music in the Fourteenth Century.* Toronto: University of Toronto Press, 1991.

Winn, James Anderson. *Unsuspected Eloquence: A History of the Relations between Poetry and Music.* New Haven, Conn.: Yale University Press, 1981.

Wiora, W. "Jubilare sine verbis." In *In memoriam Jacques Handschin,* ed. H. Anglès et al. Strasbourg: P. H. Heitz, 1962.

Witts, Richard. "How to Make a Saint: On Interpreting Hildegard of Bingen." *Early Music* 26 (1998): 479–85.

Wood, Elizabeth. "Sapphonics." In *Queering the Pitch: The New Gay and Lesbian Musicology,* ed. Philip Brett, Elizabeth Wood, and Gary Thomas, pp. 27–66. New York: Routledge, 1994.

Woods, Gregory. *Articulate Flesh: Male Homo-eroticism and Modern Poetry.* New Haven and London: Yale University Press, 1987.

Wright, Craig. "Leoninus, Poet and Musician." *JAMS* 39 (1986): 1–35.

——. *Music and Ceremony at Notre Dame of Paris, 500–1500.* Cambridge: Cambridge University Press, 1989.

Wright, Rosemary Muir. "Sound in pictured silence. The significance of writing in the illustration of the Douce Apocalypse." *Word and Image* 7 (1991): 239–74.

Yardley, Anne Bagnall. "'Ful weel she soong the service dyvyne': The Cloistered Musician in the Middle Ages." In *Women Making Music,* ed. Jane

Bowers and Judith Tick, pp. 15–38. Urbana: University of Illinois Press, 1986.

Young, Karl. "Chaucer and Peter Riga." *Speculum* 12 (1937): 299–303.

Yudkin, Jeremy. "The *Copula* According to Johannes de Garlandia." *Musica Disciplina* 34 (1980): 67–84.

——. "The Anonymous of St. Emmeram and Anonymous IV on the *Copula*." *Musical Quarterly* 70 (1984): 1–22.

Yunck, John A. *The Lineage of Lady Meed: The Development of Mediaeval Venality Satire*. Notre Dame, Ind.: University of Notre Dame Press, 1963.

Zieman, Katherine. "Chaucer's *Voys*." *Representations* 60 (1997): 70–91.

Ziolkowski, Jan. *Alan of Lille's Grammar of Sex: The Meaning of Grammar to a Twelfth-Century Intellectual*. Cambridge, Mass.: Medieval Academy of America, 1985.

Zumthor, Paul. *La poésie et la voix dans la civilisation médiévale*. Paris: PUF, 1984.

——. *La lettre et la voix de la "littérature" médiévale*. Paris: Seuil, 1987.

Index

Bingen, 88–89, 116, 125–29; hybrid lute-harp in *Garden of Earthly Delights* (Hieronymous Bosch), 254; incarnation of Christ as form of inversion, 163–67, 320–21; Leonin/Leoninus, *see* Leonin/Leoninus; lesbianism as opposed to homoeroticism, 128–29; marriage, homoerotics of, 330–43; misogynistic interpretations of Orpheus myth, 330–43; musical more than genital nature of, 181; Notre Dame polyphony and, *see* Notre Dame polyphony and homoerotic desire; Orpheus myth and, *see* Orpheus; "Philomena praevia," 228–29; polyphony and, *see* Polyphony and homoerotic desire; sexual nature of entire body rather than genital contact alone, 128–29, 181, 303, 380n92; Virgin Mary, homoerotic nature of devotion to, 125–26

Homophobia, rise of, 153

Homosocial musical cultures, 88–89

Honorius Augustodunensis, 217, 234–35, 243

Horologium Sapientiae (Henry Suso), xviii

House of Fame (Geoffrey Chaucer), 262, 295, 334

Hrotsvit of Gandersheim, 27

Hugh of St. Victor, 15, 199, 233–34, 290

Human music, 13–15, 17, 45, 93, 243, 288–91, 355–57

Humphrey, Duke of Gloucester, 332–38

Huot, Sylvia, 180, 322

Hurston, Zora Neale, 354–57

Hyacinthus, accidental slaying of, 298, 299

Images of music, visual, 1–2, 198–201, 237, 242–43

Incarnation of Christ: inversion, incarnation as form of, 163–67, 320–21; music itself and incarnation, analogy drawn between, 165–66; Orpheus and harp allegory in Arnulf's *Ovide Moralisé*, 316–17; "Philomena praevia," 225–26

Inferno (Dante), 214–16

Instrumental music, medieval theory of, 15–16

Isidore of Seville, 27, 295, 297, 344, 346, 350

Jacqueline, Countess of Hainault, 337–38

Jacques de Liège, 179

Jacques de Vitry, 216–18, 222

Jaeger, C. Stephen, 150

Jauss, Hans Robert, 346

Jean de Meun, 300–301, 312

Jerome, 30

Jesse, *virga* or stem of, 116–25

Jesus, *see* Christ

Jewish nonbelonging depicted as somatic dissonance in *Prioress's Tale*, 265, 282–83, 285–86, 290–91

Joachim of Fiore, 210, 318

Johannes de Garlandia, 169

Johannes Tinctoris, 361n1

John of Brabant, 337–38

John of Salisbury, 157–60, 161, 179, 180

Johnson, James Weldon, 352–54

Johnson, Mark, 12

John the Deacon, 273

John the Scot, 255

John VIII (Pope), 273

John XXII (Pope), 180

Jonah's Gourd Vine (Zora Neale Hurston), 354–57

Jordan, Mark, 167

Jubal and Tubalcain, sons of Lamech, and musicality of passion and crucifixion, 202–8

Jubilus, Augustine of Hippo's account of, 76–77

Justina, 71–72

Juvenal, 155, 157

Figurae: Reading Medieval Culture

Bruce Holsinger, *Music, Body, and Desire in Medieval Culture*

Rainer Warning, *The Ambivalences of Medieval Religious Drama*

Virginia Burrus, *Begotten, Not Made: Conceiving Manhood in Late Antiquity*

Peter S. Hawkins, *Dante's Testaments: Essays in Scriptural Imagination*

Daniel Boyarin, *Dying for God: Martyrdom and the Making of Christianity and Judaism*

Catherine Brown, *Contrary Things: Exegesis, Dialectic, and the Poetics of Didacticism*

Paul Freedman, *The Image of the Medieval Peasant as Alien and Exemplary*

James F. Burke, *Desire Against the Law: The Juxtaposition of Contraries in Early Medieval Spanish Literature*

Armando Petrucci Translated by Michael Sullivan, *Writing the Dead: Death and Writing Strategies in the Western Tradition*

Renate Blumenfeld-Kosinski, *Reading Myth: Classical Mythology and Its Interpretations in Medieval French Literature*

Paul Saenger, *Space Between Words: The Origins of Silent Reading*

David Wallace, *Chaucerian Polity: Absolutist Lineages and Associational Forms in England and Italy*

Sylvia Huot, *Allegorical Play in the Old French Motet: The Sacred and the Profane in Thirteenth-Century Polyphony*

Ralph Hanna III, *Pursuing History: Middle English Manuscripts and Their Texts*

Theresa Tinkle, *Medieval Venuses and Cupids: Sexuality, Hermeneutics, and English Poetry*

Edited by Seth Lerer, *Literary History and the Challenge of Philology: The Legacy of Erich Auerbach*